Introduction to Development Economics

Development Economics is arguably the most important field with economics. Charged with analysing and criticising the way economics develop and grow, development economists play a vital role in attempting to reduce inequality across the world. The fourth edition of this excellent textbook introduces students to this vital field.

All of the popular aspects of earlier editions are retained with new additions such as the introduction of endogenous growth theory and a new chapter on structural adjustment and growth. Defined, this is growth that occurs from within the economy, which is reliant on improvements in education, health, trade and technology.

With vastly improved and updated pedagogical features such as new topical case studies and questions for discussion, Subrata Ghatak introduces what can be a difficult subject with a welcome clarity.

Subrata Ghatak is Research Professor in Economics and Director of Research Studies in Economics at Kingston University, England. He has also acted as a Consultant to many international agencies including the United Nations and the World Bank and has written nine books and contributed numerous articles in leading international economic journals.

Introduction to Development Economics

Fourth edition

Subrata Ghatak

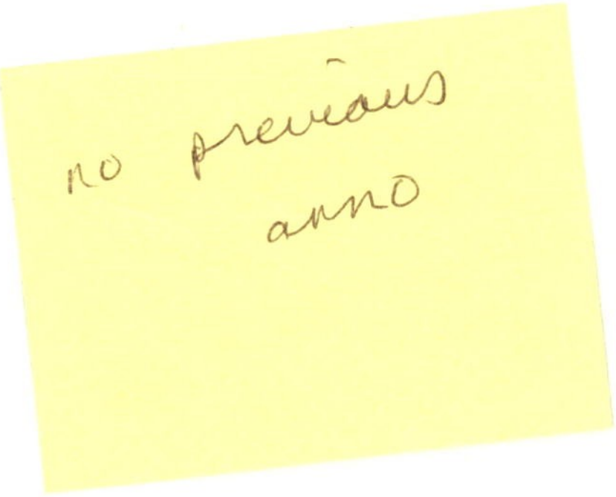

LONDON AND NEW YORK

First published 2003
by Routledge
11 New Fetter Lane, London EC4P 4EE

Simultaneously published in the United States and Canada
by Routledge
29 West 35th Street, New York, NY 10001

Routledge is an imprint of the Taylor & Francis Group

Typeset in Times by BC Typesetting Ltd, Bristol
Printed and bound in Great Britain by
TJ International Ltd, Padstow, Cornwall

British Library Cataloguing in Publication Data
A catalogue record for this book is available from the British Library

Library of Congress Cataloging in Publication Data
A catalog record has been requested

ISBN 0-415-09722-3 (hbk)
ISBN 0-415-09723-1 (pbk)

Contents

Preface to the fourth edition xi
Preface to the third edition xii
Preface to the second edition xiii
Preface to the first edition xiv
Acknowledgements xvi

1 INTRODUCTION 1

1.1 Introduction 1
1.2 Characteristics of the less developed countries 1
1.3 Types of markets in less developed countries 20
1.4 Production conditions in less developed countries 20
1.5 Growth and development 23
1.6 Human development index 26
Appendix 1.1 Measurement of income inequality 28
Appendix 1.2 A note on production functions 30

PART I
The economic theory of growth and development 35

2 GROWTH THEORIES AND THEIR RELEVANCE TO LESS DEVELOPED COUNTRIES 37

2.1 Introduction 37
2.2 Classical scenario 37
2.3 The Keynesian theory and less developed countries 39
2.4 The Harrod–Domar model and its applications 42
2.5 The neoclassical theory and less developed countries 43
2.6 Marx's theory and less developed countries 47
2.7 The Kaldor–Mirrlees model 52
2.8 The neoclassical growth accounting formula and the new endogenous growth theory 55
2.9 Differences in economic growth 60

Appendix 2.1 The basic equations of the neoclassical economic growth model 71
Appendix 2.2 Endogenous growth models 73

3 DUAL ECONOMY MODELS 79

3.1 Introduction 79
3.2 The 'surplus' labour and its contribution to development 79
3.3 The Fei–Ranis model 83
3.4 The Jorgenson model 87
3.5 Some extensions of the dual economy models: the Dixit–Marglin model 90
3.6 The Kelly et al. *model* 91
3.7 Dual economy models: a critique 91
Appendix 3.1 Employment and growth 94

Part II
Investment, saving, foreign resources and industrialization in less developed countries 97

4 ALLOCATION OF RESOURCES: INVESTMENT CRITERIA 99

4.1 The need for investment criteria in less developed countries 99
4.2 The capital turnover criterion 100
4.3 The social marginal productivity criterion 101
4.4 The maximization of the rate of creation of investible surplus principle 101
4.5 The reinvestible surplus criterion 103
4.6 Balanced and unbalanced growth 109
Appendix 4.1 The dichotomy between savings and output maximization and its solution 112

5 DOMESTIC RESOURCES FOR DEVELOPMENT 115

5.1 Introduction 115
5.2 The nature of money markets in less developed countries 115
5.3 Money and economic growth 116
5.4 Inflation and economic growth 117
5.5 Financial liberalization in LDCs: causes and consequences 124
5.6 Objectives of fiscal policy in less developed countries 126
5.7 Fiscal policy and growth 127
5.8 Deficit financing and less developed countries 131
5.9 The tax structure in less developed countries 132
5.10 Taxation and domestic resource mobilization in less developed countries: the evidence 138

5.11 *Tax reforms in less developed countries in the 1980s* 140
5.12 *Budgetary deficits and Ricardian equivalence: the case of India* 141

6 FOREIGN RESOURCES AND ECONOMIC DEVELOPMENT 146

6.1 *Introduction* 146
6.2 *The concept of foreign resources* 146
6.3 *Criteria for distribution of foreign resources* 147
6.4 *Different types of foreign resource* 150
6.5 *Dual-gap analysis and its evaluation* 154
6.6 *Gains and losses of investment by multinational corporations in less developed countries: some theoretical issues* 157
6.7 *Private foreign investment and the transfer of technology to less developed countries* 162
6.8 *Special drawing rights and the 'link'* 170
6.9 *Foreign aid and economic growth* 176
Appendix 6.1 Less developed countries and world trade 180

7 INDUSTRIALIZATION, PROTECTION AND TRADE POLICIES 190

7.1 *Major reasons for industrialization in less developed countries* 190
7.2 *The role of tariffs in economic development* 290
7.3 *The optimum tariff argument* 191
7.4 *The infant industry argument* 193
7.5 *Distortions in the factor markets* 196
7.6 *The balance of payments argument* 197
7.7 *The employment argument* 197
7.8 *'Nominal' and 'effective' rates of protection* 198
7.9 *The 'cost' of protection* 203
7.10 *Economic growth and trade* 205
7.11 *Terms of trade between developed countries and less developed countries* 206
7.12 *Export instability and economic growth in less developed countries* 208
7.13 *The role of the United Nations Conference on Trade and Development and some trade policies to help less developed countries* 210
7.14 *Non-tariff barriers and the generalized system of preferences* 212
7.15 *Regional co-operation among less developed countries* 213
7.16 *Trade liberalization and industrialization* 214
7.17 *The North–South models and intra-industry trade* 219
7.18 *Conclusion* 220
Appendix 7.1 Indices of instability of exports 223

Part III
Sectoral development and planning 227

8 SECTORAL ALLOCATION OF RESOURCES: AGRICULTURE 229

8.1 *Introduction* 229
8.2 *The role of agriculture in economic development* 229
8.3 *The concept of 'marketed surplus'* 231
8.4 *A model to mobilize agricultural surplus* 235
8.5 *Acreage response to prices* 238
8.6 *Marketed surplus, size-holdings and output* 238
8.7 *Limitations of price policy and some alternatives* 244
8.8 *Conclusion* 245

9 GREEN REVOLUTION AND INCOME DISTRIBUTION 246

9.1 *Introduction* 246
9.2 *The nature of the Green Revolution* 246
9.3 *Causes of the Green Revolution* 251
9.4 *Effects of the Green Revolution on income: a simple theory* 255
9.5 *Effects of the Green Revolution on relative factor shares* 255
9.6 *Problems and prospects of the Green Revolution* 258
9.7 *The basic needs approach* 260
9.8 *Growth theory and basic needs* 262
9.9 *A note on famines* 265

10 POPULATION, POVERTY, INCOME DISTRIBUTION, EMPLOYMENT AND MIGRATION 271

10.1 *Population and economic development* 271
10.2 *Population explosion in less developed countries and the theory of demographic transition* 273
10.3 *Low-level equilibrium trap* 274
10.4 *Fertility and population growth in less developed countries* 275
10.5 *Poverty and income distribution* 281
10.6 *Income inequality* 281
10.7 *Absolute poverty* 284
10.8 *Redistribution with growth* 287
10.9 *The employment problem* 289
10.10 *The Todaro model* 291
10.11 *Migration theory and evidence: an assessment* 296
10.12 *Stark's model* 298
10.13 *Employment policy* 299

10.14 Poverty, inequality and financial development 300
Appendix 10.1 The definition of a poverty line 304
Appendix 10.2 Migration 306
Appendix 10.3 Schultz's model of the household production approach to fertility 307
Appendix 10.4 Poverty and nutrition 310

11 DEVELOPMENT PLANNING 311

11.1 Concept of economic planning 311
11.2 Types of planning 311
11.3 Economic models and economic planning 312
11.4 The case for and against planning 313
11.5 Development planning models 314
11.6 Application of the Harrod–Domar model in development planning: India's first five year plan 316
11.7 A two-sector Harrod–Domar model for planning: the Kenyan case 317
11.8 Feldman–Mahalanobis sectoral planning and the Indian second five year plan 318
11.9 Macroeconometric models in development planning 320
11.10 Input–output analysis in development planning 322
11.11 Linear programming and development planning 326
11.12 Micro-planning: aims of cost–benefit analysis 331
11.13 The Little and Mirrlees method of project evaluation in less developed countries 335
11.14 The United Nations Industrial Development Organization (1972) guidelines 340
11.15 Social accounting and development planning by Barbara M. Roberts 343
Appendix 11.1 The Feldman–Mahalanobis model 347

12 STRUCTURAL ADJUSTMENT AND DEVELOPMENT 351

12.1 Structural adjustment and economic growth 351
12.2 The structural adjustment and stabilization policies of the IMF 351
12.3 Trade adjustment 353
12.4 Structural adjustment, stabilization and trade policies 354
12.5 Exchange rate and trade reforms 356
12.6 Structural adjustment programmes: the experience of sub-Saharan African countries 359
12.7 Conclusion 361

Part IV
A new deal in commodity trade? 363

13 THE NEW INTERNATIONAL ECONOMIC ORDER 365

13.1 Introduction 365
13.2 The evolution of the new international economic order 366
13.3 The main objectives of a new international economic order 368
13.4 The theory of commodity price stabilization: demand/supply shifts 369
13.5 Commodity price stabilization: gains and losses 371
13.6 Implications of international commodity agreements, buffer stocks and compensatory finances 373
13.7 Conclusion 375

14 THE INTERNATIONAL DEBT CRISIS
with Nigel M. Healey 378

14.1 Introduction 378
14.2 The evolving debt position of the developing world 378
14.3 Why do developing countries become indebted? 381
14.4 Sources of external finance 382
14.5 Why do debt servicing problems arise? 383
14.6 The external dimensions of the 1982 crisis 384
14.7 Phase one: 'muddling through' the debt crisis, 1982–9 385
14.8 Phase two: debt forgiveness and the Brady Plan 391

15 ENVIRONMENT AND DEVELOPMENT 398

15.1 Introduction 398
15.2 Deforestation and macroeconomic environment 399
15.3 The 'tragedy of the commons' 401
15.4 Externalities, natural resource degradation and economic policies 402
15.5 A case study: the importance of fuelwood in household energy consumption 406
15.6 An alternative farming system: alley cropping in humid West African agriculture 412
15.7 Conclusion 413

Bibliography 416
Index 452

Preface to the fourth edition

Ever since the publication of the third edition of *Introduction to Development Economics* a few years ago, development economics continues to be an exciting field as existing theories and evidence are reviewed. Simultaneously, new theories and techniques for testing them are suggested.

Students and teachers who are familiar with the third edition of this book will observe some important changes. The chief objective of the fourth edition has been, as in previous editions, to strike a fair balance between theories (old and new) and the realities of economic growth and development in less developed countries (LDCs). In this edition, major revisions have been made to update the statistics and to include new theoretical issues and empirical evidence. The fourth edition utilizes data published as recently as 2002 by the World Bank, International Monetary Fund and other sources.

In the light of many comments that I have received from colleagues and readers, I have included a new chapter on the important issue of structural adjustment and economic growth. Sections on economic, trade and financial liberalization have been extensively revised. Similarly, the section on human development has been expanded to include a rigorous analysis of the Human Deprivation Index. The chapter on the international debt crisis has been rewritten to reflect contemporary arguments about the role of international financial institutions. The appendix of Chapter 2 now comprises an extensive and technical descriptions of the 'old' and 'new' endogenous theories of economic growth.

In writing the fourth edition I am indebted to many students, lecturers, anonymous reviewers and colleagues. I am specially grateful to Dr Barbara Roberts, Professor Nigel Healey, Alan Mulhern and Truc and DieuLinh Nguyen for their excellent help. I am equally grateful to Robert Langham and Terry Clague of Routledge for their patience and kind co-operation.

S.G.

Preface to the third edition

My main aim in this edition has been, as before, to achieve a reasonable balance between new theories of economic growth and realities of economic development in less developed countries (LDCs). Many old chapters have been extensively revised. Since readers may be particularly interested in understanding the basic concepts of the 'new' view of growth and economic development, I have written a short section on the theories of endogenous growth. The discussion in the section on the human development index is also new. Two new chapters have been added: one on the environment and development and the other, on the international debt crisis, is written by my valuable colleague, Nigel Healey. Sections on trade, tax reforms and financial liberalization in the 1980s in many LDCs have been extensively revised. Similarly, recent issues on migration in LDCs have been critically evaluated. To facilitate reading, I have relegated some technical and mathematical sections as appendices to the different chapters. Many new tables have been used to provide information on the recent events in LDCs. In the preparation of this edition, I am grateful to many colleagues and students. I am particularly grateful to Barbara Roberts, Ziggy MacDonald, Steve Wheatley Price and Dawn Homer for their help. I am also indebted to Alan Jarvis of Routledge for his patience and excellent co-operation.

Subrata Ghatak
University of Leicester

Preface to the second edition

The appearance of the revised edition of my book on development economics permits me to take account of the constructive criticisms and comments received from many people. In particular, I have added two new chapters: one on the 'Green Revolution and income distribution' (Chapter 9); the other on 'The new international economic order' (Chapter 12). I felt obliged to write these two chapters in view of important changes that have taken place since I wrote the first edition of my book. I hope readers will find these additions useful. New material has been incorporated in many chapters but certain topics have been dropped in keeping with the changing emphasis in development theory and policy discussion. As before, my main objective has been to achieve a reasonable balance between economic theory and economic realities in less developed countries.

I have also added appendices at the end of many chapters to clarify a number of issues which have been discussed in the text. Readers who might view some arguments in the text as being rather concise and terse should find the appendices particularly useful. However, I have also maintained the previous edition's level of maturity, restricting the text to material that requires only the background in economic theory and quantitative methods provided by the standard course on principles of economics in most universities and colleges.

I wish to thank Pat Gibbs and Charlotte Kitson for typing parts of the manuscript in record time. I also thank Clement Aysia, Nicholas Brealey and Walter Allan for their help and for forbearance.

Subrata Ghatak
University of Leicester

Preface to the first edition

The economic development of the less developed countries (LDCs) presents many important and interesting problems to students and teachers of economics. These problems are many in number and diverse in nature; it is hoped that this book will provide an analytical framework to deal with some of these major problems. It is generally known that many issues related to the economic development of the LDCs are not purely economic. Political, social and cultural factors work alongside the economic factors when the economies of the LDCs go through a process of growth and structural change. However, the problems which are dealt with in this book are mainly economic and further reference has been made in some cases to broader and very diverse institutional issues which a 'kindred spirit' may wish (rather hopefully) to explore. This explains the reason for adopting a framework of analytical economics for the discussion of most issues raised in this book.

Although some useful books on development economics are available at present, one major reason for writing this book is to strike a greater balance between theory and practice. Thus, whenever possible, the existing theories on growth and development are evaluated in terms of the economic realities of the LDCs. The other important aspect of this book is that an attempt has been made to quantify the available evidence with the use of basic statistical tools such as regression analysis. Next, given the importance which is usually attached to planning in the LDCs, a comprehensive chapter on both *macro-* and *micro-planning* with special reference to the application of cost–benefit analysis to project appraisal has been added. The role of agriculture with special reference to the supply response of farmers has been particularly emphasized. Protection, in theory and practice, has been critically discussed. Topics of current interest like the transfer of technology, the role of the multinational corporations and the new international economic order have received due attention. Also population problems, particularly the problems of controlling fertility, poverty, income distribution, rural–urban migration and employment have been analysed carefully. Thus, the chief aim of this book is to provide a comprehensive textbook based upon rigorous qualitative and quantitative analysis.

This book is aimed chiefly at third year undergraduates taking courses in the field of development economics. Some understanding of macroeconomics and microeconomics, welfare economics, elementary mathematics and statistics is assumed, though care is taken to explain complicated and technical issues in simpler ways. It is hoped that this book will also provide background reading for postgraduate courses in development economics.

The manuscript was written mainly between 1977 and 1978 while I was teaching economics at Leicester University. I received valuable and constructive comments from many people during the course of my writing. I am particularly indebted to Professor David Pearce for all his valuable comments and for his generous help and encouragement despite his very busy schedule. I am grateful to my colleague, Leo Katzen, who has not only read the entire manuscript and made many valuable suggestions for the improvement of the book, but has also been kind enough to write jointly with me Chapter 7 on 'Population, poverty and income distribution, employment and migration'; my thanks are also due to Paul Hallwood who has kindly read the entire manuscript and offered many useful comments. Thanks are also due to Peter Ayre, Ian Bradley, Anita Ghatak, Martin Hoskins, Homi Katrak, Lionel Needleman, Howard Rees, Frances Stewart and Kerry Turner for their useful comments on different chapters of this book. On a wider academic front, I have drawn material from the works of Adelman, Chenery, Corden, Hicks, Johnson, Kuznets, Meier, Myrdal, Amartya Sen, Streeten, Thirlwall and Todaro. I feel, therefore, that it is only fair to acknowledge my debt to their writings. I would like to pay tribute to Jeanne Cretney for her skill and patience, and for providing me with the necessary secretarial assistance. Also Joan Cook, Dorothy Logsdon, Elaine Humphreys and Pat Greatorex who have been kind enough to type the manuscript. Anna Cooknell and Janut Westerman have taken the trouble of drawing the diagrams. Mr M. Ramady has also helped me in the preparation of the index. To all of them, I remain very thankful. I would also like to thank the editors of the *Oxford Bulletin of Economics and Statistics* for granting permission to reproduce material from articles of mine which were originally published in that journal.

My wife Anita and my baby daughter Churni had to pay the inevitable price of being rather neglected during the last two years. I am happy to say that they have paid this price very willingly (though not always silently). As a tiny compensation, this book has been dedicated to them and to my elder brother, Debaprasun, and his son, Souma.

For all errors in this book which unfortunately remain, I take full responsibility.

Acknowledgements

We are grateful to the following for permission to reproduce copyright material. Addison-Wesley Publishing Company for a figure from *Linear Programming* by George Hadley; Basil Blackwell & Mott Ltd for figures from 'Marketed surplus in Indian agriculture: theory and practice' from *Oxford Bulletin of Economics and Statistics* 37 (1975) by S. Ghatak and a summary of a novel *Choice of Techniques* plus figures by A.K. Sen; Cambridge University Press for an extract from 'The development of a dual economy' by D. Joijenson from *Economic Journal* (1961) and a table and equations from *Exports and Economic Growth of Developing Countries* by A. Maizels (1968); Cornell University Press for a table from *Agricultural Development and Economic Growth* edited by B.F. Johnston and H.M. Southworth; the *Economic Record* and the author Professor I.G. Williamson for an equation from 'Personal savings in developing nations' in *Economic Record* (1968); Frank Cass & Co. Ltd for a summary of 'Determinants of use of special drawing rights by developing nations' and equations by Danny M. Leipziger in *Journal of Development Studies* 11 (1975) and a summary of 'The informal link between SDR allocation and aid: a note' by Graham Bird in *Journal of Development Studies* 12 (1976); George Allen & Unwin Publishers Ltd for a summary of a model in *The Economic Theory of Fiscal Policy* by Alan Peacock and G.K. Shaw (1971); Harvard University Press for extracts from 'International aid for underdeveloped countries' by Paul Rosenstein-Roden from *Review of Economics and Statistics* and a figure from 'The pricing of food in India' by M. Khusro in *Quarterly Journal of Economics* (1967); Heinemann Educational Books Ltd and Basic Books Inc. for two summaries from *Project Appraisal and Planning for Developing Countries* by I. Little and J. Mirrlees (1974); International Association for Research in Income and Wealth for a summary of 'Aspects of poverty in Malaysia' by S. Anand in *Review of Income and Wealth* 23; International Labour Office for a summary of 'The difference models on migration' from *International Migration in Developing Countries: A Review of Theory, Evidence, Methodology and Research Priorities* by Michael P. Todaro; International Monetary Fund for equations from 'Monetary analysis of incomes and imports and its statistical application' by J.J. Polack and L. Boissoneault in *IMF Staff Papers* (1959–60); Richard D. Irwin Inc. for a diagram from *Development of the Labour Surplus Economy* by J. Fei and G. Ranis; the author Baron N. Kaldor for a brief summary of 'A new model of economic growth' by N. Kaldor and J. Mirrlees in *Review of Economic Studies* and a brief summary of the equations in 'Alternative theories and distribution' by N. Kaldor from *Review of Economic Studies* (1955–6); Lexington Books for a summary of 'The indices of instability' from *Trade and Economic Development* by O. Knudsen and A. Parnes (1975); Macmillan Publishers for a table

'Determinents of fertility: a micro-economic model of choice' by Paul Schultz in *Population Factors in Economic Development* edited by A.J. Coale (1976); Macmillan Publishing Company for a figure from *Economic Dynamics*, second edition, by W.J. Baumol; Oxford University Press for a summary and figures from 'Conflicts between output and employment objectives in developing countries' by F. Stewart and P. Streeten from *Oxford Economic Papers*, a table from 'Industry and trade in developing countries' by I. Little, T. Scitovsky and M. Scott (1970), a summary of 'Overpricing in Chile' in *Intercountry Income Distribution and Transnational Enterprises* by C. Vaitsos (1974), tables from *Redistribution with Growth* by H. Chenery *et al.* (1974); Oxford University Press Eastern Africa for equations from *Development Planning* by M. Todaro (1971); Penguin Books Ltd and the author Professor W. Elkan for a figure from *An Introduction to Development Economics* (1976); Praeger Publishers and the author Professor Biehl for a summary of 'The measurement of fiscal performances in developing countries' in *Quantitative Analysis in Public Finance* (1969) edited by Alan Peacock; Prentice-Hall International for figures from *International Economics: Analysis and Issues* by Charles Staley (1970); Stanford University Press for equations from *Theories of Economic Growth and Development* by I. Adelman (1962); the *Economic Record* and the author T.W. Swan for a figure from 'Economic growth and capital accumulation' in *Economic Record (1956);* the Johns Hopkins University Press for a table from *Indirect Taxation in Developing Economies* by John Due (1970) and a table from *The Structure of Protection in Developing Countries* by Bela Balassa (1971); the *Manchester School* and the author Professor W.A. Lewis for a summary of the Lewis model in 'Economic development with unlimited supplies of labour' from *Manchester School of Economic and Social Studies;* the University of Bombay for a summary and equations from 'What kind of macro-econometric models for developing economies?' by L. Klein in *Indian Economic Journal* 13 (1965); the University of Chicago Press for a summary of 'Growth, stability and inflationary finance' by Robert A. Mundell in *Journal of Political Economy* 73; the University of Delhi for a diagram from 'Ratio of interchange between agricultural and manufactured goods in relation to capital formation in underdeveloped economics' by D. Narain in *Indian Economic Review* (1957); United Nations Industrial Development Organization for an equation from *Guidelines for Project Evaluation* by A. Sen, P. Dasgupta and S. Marglin (1972); the University of Kent for equations from 'Reconciling the conflict between employment and saving and output in the choice of techniques in developing countries' by A.P. Thirlwall; Weidenfeld & Nicolson Ltd for figures from 'Saving and foreign exchange constraints' by V. Josh in *Unfashionable Economics* (1970); Yale University for a table 'Evidence on African small-holder supply elasticities' from 'Small-holder decision making tropical African evidence' by G.K. Helleiner in *Agriculture in Development Theory* edited by Lloyd Reynolds (1975).

1 Introduction

1.1 Introduction

The problems of the economic development of the poor countries of today's world is one of the most widely discussed topics of our time. Experts in various fields such as economics, politics, sociology and engineering have held different views about the nature of underdevelopment and poverty, its causes and its remedies. It has now been fully recognized that the nature and causes of the 'poverty of the nations' are very complex and the remedies are neither easy nor quick. The understanding of the problem of underdevelopment requires a good knowledge of certain basic characteristics of the less developed countries (henceforward to be referred to as LDCs). The analysis of these characteristics will shed some light on the peculiar economic and social conditions of production, consumption and distribution of income and wealth in the LDCs, which will help us to draw some policy implications.

1.2 Characteristics of the less developed countries

1.2.1 Low per capita *real income*

Low *per capita* real income is generally regarded as one of the main indicators of the socioeconomic conditions of the LDCs. A comparison with the economically developed countries (DCs) is striking (see Tables 1.1–5). It shows very clearly the difference between the DCs and the LDCs. If the *per capita* income of the United States and India are considered, it is clear that an average Indian earned about 1.5 per cent of the income of an average American in 1999. Most of the LDCs exhibit this very low ratio of income to population. It shows the relatively low level of national income in most LDCs, or a high level of population, or both. Low *per capita* real income is a reflection of low productivity, low saving and investment and backward technology and resources, while the level of population is determined by complex socioeconomic factors. Hence, the importance of population in relation to national income in the LDCs can hardly be overemphasized, and this is discussed in the next section.

1.2.2 Population

Most LDCs generally experience a high population growth rate or, where the population growth rate is not very high *in comparison with other LDCs,* the size of the population may be very high (e.g. China and India). LDCs usually experience high birth rates

Table 1.1 LDCs' economic performance, 2000–1

Country	Gross domestic product (average annual % growth)		Exports of goods and services (average annual % growth)		Imports of goods and services (average annual % growth)		GDP deflator (% growth)		Current account balance (% of GDP)		Gross international reserves	
	2000	2001	2000	2001	2000	2001	2000	2001	2000	2001	US$ million 2001	Months of import coverage 2001
Algeria	2.4	3.6	7.4	−1.1	7.0	17.2	23.7	5.3	–	12.3	17,863	13.1
Argentina	−0.5	−1.7	2.0	5.2	−0.5	−1.8	1.1	−0.1	−3.1	−2.8	20,964	5.3
Armenia	6.0	9.6	16.6	12.7	10.0	−1.8	−1.3	4.0	−14.6	−15.2	337	4.7
Azerbaijan	11.1	8.5	17.8	16.4	8.9	25.3	13.0	3.5	−2.8	−13.5	679	2.8
Bangladesh	5.9	6.0	8.6	17.3	5.7	17.8	1.9	3.4	0.0	−2.7	1,653	1.8
Bolivia	2.4	0.0	6.1	6.1	1.3	0.2	3.7	3.5	−5.6	−4.8	1,034	5.4
Brazil	4.5	2.0	11.0	8.6	13.8	5.0	8.5	6.0	−4.1	−4.3	27,078	3.5
Bulgaria	5.8	4.5	24.2	7.9	14.6	5.3	5.6	7.0	−5.8	−6.0	3,423	4.5
Cameroon	4.2	5.3	−4.9	1.9	16.0	11.4	3.5	3.0	−1.7	−2.0	11	0.0
Chile	5.4	3.2	7.5	18.2	10.1	16.4	4.0	4.1	−1.4	−2.1	16,331	8.0
China	7.9	7.3	32.0	5.0	24.8	13.0	0.9	2.0	1.9	1.6	185,662	7.4
Colombia	2.8	1.8	5.3	1.5	5.8	18.1	10.7	11.1	0.4	−2.7	9,185	5.8
Congo. Rep.	7.9	3.1	9.1	−1.5	17.3	0.2	46.4	−12.4	–	−14.4	–	–
Costa Rica	1.7	0.6	−0.5	−4.2	−5.0	2.0	7.1	10.0	–	−5.5	1,003	1.4
Côte d'Ivoire	−2.3	−1.5	−1.9	−2.7	1.0	−1.8	−0.1	2.9	−0.1	−5.0	–	–
Croatia	3.7	4.0	8.7	7.1	4.2	10.3	6.5	5.4	−2.1	−4.4	4,422	4.6
Dominican Rep.	7.8	2.0	8.7	4.4	14.5	0.1	7.7	6.0	−5.2	−2.4	850	1.1
Ecuador	2.3	4.6	−0.2	0.0	18.7	31.1	105.9	18.0	–	−0.2	1,408	2.3
Egypt, Arab Rep.	5.1	3.3	10.3	6.5	2.5	−3.8	5.8	3.1	−1.2	0.0	–	–
El Salvador	2.0	2.0	15.8	−2.6	14.8	1.6	3.9	3.7	−3.2	−6.5	1,710	4.1
Estonia	6.4	4.2	3.5	4.8	3.8	4.5	5.3	−0.5	−6.3	−5.5	1,272	2.8
Ghana	3.7	4.0	−2.3	0.3	−17.3	2.0	27.2	34.6	−7.9	−12.4	431	1.4
Guatemala	3.3	1.9	4.8	1.1	2.6	2.7	5.5	7.3	−5.5	−4.5	2,152	4.5
Honduras	4.8	2.5	14.6	−3.1	8.0	4.0	9.0	9.5	−3.4	−4.7	1,386	4.7
India	5.2	4.5	5.0	−1.6	5.0	2.9	5.3	6.0	−0.6	−1.2	42,636	6.2
Indonesia	4.8	3.3	16.1	−3.3	18.2	6.0	11.0	10.0	5.2	2.6	30,085	5.4
Iran, Islamic Rep.	5.4	5.1	11.8	−4.5	14.2	20.2	22.3	16.9	12.1	6.9	22,886	11.8
Jamaica	0.8	1.5	4.4	1.8	4.3	1.9	10.6	8.8	−3.7	−5.5	1,451	–
Jordan	3.9	3.5	2.1	14.1	13.0	12.4	−0.6	1.1	0.7	−2.7	3,226	5.7

Kazakhstan	9.6	13.2	23.9	−3.0	10.9	22.0	17.5	11.6	5.9	−5.0	2,508	2.7
Kenya	−0.2	2.0	8.6	3.1	18.1	1.4	6.8	5.0	−2.3	−8.0	743	2.2
Latvia	6.6	7.0	12.8	6.5	4.8	6.1	4.3	2.4	−6.9	−6.8	–	–
Lithuania	3.9	3.8	12.9	10.2	4.5	8.1	2.1	0.8	−6.0	−6.0	–	–
Macedonia, FYR	4.3	−4.6	19.2	–	33.0	–	8.0	6.0	−3.0	–	–	–
Malawi	1.7	2.8	−5.3	11.1	−18.2	6.0	24.5	28.0	−30.8	−10.8	–	–
Malayasia	8.3	1.1	26.2	3.0	16.3	1.3	4.7	3.0	–	6.2	–	–
Mauritius	8.0	5.5	5.5	6.3	0.7	5.9	0.0	12.1	−0.8	0.8	982	3.5
Mexico	6.9	0.9	16.0	−2.4	21.4	−3.4	10.9	7.0	−3.2	−3.1	39,463	2.3
Moldova	1.9	6.1	7.5	16.4	30.6	12.3	27.0	12.0	−9.4	−8.0	227	2.4
Morocco	0.9	6.5	4.4	1.4	7.8	2.3	1.6	2.5	−1.4	−0.8	7,018	6.2
Nicaragua	4.3	3.0	11.5	2.2	−8.5	0.3	11.6	8.2	−20.6	−30.5	539	3.0
Nigeria	3.8	2.9	−1.6	1.9	16.0	16.9	25.4	6.9	17.0	−4.0	–	–
Pakistan	4.4	3.4	16.0	7.2	−2.3	6.2	3.7	5.5	−3.6	−3.3	2,080	1.7
Panama	2.7	2.0	5.7	4.8	−0.8	−3.7	0.8	1.6	−9.4	−6.0	743	1.5
Papua N. Guinea	0.3	3.0	2.4	2.3	–	–	15.6	7.7	−0.2	−5.9	442	1.8
Paraguay	−0.3	−0.5	−31.6	1.7	−11.7	−1.4	8.9	9.0	−4.0	−2.7	936	3.3
Peru	3.1	0.5	7.9	1.1	3.6	7.4	3.6	1.5	−3.0	−2.6	8,732	8.6
Philippines	4.0	2.5	6.6	−12.3	0.2	−6.7	6.7	8.3	12.2	7.8	16,574	4.5
Poland	4.0	1.1	6.0	–	−2.5	–	7.2	6.0	−6.3	–	28,004	6.4
Romania	1.6	4.5	23.9	11.7	29.1	21.0	45.3	35.0	−3.7	−4.7	4,591	3.4
Russian Federation	8.3	5.5	4.3	2.6	17.5	16.5	37.1	20.5	16.7	11.4	40,806	6.2
Slovak Republic	2.2	2.8	15.9	7.0	10.2	13.0	6.5	6.4	−3.6	−8.5	6,441	4.4
South Africa	3.1	2.5	8.2	3.1	7.4	9.2	6.5	6.0	−0.4	−0.3	15,532	5.1
Sri Lanka	6.0	2.5	7.2	8.3	12.9	0.9	7.1	13.5	−6.2	−4.0	1,050	1.5
Syrian Arab Rep.	2.5	0.8	21.4	–	11.0	–	1.1	2.0	6.3	0.6	3,264	–
Thailand	4.3	1.6	15.4	−0.1	20.4	−2.1	1.8	2.0	7.7	4.7	30,141	4.5
Trinidad & Tobago	4.8	4.5	1.2	−2.1	16.2	14.3	9.8	3.4	–	3.7	1,849	4.3
Tunisia	4.7	5.4	6.6	6.8	9.6	6.3	2.4	2.5	−4.2	−4.3	2,442	2.7
Turkey	7.2	−6.5	10.5	10.2	33.4	−20.1	50.6	60.7	−4.9	1.3	18,938	4.1
Uganda	3.5	6.0	−0.7	10.1	6.3	6.6	3.3	5.5	−13.9	−13.4	858	5.0
Ukraine	5.8	7.0	13.8	10.2	17.5	11.5	25.3	11.3	4.7	2.8	2,980	1.7
Uruguay	−1.3	−1.2	4.0	0.8	−0.9	−6.0	3.6	5.1	−3.0	−2.9	2,800	6.8
Uzbekistan	4.0	3.8	−5.6	1.5	−6.2	8.6	44.3	42.8	2.4	−0.5	1,160	4.2
Venezuela, RB	3.2	3.3	5.8	−3.7	19.5	3.3	26.8	9.6	11.1	5.1	16,401	7.4
Zambia	3.5	5.0	4.9	26.7	7.2	21.6	18.1	24.9	0.0	−20.3	–	–
Zimbabwe	−4.9	−8.1	−16.6	−3.8	−21.6	−2.5	59.9	70.0	0.0	−1.0	–	–

Note: Data for 2001 are the latest preliminary estimates, and may differ from those in earlier World Bank publications.

Source: World Bank staff estimates.

Table 1.2 Key macroeconomic indicators

Country	Nominal exchange rate: Local currency per $	Nominal exchange rate: % change		Real effective exchange rate (1995 = 100)		Money and quasi money (annual % growth)		Gross domestic credit (annual % growth)		Real interest rate (%)		Short-term debt[a] (% of exports)
	2001	2000	2001	2000	2001	2000	2001	2000	2001	2000	2001	2000
Algeria	77.8	8.7	3.3	107.7	113.2	13.2	–	−19.5	–	−11.0	9.5	1.0
Argentina	1.0	0.0	0.0	–	–	1.5	−16.5	−2.7	2.9	9.8	50.0	73.8
Armenia	561.8	5.4	1.7	108.7	91.6	38.6	15.2	12.3	−1.6	33.4	26.7	7.9
Azerbaijan	4,775.0	4.3	4.6	–	–	73.4	−10.8	13.5	−33.3	–	–	6.9
Bangladesh	57.0	5.9	5.6	–	–	19.3	15.5	13.7	17.7	13.4	15.8	3.4
Bolivia	6.8	6.7	6.7	117.9	117.7	0.4	3.4	−0.9	−3.7	29.7	20.1	23.8
Brazil	2.3	8.9	19.0	–	–	4.3	10.9	8.6	29.7	44.5	61.9	44.8
Bulgaria	2.2	7.7	5.7	120.7	128.1	28.8	–	9.8	–	5.6	–	5.8
Cameroon	744.3	8.0	5.6	95.7	100.4	19.1	17.2	−0.8	5.3	17.9	20.7	48.7
Chile	656.2	8.0	14.6	106.0	90.8	6.2	11.3	13.9	14.5	10.4	10.4	10.7
China	8.3	0.0	0.0	107.6	109.6	12.3	14.5	10.9	8.1	4.9	5.9	5.9
Colombia	2,301.3	16.7	5.2	95.6	101.1	14.8	18.9	12.1	13.2	7.3	20.7	15.9
Congo. Rep.	744.3	8.0	5.6	–	–	58.5	6.4	−28.1	16.4	−16.6	20.7	40.0
Costa Rica	341.7	6.7	7.4	106.8	114.5	18.4	8.6	22.0	3.3	16.6	23.8	12.0
Côte d'Ivoire	744.3	8.0	5.6	96.5	100.6	−1.9	2.1	−4.5	−7.2	–	–	22.9
Croatia	8.4	6.7	2.5	98.9	104.3	29.1	29.2	9.3	25.8	5.3	8.5	7.3
Dominican Rep.	17.2	3.9	2.9	110.3	116.2	17.4	27.6	20.5	23.1	17.7	24.3	10.8
Ecuador	25,000.0	23.5	0.0	73.3	113.1	11.1	31.0	−6.8	30.7	−43.5	15.0	13.3
Egypt, Arab Rep.	4.5	8.2	21.7	–	–	11.6	–	11.1	–	7.0	–	19.0
El Salvador	8.8	0.0	−0.1	–	–	1.0	–	3.1	–	9.7	–	20.5
Estonia	17.7	8.1	5.2	–	–	25.7	23.0	27.2	24.4	2.2	9.4	19.2
Ghana	7,190.0	99.4	2.0	81.1	88.4	38.4	–	50.4	–	–	–	23.6
Guatemala	8.0	−1.2	3.5	–	–	35.5	9.4	13.5	−15.4	14.6	19.0	28.8
Honduras	15.9	4.4	5.2	–	–	24.4	13.0	29.8	13.3	16.4	23.4	12.5
India	48.2	7.5	3.1	–	–	15.2	14.6	16.0	12.4	7.8	12.0	4.5
Indonesia	10,400.0	35.4	8.4	–	–	15.9	13.0	26.2	8.1	6.7	19.2	30.5
Iran, Islamic Rep.	1,751.0	29.1	−22.6	297.7	360.7	22.4	26.5	12.8	15.1	–	–	12.2
Jamaica	47.3	10.0	4.1	–	–	13.0	13.2	−1.8	−20.6	11.6	19.5	16.5
Jordan	0.7	0.0	0.0	–	–	7.6	–	1.8	–	12.4	–	12.1
Kazakhstan	150.2	4.6	3.9	–	–	45.0	35.9	70.6	6.0	–	–	4.9

Kenya	79.0	7.0	–0.4	–	–	4.5	4.5	1.3	2.8	14.5	19.8	29.2
Latvia	0.6	5.2	4.9	–	–	27.0	17.8	43.1	31.8	7.2	9.3	35.8
Lithuania	4.0	0.0	0.0	–	–	16.5	21.4	–3.1	5.8	9.8	7.0	21.0
Macedonia, FYR	68.6	9.9	–2.3	72.8	74.0	21.4	–	–17.2	–	10.1	–	4.5
Malawi	67.3	72.4	–16.0	112.7	146.4	41.4	4.4	24.4	9.9	23.0	56.2	15.7
Malayasia	3.8	0.0	0.0	86.6	92.7	9.9	6.7	9.6	7.5	1.9	6.7	4.1
Mauritius	30.4	9.5	9.0	–	–	9.2	9.3	4.8	12.7	20.8	21.0	28.8
Mexico	9.1	0.6	–4.5	–	–	–4.2	5.7	–2.6	–3.5	6.6	13.9	9.8
Moldova	12.9	6.8	4.5	109.8	105.9	41.7	40.5	14.4	20.4	5.3	27.1	3.4
Morocco	11.6	5.3	8.9	108.2	101.6	8.4	14.7	11.2	3.4	11.6	–	2.0
Nicaragua	13.8	6.0	6.0	113.1	115.8	9.4	6.5	9.3	16.4	8.7	22.8	75.9
Nigeria	–	11.8	–	81.0	98.9	48.1	–	–25.3	–	–3.3	–	5.1
Pakistan	60.9	12.1	4.9	93.6	89.3	12.1	–	10.6	–	–	–	14.2
Panama	1.0	0.0	0.0	–	–	10.0	–	7.6	–	9.3	10.2	5.0
Papua N. Guinea	3.8	13.7	22.5	92.8	83.6	5.0	–0.6	–2.1	–6.2	1.7	14.7	2.2
Paraguay	4,718.1	5.9	33.8	97.1	85.0	4.8	16.4	11.7	16.7	16.4	30.5	18.2
Peru	3.4	0.6	–2.8	–	–	–0.4	1.6	–0.3	0.3	23.4	20.4	39.3
Philippines	51.4	24.0	2.8	89.8	84.9	8.1	1.5	9.3	1.8	4.0	11.9	12.0
Poland	4.0	–0.2	–3.6	121.6	134.8	11.8	–	7.2	–	12.0	–	14.4
Romania	31,597.0	42.0	21.9	107.1	111.2	38.0	48.8	15.5	33.4	–	–	2.9
Russian Federation	30.1	4.3	7.0	90.5	109.2	58.4	36.2	13.7	26.3	–9.2	17.0	13.4
Slovak Republic	–	12.1	–	109.3	107.9	15.2	–	8.2	–	7.9	–	8.0
South Africa	12.1	23.1	60.2	82.9	64.3	7.2	15.1	14.0	12.3	7.5	13.0	24.7
Sri Lanka	93.2	14.4	12.8	–	–	12.8	–	26.2	–	8.5	–	9.2
Syrian Arab Rep.	11.2	0.0	0.0	–	–	19.0	–	–7.8	–	–	–	79.6
Thailand	44.2	15.5	2.2	–	–	3.4	2.4	–7.5	–6.1	5.9	7.3	17.3
Trinidad & Tobago	6.2	0.0	–1.0	115.4	128.8	11.7	–	–6.2	–	6.1	–	17.7
Tunisia	1.4	11.2	–2.7	100.8	99.4	14.1	11.7	27.5	20.4	–	–	9.7
Turkey	1,477,524.0	24.4	116.1	–	–	40.0	95.3	75.9	134.0	–	–	49.4
Uganda	17272.4	17.3	–2.2	96.0	103.2	18.1	–	73.9	–	19.0	21.4	14.2
Ukraine	5.3	4.0	–2.4	118.4	119.7	44.4	43.2	23.1	18.8	12.9	32.3	2.3
Uruguay	14.8	7.7	18.0	113.1	110.1	7.2	11.7	1.4	1.7	43.8	51.7	42.6
Uzbekistan	–	–	–	–	–	–	–	–	–	–	–	8.3
Venezuela, RB	763.0	7.9	9.0	161.6	176.8	23.1	13.8	15.4	34.8	–1.3	23.1	4.7
Zambia	3,830.4	58.0	–7.9	113.3	120.9	73.8	–	59.5	–	17.6	46.2	8.0
Zimbabwe	55.0	44.4	–0.1	–	–	68.9	105.6	66.4	73.0	5.2	–	26.4

Note: Data for 2001 are preliminary and may not cover the entire year. [a] More recent data on short-term debt are available on a Web siite maintained by the Bank for International Settlements, the International Monetary Fund, the Organization for Economic Co-operation and Development, and the World Bank: www.oecd.org/debt.

Source: International Monetary Fund, *International Financial Statistics*; World Bank, Debtor Reporting System.

Table 1.3 Growth of output, 1980–90 and 1990–2000 (average annual %)

Country	*Gross domestic product*		*Agriculture*		*Industry*		*Manufacturing*		*Services*	
	1980–90	*1990–2000*	*1980–90*	*1990–2000*	*1980–90*	*1990–2000*	*1980–90*	*1990–2000*	*1980–90*	*1990–2000*
Afghanistan	–	–	–	–	–	–	–	–	–	–
Albania	1.5	3.3	1.9	6.0	2.1	−0.4	–	−6.6	−0.4	3.8
Algeria	2.7	1.9	4.1	3.6	2.6	1.8	4.1	−2.1	3.0	1.9
Angola	3.4	1.3	*0.5*	−1.5	*6.4*	3.7	*−11.1*	−0.4	*1.3*	−2.0
Argentina	−0.7	4.3	0.7	3.4	−1.3	3.8	−0.8	2.8	0.0	4.5
Armenia	–	−1.9	–	0.4	–	−7.9	–	−4.3	–	6.7
Azerbaijan	–	−6.3	–	*0.6*	–	*−2.8*	–	*−21.1*	–	*2.3*
Bangladesh	4.3	4.8	2.7	2.9	4.9	7.3	3.0	7.2	4.4	4.5
Belarus	–	−1.6	–	−4.1	–	−1.9	–	−0.8	–	−0.5
Benin	2.5	4.7	5.1	5.8	3.4	4.1	5.1	5.8	0.7	4.1
Bolivia	−0.2	4.0	–	3.3	–	4.0	–	–	–	4.3
Bosnia & Herz	–	–	–	–	–	–	–	–	–	–
Botswana	10.3	4.7	3.3	0.8	10.2	2.9	8.7	4.1	11.7	6.9
Brazil	2.7	2.9	2.8	3.2	2.0	2.6	1.6	*2.1*	3.3	3.0
Bulgaria	3.4	−2.1	−2.1	0.4	5.2	−3.7	–	–	4.5	−1.3
Burkina Faso	3.6	4.9	3.1	4.2	3.8	5.9	2.0	7.0	4.6	4.6
Burundi	4.4	−2.6	3.1	−1.6	4.5	−5.6	5.7	*−8.0*	5.6	−2.0
Cambodia	–	4.8	–	1.9	–	8.3	–	*8.2*	–	6.9
Cameroon	3.4	1.7	2.2	5.6	5.9	−0.8	5.0	1.4	2.1	0.2
Central African Rep.	1.4	2.0	1.6	3.9	1.4	0.8	5.0	0.0	1.0	−0.5
Chad	6.1	2.2	2.3	4.4	8.1	2.2	–	–	6.7	1.2
Chile	4.2	6.8	5.9	1.5	3.5	6.0	3.4	4.6	2.9	5.6
China	10.1	10.3	5.9	4.1	11.1	13.7	11.1	13.4	13.5	9.0
Hong Kong, China	6.9	4.0	–	–	–	–	–	–	–	–
Colombia	3.6	3.0	2.9	−2.2	5.0	1.7	3.5	−2.3	3.1	4.3
Congo, Dem. Rep.	1.6	*−5.1*	2.5	*2.9*	0.9	*−11.7*	1.6	*−13.4*	1.3	*−15.2*
Congo, Rep.	3.3	−0.4	3.4	1.3	5.2	2.6	6.8	−2.8	2.1	−3.9
Costa Rica	3.0	5.3	3.1	4.1	2.8	6.2	3.0	6.7	3.3	4.7
Côte d'Ivoire	0.7	3.5	0.3	3.6	4.4	5.1	3.0	3.8	−0.3	2.6
Croatia	–	0.6	–	−2.0	–	−2.5	–	−3.3	–	0.9
Cuba	–	*4.2*	–	*5.2*	–	*6.6*	–	*6.3*	–	*2.5*
Czech Rep.	–	0.9	–	3.3	–	−0.8	–	–	–	1.8
Dominician Rep.	3.1	6.0	−1.0	3.7	3.0	7.1	2.3	4.9	4.2	5.9
Ecuador	2.0	1.8	4.4	1.7	1.2	2.7	0.0	2.1	1.7	1.3
Egypt, Arab Rep.	5.4	4.6	2.7	3.1	3.3	4.9	–	6.3	7.8	4.5
El Salvador	0.2	4.7	−1.1	1.3	0.1	5.3	−0.2	5.3	0.7	5.4
Eritrea	–	*3.9*	–	*−1.0*	–	–	–	–	–	–
Estonia	2.2	−0.5	–	−3.1	–	−3.2	–	*2.5*	–	1.8
Ethiopia	*1.1*	4.7	*0.2*	2.1	*0.4*	6.1	*−0.9*	6.6	*3.1*	7.1
Gabon	0.9	2.8	1.2	−1.4	1.5	2.5	1.8	*0.6*	0.1	3.9
Gambia	3.6	3.1	0.9	2.7	4.7	1.1	7.8	1.0	2.7	4.3
Georgia	–	−13.0	–	*1.7*	–	*5.1*	–	*3.2*	–	*15.6*
Ghana	3.0	4.3	1.0	3.4	3.3	2.6	3.9	−3.3	5.7	5.7
Greece	0.9	2.1	−0.1	*0.5*	1.3	*1.1*	–	–	0.9	*2.4*
Guatemala	0.8	4.1	1.2	2.8	−0.2	4.3	0.0	2.8	0.9	4.7
Guinea	–	4.3	–	4.3	–	4.7	–	4.1	–	3.6
Guinea-Bissau	4.0	1.2	4.7	3.9	2.2	−3.1	–	−2.0	3.5	−0.6
Haiti	−0.2	−0.6	−0.1	−3.3	−1.7	1.2	−1.7	−10.8	0.9	0.2
Honduras	2.7	3.2	2.7	2.0	3.3	3.7	3.7	3.9	2.5	3.8
Hungary	1.3	1.5	1.7	−2.2	0.2	3.8	–	*7.9*	2.1	1.4
India	5.8	6.0	3.1	3.0	6.9	6.4	7.4	7.0	7.0	8.0
Indonesia	6.1	4.2	3.6	2.1	7.3	5.2	12.8	6.7	6.5	4.0
Iran, Islamic Rep.	1.7	3.5	4.5	3.8	3.3	−3.8	4.5	4.7	−1.0	9.2
Iraq	−6.8	–	–	–	–	–	–	–	–	–
Israel	3.5	5.1	–	–	–	–	–	–	–	–

Table 1.3 (continued)

	Gross domestic product		*Agriculture*		*Industry*		*Manufacturing*		*Services*	
Country	*1980–90*	*1990–2000*	*1980–90*	*1990–2000*	*1980–90*	*1990–2000*	*1980–90*	*1990–2000*	*1980–90*	*1990–2000*
Jamaica	2.0	0.5	0.6	1.9	2.4	−0.5	2.7	−1.9	1.8	1.1
Jordan	2.5	5.0	6.8	−2.0	1.7	4.7	0.5	5.4	2.3	5.0
Kazakhstan	–	−4.1	–	−7.9	–	−9.0	–	–	–	2.8
Kenya	4.2	2.1	3.3	1.3	3.9	1.7	4.9	2.1	4.9	3.3
Korea, Dem. Rep.	–	–	–	–	–	–	–	–	–	–
Korea, Rep.	8.9	5.7	3.0	2.0	11.4	6.3	12.1	7.5	8.4	5.7
Kuwait	*1.3*	*3.2*	*14.7*	–	*1.0*	–	*2.3*	–	*2.1*	–
Kyrgyz Rep.	–	−4.1	–	1.5	–	−10.4	–	−14.3	–	−6.4
Lao PDR	*3.7*	6.5	*3.5*	4.9	*6.1*	11.0	*8.9*	11.7	*3.3*	*6.5*
Latvia	3.5	−3.4	2.3	−7.0	4.3	−8.4	4.4	−7.8	3.3	2.5
Lebanon	–	6.0	–	*1.8*	–	*−1.6*	–	*−4.3*	–	*4.1*
Lesotho	4.5	4.1	2.8	1.8	4.9	5.9	8.5	6.6	4.0	4.4
Liberia	*−1.7*	–	*1.2*	–	*−6.0*	–	*−5.0*	–	*−0.8*	–
Libya	*−5.7*	–	–	–	–	–	–	–	–	–
Lithuania	–	−3.1	–	−1.1	–	−7.0	–	−8.5	–	−0.3
Macedonia, FYR	–	−0.8	–	0.3	–	−2.5	–	−4.4	–	0.7
Madagascar	1.1	2.0	2.5	1.4	0.9	2.4	*2.1*	*0.6*	0.3	2.5
Malawi	2.5	3.8	2.0	7.6	2.9	1.6	3.6	−2.1	3.3	3.4
Malaysia	5.3	7.0	3.4	0.3	6.8	8.6	9.3	9.8	4.9	7.2
Mali	0.8	3.8	3.3	3.2	4.3	6.6	6.8	3.0	1.9	2.9
Mauritania	1.8	4.2	1.7	5.0	4.9	2.4	*−2.1*	−0.5	0.4	4.9
Mauritius	6.2	5.3	2.9	−0.9	10.3	5.5	11.1	5.6	5.5	6.4
Mexico	1.1	3.1	0.8	1.8	1.1	3.8	1.5	4.4	1.4	2.9
Moldova[a]	2.8	−9.7	–	−13.7	–	−16.7	–	–	–	*1.9*
Mongolia	*5.4*	1.0	*1.4*	3.2	*6.6*	−0.5	–	–	*8.4*	0.1
Morocco	4.2	2.3	6.7	−0.9	3.0	3.2	4.1	2.7	4.2	2.8
Mozambique	−0.1	6.4	*6.6*	5.5	*−4.5*	14.0	–	*17.6*	*9.1*	1.7
Myanmar	0.6	*6.6*	0.5	*5.3*	0.5	*10.1*	−0.2	*7.0*	0.8	*6.8*
Namibia	1.3	4.1	2.5	4.1	−0.1	*2.3*	3.3	*2.7*	2.1	*4.6*
Nepal	4.6	4.9	4.0	2.5	8.7	7.2	9.3	9.2	3.9	6.2
Nicaragua	−1.9	3.5	−2.2	5.7	−2.3	4.2	−3.2	1.8	−1.5	1.8
Niger	−0.1	2.4	1.7	3.2	−1.7	2.0	*−2.7*	2.6	−0.7	1.9
Nigeria	1.6	2.4	3.3	3.5	−1.1	1.0	0.7	1.2	3.7	2.9
Oman	8.4	*5.9*	7.9	–	10.3	–	20.6	–	5.9	–
Pakistan	6.3	3.7	4.3	4.4	7.3	3.9	7.7	3.5	6.8	4.4
Panama	0.5	4.1	2.5	2.0	−1.3	5.4	0.4	2.8	0.7	4.0
Papua N. Guinea	1.9	4.0	1.8	3.7	1.9	5.5	0.1	5.6	2.0	3.0
Paraguay	2.5	2.2	3.6	2.5	0.3	3.2	4.0	0.7	3.1	1.6
Peru	−0.1	4.7	3.0	5.8	0.1	5.4	−0.2	3.8	−0.4	4.0
Philippines	1.0	3.3	1.0	1.6	−0.9	3.3	0.2	3.0	2.8	4.1
Poland	–	4.6	–	−0.2	–	4.2	–	–	–	*4.1*
Portugal	3.1	2.7	2.8	−0.3	3.2	3.2	–	–	2.3	2.3
Puerto Rico	4.0	*3.1*	1.8	–	3.6	–	3.6	–	4.6	–
Romania	0.5	−0.7	–	−0.6	–	−0.8	–	*−2.8*	–	−0.5
Russian Federation	–	−4.8	–	*−6.0*	–	−7.6	–	–	–	*−1.0*
Rwanda	2.2	−0.2	0.5	−2.3	2.5	2.8	2.6	6.6	5.5	−0.1
Saudi Arabia	0.0	1.5	13.4	*0.7*	−2.3	*1.5*	7.5	*2.7*	1.3	*2.0*
Senegal	3.1	3.6	2.8	1.9	4.3	4.8	4.6	4.0	2.8	3.8
Sierra Leone	1.2	−4.3	3.1	−0.1	1.7	−6.2	–	*5.0*	−2.7	−10.3
Slovak Rep.	*2.0*	2.1	*1.6*	1.2	*2.0*	−2.7	–	*4.1*	*0.8*	6.5
Slovenia	–	2.7	–	*−0.1*	–	*2.9*	–	*4.0*	–	*3.9*
Somalia	2.1	–	3.3	–	1.0	–	−1.7	–	0.9	–
South Africa	1.0	2.0	2.9	0.6	0.7	1.0	1.1	1.2	2.4	2.6

continued on next page

Table 1.3 (continued)

Country	*Gross domestic product*		*Agriculture*		*Industry*		*Manufacturing*		*Services*	
	1980–90	*1990–2000*	*1980–90*	*1990–2000*	*1980–90*	*1990–2000*	*1980–90*	*1990–2000*	*1980–90*	*1990–2000*
Sri Lanka	4.0	5.3	2.2	1.9	4.6	7.0	6.3	8.1	4.7	6.0
Sudan	0.4	8.1	−0.6	11.3	*1.3*	7.7	3.4	4.0	*1.9*	6.3
Swaziland	6.5	3.3	2.5	1.0	11.2	3.9	14.0	3.0	4.9	3.5
Syrian Arab Rep.	1.5	5.8	−0.6	5.3	6.6	9.9	–	10.8	1.6	4.6
Tajikistan	*2.0*	−10.4	*−2.8*	−5.8	*5.5*	−16.6	*5.6*	−12.6	*3.4*	−0.4
Tanzania[b]	–	2.9	–	3.2	–	3.1	–	2.7	–	2.7
Thailand	7.6	4.2	3.9	2.1	9.8	5.3	9.5	6.4	7.3	3.7
Togo	1.7	2.3	5.6	4.0	1.1	2.8	1.7	2.9	−0.3	0.4
Trinidad and Tobago	−0.8	3.0	−5.9	1.9	−5.5	3.4	−10.1	5.9	6.7	2.7
Tunisia	3.3	4.7	2.8	2.4	3.1	4.6	3.7	5.5	3.5	5.3
Turkey	5.4	3.7	1.3	1.4	7.8	4.1	7.9	4.8	4.4	3.7
Turkmenistan	–	−4.8	–	−5.7	–	−3.2	–	–	–	−5.8
Uganda	*2.9*	7.0	*2.1*	3.7	*5.0*	12.3	*3.7*	13.6	*2.8*	7.9
Ukraine	–	−9.3	–	−5.8	–	−11.4	–	−11.2	–	−1.1
United Arab Emirates	−2.1	*2.9*	9.6	–	−4.2	–	3.1	–	3.6	–
Uruguay	0.5	3.4	*1.8*	2.8	*1.2*	1.1	*1.7*	−0.1	*2.4*	4.6
Uzbekistan	–	−0.5	–	0.1	–	−3.2	–	–	–	0.3
Venezuela, RB	1.1	1.6	3.1	1.4	1.7	2.9	4.4	0.9	0.5	0.4
Vietnam	*4.6*	7.9	*4.3*	4.8	–	12.1	–	–	–	7.7
West Bank and Gaza	–	*2.8*	–	*−4.2*	–	*0.8*	–	*3.6*	–	*2.8*
Yemen, Rep.	–	5.8	–	5.1	–	7.9	–	4.4	–	5.1
Yugoslavia, Fed. Rep.	–	*0.6*	–	–	–	–	–	–	–	–
Zambia	1.0	0.5	3.6	3.9	1.0	−4.0	4.1	1.2	−0.2	2.6
Zimbabwe	3.6	2.5	3.1	4.3	3.2	0.4	2.8	0.4	3.0	3.1
World	**3.3 w**	**2.7 w**	**2.5 w**	**1.4 w**	**3.1 w**	**1.5 w**	**– w**	**– w**	**– w**	**2.9 w**
Low income	4.5	3.2	3.0	2.5	5.5	2.7	7.8	2.6	5.5	5.1
Middle income	3.3	3.6	3.5	2.0	3.6	3.9	4.6	6.2	3.6	3.9
Lower middle income	4.1	3.6	4.2	2.1	5.9	4.1	7.0	8.9	5.5	4.3
Upper middle income	2.7	3.6	2.7	1.9	2.6	3.7	3.6	*4.1*	3.0	3.7
Low and middle	3.5	3.5	3.4	2.2	3.9	3.7	4.9	5.7	3.9	4.1
income			4.4	3.1	9.3	9.3	10.4	9.9	8.6	6.4
East Asia and Pacific	7.9	7.2								
Europe and Central Asia	–	−1.5	–	−2.3	–	−3.8	–	–	–	*1.6*
Latin American and Carib.	1.7	3.3	2.3	2.3	1.4	3.3	1.4	*2.6*	1.9	3.4
Middle East and N. Africa	2.0	3.0	5.2	2.6	0.3	*0.9*	–	3.8	2.4	*4.5*
South Asia	5.6	5.6	3.2	3.1	6.8	6.2	7.0	6.6	6.5	7.1
Sub-Saharan Africa	1.6	2.5	2.3	2.8	1.2	1.6	1.7	1.6	2.4	2.6
High income	3.3	2.5	1.4	*0.0*	2.9	*0.7*	–	–	–	–
Europe EMU	2.4	1.9	1.1	1.3	1.6	1.0	–	*1.2*	2.9	2.2

Notes: [a] Excludes data for Transnistria. [b] Data cover mainland Tanzania only. Italic figures indicate slightly different period.

Source: World Bank 2002.

but the advancement of medical science has led to a significant reduction in the death rates (except in some African countries). This has engendered a situation which has been generally termed 'population explosion'. One of the main implications of such population explosion has been the growth of the proportion of people who live on the subsistence level or 'poverty line', defined as the line of minimum calorie intake to stay alive in LDCs. Another aspect of population growth has been the growth of the proportion of unemployed people in the LDCs who tend to migrate, chiefly from the villages to the cities, in search of a livelihood.

1.2.3 Unemployment, underemployment and disguised unemployment and low productivity

Large-scale unemployment is a common feature of most LDCs. Factors like population pressure, the absence of job opportunities, either because of the low level of economic activity or because of the poor growth rate or both, the choice of techniques which are capital rather than labour intensive, education which is unrelated to economic needs, rigid wages set without much regard to the social opportunity cost of labour and lack of investment could all explain such unemployment problems. The phenomenon of underemployment noticed in many LDCs is a situation whereby the type of employment has not much relation to the qualification of the employees, wages are above the marginal productivity of labour and a large portion of labour-hours remains unused. Disguised unemployment is supposed to occur when the employment of an additional unit of labour does not add anything to production. The reason for employment could be, say, family considerations rather than profit maximization. Reliable information about actual unemployment in the LDCs is difficult to obtain, but most data suggest that the proportion of unemployment in the LDCs varies between 8 per cent and 35 per cent (Turnham and Jaegar 1971). The unemployed and the underemployed together in the LDCs would probably be about 30 per cent of the total work force (Todaro 1981). However, most data on labour utilization in the LDCs are rather weak, particularly in the rural areas. Both the quantity and quality of information are better for industrial employment which in most LDCs varies between 5 per cent and 25 per cent. Substantial difficulties are involved in the measurement of the actual level of underemployment and disguised unemployment in LDCs in the light of the production conditions and objective functions of these economies. Owing to the nature of the agricultural production cycle, work is sometimes available for six months in a year when labour shortage rather than labour surplus may be observed, particularly during the sowing and harvesting seasons in agriculture. Such seasonalities must be accounted for in the estimation of unemployment. Also, if *family* income or output rather than profit maximization is regarded as the objective condition, then the comparison between the marginal product of labour and wages becomes less meaningful.

Labour in the LDCs is relatively abundant in relation to capital and the productivity of labour is usually low in most LDCs in comparison with such productivity in the DCs. Such low productivity is the outcome of the paucity of capital and other resources, backward technology, lack of proper education, training and skill, and poor health and nutrition.

Table 1.4 Structure of output, 1990 and 2000 (% of GDP)

	Gross domestic product (US$ million)		*Agriculture value added*		*Industry value added*		*Manufacturing value added*		*Services value added*	
Country	*1990*	*2000*	*1990*	*2000*	*1990*	*2000*	*1990*	*2000*	*1990*	*2000*
Afghanistan	–	–	–	–	–	–	–	–	–	–
Albania	2,102	3,752	36	51	48	26	42	12	16	23
Algeria	62,045	53,306	11	9	48	60	11	8	40	31
Angola	10,260	8,828	18	6	41	76	5	3	41	18
Argentina	141,352	284,960	8	5	36	28	27	18	56	68
Armenia	4,124	1,914	17	25	52	36	33	24	31	39
Azerbaijan	9,837	5,267	–	19	–	38	–	7	–	43
Bangladesh	30,129	47,106	29	25	21	24	13	15	50	51
Belarus	35,203	29,950	24	15	47	37	39	31	29	47
Benin	1,845	2,168	36	38	13	14	8	9	51	48
Bolivia	4,868	8,281	26	22	20	15	17	13	54	63
Bosnia & Herz.	–	4,394	–	12	–	26	–	16	–	62
Botswana	3,766	5,285	5	4	56	44	5	5	39	52
Brazil	464,989	595,458	8	7	39	29	*25*	24	53	64
Bulgaria	20,726	11,995	18	15	51	28	–	17	31	58
Burkina Faso	2,765	2,192	32	35	22	17	16	12	45	48
Burundi	1,132	689	56	51	19	18	13	*9*	25	31
Cambodia	1,115	3,183	56	37	11	20	5	*6*	33	42
Cameroon	11,152	8,879	25	44	29	20	15	11	46	36
Central African Rep.	1,488	963	48	55	20	20	11	9	33	26
Chad	1,739	1,407	29	39	18	14	14	11	53	47
Chile	30,323	70,545	9	11	41	34	20	16	50	56
China	354,644	1,079,948	27	16	42	51	33	35	31	33
Hong Kong, China	74,784	162,642	0	*0*	25	*14*	18	*6*	74	*85*
Colombia	40,274	81,283	17	14	38	31	21	14	45	56
Congo, Dem. Rep.	9,348	*5,584*	30	–	28	–	11	–	42	–
Congo, Rep.	2,799	3,215	13	5	41	71	8	3	46	24
Costa Rica	5,713	15,851	18	9	29	31	22	24	53	59
Côte d'Ivoire	10,796	9,370	32	29	23	22	21	19	44	48
Croatia	*18,156*	19,031	10	9	34	33	28	23	56	58
Cuba	–	–	–	7	–	46	–	37	–	47
Czech Rep.	34,880	50,777	6	4	49	41	–	–	45	55
Dominician Rep.	7,074	19,669	13	11	31	34	18	17	55	55

Ecuador	10,686	13,607	13	10	38	40	19	17	49	50
Egypt, Arab Rep.	43,130	98,725	19	17	29	34	18	19	52	49
El Salvador	4,807	13,211	17	10	26	30	22	23	57	60
Eritrea	*437*	608	*29*	*17*	*19*	*29*	*13*	*15*	*52*	*54*
Estonia	6,760	4,969	17	6	50	*27*	42	16	34	67
Ethiopia	6,842	6,391	49	52	13	11	8	7	38	37
Gabon	5,952	4,932	7	6	32	53	6	4	50	40
Gambia	317	422	29	38	13	13	7	5	58	49
Georgia	12,171	3,029	32	32	33	13	24	7	35	55
Ghana	5,886	5,190	45	35	17	25	10	9	38	39
Greece	84,075	112,646	11	*8*	28	*24*	–	*12*	61	*68*
Guatemala	7,650	18,988	26	23	20	20	15	13	54	57
Guinea	2,818	3,012	24	24	33	37	5	4	43	39
Guinea-Bissau	244	215	61	59	19	12	8	10	21	29
Haiti	2,981	4,050	32	28	21	20	15	7	48	51
Honduras	3,049	5,932	22	18	26	32	16	20	51	51
Hungary	33,056	45,633	15	*6*	39	*34*	*23*	*25*	46	*61*
India	316,891	456,990	31	25	28	27	17	16	41	48
Indonesia	114,427	153,255	20	17	38	47	18	26	42	36
Iran, Islamic Rep.	120,404	104,904	24	19	29	22	12	16	48	59
Iraq	48,657	–	–	–	–	–	–	–	–	–
Israel	52,490	110,386	–	–	–	–	–	–	–	–
Jamaica	4,239	7,403	6	6	43	31	20	13	50	62
Jordan	4,020	8,340	8	2	28	25	15	16	64	73
Kazakhstan	40,304	18,230	*27*	9	*45*	43	*9*	18	*29*	48
Kenya	8,533	10,357	29	20	19	19	12	13	52	61
Korea, Dem. Rep.	–	–	–	–	–	–	–	–	–	–
Korea, Rep.	252,622	457,219	9	5	43	43	29	31	48	53
Kuwait	18,428	37,783	1	–	52	–	12	–	47	–
Kyrgyz Rep.	2,951	1,304	34	39	36	26	28	6	30	34
Lao PDR	865	1,709	61	53	15	23	10	17	24	24
Latvia	12,490	7,150	22	4	46	25	34	14	32	70
Lebanon	2,838	16,488	–	12	–	22	–	10	–	66
Lesotho	615	899	24	17	33	44	14	16	43	39
Liberia	–	–	–	–	–	–	–	–	–	–
Libya	–	–	–	–	–	–	–	–	–	–
Lithuania	13,254	11,314	27	8	31	33	21	21	42	59
Macedonia, FYR	4,472	3,573	9	12	46	33	36	21	46	55
Madagascar	3,081	3,878	32	35	14	13	12	–	53	52
Malawi	1,881	1,697	45	42	29	19	19	14	26	39

continued on next page

Table 1.4 (continued)

Country	Gross domestic product (US$ million)		Agriculture value added		Industry value added		Manufacturing value added		Services value added	
	1990	*2000*	*1990*	*2000*	*1990*	*2000*	*1990*	*2000*	*1990*	*2000*
Malaysia	44,024	89,659	15	11	42	45	24	33	43	44
Mali	2,421	2,298	46	46	16	17	9	4	39	37
Mauritania	1,020	935	30	22	29	31	10	9	42	47
Mauritius	2,642	4,381	12	6	32	32	24	24	56	62
Mexico	262,710	574,512	8	4	28	28	21	21	64	67
Moldova[a]	10,567	1,286	31	28	39	20	–	16	30	52
Mongolia	–	969	17	33	30	19	–	5	52	48
Morocco	25,821	33,345	18	14	32	32	18	18	50	54
Mozambique	2,463	3,754	37	24	18	25	10	13	44	50
Myanmar	–	–	57	*60*	11	*9*	8	*7*	32	*31*
Namibia	2,530	3,479	11	*11*	35	*28*	13	*11*	54	*61*
Nepal	3,628	5,497	52	40	16	22	6	10	32	37
Nicaragua	1,009	2,396	31	32	21	23	17	14	48	45
Niger	2,481	1,826	35	39	16	18	7	7	49	44
Nigeria	28,472	41,085	33	30	41	46	6	4	26	25
Oman	10,535	*14,962*	3	–	58	–	4	–	39	–
Pakistan	40,010	61,638	26	26	25	23	17	15	49	51
Panama	5,313	9,889	9	7	15	17	9	8	76	76
Papua N. Guinea	3,221	3,818	29	26	30	44	9	9	41	30
Paraguay	5,265	7,521	28	21	25	27	17	14	47	52
Peru	26,294	53,466	7	8	23	27	15	14	70	65
Philippines	44,331	74,733	22	16	34	31	25	23	44	53
Poland	58,976	157,739	8	4	50	36	–	*21*	42	60
Portugal	70,863	105,054	9	4	31	31	–	*19*	60	66
Puerto Rico	30,604	–	1	–	42	–	40	–	57	–
Romania	38,299	36,719	20	13	50	36	–	27	30	51
Russian Federation	579,068	251,106	17	7	48	39	–	–	35	54
Rwanda	2,584	1,794	33	44	25	21	19	12	42	35
Saudi Arabia	104,670	173,287	6	*7*	50	*48*	8	*10*	43	*45*
Senegal	5,698	4,371	20	18	19	27	13	18	61	55
Sierra Leone	897	636	47	47	20	30	4	5	33	23
Slovak Rep.	15,485	19,121	7	4	59	31	–	22	33	65
Slovenia	*12,673*	18,129	*6*	3	*46*	38	*35*	28	*49*	58
Somalia	917	–	65	–	–	–	5	–	–	–

South Africa	111,997	125,887	5	3	40	31	24	19	55	66
Sri Lanka	8,032	16,305	26	20	26	27	15	17	48	53
Sudan	13,167	11,516	–	37	–	18	–	9	–	45
Swaziland	842	1,478	14	17	43	44	35	33	44	39
Syrian Arab Rep.	12,309	16,984	28	24	24	30	20	27	48	46
Tajikistan	4,339	991	33	19	38	26	25	23	29	55
Tanzania[b]	4,259	9,027	46	45	18	16	9	7	36	39
Thailand	85,345	122,166	12	10	37	40	27	32	50	49
Togo	1,628	1,219	34	38	23	22	10	10	44	40
Trinidad and Tobago	5,068	7,312	3	2	46	43	9	8	51	55
Tunisia	12,291	19,462	16	12	30	29	17	18	54	59
Turkey	150,721	199,937	18	16	30	25	20	15	52	59
Turkmenistan	8,129	4,404	32	27	30	50	–	40	38	23
Uganda	4,304	6,170	57	42	11	19	6	9	32	38
Ukraine	91,327	31,791	26	14	45	38	36	34	30	48
United Arab Emirates	34,132	*46,481*	2	–	64	–	8	–	35	–
Uruguay	9,287	19,715	9	6	35	27	28	17	56	67
Uzbekistan	*23,673*	7,666	33	35	33	23	–	10	34	42
Venezuela, RB	48,593	120,484	5	5	50	36	20	14	44	59
Vietnam	6,472	31,344	37	24	23	37	19	*18*	40	39
West Bank and Gaza	–	4,359	–	8	–	27	–	15	–	66
Yemen, Rep.	4,828	8,532	24	15	27	46	9	7	49	38
Yugoslavia, Fed. Rep.	–	8,449	–	–	–	–	–	–	–	–
Zambia	3,288	2,911	21	27	51	24	36	13	28	49
Zimbabwe	8,784	7,392	16	18	33	25	23	16	50	57
World	**21,816,968 t**	**31,492,776 t**	**7 w**	**5 w**	**36 w**	**31 w**	**– w**	**22 w**	**57 w**	**64 w**
Low income	890,673	1,048,306	29	24	30	32	18	18	41	44
Middle income	3,518,514	5,513,236	13	9	39	36	*25*	25	47	55
Lower middle income	1,656,455	2,347,172	21	13	40	41	27	27	39	45
Upper middle income	1,879,581	3,170,508	9	7	39	32	*24*	23	52	62
Low and middle income	4,403,910	6,560,552	16	12	38	35	23	32	46	54
East Asia and Pacific	927,056	2,059,121	20	13	40	46	28	–	40	41
Europe and Central Asia	1,252,935	942,079	17	10	44	35	–	21	39	57
Latin American and Carib.	1,132,901	2,000,535	9	7	36	29	*23*	*14*	55	64
Middle East and N. Africa	401,331	659,692	15	*14*	39	*37*	12	16	47	*48*
South Asia	404,744	596,794	31	25	27	26	17	14	43	49
Sub-Saharan Africa	297,641	322,730	18	17	34	30	17	–	48	53
High income	17,413,841	24,927,330	–	–	–	–	–	*21*	–	–
Europe EMU	5,539,185	6,048,446	4	2	34	29	*25*		62	68

Notes: [a] Excludes data for Transnistria. [b] Data cover mainland Tanzania only. Italic figures indicate slightly different period.

Source: World Bank.

Table 1.5 Structure of demand, 1990 and 2000 (% of GDP)

Country	*Household final consumption expenditure*		*General government final consumption expenditure*		*Gross capital formation*		*Exports of goods and services*		*Imports of goods and services*		*Gross domestic savings*	
	1990	*2000*	*1990*	*2000*	*1990*	*2000*	*1990*	*2000*	*1990*	*2000*	*1990*	*2000*
Afghanistan	–	–	–	–	–	–	–	–	–	–	–	–
Albania	61	92	19	11	29	19	15	19	23	40	21	–3
Algeria	57	42	16	14	29	24	23	42	25	22	27	44
Angola	36	17	34	39	12	28	39	90	21	74	30	44
Argentina	77	71	3	14	14	16	10	11	5	11	20	15
Armenia	46	96	18	12	47	19	35	23	46	51	36	–8
Azerbaijan	–	59	–	12	–	26	–	41	–	38	–	28
Bangladesh	86	78	4	5	17	23	6	14	14	19	10	18
Belarus	47	59	24	20	27	23	46	68	44	69	29	21
Benin	87	82	11	12	14	20	14	15	26	29	2	6
Bolivia	77	74	12	16	13	18	23	18	24	25	11	11
Bosnia & Herz.	–	110	–	–	–	20	–	27	–	58	–	–10
Botswana	39	*58*	24	*28*	32	*20*	55	*28*	50	*33*	37	*14*
Brazil	59	63	19	18	20	21	8	11	7	12	21	19
Bulgaria	60	71	18	18	26	17	33	58	37	64	22	11
Burkina Faso	77	76	15	15	21	28	13	11	26	30	8	9
Burundi	95	93	11	13	15	9	8	9	28	24	–5	–6
Cambodia	91	92	7	–	8	15	6	40	13	47	2	8
Cameroon	67	69	13	10	18	16	20	31	17	27	21	20
Central African Rep.	86	81	15	11	12	11	15	13	28	16	–1	8
Chad	89	91	10	8	16	17	13	17	29	32	0	1
Chile	62	63	10	12	25	23	35	32	31	31	28	25
China	50	47	12	13	35	37	18	26	14	23	38	40
Hong Kong, China	57	58	7	10	27	28	134	150	126	145	36	32
Colombia	66	67	9	19	19	12	21	22	15	20	24	14
Congo, Dem. Rep.	79	–	12	–	9	–	30	–	29	–	9	–
Congo, Rep.	62	28	14	11	16	24	54	79	46	42	24	61
Costa Rica	61	67	18	13	27	17	35	48	41	46	21	19
Côte d'Ivoire	72	71	17	10	7	12	32	46	27	39	11	19
Croatia	*74*	57	*24*	26	14	22	*78*	45	*86*	51	–21	16
Cuba	–	70	–	23	–	10	–	16	–	18	–	7
Czech Rep.	49	54	23	20	25	30	45	71	43	75	28	26
Dominician Rep.	80	78	5	8	25	24	34	30	44	39	15	14

Ecuador	69	62	9	9	17	17	33	42	27	31	23	28
Egypt, Arab Rep.	73	73	11	10	29	24	20	16	33	23	16	17
El Salvador	89	88	10	10	14	17	19	28	31	43	1	2
Eritrea	*98*	*132*	*33*	–	*5*	38	*20*	16	*57*	86	*–31*	–32
Estonia	62	58	16	21	30	26	*60*	84	*54*	88	22	21
Ethiopia	74	78	19	23	12	14	8	15	12	331	7	–1
Gabon	50	62	13	10	22	26	46	37	31	35	37	28
Gambia	76	83	14	13	22	17	60	48	72	61	11	4
Georgia	65	82	10	13	31	15	40	37	46	47	25	5
Ghana	85	81	9	15	14	24	17	49	26	70	5	3
Greece	72	*71*	15	*15*	23	*22*	18	*20*	28	*29*	13	*14*
Guatemala	84	84	7	7	14	17	21	20	25	28	10	9
Guinea	73	77	9	6	18	22	31	26	31	31	18	17
Guinea-Bissau	87	95	10	14	30	18	10	32	37	58	3	–9
Haiti	93	*100*	8	7	12	11	16	12	29	27	–1	–4
Honduras	66	66	14	13	23	35	36	42	40	56	20	21
Hungary	61	64	11	10	25	31	31	63	29	67	28	26
India	66	65	12	13	25	24	7	14	10	17	22	21
Indonesia	59	67	9	7	31	18	25	39	24	31	32	26
Iran, Islamic Rep.	62	52	11	14	29	20	22	35	24	21	27	34
Iraq	–	–	–	–	–	–	–	–	–	–	–	–
Israel	56	59	30	29	25	19	35	40	45	47	14	12
Jamaica	62	68	14	16	28	27	52	44	56	55	24	16
Jordan	74	81	25	25	32	20	62	42	93	69	1	–6
Kazakhstan	*52*	63	*18*	11	*32*	14	*74*	59	*75*	47	*30*	25
Kenya	67	78	19	18	20	13	26	26	31	36	14	4
Korea, Dem. Rep.	–	–	–	–	–	–	–	–	–	–	–	–
Korea, Rep.	53	58	10	10	38	29	29	45	30	42	37	31
Kuwait	57	41	39	22	18	11	45	57	58	31	4	37
Kyrgyz Rep.	71	77	25	19	24	16	29	43	50	55	4	4
Lao PDR	–	*82*	–	*5*	–	*24*	–	*36*	–	*48*	–	*13*
Latvia	53	63	9	19	40	27	48	46	40	54	39	19
Lebanon	140	88	25	19	18	18	18	13	100	38	–64	–7
Lesotho	139	101	14	18	53	40	17	28	122	88	–53	20
Liberia	–	–	–	–	–	–	–	–	–	–	–	–
Libya	–	–	–	–	–	–	–	–	–	–	–	–
Lithuania	57	64	19	21	33	21	52	45	61	52	24	14
Macedonia, FYR	72	82	19	18	19	17	26	45	36	62	9	0
Madagascar	86	87	8	7	17	16	17	25	27	35	6	6
Malawi	72	82	15	17	23	13	24	26	33	38	13	1

continued on next page

Table 1.5 (continued)

Country	*Household final consumption expenditure*		*General government final consumption expenditure*		*Gross capital formation*		*Exports of goods and services*		*Imports of goods and services*		*Gross domestic savings*	
	1990	*2000*	*1990*	*2000*	*1990*	*2000*	*1990*	*2000*	*1990*	*2000*	*1990*	*2000*
Malaysia	52	43	14	11	32	26	75	125	72	104	34	47
Mali	80	79	14	13	23	23	17	25	34	40	6	7
Mauritania	69	68	26	17	20	30	46	41	61	57	5	15
Mauritius	65	66	12	12	31	26	65	64	72	67	24	22
Mexico	70	68	8	11	23	23	19	31	20	33	22	21
Moldova[b]	*58*	89	*15*	16	25	22	49	50	51	77	23	−5
Mongolia	58	66	32	20	38	30	24	65	53	82	9	14
Morocco	65	63	15	19	25	24	26	31	32	37	19	18
Mozambique	101	79	12	12	16	34	8	15	36	39	−12	10
Myanmar	89	87	–	–	13	*13*	3	*0*	5	*1*	11	*13*
Namibia	46	*54*	28	*29*	35	24	47	*49*	56	*56*	26	*17*
Nepal	83	75	9	9	18	24	11	24	21	32	8	16
Nicaragua	59	88	43	19	19	34	25	40	46	81	−2	−7
Niger	84	84	15	13	8	11	15	15	22	23	1	3
Nigeria	56	45	15	21	15	23	43	52	29	41	29	34
Oman	27	–	38	–	13	–	53	–	31	–	35	–
Pakistan	74	77	15	11	19	16	16	16	23	19	11	12
Panama	60	61	18	15	17	30	38	33	34	39	21	24
Papua N. Guinea	59	*66*	25	*13*	24	*18*	41	*45*	49	*42*	16	*21*
Paraguay	77	83	6	10	23	22	33	20	39	35	17	7
Peru	74	71	8	11	16	20	16	16	14	18	18	18
Philippines	72	63	10	13	24	18	28	56	33	50	18	24
Poland	48	64	19	16	26	27	29	27	22	34	33	20
Portugal	62	63	16	20	28	28	33	31	40	43	21	16
Puerto Rico	–	–	–	–	–	–	–	–	–	–	–	–
Romania	66	74	13	13	30	19	17	34	26	40	21	14
Russian Federation	49	46	21	16	30	17	18	46	28	25	30	38
Rwanda	84	88	10	12	15	15	6	8	14	24	6	−1
Saudi Arabia	40	33	31	27	20	16	46	50	36	26	30	40
Senegal	76	79	15	10	14	20	25	31	30	40	9	11
Sierra Leone	82	91	10	17	9	8	24	17	25	33	8	−8
Slovak Rep.	54	53	22	19	33	30	27	74	36	76	24	28
Slovenia	*55*	55	*19*	21	*17*	28	*84*	59	*74*	63	*26*	24
Somalia	*112*	–	–	–	16	–	10	–	38	–	−12	–

South Africa	63	64	20	18	12	15	24	29	19	26	18	18
Sri Lanka	76	72	10	10	23	28	29	40	38	51	14	17
Sudan	–	85	–	–	–	14	–	17	–	16	–	15
Swaziland	62	75	18	20	20	20	76	66	76	81	21	4
Syrian Arab Rep.	69	62	14	13	17	21	28	38	28	35	17	24
Tajikistan	74	76	9	8	25	20	28	81	35	85	17	16
Tanzania[c]	81	84	18	7	26	18	13	15	37	23	1	9
Thailand	57	60	9	9	41	23	34	67	42	59	34	31
Togo	71	83	14	11	27	21	33	36	45	50	15	6
Trinidad and Tobago	59	56	12	12	13	19	45	65	29	52	29	32
Tunisia	58	60	16	16	32	27	44	44	51	48	25	24
Turkey	69	69	11	14	24	24	13	24	18	31	20	17
Turkmenistan	49	34	23	16	40	40	–	63	–	53	28	49
Uganda	92	87	8	11	13	18	7	10	19	26	1	3
Ukraine	57	58	17	19	27	19	28	61	29	57	26	23
United Arab Emirates	39	–	16	–	20	–	65	–	40	–	45	–
Uruguay	70	75	12	13	12	14	24	19	18	21	18	12
Uzbekistan	61	64	25	20	32	11	29	44	48	39	13	17
Venezuela, RB	62	63	8	7	10	18	39	29	20	17	29	30
Vietnam	86	69	8	6	13	27	26	–	33	–	6	25
West Bank and Gaza	–	92	–	32	–	33	–	14	–	71	–	−24
Yemen, Rep.	74	58	17	14	15	19	14	50	20	41	9	28
Yugoslavia, Fed. Rep.	–	79	–	25	–	14	–	32	–	50	–	−4
Zambia	64	86	19	11	17	18	36	31	37	46	17	3
Zimbabwe	63	63	19	24	17	13	23	30	23	31	17	12
World	**59 w**	**61 w**	**17 w**	**17 w**	**24 w**	**22 w**	**20 w**	**23 w**	**20 w**	**23 w**	**24 w**	**23 w**
Low income	66	67	12	12	24	20	17	28	20	28	21	20
Middle income	59	59	14	15	26	24	21	32	20	29	27	26
Lower middle income	56	54	13	14	31	26	22	36	22	30	30	32
Upper middle income	61	62	15	15	23	22	21	29	19	28	24	23
Low and middle income	60	60	14	14	26	23	21	31	20	29	26	26
East Asia and Pacific	54	54	11	11	35	30	26	42	26	37	35	35
Europe and Central Asia	55	58	18	16	28	21	23	44	24	39	26	26
Latin American and Carib.	65	66	13	15	19	20	14	17	12	18	21	19
Middle East and N. Africa	57	51	20	18	24	20	33	38	35	28	23	30
South Asia	69	68	12	12	24	23	9	15	13	18	20	20
Sub-Saharan Africa	66	66	17	17	15	17	27	32	26	32	16	17
High income	59	*61*	18	*17*	23	*22*	20	*22*	20	*22*	24	*22*
Europe EMU	56	57	20	20	23	22	28	34	28	33	24	23

Notes: [a] Data on general government final consumption expenditure are not available separately; they are included in household final consumption expenditure. [b] Excludes data for Transnistria. [c] Data cover mainland Tanzania only. Italic figures indicate slightly different period.

Source: World Bank.

1.2.4 Poverty

Evidence from the LDCs with regard to the level of poverty suggests that a very significant proportion of their populations earn a level of income which varies between $50 and $75 per annum at 1990 prices. This income is regarded as the minimum level for bare survival in the LDCs. It has been estimated that about 1.4 *billion* people, which accounts for about 35 per cent of the world's population, lived at 'subsistence level' by the end of 1990. This figure is staggering and more recent evidence may well suggest that the present situation might have deteriorated further. People who live on the poverty line in the LDCs usually reside in the rural areas. This raises the problem of income distribution not only among the rich and the poor countries but also within the LDCs themselves.

1.2.5 Income distribution

The pattern of income distribution within the LDCs shows considerable variation. In general, there is evidence to suggest that the pattern of income distribution tends to be more unequal in most LDCs in comparison with the DCs (Ahluwalia 1974). However, the hypothesis that the high rates of growth of income in the LDCs will always have an adverse effect on relative equality has been rejected on the basis of some evidence from the LDCs (Ahluwalia 1974). But this evidence does not alter the proposition that many LDCs experience severe inequalities in income distribution although some suffer less than others. In any case, evidence from forty-four LDCs suggest that, on average, only about 6 per cent of national income accrues to the poorest 20 per cent of the population, whereas 30–56 per cent of national income is obtained by the highest-paid 5–20 per cent of the population. In some LDCs such inequalities are extreme. For instance, in Jamaica the poorest 20 per cent of the population obtain only 2.2 per cent of national income, whereas the highest-paid 20 per cent obtain about 62 per cent of such income. In Iraq, Gabon and Colombia, the share of the poorest 20 per cent and richest 20 per cent in national income is 2 per cent and 68 per cent, 2 per cent and 71 per cent, 2.2 per cent and 68.1 per cent respectively (Jarvis 1973; see also Todaro 1981). However, some of the LDCs like Taiwan (1964), South Korea (1970) and Sri Lanka (1969–70) show low inequality as measured by the Gini coefficients which stood at 0.32, 0.36 and 0.37 respectively for these countries (Ahluwalia 1974; see also Appendix 1A). It is important to note that the technological progress in agriculture in some LDCs – sometimes called the 'Green Revolution' – has led to a substantial rise in farm income and profits among the richer section of the peasants who have easy access to the crucial inputs like fertilizers, irrigation facilities, better seeds, credit and marketing facilities. This has simply heightened the problem of the distribution of such gains more equally, particularly among the poorer section of the rural population who depend mainly on agriculture for their livelihood. It has sometimes been regarded as the 'second-generation' problem of the green revolution which requires urgent attention in the LDCs for maintenance of both economic and socio-political stability (see Chapter 9).

1.2.6 Predominance of agriculture in the national economy

Agriculture usually dominates the economies of many LDCs. It generally accounts for 45–90 per cent of the total output and about 60–95 per cent of total employment. Clearly, the economic growth and development of these countries will be closely tied to the general development of agriculture. Unfortunately, many LDCs, in order to promote rapid economic growth, neglected agriculture and decided to promote industrialization as quickly as possible. The need for industrialization in the 'basic' sectors of the LDCs is generally understood and recognized. What is less clearly understood in most LDCs is that a basic industry cannot be built without a basis. Such a basis is usually provided by a well-developed agricultural sector which would supply 'wage goods', food, raw materials, labour, markets and foreign exchange for the development of both the industrial and agricultural sectors. This balanced growth between agriculture and industry received inadequate attention from the planners and policy makers of most LDCs with the result that most developments have accrued to the urban rather than the rural sector where the overwhelming majority of the total population live in the LDCs – a phenomenon which has been described as the 'urban bias' (Lipton 1968a). It is suggested that this 'urban' rather than 'rural' bias could explain why poor people stay poor in most LDCs. Resources are usually directed for the growth of 'modern' industrial sectors and, whatever the gains in real income that accrue to the economy, are usually distributed within the modern sector while the poor, rural sector is driven into further impoverishment and deprivation of resources (Lipton 1977). In 1980 the American agricultural labourer produced, on average, output worth $7.11; his counterpart in Africa and Asia produced output worth only $0.21.

Agriculture in many LDCs is characterized by high pressure on land, use of very backward technology, low saving and investment and hence poor productivity. A large majority of the peasants live in abject poverty and the rate of literacy is also very poor. The land is usually scattered and fragmented and the distribution of land ownership is haphazard in most cases. The use of modern technology like better seeds and chemical fertilizers is largely unknown in many parts although there are pockets of agriculture where modern farming methods, particularly the use of better seeds and fertilizers, have made some progress. However, the availability of adequate water supply remains an important bottleneck in the development of agriculture in many LDCs. It has been demonstrated that, without adequate water supply, the adoption of modern farming methods, like the use of fertilizers, is likely to show signs of diminishing returns (Ishikawa 1967). It seems reasonable to suggest that the future development strategy for many LDCs could involve a recasting of priorities, and the development of the agricultural sector requires most serious consideration.

1.2.7 Foreign trade

Foreign trade generally forms a rather small part of the national income in many LDCs. There are some exceptions, however, e.g. Hong Kong, Singapore, Malaysia, Thailand and Taiwan. The pattern of foreign trade for most LDCs is usually characterized by former colonial trade relationships. This means that just as the former colonies used to export the primary commodities and raw materials to the imperial countries at the centre and import from them the finished products, so today's LDCs are chiefly net exporters of primary products and net importers of industrial goods. In a way, such a trading relationship is dictated by economic history since most LDCs of today were under the political domination of today's DCs. Also, the pattern of trade reflects the pattern of production and resource mobilization in the LDCs and DCs. Primary exports from the LDCs chiefly consist of agricultural goods (e.g. jute and tea from India, coffee from Brazil, tea from Sri Lanka, cocoa from Ghana). The income from such exports sometimes fluctuates quite sharply because of either demand or supply conditions or both (see Chapter 13). These goods are generally exported to only a few markets – a phenomenon which is regarded as 'market or geographic concentration', where the export of a few goods is known as 'commodity concentration'. The fluctuation in export earnings is related to the fluctuation in the production cycles of agricultural goods on the *supply* side. Also, the development of many synthetic products has largely reduced the *demand* for primary goods from the LDCs. Note that the demand for a primary product is not usually price and income-dependent. This implies that although there has been significant increase in the income (both total and *per capita*) of DCs in the last hundred years, the demand for the primary product has increased less than proportionately and this has contributed to the decline in the export earnings of LDCs. Similarly, when the prices of primary goods fell, demand did not rise in equal proportion and again the export revenue of the LDCs was lost. There is some evidence to suggest that the ratio of export prices to import prices (the terms of trade) secularly moved against the LDCs *vis-à-vis* the DCs (though not in all periods) over the twentieth century, but this has been debated (see Chapter 7). Fluctuations in foreign exchange earnings of the LDCs are also observed, though their causes and consequences are still very much open to discussion. However, schemes for the stabilization of the export earnings of the LDCs have received major attention in the United Nations Conference on Trade and Development (UNCTAD) as well as in the present north–south dialogue (1977) through the funding of a commodity butter stock scheme (see Chapter 13).

1.3 Types of markets in less developed countries

After discussing the major features of the LDCs, it is useful to look at the operation of the different forms of markets in the LDCs. In traditional economic theory it is generally argued that, given the free operation of market forces, free competition will ensure the optimum or most efficient allocation of all the existing resources and the situation will be Pareto optimal, i.e. it will be impossible to increase the welfare of any one individual without reducing the welfare of others. However, in most LDCs the market or the 'invisible hand' does not always operate very smoothly and indeed instances of market 'failure' are rather frequent. An analysis of the production conditions in different market forms in the LDCs is necessary to illustrate the point.

1.4 Production conditions in less developed countries

Let us assume, in line with standard economic theory, that total output produced within a country (Q) is given by land (L_a), labour (L), capital (K) and organization (R). More formally

$$Q = f(L_a, L, K, R)$$

Resource allocation will be optimal at the point where the marginal productivity of the different factors is equal to the factor prices (see Appendix 1.2). Such an allocation would also be socially most efficient as long as there is no difference between the social and the private costs of production. Private profits in a competitive economy will be maximized by applying the standard rule of equating marginal cost of producing the goods to prices (which, under free competition, are also equal to marginal revenue), and if there is no difference between private profit and social benefit, social welfare will also be maximized. It is contended that this 'if' is a big 'if' because markets in most LDCs are neither free nor homogeneous and hence the application of the marginal principles to LDCs will not achieve their objectives. The nature of this criticism can be understood more clearly if the different types of markets in the LDCs are briefly discussed.

1.4.1 Land

Land in most LDCs is one of the major inputs, if not the major input, of production. The pattern of land ownership in most LDCs suggests that a great proportion of cultivated land is held by a small minority of landowners, whereas a great majority of the peasants frequently hold a small proportion of such land. Given the predominance of agriculture in the economies of the LDCs, and the fact that land is usually the most important form of asset to be held, particularly in the rural areas, the impact of haphazard distribution of land on income distribution can easily be realized. The system of land ownership is also very complicated and a distinction is generally made between (1) owner-cultivators; (2) the sharecroppers who provide, say, bullocks and ploughs for cultivation for some return from cultivation; (3) the tenants; and (4) the agricultural labourers who are usually hired and fired with the fluctuations of production cycles in agriculture. Obviously, the sharecroppers, tenants and agricultural labourers will not have much incentive to work when the returns from labour are generally low and fixed and when they are not the legal landowners. Land is generally fragmented, differing in soil structure, fertility and productivity. Many cultivators who own big plots of land are absentee landlords who take little interest in investment in the land, pay low wages to the hired labourers and could easily become the agents of 'exploitation'. The legal records of title to land are very difficult to obtain in most LDCs. In most cases, very backward techniques are used for production and the returns from land are usually low. Although the peasants are not generally unresponsive to economic opportunities, the lack of better inputs could lower such returns. But even if the inputs are provided, these may be available only to a certain class of farmers without showing tangible benefits for the vast majority of the peasants. The land market is far from free.

Adverse weather conditions usually aggravate the dire poverty of the tenants and landless labourers, and some small peasants are forced to sell the land and go into debt. Under such circumstances, it is no surprise that the 'Indian peasants are born in debt, live in debt and die in debt'. All this could well imply the urgent necessity to introduce major institutional changes and land reform in many LDCs.

1.4.2 Labour market

Most LDCs experience high growth rates of population which add to the flow of labour supply every year. The labour market is far from homogeneous. Lack of skilled labour is observed in many African and some Asian countries. The supply of labour tends to exceed its demand by a significant amount which results in unemployment – open, disguised or underemployment. Labour is primarily engaged in agriculture and services. The mobility of labour between the different regions is not high. Wages tend to differ significantly between the industrial urban and the rural agricultural areas, and migration usually occurs in substantial numbers from the villages to the towns. The level of wages usually paid in the LDCs does not bear any close relationship to the marginal productivity of labour, particularly in the rural areas. In many cases such wages are administered either by custom or by legislation, rather than being market determined. Lack of proper educational facilities, poor health and standards of nutrition, and paucity of both physical and social capital could account for the low productivity that is often observed in the labour market in most LDCs.

1.4.3 Capital market

The capital market in the LDCs is often narrow and difficult to measure. Usually, buildings, machinery and equipment are treated as parts of capital. The definition of capital is always difficult and such a definition can only be broad in the context of the LDCs because even the provision of some consumer goods could increase the flow of future income. Thus, the provision of education, shelter, transport and health services could easily add to the flow of future income and could be regarded as important elements of social capital.

Capital is one of the most scarce and important inputs in the LDCs and thus most LDCs have given major emphasis to the role of capital formation for economic growth. Low income generates low saving, low investment, low productivity and low income and the 'vicious' circle is complete. The market for capital is assuredly characterized by duality, with the organized urban sector using sophisticated means to borrow and lend capital, whereas the unorganized rural sector remains outside the control of modern business practices. The money market is also characterized by 'financial dualism' (Myint 1971), where the organized sector uses modern banking and financial methods of transaction, and the unorganized rural money markets are generally dominated by the 'unholy' trinity of the 'landlords-cum-merchants-cum-moneylenders' who frequently, acting as monopolists and monopsonists, could be the agents of 'exploitation'. The flow of funds between the two sectors is rather limited.

The capital scarcity in the LDCs usually accounts for its limited use. The duality and the complex structure of the capital market suggest the difficulty that lies in its treatment as a homogeneous unit (for details see Ghatak 1995).

1.4.4 Organization

The lack of entrepreneurship is regarded as one of the major bottlenecks in the development of the LDCs. Where the entrepreneur class existed, governments did not provide sufficient incentives for its prosperity. Lack of proper education and managerial skill went hand-in-hand in most LDCs and, even where the resources were available, proper organization for the mobilization of such resources was inadequate. Motivation, culture, attitude, resources, institutions and public policy all had varying roles to play in shaping the types of organization that most LDCs have today (Myrdal 1968).

1.4.5 Commodity market

The commodity markets in most LDCs are also characterized by duality. This is so because in parts of such markets (e.g. in agriculture) barter forms of transaction, rather than monetary transactions, take place. This makes the estimation of the value of the product quite difficult without the use of some 'shadow' or imputed prices. There are other difficulties with regard to the weights which should be attached to the evaluation of non-traded outputs. With the expansion of money income, barter forms of transactions are probably on the wane in many LDCs, though their presence still adds to the problems of proper evaluation of the products.

It is in the light of these complex features of the market in LDCs that their 'growth' and 'development' should be judged – a distinction to which we now turn.

1.5 Growth and development: is *per capita* real income a valid index?

The terms 'growth' and 'development' are usually used to mean the same thing. A growth of the *per capita* income is supposed to contribute to a general rise in the standard of living of the people in general. But growth and development need not be the same. For instance, Kuwait's *per capita* real income may be the highest in the world and yet the standard of living of an 'average' Kuwaiti may not be the same as that of an 'average' American. In other words, *per capita* real income figures are derived by dividing the total real national income by the total population to obtain an average figure and these averages can be misleading. Thus, the distribution of income must be taken into account before something can be said about the general level of development. A country's gross domestic product (GDP) may grow at a very fast rate and yet only a small proportion of its population could be the beneficiaries of such growth, while the masses of its population may not experience any improvement in their standard of living. There may be growth but no development. Instances are not rare and these are cited in the chapter on income distribution (Chapter 10).

Second, a fast growth rate in total output may indicate a healthy state of the economy, but if population growth rate matches the output growth rate, then *per capita* growth rate is negligible. Here also growth without development is possible. The important variable which is hindering the 'development' in this case is the growth of population.

Third, the use of *per capita* real income or consumption data, converted into the foreign exchange rate, may not always be an adequate index to measure development in a world of floating exchange rates (for an index of the real GDP adjusted for changes in terms of trade, see Summers and Heston 1984, 1991). Also, the expression of *per capita* real income in terms of official exchange rates may not be very meaningful if such rates remain highly overvalued – a frequently observed phenomenon in the LDCs.

Fourth, growth without development is supposed to be the feature of 'dual' societies in the LDCs (Boeke 1953). Such 'dual' societies are characterized by contrasts between the very rich and the very poor, between the towns and villages, between different social classes and so on. Prima facie, it is not easy to argue that dualism is the cause or effect of underdevelopment. If dualism is interpreted as class distinction and inequalities in income distribution, then its presence could be observed even in many economically developed countries.

Finally, the quality of life is to be regarded as an important index of development. It is contended that such quality is not adequately reflected in the index of *per capita* income growth. A country (X) may have a lower *per capita* real income than the other (Y), but the quality of life enjoyed by the citizens of X may be better than that of Y. Here the problem is one of setting up a composite index to measure the 'quality' of life. Several factors are involved in the measurement of such 'quality', e.g.

1 education and literacy rates;
2 life expectancy;
3 the level of nutrition as measured by calorie supply per head or by some such index;
4 consumption of energy per head;
5 consumption of iron and steel per head;
6 consumption of consumer durables *per capita*;
7 the proportion of infant mortality per thousand of the live population.

It is clear that some of the factors mentioned above should be measured in terms of 'non-monetary' rather than monetary indicators. In fact, attempts have been made to compare the standard of living in different countries by using non-monetary indicators. Here the aim was to test a significant statistical correlation between the non-monetary and aggregate national income indices in order to forecast the real consumption per head which is supposed to be a better indicator of quality of life (see Beckerman 1966 for details). Some other non-monetary variables which are supposed to explain *per capita* consumption are (1) stock of radios and telephones; (2) consumption of meat; (3) number of letters sent, etc. (Duggar 1968). The final forecasts are then compared with the national accounts data on private consumption converted in official exchange rates. The results of the study by Beckerman show some major differences between monetary and non-monetary indicators of *per capita* consumption. The results also show that, while the highest 10 per cent of the world population accounted for 35.2 per cent of world consumption, the poorest 10 per cent obtained only 1.6 per cent of global consumption. These results simply highlight the gulf between the rich and poor countries (Beckerman and Bacon 1970).

The 'quality' of life could also be measured by looking at the social and political developments of different countries (Adelman and Morris 1967). It is generally assumed by development economists that an increase in investment, industrialization, agricultural productivity and economic growth will be closely related to the rise in the extent of economic and political participation by the people. However, events in many LDCs tend to suggest that a fast rate of economic growth has been associated with greater inequality in income distribution and a decline in people's participation. Indeed, if the *per capita* real income growth rate is less than 3.5 per cent, the relative share of the poor sections tends to fall. After adjusting for population growth this calls for an income growth rate higher than 5.5 per cent which few LDCs have achieved so far. Also, higher growth rates are a necessary but not sufficient condition for raising the share of the poor (Adelman 1975). Hence, to achieve greater political and economic quality, the case for socio-political and institutional changes has been strongly advocated. 'Without new institutions and policies specifically designed to improve the lot of the poor, there is no realistic chance of social justice in the underdeveloped world of our time' (Adelman and Morris 1973: 202). Very few, now, would dispute this statement. The lack of major structural and institutional changes could only enrich the 'new elites' in the LDCs without developing the standard of living of the poor. If the economic differences between the rich and poor countries appear like *A Tale of Two Cities,* then such a tale could also be heard loudly even within many LDCs.

The above analysis suggests that the *per capita* real income growth rate is not a very satisfactory measure of economic 'development' and that it needs to be supplemented by other indices such as *per capita* real consumption, monetary, non-monetary, demographic and socio-political variables, e.g. life expectancy, infant mortality, education, literacy, distribution of income among the different classes, and the level and extent of people's participation in government and the degree of decentralization of economic and political power. The construction of such an index is very much an important topic of future research. On the other hand, although the level and rate of *per capita* real income growth is an imperfect index, it is difficult to believe that significant development could take place without a rise in *per capita* real income. This probably accounts for the great importance that is usually attached to the nature and changes of the level of *per capita* real income to measure growth and development in the economic literature.

It is perhaps useful to note that, if past growth rates continue into the future (and assuming for the moment that it is misleading to compare cross-country gross national product (GNP) *per capita* statistics), the 'economic distance' between the rich and poor nations is very unlikely to be closed. Morawetz (1977) suggests that among the fastest growing LDCs only eight will close the gap within a hundred years, and only sixteen will close it within a thousand years.

It is well acknowledged that exchange rate conversions of the GDPs of countries to a single currency (e.g. the pound or US dollar) do not always offer a solid foundation for international comparison. In one study, measuring the purchasing power parities of different currencies demonstrates very clearly that the ratio of purchasing power and GDP of the currencies of LDCs is *systematically* larger than their exchange rates, compared with the purchasing power/exchange rate relationship of DCs (Kravis *et al.* 1978). It is interesting to point out that the study by Kravis *et al.* reveals that the GDP per head of Bangladesh is about *three times* higher if shown in *real* GDP figures (i.e. in terms of purchasing power parity) than if stated in terms of 'nominal' GDP figures (i.e. in terms of conversion into dollar exchange rates). Thus in 1970 the *per capita* GDP of Bangladesh was US$90 expressed in exchange rate terms. When converted in terms of purchasing power parities, it stood at $250.

A more fundamental question can be asked as to whether the historical process often described as growth can be really understood in terms of increase in *per capita* income and individual welfare (see Guha 1981 for an interesting analysis). Guha argues that a larger bundle of goods will obviously leave the individual happier given an invariant and unsaturated utility function. Given a single or a Hicksian composite commodity, the assumptions of stability of tastes and non-satiety make this definitionally true. However, all observed growth processes have been accompanied, if not caused, by changes in preferences. 'The demonstration effect is a potent force behind most growth processes.' If this is true, the higher consumption levels due to growth may yet leave people more dissatisfied than ever. Witness the significant and positive correlation between *per capita* income and suicide rate per thousand of population. Guha argues that processes which we generally understand as growth produce improvements in different biological indices – 'notably life expectancy'. 'Indeed, biological improvement might be described as the necessary and sufficient condition for economic growth in a closed population. Increase in welfare, on the other hand, is not only a disputable criterion, but may not even be a scientifically meaningful one' (Guha 1981: 126). Clearly, economic development has a number of biological implications, e.g. the control of epidemics, improvements in nutritional standards, etc. But these are best summed up in the growth of life expectancy.

If this statement is true, then it is possible to understand the lack of any significant and direct association between economic growth and individual welfare. It is of interest to note that a very high productivity in many sectors in DCs does not imply a net increase in welfare but an 'indispensable adaptation' to the complex problems of urban-industrial living (see for example Wilkinson 1972). Thus, the inherent demographic features of economic development require a series of adaptations 'which multiply many measurable outputs manifold without necessarily adding to utility' (Guha 1981: 127). It is clearly interesting and refreshing to consider economic development as the adaptive response of the human species to its environment.

1.6 Human development index

It has been mentioned that a rise in *per capita* income is a necessary but not sufficient condition to measure economic or human development. In 1990 the United Nations Development Programme (UNDP) published a human development index (HDI) – a new yardstick that provides a broad method by which inter-country and inter-temporal comparisons of living standards can be undertaken. Since it has been widely acknowledged that national accounting concepts do not capture all aspects of economic welfare, e.g. environmental pollution and quality of life, social justice, etc., and neglect the important issue of non-marketed goods in LDCs (e.g. agricultural goods consumed by producers), the need for constructing an HDI is overwhelming. Of course, purely in economic terms, one of the useful ways to judge inter-country standards of living would be to consider the purchasing power of a country's currency over GDP rather than make a simple conversion of the domestic *per capita* income into US dollars at a certain exchange rate (Summers and Heston 1988, 1991). The Penn World data sets present time-series national accounting data which are denominated in a common set of prices in a common currency. The importance of this research is that it enables real quantity comparisons to be made both over time and between countries.

Penn World Tables (Summers and Heston 1991) provide a meaningful basis of comparative economic development. They do not provide the exact index of the physical quality of life (PQLI). The PQLI is generally based on three indicators: (1) infant mortality IM, (2) life expectancy e, (3) basic literacy L, i.e.

$$\text{PQLI} = f(\text{IM}, e, L)$$

To construct the PQLI, we can write

$$\text{PQLI} = (\text{IMI}, e\text{I}, L\text{I})/3$$

where IMI is an index of IM, eI is an index of e and LI is an index of L.

The last equation could be rewritten as

$$\text{PQLI} = 0.33\text{IMI} + 0.33e\text{I} + 0.33L\text{I}$$

where 0.33 is the (equal) weight applied to each of the separate indicator indices. In the HDI proposed by the UNDP, we have

$$\text{HDI} = g(Y, L, e)$$

where Y is *per capita* income, L is the literacy rate and e is life expectancy at birth. Thus the HDI according to the UNDP comprises GNP *per capita*, longevity and education. The index varies between 0 and 1: the nearer to 1, the higher the level of human development. Despite the well-known measurement problems, it is argued: 'The conceptual and methodological problems of quantifying and measuring human development become more complex for political freedom, personal security, interpersonal relations and the physical environment. . . . Special effort must go into developing a simple quantitative measure to capture the many aspects of human freedom' (UNDP 1990: 13).

Human development has two facets: (1) actual *achievement* and (2) shortfall from a target or a measure of *deprivation* – an index which 'emphasises the magnitude of the tasks that still lie ahead' (UNDP 1990: 14). The construction of the index of deprivation indicator (DI) is as follows:

$$\text{DI}_{Y_j} = \frac{\max Y - Y_j}{\max Y - \min Y}$$

$$\text{DI}_{e_j} = \frac{\max e - e_j}{\max e - \min e}$$

$$\text{DI}_{L_j} = \frac{\max L - L_j}{\max L - \min L}$$

where DI_{Yj}. and DI_{ej} and DI_{Lj} are the DI for the jth country for income, life expectancy at birth and literacy respectively. Max Y, max L and max e are the maximum values for Y, L and e respectively. Y_j, e_j and L_j are the actual values for income, life expectancy at birth and literacy respectively for the jth country.

Suppose we wish to calculate the DI for Papua New Guinea (PNG) (country j). Let the highest *per capita* GDP be \$17,620 for the United States and the lowest be \$200 for Zaire (according to the Penn World data set based on purchasing power parity for 1990). Let the *per capita* GDP be \$700.00 for PNG. Then for PNG the DI can be calculated as follows:

$$\text{DI}_{Y_{\text{PNG}}} = \frac{17{,}620 - 700}{17{,}620 - 200} = 0.97$$

Note that UNDP does not employ the logs of all income data. Transformation of all data into logarithms would produce different values of DI_Y (see, for example, Doessel

Table 1.6 Prosperity ranked by HDI versus GNP

Country	*Rank on HDI*	*HDI*	*Rank on GNP per capita*	*Ranks based on 160 countries*	
				HDI	*GNP per capita*
Japan	1	0.981	1	2	3
United Kingdom	2	0.962	3	10	21
Germany	3	0.955	2	12	10
Republic of Korea	4	0.871	6	34	39
Singapore	5	0.848	4	40	25
Brazil	6	0.739	7	59	54
Saudi Arabia	7	0.687	5	67	33
Thailand	8	0.685	8	69	79
Sri Lanka	9	0.651	10	76	120
China	10	0.612	11	79	130
Cameroon	11	0.313	9	118	88
Tanzania	12	0.268	14	126	158
Uganda	13	0.192	13	133	141
Sierra Leone	14	0.062	12	159	145

Sources: UN *Human Development Report 1992*, World Bank; Smith (1993).

and Gounder 1994). An average DI has been constructed by the UNDP as follows:

$$\mathrm{DI} = 0.33\mathrm{DI}_{Y_j} + 0.33\mathrm{DI}_{e_j} + 0.33\mathrm{DI}_{L_j}$$

Finally, to obtain the HDI, the value of DI is subtracted from 1, i.e.

$$\mathrm{HDI} = 1 - \mathrm{DI}$$

Clearly, the HDI will vary between 0 and 1. Rankings of the same country could be different according to the HDI and GNP *per capita* index. Table 1.6 shows how big a gap emerges in the two ranking systems for some countries. For instance, China, Sri Lanka and Tanzania are ranked much higher in terms of the HDI than on a GNP *per capita* basis. On the other hand, Cameroon and Saudi Arabia are countries where HDI lags behind GDP *per capita.* Interestingly, the UK is ranked above Germany when we use the HDI rather than GNP *per capita* of the two countries (Smith 1993).

Appendix 1.1 Measurement of income inequality

Several methods to estimate how inequality could be described are available. Here we shall briefly state the major ones.

1 The first method is to estimate the ratio of incomes obtained by, say, the bottom 3 per cent of the population and the top 10 per cent of the population. Such an index really shows the extent of inequality between the very rich and the very poor.
2 The other index which is frequently used to measure inequality is the 'Lorenz curve' (called after the American statistician C. Lorenz who invented it in 1905) which

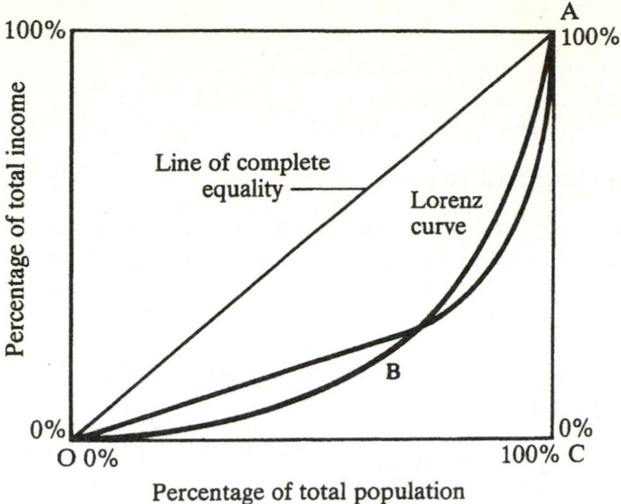

Figure A1.1.1

shows associations between percentages of *income receivers* and percentages of income. In Figure A1.1.1, the vertical axis shows different percentages of income whereas the horizontal axis measures cumulative percentages of income receivers. The diagonal line OA shows the line of *exact equality* because, at every point on it, the percentage of income receivers is equal to the percentage of income obtained. The Lorenz curve depicts the *actual* association between percentages of total income and percentages of income receivers. In the rather unlikely case when the Lorenz curve is identical with the line OA, there is no inequality. On the other hand, the further the Lorenz curve moves away from the line OA, the greater is the inequality. Note that if the Lorenz curve of a country X always lies outside that of country Y, then the inequality in distribution of income is larger in the country X in comparison with the country Y. But if they intersect each other, then it is hard to tell which country suffers from greater inequality without making subjective value judgements.

3 The most favoured index to measure inequality is the Gini coefficient or G (called after Gini who invented it in 1912) which is the ratio of area OAB to area OCA. Thus the Gini coefficient ranks according to the area between the Lorenz curve and the diagonal and it is a direct measure of income difference between every pair of incomes. Symbolically, if y is income, m is average or mean income, n is number of persons and $i = 1, 2, \ldots n$, then

$$\sum_{i=1}^{n} y_i = nm$$

and the Gini coefficient G is

$$G = \frac{1}{2} n^2 m \sum_{i=1}^{j} \sum_{j=2}^{n} |y_i - y_j|$$

Where $G = 0$, everyone gets the same income; where $G = 1$, only one person gets everything. Clearly, for most countries the actual value of G lies between 0 and 1. Note that G also shows the share of different groups of the population in income. (For details and discussions of other methods, see Sen 1973; Atkinson 1970; Pen 1971.)

Appendix 1.2 A note on production functions

A production function describes maximum output from a given set of inputs. More formally, let Q be the amount of output and $x_1, x_2, \ldots x_n$ be the inputs. Then we have

$$Q = f(x_1, x_2, \ldots x_n) \tag{A1.2.1}$$

A production function is the border of a production set. A simple production function can be given by the following relationship:

$$Q = f(K, L)$$

where K is capital and L is labour. The marginal product of labour $\text{MP}_L = \text{d}Q/\text{d}L$. Similarly, the marginal product of capital $\text{MP}_K = \text{d}Q/\text{d}K$. The marginal rate of substitution of capital for labour (to keep Q fixed on an isoquant) is given by R. Thus:

$$R = -\frac{\text{d}K}{\text{d}L}$$

The elasticity of substitution, σ, between factors is defined as follows:

$$\sigma = \frac{\text{d}(K/L)/(K/L)}{\text{d}R/R}$$

A production function is homogeneous of degree r if, putting λK instead of K and λL instead of L, a production function $f(\lambda K, \lambda L)$ is equal to $\lambda^r f(K, L)$.

It is now easy to point out that, where $r = 1$, we have constant returns to scale; where $r < 1$, diminishing returns to scale prevail; where $r > 1$, we have increasing returns to scale. A production function is linearly homogeneous where $r = 1$. Note that the elasticity of production with respect to labour is given by

$$E_L = \frac{\text{d}Q}{\text{d}L}\frac{L}{Q}$$

Similarly output elasticity with respect to capital is given by

$$E_K = \frac{\text{d}Q}{\text{d}K}\frac{K}{Q}$$

Following Cobb–Douglas, a *non-linear* production function can be written as

$$Q = AK^{\alpha}L^{\beta}$$

where $A = \alpha$, β a positive constant.

To obtain MP_L, MP_K, E_L, E_K and σ we differentiate the function with respect to L and K respectively and obtain the following equations:

$$\mathrm{MP}_L = \frac{\partial Q}{\partial L} = f_L = \beta A K^{\alpha} L^{\beta-1} = \beta \frac{Q}{L} > 0 \text{ for } K, L > 0$$

and

$$\mathrm{MP}_K = \frac{\partial Q}{\partial K} = f_K = \alpha A K^{\alpha-1} L^{\beta} = \alpha \frac{Q}{K} > 0 \text{ for } K, L > 0$$

$$E_{QL} = \frac{\partial Q}{\partial L}\frac{L}{Q} = \beta A K^{\alpha} L^{\beta-1}\frac{L}{Q} = \beta \frac{Q}{L}\frac{L}{Q} = \beta$$

$$E_{QK} = \frac{\partial Q}{\partial K}\frac{K}{Q} = \alpha A K^{\alpha-1} L^{\beta}\frac{K}{Q} = \alpha \frac{Q}{K}\frac{K}{Q} = \alpha$$

The function is homogeneous of degree $\alpha + \beta$. Hence, if $\alpha + \beta = 1$, we have constant returns to scale. When $\alpha + \beta > 1$, we have increasing returns; similarly if $\alpha + \beta < 1$, we have diminishing returns. Note that $\sigma = 1$ in the Cobb–Douglas case. The proof is simple.

$$Q = AK^{\alpha}L^{\beta}$$

Totally differentiating and setting equal to zero,

$$0 = AK^{(\alpha-1)}\alpha L^{\beta}\mathrm{d}K + AK^{\alpha}\beta L^{(\beta-1)}\mathrm{d}L$$

or

$$0 = \alpha \frac{Q}{K}\mathrm{d}K + \beta \frac{Q}{L}\mathrm{d}L$$

Therefore

$$\frac{\mathrm{d}L}{\mathrm{d}K} = -\frac{\alpha}{\beta}\frac{L}{K} = \frac{\mathrm{d}K}{\mathrm{d}L} = -\frac{\beta}{\alpha}\frac{K}{L}$$

or

$$\frac{\mathrm{d}(\mathrm{d}K/\mathrm{d}L)}{\mathrm{d}(K/L)} = -\frac{\beta}{\alpha} = \frac{\mathrm{d}R}{R}$$

Now

$$\sigma = \frac{\mathrm{d}(K/L)/(K/L)}{\mathrm{d}R/R} \qquad R = -\frac{\mathrm{d}K}{\mathrm{d}L} \qquad \frac{\mathrm{d}R}{R} = -\frac{\beta}{\alpha}$$

A simple substitution yields

$$\sigma = \frac{-\beta}{\alpha}\frac{-\alpha}{\beta} = 1$$

i.e. a 1 per cent change in the factor's relative price will bring about a 1 per cent change in factor proportions.

It is useful to remember, then, that, under perfect competition when producers maximize profit, factors will be paid according to the value of their marginal product, i.e. MP_K is profits or rental r and MP_L is wages W. For the total share of factors

$$K MP_K + L MP_L = K\alpha\frac{Q}{K} + L\beta\frac{Q}{L} = Q(\alpha + \beta)$$

One of the important implications of the neoclassical theory is that, where factors are paid according to the values of their marginal products, total product will be just exhausted. Hence the system of distribution is just. Also, when $W = MP_K$ and $r = MP_L$, the allocative efficiency in the economy is Pareto optimal. Most researchers on LDCs try to reach conclusions about their allocative efficiencies by examining the marginal principles.

The constant elasticity of substitution production function

The alternative form of production function proposed by Solow, Minhas, Arrow and Chenery (SMAC) in 1961 is known as the constant elasticity of substitution (CES) or SMAC production function. In the use of a Cobb– Douglas production function, it is assumed that the elasticity of substitution $\sigma = 1$. Also, the marginal product of any factor is assumed to be the same in alternative uses. These assumptions have not always been confirmed by empirical studies. For instance, Solow *et al.* have observed that K/L ratios change between countries much more in some industries than in others. In other words, there are factors other than marginal products which may account for changes in K/L ratios. The proposed CES production function has the following form:

$$Q = \gamma[\delta K^{-p} + (1 - \delta)L^{-p}]^{-v/p}$$

where Q is total output; $v, y > 0$; γ is the efficiency parameter; $p \neq 0$; δ is the distributive parameter: $0 \leq \delta < 1$; p is the substitution parameter: $-1 < p < \propto$; and v is the degree of the function (i.e. measures returns to scale).

To simplify the above function, let us assume that the function is homogeneous of degree one. Hence we can write

$$Q = \gamma[\delta^{-p} + (1 - \delta)L^{-p}]^{-1/p}$$

It can be shown that

$$\sigma = \frac{1}{1 + p}$$

It is obvious that, if $p = 0$, $\sigma = 1$ and the CES production function is the same as the Cobb–Douglas production function (see for example Layard and Walters 1978).

To prove this, rearrange the CES production function of degree one in the following way:

$$Q^{-p} = \delta K^{-p} + (1 - \delta)L^{-p}$$

Differentiating the above equation totally, we have

$$-pQ^{-p-1}\mathrm{d}Q = -p\delta K^{-p-1}\mathrm{d}K - p(1-\delta)L^{-p-1}\mathrm{d}L \qquad \text{(A1.2.2)}$$

Now,

$$f_L = \frac{\partial Q}{\partial L} = (1-\delta)\left(\frac{Q}{L}\right)^{1+p}$$

$$f_K = \frac{\partial Q}{\partial K} = \delta\left(\frac{Q}{K}\right)^{1+p}$$

$$\frac{f_L}{f_K} = \frac{1-\delta}{\delta}\left(\frac{K}{L}\right)^{1+p}$$

It follows that

$$\frac{K}{L} = \left(\frac{\delta}{1-\delta}\frac{f_L}{f_K}\right)^{1/(1+p)}$$

We know that

$$\sigma = \frac{\partial \log(K/L)}{\partial \log(f_L/f_K)} = \frac{1}{1+p}$$

It is easy to see now that, if $p = 0$, the CES function is equivalent to the Cobb–Douglas production function. From (A1.2.2)

$$\frac{\mathrm{d}Q}{Q^{1+p}} = \delta\frac{\mathrm{d}K}{K^{1+p}} + (1-\delta)\frac{\mathrm{d}L}{L^{1+p}}$$

If $p = 0$

$$\frac{\mathrm{d}Q}{Q} = \delta\frac{\mathrm{d}K}{K} + (1-\delta)\frac{\mathrm{d}L}{L}$$

Thus,

$$\mathrm{d}\log Q = \delta\mathrm{d}\log K + (1-\delta)\mathrm{d}\log L$$

Integrating and assuming r is the constant of integration

$$Q = rK^{\delta}L^{1-\delta}$$

This is the same function as we have in the Cobb–Douglas case.

It is useful to note that the CES production function is not always easy to apply to LDCs. If aggregation over variables is not possible then it is difficult to apply. However, the CES function can be estimated directly by using the maximum likelihood technique or indirectly by using the association between AP_L and wage rate which gives the value of σ as the coefficient for the wage rate. It is evident that the exact value of σ has important implications for analysing substitutability between factors and the pattern of income distribution. Let σ in industry be less than one in a developing country. If wages rise, the share of agricultural labour is supposed to fall. A technical progress will then shift the distribution of labour income from agriculture to manufacturing. (For details, see for example Yotopoulos and Nugent 1976.)

Questions

1 How important is *per capita* income as a measure of economic development?
2 What is a Lorenz curve? Calculate the Gini coefficient for the measurement of global income inequality.
3 Critically distinguish between economic growth and development.
4 Explain the following concepts:

   (a) Human Development Index.
   (b) Human Deprivation Index.

5 Is 'Human Development Index' a better indicator of economic development than the level of *per capita* income?

Part I

The economic theory of growth and development

2 Growth theories and their relevance to less developed countries

2.1 Introduction

The development of the theories of economic growth – or what Marshall regarded as long-run equilibrium analysis – in the last fifty years has been remarkable. Such growth may be explained partly by the desire to analyse the problems and policies for economic development of many war-ravaged countries after the Second World War and partly by the necessity to stimulate growth in many poor countries in Asia, Africa and Latin America. Sometimes, growth just happened and theorists decided to explain it. The idea of promoting growth is not new in the history of economic thought. Indeed, the classical economists envisaged a scenario to describe the process of economic growth. In this chapter we shall try to analyse the basic features of some of the major theories of economic growth and show their relevance to the problems of economic development of the LDCs. We shall start off with discussion of the classical theory of growth.

2.2 Classical scenario

The theory of growth, as stated by the classical writers such as Smith, Mill, Malthus and Ricardo, can be described in a simple way. Given a certain amount of labour (and assuming, of course, the labour theory of value), at a certain level of production, wages will be paid to each worker according to the level of subsistence and any 'surplus', i.e. the difference between total production and total consumption which is assumed to be equivalent to the total wage bill, will be accumulated by the capitalists. Such accumulation will increase the demand for labour and, with a given population, wages will tend to rise. As the wage exceeds temporarily the level of subsistence, the population will increase according to the Malthusian theory of population. With a growth of population, the supply of labour will be encouraged and wages will again fall back to the level of subsistence. But as wages become equal to the subsistence level, a surplus will emerge again to encourage accumulation and demand for labour and the whole process will be repeated again in the next phase. The dynamics of growth ends as the law of diminishing returns sets in and wages eat up the whole of production, leaving no surplus for accumulation, expansion and growth of population. The 'magnificent dynamics' ends not with a bang but a whimper. This is illustrated by Figure 2.1.

The vertical axis measures total production minus rent and the horizontal axis measures employment of labour. The line OW indicates the subsistence wage line.

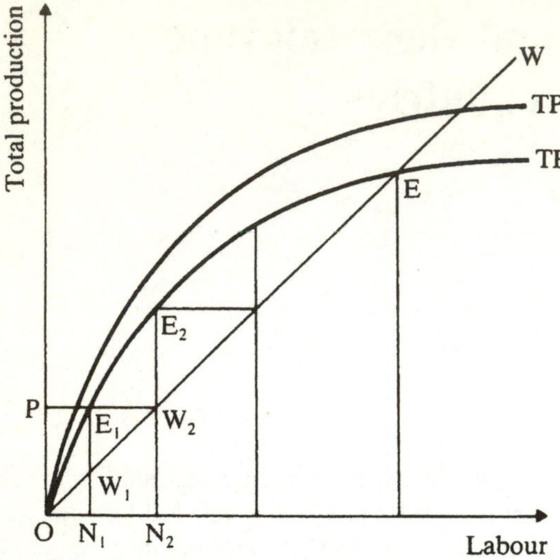

Figure 2.1

With ON_1 population, production is OP, wage per unit is N_1W_1 and surplus or profit is E_1W_1 when TP (total production) is the sum of wages and profits only. The emergence of a surplus engenders accumulation which leads to an increase in the demand for labour. Wages rise to E_1N_1 since the demand for labour rises with accumulation but population, and therefore labour supply, remain constant at ON_1. But once wages are above the level of subsistence, i.e. $E_1N_1 > N_1W_1$, growth of population is stimulated to ON_2 – thanks to the Malthusian theory of population. Once the population is ON_2, a 'surplus' emerges again, i.e. E_2W_2, as wages are driven back to the level of subsistence and the whole process is repeated until the economy reaches a point like E where the 'stationary' state is attained. As wages are equal to production, there is no surplus or accumulation or expansion and the day of doom is reached. If technical progress is introduced (a shift of TP to TP′), then note that the day of doom is postponed, but not eliminated.

2.2.1 The limitations of the classical model

1 It is important to note that the role of technical progress has been grossly underestimated in the model. The experience of the last two centuries has shown that the role of diminishing returns as the pointer to the day of doom has certainly diminished.
2 The 'iron law of wages', which suggests that wages cannot be above or below the level of subsistence because of the Malthusian law of population, has been discredited as the sole explanation of wage determination with the growth and change of the industrial structure. For one thing, the 'iron law of wages' is based only on supply whereas wages are determined both by demand and supply. For another, it does not take into account the role of trade unions in wage determination.
3 The Malthusian theory of population growth has been proved to be misleading in the light of the experience of economic growth of the economically advanced

countries of today. The Malthusian argument that, whenever wages are above the level of subsistence, people like to have more babies rather than bicycles, radios, televisions or cars seems to be invalid, both logically and empirically.

4 The classical model is too simple to account for all the complex factors which influence growth in the LDCs. For instance, labour is hardly a homogeneous input and nor is capital in the LDCs. Different types of labour and capital could affect growth differently. Accumulation need not be the sole objective function in economies where people share and share alike. Also, attitudes, culture and traditional institutional values exert varying degrees of influence on growth.

2.3 The Keynesian theory and less developed countries

It is interesting to note to what extent the Keynesian theory provides some answers to the problems of economic development of poor countries. It is significant to observe that in the classical theory money is a 'veil' and has nothing to do with the determination of real factors like output and employment; money plays no role in the equilibrium analysis of value and distribution in the classical system whereas in the Keynesian model money tends to influence the equilibrium values of output and employment. Later, however, Patinkin tried to integrate value and monetary theory by introducing the real balance effect (Patinkin 1968).

One of the main sources of conflict between the Keynesian and classical theories lies in the way the difference between demand for and supply of money should be corrected. In the classical theory, an increase in money supply will raise unwanted cash holding and, since a rational individual does not hold money for its own sake, excess money would be spent on goods and services, pushing the prices upwards, with a given level of output. The mechanism could be explained with the help of the quantity theory.

Let

$$MV = PT$$

where M is quantity of money, V is velocity, P is price level and T is total transactions. It is assumed that V and T are unlikely to change substantially, particularly in the short run since V is mainly determined by tastes and T is largely given by the technology and the real resources. In such a situation, an expansion of M will have a direct and positive impact on prices. An increase or decrease in M will increase or decrease prices. The critics, however, have argued that, if either V or T or both change with the change in M, then the direct relationship between M and P is unlikely to hold. To this, the 'new monetarists' headed by Friedman point out that as long as the demand for money remains stable an expansion of M will always lead to a rise in prices, though the effect may not be observed instantaneously. At a higher price the expansion of the money supply would be consistent with ordinary transaction demand (k) which is assumed to be a fixed proportion of income (Y), or $M = kY$.

In the Keynesian theory, an expansion of money supply will raise bond prices and reduce the interest rate, increase the level of investment and output and perhaps lead to a secondary effect on prices. Should there be excess capacity, the effect on prices of a rise in money supply will be even less. If we are concerned with an underemployment situation, prices should not be affected so long as the supply of output with respect to money supply is elastic. Thus the effect could well be on income, output and employment.

Box 2.1 Human capital and institutional design

Human capital affects the quality of the rules that govern market transactions and the enforcement of these rules. Literacy levels and technical skills vary greatly across and within countries. The poorest economies of the former Soviet Union have income levels lower than many countries in Asia and Africa but nearly universal primary education. So literacy is less of a barrier for Armenians using formal institutions than it may be for some Angolans – and it is less of a problem for today's Malaysians than it was for those of a generation ago. The rules and organizations that govern markets have to allow relevant market actors to use them easily. This argument holds within countries as well – for example, across poorer rural and richer urban areas.

The usefulness of institutions also depends on the capability of their administrators. Judges untrained in corporate law and accountancy, for instance, may not be the best arbiters of bankruptcy cases. Successful institution builders have had either to tailor institutions to prevailing administrative capacity (using, for example, simpler bankruptcy rules) or to complement institution building with a strong focus on concurrently developing technical expertise for administrators (from accountancy skills to regulatory economics).

It is difficult to see the application of Keynesian theory to the special features of an underdeveloped country, however. First, most LDCs have some form of 'dualism' in their market structure (see Chapter 1). The money market in particular tends to be affected by 'financial dualism'. The presence of the non-monetized sector also poses considerable problems as the use of monetary policies, e.g. changes in the bank rate and open market operations, is limited. Further, because of widespread illiteracy, people do not have sufficient knowledge about the financial assets which may be acquired. Nor do they have enough confidence in different forms of financial assets, so that investment is usually made in land or gold. Despite the presence of an organized and sophisticated money market, an unorganized money market, usually ruled by village moneylenders, merchants and traders, still predominates (Wai 1957; Ghatak 1976). Thus, people tend to spend more with expansion of money supply and this puts up prices in the classical fashion. This would be the case so long as the elasticity of output to the money supply is less than unity and, given the lags of response and the rigidities of the market structure, it looks as though the classical rather than the Keynesian theory would be valid for an underdeveloped country. Figure 2.2 attempts to explain this. It shows that if the money supply rises from OM_1 to OM_2, demand rises and output rises (as measured by OQ) from M_1T_1 to M_2T_2, given any excess capacity or the availability of unused resources. Beyond T_3, output does not respond to increases in money supply. Thus, if money supply rises from OM_3 to OM_4, output will remain stationary if all the resources are used up, i.e. $M_3T_3 = M_4T_4$ but prices rise as measured by P_1T_4. If money supply rises further to OM_5, prices rise to P_2T_5. The classical model is valid beyond T_3 whereas the Keynesian model operates before T_3.

It has been argued sometimes that the problem of most LDCs is not always a lack of demand (indeed, with a low income the marginal propensity to consume (MPC) should

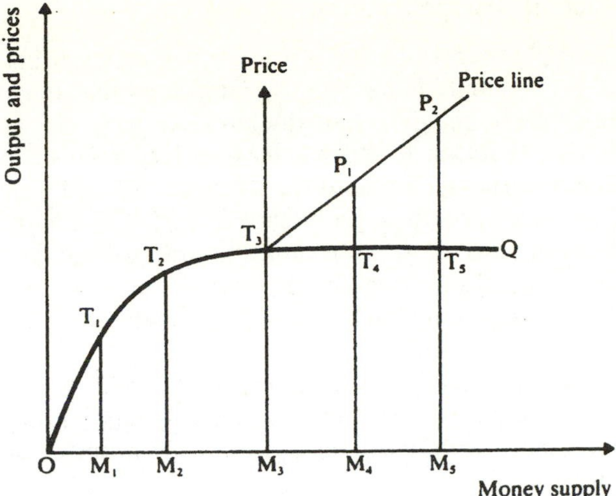

Figure 2.2

be very high), but lack of savings and proper investment. Thus absence of an array of financial assets like bonds and securities as well as of financial institutions like banks (Gurley and Shaw 1960) coupled with institutional and resource constraints plus population growth rate may well induce one to approach the problem from the supply side (Lipton 1969).

One of the major pillars of Keynesian economics is that income is generated by investment via the process of multipliers and so are consumption and *savings*. But in an LDC, given a very low elasticity of output, the Keynesian type multiplier has not much application because, with a rise in investment, the money multiplier may operate but the real income multiplier does not and hence prices tend to rise (Rao 1958; Hasan 1960). It has been argued that in LDCs there is no involuntary unemployment. Unemployment is usually disguised in the sense that although the marginal productivity of labour is zero or near zero and wages are higher than marginal productivity in underdeveloped agriculture, labour remains *employed* as the mode of production (use of *family* labour rather than *wage* labour) and objective functions in traditional agriculture (income or output rather than profit maximization) are different in developed countries. The problems of unemployment can hardly be solved in the Keynesian fashion by increasing aggregate demand. Further, to allow for a transfer of labour from agriculture to industry, an industrial base must be created. An industrial base cannot be created simply by increasing *money* income and *money* demand. Again, consumer goods industries in many LDCs do not have substantial excess capacities to cope with increased demand. Moreover, redistributive effects of inflation and shifts in the consumption function may also influence the marginal propensity to consume. It appears that the Keynesian theory of effective demand for income and employment generation via the process of multipliers loses much of its force in LDCs which experience low supply elasticities and structural rigidities.

2.4 The Harrod–Domar model and its applications

In theory, the Harrod–Domar (HD) model is a cross between the classical and the Keynesian theories of growth. Harrod and Domar rightly emphasized that the prime mover of the economy is investment and it has a dual role to play. It creates demand but it also creates capacity (Baldwin 1972). Whereas the Keynesians concentrated only upon the former, the classicists emphasized the latter. The variables chosen by Harrod and Domar are the broad aggregates, e.g. investment, capital and output. It is assumed that capital and labour are used in a *fixed* technical or behavioural relationship, and that output is related to the capital stock by the capital–output (c/o) ratio. The concept of the c/o ratio has greatly dominated theories of growth and planning for LDCs and hence justifies some special attention.

Let Y be income or output, S savings and I investment; and let $s = S/Y$, $v = I/\Delta Y$ (investment divided by incremental output or the incremental capital–output ratio) and $g = \Delta Y/Y$(rate of growth of Y). Now, with fixed v and given $S = I$ in the equation, we have

$$\frac{\Delta Y}{Y} = \frac{\Delta Y}{I}\frac{S}{Y} \quad \text{or} \quad g = \frac{s}{v} \tag{2.1}$$

Alternatively, in terms of a linear difference equation

$$\frac{Y_{t+1} - Y_t}{Y_t} = sb \tag{2.2}$$

where b is the output–capital ratio. Thus

$$Y_{t+1} = Y_t + sbY_t = (1 + sb)Y_t \tag{2.3}$$

given that the proportional growth rate of income equals the savings ratio multiplied by the output–capital ratio.

The solution to the difference equation is

$$Y_t = Y_0(1 + sb)^t \tag{2.4}$$

Although a solution to the model exists, the real problem that now emerges is related to stability. If we get away from the simple HD model where I is given by planned savings and where an investment function based on expectations is absent, we can observe the problem even in the context of the Harrodian investment function of the accelerator type. The investment level is given by the expectations of additional demand and this investment via the multiplier generates effective demand. The real issues that Harrod confronted are (1) the conditions for realizing investors' expectations; (2) the problems that emerge when the expectations are not realized.

In reality Harrod's model stands on a knife-edge because if investors expect more than the rate 'warranted' by s/v (i.e. 'equilibrium' or 'warranted' rate of growth) then the actual growth rate of demand will be greater than the anticipated rate, leading to inflation as the expectation was too low. Conversely, if the expected rate of growth is lower than the warranted growth rate, then the actual growth rate will be less than the expected rate; it will mean that the investors expected too much rather than too little deflation. 'The market thus seems to give a perverse signal to the investor and this is the source of Harrod's problem' (Sen 1970). To maintain a steady state growth rate, with labour requirements per unit of output being given, Y cannot indefinitely grow at a rate higher than n (the growth rate of labour supply, fixed by non-economic forces); thus at a steady state $g = s/v = n$; but as s, v and n are determined independently, the steady state becomes a special case (Hahn and Matthews 1964: 6). Full employment steady state growth rate stands on a 'razor's edge'.

Apart from the problem of instability, the HD model is based on a number of simplifying assumptions, e.g. one product (i.e. commodity composition of the total product is disregarded), a fixed technological relationship between capital stock and income flows, constancy of the savings ratio, absence of lags, vertical integration of the economy and no problem about inter-industrial deliveries, absence of trade, no depreciation of capital and one factor of production. But despite these restrictive assumptions (Chakravarty 1959: 39–40), the HD model has been used in many countries either as a rationale behind the planning exercises or as part of a forecasting mechanism (Myrdal 1968).

The chief appeal of this model perhaps lies in its simplicity. Given a target growth rate g^* and v, it is easy to find the level of s that must be realized to attain g^*. Again, if the sufficient level of s is not forthcoming to match a certain level of I to attain g^* then the model states the required amount that should be borrowed from abroad. The model also predicts that given v, the higher the s, the higher is g, or the lower the v with given s, the higher is g.

However, the application of the HD model is beset with numerous difficulties. We set out the major ones in the following:

1 The model is too aggregative and hence does not provide the basis for a detailed quantitative study, nor does it highlight the structural and regional problems.
2 The problem of estimation of capital is not easy in any country (Robinson 1956) and is particularly difficult in LDCs.
3 The data available on most LDCs are such as to make the reliable estimate of capital–output ratios very difficult.
4 Labour along with capital in another input in the process of production. Even in a so-called labour surplus LDC, evidence suggests that such surplus is sometimes observed only seasonally (see Sen 1975).
5 The assumption of a fixed coefficient of production may also be questioned just as it is equally possible to doubt the assumption about the absence of trade. However, the theoretical search for stability of the HD model continued and one way out was suggested by the neoclassical economists. In the following section, we shall examine the properties of the neoclassical model more closely (see also Chapter 8).

2.5 The neoclassical theory and less developed countries

Basically the answer of neoclassical economists to the instability problem is to make the capital–output ratio flexible rather than fixed. It is assumed by the neoclassicists that the production function is 'well-behaved', that there are constant returns to scale and no technical progress, and that capital is 'malleable' (i.e. capital stock can be adapted to more or less capital-intensive techniques of production; Solow 1956, 1960; Swan 1956; Hicks 1965; Meade 1961). Implicit within a 'well-behaved' production function are the assumptions that capital and labour are perfectly substitutable and factors of production are paid according to the value of their marginal products. There is perfect foresight and flexibility of wages, prices and interest rates. It is generally argued that when the warranted growth rate g is greater than the natural rate n and the economy tends to shoot through the full employment ceiling, labour becomes expensive in relation to capital. This would lead to the adoption of labour-saving techniques. Thus the capital–output ratio will rise and s/v will fall until it is equal to n. On the other hand, if $s/v < n$, there would be an excess supply of labour which would reduce real wages in comparison with real interest rate inducing the use of more labour-intensive technology which would reduce v and increase s/v until $s/v = n$. The neoclassical model thus shows with the utmost simplicity that the Harrodian 'knife-edge' problem is curable, i.e. steady state growth can be attained simply by varying the capital–output ratio. In fact equilibrium growth in a neoclassical model is consistent with the concept of dynamic disequilibrium, where output, capital stock, labour supply and investment will grow at a constant exponential rate or they do not change at all. It is the mythical 'golden age' of Mrs Robinson (Robinson 1956: 99). In a 'golden age' economy one must have

$$\bar{Q} = \bar{Q}_0 \, e^{qt} \tag{2.5}$$

$$\bar{K} = \bar{K}_0 \, e^{ht} \tag{2.6}$$

$$\bar{L} = \bar{L}_0 \, e^{nt} \tag{2.7}$$

$$\bar{I} = \bar{I}_0 \, e^{mt} \tag{2.8}$$

where Q is production, K is capital, L is labour and I is investment. h, n, m are constant growth rates. (Bars over the symbols denote 'golden age' equivalent growth margin.)

At full employment, investment must equal full employment savings and net investment should be equal to the change in capital stock.

$$I = \frac{dk}{dt} = sQ \tag{2.9}$$

We have

$$\bar{I}_0 \, e^{mt} = h\bar{K}_0 \, e^{ht} = s\bar{Q}_0 \, e^{qt} \tag{2.10}$$

For all values of t equation (2.10) can hold only when growth rates of m, Ih and q are equal to each other. Also 'golden age' growth rate can take place with the rate of technical progress, which should be capital augmenting.

One major point to emphasize here is that 'golden age' growth rate is independent of the rate of saving (see also Appendix 2.1) and this is different from the conclusion reached by Harrod and Domar. The reason is that a rise in the saving proportion will raise the growth of capital and output for a while but because of diminishing returns the original growth rate will be restored. The marginal product of capital will fall if capital rises faster than labour and that will also account for the fall in the growth rate of output. Two economies with the same growth rate of population but different levels of s will have the *same rate* of growth (though *per capita* income levels could be different) because, given $g = s/v$, whenever s rises, v also rises. Although this remarkable conclusion is partly based on the capital-malleability assumption, notice that the non-malleability of capital does not preclude the steady state solution because in the steady state the rate of profit is constant over time, and all machinery, independent of the time of its construction, will have the same labour intensity.

The neoclassical mechanism can also be explained in another way. Let us assume that output Q is produced by capital K and labour L and they bear the following relationship:

$$Q = K^{\alpha} L^{\beta} \tag{2.11}$$

In the type of production function given in (2.11) we assume constant returns to scale so that $\alpha + \beta = 1$. The increase in the stock of capital is the amount saved, sQ, where s is the saving–output or income ratio. The growth rate of capital is sQ/K per annum. Let q stand for the growth of output per annum and n stand for the growth of labour. Given equation (2.11) and after logarithmic differentiation, we derive the following equation to describe the growth rate of output:

$$q = \alpha sQ/K + \beta n \tag{2.12}$$

All savings are invested through changes in the interest rate and excess capital is sQ/K per annum. The interest rate r and the real wage rate ω are equal to the marginal productivities of capital and labour respectively so that

$$r = \alpha Q/K \tag{2.13}$$

and

$$\omega = \beta Q/L \tag{2.14}$$

In other words, the rate of profit is proportional to the output–capital ratio and the wage rate is proportional to output per unit of labour. As α and β stand for output elasticities of capital and labour respectively, the relative share of profits and wages in the economy remains constant (see section 2.8).

In Figure 2.3 the linear growth rate of capital sQ/K is taken as a function of Q/K by a line through the origin with slope equal to a given ratio of saving, say 20 per cent. This is regarded as the growth line of capital. The 'contribution' of capital to output growth is given by $\alpha sQ/K$ in another line through the origin. The growth of labour supply is assumed fixed (say 2 per cent).

The distance OA is βn (i.e. the contribution of labour to output growth). Adding the two contributions of capital and labour we get growth of output q, since $\alpha + \beta = 1$. The three lines of growth must meet at a point such as E where growth is, say, 2 per cent per annum. Output growth q lies between the growth lines of labour and capital and is divided in the proportion $\alpha : \beta$. Beyond E capital is growing faster than output and Q/K falls until E is reached; before E output is growing faster than capital and this leads to a rise of Q/K to a point such as E. In short, equilibrium at a point like E is stable (see Appendix 2.1 for a simple proof). In the HD model

$$g = s/v$$

so that any rise in the saving ratio without any change in the capital–output ratio will lead to a rise in the growth rate. But in neoclassical theory the capital–output ratio is no longer fixed and it could be raised, given a 'well-behaved' production function. Here, if

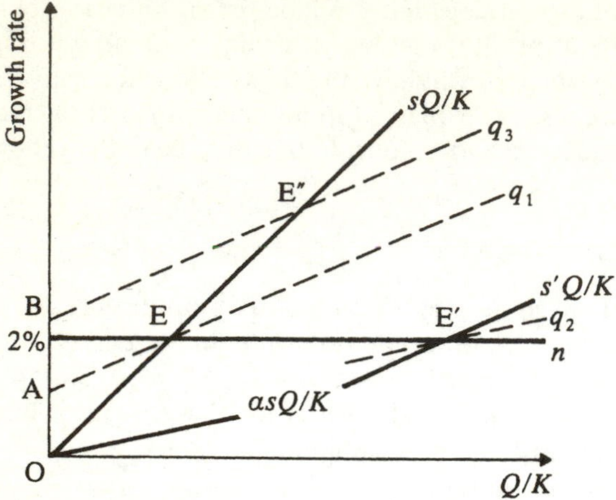

Figure 2.3

there is a rise in saving, the capital–output ratio will rise by an equal proportion and that will leave the growth *rate* unaltered. In terms of our diagram, let the saving ratio fall from 20 per cent to 10 per cent. The equilibrium is now reached at E′ where the new output growth line q_2 intersects n and $s'Q/K$. Note that the equilibrium rate of growth remains unchanged at 2 per cent which is given by the growth rate of labour and the ratio of saving gives the output–capital ratio at which equilibrium occurs. However, a rise in saving will raise the output per head and the wage rate though the output–capital ratio and the profit rate will fall. But the growth rate will remain the same.

So far we have assumed away the role of technical progress. Let us assume that technical progress is 'neutral' (i.e. neither labour nor capital augmenting) and its contribution to output growth is k per cent per annum above the contributions of capital and labour. This is given by the distance AB in Figure 2.3. The output growth line is now given by q_3 and equilibrium is attained at E″. Note that at E″ both the output–capital ratio and the profit rate are higher in comparison with E. Also *per capita* output is not only higher at E'' in comparison with E but rising constantly (given by the distance between q_3 and n). Its rate of rise is greater than m per cent (imparted by technical progress) because capital's contribution is also sustained by 'technical progress at a higher level' (Swan 1956: 337).

2.5.1 Application of the neoclassical theory to LDCs

There are reasons which make the case for application of the neoclassical model to the developing countries very doubtful. For instance, it is difficult to accept the idea of a 'well-behaved' production function in LDCs just as it is equally difficult to see the relevance of the marginal productivity theory of distribution in peasant economies characterized largely by family farming rather than wage-labour. It is equally possible to argue that given the nature of the market structure and financial mechanism in most LDCs, the neoclassical solution, i.e. equilibrium between r and the rate of profit, would be difficult to achieve. Even when equality can be achieved, it will be relevant only to the organized markets which are usually located in the urban sector without affecting much the partly monetized and unorganized rural sector. Further, land is generally excluded from the neoclassical production function. It is also difficult to define precisely the nature of capital in peasant economies given the problem of heterogeneity of capital.

The major difficulties that arise in the application of the neoclassical model stem from analysis in terms of one factor, capital, and the type of aggregation that has been highlighted. It is easy to comprehend some *ceteris paribus* assumptions but it is less easy to understand the existence of either a very well-behaved production function with indefinite substitution possibilities in LDCs and the application of the principle of marginal productivity to dictate factor shares in such a way as to attain a profit rate which is commensurate with an interest rate at a steady state. In LDCs, rainfall variability alone would rule out any unique association between marginal productivity and income shares. In fact, one can get only a probability distribution of marginal productivities, and the greater the impact of future rainfall and the smaller the knowledge of that rainfall, the greater is the probability of obtaining a misleading result by applying marginal productivity theory. Further, if the variance of rainfall is high, the risk premium will be high and the marginal value productivity equalization rule does not allow any trade-off between the variance and the expected value of profit. Moreover, factor market imperfections and inter-farm differences in output from the same inputs would be high in less developed agriculture (Lipton 1968b). Indeed, given fluctuations in weather and the subsistence living standards, the optimizing peasant needs 'survival algorithms', not profit maximization. Thus the logic of peasant economies renders the application of the marginal productivity rule difficult, partly because of the difference in the objective function and partly because of differences in institutions and social values.

There are other general criticisms of the neoclassical theory. For example, in the absence of any *specific* mechanism to bring about the equilibrium between investment and full employment saving, the balancing mechanism is supposed to be the interest rate r and an equilibrium rate of profit on investment which should be equal to r. But this conclusion must be qualified in the presence of risks and uncertainties. Again, monetary forces may determine a certain r which could lead to a choice of v inconsistent with a steady state growth. Also, the steady state profit rate may require real wages below subsistence level and hence the solution may not be feasible (see also Hall 1983).

2.6 Marx's theory and less developed countries

Marx rejected some principal features of the classical theory of economic growth and offered his own theory within a socio-historical framework in which economic forces play a major role. In Marxist theory, the law of diminishing returns has been discarded because Marx believed that the classical theory of stationary state was actually a creation of human actions rather than the end product of a natural, immutable law. For a similar reason, Marx also castigated the Malthusian theory of population.

Marx looked at economic development from a social and historical standpoint. Each stage of economic growth was regarded as the product of Hegelian dialectics of a game of contradictions where a thesis created its anti-thesis and the conflict between the two produced a synthesis. Marx also emphasized that, with capitalism, *social relations of production* are much more important than exchange relations between goods. The *social* character of labour has been stressed in particular. Marx argued that labour productivity 'is a gift, not of nature, but of history embracing thousands of centuries' (Marx 1906: 562). However, the Marxist concept of *relations of production* is rather vague. It has been interpreted as an *'organic* whole' characterized by labour organization and skill, the standing of labour in society, technological and scientific knowledge and its use in a certain environment (Bober 1950). In the Marxist analysis, these 'relations of production' determine the socio-cultural set-up of a society. Marx believed that capitalism would not end up in a quiet classical 'stationary' state; rather, it would break up with a 'bang' 'when the expropriators are expropriated'. Here, we shall only analyse the economic views in the Marxist theory, abstracting from social and institutional issues.

The Marxist model of economic growth depends on some major dynamic 'laws':

1 the law of capitalistic accumulation which says that the prime desire of the capitalists is to accumulate more and more capital;
2 the law of falling tendency of the *rate* of profit which plays a crucial role in the breakdown of the capitalistic system (this law is illustrated below);
3 the law of increasing concentration and centralization of capital which tells us that, with the growth of capitalism, cut-throat competition among capitalists will lead to the annihilation of smaller firms by bigger ones which will lead to the growth of monopoly and concentration of economic power;
4 the law of increasing 'pauperization' which implies the growth of the misery of the working class with the advancement of capitalism, reflected in wages being tied to the subsistence level coupled with a rise in the proportion of unemployed people or what Marx called the 'industrial reserve army of labour', made possible by the substitution of capital for labour in the process of technical change.

The simultaneous working of these laws would generate contradictory forces which would eventually sharpen the class conflict between capitalists and workers or between 'haves' and 'have-nots'. Capitalism would face a violent death in the final confrontation when the expropriators would be expropriated. Hence, Marx gave the clarion call: 'Workers of the world, unite', as they have nothing to lose except their 'chains'.

The Marxist notion of the falling *tendency* of the *rate* of profit plays a crucial part in the whole process of change and can now be illustrated. According to Marx, the value of a commodity (w) is given by the sum of 'constant capital' (c) or the plant and machinery *used up in production* plus the 'variable capital' (q) or the wage bill plus the 'surplus value' (s) or the value that labour produces in excess of necessary labour to produce a commodity. If the working day consists of 8 hours and only 4 hours are required to produce a commodity then for the remaining 4 hours the worker is producing a surplus value which is expropriated by capitalists (Sweezy 1942). More formally,

$$w = c + q + s$$

and

$$x = s/q$$

where x is the rate of surplus value or the rate of 'exploitation'. Thus, in the above example,

$$4 \text{ hours}/4 \text{ hours} = 100 \text{ per cent} = x$$

The rate of profit (p) in the Marxian analysis is given by

$$p = \frac{s}{q + c}$$

or

$$p = \frac{s/q}{1 + c/q}$$

Let $s/q = x$, i.e. the rate of exploitation, and $c/q = j$ or the 'organic composition of capital'. Then we have

$$p = \frac{x}{1 + j}$$

Now, it is clear that if x remained constant, p and j would be inversely correlated. A rise in j would take place as capitalism developed with continuous accumulation. Also, capitalists would substitute capital for labour whenever wages tended to rise above the subsistence level to maintain their rate of profit. The process would lead to higher unemployment among the working class and sharpen the polarization of forces. On the other hand, the crisis of capitalism would be reflected in the periodic fluctuations of growth and a falling tendency of the rate of profit. Such a falling tendency of the *rate* of profit would lead to cut-throat competition among the capitalists which, in its turn, would lead to monopoly. Eventually, the conflict between the 'immiserized proletarians' and the capitalists would toll the death knell of capitalism.

It is interesting to observe that the law of a tendency for the rate of profit to fall may not always be observed within an economic system. This can easily be demonstrated *within the Marxist model* (see Adelman 1962). We have

$$p = \frac{x}{1 + j}$$

Differentiating p with respect to time t we obtain

$$\frac{dp}{dt} = \frac{1}{1 + j}\frac{dx}{dt} - \frac{x}{(1 + j)^2}\frac{dj}{dt}$$

or

$$\frac{dp}{dt} = \frac{1}{1 + j}\left(\frac{dx}{dt} - P\frac{dj}{dt}\right)$$

Note that the profit rate will *rise* if the rate of exploitation rises more rapidly than the organic composition of capital. Even if the rise in the organic composition of capital is higher than that of the rate of exploitation, whether or not profit will fall depends on the difference between dx/dt and the *product* of profit rate and dj/dt. For profit rate to *fall*, $p\mathrm{d}_j/\mathrm{d}t$ (which is negative) must be greater than $\mathrm{d}x/\mathrm{d}t$. But a *fixed* rate of exploitation and an increase in capital intensity may not go together because a rise in organic composition of capital would raise labour productivity which would either raise the rate of exploitation (which Marx assumes away) or raise real wages (which Marx rejected). Inevitably, the internal consistency of the Marxist model has been questioned (Sweezy 1942; Adelman 1962). Further, as has been shown above very clearly, a rise in the organic composition of capital could *increase* the rate of profit with an increase of productivity and a change in technology. Under such circumstances, the intensity of competition among capitalists declines. Technical progress may be neutral or even labour-using (say, with the application of more and more seed and fertilizer in agriculture in LDCs). Thus the rise in the industrial reserve army of labour and a fall in the wage share in national income may not occur.

Other criticisms usually levelled at the Marxist model may also be mentioned briefly. It is contended that Marx's correlation between the growth of the average firm size and an increase in the degree of concentration need not always happen. However, the proportion of unemployment has increased in both DCs and LDCs in recent decades.

Empirically, wage share of national income in most DCs remained fairly constant for a long time and this phenomenon seems to have weakened the Marxist law of increasing pauperization (Kaldor 1957). On the other hand, the Marxist prediction about the increasing concentration and centralization of capital is not rejected. However, the rise in the output–capital ratios in DCs probably reflects the growth of both accumulation and real wages, a phenomenon which Marx probably did not envisage within the strict framework of his analysis (Fellner 1957).

2.6.1 Marx and the LDCs

On the problems of LDCs Marx's analysis was rather thin. Marx paid some attention to Indian economic problems. The Indian society was regarded by Marx as an assembly of small self-contained 'village systems' where people 'agglomerated in small centres by the domestic union of agricultural and manufacturing pursuits'. The socioeconomic system of India stagnated because 'these little communities [i.e. village systems] transformed a self-developed social state into never-changing natural destiny' (Marx 1853). Marx thought that British rule in India would administer an (albeit rude) shock to the static Indian society, through the introduction of modern science and technology, which would break down the static society and usher in capitalism. However, the verdict of history has been somewhat different.

The quintessence of the Marxist theory of underdevelopment is well summarized by Adelman: 'underdevelopment is the consequence of a particular adverse combination of initial conditions and structural parameters, which results in economic and social stagnation. Development can occur only as a result of an exogenous shock, the essential effect of which is to change the initial conditions in such a way that self-sustained growth takes place' (Adelman 1962: 91).

2.6.2 Neo-Marxist theory of underdevelopment

The idea that the village system of LDCs could be changed by an exogenous shock has prompted some Marxist economists of today (whom we would call neo-Marxists) to use the Marxist model to analyse problems of LDCs (for a review of theoretical contributions to post-Marxian literature see, for example, Bose 1975). There are, of course, other sociological, political and historical reasons. Here, a very brief outline of the neo-Marxist theory of underdevelopment is given.

Some neo-Marxists trace the origin of capitalism to the idea of mercantilists who believed in the principle of accumulation. Historically, the development of capitalism in Europe led to imperialism and colonialism which created a wealthy and strong centre (the imperial power) and a weak, poor periphery, which mainly consisted of colonies. The capitalistic and imperialistic development at the centre is supposed to have taken place through the exploitation of colonies at the periphery, and this is supposed to have been reflected in the movement of the ratio of export price to import price, or the terms of trade, against poor countries (Prebisch 1964). Free trade became the convenient vehicle of 'exploitation'. Hence: 'Underdevelopment, no less than development itself, is the product but also part of the motive power of capitalism' (Frank 1969, 1975; for an evaluation of the Prebisch thesis, see Chapter 7). The poor countries of today, despite their political independence, have become *economically dependent* upon the developed metropolis because of their historical past reinforced by the 'neo-colonial' ties of trade, aid and transfer of technology. As trading partners, the LDCs are dependent upon the DCs because the goods they usually produce (mainly primary commodities) are both price and income inelastic while the goods they want, they cannot produce themselves. It is argued that such a situation has led to 'unequal exchange' between the centre and periphery (Emmanuel 1972). The LDCs are further exploited and made more dependent upon the DCs with the growth of international capitalism and multinational corporations who in their global search for more profit can easily mop up 'surplus' from LDCs (and DCs as well) as they can direct their investment from low-profit to high-profit areas quite easily (Radice 1975). Productivity is likely to remain low in those LDCs from whence the 'surplus' or profit has been extracted and this could only perpetuate their poor economic conditions. The structural effects of such a system are seen in the prevention of the growth of indigenous enterprises and the perpetuation of a small market which usually caters for 'elitist' demand or the demand of the people who are included in the higher income groups in LDCs. Also, one finds the inadequate production of goods necessary for mass consumption, import of luxury goods which creates balance of payments problems and a choice of technology and products which are unsuitable for LDCs. Thus, the technology which is capital intensive (often imported) usually creates more unemployment and poverty and accentuates the existing inequalities in income distribution. The indigenous 'elite class' in collusion with international capitalism perpetuates the self-reproducing, static, neo-colonial structures of LDCs. This, in a nutshell, is the underdevelopment and dependency theory (UDT) in the neo-Marxist writings of today.

The empirical support of the neo-Marxist theory is usually derived from the experiences of the poor Asian and the Latin American countries in the last forty years. It is argued that, despite the modest growth of the real national income in these countries, both inflation and unemployment have soared. The increase in *per capita* real income has been slight, while in some cases it has actually fallen with poverty and inequality in income distribution increasing. This is regarded as the product partly of the UDT theory, partly of the so-called 'socialist' policies which consist of the manipulation of the Keynesian interventional policies rather than the restructuring of economies, say, on Chinese lines, and partly because of the unholy alliance of the international aid agencies, champions of state capitalism within the LDCs, who are against fundamental reforms and multinationals or the 'fall guys'.

2.6.3 Evaluation of the neo-Marxist theory of underdevelopment

Many of the hypotheses on the UDT, put forward by the neo-Marxist writers, are not amenable to rigorous statistical analysis. Some of them will be dealt with in subsequent chapters. Suffice now to say that the debate on the movement of the terms against LDCs remains inconclusive even today (see Chapter 7). Protection and import substitution have sometimes resulted in real income losses in LDCs, and abdication of principles of free trade, over-valuation of currency and controls of trade have actually penalized exports and agriculture and rewarded industry and urban areas in LDCs (see Chapters 7 and 8). Ironically, 'protection' has sometimes really meant the protection of the small sector of rich industrial monopoly capital at the expense of the vast agricultural sector where 70–90 per cent of people in LDCs live. However, the effects of multinationals on the economies of LDCs have been debated and the extent of 'exploitation' is not always known (see Chapter 6). It is also difficult to accept the argument that the effects of the flow of foreign resources to LDCs have *always* been harmful. The argument about the choice of wrong technology or of product does not always clearly follow from the UDT theory as such a choice is not only exogenous but also endogenous. In other words, even if multinationals wish to introduce from outside inappropriate techniques or products to LDCs, such an introduction or choice could not always be made without the internal support of recipient countries. At the theoretical level, it may be argued that the UDT defines the concept of development rather vaguely. It does not state clearly the ways to accomplish development; it is too much concerned with the analysis of how *underdevelopment* took place in the *past* rather than how *development* can be achieved in the *future;* it does not seek to estimate carefully the extent of exploitation. Naturally, statements like 'Capitalism has created underdevelopment not simply because it has exploited the underdeveloped countries, but because it has not exploited them *enough'* (Kay 1975, his italics) become difficult to evaluate. Indeed, it has been argued rather pointedly, 'Curiously enough, it is not clear that UDT provides any explanation of why more capital was not invested and accumulated in the Third World in the past, nor of why it should not now take advantage of cheap labour and soak up vast pools of unemployed people in the Third World today' (Leys 1977: 96).

2.7 The Kaldor-Mirrlees model

Kaldor has discussed two models of economic growth (1957, 1962). Here, we shall be mainly concerned with the one by Kaldor and Mirrlees (KM) in 1962. The crucial feature of the KM model is that the saving ratio can be made flexible to obtain a steady state economic growth. Unlike the neoclassical model, the capital–output ratio remains fixed. Note that Kaldor and Mirrlees discard the production function approach of the neoclassical theory and introduce a technical progress function. The neoclassical school has not specified any investment function; but in the KM model, an investment function is specified which depends upon a fixed pay-off period for investment per worker (1962). The assumptions regarding both full employment and perfect competition are dropped. Instead, Kaldor and Mirrlees start off with the assumption that total income Y is equal to the sum of wages W and profits P:

$$Y \equiv W + P \tag{2.15}$$

Total savings S are assumed to be equal to savings out of wages (S_w) and profits (S_p):

$$S = S_w + S_p \tag{2.16}$$

Note that

$$S = s_w W + s_p P \tag{2.17}$$

and

$$S_w = s_w W \tag{2.18}$$

$$S_p = s_p P \tag{2.19}$$

where s_w is the propensity to save by wage earners, s_p is the propensity to save by profit earners and S is total savings. Both s_w and s_p are assumed to be constants indicating the equality between marginal and average propensities. Now

$$Y \equiv W + P$$

and

$$S = s_w W + s_p P$$

By substitution, we have

$$S = s_w(Y - P) + s_p P \tag{2.20}$$

$$S = (s_p - s_w)P + s_w Y \tag{2.21}$$

Since it is assumed that

$$I = S \tag{2.22}$$

we have

$$I = (s_p - s_w)P + s_w Y \tag{2.23}$$

Dividing both sides of the equation by Y and rearranging we obtain

$$\frac{P}{Y} = \frac{1}{s_p - s_w}\frac{1}{Y} - \frac{s_w}{s_p - s_w} \tag{2.24}$$

Thus, the profit share of income is given by the share of investment to income. The stability of the model is given by

$$0 \leq s_w \leq s_p \leq 1$$

Notice that the flexibility of saving is achieved in the KM model by the assumption of different propensities to save by wage and profit earners. The specific value of savings necessary to obtain the solution would be given by the income distribution between income classes. Given s_p and s_w, I/Y will determine P/Y. If it is assumed that $s_w = 0$, we then obtain

$$\frac{P}{Y} = \frac{1}{s_p}\frac{I}{Y} \tag{2.25}$$

Note that if the capital–output ratio K/Y is fixed, as in the HD model, we can write

$$\frac{P}{Y}\frac{Y}{K} = \frac{1}{s_p}\frac{I}{Y}\frac{Y}{K}$$

or

$$\frac{P}{K} = \frac{1}{s_p}\frac{I}{K} \tag{2.26}$$

Since $P/K = V$, the rate of profit earned on capital, and $I/K = J$, the rate of accumulation, we have

$$V = \frac{1}{s_p}J$$

or

$$s_p V = J \tag{2.27}$$

This conclusion betrays remarkable affinity to the von Neumann case where Neumann puts $s_p = 1$. Thus, all profits are saved and in equilibrium we obtain

$$V = J(= n)$$

where n is the natural growth rate which is assumed to be given. Thus the rate of growth is given by the rate of profit which is determined by the propensity to save of the profit earners.

Kaldor's introduction of an 'alternative' theory of distribution to analyse the problem of economic growth is interesting. However, several important criticisms have been levelled at the Kaldorian theory. First, Pasinetti mentions a 'logical slip' in Kaldor's argument when he observes that, although Kaldor has allowed the workers to save, he did not permit these savings to accumulate and generate income. In a more general theorem, Pasinetti has demonstrated that on a steady state growth path the profit rate depends only on the growth rate and the propensity to save by the capitalists; it is independent of the propensity to save by the workers (see Pasinetti 1962 for the proof). However, if it is assumed that capitalists as a class have been banished and capital is owned by the workers alone, then the relevant variables in the balanced growth path will be given by s_w and n (see, for details and proof, Samuelson and Modigliani 1966; also, for a lucid analysis, Jones 1975).

Second, Kaldor's assumption about the fixed propensities to save disregards the impact of life cycle on saving and work. Third, the assumption of a fixed *class* of income receivers is regarded as unrealistic (Samuelson and Modigliani 1966). Finally, Kaldor's model fails to exhibit an explicit *behavioural* mechanism which will ensure that the *actual* distribution of income will be such as to maintain the steady state growth path.

Few empirical tests are available to assess whether the Kaldorian theory could be applied to LDCs. In one study that was conducted for the Indian economy for the period 1948–58, no positive and statistically significant relationship was observed between profit share and investment share in income (Bharadwaj and Dave 1973). However, because of imperfection of the data and the rather small number of observations, more research is necessary to draw any firm conclusion. The present emphasis on the analysis of economic growth and income distribution by Chenery *et al.* (1974) in LDCs may lead to more theoretical and empirical research in this field (see Chapter 10).

2.8 The neoclassical growth accounting formula and the new endogenous growth theory

Following the work of Solow (1956, 1957) and Dennison (1967), the neoclassical theory to compute the contribution of different inputs to the overall growth rate of an economy can be explained in a simple way. Let labour L, capital K and technology A grow by rates $\Delta L/L$, $\Delta K/K$ and $\Delta A/A$. Output grows at rate $\Delta Q/Q$.

Assume that technical progress is neither capital nor labour intensive, i.e. it is neutral, and hence the production function can be written as

$$F(L, K, A) = Af(L, K)$$

Thus, the rate of growth of output is roughly given by

$$\frac{\Delta Q}{Q} = \frac{\Delta A}{A} + \frac{\Delta f(L, K)}{f(L, K)} \tag{2.28}$$

Hence, the real output growth rate of the product of A and $f(L, K)$ is just the sum of the section of the change in output that occurs due to change in the use of labour and capital inputs and can be written in terms of the marginal productivities of labour (M_L) and capital (M_K). We can now write

$$\frac{\Delta f(L, K)}{f(L, K)} = \frac{M_L \Delta L}{Q} + \frac{M_K \Delta K}{Q} \tag{2.29}$$

Substituting (2.29) into (2.28) we have

$$\frac{\Delta Q}{Q} = \frac{\Delta A}{A} + \frac{M_L \Delta L}{Q} + \frac{M_K \Delta K}{Q} \tag{2.30}$$

Since profit-maximizing firms use labour and capital up to the amounts where $M_L = W/P$ (real wages) and $M_K = R^K/P$ (real rental price), we can write (2.30) as

$$\frac{\Delta Q}{Q} = \frac{\Delta A}{A} + \frac{W}{P}\frac{\Delta L}{Q} + \frac{R^K}{P}\frac{\Delta K}{Q} \tag{2.31}$$

Rearranging we get

$$\frac{\Delta Q}{Q} = \frac{\Delta A}{A} + \frac{WL}{PQ}\frac{\Delta L}{L} + \frac{R^K K}{PQ}\frac{\Delta K}{K} \tag{2.32}$$

Since WL/PQ (say 0.6) is the labour share of income and $R^K K/PQ$ (say 0.4) is the share of capital in income we have

$$\frac{\Delta Q}{Q} = \frac{\Delta A}{A} + 0.6\frac{\Delta L}{L} + 0.4\frac{\Delta K}{K} \tag{2.33}$$

Thus with a Cobb–Douglas type of production function such as

$$Q = AK^{\alpha}L^{\beta}$$

and assuming $\alpha = 0.6$ (i.e. elasticity of output with respect to capital) and $\beta = 0.4$ (i.e. elasticity of capital with respect to labour), we can estimate the contributions of different types of inputs, including human capital (say H) as emphasized in the 'endogenous growth' literature, to the output growth rate (see, for example, Lucas 1988; Barro 1991; Romer 1986, 1990; Mankiew *et al.* 1992). The 'augmented' neoclassical aggregate production function that includes human capital accumulation can then be written as follows:

$$Q = AK^{\alpha} + L^{\beta} + H^{\gamma} = 1 \tag{2.34}$$

2.8.1 'Endogenous growth theories' and LDCs

It is now well acknowledged that one of the major problems in the use of neoclassical growth theories is that it does not provide a satisfactory explanation of changes in technology (i.e. $\Delta A/A$) and productivity growth. In the original neoclassical growth models, the term $\Delta A/A$ is usually taken as a proxy for the *autonomous* change in productivity. It is also known as the 'residual' element to explain output growth rate, i.e. the part of output growth which is not explained by the growth rates of inputs like labour and capital. Since this 'residual' factor is assumed to be 'exogenous' and its role in the empirical studies of economic growth of DCs is found to be significant, economic growth seems to have fallen on countries like 'manna' from heaven! In other words, economic theory had very little to offer to explain the fall of such 'manna' from heaven. The absence of a sensible theory to explain the role of the 'residual' element simply underlines the measured estimate of such an input as the coefficient of our ignorance! In the late 1980s, a number of economists were prompted to analyse the nature and role of such a 'residual' element in growth theories by endogenizing it (see Romer 1986, 1990; Lucas 1988).

The origin of the endogenous growth theory can be traced back to the early 1960s when Arrow published his seminal work on 'Learning by doing' (Arrow 1962). The theory seeks to explain changes in technology by analysing the role of investment in research, training and education by firms as well as by government policies in changing economic incentives (e.g. via taxes and subsidies) to promote physical and human capital accumulation. Thus, the new theory examines how changes in government subsidies and taxes can have a *permanent* effect on the growth rate of output, and not just on the level of the output as shown by Solow.

If we stick to the orthodox neoclassical growth theory and assume that technical progress A is exogenous, then given the fact that knowledge is relatively inexpensive to input, all countries (rich and poor) should attain in the long run the same A in their production function. Thus the orthodox neoclassical growth theory indicates a 'convergence' or 'catching up' process in which LDCs acquire techniques and learn inter-temporally how to use them efficiently. In addition, LDCs with low K/L rates should have high M_K and attract foreign capital. *Eventually,* a system of convergence should produce the same *per capita* GDP. This means that countries with low *per capita* GDP should grow faster to catch up with the DCs. Thus, the correlation between *per capita* GDP and average growth rate should be negative. This is regarded as β convergence.

In practice, evidence based on data available for 1960–86 for ninety-eight countries hardly supports this view. The endogenous growth theory tried to explain such lack of convergence by introducing the role of human capital (H) (as a complementary input to physical capital) in the production function. Assume

$$Q = F(K, L, H)$$

Here note that M_K is also a function of H and hence simple K/L ratios are inadequate indicators of productivity. So despite the fact that LDCs have less capital relative to labour (i.e. M_K is supposed to be high in LDCs), the combination of low human capital stock and capital may not imply a high M_K in practice. One way to include H in the aggregate production function is to write $\Delta Q/Q = g$,

$$g = F(K, L, H)$$

and

$$g = K^{\alpha} L^{\beta} H^{\gamma}$$

i.e.

$$g = \alpha \frac{\Delta K}{K} + \beta \frac{\Delta L}{L} + \gamma \frac{\Delta H}{H}$$

If constant returns to scale prevail, we have $\alpha + \beta + \gamma = 1$. By introducing H, we can now explain the 'manna from heaven' or the residual element A. If $\alpha = \gamma \Delta H/H$ then it shows the rate of human capital accumulation in a particular country. The more a country saves and invests in human capital, the faster it grows.

Barro (1991) claims that when the *per capita* growth rate is corrected for investment in human capital, convergence occurs among the ninety-eight countries in the sample. The barrier to convergence seems to be inadequate investment in human capital among LDCs. For empirical verification of the new endogenous growth theory, investment in human capital is measured by observing the disparities in levels of education in different countries. Lucas (1988) also argues that such disparities in the levels of education and labour skills can explain a good deal of the discrepancies in growth rates across nations. Note that, with H as the argument in the production function, constant returns to scale prevail. Some countries (e.g. newly industrialized countries such as South Korea and Taiwan) could also have enjoyed increasing returns to scale due to the emergence of positive *externalities*.

Table 1.6 illustrates the sharp differences of investment in human capital in different countries of the world. It seems to imply that if, over time, LDCs accumulate enough 'human capital', they should 'converge'. Economic growth and convergence will be faster the more is saved and invested in both human and physical capital.

It is important to emphasize that in most LDCs 'public infrastructure' (PI) can be included with the aggregate production function and can help explain Solow's 'residual' element. The term PI includes roads, schools, hospitals, communication systems and health care facilities generally provided by the government. Since PI is usually funded by public saving and is not exchanged on global markets, inadequate accumulation may occur, say, in some African countries and can explain the lack of convergence among countries. In this sense, if technical progress is *endogenous*, convergence among countries' *per capita* incomes need never occur since government policies can affect output rates both positively and negatively. Not only do nations need to converge; they may well diverge (Lee *et al.* 1997)! The empirical verification of such a hypothesis remains to be tested. If it is valid, it implies a significant role for policy formulators to raise savings and investment in human capital (e.g. education, research and development). Thus, externalities from PI and increasing returns to scale may well explain convergence. Human capital accumulation, knowledge and PI can be possible elements that create externalities. For LDCs, policies formulated to raise their accumulation are very desirable.

The algebra of growth accounting can also be described in a simple way. Let the production function be continuous and homogeneous of degree one, i.e.

$$Q = F(L, K, T) \tag{2.35}$$

Where Q is aggregate real output, K is stock of capital, L is labour and T is time. Differentiating (2.35) with respect to time T, we have

$$\frac{\mathrm{d}Q}{\mathrm{d}t} = \frac{\partial F}{\partial L}\frac{\mathrm{d}L}{\mathrm{d}T} + \frac{\partial F}{\partial K}\frac{\mathrm{d}K}{\mathrm{d}T} + \frac{\partial F}{\partial T}\frac{\mathrm{d}T}{\mathrm{d}T} \tag{2.36}$$

Dividing (2.36) by Q, using K and L, we obtain

$$\frac{1}{Q}\frac{\mathrm{d}Q}{\mathrm{d}T} = \frac{1}{Q}\left(\frac{\partial F}{\partial L}\frac{\mathrm{d}L}{\mathrm{d}T}L\frac{1}{L} + \frac{\partial F}{\partial K}\frac{\mathrm{d}K}{\mathrm{d}T}K\frac{1}{K} + \frac{\partial F}{\partial T}\right) \tag{2.37}$$

Hence, we have

$$\frac{\mathrm{d}Q/\mathrm{d}T}{Q} + \frac{(\partial F/\partial L)L}{Q}\frac{\mathrm{d}L/\mathrm{d}T}{L} + \frac{(\partial F/\partial K)}{Q}\frac{\mathrm{d}K\mathrm{d}T}{K} + \frac{\partial F/\partial T}{Q} \tag{2.38}$$

Let

$$g_Q = \frac{\mathrm{d}Q/\mathrm{d}T}{Q}$$

be the growth rate of real income;

$$g_L = \frac{\mathrm{d}L/\mathrm{d}T}{L}$$

be the growth rate of labour; and

$$g_K = \frac{\mathrm{d}K/\mathrm{d}T}{K}$$

be the growth rate of capital. In a competitive economy, marginal productivity of labour $M_L = w$ (real wage rate) $= \partial F/\partial L$. Then, the wage share in national income is

$$S_L = \frac{(\partial F/\partial L)}{Q} = w\frac{L}{Q}$$

Similarly, assume that $M_K = \partial F/\partial K = \gamma$ (i.e. interest rate or rental) and the share of capital in national income is

$$S_K = \frac{(\partial F/\partial K)K}{Q}\gamma\frac{K}{Q}$$

Let

$$c = \frac{\partial F/\partial T}{Q}$$

be the contribution of the 'residual' input to the real output growth rate. Note that c is sometimes interpreted as an index of productivity growth which takes place autonomously. Thus c is sometimes regarded as an index of technical progress (for an empirical analysis for LDCs, see for example Langham and Ahmed 1981; Robinson 1971).

Substituting into equation (2.38) we can now write the growth equation in the following compact form:

$$g_Q = c + S_L g_L + S_K g_K \tag{2.39}$$

The role of productivity growth (i.e. the residual) or technical progress (c) can now be estimated as follows:

$$c = g_Q - S_L g_L - S_K g_K \tag{2.40}$$

For LDCs, owing to the problems of getting reliable data on capital, sometimes it is assumed that the share of domestic investment I in the GDP is equivalent to the incremental stock of capital, i.e.

$$\frac{\mathrm{d}K/\mathrm{d}T}{Q} = I$$

The above production function analysis can be extended to analyse the roles of structural change and foreign exchange inflows in economic growth (see Robinson 1972). The impact of structural change on the growth rate can be measured by examining the role of capital and labour transfers from the less productive to the more productive sector. The differences in marginal *revenue* products of capital and labour in different sectors (e.g. industry and agriculture) are a function not only of technological factors shown in the differences in the marginal *physical* products but also of demand factors shown in the relative output prices. As Robinson argues, a difference in productivity initiated by technical progress can be sustained by continuous changes in the demand structure that preclude a narrowing of price differential as the modern sector enlarges its output. It is shown that factor transfers to the non-agricultural sector and net foreign exchange reserves played very important roles in 'explaining' the economic growth of thirty-nine LDCs (see Robinson 1971 for details). However, for LDCs, the quality and reliability of data are sometimes open to doubt. In addition, there are market imperfections and there are cases when markets operate in a disequilibrium. The problems of aggregation and measurement are also serious in a number of LDCs. Hence, the results of production function studies should be interpreted with caution.

2.9 Differences in economic growth

2.9.1 The 'old' and 'new' endogenous theories of economic growth

It is generally acknowledged that changes of national income over a period of time are dominated by economic cycles. Interestingly, despite short-term fluctuations in output and employment, the most important fact about national income in most countries is that it grows over time. Figure 2.4 shows US *per capita* GDP between the period from 1889 to 1990. Even though this period includes the Great Depression and the two World Wars, the important empirical regularity that this figure suggests is a steady rise in US national income over many decades.

The income of an average American in 1998 was 1.8 times higher than in 1960, 3.2 times higher than in 1930 and seven times higher than in 1870. If the United States sustains its rate of growth its *per capita* income will double every thirty-five years. It is also an impressive record when compared with that of the least dynamic economics in the world, described in Table 2.1 (e.g. the Central African Republic or Guyana).

But by the standards of the growth miracles witnessed in the last three decades of the twentieth century, US growth seems slow. Table 2.1 also reports the rates of expansion for the world's most dynamic economies between 1960 and 1985. At its current rate of growth the Singapore economy doubles its income every nine years! If this rate of

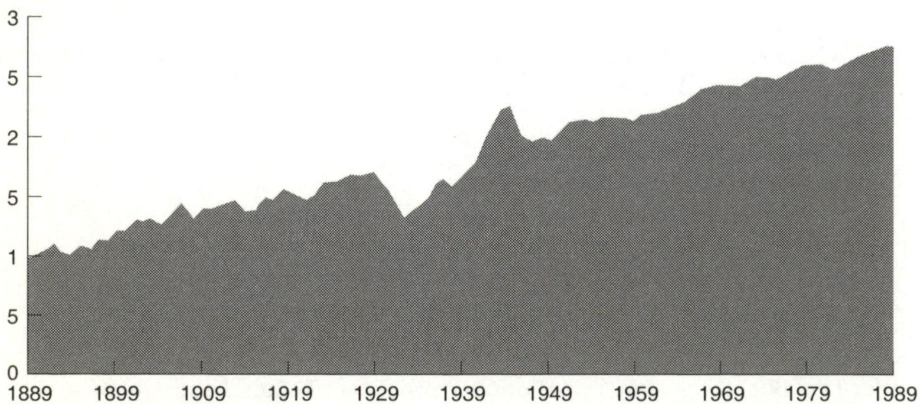

Figure 2.4 Logarithm of US *per capita* real income, 1889–1989

Source: Rebelo 1996.

Table 2.1 The world's most dynamic and least dynamic economies

Economies	*Annual rate of growth of* per capita *GDP, 1960–85 (%)*
Most dynamic	
Singapore	7.5
Hong Kong	6.5
Korea, Taiwan, Malta, Japan	5.5
Botswana, Gabon	5.0
Least dynamic	
Ghana, Zaire, Venezuela	–0.2
Burundi, Sudan, Zambia, Madagascar	–0.1
Central African Republic, Guyana	–0.5

Source: Summers and Heston (1991); Rebelo (1996).

expansion were maintained, the income level of Singapore's next generation would be 190 times higher than its current level. Whether the US economy can grow at the same rate as Singapore and why so many countries fail to develop are some of the questions that growth theory (both exogenous and endogenous) tries to answer.

2.9.2 The main motors of growth

The increase in the level of US income between 1870 and 1990 reflects the large volume of investment that took place during this period of time. Investment can take many forms: equipment investment, acquisition of new machinery, building of infrastructure, devoting time to learning how to perform a task or how to operate a new piece of equipment, trying to develop a new product, etc. Traditional growth theory, which built on the neoclassical growth model developed in the 1960s by, among others, Robert Solow, emphasized the role played by the accumulation of physical capital. Clearly the level of physical capital in the United States is much larger today than in 1870.

But the accumulation of physical capital is only part of the story. The major difference between most contemporary economies and those of a century ago is that today we have much better goods and technologies. All this, according to some, is due to technological progress. Investment in research and development (R&D), which Solow's neoclassical model treated as exogenous, has been the focus of the recent theoretical work.

The first phase of new growth models stemmed from Paul Romer's (1986, 1990) work. Romer explores the conditions under which sustainable growth is feasible when there are no exogenous increases in productivity. He, thus, focused on the most important drawback of the models of the 1950s and 1960s: their inability to explain sustained growth without assuming exogenous increases in productivity (often described as 'exogenous technical progress'). Romer's work was influenced by two observations:

1 The growth rate in the developed world shows no signs of a decline.
2 Sustained growth is feasible only when there are no decreasing returns to capital accumulation (if new investment brings down the real rate of return on capital, sustained growth is not feasible). This led him to propose a model in which there

were no diminishing returns to capital because of externalities associated with capital accumulation. These externalities meant that the productivity of an individual firm is higher, the higher the aggregate stock of capital.

Work on the link between externalities of the form proposed by Romer and growth attracted interest (Caballero and Lyons 1992; Benhabib and Jovanovic 1991).[1] However, it became clear at a theoretical level that externalities were not essential for sustainable growth (Jones and Mapinelli 1990; Rebello 1991). Probing deeper into the essence of technological progress would require more sophisticated models.

Romer also pioneered the second phase of work on growth models by proposing in 1990 a model in which private firms invested in R&D so they could create new goods that increased the efficiency of the production process (see also Grossman and Helpman 1991). This model considers the fact that private firms will only invest in R&D if there exist patents and other forms of property rights protection that allow them to appropriate the rewards to its innovation process. These patent systems create a temporary monopoly by restricting the number of users of the technology. However, the monopolistic nature of markets for new goods is necessary so that R&D investment takes place.

Aghion and Howitt (1992, 1998) and Grossman and Helpman (1991) studied the 'creative destruction' dimension of R&D investment. New, more desirable products displace the demand for older products, forcing firms with outdated technology to fail. There is, thus, a close link between technological progress, the dynamics of firm creation and firm destruction, and the behaviour of unemployment. Jobs may be less secure, spells of unemployment more frequent and opportunities for older works more scarce in an economy with fast technological progress. This link between growth and business cycles was first discussed in the writings of Schumpeter in the 1930s. However, only recently have these ideas have been incorporated in coherent models that can be used to analyse the effects of public policies (see e.g. Aghion and Howitt 1991, 1998).

Another form of investment that has gained recognition in the work of Robert Lucas (1988) is the accumulation of human capital. Developed economies invest heavily in their education system. High levels of education interact with technological progress at least at two levels. First, highly skilled individuals, who underwent long periods of formal schooling, are responsible for the vast majority of innovations. Second, the effective use of new technologies often require high levels of human capital. A powerful workstation in the hands of someone not familiar with its operating system is less useful than a small calculator.[2]

The available empirical evidence (Psacharopoulos 1985) suggests that there are high rates of return to primary and secondary education. These basic education levels involve moderate investments and build skills that are essential for a successful diffusion of technical progress. There is also evidence (Bartel and Lichtenberg 1987) that skilled workers are essential in setting up new plant and in the process of learning by doing by which new plant raises its productivity.

Formal schooling is not the only source of human capital accumulation. Arrow (1962), Stokey (1988) and Young (1991) have stressed the role of other forms of skill improvement, such as 'learning by doing' (LBD) and on-the-job training. The incentive for firms and workers to engage in this type of training depends heavily on the structure of the labour market. The high wage rates enjoyed by developed countries reflect two factors; (1) the existence of a large stock of high-technology capital goods that make the productivity of labour high; and (2) the investment by workers of time and resources to learning how to operate those technologies.

Recognizing that there are three motors responsible for economic development – technological progress, human capital accumulation and physical capital investment – does not answer the question of why some countries fail to grow. There are other constraints and, unlike the view held by the advocates of the old growth theorists, public policies matter.

2.9.3 The role of public policy

The most obvious potential source of cross-country growth differentials is public policy. Different economies choose different tax systems, financial intermediation regulations, trade policy, industrial organization policy, monetary policy, property rights protection, etc. Table 2.2, extracted from Easterly *et al.* (1993), provides some empirical support to the link between policy and growth. This table, which identifies the variables that are statistically different when we compare fast-growing and slow-growing countries, was constructed using an augmented version of the Summers and Heston (1991) data set.[3] This data set has played a critical role in the wealth of empirical work accumulated over the 1990s.[4]

Table 2.2 Variables that indicate fast or slow growth (%)

Variable	*Fast growers*	*Slow growers*
Share of investment in GDP	27	17
Secondary school enrolment rates	27	7
Primary school enrolment rates	90	52
Government expenditure/GDP	14	13
Government consumption/GDP	8	12
Inflation rate	8.4	16.5
Standard deviation of inflation	8.8	19.4
Black market exchange rate premium	4.7	75.0
Standard deviation of black market premium	6.5	105.7
Share of exports in GDP	44	29

Source: Easterly *et al.* (1994).

2.9.3.1 The importance of investment

The first three variables in Table 2.2 reflect the importance of overall investment and of resources devoted to education. Fast-growing economies devote higher shares of GDP to investment purposes and feature higher rates of enrolment in primary and secondary education.[5]

The work of A. Young (1992, 1994) has partly explained the role played by high levels of investment in the growth process. A standard explanation for the extraordinary rates of growth obtained by East Asia's 'newly industrialized countries' (NICS). (Hong Kong, Singapore, South Korea and Taiwan) is that these countries have experienced extraordinary productivity growth. This growth in productivity has often been attributed to prudent public policy that has directed public and private investment to promising sectors of activity.

Young shows that high growth rates have been the result not of huge productivity growth but of very high rates of investment. Investment as a share of GDP has been, in the 1980s and 1990s, about 30 per cent for Hong Kong and South Korea, 25 per cent in Taiwan and 40 per cent in Singapore. These countries also invested heavily in education. The fraction of the working population that has completed secondary education has increased between 1966 and 1990 threefold in Hong Kong and South Korea, by two and a half times in Taiwan and fourfold in Singapore.

The idea that high levels of investment explain most of the growth miracles in East Asia also finds support in the work of De Long and Summers (1991) and Jones (1991). Their research shows the presence of a strong link between equipment investment and growth. Their regressions suggest that the high rates of expansion in East Asia do not reflect the effectiveness of industrial organization policy. They are simply the result of high levels of investment in general, and of high levels of equipment investment in particular.

The high levels of investment in countries such as the NICs have been financed mainly by domestic savings. Hence, in the new growth theory, savings matter. The high savings rates observed in these economies have often been attributed to cultural factors. However, Carroll *et al.* (1994) found that the savings behaviour of immigrants into Canada is independent of their ethnic origin. At the same time these authors have found that immigrants from Asia spend more on education than other immigrants.

High investment in physical capital and in education must partly reflect the influence of policies that encourage investment. Table 2.2 shows that fast-growing countries have slightly higher levels of government expenditure but significantly lower levels of government consumption (which Barro 1991 has used as a proxy for wasteful government activity).

2.9.3.2 Inflation

Fischer (1993) studied the relation between high and variable rates of inflation and poor growth performance. Inflation has obvious negative effects on growth by raising the amount of time and resources used to economize on money holdings. But these direct effects of inflation are likely to be small. The private sector can always adapt to inflation by using indexation systems and by transacting in foreign currencies. Fischer (1993) stresses that high inflation is, most likely, a symptom of general uncertainty about public policy that inhibits investment. The negative association between the variability of the black market exchange rate premium and growth performance is also consistent with the well established theoretical prediction that policy variability is detrimental to growth (see Ghatak and Siddiki 2001).

2.9.3.3 Trade policy

In the old growth theory, trade does not have any role to play to change economic growth rates. However, successful countries have been much more open to trade than stagnant economies. Import substitution strategies have not paid off either in South Asia or in Latin America. Some (Grossman and Helpman 1991; Rivera-Batiz and Romer 1991) have explored this link between trade openness and growth.[6] Open economies tend to absorb better the new technologies that are essential to sustainable growth because (1) they are forced to complete with the world's most advanced countries so they cannot follow the strategy of selling poor quality goods to domestically protected markets; and (2) they can more easily adopt and develop new goods and technologies by being constantly exposed to modern products.

At a worldwide level, international trade provides incentives for countries to pursue different R&D avenues, thus avoiding the costly duplication of research effort that tends to take place when economies are isolated. Romer (1994) has also shown that the welfare cost of tariffs and other barriers to trade may be much higher than has been suggested by traditional trade analyses which take the number of goods existent in an economy as fixed. The welfare cost of impediments to trade becomes much higher when we take into account their negative impact on the number of different goods available in the economy.

A free trade policy is desirable, even in cases where the protection of certain 'infant industries' can be given a theoretical justification (e.g. Krugman 1987). In practice the mechanisms used to grant protection are likely to be manipulated by influence groups in their favour, and lead to the adoption of welfare-reducing forms of protection. Empirical evidence from many LDCs (e.g. Malaysia, Turkey, Taiwan and Hong Kong) suggests a positive and significant correlation between trade liberalization and economic growth (see Ghatak *et al.* 1995, 1997; Ghatak and Wheatley Price 1997; Ghatak and Utkulu 1998).

2.9.3.4 Financial intermediation

King and Levine (1993) argue that measures of the size of the financial intermediation system (which were not included in the construction of Table 2.2) are correlated with high growth rates. These authors found empirical evidence that accords with the predictions of theoretical models. These models emphasise the well known role of financial markets in allocating capital to its most efficient use. But they also show that financial markets perform less obvious growth-enhancing functions: they foster the specialization that is essential to growth and allow agents to pool risk, making them more willing to invest in the development of new technologies.

The modern theories and evidence suggesting that financial intermediation is important to growth is in direct contrast to Joan Robinson's view that 'where enterprise leads, finance follows' (Levine 1997).

2.9.3.5 Infrastructure investment

There is a strong relation between the fraction of GDP devoted to infrastructure and the rate of growth. The importance of infrastructure investment for productivity and growth, first examined in the work of Aschauer (1985), has been the focus of a large literature. Easterly and Rebelo (1993) have found a strong, robust association between growth and public investment in transport and communications in panel data regressions. It is difficult to discern at the macroeconomic level whether infrastructure investment causes growth or whether investment in infrastructure is simply pro-cyclical. Some microeconomic data agree, however, with theories that view infrastructure investment as an important condition of growth (Barro 1990): *ex post* private real rates of return on transport and communication investment financed by the World Bank are higher than for other types of investment (Bandyopadhyay and Devajaran 1993).

2.9.3.6 A growth menu

Table 2.2 suggests that we might be able to isolate the effect of each policy on growth to create a 'growth menu'. This is not the case, for the following reasons.

The first, stressed by Levine and Renelt (1992), is that governments that adopt good policies along one dimension also tend to adopt good policies along other dimensions, thus making the effects of an individual policy difficult to isolate. Countries that adopt good trade policy also tend to follow good policies towards financial intermediation, taxation, education, etc. In contrast, countries that adopt a particular policy discouraging investment and growth are likely to adopt other growth-hampering policies. High taxes, hefty bureaucratic obstacles to economic activity and poor protection of property rights tend to hinder the adoption of new technologies that enhance productivity. As domestic industry loses its competitiveness it becomes difficult for the government to resist subsidization schemes and impose tariffs and quotas or dual exchange rates. Subsidizing and protecting inefficient industries often leads to high public deficits and to high rates of inflation.

The second constraint to creating a growth recipe is that there is a wide range of policies, such as taxation, tariffs and property rights protection, that are important in the growth process but which are difficult to measure empirically.[7] As new data become available we might be able to make more progress in uncovering policies that are empirically correlated with good growth performance.

2.9.3.7 The political process and institutional factors

The 'creative destruction' theories suggest that not everyone is necessarily a winner in growth process. Owners of old firms, workers whose skills are specific to old technologies (watchmakers, typesetters, etc.) tend to lose in the presence of technical progress. Many suspect that countries that have been successful are those that have created *institutional* arrangements that compensated the losers and thus allowed growth to continue. In contrast, stagnant countries may have been those in which institutional arrangements favoured the protection of the *status quo*. These countries often see technological progress as a threat to which they need to respond with protectionist measures, regulation and other forms of government intervention. Many think that the differential growth rates between the 'tiger' economies of East Asia and many African countries are due to the differences in the *institutional factors* that affect economic growth.

It is difficult to explain why different countries adopt different institutional arrangements. Persson and Tabellini (1994), Alesina and Rodrick (1991) and many others have begun to explore the influence of income inequality on the policies adopted by different countries. Persson and Tabellini's theoretical work predicts that democracies with high inequality adopt aggressive tax policies to redistribute income towards the poor. These policies reduce the private incentive to invest, thereby hampering the growth process. Persson and Tabellini find empirical support for their prediction that democracies with initially low income inequalities tend to grow faster than economies featuring high income inequality and serious distributional conflicts.

The importance of distribution of income in shaping public policy regarding human capital accumulation has also been the subject of research. Saint-Paul and Verdier (1992) provide an explanation for why the extension of political rights to the poor, implemented in most democracies, has not led to a slowdown in growth through the mechanism highlighted by Persson and Tabellini (1994). In Saint-Paul and Verdier's model, redistribution can enhance the growth process when it takes place through the public provision of education, which tends to foster human capital accumulation and growth.

2.9.4 Luck and poverty traps

Some argue that public policy cannot be blamed for all the development gaps. Easterly *et al.* (1993) investigate the possibility of luck playing a role in generating different growth performances. Suppose that all countries invest in configurations of industries that yield the same real rate of return. We will find, *ex post*, that some countries did better than average while others did worse than average, even though their investment prospects looked equally promising to start with. Easterly *et al.* (1993) find support for the presence of this type of randomness in the fact that policies are highly correlated across different periods of time, while growth rates display very low correlation. This suggests that countries that followed similar policies in different periods may have obtained very different growth performances.

Another reason to believe that there are other factors besides policy affecting the course of development is that the number of countries with stagnant economies is extremely high. Easterly (1994) reports that forty-six out of eighty-seven developing countries have rates of growth that are not statistically different from zero. Can policy differences alone explain why so many countries are stagnant?

Growth theorists have also explored the possible existence of 'poverty traps', an idea that was popular in the development literature of the 1950s and 1960s (e.g. Nelson 1956). A poverty trap can arise when development prospects depend on the initial stocks of physical and human capital, and on the level of technological sophistication.

Azariadis and Drazen (1990) explore a simple but appealing form of poverty trap, for which they find empirical support. They stress that human capital may be difficult to accumulate in economies with an initially small stock of human capital. Countries with low literacy rates, in particular, often find it very costly to increase their stock of human capital. This implies that investment in human capital is often scarce. Each generation starts out with a low level of human capital and makes few investments in raising the level of skills of its children, thereby perpetuating the low-skill nature of the labour force.

Malthus predicted that steady population growth eventually leads to a reduction in the level of *per capita* income. Malthus's predictions have been regarded as fallacious in view of the sustained growth experienced by many economies in the post-war period. However, Becker *et al.* (1990) suggest that Malthusian forces might underlie the stagnation of some LDCs.

Following the work by Barro and Becker (1988) on endogenous population growth, many economists uncovered a different poverty trap that results from the interaction of fertility and capital accumulation decisions. They show that parents with a low level of education tend to have a large number of children to whom they provide low education levels. In contrast, parents with high human capital generally choose to have a small number of children to whom they provide a high level of education. At an economy-wide level these joint decisions about human capital acquisition and fertility may create a poverty trap. Countries where the level of human capital is low will tend to have high fertility rates and to invest little in education, thus remaining in a Malthusian poverty trap. Ciccone has explored yet a different poverty trap mechanism. In his model specialized human capital is complementary to specialized capital goods. A poverty trap can arise because of a co-ordination failure: new capital goods may not be developed because of lack of skilled workers to use them. At the same time workers may choose not to become skilled because they fear that the capital goods necessary to make their skill valuable will not be introduced in the economy.

2.9.5 Do levels of income converge in the long run?

One main prediction of the neoclassical growth model is that income levels should converge in the long run. Underneath this convergence prediction is the assumption that there are diminishing returns to capital – the real rate of return to capital is high in economies in which capital is scarce and low where capital is abundant.

The mechanics of convergence are quite simple. Assume that a disaster destroys part of the capital stock of any economy. When normalcy resumes, capital will be scarce and command high returns. High returns to capital encourage investment that increases the growth rate of the economy. This means that the economy will grow faster than it did before the disaster, and that in the long run it will converge to the same level of income it would have enjoyed if the disaster had not taken place. So poor countries will eventually catch up with the rich nations (see Figure 2.5). Figure 2.5, extracted from King and Rebelo (1993), shows the predictions of the neoclassical model for Japanese growth after World War II. Notice that Japan grows faster than the United States and eventually catches up with the US income level.

These convergence dynamics mean that since in poor countries the stock of physical capital is low, their economies should display high real rates of return to investment and high rates of growth. Figure 2.6, which plots the growth rate of GDP for the

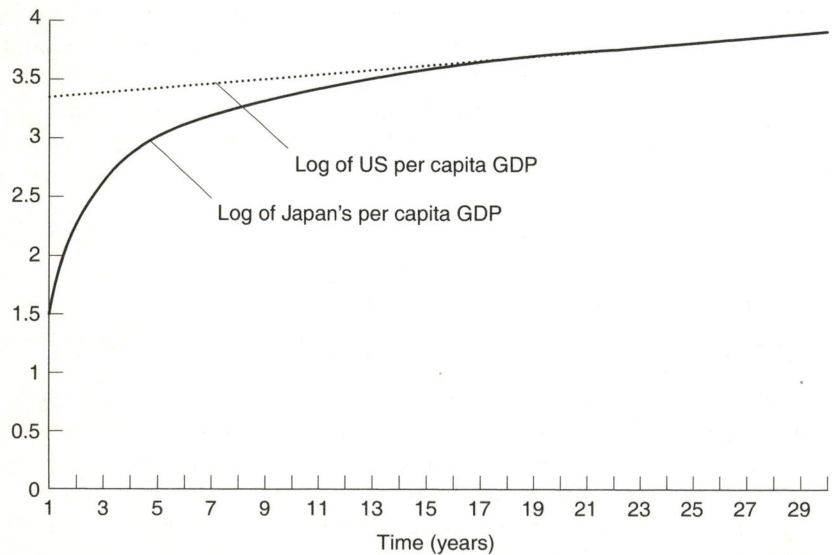

Figure 2.5 Convergence predictions, neoclassical growth model.

Source: King and Rebelo (1993)

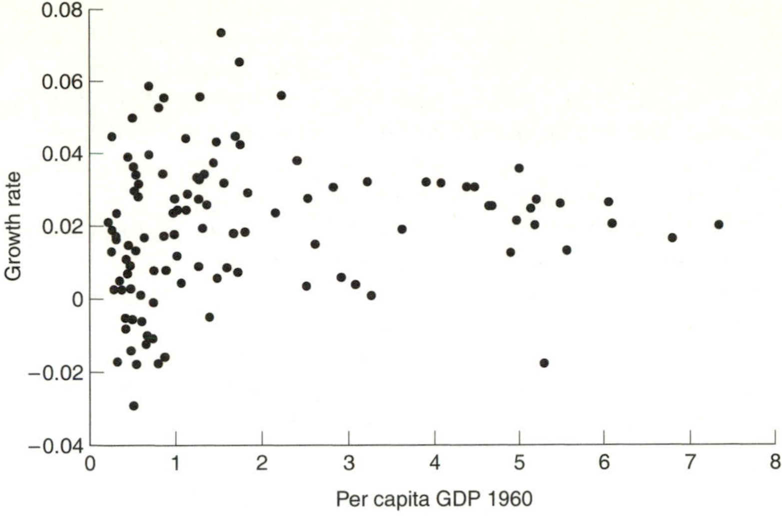

Figure 2.6 Growth rate of *per capita* GDP, 1960–85.
Source: Adapted from Rebelo (1996)

period 1960–85 against the initial level of income for a cross-section of countries from the Summers and Heston (1991) data set, shows that this convergence prediction is not borne out by the data. Poor countries do not always tend to grow faster than rich countries. The correlation between growth and the initial level of income is not negative. Furthermore, there is no evidence that real rates of return are high in poor economies (see also Lee *et al.* 1997).

This failure of a main prediction of the neoclassical growth model was one of the motivations for the development of new growth models. However, Robert Barro and Xavier Sala-i-Martin (1992, 1995), have revived the idea of convergence. They showed that convergence has occurred among the different US states, Japan and among regions of Europe, in the sense that the dispersion of income across these regions has declined over time. They also found that some convergence has taken place among OECD countries. The rate of convergence among US states and among OECD countries is 2 per cent per annum. What this means is that every year each country completes 2 per cent of the difference between its current income level and its long run income path. This rate of convergence is very slow. It means, for instance, that East Germany will take 35 years to close half the gap between its current income level and that of West Germany.

Barro and Sala-i-Martin (1995) and Mankiw *et al.* (1992) also argue that underneath Figure 2.6 one can find a more subtle notion of convergence that Barro named 'conditional convergence'. Since countries are different along many dimensions one would not expect them to converge to the same long-run path. Most likely, each country is converging to its own growth path. This means that there is convergence in growth rates but not in levels of income. If a country sees its capital stock destroyed it will grow faster and eventually catch up with the path that it was following before the shock took place. This long-term path does not, however, have to be the same for all countries. Barro argues that there is evidence of this form of convergence and that, surprisingly, the rate of convergence is also 2 per cent per year.

While much of the work on convergence has used the neoclassical growth model as its point of departure, there are other forces omitted in this model that can lead to convergence. Two obvious ones are migration and technological diffusion.

Workers tend to migrate from low-wage countries to economies where the wage rate is high. This increases the capital–labour ratio in their home country at the same time as it lowers the capital–labour ratio in the economy to which they migrate, thus reducing factor intensity differences in the two economies.

Poor countries can also raise their standard of living by adopting technologies that have been created elsewhere. This 'catching up' effect must have played an important role in the Asian growth miracles. As these countries approach the technology frontier, it will become more difficult to sustain high rates of growth.

The evidence supporting the convergence hypothesis is surprising. However, it is also clear that a convergence rate of 2 per cent per annum is a very weak force that leaves unexplained most of the cross-country diversity in growth experiences.

2.9.6 Conclusion

The growth theories developed in the 1950s and 1960s treated as exogenous the only factors responsible for long-run growth in aggregate income: population growth and technological progress. As a consequence, policies that distorted the returns to accumulation could lead to a temporary slowdown but did not affect long-term growth prospects.

In contrast, recent work on growth theory emphasizes repeatedly the idea that any factor reducing the rewards to investment by the private sector will permanently slow down the rate of economic expansion. There are abundant examples of these types of factors: high taxes, bureaucratic red tape, obstacles to financial intermediation, corruption, barriers to trade, inefficient education systems, lax patent protection, poor protection of general property rights, political instability, etc.

This list of policy variables might suggest that it is possible to trace all differences in growth experiences to differences in public policy. It is, however, likely that initial conditions, such as the stock of physical and human capital and the state of economic development, might play a role in determining the prospects for economic development. Some configurations of initial conditions, namely ones with very low levels of human capital, might lead the economy to remain in a 'poverty trap'.

Other configurations of initial conditions, namely ones with low levels of physical capital, may be associated with high rates of return and high rates of growth. The literature has revived the idea that poor countries should – everything else equal – grow at faster rates than rich countries. This tendency towards convergence is, however, weak and can easily be overwhelmed by other factors.

There are also random factors affecting growth performance. Some countries might have invested in industries that looked promising but ended up yielding low rates of return, while others were lucky in their choice of sectoral investment.

The literature has shown that a policy is neither exogenous nor chosen by a benevolent dictator. Policies are also developed by interest groups and political forces (Rebelo 1996). The institutional factors that condition the interaction between political forces can be very useful to study the mechanics of growth and development. Unfortunately, our present knowledge of the theoretical and empirical link between institutions, policy and growth is not quite remarkable. The study of such a link is a very important area of future research.

Appendix 2.1 The basic equations of the neoclassical economic growth model

The 'basic' equation in Harrod's model of economic growth is given by the growth rate of output. The 'basic' equation in the neoclassical model, however, is defined in terms of the path of the capital–labour ratio k through time. Assume, in a one-good closed (corn) economy, that income Y is equal to total consumption C plus total investment I, i.e.

$$Y \equiv C + I \tag{A2.1.1}$$

Note that in the above equation we have assumed away the presence of foreign trade and government expenditure. To change equation (A2.1.1) in *per capita* terms we divide Y, C and I by the labour force N to obtain

$$\frac{Y}{N}(t) \equiv \frac{C}{N}(t) + \frac{I}{N}(t) \tag{A2.1.2}$$

where t is time. We know that

$$Y = f(K, N) \tag{A2.1.3}$$

or

$$\frac{Y}{N} = f\left(\frac{K}{N}, \frac{N}{N}\right) \tag{A2.1.4}$$

or, in *per capita* terms,

$$y = f(k) \tag{A2.1.5}$$

Therefore, equation (A2.1.2) can be written

$$f[k(t)] = \frac{C}{N}(t) + \frac{I}{N}(t) \tag{A2.1.6}$$

Since $k = K/N$, by taking natural logarithms we can write

$$\ln k = \ln K - \ln N \tag{A2.1.7}$$

By logarithmic differentiation we have

$$\frac{1}{k}\frac{\mathrm{d}k}{\mathrm{d}t} = \frac{1}{K}\frac{\mathrm{d}K}{\mathrm{d}t} - \frac{1}{N}\frac{\mathrm{d}N}{\mathrm{d}t} \tag{A2.1.8}$$

We know that the growth rate of capital stock $(\dot{K}/K)$ net of growth rate of labour $(\dot{N}/N)$ gives the growth rate of the capital–labour ratio, i.e.

$$\frac{\dot{k}}{k} = \frac{\dot{K}}{K} - \frac{\dot{N}}{N} \tag{A2.1.9}$$

Let us assume that

$$\dot{N}/N = n \tag{A2.1.10}$$

Then, equation (A2.1.9) can be stated as

$$\frac{\dot{k}}{k} = \frac{\dot{K}}{K} - n \tag{A2.1.11}$$

If we multiply both sides by K/N or k we get

$$\frac{\dot{k}}{k}k = \frac{\dot{K}}{K}\frac{K}{N} - n\frac{K}{N} \tag{A2.1.12}$$

$$\dot{k} = \frac{\dot{K}}{N} - n\frac{K}{N} \tag{A2.1.13}$$

$$\dot{k} = \frac{\dot{K}}{N} - nk \tag{A2.1.14}$$

$$\frac{\dot{K}}{N} = \dot{k} + nk \tag{A2.1.15}$$

We know that in a neoclassical model

$$\dot{K} = I \tag{A2.1.16}$$

Therefore

$$\frac{\dot{K}}{N} = \frac{I}{N} \tag{A2.1.17}$$

Substituting equation (A2.1.17) into equation (A2.1.6) and ignoring t we obtain

$$f(k) = \frac{C}{N} + \dot{k} + nk \tag{A2.1.18}$$

From equation (A2.1.18) it follows that output per head is the sum of consumption per head (C/N), a proportion of investment which rises, i.e. $\dot{k}$, and a proportion of investment which keeps the K/N ratio fixed in the face of a growing work force, nk.

From (A2.1.18) we get

$$\dot{k} = f(k) - \frac{C}{N} - nk \tag{A2.1.19}$$

Since $f(k) = y = Y/N$, equation (A2.1.19) can be written as

$$\dot{k} = \frac{Y}{N} - \frac{C}{N} - nk \tag{A2.1.20}$$

or

$$\dot{k} = \frac{S}{N} - nk \tag{A2.1.21}$$

where S is total saving ($= Y - C$).

In the neoclassical theory a proportional saving function is assumed. Thus

$$S = sY \tag{A2.1.22}$$

Substituting equation (A2.1.22) into equation (A2.1.21) we have

$$\dot{k} = s\frac{Y}{N} - nk \tag{A2.1.23}$$

or

$$\dot{k} = sf(k) - nk \tag{A2.1.24}$$

since $Y/N = y = f(k)$.

Equation (A2.1.24) has been regarded as the basic or fundamental equation of neoclassical theory. If we examine the right-hand side of the equation closely we find that $sf(k)$ is just savings per head and this is also equal to investment per head. The next term, nk, simply keeps the K/N ratio fixed as explained above. In other words, k or the rate of change in the capital–labour ratio is given by savings or investment per head net of the amount needed to keep the capital–labour ratio fixed in the face of a growing population. It is clear that when investment (or saving) per head is greater than nk the stock of capital will grow faster than that of labour and there will be a rise in the capital–labour ratio. If the saving per head is less than nk, the labour force will grow faster than the stock of capital and the capital–labour ratio falls. This is illustrated in Figure A2.1.1. The vertical axis measures y or output per head and the horizontal axis measures k or capital per head. The lines $nk, f(k)$ and $sf(k)$ have already been explained. Below the point 0 we show the line of capital accumulation. Equilibrium is attained at E where $sf(k) = nk$. Before E, $sf(k) > nk$ and hence k rises until E is reached. Beyond E, $nk > sf(k)$ and k falls and once again the economy moves back to E. Thus, the equilibrium at E is stable.

Appendix 2.2 Endogenous growth models

Research and development models

Framework and assumptions

In this framework, we have a research and development (or R&D) sector and a model of the production of new technologies. We also need to model the allocation of resources between conventional goods production and R&D.

To simplify, assume first that both the R&D and goods production functions are generalized Cobb–Douglas functions. Following the Solow model, a fraction of output is saved and another fraction of the labour force and capital is used in the R&D sector as exogenous and constant. These assumptions do not change the model's main implications.

The specific model we consider is a simplified version of the models of R&D and growth developed by Romer (1990), Grossman and Helpman (1991) and Aghion and Howitt (1992). There are two sectors, a goods-producing sector where output is produced and an R&D sector where additions to the stock of knowledge are made. Fraction 1 of the labour force is used in the R&D sector and fraction $1 - a_L$ in the

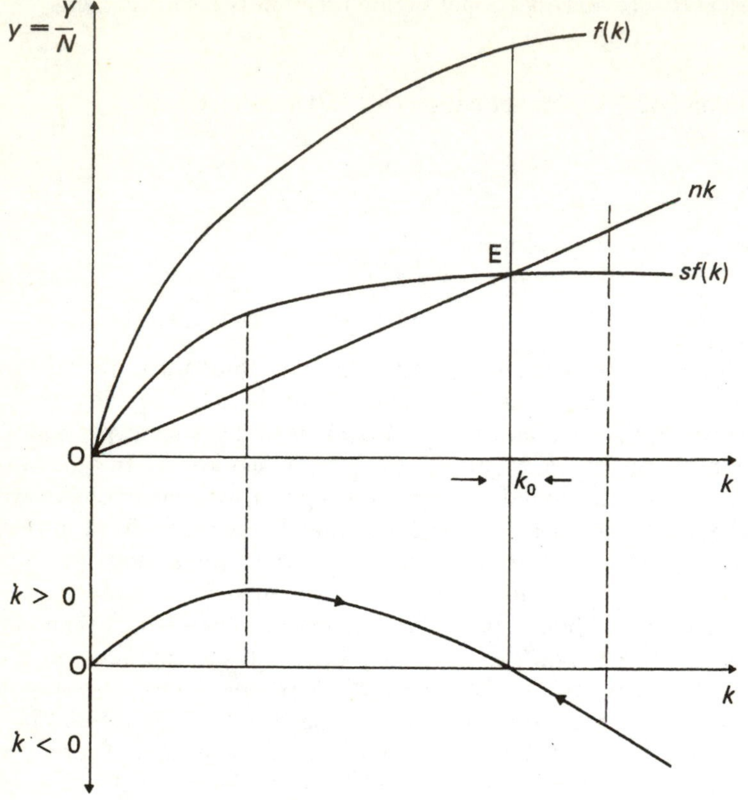

Figure A2.1.1

goods-producing sector; similarly, fraction a_K of the capital stock is used in R&D and the rest in goods production. Both sectors use the full stock of knowledge. Since the use of an idea or a piece of knowledge in one place does not prevent it from being used elsewhere [non-rivalry among inputs] we do not have to consider the division of the stock of knowledge between the two sectors.

The total output produced [PF] at time t is thus

$$Y(t) = [(1 - a_k)K(t)]^{\alpha}[A(t)(1 - a_L)L(t)]^{1-\alpha} \qquad 0 < \alpha < 1 \qquad \text{(A2.2.1)}$$

Note that equation (A2.2.1) implies constant returns to capital and labour: with a given technology, doubling the inputs doubles the amount of output.

The production of new ideas depends on the quantities of capital and labour engaged in research and technology:

$$\dot{A}(t) = G(a_k K(t), a_L L(t), A(t)) \qquad \text{(A2.2.2)}$$

Under the assumption of generalized Cobb–Douglas production, this becomes

$$\dot{A}(t) = B[a_k K(t)]^{\beta}[a_L L(t)]^{\gamma} A(t)^{\theta} \qquad B > 0, \beta \geq 0, \gamma \geq 0 \qquad \text{(A2.2.3)}$$

Where B is a shift parameter.

Notice that the production function for knowledge is not assumed to have constant returns to scale to capital and labour. In addition, there does not appear to be any strong basis for restricting how increases in the stock of knowledge affect the production of new knowledge; thus no restriction is placed on θ in (A2.2.3). If $\theta = 1$, $\dot{A}$ is proportional to A; the effect is stronger if $\theta \geq 1$.

As in the Solow model the saving rate is exogenous and constant. In addition depreciation is set to zero for simplicity. Thus

$$\dot{K}(t) = sY(t) \tag{A2.2.4}$$

Finally, we continue to treat population growth as exogenous:

$$\dot{L}(t) = nL(t) \qquad n \geq 0 \tag{A2.2.5}$$

This completes the description of the model.

The model without capital: the dynamics of knowledge accumulation

With no capital in the model, the production function for output (equation A2.2.1) becomes

$$Y(t) = A(t)(1 - a_L)L(t) \tag{A2.2.6}$$

Similarly, the production function for new knowledge (equation A2.2.3) is now

$$\dot{A}(t) = B[a_L L(t)]^{\gamma} A(t)^{\theta} \tag{A2.2.7}$$

Population growth continues to be described by equation (A2.2.5).

Equation (A2.2.6) implies that output per worker is proportional to A, and thus that the growth rate of output per worker equals the growth rate of A. We therefore focus on the dynamics of A, which are given by (A2.2.7). The growth rate of A denoted g_A is

$$g_A(t) \equiv \frac{\dot{A}(t)}{A(t)} = Ba_L^{\gamma} L(t)^{\gamma} A(t)^{\theta - 1} \tag{A2.2.8}$$

Since B and a_L are constant, whether g_A is rising, falling or constant depends on the behaviour of $L^{\gamma} A^{\theta - 1}$. In particular, equation (A2.2.8) implies that the growth rate of g_A is γ times the growth rate of L plus $\theta - 1$ times the growth rate of A. Thus

$$\dot{g}_A(t) = [\gamma n + (\theta - 1)g_A(t)]g_A(t) \tag{A2.2.9}$$

The initial values of L and A and parameters of the model determine the initial value of g_A.

The production function for knowledge, (A2.2.7), implies that g_A is always positive. Thus g_A is rising if $\gamma n + (\theta - 1)g_A$ is positive, falling if this quantity is negative, and constant if it is zero. g_A is therefore constant when

$$g_A = \frac{\gamma n}{1 - \theta} \equiv g\dot{A} \tag{A2.2.10}$$

To describe further how the growth rate of A behaves (and thus to characterize the behaviour of output per worker), we must distinguish among the cases $\theta < 1$, $\theta > 1$, and $\theta = 1$.

Equation (A2.2.9) implies that, when θ is less than 1,

$$\dot{k}(t) = \frac{\dot{K}(t)}{A(t)L(t)} - \frac{K(t)}{[A(t)L(t)]^2}[A(t)\dot{L}(t) + L(t)\dot{A}(t)]$$

$$= \frac{s_K Y(t)}{A(t)L(t)} - \frac{K(t)}{A(t)L(t)}\left[\frac{\dot{L}(t)}{L(t)} + \frac{\dot{A}(t)}{A(t)}\right]$$

$$= s_K y(t) - (n+g)k(t) \qquad \text{(A2.2.11)}$$

$$= s_K k(t)^{\alpha} h(t)^{\beta} - (n+g)k(t) \qquad \text{(A2.2.12)}$$

The dynamics of knowledge and capital

As mentioned above, when the model includes capital there are two endogenous stock variables, A and K. Paralleling our analysis of the simple model, here we focus on the dynamics of the growth rates of A and K. Substituting the production function,

$$\dot{K}(t) = s(1-a_k)^{\alpha}(1-a_L)^{1-\alpha}K(t)^{\alpha}A(t)^{1-\alpha}L(t)^{1-\alpha} \qquad \text{(A2.2.13)}$$

Dividing both sides by $K(t)$ and defining $c_K = s(1-a_k)^{\alpha}(1-a_L)^{1-\alpha}$ gives us

$$g_k(t) \equiv \frac{\dot{K}(t)}{K(t)} = c_K\left[\frac{A(t)L(t)}{K(t)}\right]^{1-\alpha} \qquad \text{(A2.2.14)}$$

Similarly, dividing both sides of equation (A2.2.3) by $A(t)$ yields an expression for the growth rate of A:

$$g_A(t) = c_A K(t)^{\beta} L(t)^{\gamma} A(t)^{\theta-1} \qquad \text{(A2.2.15)}$$

Learning by doing

Arrow (1962) has shown that after a new aeroplane design is introduced, the time required to build the frame of the marginal aircraft is inversely proportional to the cube root of the number of aircraft of that model that have already been produced; this improvement in productivity occurs without any evident innovations in the production process. Hence, the accumulation of knowledge occurs in part not as a result of deliberate effort but as a side effect of conventional economic activity. This type of knowledge accumulation is known as *learning by doing* (LBD).

When LBD is the source of technological progress, the rate of knowledge accumulation depends not on the fraction of the economy's resources engaged in R&D but on how much new knowledge is generated by conventional economic activity. Analysing LBD therefore requires some slight changes in our model. All inputs are now engaged in goods production; thus the production function becomes

$$Y(t) = K(t)^{\alpha}[A(t)L(t)]^{1-\alpha} \qquad \text{(A2.2.16)}$$

The simplest case of LBD is when learning occurs as a side effect of the production of new capital. As the increase in knowledge is a function of the increase in capital, the stock of knowledge is a function of the stock of capital. Thus there is only one stock variable whose behaviour is endogenous. Making our usual choice of a power function, we have

$$A(t) = BK(t)^{\phi}, \quad B > 0, \quad \phi > 0 \tag{A2.2.17}$$

Equations (A2.2.16–17), together with (A2.2.4–5) describing the accumulation of capital and labour, characterize the economy.

To analyse the properties of this economy, begin by substituting (A2.2.17) into (A2.2.16); this yields

$$Y(t) = K(t)^{\alpha} B^{1-\alpha} K(t)^{\phi(1-\alpha)} L(t)^{1-\alpha} \tag{A2.2.18}$$

Since $K(t) = sY(t)$, the dynamics of K are given by

$$\dot{K}(t) = sB^{1-\alpha} K(t)^{\alpha} K(t)^{\phi(1-\alpha)} L(t)^{1-\alpha} \tag{A2.2.19}$$

In this model of knowledge accumulation without capital ('The model without capital', above) the dynamics of A are given by $\dot{A}(t) = B[a_L L(t)]^{\gamma} A(t)^{\theta}$ (see equation A2.2.7).

Once again, a case that has received particular attention is $\phi = 1$ and $n = 0$. In this case, the production function (equation A2.2.18) becomes

$$Y(t) = bK(t), \quad b = B^{1-\alpha} L^{1-\alpha} \tag{A2.2.20}$$

Capital accumulation is therefore given by

$$\dot{K}(t) = sbK(t) \tag{A2.2.21}$$

Because the productioin function in these models is written using the symbol A rather than the b used in (A2.2.26), these models are often referred to as $Y = AK$ models.

A model of human capital and growth: assumptions

The PF is given by

$$Y(t) = K(t)^{\alpha} H(t)^{\beta} [A(t)L(t)]^{1-\alpha-\beta}, \qquad \alpha > 0, \beta > 0, \alpha + \beta < 1 \tag{A2.2.22}$$

where H is the stock of human capital. L continues to denote the number of workers; thus a skilled worker supplies both one unit of labour and some amount of H. Note that equation (A2.2.22) implies that there are constant returns to K, H and L together.

We make our usual assumptions about the dynamics of K and L:

$$\dot{K}(t) = s_K Y(t) \tag{A2.2.23}$$

$$\dot{L}(t) = nL(t) \tag{A2.2.24}$$

where we now use s_K to denote the fraction of output devoted to physical capital accumulation, and where we again assume no depreciation for simplicity. In addition, because our goal here is not to explain worldwide growth, the model follows the Solow model and assumes constant and exogenous technological progress:

$$\dot{A}(t) = gA(t) \tag{A2.2.25}$$

Finally, for simplicity, human capital accumulation is modelled in the same way as physical capital accumulation:

$$\dot{H}(t) = S_H Y(t) \tag{A2.2.26}$$

where S_H is the fraction of resources devoted to human capital accumulation.

Notes

1 An assessment of the empirical evidence on externalities in the US manufacturing sector is provided by Burnside (1995).
2 Kleenow (1994) discusses the limitations of growth models that rely on human capital as their sole engine of growth. He argues that measures of human capital cannot explain the differences in total factor productivity in a panel of US industries. Technological differences, not differences in human capital, seem to be the essential determinant of industrial productivity.
3 Fast-growing countries were defined as those whose growth rates exceed the cross-country average plus one standard deviation. Slow-growing countries are those whose growth rates are below the average minus one standard deviation.
4 This data set corrects the national income accounts of a large sample of countries for deviations relative to 'purchasing power parity'. When we translate the *per capita* income of India into US dollars using the exchange rate, we are implicitly assuming that 'purchasing power parity' holds. That is, we are assuming that the prices of all goods are the same in India as in the United States. This assumption is grossly counterfactual, thus making it difficult to compare real incomes across countries. The Summers and Heston (1991) data set uses information on prices in several countries to surmount this problem.
5 The data set employed to construct this table did not include information on R&D expenditure or on technology adoption.
6 Grossman and Helpman (1991) revisit many of the themes of trade theory in a dynamic context that highlights the role of technical progress. In particular they study the forces that determine a country's comparative advantage.
7 Evidence on the relations between these policies and growth is provided by Easterly and Rebelo (1993) and Knack and Keefer (1994).

Questions

1 Critically evaluate the 'classical' theory of economic growth.
2 What are the major ingredients of the neoclassical growth theory? What are the implications of the neoclassical growth theory for less developed countries?
3 What is 'growth accounting'? How could a 'production function' be used to calculate the sources of growth?
4 Explain the major differences between the 'exogenous' and the 'endogenous' growth theory for developing countries?
5 How useful is the 'Harrod–Domar' model for growth accounting in developing countries?

3 Dual economy models

3.1 Introduction

The growth models examined in Chapter 2 are highly aggregated in the sense that no attempt has been made to distinguish between different sectors of the economy, e.g. agriculture and industry. However, since the economies of LDCs are regarded as far less homogeneous than those of DCs, it is sometimes argued that the case of LDCs should be analysed in terms of 'dual economy' models. Unlike the DCs, the LDCs do not suffer from a labour supply constraint. The problem in LDCs is thus to transfer 'surplus' labour from unproductive to productive employment to promote growth. Such a problem was first tackled by Lewis (1954).

3.2 The 'surplus' of labour and its contribution to development

3.2.1 Lewis's model with 'unlimited' supply of labour

Surplus labour – *à la* Lewis (1954) – is defined as that part of the labour force that can be removed without reducing the total amount of output produced, even when the input of other factors remains constant. Lewis assumed a dual economy – a modern exchange sector and an indigenous subsistence economy. The capitalist sector uses reproducible capital and pays capitalists for the use thereof but the subsistence sector uses non-reproducible capital. Output per head is higher in the organized sector in comparison with the indigenous sector. Lewis argues that many poor countries such as India, Egypt and Jamaica have unlimited supplies of labour, but parts of Africa and Latin America may have a shortage of male labour. Unlimited supplies of labour exist in the subsistence sector since the supply of labour is greater than the demand for labour at the subsistence wage, i.e. the marginal product of labourers in the subsistence economy is negligible or zero, or at least below the subsistence wage.

This peculiar feature is regarded as disguised unemployment, implying that if some workers from the agricultural sector obtained alternative jobs, the rest (assuming they work harder and are willing to do so) could maintain, and in some cases increase, output. No unemployment benefit exists, so the costs of maintaining the disguised unemployment/underemployed fall on the working population.

3.2.2 Surplus labour and the growth of the economy

Surplus labour can be used instead of capital in the creation of new industrial investment projects, or it can be channelled into nascent industries, which are labour intensive in their early stages. Such growth does not raise the value of the subsistence wage, because the supply of labour exceeds the demand at that wage, and rising production via improved labour techniques has the effect of lowering the capital coefficient.

Although labour is assumed to be in surplus, it is mainly unskilled. This inhibits growth (the same as land or capital scarcities) since technical progress necessary for growth requires skilled labour. But should there be a labour surplus and a modest capital, this bottleneck can be broken through the provision of training and education facilities.

The utility of unlimited supplies of labour to growth objectives depends upon the amount of capital available at the same time. Should there be surplus labour, agriculture will derive no productive use from it, so a transfer to a non-agricultural sector will be of mutual benefit. It provides jobs to the agrarian population and reduces the burden of population from land. Industry now obtains its labour. Labour must be encouraged to move to increase productivity in agriculture. To start such a movement, the capitalist sector will have to pay a compensatory payment determined by the wage rate which people can earn outside their present sector, plus a set of other factors which include the cost of living in the new sector and changes in the level of profits in the existing sector. The margin capitalists may have to pay is as much as 30 per cent above the average subsistence wage, say WW_1 in Figure 3.1 which represents the capitalist (or industrial) sector. The marginal revenue product of labour in the subsistence sector is shown by NR; OW is the industrial wage. Given the profit maximization assumption, employment of labour within the industrial sector is given by the point where marginal product is equal to the rate of wages, i.e. OM.

Since the wages in the capitalist sector depend on the earnings of the subsistence sector, capitalists would like to keep down productivity/wages in the subsistence

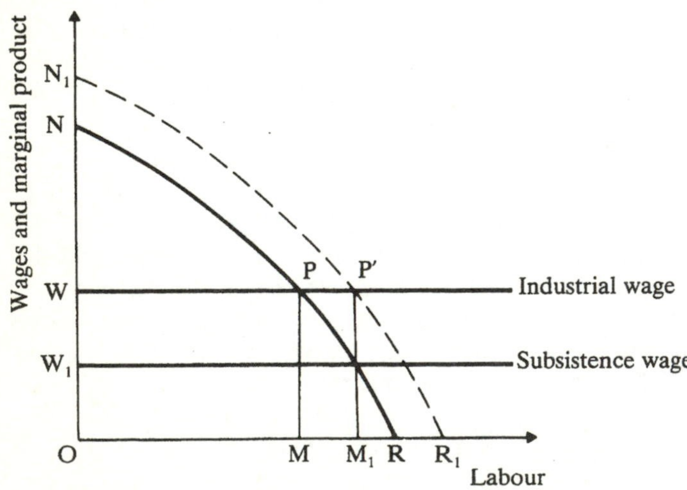

Figure 3.1

sector, so that the capitalist sector may expand at a fixed wage. In the capitalist sector labour is employed up to the point where its marginal product equals wage, since a capitalist employer would be reducing his surplus if he paid labour more than he received for what is produced. But this need not be true in subsistence agriculture as wages could be equal to average product or the level of subsistence.

The total product labour (ONPM in Figure 3.1) is divided between the payments to labour in the form of wages, OWPM, and the capitalist surplus, NPW. The growth of the capitalist sector and the rate of labour absorption from the subsistence sector depend on the use made of capitalist surplus.

When the surplus is reinvested, the total product of labour will rise. The marginal product line shifts upwards to the right, say to N_1 R_1. Assuming wages are constant, the industrial sector now provides more employment. Hence employment rises by MM_1. The amount of capitalist surplus goes up from WNP to WN_1P'. This amount can now be reinvested and the process will be repeated and all the surplus labour would eventually be exhausted.

When all the surplus labour in the subsistence sector has been attracted into the capitalist sector, wages in the subsistence sector will begin to rise, shifting the terms of trade in favour of agriculture, and causing wages in the capitalist sector to rise. Capital accumulation has caught up with the population and there is no longer scope for development from the initial source, i.e. unlimited supplies of labour. When all surplus labour is exhausted, the supply of labour to the industrial sector becomes less than perfectly elastic. It is now in the interests of producers in the subsistence sector to compete for labour as the agricultural sector has become fully commercialized. Note that it is the increase in the share of profits in the capitalist sector which ensures labour surplus is continuously utilized and eventually exhausted. Real wages will tend to rise along with increases in productivity and the economy will enter into a stage of self-sustaining growth.

3.2.3 Criticism of Lewis's model

Several criticisms are levelled at Lewis's theory of dual economic growth:

1 Economic development takes place via the absorption of labour from the subsistence sector where the opportunity costs of labour are very low. However, if there are positive opportunity costs, e.g. loss of crops in times of peak harvesting season, labour transfer will reduce agricultural output.
2 Absorption of surplus labour itself may end prematurely because competitors may raise wage rates and lower the share of profit (Mabro 1967). It has been shown that rural–urban migration in the Egyptian economy was accompanied by an increase in wage rates of 15 per cent and a fall in profits of 12 per cent (Mabro 1967). Wages in the industrial sector were forced up directly by unions and indirectly through demands for increased wages in the subsistence sector, as payment for increased productivity. In fact, given the urban–rural wage differential in most poor countries, large-scale unemployment is now seen in both the urban and the rural sectors.
3 The Lewis model underestimates the full impact on the poor economy of a rapidly growing population, i.e. its effects on agricultural surplus, the capitalist profit share, wage rates and overall employment opportunities. Similarly, Lewis assumed that the rate of growth in manufacturing would be identical to that in

agriculture, but if industrial development involves more intensive use of capital than labour, then the flow of labour from agriculture to industry will simply create more unemployment.

4 Lewis seems to have ignored the balanced growth between agriculture and industry. Given the linkages between agricultural growth and industrial expansion in poor countries, if a section of the profit made by the capitalists is not devoted to agricultural development, the process of industrialization would be jeopardized.

5 Possible leakages from the economy seem to have been ignored by Lewis. He assumes boldly that a capitalist's marginal propensity to save is close to one, but a certain increase in consumption always accompanies an increase in profits, so the total increment of savings will be somewhat less than increments in profit.

Whether or not capitalist surplus is used constructively will depend on the consumption – saving patterns of the top 10 per cent of the population. But capitalists alone are not the only productive agents of society. Small farmers producing cash crops in Egypt have shown themselves to be quite capable of saving the required capital. The world's largest cocoa industry in Ghana is entirely the creation of small enterprise capital formation (Elkan 1973).

6 The transfer of unskilled workers from agriculture to industry is regarded as almost smooth and costless, but this does not occur in practice because industry requires different types of labour. The problem can be solved by investment in education and skill formation: but the process is neither smooth nor inexpensive.

3.2.4 Empirical tests of Lewis's model

1 Empirical evidence does not always provide much support for the Lewis model. Schultz (1964) in an empirical study of village India during the influenza epidemic of 1918–19 showed that agricultural output declined, although his study does not prove 'whether output would have declined had a comparable proportion of the agricultural population left for other occupations in response to economic incentive' (Sen 1975; also 1966, 1967). Again disguised unemployment may be present in one region/sector of the economy but not in others. Further, empirically it is important to know not only whether the marginal productivity is equal to zero, but also the amount of surplus labour and the effect of its withdrawal on output.

2 Schultz did not distinguish between summer (*Kharif*) and winter (*Rabi*) seasons of agricultural production (Mehra 1966). A study of India has shown that summer agricultural output (which followed the epidemic) did not actually fall. The fall in output observed by Schultz was mainly due to some random elements like weather conditions. However, the fact that the summer output did not fall even when there was a substantial reduction of labour tends to support the hypothesis of Lewis. In fact, an analysis of farm data (which is much more interesting than the results deduced from the aggregated data) reveals that, while in some farms marginal productivity of labour may be positive, in others it could be zero or statistically insignificant (Desai and Mazumdar 1970).

3 Lewis did not pay full attention to the pattern of seasonality of labour demand in traditional agriculture. It has been established that labour demand varies considerably and such demand is at its peak during the sowing and harvesting seasons (Mehra 1966). Thus, during some months of the year, the marginal productivity of labour could be much above zero.

4 The Lewis model was applied to the Egyptian economy (Mabro 1967) and despite the proximity of Lewis's assumptions to the realities of the Egyptian situation during the period of study, the model failed (a) because Lewis seriously underestimated the rate of population growth and (b) because the choice of capital intensity in Egyptian industries did not show much labour-using bias and, as such, the level of unemployment did not show any tendency to register significant decline.
5 The validity of the Lewis model was again called into question when it was applied to Taiwan (Ho 1972). It was observed that, despite the impressive rate of growth of the economy of Taiwan, unemployment did not fall appreciably and this is explained again with reference to the choice of capital intensity in industries in Taiwan. This raised the important issue whether surplus labour is a necessary condition for growth.

3.3 The Fei–Ranis model

Among many points that have been made about the Lewis model, it has been emphasized that Lewis did not pay enough attention to the importance of agriculture in promoting industrial growth. Also it is argued that an increase in productivity (surplus of agriculture) should precede mobilization of labour. Indeed, Fei and Ranis (FR) observed the above mentioned points and tried to develop a dual economy model involving three stages of growth (1964).

The first stage of the FR model is very similar to that of Lewis. Disguised unemployment is supposed to exist as the elasticity of labour supply is infinity and the marginal product of labour is zero. In the second stage, it is shown that rising productivity in agriculture is the foundation for industrial growth necessary to sustain the third stage. In the second stage, it is argued that labour surplus may exist as average product (AP) which is higher than the marginal product (MP) and is not equal to the subsistence level of wages (see Figure 3.2); instead it is increasing. Note that the labour supply curve in Figure 3.2(a) is perfectly elastic between S and T.

In phase I, in terms of Figure 3.2(c)

$$AL = MP = 0$$

and

$$AP = AB$$

Following the analysis of Lewis, Fei and Ranis argue that AD units of labour can be withdrawn from the agricultural sector without changing the agricultural output.

In phase II, AP > MP, but after AD, MP begins to rise (Figure 3.2(c)). The growth of the labour force in the industrial sector rises from zero to Of (Figure 3.2(a)). The AP of labour in the agricultural sector is given by BYZ (Figure 3.2(c)). After AD as migration takes place from agriculture to industry, MP > 0 but AP falls and that would imply a rise in real wages for industrial labourers because of the scarcity of the food supply. An increase in real wages will reduce profit and the size of the 'surplus' which could have been reinvested to promote industrialization. However, should there be a 'surplus' and as long as it can be used for investment rather than consumption and distributed evenly between agriculture and industry, growth can still be raised without reducing the rate of growth of industrialization. Investment in industry will

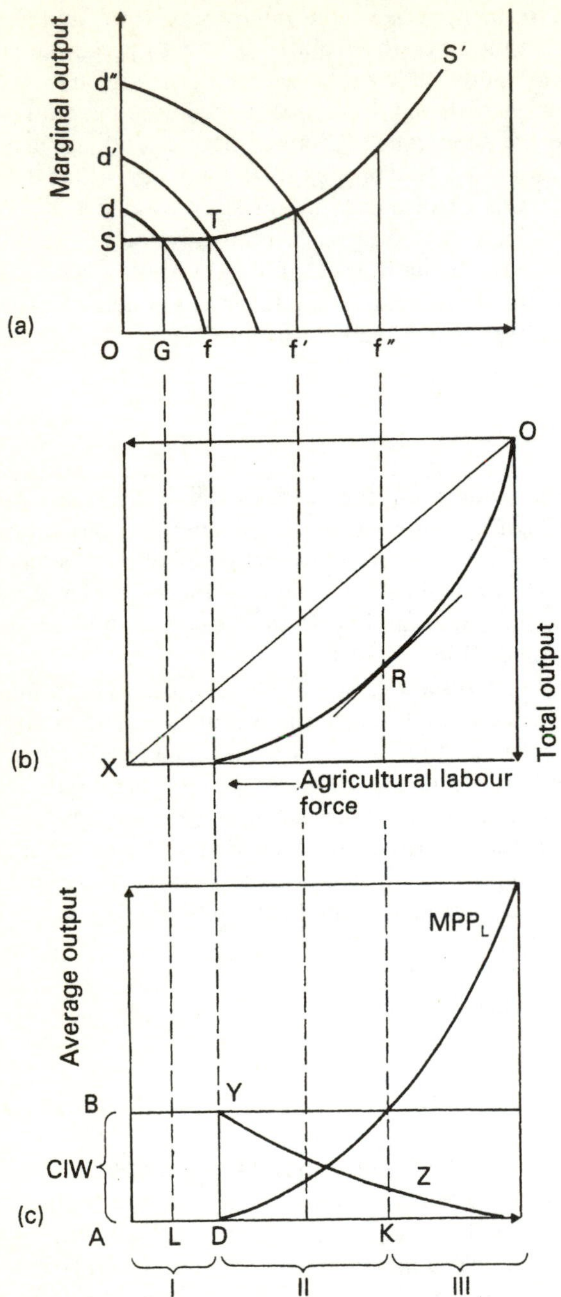
Marginal output
d″
d′
d
T
S
S′
(a)
O
G
f
f′
f″
O
R
Total output
(b)
X
Agricultural labour force
Average output
MPP$_L$
B
Y
CIW
Z
(c)
A
L
D
K
I
II
III

Figure 3.2

shift the MP outwards (in Figure 3.2(a) from df to d′f′ and then to d″f″) and this will enable the agricultural sector to get rid of labour until MP = real wages = AB = constant institutional wages (CIW), which is measured by the slope of OX at equality with AP (see Figure 3.2b). MP = CIW where the tangent to the total output line ORX at R is parallel to OX. This is regarded as a point of commercialization in the FR model because the economy is fully commercialized now in the absence of 'open' or 'disguised' (i.e. people who are unproductive but employed) unemployment. The amount and time to reallocate labour will depend upon

1 the rate of growth of industrial capital stock which is given by the growth of profits in industries and the growth of surplus generated within the agricultural sector;
2 the nature and bias of technical progress in industry;
3 the rate of growth of the population.

It is important that the rate of labour transfer is in excess of the rate of growth of the population.

The three phases of labour transfer can now be easily described.

1 In phase I we have MP = 0 and surplus labour is given by AD.
2 In phase II we have CIW > MP > 0 and open and disguised unemployment is given by AK.
3 In phase III MP > CIW and the economy is fully commercialized and disguised unemployment is exhausted. The supply curve of labour is now steeper and both industry and agriculture start bidding equally for labour.

Thus, we find that whereas Lewis has failed to offer a satisfactory analysis of this subsistence sector and ignored the real impact of population growth and the choice of capital intensity on the process of surplus labour absorption, Fei and Ranis emphasized that the agricultural sector must also grow in line with industrial growth if the mechanism that Lewis described was not to grind to a halt. Thus, three major points are highlighted in the FR model.

1 The growth of agriculture is as important as the growth of industry.
2 The growth of agriculture and industry should be balanced.
3 The rate of labour absorption must be higher than the rate of population growth to get out of the Malthusian nightmare.

Fei and Ranis argued that surplus can be extracted by the investment activities of landlords and by the fiscal measures of the government. However, 'leakages' could exist because of the costs of transferring labour (both private and social, like transport costs and building of schools and hospitals, etc.), increased *per capita* consumption of agricultural output and the maintenance of a 'permanent' gap between urban and rural wages. However, productivity in agriculture may not rise even if higher *per capita* incomes were not consumed. This could happen if the supply curve of labour is backward bending, i.e. peasants reduce their work effort as their incomes rise.

It may be pointed out, however, that if *per capita* income rises, consumption patterns may change without an increase in food consumption. Further, the case of a backward-bending supply curve of labour hardly has any empirical basis (Blake 1962).

3.3.1 Evaluation of the Fei–Ranis model

Although the FR model is an improvement on the Lewis model in the sense described above, a number of criticisms have been levelled at it.

1 It is assumed in the FR model that MPL = 0 and the transfer of labour from agriculture will not reduce output in the agricultural sector in phase I. But it has been shown (Berry and Soligo 1968) that agricultural output in phase I of the FR model will not remain constant and may fall under different systems of land tenure (e.g. peasant proprietorship, sharecropping etc.) except under the following three cases.

   (a) Leisure is an inferior good.
   (b) There is leisure satiation.
   (c) Leisure and food are perfect substitutes with a constant marginal rate of substitution for all real income levels.

   If MPL > 0, leisure satiation is ruled out, and if MPL = 0 complete substitution between leisure and food is not a sufficient condition for fixed output. The only sufficient condition is that leisure is an inferior good whatever the value of MPL may be positive (see Figure 3.3). Let food be measured on the vertical axis and leisure along the horizontal axis. I_0, I_1 are the indifference curves between food and leisure of the agriculturist within the 'potentially feasible' set of consumption points. OS is the subsistence level of food consumption without which labour in the agricultural sector will not live. OG is the maximum leisure and thus labour input is measured from right to left as the origin in this case is G. The falling slope of the transformation curve SAG implies that the agricultural worker is using up more leisure to the same units of land. The marginal rate of transformation between leisure and food is zero at a point like A. At A, MPL = 0, and when the indifference curve is tangent at this point to the transformation curve, leisure satiation is obtained as the marginal rate of substitution between food and leisure is zero. Let OS be the subsistence level of income. When the wage rate is given, the transformation curve is GH and its slope is the fixed wage rate. Now, if one labourer is transferred from the agricultural sector and his land is distributed equally among the remaining labourers, SAG shifts to RTG. At T, MPL = 0 and the APL per hour is the same as at A, given constant returns to scale. Let us assume that MPL = 0 where agriculturists are living at the subsistence level. In order to maintain the same level of output, when SAG shifts to RTG, the indifference curve going through T must be flat (see also Sen 1966). But this would imply 'leisure satiation' (as explained above), or leisure as a very inferior commodity (i.e. the indifference curve going through A may not be absolutely flat, though the one which goes through T must be so). Leaving these conditions which Berry and Soligo consider as exceptional, total output would decline. Per capita output remains the same, though, because otherwise consumption will be less than the level of subsistence, and labour input per head may either increase or decrease (see Berry and Soligo 1968 for details of the different types of case).

2 It has been mentioned already that whether or not MPL = 0 is an empirical issue. Given the seasonality in the food production in LDCs, it is more likely that MPL would be greater than zero, particularly during the sowing and harvesting seasons. The Japanese data, even for the pre-First World War period, did not show the existence of an unlimited supply of labour (Jorgenson 1966).

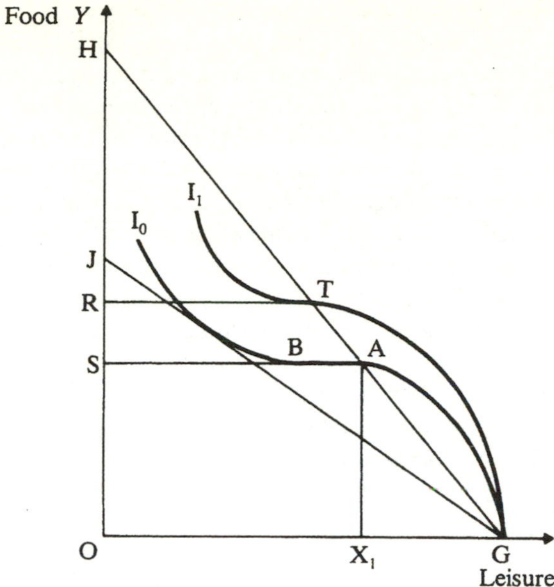

Figure 3.3

3 In the FR model, output is mainly determined by land and labour inputs, and the role of capital has been neglected. It has been shown that capital plays an important role in determining output, particularly when one considers the technological changes in agriculture in LDCs – sometimes called the 'Green Revolution' (see for example Brown 1971; Byres 1972; Frankel 1971; Griffin 1974, 1976; Ghatak and Ingersent 1984; for details see Chapter 9).

4 Fei and Ranis ignored the role of foreign trade as they assumed a closed-economy model. It is observed in the process of the economic development Japan imported cheap farm products to improve her terms of trade. It may be pointed out that the relaxation of a closed economy assumption will soften the balanced growth constraint.

5 One of the major reasons to account for the sluggish expansion of the industrial sector in the LDCs could have been the very low productivity rises in subsistence agriculture. In such a situation, the rise in surplus from agriculture is a much more important determinant of non-agricultural employment than the reinvestment of surplus (Jorgenson 1966). Indeed, this is the essence of the dual economy model as developed by Jorgenson (1961), who argues that for the improvement of the modern sector (i.e. the non-agricultural sector of the LDCs), it is imperative that the surplus must be generated and that *it should persist*. We now turn to the discussion of the Jorgenson model in the next section.

3.4 The Jorgenson model

Jorgenson distinguishes between the modern (say industrial) and the backward (say agricultural) sector of the economy. Production in the backward sector is determined by land and labour and such a production function is subject to diminishing returns.

In the modern sector, output is given by labour and capital and the function is subject to constant returns to scale. It is assumed that technical progress is neutral. Population growth is determined by *per capita* food supply and the net rate of reproduction (i.e. birth rate minus the death rate). Given these assumptions, Jorgenson argues that 'surplus' in agriculture (food production net of consumption) releases labour to be employed in industry and the growth rate of industrial employment is given by the growth of the surplus. After the initial investment, growth of accumulation is given by the growth of labour in the industrial sector and the terms of trade between the agricultural and the industrial sectors, though industrial real wages could be more than agricultural real wages to allow for labour migration. The gap is proportional to industrial wages and is stable in the long run. This gap also determines the terms of trade between the two sectors and the investment rate in the modern sector. It is assumed that the economy is closed. The model can then be formally described as follows.

Let Y be agricultural production, L_{a} total land available and P total population. Let the production function be of the Cobb–Douglas type, i.e.

$$Y = e^{\alpha t} L_{\mathrm{a}}^{\beta} P^{1-\beta} \tag{3.1}$$

where $e^{\alpha t}$ is the change in output due to technical progress. Since land is assumed to be fixed

$$Y = e^{\alpha t} P^{1-\beta} \tag{3.2}$$

Now

$$y = Y/P = e^{\alpha t} P^{-\beta} \tag{3.3}$$

where y is *per capita* agricultural output. Differentiating with respect to time and dividing by y, we obtain

$$\frac{\dot{y}}{y} = \alpha - \beta \frac{\dot{P}}{P} \tag{3.4}$$

Let

$$\frac{\dot{P}}{P} = \eta$$

Then

$$\frac{\dot{y}}{y} = \alpha - \beta\eta \tag{3.5}$$

or

$$\dot{y} = (\alpha - \beta\eta)y \tag{3.6}$$

The general solution is then

$$y(t) = e^{(\alpha - \beta\eta)^t} \gamma(0) \tag{3.7}$$

which specifies the situation where *per capita* income growth, $\alpha - \beta\eta > 0$, would be obtained for any positive level of output. In a backward economy, β (i.e. diminishing returns to labour in agriculture) is assumed to remain fixed. Hence, public policy should be used to alter either α (i.e. the rate of technical progress) or η (i.e. the maximum growth rate of the population), or both. An increase in output per head would be assumed as long as $\alpha > \eta$. Where $\alpha = \eta$, a 'low-level equilibrium' is obtained.

In the industrial sector, the production function is given by

$$Q = (C, L, t) \tag{3.8}$$

where Q is total industrial output, C is capital, L is industrial labour and t is time, as technical progress is expected to be rapid in industry. Let

$$Q = A(t)C^{\gamma}L^{1-\gamma} \tag{3.9}$$

Let

$$\dot{A}/A = \lambda$$

or

$$\dot{A} = A\lambda \tag{3.10}$$

A little manipulation shows that

$$\dot{q} = e^{\lambda t}C^{\gamma} \tag{3.11}$$

where q is output per head: Q/L.

Again differentiating with respect to time and dividing through by q:

$$\frac{\dot{q}}{q} = \lambda + \gamma\frac{\dot{C}}{C} \tag{3.12}$$

To promote growth and to escape stationary equilibrium of a backward economy, it is necessary to accumulate capital. But to promote accumulation, it is imperative to extract positive agricultural surplus. Hence $\alpha - \beta\eta > 0$ is a necessary and sufficient condition for generating agricultural surplus and the generation of surplus is vital for industrialization. Jorgenson argues that the surplus should not only be extracted but it must persist to avoid any slipping back to the stationary state.

The Lewis and FR models predict a fall in the capital–output ratio at a given rate (λ/β). Also given the assumption that capitalists save all of their income, the Lewis and FR models predict rising growth rates of output and employment as capital grows over time. In the Jorgenson model, growth rates of output and capital would be the same and employment in the modern sector would rise less rapidly than the rise in capital and output. (For a modification of Jorgenson's analysis, see Dixit 1969; Kelly *et al.* 1972.)

3.4.1 Evaluation of the Jorgenson model

Despite the elegance of the Jorgenson model, several criticisms of it can be made. First, Jorgenson ignores the role of capital in his agricultural production function. Empirical evidence does not always support this assumption (see, for example, the Japanese case (Nakamura 1965), the Indian case (Shukla 1965) and the Egyptian case (Hansen 1968)). Indeed, in some cases capital has played a significant role in raising agricultural output. Second, although the production relations between the modern and the backward sectors are considered to be different, no such difference in tastes (i.e. demand) is recognized. Also, most writers on the dual economy including Jorgenson have ignored the 'spatial' effects of structural change. Third, it has been shown that once the assumptions regarding taste and technology are altered the predictions of the Jorgenson model (and indeed those of the Lewis and FR models also) lose their generality (Kelly *et al.* 1972). Fourth, the neoclassical features of the Jorgenson model have their usual limitations. Fifth, although there may be some truth in the observations of Jorgenson (1966) and also of Schultz (1964) that the marginal productivity of labour in agriculture is unlikely to be zero, particularly in the sowing and harvesting seasons, the point is not important for finding out the proper shadow price in a surplus labour economy. What is relevant to determine the shadow price is the difference between the 'marginal productivity of the employed and the marginal productivity of the unemployed' (Marglin 1976: 11) because 'whenever a gap exists between a worker's marginal productivity and his opportunity cost, a labour surplus exists in the sense that is relevant for valuation of inputs and outputs. Shoeshine boys, pedicab drivers and farmers are surplus if output would be increased by transferring men from these services and from agriculture to industry' (Marglin 1976: 11).

3.5 Some extensions of the dual economy models: the Dixit–Marglin model

The dual economy models have been extended to include dynamic behaviours. These models are fairly complex as they deal with dynamic optimization problems (see Dixit 1968; Marglin 1976). Here we summarize their main features only.

In the Lewis and FR models, the supply curve of labour is assumed to be perfectly elastic at a given real wage rate W which is fixed either by the subsistence level or by institutional considerations. At full employment, APL $< W$, given the paucity of capital. Marglin (1976) has shown that in an economy with the features described by Lewis and Fei and Ranis, over a *finite* planning horizon, a dynamic optimal employment policy maximizes neither output nor surplus, but is in between, and the rule to pursue a dynamic investment policy is that the demand price of investment should be greater than the marginal utility of consumption. The rule in the neoclassical theory is that the demand price of investment should be equal to the marginal utility of consumption. However, as Dixit (1968) points out, in Marglin's analysis labour surplus and subsistence consumption persist and it is expected that the economy would attain full employment within a *given finite* time horizon. In Dixit's model, both consumption and full employment appear as constraints.

The optimal growth path for a subsistence economy consists of different phases. By the end of phase I, enough capital accumulation takes place and APL $> W$, but unemployment is allowed to persist. In phase II, full employment prevails but W is equal to *per capita* consumption, i.e. investment is allowed to take place at the cost of consumption. As phase II ends after a given time, *per capita* consumption is allowed to rise as the economy enters the neoclassical era. However, Dixit does not pay much attention either to the agricultural sector or to the terms of trade between agriculture and industry and marketed surplus. There are political and institutional constraints which can affect the solutions (Marglin 1976).

3.6 The Kelly *et al.* model

In a *general* theory of growth in dual economies, Kelly *et al.* (1972) have tried to analyse the problems of transition and technological dualism in agricultural and industrial production, bias in technical progress, difference in consumption patterns and migration. The basic model consists of fourteen equations and fourteen variables. A useful feature of the model is the inclusion of demand analysis based on the work of Stone (1964) and Geary's (1951) linear expenditure system. The other interesting feature of the model is the analysis of demographic dualism. Simulation techniques are used to test the model mainly in the light of the experience of Japan under the Meiji imperial dynasty.

In contradistinction to the Jorgenson model, Kelly *et al.* assume that both sectors use labour *and* capital. Given the parameter values and initial conditions, time paths of the endogenous variables are observed (e.g. declining labour share, fixed rate of technical progress, falling growth rate of output, etc.). The choice of initial values is dictated by the experience of the writers in the Philippines and the simulation is carried out for the case of Meiji Japan. The writers claim that the model performed very well.

Given the 'satisfactory' performance of the model, it is implied that land is *not* a significant variable affecting output. This is surprising. The writers have ignored the role of foreign trade which is regarded by some as one of the major engines of growth. However, the authors' attempt to explore the sensitivity of the key variables to different parameters merits serious attention. It is of interest to note that shifts in demand parameters have significant effects on growth and structural change. In the disequilibrium model also, the sensitivity analysis of the relationship between economic change and demand is interesting. But the analysis of the terms of trade is very sketchy. Despite these criticisms, it should be pointed out that the authors have adopted an interesting approach to analysing the problems of dual economies, though the choice of a neoclassical framework of analysis and the experience of Meiji Japan to test the model must be viewed with caution (for details see Ghatak and Ingersent 1984).

3.7 Dual economy models: a critique

The growth models considered in Chapter 2 are highly aggregative and some economists (Lewis 1954; Fei and Ranis 1961, 1964; Jorgenson 1961, 1967; Dixit 1968, 1971; Kelly *et al.* 1972) began to analyse the problems in terms of two sectors, namely agriculture and industry. Briefly, the so-called traditional non-capitalist agricultural sector is supposed to be unresponsive to economic incentives and here the leisure preferences are imagined to be high; production for the market does not take place and producers apparently do not follow profit-maximizing rules: 'disguised' or open unemployment is supposed to prevail throughout the rural sector and indeed the marginal productivity of labour is expected to be zero, and in some cases negative (Nurkse 1953). Income is equal to subsistence level (Leibenstein 1957: 154) partly determined by physiological and partly by cultural levels (Lewis 1954). Further, capital has no role to play in agricultural production (Jorgenson 1967: 291). Two sectors are linked by the influx of surplus homogenous labour from agriculture to industry. Nothing happens to the transfer of savings or capital and growth takes place when demand rises as a result of ploughing back of profits by the capitalists into reinvestment. The backward sector is eventually 'modernized' with the transfer of all surplus labour from agriculture.

The extension of the Lewis model by Fei and Ranis (1964) also suffers from some limitations. First, no attempt is made by Fei and Ranis to account for stagnation. Second, no clear distinction is made between family-based labour and wage-based labour and nothing is said about the process of self-sustaining growth. The investment function is not specified and money, price, foreign exchange as well as terms of trade between agriculture and industry are ignored.

The dual economy model of Jorgenson is based on familiar neoclassical lines but this hardly helps us to accept it as a more sound theory or, better, in terms of its predictive capacity. For example, Jorgenson considers land and labour only in terms of their agricultural production function and ignores the role of scarce capital. Jorgenson assumes that a surplus arises when agricultural output per head is greater than the income level at which the population growth rate is at its 'physiological maximum'. This is difficult to comprehend because a clear definition of physiological maximum is lacking and a surplus may exist even before the point at which income corresponding to this maximum is reached. Jorgenson, like Fei and Ranis, neglects the role of money and trade. No capital formation takes place in agriculture in Jorgenson's model; no attempt is made to analyse the problems of disguised unemployment in agriculture and it is assumed that the industrial wage is equal to the marginal productivity of labour. The shortcomings of the Jorgenson model *vis-à-vis* the FR model lie in the assumption of a 'Malthusian response mechanism and a zero income elasticity of the demand for food' (Hayami *et al.* 1971: 22–3). Population growth in LDCs is not always determined by consumption per head. Also, the case for a zero income elasticity of the demand for food is not well supported in practice (NCAER 1972). (For an extension of the Jorgenson model, see Ramanathan 1967, where some of the restrictive assumptions are relaxed.) In both the FR and Jorgenson models, it is implicitly assumed that technical progress would be of a labour-augmenting type. This may not happen in practice (Krishna 1975). The Lewis and FR models suffer from an additional weakness in laying the emphasis only on accumulation and not on technical progress. If growth in the Lewis–FR fashion means rise in income and if the marginal propensity to consume food is positive for any group of income recipients, then, with given output, food prices will rise which will raise wages and reduce profits and growth. Thus any type of accumulation increases industrial wages and at no phase is the supply of labour to industry infinitely elastic (Guha 1969).

The earlier dual economy models failed to specify the precise relationship between two sectors (Dixit 1968, 1971). It is contended that to take care of the interdependence between terms of trade and the supply price of labour, a general equilibrium analysis may be necessary. Dixit implies that the important factors that affect the shadow price of labour are the degrees of suboptimality of savings (the shadow price of savings in terms of consumption) as well as the price and income elasticities of the demand for food.

In general equilibrium analysis, if the interdependences are to be dealt with simultaneously, it becomes difficult to see how the results rest on the premises or whether the 'tail is wagging the dog'. Again, Dixit's assumption that the only activity which can be undertaken in the traditional sector is food production is not easy to accept. The traditional sector also enters into non-agricultural activities; market wages and the shadow price of labour could be different because of taxes which may be influenced by the elasticity of marketed surplus. In any case, Dixit does not give much emphasis to the agricultural sector in his earlier model. Thus, the closed economy models of the dual economy may be misleading (Newbery 1974: 41) and the empirical estimation of a general equilibrium model is very difficult.

It seems that although the writers on the dual economy models adopted a useful approach to analyse the problems of LDCs, most of their work is devoid of any rigorous empirical analysis. An attempt has been made (Kelly *et al.* 1972) to test a modified neoclassical dual economy model with particular reference to Japan by using simulation techniques. It seems that the Japanese case is not very typical (Ishikawa 1967) of LDCs. The other familiar neoclassical premises on which the model rests do not seem to be very appropriate. These include full employment, wage-labour and neglect of land as an input in the production function. The absence of foreign trade and lags in the economic system is also disturbing.

Although the dual economy models originated from the unnecessary neglect of agriculture the models themselves do not perform very well, not only because they are based on certain simple and sometimes incorrect assumptions but also because they fall in their predictive power. First, the division of the sectors into two completely independent compartments is dubious. Second, almost all the empirical evidence available at present suggests that farmers in LDCs respond to price incentives in a way which is very similar to the response that one finds in developed countries (Bauer and Yamey 1959; Behrman 1968; Krishna 1963; Ghatak 1975a). Third, it is doubtful whether disguised unemployment prevails throughout the year. Seasonal unemployment is easily observed in many poor countries. But employment in non-farm work is also observed in some countries (Griffin 1969). Evidence also suggests that in some countries surplus labour could disappear at times of sowing and harvesting (Jorgenson 1966; Schultz 1964; Marglin 1976). Fourth, wages could be higher than marginal products only when non-farming activities are wholly absent, no employment is offered outside the joint family farm and if no labour is hired (Berry and Soligo 1968). But the experience of Latin America, the case of migrant labour in Africa and the fact of hiring labour during sowing and harvesting seasons of main crops in India would not always support the zero marginal productivity theory. It is shown that all farms are not characterized by zero marginal productivity of labour (Mathur 1964). Fifth, the case of a backward-bending supply curve of labour (Boeke 1953: 40; Higgins 1968) in LDCs may also be debated.

If people live at subsistence level, it is only natural that they should seek to attain their survival algorithms and the trade-off between income and leisure would not be observed until a critical minimum income level is reached where the basic wants are satisfied. We shall elaborate this point in the next chapter. Sixth, the theory that only the capitalists in the urban sector can save is questioned (Bergan 1967). After investigating saving behaviour in Pakistan and Bangladesh, Bergan concludes that 'rural areas . . . appear to have contributed at least three-fourths of total savings of the country'. Similarly, despite the fact that the Egyptian situation conformed well to some basic assumptions of the Lewis model, its application shows very poor predictive power partly because of the underestimation of population growth rate, the nature of manufacturers and the behaviour of capitalists (Mabro 1967: 341–77; Kanbur and McKintosh 1987; Ghatak 1991).

The predictions of the dualistic theories are threefold: (1) aggregate *per capita* income should increase; (2) *per capita* rural income would remain fixed; (3) the rate of population growth would be the same as the growth rate of agriculture. Facts from most LDCs show otherwise. In Africa (north of the Sahara) between 1960 and 1967 *per capita* income fell by 0.3 per cent per year. Per capita rural income also fell in some parts of India (Bardhan 1970a, b), in Spanish America (Griffin 1969) and in Pakistan (Bose 1968). Between 1957 and 1966 the growth rate of the population was greater than the growth rate of food production in many countries (Griffin 1969: 26). The models thus seem to be static and not historical. However, more research is necessary to draw firm conclusions about the utilities of the dual economy models. (For an advanced analysis, see McKintosh 1975, 1978.)

Appendix 3.1 Employment and growth

Within the Lewis and FR models, it is possible to demonstrate that the accumulation of surplus or profits by capitalists need not always raise the level of employment in the industrial sector (see Figure A3.1.1). The vertical axis measures the real wage and the marginal productivity of labour (MPL) and the horizontal axis measures the employment of labour. Initial equilibrium is reached at a point like E where the MPL = OW(real wage). The line WW′ is infinitely elastic because it is assumed that the supply of labour is unlimited at a subsistence level of wage or OW. The wage bill

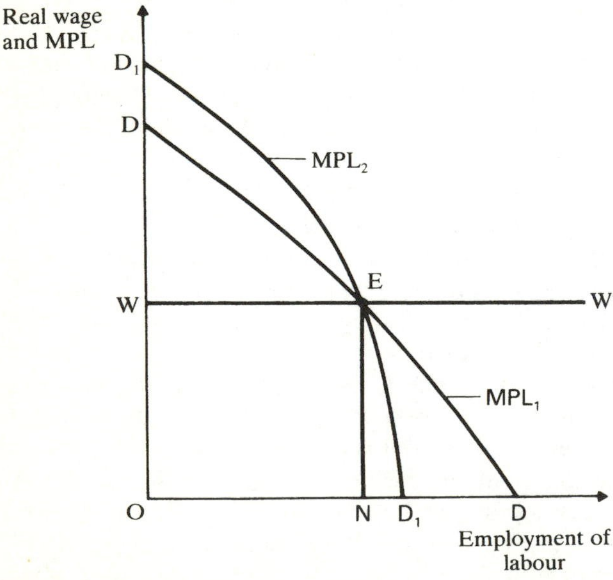

Figure A3.1.1

is given by OWEN and surplus or profits are equal to DWE. If the capitalist decides to choose capital-intensive (i.e. labour-*saving*) techniques of production, labour productivity rises, as shown by the shift of the demand or MPL curve of labour from DD or D_1D_1 but neither wages nor employment rise as the equilibrium is still attained at E. However, the profits of capitalists are greater after the introduction of labour-saving techniques and the area $WD_1E > WDE$. This may also be regarded as an illustration of growth without 'development'.

Questions

1 Explain the following concepts:

   (a) 'Surplus labour'.
   (b) 'Disguised unemployment'.
   (c) 'Dual economy models'.

2 Analyse the implication of the existence of 'disguised unemployment' in underdeveloped agriculture.
3 What are the major features of the 'dual economy model' of A.W. Lewis? What are the limitations of the Lewis model?
4 In what sense, is the Fei–Ranis model is an improvement on the Lewis model?
5 Evaluate the major contributioins of Jorgenson to the development of the 'dual economy model'.

Part II

Investment, saving, foreign resources and industrialization in less developed countries

4 Allocation of resources: investment criteria

4.1 The need for investment criteria in less developed countries

In the traditional static economic theory, allocation of resources is regarded as optimal or efficient when any transfer of resources between different sectors will not raise real national income any further. The principle to obtain such a point of optimality is to equate marginal productivities of different inputs in alternative activities. However, the peculiar characteristics of the LDCs generally account for a separate discussion of the investment criteria. For example, the different markets (product, labour, money, etc.) in the LDCs are so imperfect that the market prices of resources, i.e. wages and interest, do not reflect their true social opportunity costs. Thus, market prices may give wrong 'signals' for allocating resources and, given the divergences between the marginal private net benefits (net of costs) and marginal social net benefits (net of costs), the use of marginal principles will result in misallocation of resources. Second, the LDCs may not be interested in the *static* principles of resource allocation.[1] Given these principles, the LDCs may wish to maximize immediate rather than future output and consumption. But this may not lead to the attainment of a future optimal level. Third, it is normal in the application of the static principles that the existing distribution of income is assumed to be optimal and remains unaltered by the choice of development strategy. This is questionable if the choice of a strategy leads to maximum output but a more uneven distribution of income. That this can occur in practice has been shown in the process of 'Green Revolution' in many LDCs. Fourth, the question of externalities in many sectors could well lead to divergences between social and private costs.

Problems of investment criteria in LDCs are also related to macro and micro level decision-making processes. However, these processes could be, and sometimes are, interrelated. Thus, the planners may have to decide on the *sectoral* allocation of investments. Next, within the different sectors, given the resources, decisions regarding the choice of *projects* should be made: finally, the project managers must also decide the *techniques* of production, given the relative prices of different inputs. The choice of techniques could easily be influenced by the sectoral allocation of resources. Likewise, project allocation could be influenced by sectoral allocation. Again the choice of techniques may influence project allocation.

The debate among the different schools advocating different investment criteria has generally centred round the question of allocating scarce inputs in the LDCs (usually capital and sometimes foreign exchange) in the most efficient way to attain the best combination between present and future consumption, subject to the economic and social constraints. Since the arguments are different, and each has some merits and limits, we will proceed to discuss them in turn.

4.2 The capital turnover criterion

The problems of investment strategies in most LDCs centre round the choice of values of the different variables of the Harrod–Domar growth model to maximize growth rates. Assuming that S is the saving–income ratio and C is the capital–output ratio, the Harrod–Domar model states that $g = S/C$ where g is the rate of growth of output (see Chapter 2). It is obvious from this equation that to raise the growth rate we are required either to raise S or to lower the value of C. Given such policy options, Polak (1943) and Buchanan (1945) argued that given the scarcity of capital in LDCs the Harrodian C should be minimized. This is known as the capital turnover criterion. The marginal capital–output ratio (i.e. the capital coefficient) shows the additional investment needed to obtain an additional unit of output. Usually, historical experience dictates the past values of the capital–output ratio though one can make allowance for the future. Total needs for capital can be obtained by the use of an aggregate capital–output ratio and sectoral output ratios could be used to estimate the needs for capital in various sectors. According to Polak and Buchanan, those investment projects should be chosen which have a low C, i.e. a high rate of capital turnover.

The merits of this line of argument are as follows.

1 Given some capital scarcity in LDCs, a high capital turnover criterion would lead to an efficient allocation of resources.
2 Since the rate of population growth and sometimes the size of the population are very high, the supply of labour in most cases is greater than demand, particularly in unskilled work. The choice of the capital turnover criterion would lead to the adoption of labour-intensive techniques of production and this would help to alleviate the problem of unemployment.
3 Since many LDCs suffer from a balance of payments constraint because of their high demand to import modern technology from the developed countries, the use of the capital turnover criterion will reduce such demand and ease the pressure on foreign exchange.

However, the theory is criticized on many grounds. We mention the major arguments.

1 The use of this criterion ignores the externalities arising out of investments. Given the complementarities of different projects, a project which involves a higher capital–output ratio need not be assigned always a lower priority.
2 The time element plays a crucial role because quick-yielding projects with a lower capital–output ratio in the short run do not necessarily have a lower ratio in the long run.
3 In some projects, particularly within the agricultural sector in LDCs, fixed capital may form a small proportion of total inputs of working capital. The fixed capital–output ratio may fluctuate substantially because of factors other than capital investment.
4 The use of the capital turnover criterion may go against the objective of maximizing the rate of economic growth if resources such as skill and management are scarce.

4.3 The social marginal productivity criterion

It has been contended mainly by Kahn (1951) and Chenery (1953) that, in allocating investment, it is necessary to consider the total net contribution of the marginal unit of investment to national output (i.e. the social marginal productivity (SMP)) and not merely that portion of the contribution (or of its costs) which may accrue to the private investor. Efficient allocation consists of maximizing the value of national product and the principle to obtain this objective is to equate the SMP of capital in different uses. Where the social opportunity cost of labour is zero there is no difference between the capital turnover criterion and the SMP criterion. More formally the SMP criterion may be defined as follows:

$$\mathrm{SMP} = \frac{V}{K} - \frac{C}{K}$$

where V is the annual value of total output, C is the total annual cost of amortization and K is total investment. To adjust for the total net effect on the balance of payments (B), the above equation can he rewritten as

$$\mathrm{SMP} = \frac{V}{K} - \frac{C}{K} + \frac{\mathrm{VB}}{K}$$

where VB is the variation in income because of a change of one unit in the balance of payments.

Like the capital turnover criterion, the SMP principle also suffers from the following major criticisms.

1 The SMP principle ignores the multiplier effects on future income levels.
2 The SMP criterion does not make due allowance for the changes in the nature and quality of factors of production such as population and labour that may take place as a result of present investment.
3 In the labour-surplus economies where the opportunity cost of labour may be zero, the SMP criterion is open to the same criticisms as can be levelled against the capital turnover criterion.

Until now we have been discussing the main strengths and weaknesses of the arguments which are advanced to the theory of maximizing current national income. We now turn to discussion of the theory which aims at maximizing future rates of growth.

4.4 The maximization of the rate of creation of investible surplus principle

The maximization of the rate of creation of investible surplus (MRIS) criterion is chiefly advocated by Galenson and Leibenstein (1955). Their main objective is to maximize *per capita* real income at a future point of time. Galenson and Leibenstein emphasize the role of capital accumulation to achieve a higher rate of growth. Their main argument rests on the following premises. First, national income can be divided into two parts: wages and profits. Second, wage earners savings are zero but profit earners total income is available for investment. Third, one production function, which makes output per unit of labour a function of capital per unit of labour, prevails in the whole economy.

Given these assumptions, maximization of *per capita* real income at some future point of time would require an increase of capital per unit of labour at present. This implies the maximization of investment at each preceding period which in turn requires that profit share in national income should be maximized (or wage share be minimized). The implication is to choose those projects which involve higher capital intensity, i.e. where the capital–labour ratio is highest. Allocation efficiency is achieved by distributing the available capital in different uses in such a way that 'the marginal *per capita* reinvestment quotient' of capital is equal in different projects.

4.4.1 Evaluation of the MRIS criterion

1 Per capita real income maximization at some future point of time has not been considered as a very realistic goal (Eckstein 1957). It is argued that governments should be concerned with the welfare to be enjoyed at each period in future, with the entire future growth of the system.
2 There is not enough evidence to assume that the propensity of the workers to save will be zero and that of the profit earners will be equal to one. Even if it is assumed that the only savers are profit earners, maximization of profit does not necessarily imply maximization of the capital–labour ratio (Moses 1957; Bator 1957).
3 Maximum use of capital in some projects may well reduce the rate of profit particularly where we do not assume that production is the same function of capital for all sectors.
4 In labour-surplus economies as well as in LDCs characterized by large unemployment and underemployment, maximization of employment may well be a social and political objective (Brahmananda and Vakil 1956). Realization of such an aim may well call for the use of the capital turnover rather than the MRIS principle.
5 Many LDCs do not have markets large enough to support capital-intensive industry on an economic basis.
6 Unless a balance is struck between increases in the production of capital goods and of consumer goods, supply inelasticities in the production of consumer goods could lead to inflation.[2]

The capital-intensive industries in some LDCs have been set up by disregarding the doctrine of comparative cost advantage and by upholding the argument of protecting the infant industry. Sometimes the output of these protected industries is inferior in quality and their prices are higher than world prices. When these industries are protected *sine die*, the benefits of obtaining a high reinvestment quotient in these industries must be offset by the high price paid by those industries which use their product and the consequent reduction in their reinvestment quotient. This argument is not without empirical foundation as has been shown in connection with the construction of a fertilizer plant near Paradeep in India (Sara 1975).

However, all these criticisms do not necessarily invalidate one of the major points in the Galenson–Leibenstein thesis: the use of the SMP criterion may lead to a choice of projects and would imply a given income distribution which could affect savings rate. Eckstein (1957) argues that the use of fiscal policies may be necessary in such cases to obtain desired savings instead of banking upon planned investment based on a reinvestment criterion. But given the limitations of fiscal policy in raising savings Eckstein has proposed that projects with the highest marginal growth contribution

(MGC) should be selected, where MGC is given by the project's direct contribution to consumption plus the present value of the future consumption stream rendered possible by the growth of capital. However, the limitations of Eckstein's theory are obvious. For one thing, population is regarded as an exogenous variable; for another, income distribution is regarded as optimal throughout the analysis. Eckstein admits that, where the government cannot achieve a satisfactory level of investment by fiscal means, those projects should be favoured which yield high rates of reinvestment. Next, if the time horizon is infinite, it is unreasonable to assume that the only critical factor in growth is capital at every period in the future. Moreover, the need to direct all reinvestments to a single project can also be questioned (Meier 2001).

We now turn to the alternative criterion proposed by Sen and Dobb.

4.5 The reinvestible surplus criterion

The criteria suggested by Dobb (1960) and by Sen (1968) are rather similar. For brevity, we shall consider only the proposed criterion as developed by Sen.

In the Sen model the economy is divided into two sectors: one is modern, the other is backward. The modern sector is again subdivided into two parts: one sector (A) is producing machinery with only labour; the other sector (B) is producing corn by using machinery and labour. In the backward sector corn (i.e. a consumer good) is produced by labour alone. Labour productivity in the modern sector A is given by the capital intensity of the technology applied there where the capital intensity is given by the total number of man-years necessary in sector A to turn out enough machinery for one unit of labour in sector B. Sen assumes that wages in the modern sector are determined by the corn output produced by sector B. But since it takes some time to set up the modern sector, wages in the modern sector would have to be paid out of the 'surplus' in the backward sector.

Sen then distinguishes between the following aims: (1) maximization of current output (i.e. corn); (2) maximization of the rate of growth of output; (3) maximization of the undiscounted flow of output over a finite period of time. The choice of capital intensity will differ according to the nature of the objective. Sen describes how a conflict can arise between the current output maximization principle and the criterion to maximize the *rate of growth of output* (see Figure 4.1). Let the vertical axis measure output (corn) and the horizontal axis measure the employment of labourers. In the south-east corner the combination of labour and capital is measured. The curve OQ is the production function and OW is the given wage line which shows wage bills at various levels of employment. At point E, we obtain maximum output (EL) and employment of OL which would work with OK amount of capital; the degree of capital intensity is given by the tangent of the angle OLK. Labour productivity is given by the tangent of the angle $P_{1n}OL$. Note that at E we find that the capital turnover and the SMP criteria are satisfied. But if the objective is to maximize the reinvestible surplus to obtain a higher rate of growth, the point to choose is E_1, where AB is tangent to OQ and parallel to OW. Maximum surplus is shown by E_1S_1. It is easily observed that if the Galenson–Leibenstein criterion (i.e. MRIS) is followed, the point E_1 rather than E would be chosen, capital intensity would be higher at E_1 than at E (i.e. the tangent of the angle OL_1K is greater than that of OLK) and labour productivity would also be higher (i.e. the tangent of the angle $P_{2n}OL$ is greater than that of $P_{1n}OL$). Given similar diagrams, it is also possible to show that maximization of

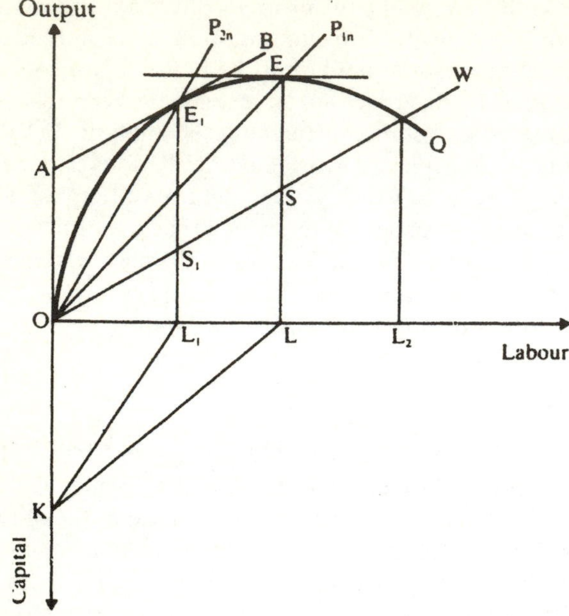

Figure 4.1

current output may lead to the emergence of a negative surplus. However, maximization of output need not mean maximization of employment as can be shown by the difference between OL and OL_2. In fact, employment expansion beyond OL_2 leads to the emergence of negative 'surplus' ('eating' the railways!).

The moral of the above exercise is to show clearly that there is a basic conflict between maximizing consumption at present (by using the capital turnover or SMP criterion) or in future (by applying the MRIS criterion) (see Figure 4.2). Let Pp' be the production possibility frontier for an LDC. If all the resources are allocated to the production of investment goods, OP of capital goods would be produced; on the other hand, if all the resources are spent on the production of consumer goods, Op' of consumer goods would be produced.[3] Obviously, society will choose to produce some combination of both the goods. However, lines Og and Og_1 represent different growth rates (4 per cent and 6 per cent respectively). Assume that the economy is growing along Og. But if a higher growth rate (say Og_1) is regarded as desirable, it requires a cut in consumption goods by cd which would allow resources to be released for the production of more investment goods to take the economy to F; given a rise in the production of investment goods, the growth rate will be higher, i.e. 6 per cent instead of 4 per cent. But present consumption must be sacrificed to obtain the higher growth path, though the choice of a higher growth path at present will ensure higher consumption in the future as well (see also Appendix 4.1).

As one of the solutions to the dilemma, Sen has proposed that since the choice of investment criterion depends upon the time horizon of output generation, the time preference and the social welfare function (assuming that such a function is available to the planners), the best way of looking at the problem would be to derive the alternative time series of consumption obtained by following different criteria. The point

Box 4.1

Amartya Sen

Nobel Prize winner Amartya Sen has made a huge contribution to development economics. Sen brought clarity to the problem of whether developing countries should use more labour-intensive methods of production than would be profitable at the market wage rate. In so many developing countries, labour is an abundant factor of production whilst capital is very scarce. It is tempting therefore to suggest that labour-intensive means of production are the most productive. This thinking ignores the fact that savings rates may well be lower if more money is paid out in low wages, thus creating a vicious circle where capital remains scarce. One of Sen's contributions was to create a clear analytical framework in which these issues could be discussed, i.e. he refined the use of a 'shadow cost' model to take into account the full economic cost of hiring an extra worker. Another of Sen's key contributions has been to legitimize the investigation of topics like famine, which beforehand were considered to be outside economics' concerns.

Atkinson, A. 'The contributions of Amartya Sen to welfare economics', *Scandinavian Journal of Economics* 101 (2), 1999.

can be shown clearly in Figure 4.3. Let the vertical axis measure the growth of output of consumer goods and the horizontal axis measure time. Output can be produced by either technique K or technique L. Technique K produces less output now than technique L but after B the rate of growth of output under technique K is such as to compensate for the initial loss of output by the year T_1. It is assumed that the area $AA'B = BCC'$. Although the use of technique L generates more output in the current period, it yields progressively less and less in future, given the slope of the curve AL. Now if society is prepared to wait until period T_2 (say for thirty years), consumption sacrificed at present could be made up by that time and after T_2

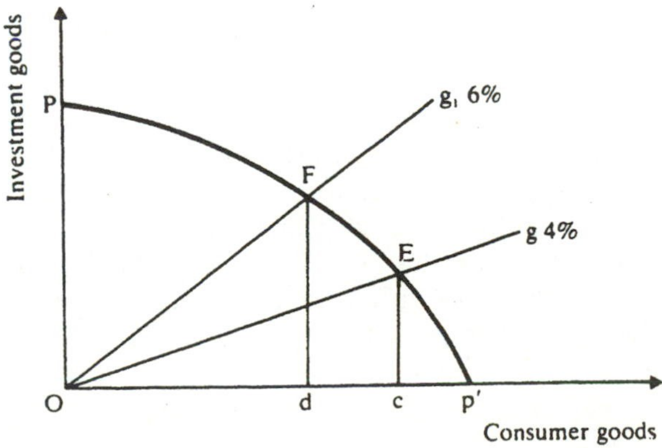

Figure 4.2

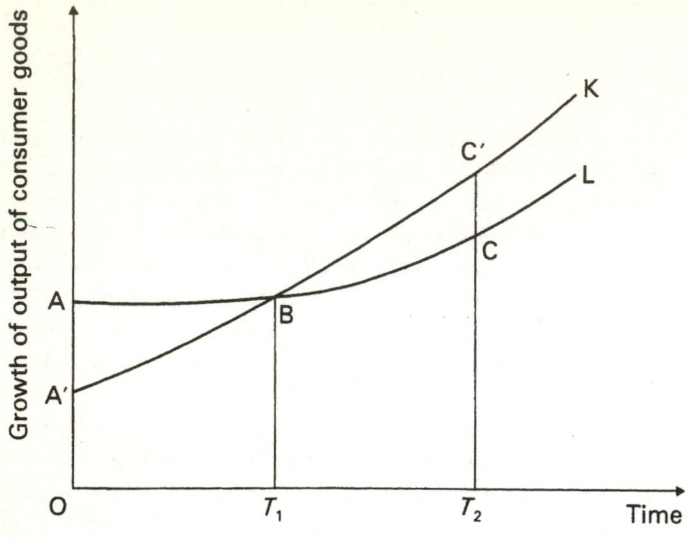

Figure 4.3

society would enjoy higher output and consumption by choosing technique K. But if the social welfare function is such that society values present output and consumption more than future output and consumption, then society may well choose technique L.

4.5.1 Evaluation of the reinvestible surplus criterion

The choice between maximization of output and maximization of employment is more complex than the previous analysis would suggest. Output is a heterogeneous concept; so is employment (Stewart and Streeten 1972). Since both output and employment change over time and since present output and employment may affect future levels, both intra- and inter-temporal weighting is very important. It is possible to state that generation of more output (with given capital and technology) will require more labour and to that extent the conflict between the objectives to maximize employment and output is more apparent than real. However, the conflict between the two objectives would be more real if it is assumed that a new technology is chosen. The example given by Stewart and Streeten (1972) can be cited. Suppose £100,000 is the amount of money available for investment in a textile industry. Let the capital–output ratio be 2.5 if advanced technology is used; if the capital cost per work place is given as £1,000, then additional output would be worth £40,000 and additional employment would be 100. But if a traditional hand-spinning technique is used, where the capital–output ratio is 5.0 and the cost per work place is given as £100, then additional employment would be 1,000 but the value of additional output would be only £20,000. Note that in this case, although the capital–labour ratio is lower, the capital–output ratio is higher than for the more capital-intensive modern method. This is because a large-scale capital-intensive technique can economize on capital since economies of scale occur and this leads to a fall in capital cost in relation to output (Kaldor 1965; Amin 1969).

It is also necessary to point out that output is likely to rise with extra employment (unless labour is wholly unemployed in which case it should not be employed, at least not in the organized profit-maximizing modern sector, in the first place) and the level of employment will be largely given, *inter alia,* by the level of wages. In the Dobb–Sen model (see Figure 4.1) it is assumed that wages are fixed and this helps to explain the dichotomy between employment and output maximization. But if the real wages are allowed to fall, the conflict between the two objectives will be minimized. Evidence suggests that more labour-intensive methods like traditional spinning could also save more capital per unit of output in comparison with modern factor methods (Bhalla 1964). So long as indigenous materials could be used by the unemployed labour without involving a diversion of resources, an increase in employment will also lead to a rise in output. (See Appendix 4.1 for a simple proof.)

It is usually assumed that higher consumption rather than saving will follow the use of labour-intensive rather than capital-intensive techniques of production and this will lower the growth rate for the economy as a whole. A conflict then occurs between macro and micro concepts of efficiency (Meier 2001). But such an argument rests on the following premises:

1 Wages are independent of the choice of techniques.
2 All wages are consumed and all profits are saved.
3 Fiscal policy is inadequate to raise taxes to obtain the desired savings ratio and real wages are unlikely to be reduced even when inflation takes place in many LDCs.

Given these premises, the impact of the choice of increasing capital intensity on growth and employment within the neoclassical theory can easily be analysed using Figure 4.4. The horizontal axis measures the capital–labour ratio (C/L) and the vertical axis measures output per unit of labour (Q/L). The production function is given by OP and it shows that, for any output, present employment is maximized by using the most labour-intensive technology and this is reflected in a move *towards the origin* in the diagram. However, employment growth will be given by output growth at a given

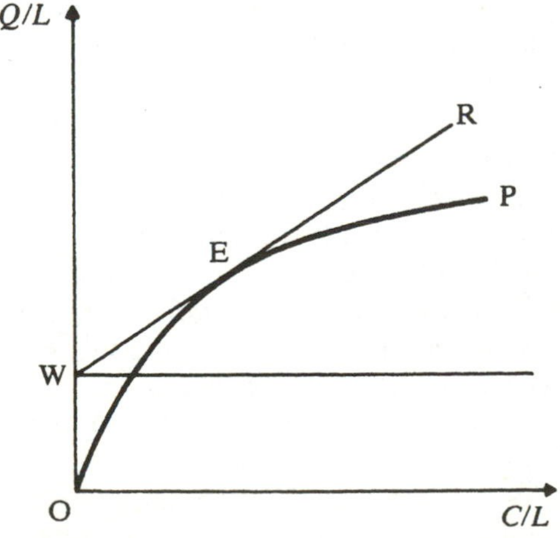

Figure 4.4

capital intensity (assuming away technical progress or even assuming *neutral* technical progress). Given assumption (2) above, output- and employment-maximizing technologies will be determined by the level of wages. Let wages be OW and, given assumption (1), the rate of growth of the economy is shown by the slope of WR to the production function. The highest growth rate is reached at E but this is not the point at which maximum employment is obtained since we have moved further from the point of origin. If the techniques of production to optimize the growth rates of employment and of output are the same, the conflict between them disappears. The conflict will be aggravated if real wages rise.

Evidence suggests that wages are related to labour productivity, the scale of activity and the choice of technology, and that small enterprises which usually adopt more labour-intensive methods (i.e. lower C/L) also offer a lower level of wages (Dhar and Lydall 1961; Shetty 1963; Okita 1964). Thus the choice of technique is not independent of the scale of operation and the level of wages. Also it is not wholly realistic to assume that all profits would be saved. A part of them may be frittered away in conspicuous consumption. Besides, foreign and multinational enterprises repatriate some profits, interest and royalties, which clearly reduces reinvestible funds. The implicit assumption in the Sen–Dobb model is that all profits would be saved because profits would accrue to the public sector and the means of production would be owned by the state. This may be questioned because most LDCs have mixed economies. Further, the inability of the government to raise savings by manipulating fiscal and wage policies is viewed with scepticism when the same government is able to sacrifice present consumption and employment by choosing certain techniques (Stewart and Streeten 1972). Moreover, choice of techniques could be influenced by the degree of competition. In a competitive economy, to maintain or maximize profits, producers will try to minimize costs and look for an optimum combination of factors of production, while in a protected economy, the producers are under no such compulsion to reduce costs by introducing technical progress or by choosing the optimal proportions. It is worth mentioning that despite labour abundance and capital scarcity in many LDCs, neither domestic nor foreign enterprises have shown much interest in taking advantage of the existing factor–cost ratios.

Some other points are also worth emphasizing in this connection. First, the problem of investment allocation cannot be viewed only in static terms. It is important to observe the dynamic optimal growth paths. It has been shown (Srinivasan 1962) that such an optimal sustainable *per capita* consumption growth path exists for an economy consisting of two sectors – one sector producing consumer goods, the other capital goods. Others have also tried to analyse the theoretical properties of such growth paths (Findlay 1966; Dixit 1968; Bose 1968; Uzawa 1962).

Second, the choice of optimum technology is a rather complex issue. Different sectors may require different intensities which would be optimal; e.g. an optimal technology for agriculture may require the use of labour-intensive technology whereas such an optimality may be reached in choosing a capital-intensive method in generating power and electricity. Thus *micro* concepts of optimality should not be confused with the macro objective of maximizing output growth rate by utilizing all the inputs which could be obtained. To achieve overall *consistency* in resource allocation, investment planning or programming is necessary. The use of input–output tables and programming models would be quite useful in such cases.

Third, different technologies embody different types of externalities which are not usually considered within a static analysis. Such externalities could arise because of the economies of scale in industries. Due regard to the externalities in a dynamic analysis may well influence the choice of techniques. Finally, the pattern of income distribution would be different with different technologies. A labour-intensive technology (say, a seed–fertilizer revolution in the agriculture of LDCs which could be labour using) could raise total and per acre output, but because of higher employment and the higher marginal propensity of agriculturalists to consume, the saving–income ratio may fall, leading to a fall in the growth rate. It is, of course, assumed that higher savings and investment, rather than higher consumption, lead to a higher rate of growth. Mirrlees (1975), on the other hand, has argued that growth can be increased by increased consumption. This line of argument is not new altogether as it has been shown before (Leibenstein 1957) that an increase in consumption in LDCs will mean better nutrition, greater efficiency and higher productivity of labourers in LDCs. The empirical tests of such models have hardly been carried out either to accept or to reject such theories.

Empirical evidence suggests that choice of techniques does exist in many LDCs in manufacturing, metalworking and textile industries (Bhalla 1975). Similarly, cost of production and thus the choice of technique is influenced not only by prices but also by the scale of production. Also, relative factor-price differences between rural and urban areas in an LDC may influence the choice (Stewart 1975). Again, substitution possibilities between different types of labour and between labour and working capital, as well as the choice of products, can affect the final choice of technology.

4.6 Balanced and unbalanced growth

A lively debate has taken place between the advocates of balanced and unbalanced growth as strategies for economic development in the 1950s and 1960s, though after numerous qualifications of both versions the merit of the initial debate and distinction has been considerably diminished. It now appears that both schools of thought have considerable grounds in common and the division between them is more apparent than real. Here we shall first analyse the arguments of the proponents of balanced growth (BG) and this will be followed by analysis of the theory of unbalanced growth (UBG). In conclusion it will be argued that the two theories instead of being substitutes are really complementary to one another.

As one of the main champions of BG, it was Rosenstein-Rodan (1943) who was the first to point out the need to achieve growth by a 'big push' in east and south-east Europe. His arguments mainly rest on the desirability of surmounting the indivisibilities in both demand and supply. The emergence of external economies from the use of 'lumpy' social capital helps to remove the indivisibilities on the supply side. The bottlenecks on the demand side imposed by the narrow size of the markets could be removed if a number of industries could be set up simultaneously, each catering for the other. In Figure 4.5 it is shown that, given the demand and average cost curves D_1, D_2, and C_1, C_2 respectively for two industries, a clear loss is indicated. But the establishment of the industries simultaneously helps to shift the demand curve to D'_1 and D'_2 and with given cost curves both of them would be viable. A 'big push' or massive investment in many projects will enable the economy to remove the difference between social and private marginal product and the industries themselves, once set up,

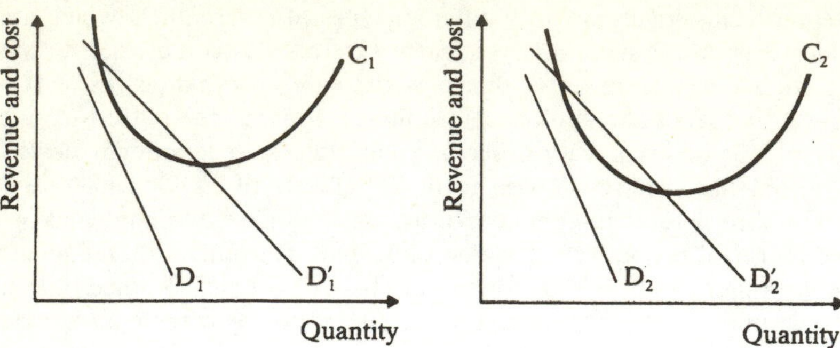

Figure 4.5

would be viable as they would not experience either supply or demand constraints. Nurkse (1953) has spoken about the case for BG mainly on grounds of demand creation since it is assumed that the LDCs would not be able to raise their exports substantially. Lewis (1955) has argued for BG mainly because he wanted to avoid excess capacities and waste. He has pointed out the need to maintain the terms of trade constant between different sectors so that the growth of any sector need not be adversely affected by an adverse movement of the terms of trade against it. The other point that Lewis has emphasized is that the relative rates of growth of each sector will be given by the income elasticities of the demand for their goods. Such a policy would overcome the bottlenecks that might emerge in the process of growth. Here Lewis has emphasized the vertical nature of production of the supply side while Rosenstein-Rodan and Nurkse have emphasized the horizontal interdependence of consumption (Mathur 1966).

4.6.1 The arguments against balanced growth

Several arguments have been advanced against the BG doctrine. Thus, Fleming (1955) has pointed out that if most industries expand at the same time, then assuming fixity of supply of factors and their full employment, inflation would take place. However, it may be mentioned that the supply of factors may not remain fixed over time and in many countries labour is hardly fully employed and BG need not lead to inflation (Nath 1962).

Bauer and Yamey (1957) have also criticized the doctrine of BG on the grounds that it unrealistically assumes that the supply of food is elastic. But if BG means a balanced development of both industry and agriculture then the criticism will lose its strength. Bauer and Yamey have also argued that 'any industry which is able to compete in the export market would be established independently of the schemes of balanced industrialization'. But this argument will be weakened if the external economies of production, which would emerge by setting up many industries to increase the competitiveness of the export industries, are taken into account (Nath 1962).

Other criticisms of the BG theory are advanced by Hirschman (1958b) and Streeten (1959) but these points of view could best be analysed in the context of the theory of UBG.

4.6.2 An evaluation of unbalanced growth theory

The case for UBG, according to its champions, rests primarily on the necessity to economize on the use of resources. For example, it is argued that since most LDCs experience a shortage of entrepreneurs, it is very difficult for them to attain BG (Bauer and Yamey 1957; Kindleberger 1956) and as such growth should be unbalanced because it helps the LDCs to economize 'genuine decision-making' (Hirschman 1958b: 63). Next it is argued that growth should take place through shortages and excesses as it is assumed that every challenge would generate its own response. This is very much like the operation of Say's law in reverse: that demand creates its own supply. In fact, Streeten (1959) argued that technical progress in economic history has taken place mostly as an answer to the bottlenecks generated in the path of economic progress. Next, it is said that the case for UBG rests on the strong positive correlation between the growth rate of industrial output and that of its productivity (Scitovsky 1959; Streeten 1959). Assuming that such a correlation is present, *a priori*, such an event does not necessarily destroy the case for BG, nor does it support the case for UBG. It has also been argued that BG would require planning and most LDCs do not have either the requisite skill or the necessary reliable and adequate information to formulate such plans. Moreover, planning may involve huge costs in real terms (e.g. lengthy decision-making processes, 'red tape', favouritism) and monetary terms (e.g. the financial costs of setting up the whole planning department plus its operational costs). Further, given the scarcity of resources in LDCs, all waste or external diseconomies should be minimized as far as possible. Thus, development via the creation of excess capacities in social capital in comparison with the output produced by direct productive activities is regarded as wasteful and the balance between the growth of output and social capital is regarded as irrelevant as it reduces induced investment (Hirschman 1958b). Hirschman has obviously considered the growth path via 'shortages' (i.e. where output from direct productive activities is rising faster than social capital) as more efficient as it is likely to achieve greater induced investment.

The need to minimize external diseconomies is evident in LDCs. But Hirschman's analysis does not provide a convincing case for maximizing induced investment. It is known, as in Italy, that the creation of social capital is not enough to promote growth. Nor is it certain that induced private investment would be forthcoming, particularly in the creation of social capital whenever there are shortages (Thirlwall 1974). It is much more difficult to say, with empirical evidence, that the choice of the UBG path is 'efficient' or optimal in terms of resource use. The strength of the UBG theory rests on the implicit assumption of elastic supply for many LDCs but this is not a very realistic assumption. Next, the lack of balance between demand and supply could easily lead to inflation, with all its undesirable consequences (e.g. devaluation and its unfavourable impact on the balance of payments when the marginal propensity to import is high, the price and income elasticities of demand for exportables are low and there are regressive effects on income distribution). Again, following the UBG theory, if resources are concentrated on the production of only a few commodities, the effects may not always be desirable. For example, from the standpoint of the balance of payments, there is always the danger of putting 'all the eggs in one basket' and thereby suffering due to the lack of trade diversification. Finally, although it is possible to cite forward linkages (percentage of output used as inputs in other activities) and backward linkages (percentage of output bought from other sectors) in the manufacturing sector of the LDCs, such linkages are few between industry and agriculture in many poor countries.[4]

4.6.3 A reconciliation between BG and UBG theories

The above discussion shows that the two theories cover a lot of common ground and, if several qualifications of the different arguments of these two schools are taken into consideration, it is possible to suggest that the two theories, instead of being substitutes, are really complementary to one another. This is clearly reflected in the statement of Streeten (1959):

> choose projects which, (i) while advancing some sectors, concentrating the pressure or unbalance on groups and sectors whose response to a challenge is likely to be strongest; (ii) while creating bottlenecks also break them; (iii) while providing products and services for industry, agriculture and consumers, also induce new developments to take place in other directions, directly and indirectly related to them; (iv) while providing a new product or service require consequential investment in other lines.

Again, to reap the benefits of externalities, it may be necessary to undertake large investments and this approach need not be inconsistent with the idea of concentrating resources in a few sectors. If unbalanced growth is defined not so much in terms of shortages as in terms of concentration on certain activities, according to comparative advantage or the existence of increasing returns, balanced and unbalanced growth can be complementary strategies (Thirlwall 1974). Similarly, the economies mainly dominated by private enterprises also recognize the need to strike a balance between present and future demand and supply and use planning and programming tools to obtain such balance. Although the concept of planning is normally associated with the doctrine of balanced growth, such a concept by itself need not mean total state control and ownership as planning may involve licensing, the issue of directives and the offer of subsidies to private enterprises. Historically, although economic development followed an uneven path, the need to obtain BG as an objective was seldom refuted. The supporters of BG theory would not find it difficult to accept that the differences in demand and supply of goods could be partially adjusted by the differences in elasticities in demand with respect to prices, and producers do respond in some cases to relative output and input prices. As regards the desirability of creating social overheads, it is interesting to point out that both Streeten and Nurkse have emphasized the need to build up supply in excess of demand and, here again, the difference between the two schools is negligible.

Appendix 4.1 The dichotomy between savings and output maximization and its solution

The conflict between savings and output maximization can be shown with the help of the following equations. Let the production function be

$$Q = \alpha N - \beta N^2 \tag{A4.1.1}$$

Let the investible surplus be given by

$$S = \alpha N - \beta N^2 - wN \tag{A4.1.2}$$

Where Q is output, S is investible surplus, N is labour employed and w is the rate of wage per unit of labour employed.

To maximize surplus, we differentiate equation (A4.1.2) with respect to N and set it equal to zero:

$$\frac{dS}{dN} = \alpha - 2\beta N - w = 0 \tag{A4.1.3}$$

$$\alpha - 2\beta N = w$$

$$N = \frac{\alpha - w}{2\beta} \tag{A4.1.4}$$

To obtain the highest level of output, we differentiate (A4.1.1) with respect to N. Thus

$$\frac{dQ}{dN} = \alpha - 2\beta N = 0 \tag{A4.1.5}$$

$$N = \frac{\alpha}{2\beta} \tag{A4.1.6}$$

Note that the difference between (A4.1.4) and (A4.1.6) will tend to disappear as w falls to zero. Models which emphasize the dichotomy between employment and output maximization usually assume wages as given (see Thirlwall 1976b). It is easy to show that this dichotomy also disappears if we have a Cobb–Douglas production function, i.e. $Q = AN^{\alpha}K^{\beta}$ where K is capital.

Notes

1 Note that the traditional theory may incorporate *some* time dimension.
2 The implication here is that maximizing the capital–labour ratio is the same as adopting capital goods industries. This need not be the case. It has been argued that capital goods industries could be relatively more labour intensive than some other forms of industries (see Pack and Todaro 1969).
3 In an open economy it is not necessarily a question of allocating resources for the *production* of consumer and investment goods: rather, it could be a problem of allocating *expenditure* on such goods.
4 However, in both China and Taiwan, there are important links between the agricultural sector and rural industry.

Questions

1 Why do we need different investment criteria for developing countries?
2 What are the differences between the 'capital turnover' and the 'social marginal productivity' criteria?
3 Evaluate the principle of maximization of the rate of creation of investible surplus.

4 Explain the dichotomy between:

(a) Maximization of *current* output.
(b) Maximization of *the rate of growth* of output.

How valid is the dichotomy if labour markets are flexible?

5 How valid is the distinction between 'balanced' and 'unbalanced' growth for developing countries?

5 Domestic resources for development

5.1 Introduction

Most LDCs mainly depend upon domestic resources for their development. Foreign resources and trade also play some part in financing the economic development of the LDCs, but a more comprehensive discussion of their role will follow later (see Chapters 6 and 7). At the outset, it is necessary to emphasize the importance of shifting funds from low to high productivity users and also the need for small farms and other businesses to have working balances and funds for new (and replacement) investment. Here we shall chiefly examine the roles of (1) monetary, (2) inflationary and (3) fiscal policies in financing growth. We shall first analyse some features of the money markets of the LDCs.

5.2 The nature of money markets in less developed countries

It is important to stress at the outset the nature of money markets in LDCs. Such a money market is distinguished by its *duality,* with its *organized* and *unorganized* sectors, with different business practices and interest rates (Wai 1957; Myint 1971; Ghatak 1976, 1995). The organized sector usually comprises the commercial and co-operative banks, the central bank and other governmental agencies like the agricultural finance corporations. The unorganized sector mainly comprises the money lenders, indigenous bankers, landlords, traders and merchants. The organized money market tends to be highly sophisticated and specialized with its developed bill-market. Funds sometimes flow between the organized and unorganized sectors but their links with one another seem to be very weak. Note that the organized markets are far from homogeneous in LDCs and this implies the presence of many interest rates within the rural money markets. The main features that distinguish the unorganized sector from the organized sector are as follows:

1 informality in dealings with customers and personal contact with borrowers;
2 flexibility of loan operations and simple systems of maintaining accounts;
3 absence of specialization, i.e. blending moneylending with other economic activities;
4 secrecy in financial dealings.

5.2.1 The role of a money market in LDCs

A money market usually caters for the demand and supply of *short-run* loanable funds. In this context, several useful functions of a money market can be mentioned. First, by allocating saving to investment, it tends to allocate resources more efficiently. Second, it tends to establish an equilibrium between demand for and supply of funds. Third, by promoting liquidity and ensuring the safety of financial assets, it promotes saving and investment. This is important in LDCs where savings and investment habits leave much room for improvement. In the rural sector, very frequently, savings consist of bullion-hoarding and land-holding rather than the holding of financial assets. Thus, even if there is ability to save, in the absence of a developed money market the economy is deprived of an array of financial assets which could lead saving into productive investment (Gurley and Shaw 1960: 49, also 1967). Fourth, a money market ensures the flow of funds from one sector to another and thus encourages financial mobility. Fifth, a developed money market is essential for implementing the monetary policies (e.g. the bank rate and open market operations) of the central bank. Also, a developed money market is crucial for providing elasticity in the flow of funds.

The dualism in the money markets in LDCs has had certain effects. First, it has led to restricted use of cheques. Second, to supplement the credit needs of the economy, especially of the rural sector, it has led to the growth of different types of instruments of credit. This, again, has reduced the use of bank credit. Third, it has restricted the volume of monetary transactions and perpetuated non-monetized transactions. Fourth, the absence of a well-developed money market has deprived the economy of necessary financial assets with which savings could have been more efficiently tapped and converted into investment for raising the level of development. Last, but not least, the presence of the 'financial dualism' has perpetuated some age-old customs, like gold-hoarding, which have restricted the use of available resources for productive investment.

5.3 Money and economic growth

It is now easy to see how a process of monetary expansion can aid the growth of LDCs. First, money replaces barter transactions which are frequently wasteful and time-consuming to strike the right balance between demand and supply. Notice that the relative cost of printing money is small. Second, money as a medium of exchange induces specialization and increases productivity. Specialization in the production of specific crops in a peasant economy would increase the interdependence and exchange among the various sectors and increasing monetization (i.e. increase in the ratio of monetary transactions (M) to total transactions (T), an increase in M/T) could only facilitate this process of increasing productivity. Third, in a developing country, to match increasing output and the demand for money, it is necessary to increase money supply. Fourth, if barter transactions are replaced by monetary transactions, then real resources will be released to promote growth. In fact, increasing monetization would require the promotion of banking and credit institutions which could help considerably the promotion of saving, investment and growth (Kaldor and Mirrlees 1962; Wai 1972; Wallich 1969). Fifth, money can also act as a store of value, and the government by incurring public debt can provide alternative channels to mobilize enough saving to achieve equality between the natural rate and the warranted growth rate of capital (Tobin 1965).

It has been argued that empirical evidence for some Latin American and Asian countries suggests positive and significant correlation between money supply and real output growth between 1959 and 1966 (Fan 1970). However, a high rate of inflation tends to exert a negative influence on real income growth. This analysis is plausible; but, here again, it is important to point out that the low value of R^2 (i.e. the proportion of explained variation to total variation of real output growth) reduces the predictive power of the model. For the Latin American countries, Fan calculates the critical rate of increase of money supply as 16.5 per cent per annum beyond which monetary expansion would be inflationary. However, these figures should be treated with due caution because the models on which they are based may be wrongly specified and the predictive power of these models is limited.

For the LDCs, evidence suggests a positive and significant relationship between the ratio of investment to income and the growth of *per capita* income (Thirlwall 1974). A similar relationship between investment ratio and the growth of real income is observed by others (Hill 1964; Modigliani 1970). However, evidence from some Asian countries suggests that, if saving is treated as a function of income, then it is also possible to find a positive and significant relationship (Williamson 1968). This is indicated in the following equation:

$$S/N = -9.45 + 2.03Y/N$$

$$(1.31)(0.010)$$

$$R^2 = 0.829$$

(figures in parentheses are the standard error). S is total saving, N is population and Y is total income. About 83 per cent of the total variation in saving per head is explained by income per head and the value of the income per head coefficient is statistically highly significant. However, at a very high level of income this strong and positive relationship could weaken.

The above discussion shows the relationship between monetary expansion, saving, investment and economic growth. It has been mentioned that an expansionary monetary programme in an LDC could be inflationary beyond a certain level, given the supply inelasticities. The effects of such inflationary finance on growth will now be analysed.

5.4 Inflation and economic growth

It is tempting for the LDCs to resort to inflation as a major 'tax' to finance their public expenditure to promote economic development, particularly when the tax revenue as a proportion of GNP is low and tax elasticity with respect to income is not always greater than unity. Given certain demand for money assumptions, inflation can raise revenues. Second, by increasing profitability of industries, inflation can provide incentives to investment. Third, the government will be less obliged to depend upon foreign resources if it can raise more revenue at home. Fourth, it has been argued that inflationary financing could promote the growth of banks and other financial institutions. These agencies may induce the public to hold financial rather than physical assets and thus release real resources for economic growth (Thirlwall 1974). This, however, is a rather dubious argument because, at times of high inflation, people may be induced to hold more physical rather than financial assets.

On the debit side, inflation could easily distort the efficient allocation of resources and reduce real growth. Second, a high level of inflation will reduce a country's competitive power in the export market and it may eventually price itself out. The LDCs which suffer from a chronic balance of payments deficit, therefore, should exercise greater caution in the use of inflationary policies. Third, inflation may make the distribution of income more unequal. Many LDCs experience significant inequalities in the distribution of income and, as such, inflationary financing, which often tends to redistribute income in favour of profits rather than wages, may arouse public hostility. However, it may be argued that, even if inflation promotes more inequality, it tends to raise profit share and thereby the saving ratio in national income and this could have a beneficial effect on growth. Critics argue that consumption could also have a favourable effect on growth in the LDCs (Mirrlees 1975; Foxley 1976; Bliss and Stern 1976). Fourth, a high level of inflation could easily shake people's confidence in the currency and this could induce greater holding of physical rather than financial assets with detrimental effects on growth. Finally, hyperinflation could only have disastrous consequences on the currency and financial system without conferring much significant benefit on the real growth of a country.

On balance, the weight of the arguments seem to be in favour of a mild degree of inflation for promoting growth (Ghatak 1995). The mechanism has been illustrated by Mundell (1965) and his model will be analysed next.

5.4.1 Mundell's model of inflation and growth

Mundell starts off with the basic quantity theory equation to show the relationship between inflation and economic growth (Mundell 1965). Thus, we have

$$MV = PQ \tag{5.1}$$

where M is money supply, P is price level, V is velocity and Q is total output.

If we differentiate (5.1) with respect to time t we have

$$\frac{1}{V}\frac{\mathrm{d}V}{\mathrm{d}t} = p + g - m \tag{5.2}$$

where p is the rate of growth of prices, i.e. $(1/p)\,\mathrm{d}P/\mathrm{d}t$; g is the rate of growth of quantity, i.e. $(1/Q)\,\mathrm{d}Q/\mathrm{d}t$; and m is the rate of growth of the money supply, i.e. $(1/M)\,\mathrm{d}M/\mathrm{d}t$.

Let us assume that

$$Q = \beta K \tag{3.5}$$

where β is the output–capital ratio or productivity of capital and K is the total stock of capital. It is implicitly assumed that labour is in 'surplus' because output Q simply depends on capital K. Differentiating (5.3) with respect to t we obtain

$$\frac{\mathrm{d}Q}{\mathrm{d}t} = \beta\frac{\mathrm{d}K}{\mathrm{d}t} \tag{5.4}$$

Let us assume that all public investments are financed by the banks and the true value of public investment is

$$\frac{G}{P} = \frac{1}{P}\frac{\mathrm{d}B}{\mathrm{d}t} = \frac{\mathrm{d}K}{\mathrm{d}t} \tag{5.5}$$

where G is public investment and B is bank reserves.

The association between B and M is given by

$$B = rM \tag{5.6}$$

where r is the fractional reserve ratio. Differentiating (5.6) with respect to time we have

$$\frac{\mathrm{d}B}{\mathrm{d}t} = r\frac{\mathrm{d}M}{\mathrm{d}t} \tag{5.7}$$

Substituting into (5.5), we have

$$\frac{\mathrm{d}K}{\mathrm{d}t} = r\frac{1}{P}\frac{\mathrm{d}M}{\mathrm{d}t} \tag{5.8}$$

Making the necessary substitution between (5.8) and (5.4), we obtain

$$\frac{\mathrm{d}Q}{\mathrm{d}t} = r\beta\frac{1}{P}\frac{\mathrm{d}M}{\mathrm{d}t} \tag{5.9}$$

Dividing (5.9) by Q, we have

$$\begin{aligned}\frac{1}{Q}\frac{\mathrm{d}Q}{\mathrm{d}t} &= r\beta\frac{1}{PQ}\frac{\mathrm{d}M}{\mathrm{d}t} \\ &= r\beta\left(\frac{1}{M}\frac{\mathrm{d}M}{\mathrm{d}t}\right)\frac{M}{PQ}\end{aligned} \tag{5.10}$$

Equation (5.10) gives the relationship between the rate of output growth and the growth of the money supply. Recalling (5.2), we can now write

$$g = \frac{r\beta}{V}m \tag{5.11}$$

If V is constant, we can rewrite (5.2) as

$$p = m - g \tag{5.12}$$

Substituting into (5.11), we have

$$p = \left(1 - \frac{r\beta}{V}\right)g \tag{5.13}$$

or

$$p = \left(\frac{V}{r\beta} - 1\right)g \tag{5.14}$$

Equations (5.13) and (5.14) show the relationship between p, m and g which could be promoted by deficit financing.

Note that $1/V$ is the *planned* money–income ratio. If the government decides to spend r units on investment goods and if prices are stable, then such spending would raise output by $r\beta$. However, if output rises by one unit and money demand rises by $1/V$, a rise in output of $r\beta$ would raise money demand by $r\beta/V$ units, while money supply rises by one unit. Thus whether or not deficit financing is inflationary or deflationary will depend upon

$$V \gtrless r\beta$$

Deficit financing could be inflationary since in general both r and β are less than 1 but $V > 1$.

To find out more about the actual working of the model, let us assume that $V = 4$, $\beta = 0.33$ and $r = 0.4$. Solving equation (5.14) we find that

$$p = 29.303g$$

Thus a 29 per cent inflation is necessary to increase the growth rate by 1 per cent. Note that given the capital–output ratio, i.e. $1/\beta$ or 3.03, a rise of about 10 per cent (i.e. 29.303/3.03) in prices is necessary to raise savings by 1 per cent.

It may be argued that V would not remain constant if inflation tends to be excessive; rather it should rise with inflation. More formally,

$$V = V(P) \tag{5.15}$$

and

$$\frac{\mathrm{d}V}{\mathrm{d}P} > 0$$

Imagine that the relationship between V and P is linear. Thus,

$$V = V_0 + \alpha P \tag{5.16}$$

where V_0 is the velocity with no inflation. This equation is coupled with the equation

$$P = \left(\frac{V}{r\beta} - 1\right)g \tag{5.17}$$

to obtain

$$P = \frac{V_0 - r\beta}{r\beta - \alpha g}g \tag{5.18}$$

It is clear from equation (5.18) that P/g rises with a rise in g. At the limit inflation would be infinite and the growth rate can no longer be promoted by inflation. The optimal credit-financed rate of growth (g^*) is then

$$g^* = \frac{r\beta}{\alpha} \tag{5.19}$$

Using equation (5.14) and assuming with Mundell that $V_0 = 3$, $\beta = 0.5$ and $r = 0.3$,

$$P = \frac{57}{3 - 20\alpha g} g$$

and if $\alpha = 0$, $P = 19g$, i.e. prices should rise by 19 per cent per annum to increase growth by 1 per cent per annum. If $\alpha = 10$, then

$$P = \frac{57g}{3 - 200g}$$

i.e. a 1.5 per cent growth per annum would be related to infinite inflation.

Thus, to raise growth rate g by 1 per cent per annum the necessary rate of price increase would be 57 per cent per annum.

Some of the limitations of the Mundell model may now be mentioned.

1 Mundell's assumption that the output–capital ratio, or β, would remain fixed during the process of economic development is questionable when the whole structure of the economy could undergo important changes. Indeed, if credit financing can increase capacity utilization, the output–capital ratio will rise.
2 Should the credit-financed public investment displace private investment rather than consumption, the rate of growth may be adversely affected.
3 The model is closed; but if the role of foreign trade is included, then output–capital ratios could be raised by importing capital by credit-financed government investment (Thirlwall 1974).
4 If inflation is high, velocity is likely to change. This would imply that, for achieving a certain growth rate, a much higher rate of inflation will be needed. From the standpoint of policy formulation, it is almost preposterous to assume that a government would allow prices to rise by 57 per cent per annum to increase the growth rate by 1 per cent per annum.
5 It is argued that the value of r should depend upon the proportion of money holdings supported by government securities rather than the ratio of bank reserves to money supply, as implied by Mundell. A proportion of the expansion of bank deposits will reflect the purchase of government securities, and to this extent the need for borrowing from the central bank for any given expenditure requirement is reduced (Thirlwall 1974: 139). The former is generally higher than the latter (0.5 as against 0.3 in LDCs).
6 To the extent that growth in the LDCs is constrained by a lack of demand (Bottomley 1971), credit-financed investment, particularly in projects where the fruition lags are small, could have a favourable impact on growth without seriously disturbing price stability.

Empirical evidence for LDCs shows that, although inflation has a positive effect on saving, such impact, in most cases, is statistically insignificant. The relationship between inflation and investment appears to be positive and significant. This could partly be explained by the impact of inflation on a higher level of imports of investment goods. However, inflation beyond a certain rate (an 'optimal rate') is bound to affect adversely not only investment but also the rate of exchange, balance of payments

Box 5.1 International track records on fiscal deficits and inflation

As Figures 1–2 show, fiscal deficits in the industrial countries as a whole rose progressively for two decades starting in the early 1960s, stabilized briefly in the late 1980s, and then began to grow again. Persistently high deficits have boosted public debt (even before unfunded pension liabilities are included) from about 40 per cent of GDP in 1980 to 70 per cent in 1995. Developing countries in the aggregate have shown considerable improvement in fiscal discipline, although with substantial variation. Fiscal deficits started falling in the early 1980s, mainly because of expenditure cuts.

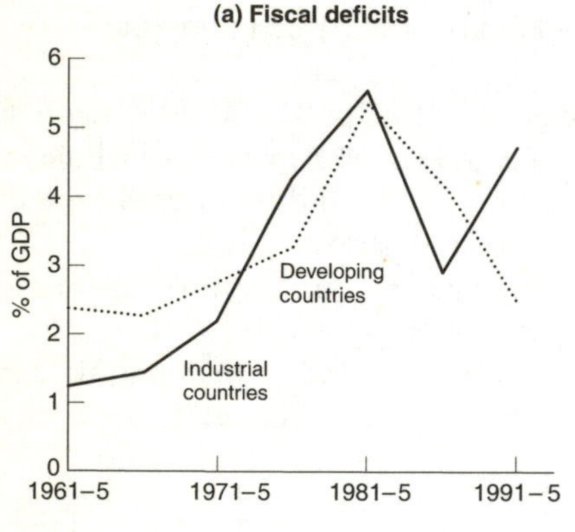

Figure 1

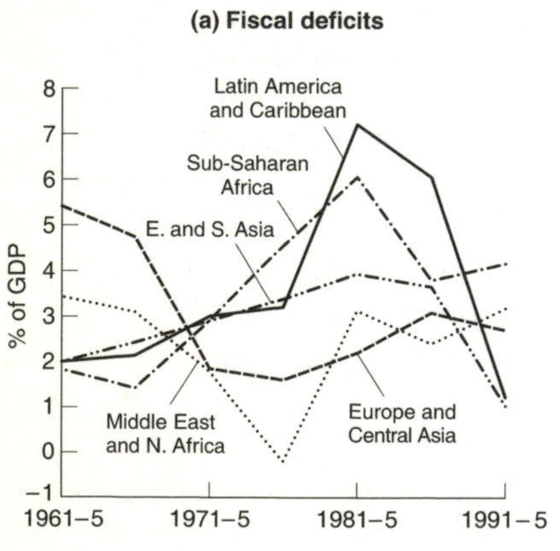

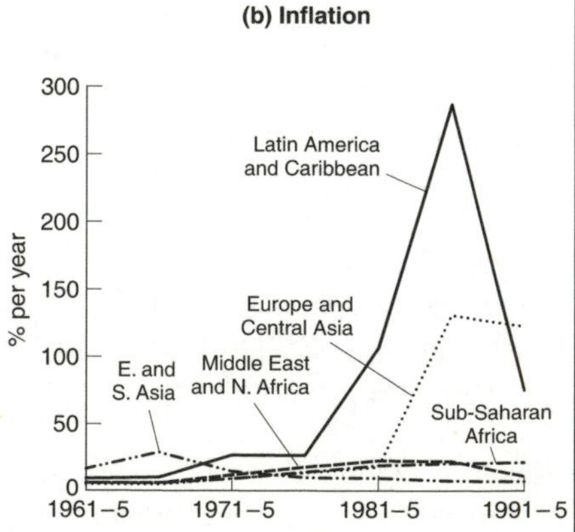

Figure 2

continued on next page

Box 5.1 continued

However, this aggregate picture reflects mainly successes in Asia and Latin America, where sustained and dramatic deficit reductions have been achieved. By contrast, in the first half of the 1990s neither the African nor the Middle Eastern countries were able to follow through on deficit reductions achieved in the second half of the 1980s.

Inflation rates have varied across regions even more than have fiscal deficits. The inflationary episode of the 1970s and early 1980s spread quickly around the world. The cool down of inflation that started in the industrial countries in the early 1980s has begun to take hold, but with a lag. In the developing countries inflation began to moderate in the early 1990s, but not everywhere. In some developing regions, inflation rates are showing signs of convergence toward those of the industrial countries.

and the level of unemployment. Existing information also supports this intuitive judgement (Thirlwall 1974).

Further evidence suggests that an inflation tax is feasible in the case of many LDCs. But inflation may have an important adverse impact on allocation of resources in LDCs in particular with fixed foreign exchange and interest rates (Newlyn 1977). Whether inflation as a deliberate policy is desirable or not depends on whether the effect of inflation on resource mobilization is greater than its impact on efficiency. 'A full assessment would require one to compare the costs involved with the costs associated with distortions introduced by other taxes which would be needed to replace the revenue lost from the inflation tax' (Ayre 1977). Among other costs of inflation note that it distorts the real rates of return between the different sectors and between the different types of financial assets since in many LDCs, while inflation goes on, nominal interest and exchange rates are kept constant and 'financial repression' occurs (McKinnon 1973; Shaw 1973; Ghatak 1995), resulting in a reduction in the demand for real balances. A change in the financial structure of the LDCs is thus regarded as an important factor in promoting economic growth (Galbis 1977; McKinnon 1973; Shaw 1973). The development policies in many LDCs are supposed to have resulted in 'shallow finance' rather than 'deepening' finance or financial 'liberalization' which, *inter alia*, 'matters' in promoting economic growth (Shaw 1973). If inflation takes place, although nominal finance rises, real finance does not rise by the same proportion since it is taxed away by inflation and this state is considered as shallow finance. If finance is shallow as a proportion of income, the real rates of return tend to be very low or even negative. When finance is deepening (one index of which is an increase of liquidity reserves; other indices include an increase in the accumulation of average balances of liquid assets – which would prevent waste of resources in barter transactions – in all markets, an increase in the proportion of financial assets in income or wealth, and greater diversification of financial assets), government tends to be less dependent on taxes and foreign savings, capital flight is reversed, velocity falls, and real savings grow in financial rather than physical assets and pave the way for a greater integration between the organized and unorganized money market. As the real size of the monetary system grows, the differences between the interest rates in the organized and unorganized money markets tend to diminish and real rates of interest tend to rise, reflecting more accurately the opportunity cost of capital (as capital is generally the scarcer input in relation to labour in LDCs). Higher real rates are likely to raise real savings and real growth. An increase in real rates would also help for choosing a more appropriate technology (usually labour intensive in this case) with a higher level of employment and a more egalitarian system of income distribution. It is argued that as long as an interventionist policy keeps the nominal interest rates and foreign exchange rates fixed and a state of 'financial repression' prevails, 'the costs in both inefficiency and corruption are high' (Shaw 1973: 12).

Evidence suggests that between 1963 and 1968, while Uruguay experienced a rise in nominal money supply (which included the time and savings deposits) of 710 per cent its real value actually fell by 55 per cent. During the same period in Ghana, the index of nominal money supply (as defined above) rose from 1.00 to 1.63 while the index of real value remained almost constant. Real output and real consumption fell sharply in Uruguay with severe repercussions upon its financial system and exchange rates. The economy of Ghana also received a considerable setback. On the other hand, in Iran and Thailand where a process of financial deepening took place, i.e. growth in nominal money supply almost matched the increase in real finance, in the same period a rise in both real income and consumption was observed (Shaw 1973: 5).

The complexity of this discussion is now clear. A realistic policy of financial reform is called for to promote real saving and growth and employment in the LDCs. Rates of interest should be raised to reflect more correctly the relative scarcity of capital and this would have beneficial effects upon the choice of technology, employment and income distribution. Although the attraction of an inflation tax is obvious in situations where the real values of revenues from other taxes are falling with rising prices (see Bird 1977 who shows how the real revenue from land tax in Japan was much less than its nominal value in the late nineteenth century) and when 'inflation is a taxation *without representation*', which even the weakest government could enforce upon its people (Keynes 1930), it could be used only in moderate amounts to mobilize resources (say, not more than 10–15 per cent depending upon the country) and great caution is needed to handle it before it gets out of hand.

5.5 Financial liberalization in LDCs: causes and consequences

The controversy over the relative merits and demerits of financial liberalization (FL) in less developed countries (LDCs) is now well documented. The advocates of the FL school consider the rise in the *real* interest rates (nominal interest rate minus the rate of inflation) in LDCs as an essential tool to promote savings, investment and the output growth rate. But the 'structuralists' point out that such a rise in real interest rates could lead to a fall in investment, lower output and higher inflation, particularly when such rates account for a major proportion of the total production costs and funds could be diverted from the unorganized (UMM) to the organized money market (OMM) (see e.g. Fry 1997a; Gelb 1989; Ghatak 1995; McKinnon 1973, 1976; Shaw 1973; Taylor 1983; Van Wijnbergen 1983a, b). Besides, savings could be *insensitive* to interest rates. There is some evidence to indicate that the radical liberalization programmes have not always been successful in the 'Southern Cone' (see e.g. Corbo and de Melo 1985).

It is not easy to decide in favour of either of these two conflicting theories on purely theoretical grounds without a proper empirical investigation. Thus, it is important to set up an empirical model to examine the validity of the two conflicting theories in the light of the experience of LDCs.

The major arguments in favour of financial liberalization (FL) for promoting economic growth of an LDC are well known (for details see McKinnon 1973; Fry 1997). Assume that in a 'financially repressed regime' (FRR) the real interest rate (r, the difference between the nominal interest rate (d) and the rate of inflation) is very low, as it is administered rather than market-determined and so generates only relatively small savings. The main rationale for keeping r very low, if not negative, as evidenced in the case of many LDCs, is the belief that such low r stimulates large-scale investment activity. However, investment is generally savings constrained under an FRR and investors generally depend on self-financing. Thus, they try to build up a 'conduit' of funds to finance their investment projects by accumulating higher amounts of real money balances, M/P. With FL, *r will* rise and so will both savings and investment. The market is fully liberalized when, at a market-determined real rate of interest, savings and investment are at equilibrium. *As r rises, some inefficient forms of investment, usually measured by the capital–output ratio, will improve. Allocation of resources will be better with rationed savings and growth rate of output will be stimulated* (Gelb 1991). Besides, when real interest rates are negative, there is no incentive to use capital efficiently; since excess capacity is costless, plants are built with far more capacity than is necessitated by current production plans. Moreover, empirically it has been shown that for many LDCs a rise in r is associated with a rise in the incremental output–capital ratio (Fry 1997).

Several points should be noted with regard to the operation of this policy. First, there are limits to FL. If the expected rate of inflation in an LDC is very high, then, to keep the real rate of interest positive, authorities must also keep nominal interest rates (d) still higher.

Such a high rate has many undesirable consequences. For instance, small firms will be vulnerable to high interest rates if a very high proportion of their working capital depends on borrowed funds. Thus a high r may actually reduce the level of investment and output (see, for example, Wijnbergen 1983a). For small firms a high rate is particularly problemetical, as amortization is accelerated. Second, the sequencing of liberalization is quite important. It implies that the liberalization of the money market should be followed rather than preceded by the liberalization of the trade sector. Otherwise the economy may suffer from severe balance of payments problems. Third, in a system of mark-up pricing where d is an important element of total cost FL can lead to accelerating inflation. The actual validity of such a proposition is, of course, a matter of empirical verification. Further, FL policy without fiscal control of budgetary or external account could easily raise question marks about policy credibility. Finally, the FL school pays little attention to the role the UMM can play in LDCs. If funds flow between the OMM and the UMM, an increase in interest rates in the OMM will drive up the interest rate in the UMM, given constraints on lending in the OMM. Firms which borrow largely from the UMM will be forced to cut back production and employment because of the increase in the cost of borrowing and output will fall.

Structuralists, however, assume that the UMM works efficiently (Wijnbergen 1983a, 1985). Further, changes in the interest rates of the UMM, caused by changes in rates in the OMM, could critically depend upon a free flow of funds between the two markets. The nature of links between the two types of market is a testable hypothesis. Indeed, for India, it has been shown that the link is positive but rather weak (see Ghatak 1975a). Next, a rise in investment and output because of a rise in *r* generally implies a substitution effect on investment which may or may not be valid. Finally, the positive effects of FL can be observed only in the long run. The exact length of the lag depends upon the nature of the financial intermediation, the interaction between the real and monetary sector and the supply response – all of which could vary from one country to another.

In some cross-country studies, real interest rates were found not to exert a significant effect on savings. On the other hand, some country-specific studies found that the real rate of interest had a positive effect on savings (Ghatak 1997). King and Levine (1993) and Levine (1997) found a strong correlation between the degree of financial development and growth, investment and efficiency of capital. Some used time-series data to show that the causality between financial depth – as measured by, say, the ratio of bank deposits to GDP – and growth varies across countries (Demetriades and Hussein 1996). In some countries, financial development caused economic growth (e.g. Honduras and Sri Lanka); in others, the causality ran the other way round (e.g. Pakistan and Turkey). Sometimes the relationship is bi-directional (Guatemala, India, Korea, Thailand). Others developed an index of FL depicting mostly the deregulation of interest rates for fifty DCs and LDCs for the period 1980-95 and observed that banking crises are more likely to occur in liberalized financial systems. The results are more robust for countries with weaker financial institutions, lack of financial supervision and contract enforcement. The other point to remember is that FL via interest rate liberalization may raise interest rate payments on the public debt and thus lead to a higher fiscal deficit. Arestis and Demetriades (1997) even reported a weak but positive effect of financial repression on economic growth. Clearly, a more definitive judgement can be reached with more information and better specification of the models which explicitly allow the role of financial institutions in economic growth. It is important to remember that FL by itself is unlikely to boost economic growth if it is not supported by appropriate and prudent macroeconomic stabilization policies (e.g. low and stable budget deficit as a proportion of the GDP and trade reforms to eliminate distortions in exchange rates) and sound, accountable financial institutions.

5.6 Objectives of fiscal policy in less developed countries

The major objectives of fiscal policy in LDCs are as follows:

1 to raise revenue for the government;
2 to stabilize prices by changing aggregate demand;
3 to promote economic growth by mobilizing 'surplus';
4 to promote foreign investment should it be considered desirable;
5 to change the pattern of income distribution according to some social objectives, e.g. more equal distribution of income;
6 to minimize the adverse effects on resource allocation.

Most governments in LDCs try to achieve a combination of some of these major objectives. The main instruments to attain the targets are usually taxation, expenditure and deficit finance. Each of these will be examined in turn, but first it is necessary to discuss briefly the role of fiscal policy in promoting growth.

5.7 Fiscal policy and growth

The role of fiscal policy in promoting economic growth is fairly well known. In the classical period, however, it was believed that the very best of all principles of government finance was to tax little and spend little. With the development of what is known as the 'balanced budget multiplier' (BBM) this attitude has altered. The BBM states that if the tax (ΔT) and expenditure (ΔG) by the government rise by, say, £100 million, national income (ΔY) will also rise by £100 million.

More formally, let

$$Y = C + I + G \tag{5.20}$$

where I is autonomous investment (fixed), C is consumption ($C = bY$), Y is income and G is government expenditure. Then

$$\Delta Y = \Delta C + \Delta G \tag{5.21}$$

The effect of a change in public expenditure is then

$$\Delta Y = \frac{1}{1-b} \Delta G \tag{5.22}$$

where b is the marginal propensity to consume (MPC) and $1/(1-b)$ is the multiplier. Then

$$\frac{\Delta Y}{\Delta G} = \frac{1}{1-b} \tag{5.23}$$

Next, to find out the effect of changes in taxes (ΔT) on income (Y), note that when taxes are raised, consumption is likely to fall, *but not by the full amount of the change in tax* (ΔT). In fact, consumption will fall by the product of MPC and ΔT. Thus

$$\Delta C = -b\,\Delta T \tag{5.24}$$

Using the multiplier theory we have

$$\Delta Y = \frac{1}{1-b} \Delta C \tag{5.25}$$

By substitution

$$\Delta Y = \frac{b\,\Delta T}{1-b} \tag{5.26}$$

or

$$\frac{\Delta Y}{\Delta T} = -\frac{b}{1-b} \tag{5.27}$$

Combining the effects of public expenditure and taxes on income, we have

$$\frac{\Delta Y}{\Delta G}+\frac{\Delta Y}{\Delta T}=\frac{1}{1-b}-\frac{b}{1-b}=\frac{1-b}{1-b}=1 \tag{5.28}$$

The result indicates that the effects of, say, a positive change in government tax and expenditure will have an equal and positive effect on national income.

The BBM theory, as described above, does not include the role of foreign trade. It assumes a constant MPC which may not be valid particularly when the economy of an LDC is developing rapidly. Nor is there enough empirical reason to believe that there would always be a one-to-one correspondence between changes in taxes and expenditure and changes in income, particularly if the economy experiences serious bottlenecks on the supply side, a common problem for many LDCs. However, the general prediction of the theory about the expansionary role of fiscal policy has been of special interest to the LDCs. Here more empirical research is necessary to draw firm conclusions. The BBM theory, within its limitations, has the very interesting implication that, *without a budget deficit,* income could be expanded only if the budget size is large enough. In the next section we relax the assumption regarding the closed economy and introduce trade in our model.

5.7.1 Fiscal policy in an open economy

In an open economy, for one country, the basic Keynesian income equation could be written as follows (see Morss and Peacock 1969 for details):

$$Y = C + I + G + (X - M) \tag{5.29}$$

where X is exports and M is imports. Let

$$C = a + bY_{\mathrm{d}} \tag{5.30}$$

$$M = c + dY \tag{5.31}$$

$$Y_{\mathrm{d}} = Y - eY - T \tag{5.32}$$

$$T = fY \tag{5.33}$$

where e is the fraction of income which goes to the corporate sector. Assuming fixed I_0, G_0 and X_0 and by substitution we have

$$Y = \frac{a - c + I_0 + G_0 + X_0}{1 - b + d + be + bf} \tag{5.34}$$

where the multiplier is

$$k = \frac{1}{1 - b + d + be + bf} \tag{5.35}$$

For another country similar multipliers could be observed. If we allow the government expenditure to vary, then its effect could now be predicted on the level of income. It is possible, however, to modify some other assumptions. For instance, X_1 can be regarded as a function of income in country 2 (Y_2) net of taxes in country 2 (T_2). More formally

$$X_1 = g_2 Y_2(1 - T_2) \tag{5.36}$$

Similarly, the import equation could also be related to disposable rather than nominal income. In such cases, an autonomous rise in marginal propensity to import in country 2 will tend to raise income in country 1. In the same way, income expansion in country 1 will tend to raise exports from country 2. The determination of income in country 1 will now depend upon income, the marginal propensity to import and taxes in country 2. It seems that a more comprehensive discussion could only be made in terms of fiscal, monetary and exchange rate policies (for details, see Peacock and Shaw 1974). This may require a complicated exercise in the estimation of the actual parameters to predict the effects of changes in taxes and expenditure on national income. The relationship between fiscal policy and growth will now be discussed.

5.7.2 The Peacock and Shaw model

The relationship between fiscal policy and growth can best be analysed within a Harrod–Domar (HD) framework rather than a neoclassical framework. Recalling the HD equation for growth (see Chapter 2) we have

$$y = s/v$$

where y is the growth rate of output, s is the saving ratio and v is the capital–output ratio. It is easily observed that fiscal policy, by raising s, can raise growth. But no such role could be played by fiscal policy within a slow-type of neoclassical theory as the population growth rate n will determine the growth rate. A change in taxation or public expenditure could change saving, but this would also change the capital–output ratio v with no change in growth *rates* (R. Sato 1963; 1967). The present discussion within the HD model is based on the analysis of Peacock and Shaw (1974).

Let us assume that on the supply side output capacity Y_t^c in period t is given by private investment and government expenditure in the past period (i.e. I_{t-1} and G_{t-1} respectively). Thus we have

$$\Delta Y_t^c = \beta(I_{t-1} + \rho G_{t-1}) \tag{5.37}$$

where β is the output–capital ratio and ρ is the proportion of government expenditure that consists of investment.

Let the equation for the demand side be

$$Y_t = C_t + I_t + G_t \tag{5.38}$$

Let

$$C_t = bY_t(1 - T_y) \tag{5.39}$$

and

$$I_t = I_{t-1} = I_{0t} \text{ (fixed)} \tag{5.40}$$

Box 5.2 The financial revolution versus the industrial revolution

It is commonly believed that technological development in England during the late eighteenth century was the driving force behind the industrial revolution and modern economic growth. An alternative perspective gives more emphasis to the significance of institutional change and particularly to the role of financial institutions in the process. For example, some argue that capital market improvements, which mitigated liquidity risk, were the primary cause of the industrial revolution. Many of the inventions already existed but required large injections and long-term commitment of capital, which was not possible without further development of financial markets. The industrial revolution had to wait for the financial revolution.

As in England, a sophisticated financial system developed in the United States before its industrial revolution in the nineteenth century. The Dutch Republic, long before its remarkable growth in the seventeenth century, had a financial revolution that involved institutional innovations such as the adoption of negotiable international bills of exchange to finance the economy's external trade, negotiable securities to finance the public debt, a convenient payment system, a stable currency, a strong private banking system, and securities markets.

where T_y is the given rate of income tax. Let

$$G_t = gY_t \tag{5.41}$$

Then the level of income equilibrium is given by

$$Y_t = \frac{I_{0t}}{1 - b + bT_y - g} \tag{5.42}$$

A variation in investment will be reflected in income changes via changes in demand. Thus

$$\Delta Y_t = \frac{\Delta I_t}{1 - b + bT_y - g} \tag{5.43}$$

To maintain the equilibrium in the economy, the supply side or capacity output must be equal to money demand. That is

$$\Delta Y_t^c = \Delta Y_t \tag{5.44}$$

i.e.

$$\beta(I_{t-1} + \rho G_{t-1}) = \frac{\Delta I_t}{1 - b + bT_y - g} \tag{5.45}$$

Dividing by Y_{t-1},

$$\frac{\Delta Y_t}{Y_{t-1}} = \frac{\beta I_{t-1}}{Y_{t-1}} + \frac{\beta \rho G_{t-1}}{Y_{t-1}} = \frac{\Delta I_t/(1 - b + bT_y - g)}{I_{t-1}/(1 - b + bT_y - g)} \tag{5.46}$$

Note that

$$\frac{G_{t-1}}{Y_{t-1}} = g \quad \text{and} \quad \frac{I_{t-1}}{Y_{t-1}} = 1 - b + bT_{\text{y}} - g \tag{5.47}$$

so that we have

$$\frac{\Delta Y_t}{Y_{t-1}} = \beta(1 - b + bT_{\text{y}} - g + \rho g) = \frac{\Delta I_t}{I_{t-1}} \tag{5.48}$$

In other words, in order to utilize capital stock fully, the necessary growth of demand must be equal to the required investment growth which in itself is functionally related to changes both in taxes and in public expenditure. Should the actual growth be less than desired growth, actual growth could be raised by inducements to invest or to lower the desired growth by altering fiscal policies. Thus changes in taxes or public expenditure would considerably influence the equality between desired and actual growth rate. For LDCs it is of prime importance to utilize fully both capital and *labour*. In this sense, the HD model loses some of its appeal for devising fiscal policies for the LDCs, though the advocates of 'prior saving' theory may find it useful.

5.8 Deficit financing and less developed countries

Deficit financing (DF) has played an important role in many LDCs. Given the inability of their governments to mobilize enough resources to achieve a desired rate of growth, unreliability of foreign investment and lack of tax elasticity, the temptation to adopt DF is understandable. The impact of money supply on prices, saving and growth has already been discussed. It remains to be pointed out that for DF to be effective in the LDCs the supply of output must be elastic with respect to demand. Otherwise, inflation is inevitable. To count the net benefit of DF, it is necessary to examine the costs of inflation against the possible gains in resource mobilization. Among these costs, the most important are (1) distortions of real rates of return; (2) inefficiency in allocation; (3) inequalities in income distribution; and (4) an increase in imports and unemployment. Among the possible benefits are the stimulus to profitability and investment, greater utilization of capacity because of increased demand and consequent lowering of the costs of production should there be excess capacity, and a larger investment provided that private investment was not forthcoming in any case. The other points which have been mentioned in its favour are, first, if an increase in money supply can stimulate growth, its presence can be tolerated. Here it is important to find the 'optimal' level of money supply. Second, if income distribution becomes more unequal because of DF, then a rise in profit share will stimulate investment. If, however, profits are not reinvested, then growth is likely to suffer. Also, if private saving is not forthcoming spontaneously, government may resort to DF for generating more savings (Oyejide 1972).

If the aggregate supply is very inelastic, then the different effects of DF can be shown with the help of Figure 5.1. In quadrant I, the Keynesian income–expenditure equilibrium is shown at F. A tax cut or a rise in public expenditure or both will stimulate monetary demand and this is shown by the shift of the expenditure line from E to E'. A rise in aggregate demand raises the price level from P to P_1 in quadrant II. In quadrant III, the effect of such a rise in domestic prices is shown on imports and the

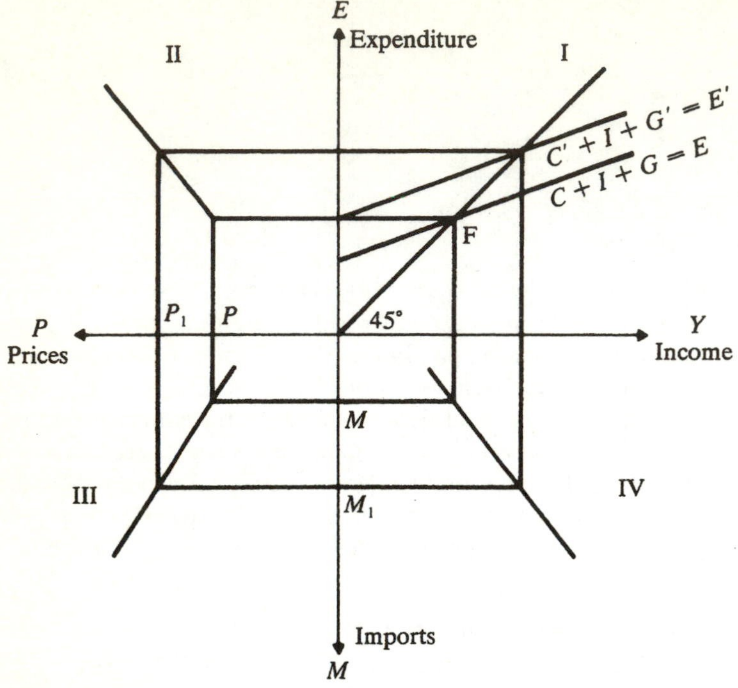

Figure 5.1

balance of payments. Thus imports tend to rise from M to M_1. Quadrant IV shows the relationship between a change in money income and imports and this relationship is assumed to be positive. The fall of unemployment is virtually nothing if supply does not respond to changes in demand. Indeed, as the rates of inflation increase with demand stimulation, unemployment may actually rise. This has led some to conclude that in LDCs, since a 'money' multiplier rather than a 'real' multiplier operates, the Keynesian theory has a very limited role to play (Rao 1958; Hasan 1960). On the other hand, supporters of the DF theory argue that as long as public expenditure takes place in quick-yielding investment with a short fruition lag and/or if DF of such investment could reduce the capital–output ratio either through the choice of appropriate technology or by greater utilization of existing excess capacity, then growth rate could indeed rise. The empirical evidence available so far does not lead to any firm conclusions. The DF, generating a moderate rate of inflation, may help to promote growth, but once again the evidence seems to weigh against the use of a high rate of inflation. To what extent there is a direct and significant correlation between DF, inflation and growth in the LDCs is a very important area for future research.

5.9 The tax structure in less developed countries

The tax structures of most LDCs are narrowly based, inelastic with respect to changes in income and greatly dependent upon indirect rather than direct taxes. Thus, if fiscal policy is to play a more vigorous role to promote revenue, growth and stability (both economic and political), it is imperative that the tax base should be broadened, that the tax revenue should be more elastic with respect to income (i.e. say, a 1 per cent increase in income should lead to a more than 1 per cent rise in taxes) and that there should be a *relative* expansion of the role of direct taxes in comparison with indirect taxes. The last point, however, has been debated considerably while the soundness of the first two arguments has not been questioned. A brief discussion of the different types of direct and indirect taxes may therefore be of some interest.

5.9.1 Direct taxes in LDCs

The major direct taxes in LDCs consist of income tax, corporation tax, wealth tax and property tax. Usually in LDCs, the proportion of direct taxes in total tax is much lower than that of indirect taxes, and direct taxes on agricultural income are generally very low. As regards income tax, its marginal rates are sometimes very high in countries like India and Sri Lanka and this, although regarded as desirable by some on the grounds of ability to pay and social justice, has been criticized by others because of its adverse effects on saving and work effort. Second, with the growth of agriculture from the late 1960s in many Asian countries and the emergence of a 'kulak' or relatively well-off class of peasants who have been the main beneficiaries of the 'Green Revolution', it is argued that agricultural income taxation should be made progressive. However, most governments in South Asia as well as in other LDCs did not raise the proportion of agricultural income taxes to total taxes by more than 5 per cent. The high marginal tax rates plus administrative corruption have resulted in large-scale tax evasion and revenue losses.

In order to widen the tax base, Kaldor (1956a) in his tax reform proposal for India suggested the imposition of expenditure tax, wealth tax, gift tax and property tax. Of these, the *expenditure tax* is very novel. It implies a tax on income minus saving, i.e. spending. The main reasons for it are (1) restriction of consumption and increase of saving; (2) avoidance of the difficulty of identifying 'income' in the LDCs; and (3) the fulfilment of the canon of ability to pay with social justice without reduction of saving and capital formation.

The Indian government accepted the proposal, imposed the tax but repealed it, reimposed it and repealed it again! Apart from India the only other country which imposed it was Sri Lanka which also withdrew it soon after its imposition. One of the reasons for such loss of enthusiasm about expenditure tax is intuitive. As Prest says, 'the notion that there is a large amount of luxurious consumption expenditure in these countries which can be curtailed by very simple tax legislation, thereby releasing vast sums of money for domestic capital purposes, is singularly superficial' (Prest 1972: 80–1). Second, the assessment of expenditure is unlikely to be simple as it is now necessary to measure both income and saving and the administrative costs of expenditure tax are likely to be large. Third, evidence from India and Sri Lanka suggests that the revenue effect was small and, given the administrative cost of collection, such small revenue was inadequate to justify the high cost of collection. Fourth, in India it became very difficult to differentiate between business and personal expenditure and this simply highlights the problem of administration (Chelliah 1969). However, as a supplement rather than a substitute for income tax, the expenditure tax could still be introduced in the LDCs as long as the tax is simple and economical to operate.

Other forms of direct taxation which could increase the tax base include wealth tax, gift tax, profits tax and some other forms of company taxation. Although these taxes could increase the tax base in LDCs, empirically their revenue effect turned out to be smaller than was expected in some South Asian countries. Marginal rates of corporation and profit taxes were deliberately kept low in some LDCs to reduce their disincentive effect on saving and capital formation. The other reason for keeping business taxes low in LDCs is to attract foreign investment. On the other hand, from the point of view of administration and convenience of collection, higher revenue could be raised with less difficulty via increases in the rates of company taxes. However, the income of companies is not a large proportion of the national income in LDCs. Also, high company tax rates could inhibit the development of new enterprises. In addition, few LDCs would take the risk of destroying incentives to invest by raising company tax rates too high. However, given high rates of company taxes in some DCs, the LDCs could effectively raise revenue by raising rates of company taxes as long as there is a positive difference between company tax rates in DCs and LDCs.

Land tax has been considered as one of the major instruments for mobilizing surplus from agriculture. The case of land tax in Japan during the nineteenth century has usually been cited as important evidence in favour of such tax as it contributed a significant proportion of total tax revenue, though its importance may have been exaggerated (Sinha 1969) and its real impact may have been reduced because of inflation (Bird 1977). The main reasons in favour of land tax are as follows.

1 In the LDCs, although it is possible to conceal income and its sources, it is difficult to conceal land and hence the task of assessment becomes easier.
2 A tax on land will not make it move from one country to the other, but a tax on some other types of capital might.
3 Land tax could be formulated in such a way as to encourage the farmers to undertake the cultivation of more land or to cultivate land more intensively where land is scarce. The evidence from Chile supports this argument (Furtado 1970: 52).
4 The importance of land in comparison with other forms of capital assets in LDCs implies that a land tax would broaden the tax base.
5 From the standpoint of equity, if a tax on large land-holdings forces the landowners to sell some parts of their land to the small farmers, then this could be regarded as a more equitable distribution of wealth.
6 From 5 it can be argued that if the productivity of land per acre and size-holding are inversely related (a phenomenon which is supposed to have been observed in India), then from the point of view of *efficiency*, a tax on large land-holding is all the more desirable. Also, since small-scale farms tend to be more labour intensive than capital intensive, employment may increase.
7 In a subsistence economy, a land tax should increase the demand for money. Farmers would thus be induced to raise their marketed surplus and greater 'real' surplus could be mobilized to promote economic growth.

The main drawbacks in the land tax system can now be mentioned.

1 Fragmentation of land and lack of a clear legal idea about land ownership in most LDCs could make the administration of land tax very difficult.

2 There are important problems of assessment of land taxes in the LDCs with reference to the value of output or the value of capital or potential productivity of land or by some other index.
3 If the tax is a fixed proportion of per hectare land-holding without due regard to its productivity, then total revenue might not be high.
4 The information about land-holding and title deeds in most LDCs is rather poor and sometimes out of date. This makes the task of land tax administration very difficult.
5 Given the political importance of the well-off class among the landowners, many LDCs have found the introduction of land taxation to be very difficult.

On balance, the arguments in favour of land tax seem to outweigh those against it. Where political will exists, the case for a land tax in one form or other deserves serious consideration. If its imposition requires some institutional reforms, then such reforms also merit urgent attention. Different types of land taxation could also be introduced. For instance, in Nicaragua, such a tax is related to the fertility of land. Also, in Honduras and Guatemala, the tax rates on land tend to rise if the land is unused (Bird and Oldman 1975). The principle of self-assessment has also gained attention. The main point to emphasize is that wherever there is an appreciation in the capital value of land, such gains, like any other capital gains, should be taxed. The spread of the 'Green Revolution' in many LDCs has enhanced the capital values of land. Given a rise in farm income and profit and the narrow base of direct taxes, it is both necessary and desirable to tax the main beneficiaries of such 'revolution' not only from the standpoint of mobilizing surplus for capital formation but also to promote social justice.

5.9.2 Indirect taxes in LDCs

Indirect taxes in LDCs usually consist of sales taxes, excise taxes and customs duties. Sometimes, marketing boards offer less than international prices to the domestic producers, the differential being the tax. Tariffs on imports are also recognized as an important type of indirect tax. Value-added tax and payroll taxes are now increasingly regarded as important types of indirect taxation for LDCs. The indirect taxes are generally borne by the consumers and as such they are sometimes regarded as consumption-based taxes.

The overwhelming importance of indirect taxes as a proportion of total tax revenue is clearly shown in Table 5.1. Countries earning less than $100 *per capita* collect 68 per cent of total tax revenue in indirect taxes, whereas DCs usually collect about 32 per cent of their total tax revenues by such taxes. The main reasons for such heavy dependence can easily be pointed out.

1 The revenue that could be raised by indirect taxes is likely to be greater in comparison with revenue that could be obtained by imposing direct taxes. This is clear given the narrow tax base and low income of most people in LDCs.
2 Since the indirect taxes are less difficult to collect and relatively easier to administer than direct taxes, this form of taxation has wide appeal in LDCs.

Table 5.1 Reliance on indirect taxes by per capita GNP class

Estimated per capita GNP (US$)	*No. of countries included*	*Indirect taxes as percentage of total tax revenue (average)*
Developing countries		
100 or less	20	68
101–200	11	64
201–500	19	64
501–850	9	50
Highly developed countries		
Over 850	15	32

Source: Due (1970).

3 It is argued that, compared with, say, income taxes, indirect taxes as they are related to spending rather than earning should have less adverse effect on saving and investment. Since indirect taxes are based on consumption, they can directly affect demand.
4 In most LDCs, the proportion of wages and salaries in national income is quite low. This would obviously limit any potential expansion of the direct tax base. However, in theory the elasticity of tax revenue from indirect taxes is unlikely to be greater than one in LDCs as consumption does not grow as fast as income. In practice, revenue elasticities of sales tax and excise duties in LDCs are estimated to be 2.4 per cent, as against 1.5 per cent in the case of income taxes (Chelliah 1971).
5 Indirect taxes could be made 'progressive' to the extent that 'luxury goods', home-produced or imported, are subjected to a higher level of excise or import duties. When these taxes are levied on luxury imports, the foreign exchange constraint is eased.

Criticisms of indirect taxes in LDCs are generally made on the following grounds:

1 Indirect taxes are usually regarded as regressive. If the objective of the LDCs is to minimize the inequalities in the distribution of income and wealth, then such taxes are unlikely to be very effective policy instruments, despite steep taxes on 'luxuries'.
2 Indirect taxes do not direct investment and production in the socially most desirable channels as they distort optimal choice.
3 Consumers' choice is always distorted because of indirect taxes and a loss of consumer surplus and social welfare is indicated.
4 Customs duties, which sometimes form a significant source of tax revenue in the LDCs, become increasingly inadequate as a means of raising sufficient revenue over time as domestic production rises. In an advanced stage of economic development, imports of investment goods form the bigger share of the total imports in comparison with imports of luxury products. When customs duties are increased, the undesirable aspects of high level protection may well emerge. For example, the production of 'luxury' goods would be profitable and investment may well take place in luxury industries rather than in other socially more desirable channels.

5 In many LDCs, several exportables are subject to taxes. Although these taxes are simple to administer, this form of taxation has adverse effects on exports as it raises prices in the international market.
6 Sales tax – single stage or multi-stage – and excise duties are often regarded as important types of indirect taxes which are quite productive and easy to operate in the LDCs. But here also the point could be made that once a large variety of goods is produced with a general increase in production, sales tax and excise duties become very complicated and difficult to administer.

Given these arguments, it seems that although the indirect taxes in general do not always satisfy the principle of equity or ability, most LDCs will continue to bank upon them heavily in the near future, given their tax elasticity, revenue effect, administrative simplicity and broad base. Recently, the introduction of value-added tax (VAT) has been advocated and this is discussed in the next section.

5.9.3 The case for and against VAT in the LDCs

While under a system of single-stage sales taxation total tax revenue is obtained at only one point in the channels of production or distribution, under VAT a tax could be imposed on different stages in such channels, but only to the amount of value added. The service sector may be exempted from the purview of VAT. The very poor farmers in LDCs need not pay VAT. It is argued that VAT is superior to other forms of sales tax because it is neutral among different types of organization of production and distribution whereas the sales tax could increase vertical integration among firms since it applies to every stage of sale of the product – from the point of its initial production to the point of its ultimate consumption. It is clear that under such circumstances a firm would avoid paying taxes if it were the producer of the intermediate goods (Due 1976). Thus, the inducement to the growth of monopoly is strengthened which could result in lower output, higher prices and inefficiency in resource allocation. Evidence from Chile seems to support this argument.

Second, the adverse effects of indirect taxes on exports would be avoided if the amount of VAT could be worked out at the export points and given back to the exporters. Similarly, if the aim is import substitution, VAT may be formulated in such a way as to exclude imports of capital goods.

Third, within a trading block, or common market, fiscal policy needs a certain degree of harmonization of tax instruments and very often VAT plays a more useful role than the different types of sales tax in different countries. This is witnessed in the case of the European Union countries.

Fourth, the sales taxes discriminate in favour of imports compared with home-produced goods because the latter go via a greater number of sales within an economy than do imports. Again, the imposition of VAT will have neutral effects on imports and home production because, at every transaction of importable goods which adds to the value, the goods would be subject to VAT.

Lastly, VAT makes cross-checking possible. Indeed, VAT has the merit of providing incentive to firms to report non-payment of taxes by other firms if they are allowed some tax credit.

However, the differences between sales tax and VAT are not large. The final choice between VAT and sales tax would depend upon the following factors:

1 The relative importance of retail as against wholesale trade – if the latter is more significant and the large firms operate, the case for VAT will be strengthened;
2 If the size of revenue needed from tax is small, then a sales tax might be preferred to VAT;
3 If an LDC strongly desires import substitution via large-scale import of capital goods, then the greater will be the pressure to exempt such goods from taxes and the stronger will be the case for VAT.

The arguments against VAT can now be summarized.

1 VAT can make the tax structure very complicated, given the lack of skilled manpower in many LDCs, its actual implications may be misinterpreted.
2 VAT could be difficult to administer given large-scale illiteracy in the LDCs.
3 Under VAT, a certain degree of 'tax morality' is assumed on the part of the tax-paying firms and this could be lacking in many parts of the underdeveloped world.

In the light of the above arguments, it seems fair to conclude that where administrative machinery permits, the case for VAT rests chiefly on its neutral effect on production and distribution. Extended to the retail level, it would be broad-based to raise a significant amount of revenue. From the standpoint of equity and ability to pay, several modifications could be introduced to VAT for a more egalitarian distribution of income and wealth. For example, exemptions from paying VAT might include the small farmer, primary education and rural health services, particularly for the poorer class of peasant who could be wholly excluded from the scope of VAT. If the great reliance on indirect taxes in the LDCs is likely to continue both as an instrument of earning revenue and an instrument for stabilization, then VAT for the LDCs merits serious consideration.

5.10 Taxation and domestic resource mobilization in less developed countries: the evidence

The tax system in LDCs is 'perhaps . . . the most pervasive and far-reaching policy instrument available to the government' (Bird 1983). The demand for generating greater tax revenue in LDCs emanates from the necessity to finance public investment projects. The desire to raise more revenue, however, could be in conflict with equity objectives as taxes affect income distribution, provision of public goods and services, and general programmes of stabilization. Given a variety of objectives, tax systems vary significantly across LDCs. Gemmell (1987b) shows that the main differences between the DCs and the LDCs are (1) the greater share of tax revenue from income and profit taxes and social insurance payments in the former group and (2) the greater importance of various trade taxes in the latter group. Further, LDCs generally implement a more complex set of consumption and excise taxes than DCs and frequently offer subsidies on basic wage goods. Some African countries use marketing boards to tax exports of mainly agricultural goods. Other LDCs are now using sales and VAT (for details, see Goode 1984; Chelliah *et al.* 1975).

During 1966 and 1975 most LDCs experienced rising tax ratios as income *per capita* increased (Tait 1988). Most statistical results suggest that tax buoyancies generally exceed elasticity estimates, showing the prevalence of discretionary tax increases and improvements in collection and administration. Income and consumption tax elasticities are greater than trade tax elasticities (Greenaway 1984). Income tax elasticities fell as income rose.

Previous ideas that LDC tax systems are generally regressive but could be used for speeding up an economy's growth rate have been altered considerably (see, for example, Gemmell 1987b; Toye 1979; Ahmad and Stern 1984, 1989; Newbery and Stern 1987). The current applied normative analysis of 'tax reform' – developed by Ahmad and Stern (AS) – provides a method of evaluating the welfare effects of tax changes in LDCs. Ahmad and Stern assume a social welfare function W which is a function of utilities of households (which are given by prices of goods). The government raises revenue by taxing goods and services. Factor incomes and producer prices are constant. Under competitive conditions, indirect taxes are fully reflected in prices of goods. For tax reform, the problem is to analyse tax changes which raise social welfare for a fixed or greater tax revenue, or vice versa. If tax systems in LDCs are non-optimal, then there must be some welfare-improving tax alterations. In a two-goods, two-taxes case, rises in both tax rates increase revenue but reduce social welfare. One combination of tax rates provides fixed revenue; the other results in fixed social welfare. Necessary tax changes are obtained by Ahmad and Stern by observing the marginal cost α_1, in terms of welfare, of one extra unit of revenue raised by the tax on one of the two goods. This is then compared with the marginal cost of raising an extra unit of revenue by the tax on the other good, $\alpha_j (i, j = 1, 2)$. If $\alpha_i < \alpha_j$, welfare increases by raising taxes on $i(t_i)$ and decreasing t_j, (taxes on j). Ahmad and Stern define α as

$$\alpha = \frac{\partial W}{\partial t_i} \frac{\partial R}{\partial t_i}$$

Clearly, $\partial R/\partial t_i$ is given by a vector of tax rates and the elasticity of demand to tax changes. The measurement of $\partial W/\partial t_j$ (changes in social welfare due to changes in tax rates) depends on the availability of information about consumption of households and the welfare weights attached to each household's utility in the welfare function. The ranking of α_is turned out to be quite sensitive to assumed 'inequality aversion' in India (Ahmad and Stern 1984). Ahmad and Stern found that the present tax structure in India is optimal with no inequality aversion. For each inequality aversion, there was always at least one welfare-raising tax reform.

Despite the importance of price signals in LDCs, the effects of taxes on prices are too marginal to have a major impact on incentives for growth. Even a more progressive tax system has minor effects on income distribution. Most LDCs depend very heavily on import duties (tariffs) as a revenue source. Such high duties provide strong incentives for smuggling or evading tariffs (see, for example, the Colombian case study reported in Gillis *et at* 1987). Taxes, however, influence incentives to save and invest. In most LDCs, expenditure-based taxes are regarded as more inducive for growth in private savings than are income-based taxes. Changes in taxes are also regarded as instruments for macroeconomic stabilization programmes. Since agriculture plays a special role in LDCs, the incidence of land or agricultural income tax and export crop subsidies should be analysed in a general equilibrium framework (Newbery and Stern 1987; Ahmad and Stern 1989). It is concluded that advice on tax policy should be based on the results of *individual* country studies, given enormous cross-country variations in the tax systems in LDCs (Gemmell 1987).

5.11 Tax reforms in less developed countries in the 1980s

The problem of tax reform in LDCs is to observe tax alterations which will raise social welfare but leave tax revenue constant or vice versa. When current taxes are suboptimal (as they are in most LDCs), then there must be one (if not many) welfare-raising tax reforms. This is shown in Figure 5.2 where two taxes t_i and t_j are measured on the vertical and horizontal axes respectively. The line AA′ shows combinations of the two tax rates providing some tax revenue while BB′ yields associations of t_i and t_j holding social welfare fixed. When both rates rise, tax revenue increases but welfare falls. Clearly, the area OAB in the figure depicts desirable changes in tax rates since both revenue and welfare rise in that area (i.e. $\partial R > 0$, $\partial V > 0$).

The aims of taxation should be similar in both DCs and LDCs (i.e. to increase resources for public expenditure in a way that is efficient, equitable and feasible); the main differences in the two types of tax structure lie in the constraints facing governments: the weakness of administration, limited experience with taxation, poor accounting, the low level of monetization in the economy, the high share of agriculture and the fact that 'tax handles' are generally few in number relative to developed countries will have a different structure and emphasis (Burgess and Stern 1993). In view of growing public debt in LDCs (for example Buiter and Patel 1992), it is acknowledged that such expenditure should be checked to tackle the insolvency problem of many LDC governments. However, some cuts in government expenditure, sometimes advocated by some international lending agencies, could have a disastrous effect on the rate of economic growth of many poor countries. In particular, it is necessary to focus on the composition of public expenditure before deciding on cuts. In addition, given the narrow bond market and the limited ability of LDC governments to finance deficits by selling bonds, and the inflationary effects of money finance, there are not very many real substitutes for taxation to increase revenue for the governments to avoid the insolvency problems.

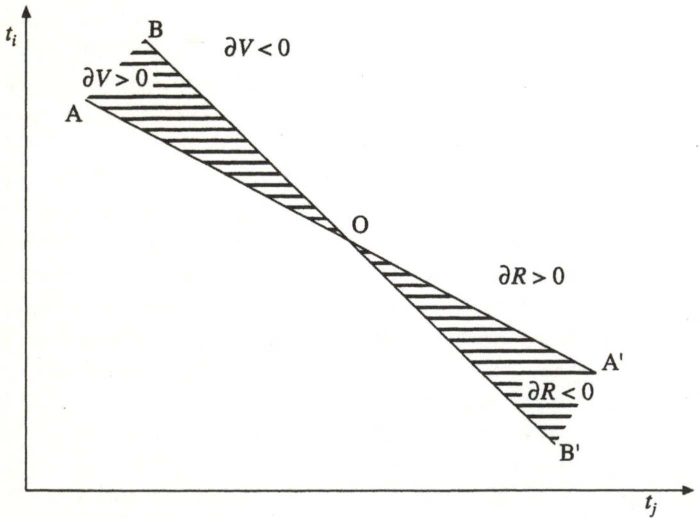

Figure 5.2 Welfare-enhancing tax reform.

Sources: Ahmad and Stern (1987); Gemmell (1987)

After examining the evidence from a large number of LDCs which have attempted tax reform in the recent past, Burgess and Stern (1993) argue that tax reform was most likely to come about when some or all of a number of requirements existed: (1) serious pressure to raise revenue; (2) a willingness to move away from high rates and a narrow base for revenue; (3) large-scale tax evasion; (4) 'irrational' and serious complications; and (5) an alteration of economic policy, say, due to the adoption of macroeconomic stabilization and/or trade liberalization programmes. It has also been shown that there are *feasible* revenue-increasing instruments for LDCs which work well. A strong case is made to move away from direct to *indirect taxes* (chiefly to VAT) as 'theoretically attractive, administratively reliable and politically possible'. Further, given the overall detrimental effects of trade taxes, there is a case to 'move away from reliance on foreign trade taxes to greater use of direct taxes'.

5.12 Budgetary deficits and Ricardian equivalence: the case of India

The causes and consequences of rising government deficits have received major attention in both industrially developed countries (DCs) and less developed countries (LDCs) (Barro, cited in Ghatak and Ghatak 1996; Buiter and Patel 1992). The theory of funding government deficit has been widely discussed in the context of the Ricardian equivalence (RE) theorem (Seater, cited in Ghatak and Ghatak 1996). Put simply, the RE theorem states that it is inconsequential whether a government budget deficit is financed by debt issue or by tax increases, since under certain conditions the impact of government purchases on aggregate demand is impervious to the mode of financing fiscal deficits. Such 'equivalence' arises because economic agents, being fully aware of the path of future fiscal policies, consider today's deficit financing as tomorrow's tax liabilities. Therefore, Barro claims, if (1) capital markets are perfect and consumers do not face any borrowing constraints, (2) both private and public sectors have the same planning, horizons and (3) taxes are non-distortionary, the RE theorem will be validated.

However, empirical evidence from DCs has not always substantiated the RE theorem. LDCs in general, and India in particular, are characterized by imperfect capital and credit markets (Ghatak 1995). Given such market imperfections, the RE theorem cannot be expected to be validated for India. But rigorous empirical tests are necessary for policy implications, as India's growing public debt and deficits in recent times have been a matter of particular concern (Buiter and Patel 1992; Gupta 1992, cited in Ghatak and Ghatak 1996). If the RE theorem is invalidated, a growing deficit financed by issuing bonds instead of by taxation will tend to raise private consumption owing to the wealth effects. This, if full employment prevails, will displace private investment or other interest-sensitive forms of private spending. In other words, invalidation of the RE theorem may imply crowding out. Apart from crowding out, tax smoothing and potential inflationary consequences of monetization of public debt are the main reasons for concern regarding the rising debt burden in India (Buiter and Patel 1992).

The following symbols are used to explain RE: C, private consumption; Y, income; G, government expenditure; T, taxes; B, government bonds; W, private wealth defined as money and bond holdings; $G2$, government spending, including interest payment on bonds; d, total government deficit; RB, interest payment on bonds; and I, investment, all should be measured in *per capita* terms and at constant prices; r, the long-term real interest rate; t, the time subscript; m, the number of lags in relevant equations.

5.12.1 Different forms of the Ricardian equivalence theorem and the crowding-out hypothesis

Different formulations to test the RE theorem and the crowding-out hypothesis used in the literature are summarized below:

$$C_t = a_0 + a_1 Y_t + a_2 G_t + a_3 T_t + a_4 W_t \tag{5.49}$$

$$C_t = a(Y_t - T_t - d_t), \quad 0 < a < 1 \tag{5.50}$$

where

$$d_t = G_t + RB_t - T_t \tag{5.51.1}$$

implies that

$$d_t = G2_t - T_t \tag{5.51.2}$$

Definitions (5.51.1–2) explain that total government deficit is primary deficit plus interest payments on bonds, and primary deficit is non-interest outlays minus total revenue. 'If there is a primary deficit in the budget, then the total government deficit will keep growing as the debt grows because of the deficit, and interest payments rise because the debt is growing' (Dornbusch and Fischer 1994: 580, cited in Ghatak and Ghatak 1996). Equation (5.50) has been rewritten in different forms with the implied restrictions on coefficients and by using the two expressions for government deficit given in (5.51.1–2). For instance, the equation

$$C_t = a_1 Y_t + a_2 T_t + a_3 d_t \tag{5.52}$$

was estimated by Buiter and Tobin (1979, cited in Ghatak and Ghatak 1996) subject to the set of restrictions given by

$$0 < a_1 < 1,\ a_2 < 0,\ a_3 < 0,\ a_1 = |a_2| \quad \text{and} \quad a_2 = a_3 \tag{5.53}$$

If all three coefficients a_1, a_2 and a_3, are statistically significant and the set of restrictions (5.53) is satisfied, then the RE theorem is supported. The definition of deficit (5.51.2) is used by Kormendi (1983, cited in Ghatak and Ghatak 1996) in the 'augmented consolidated approach', in the form

$$C_t = a_1 Y_t + a_2 T_t + a_3 G2_t \tag{5.54}$$

and is also used by Boskin (1988, cited in Ghatak and Ghatak 1996) to test the RE theorem, in the form

$$C_t = a_1(Y_t - G2_t) + a_2 d_t \tag{5.55}$$

In (5.54), the Re theorem is supported if a_2 is statistically insignificant. Deficits have no effect on current consumption because rational consumers base their consumption decisions on lifetime income, which depends on the present value of government expenditures and not on the timing of tax collections. In (5.55), the RE is invalidated if a_2 is positive and statistically significant. From (5.51.2) and (5.55) it is apparent that Boskin imposes the *a priori* restriction that the coefficients of tax and government spending are equal, though opposite in sign. But such restrictions should be tested, because they are not justified on *a priori* grounds. To yield joint tests of the RE theorem and crowding-out hypotheses, equation (5.50) can be rewritten as

$$C_t = a_1 Y_t + a_2 G_t + a_3 RB_t \tag{5.56}$$

subject to the set of restrictions (5.53), and as

$$C_t = a_1 Y_t + a_2 G2_t, \quad 0 < a_1 < 1 \tag{5.57}$$

using definitions of d_t.

If $a_2 < 0$ is statistically significant, then government consumption crowds out private consumption. Crowding out is said to occur when an increase in government expenditure leads to a reduction in private consumption, private investment, or in net exports. Deficit financing, by means other than taxation, raises real interest rates which, in turn, reduce private investment or any other interest-sensitive form of private spending (Buiter and Patel 1992; Yellen 1989, cited in Ghatak and Ghatak 1996). Because our primary objective is to test the RE theorem for India, the crowding-out effect has been tested only in two forms: (1) as indicated in equation (5.57) and (2) by regressing real *per capita* investment on real interest rates, real *per capita* income and government spending, as in the following:

$$I_t = \alpha_0 + \alpha_1 Y_t + \alpha_2 r_t + \alpha_3 G2_t \tag{5.58}$$

The expected signs of the coefficients in (5.58) are $\alpha_1 > 0$ and $\alpha_2, \alpha_3 < 0$.

It is apparent that the Buiter–Tobin type of approach, as summarized above, is based on *ad hoc* consumption behaviour. Therefore, further versions of the RE theorem were developed and tested by modifying consumption behaviour along the lines of permanent income and life-cycle ideas.

Following Seater and Mariano (1985, cited in Ghatak and Ghatak 1996) Gupta (1992) separated income and government spending into permanent and transitory components, by estimating the former, using a three-year moving average of actual components. This Friedmanian approach to income and spending was further pursued by Aschauer (1985, cited in Ghatak and Ghatak 1996). Aschauer used a consumption function based on a model of intertemporal utility maximization subject to budget constraints. With a quadratic utility function, a 'typical' family maximizes the net present value of consumption utility in current and future periods. Then Euler's equation is given as

$$E_{t-1} C_t^* = a + b C_{t-1}^* \tag{5.59.1}$$

where C^* is the effective private consumption, and E is the expectations operator.

Effective private consumption is actual personal consumption plus consumption induced by government spending, as given by

$$C_t^* = C_t + \theta G2_t \tag{5.59.2}$$

Government spending in equation (5.59.2) influences family utility and every unit of $G2$ is expected to provide the same utility as the θ units of private consumption. The parameters a and b are derived as non-linear functions of the discount rate and the real rate of interest.

If we lag equation (5.59.2) by one period and substitute into (5.59.1), then we obtain

$$E_{t-1}C_t^* = a + b\theta G2_{t-1} \tag{5.59.3}$$

If we assume that expectations are formed at time $t-1$, and take the expectations of equation (5.59.2), then we obtain

$$E_{t-1}C_t^* = C_t + \theta E_{t-1}G2_t \Rightarrow C_T = E_{t-1}C_t^* - \theta E_{t-1}G2_t \tag{5.59.4}$$

With the rational expectations hypothesis, actual consumption is expected consumption plus an error, u, which is purely random (Maddala 1992: 432). If we take this into account, and substitute (5.59.3) into (5.59.4), then we obtain

$$C_t = a + bC_{t-1} + b\theta G2_{t-1} - \theta E_{t-1}G2_t + u_t \tag{5.59.5}$$

The expected value of government spending, including interest payment on bonds, is assumed to be given by past values of itself and those of the government deficit:

$$E_{t-1}G2_t = \gamma + \varepsilon(L)G2_t + \omega(L)d_t \tag{5.59.6}$$

where ε and ω are two suitable polynomials in L, the lag operator implies

$$E_{t-1}G2_t = \gamma + \varepsilon_1 G2_{t-1} + \varepsilon_2 G2_{t-2} + \cdots + \omega_1 d_{t-1} + \omega_2 d_{t-2} + \cdots \tag{5.59.7}$$

If we then substitute (5.59.7) into (5.59.5), we obtain:

$$C_t = (a - \theta\gamma) + bC_{t-1} + \theta(b - \varepsilon_1)G2_{t-1} - \theta\varepsilon_2 G2_{t-2} - \theta\varepsilon - 3G2_{t-3}$$
$$- \cdots - \theta\omega_1 d_{t-1} - \theta\omega_2 d_{t-2} - \cdots - +u_t \tag{5.59.8}$$

The final model for estimation is given below by (5.59.9–10), with cross-equation restrictions on the parameters such as those given in equation (5.59.11). To save on degrees of freedom, we can take the case of equations (5.59.9–10), in which there are only two lags of $G2$ and d. Using the rational expectations rule again, actual government spending is expected government spending plus a random error, $\nu_t \Rightarrow$:

$$G2_t = \gamma + \varepsilon G2_{t-1} + \varepsilon_2 G2_{t-2} + \omega_1 d_{t-1} + \omega_2 d_{t-2} + \nu_t \tag{5.59.9}$$

Substitution of (5.59.7) in the two-period lag case into (5.59.5) yields:

$$C_t = \delta + bC_{t-1} + \eta_1 G2_{t-1} + \eta_2 G2_{t-2} + \mu_1 d_{t-1} + \mu_2 d_{t-2} + u_t \tag{5.59.10}$$

where

$$
\begin{aligned}
\delta &= a - \theta\gamma \\
\eta_1 &= \theta(b - \varepsilon_1) \\
\eta_2 &= -\theta\varepsilon_2 \\
\mu_1 &= -\theta\omega_1 \\
\mu_2 &= \theta\omega_2
\end{aligned} \qquad (5.59.11)
$$

The cross-equation restrictions in (5.59.11) are dictated by the rational expectations theorem. If these restrictions hold, then the RE theorem under rational expectations will be empirically validated. Aschauer estimates (5.59.9–10) under the restrictions imposed by (5.59.11) and then estimates the unrestricted form of (5.59.10) to test the violations of restrictions imposed by (5.59.11).

5.12.2 Conclusion

The time-series data for India 1950–86 consistently reject the RE theorem and provide evidence that tax cuts increase consumption. The conclusion is based on multi-cointegration analysis and estimation of the error correction and rational expectations models. The lack of evidence in favour of the RE theorem is not surprising. Imperfect credit markets, liquidity constraints, differential borrowing rates and finite horizons can all invalidate the proposition (for details see Ghatak and Ghatak 1996).

Questions

1 Explain the major features of money markets in developing countries.
2 What is the role of monetary expansion in promoting economic growth in developing countries?
3 Critically evaluate the relationship between inflation and economic growth. How useful is inflation in promoting economic growth in less developed countries?
4 Discuss the role of fiscal policy in economic development.
5 What are the major features of the tax system in LDCs? How would you reform it?
6 Explain the concept of 'Ricardian Equivalence'. What is the validity of this concept for LDCs?

6 Foreign resources and economic development

6.1 Introduction

Foreign resources have played an important role in the economic development of many economically advanced countries of today. For example, between 1870 and 1914 the ratio of capital inflow to gross domestic capital formation was about 40 per cent in Canada. The same ratio for Australia was about 37 per cent between 1861 and 1900, and for Norway it was 29 per cent between 1885 and 1914 and 31 per cent between 1920 and 1929 (Hagen 1975). Even in countries like Japan and the United States, where such ratios were lower during their early stages of economic development, foreign capital played a significant role. The LDCs of today are more or less at the same stage of economic development as the DCs in the eighteenth and nineteenth centuries. It is generally contended that foreign resources could play a vital role in promoting economic development in the LDCs. This is explained in terms of concepts such as 'the savings gap' and 'the foreign exchange gap'. But at the outset it is necessary to clarify certain key terms in the definition of foreign resources.

6.2 The concept of foreign resources

The flow of foreign resources (FR) can be of many types and it is important to know the different elements. First, there are institutions (e.g. Oxfam, War on Want, etc.) which provide *grants* to many countries to alleviate the after-effects of a natural disaster such as famine, flood or earthquakes. Such grants need not be repaid by the recipient countries, nor do they carry any interest charges. Indeed, grants are genuine 'aids' but they usually form a tiny fraction of the total inflow of FR. Second, some *loans* are given, chiefly by the international lending agencies (e.g. the World Bank) at interest rates which are lower than those in the market. Here the foreign resources are provided on 'soft' terms which reflect a desire to 'aid' the receiving countries. Where the loans are granted to the LDCs at a concessionary rate for very long periods (say, forty to fifty years), the inflow of FR takes the character of genuine foreign aid as the net present value of FR provided at a concessionary rate and to be repaid fifty years hence would be almost the same as the value of grants.

However, *foreign private investments* in the LDCs are not exactly 'foreign aid' as they are made on commercial terms. Foreign private investment usually carries commercial interest rates and does not stem from altruistic motives. Foreign private investment usually forms a significant proportion of the total inflow of FR. *Government lending* could be carried out on a bilateral or multilateral basis. Sometimes, several governments could set up a consortium to provide FR to a country or countries (e.g. Aid-India or Aid-Pakistan Consortium). Such lending could carry commercial terms; but frequently these loans are provided at concessionary rates and they have to be repaid after a long period. Sometimes, grace periods are offered to relieve the burden of debt repayments. It seems clear that *all* FR are not 'aid' or charities, some parts of them being international lending on a commercial basis (see Tables A6.1–2).

6.3 Criteria for distribution of foreign resources

Several criteria for allocating FR are discussed in the literature. Some of them can be highlighted here.

First, FR are usually given for *political* reasons. It is generally the case that FR will not be given to one's enemies (Little and Clifford 1965). A large part of American aid to the LDCs is allocated on the grounds of keeping intact America's political interest as far as possible. Usually it takes the form of giving aid to 'friendly' countries. The 'friendly' countries are usually those which would help the United States to protect itself against the danger of the spread of communism. Similarly, a large part of the flow of Soviet FR is motivated by political factors.

Second, FR are supposed to replenish the dearth of domestic saving in the LDCs. Generally, the difference between planned investment (I_p) and planned saving (S_p) is taken as an indication of the FR (F) that are necessary to attain a target rate of economic growth. In other words,

$$F = I_p - S_p$$

Indeed, in many development planning models, a target level of investment is specified to achieve a certain rate of growth of income and then an estimate of planned savings is made. When the planned investment exceeds planned savings the gap is sought to be made up by FR.

In this 'savings gap' type of analysis, the implicit assumption is that all FR would be used for domestic investments. This need not always be true and the point has been made that it is possible to see the coexistence of both a 'savings gap' and a 'foreign exchange' or 'trade' or 'bottleneck' gap where such a gap (say T_g) is given by the difference between imports (M) and exports (X). Thus

$$T_g = M - X$$

The equilibrium relationship between the 'savings gap' and the 'trade gap' can be expressed as

$$I_p - S_p = M - X$$

These two gaps need not be equal *ex ante,* though *ex post* they must be equal because of the method of national accounting. Any excess of investment over savings could only be financed by an excess of imports over exports *ex post*. It is contended that where the trade gap predominates over the savings gap, a supply of FR could have a positive effect on growth and as such FR should be provided after careful estimation of these two gaps (McKinnon 1964; Chenery and Strout 1966). A more detailed discussion will be made later.

Third, the other criterion which is sometimes advocated is known as 'absorptive capacity' (Rosenstein-Rodan 1961). There are some difficulties in the actual estimation of 'absorptive capacity' as the concept is not usually regarded as very clear. Basically, it means a country's ability to absorb capital and to use it in a productive way. Such 'productive' use of capital is measured by positive 'reasonable' rates of return on total investment. Obviously, 'absorptive capacity' would depend upon the level of income and its growth rate, the supply of skill and the level of average and marginal rates of savings. If the principle of providing FR is to step up the process of capital formation in the LDCs, then such a principle is more likely to be met in those LDCs where the *marginal* rates of savings are much higher than the average. It may be pointed out that the absorptive capacity of an economy depends, *inter alia,* upon the nature of the infrastructure of an economy. An economy with a poor system of transport and communication, with managerial skill handicapped further by lack of proper training and educational facilities, is likely to have a low absorptive capacity.

Some rough indices to measure absorptive capacity have been proposed (Rosenstein-Rodan 1961). None of them is free of subjective bias in its construction. One such index is the *rise in the volume of investment* in the last five or more years. The second index consists of the measurement of *increases in savings* in the past few years. It is of particular interest to note here the difference between marginal and average rates of savings. The third index is to examine the structure of development and administration of a country. Here the judgement is likely to be subjective. The method of finding out the necessary FR can then be stated as follows:

$$\mathrm{FR} = (ky - s)\sum Y + 5Y_0(s - S_0/Y_0) \tag{6.1}$$

where FR is the required foreign resources, k is the capital–output ratio, Y is the national income, y is the growth rate of Y, s is the marginal rate of savings, S_0/Y_0 is the average rate of savings, S is total savings and S_0 is initial total savings.

To examine the degree of responsiveness of FR to the parameters mentioned above we differentiate to obtain the following:

$$\frac{\partial \mathrm{FR}}{\partial k} = y\sum Y \tag{6.2}$$

$$\frac{\partial \mathrm{FR}}{\partial s} = -\sum Y + 5Y_0 \tag{6.3}$$

$$\frac{\partial \mathrm{FR}}{\partial (S_0/Y_0)} = -5Y_0 \tag{6.4}$$

Now the increase in national income, Y, is given by

$$\sum_0^4 Y_t = Y_0 \frac{(1+y)^5 - 1}{y} \tag{6.5}$$

For a fixed y with given k, a proportion ky of Y is needed for investment I in each year. Hence we have

$$\sum I_t = ky \sum Y \tag{6.6}$$

Let

$$S_t = sY_t - c \tag{6.7}$$

$$\sum S_t = s\sum Y_t - \sum c \tag{6.8}$$

Now

$$\text{FR} = \sum I - \sum S \tag{6.9}$$

and, ignoring time t,

$$\begin{aligned} \text{FR} &= ky\sum Y - s\sum Y + \sum c \\ &= (ky - s)\sum Y + \sum c \end{aligned} \tag{6.10}$$

Notice that since

$$c = s - \frac{S_0}{Y_0} Y_0$$

equation (6.10) could be used to obtain equation (6.1). This criterion emphasizes that the major aim for allocating FR is to promote 'self-sustaining growth' without cross-country comparisons.

Several criticisms have been levelled at the criterion of granting FR according to absorptive capacity. First, if the FR are to be allocated on the basis of past productivity of investment, then the poorest LDCs, who are in greatest need because of population pressure, are likely to get very little, as the application of this principle is tantamount to backing the winners. Second, past returns on investment are not always the most reliable indicators of the productivity of investment in future. Third, savings and output–capital ratios are likely to alter during the process of development. Fourth, the application of the principle of absorptive capacity does not make proper allowance for the different patterns of distribution of economic resources in different countries. Finally, if it is argued that the principle of distribution of FR is to raise the absorptive capacity of the LDCs rather than to accept it as given, then again there arises a case to devise certain other principles.

Next, the flow of FR is sometimes guided by historical factors. Much of the FR flowing from France and Britain goes to their former colonies. The provision of FR in such cases is sometimes regarded as imperialistic or neo-imperialistic (Hayter 1971).

The other criterion which is said to have been applied in distributing FR is the maintenance and promotion of the private sector of the economy. Japan, Germany and the United States have sometimes maintained that resources would be provided in certain LDCs so long as the private sector could be allowed to operate freely. This criterion is really derived from the political and ideological reasons for providing FR.

The 'efficiency' criterion for allocating FR has received considerable attention. The system seems to be strikingly simple and important as it upholds the pragmatic view that FR should be distributed on the basis of their most efficient use. In practice, its application is not so simple. First, it is necessary to construct a sound index of efficiency. Second, the principle of achieving maximum efficiency may run counter to the achievement of some other objective, e.g. maximization of employment or more equality in the distribution of income. Further, as Eckaus contends: 'Within any one country one could determine whether resources were being allocated and used efficiently if prices did accurately reflect relative scarcities and goals. The "if" is a big one, however' (Eckaus 1970: 158). Here, one solution of the problem lies in the application of cost–benefit analysis after making due corrections for distortions in the product and the factor markets. An index for measuring the productivity of FR has been made (Adelman and Morris 1968). But here the major problem lies in its application to different countries as factor efficiencies are likely to be different in different LDCs.

Sometimes, the principle of *stability*, chiefly in prices and in trade balances, has been regarded as the appropriate condition for allocating FR. Such a principle usually finds favour with the international organizations such as the International Monetary Fund (IMF). But this principle is really the application of the doctrine of efficiency at the national level. Notice that the application of this principle implicitly assumes that stability should be given high priority in national development policy.

The above discussion suggests the difficulties which are inherent in finding out an appropriate value-free index to measure the performance of FR on growth and development of the LDCs not only at a point in time, but also over time. Any decision regarding the most desirable direction of development is likely to be subjective. However, these subjective judgements could be stated clearly. A more composite index for measuring the effects of FR on not only saving, investment, capital–output ratios, but also on development in general, could be built. Any conflict between objectives like efficiency and self-help could be minimized if some of the criteria are treated as *constraints* (e.g. maximization of the growth rate subject to a minimum level of consumption and more equal distribution). Also, a clearer picture of the different types of growth paths with FR and their implications regarding inter-temporal saving and consumption for different generations could help to identify the 'appropriate' criteria within a country and among different countries. However, the provision of FR without any political or ideological consideration is unlikely to occur in practice.

6.4 Different types of foreign resource

6.4.1 Tied and untied foreign resources

The allocation of FR can assume different forms. They can be *tied* to the imports from donor countries (i.e. tying by sources); alternatively, their use could be linked to a specific project (i.e. tying by end use). The reasons for such tying are not difficult to understand from the point of view of the donor country. First, tying helps to increase the exports of the donor countries and protects their income and employment. However, such an argument is inconsistent with humanitarian motives for transferring resources. Second, tying of resources by some deficit donor countries may increase pressure in surplus donor countries to similar tying because tying by the deficit countries is supposed to enhance their relative share in the competitive market for exports. Such a phenomenon is regarded as 'competitive aid-tying'. Third, tying is supposed to result in efficient utilization of resources. Fourth, project tying is supposed to be effective as the projects could be identified easily. Also, such tying is expected to enhance the reputation of the donor countries. Fifth, when resources are tied both by sources and by uses, then it creates a monopolistic situation in favour of the donor country which it can easily exploit.

It is easy to see from the above why tying of resources has created so much resentment among the recipient countries. First, tying does not help the recipient countries to obtain resources at the cheapest prices. In many instances, prices paid by the LDCs are much above their world prices (Haq 1965). Second, tying will not necessarily improve the balance of payments of the donor country if the cause of such deficit is an excess demand for resources. Third, the objective of tying resources will be defeated if a recipient country decides to spend on goods and services of the donor country, from its total reserves of foreign earnings, a fraction which is greater than or equal to the value of tied resources (Bhagwati 1970). Fourth, resources may be tied to the construction of a specific project which does not satisfy the objective of the national plan. Fifth, in the event of a double-tying (i.e. both by sources and by end use), the monopolistic position of the lender may result in a situation which could be less than optimal from the point of view of the recipient country. Sixth, costs of tying of resources have been regarded as considerable for some LDCs (Bhagwati 1970). Seventh, the informal agreements about servicing over the life of the capital projects as well as some indirect costs of tying (e.g. carrying the cargo in the ship of the donor country which charges a higher than international price for freight) may well reduce the true value of the tied FR.

In view of the harmful effects of tying FR, some proposals have been made to untie them. First, all resources should be untied as to their source. The difficulty in implementing this proposal from the point of view of the country which provides FR to the LDCs and at the same time suffers from a balance of payments deficit is understandable if tying has an important balance of payments effect. Second, should the volume of international liquidity be raised to improve the balance of payments position of a deficit country transferring resources to the LDCs, then the task of untying would be less difficult. Third, greater co-ordination among the donor countries is necessary for untying FR. Fourth, double-tying should be avoided whenever possible as it is likely to maximize monopoly gains of the donor countries. Fifth, the LDCs should try to promote international tendering of projects to find out roughly the competitive or world price. It is observed that the excess costs imposed on some LDCs were about 50 per cent when such costs are measured by the ratio of the difference between the highest bid price and the successful bid price. Finally, the donor country could treat such excess cost on the recipient country as an export subsidy rather than a transfer of resources. However, in the absence of a concerted effort among the economically advanced countries, the prospect of untying of FR does not seem very bright, particularly after the oil crises of 1973 and 1979, when many industrialized countries went into a recession and faced considerable balance of payments deficits.

6.4.2 Foreign resources for projects or plans

Sometimes FR are given to a particular project or projects in LDCs. The point has been made that such FR may fail to promote the basic objective of the national plan and hence it is necessary to work at the problem of financing the plan rather than the projects. It is clear that such a problem could only arise if the aim in the national plans is different from the one in the project. But to the extent that projects included in the plan are so selected as to achieve some national objectives, the problem of financing the plan or the project disappears and the possibility of switching arises.

Donor countries may reveal their preference for financing the projects rather than the plans if the national plans are likely to be revised suddenly with frequent changes in the government (Singer 1965). Second, if the resources given by the donor country form a small proportion of planned investment, project financing could be considered as more attractive than the financing of the plan. Third, projects are easily identifiable from the point of view of the donor country. Fourth, financing of marginal projects (e.g. projects which might not have been included in the plan without FR) by FR has some advantages.

Financing of the plan has the advantage of generating greater effort in the recipient country. Second, it could improve the relationship between the lending and the borrowing country which is certainly an important goal of supply resources. Third, plans are supposed to achieve the overall development of a country and their financing is regarded as preferable by some of the recipient countries. However, since there are now very few countries which would allow projects to be set up without analysing their impact on the national plan, the discussion of project versus plan financing seems rather academic. More important, however, is the discussion of the relative advantages and disadvantages of bilateral (BL) and multilateral (ML) financing to which we now turn.

6.4.3 Bilateral and multilateral financing

The BL flow of FR is usually advocated on the following grounds:

1 BL financing could be tied while a large part of ML financing is untied.
2 The donor country can keep 'operational control' with less difficulty in the case of BL financing.
3 Effective utilization of FR is more likely to take place if financing is BL rather than ML.
4 Politically, BL rather than ML financing is more likely to be acceptable to the electorate.

Notice that the advantages from the standpoint of the donor country are not always so from the point of view of the recipient country. The major criticisms levelled at BL financing can be summarized as follows:

1 BL financing is generally used to extend political influence over the LDCs; it is regarded as an instrument for 'buying' friends.
2 BL financing is not always meant for the economic development of a country because, more often than not, 'strings' are attached to it.
3 Even without the 'strings', BL financing is regarded as morally indefensible since 'extended in the wrong way, generosity can be perceived by its intended beneficiary as insulting and contemptuous. The problem of BL financing is psychological and political rather than managerial' (Fulbright 1966).

Despite these criticisms of BL financing, it is difficult to switch over from BL to ML financing. For one thing, such a switch is likely to reduce the supply of FR simply because many donors, while supplying resources, like to exercise some leverage over their use. Such leverage is unlikely to be strong if financing is ML. For another, sometimes BL flows take place on grounds of moral responsibility (e.g. between the donors and their excolonies). However, BL and ML financing has the advantage of increasing the total volume of FR. Also, ML financing properly co-ordinated could eliminate the inefficiencies in the use of resources. Further, the problem of debt-servicing, which is worrying many LDCs, particularly after the oil crisis of 1979, can be better tackled if financing is ML rather than BL. It is pointed out, however, that ML financing is unlikely to be optimum for several reasons (Balogh 1967). First, there is absence of co-ordination among different donors and between donors and recipient countries. Second, absence of skilled manpower may aggravate the problem. Third, the decentralized and democratic controls of the present institutions are not always exercised. But these arguments are not very compelling in the sense that, instead of forming a case against ML financing as such, they could be directed towards rehabilitating the different agencies engaged in ML financing. The formation of a single agency could avoid many of these criticisms. On the other hand, the creation of a single agency has its own problems. For instance, donors may be less willing to contribute to a single international agency and this could reduce the flow of FR. Also, there are many practical difficulties in the operation of a single monolithic agency. One of the compromises could be the BL resource transfer within the ML framework (Rosenstein-Rodan 1968).

Under this 'consortium' approach, an international agency can be set up for consultation and co-ordination of the transfer of FR to LDCs. Donor countries may be allowed to transfer FR bilaterally but according to certain principles which are agreed upon internationally within the 'consortium'. A group of highly skilled people within the 'consortium' could try to overcome the problems of proper evaluation of the projects.

However, multilateralization of BL flows of FR has its drawbacks. The major point to note is that, if donor countries agree upon certain international principles for transfer of FR, then they are no longer willing to exercise their own controls over the flow of resources. But this is the real point in sticking to BL transfers. It on the contrary, the international agency fails to discard the 'strings' attached to BL flows, then one could easily raise doubts about having such an agency in the first place.

The ML agencies have gained considerable support because of their activities in the field of debt-servicing, granting of long-term loans with low interest rates and easy terms of repayments (Pearson 1969). It is argued that they try to apply rational economic criteria as far as possible in effecting the flow of FR. All this is commendable. However, it must be mentioned that the voting power within the international ML agencies is closely related to the contributions of the rich nations to the ML agencies. Some of the practices of the World Bank in Latin America have greatly reduced its credibility as a neutral agency (Hayter 1971). Here is a case to apply the principles of some agencies of the United Nations who try to maintain a more neutral character.

The above discussion is carried out under the implicit assumption that FR play an important role in the process of economic development. Such a role will now be examined in detail within the framework of 'dual gap' analysis.

6.5 Dual-gap analysis and its evaluation

The 'dual gap' consists of two parts: (1) the savings gap – investment – savings (i.e. $I = S$); and (2) the trade gap or the difference between imports M and exports X (i.e. $M - X$). In national income accounting, *ex post* the two gaps must be identical, though *ex ante* they need not be so. Notice that the two gaps cannot be added together. The algebraic representation of dual-gap analysis can be described following the analysis of Chenery and Strout (1966) and Maizels (1968).

$$C + I + X \equiv Y + M \tag{6.11}$$

$$C + S \equiv Y \tag{6.12}$$

$$S + \text{FR} \equiv I \tag{6.13}$$

$$M \equiv X + \text{FR} \tag{6.14}$$

where C is consumption, I is investment, X is exports, Y is GDP, M is imports, S is savings and FR is the net inflow of foreign resources. The first three are independent identities and the fourth equation can be determined when the three others are given. Since there are seven variables, four more equations should be added to three independent identities to make the system determinate. Thus, the following five structural equations are suggested of which only four work at any particular period of economic growth.

So we have

$$Y_t' = Y_0(1 + g')^t \tag{6.14}$$

where Y_t' is the target GDP at the target year t, Y_0 is the GDP at the initial year 0 and g' is the target growth rate.

Planned investment I_t' is given by

$$I_t' = kg'Y_t' \tag{6.16}$$

where k is the incremental capital–output ratio.

Exports in the year t are given by

$$X_t = X_0(1 + x)^t \tag{6.17}$$

where x is the growth rate of exports which is regarded as exogenous or given.

Planned savings S_t' would be equal to

$$S_t' = s_0 + s_1'Y_t' \tag{6.18}$$

where s_1' is the planned marginal propensity to save.

Similarly, planned minimum imports M_t' to sustain Y_t' would be given by

$$M_t' = m_0 + m_1'Y_t' \tag{6.19}$$

where m_1' is the marginal 'necessity' to import.

When planned investment is greater than planned savings, i.e. $I' - S'$, the savings gap exists; when planned imports are greater than planned exports, i.e. $M' - X$, a

Table 6.1 Solution of Chenery–Strout model without skill constraint

Variables	*Trade-limited growth*[a]	*Savings-limited growth*[b]	
Y'_t	$Y_0(1+g')^t$	$Y_0(1+g')^t$	(6.20)
I'_t	$kg'Y'_t$	$kg'Y'_t$	(6.21)
S'_t	$(kg'-m'_1)Y'_t+X_t-m_0$	$s_0+s'_1Y'_t$	(6.22)
X_t	$X_0(1+x)^t$	$X_0(1+x)^t$	(6.23)
M_t/M'_t	$m_0+m'_1Y_t$	$(kg'-s'_1)Y'_t+X_t-s_0$	(6.24)
C_t	$(1-kg'+m'_1)Y'_t-X_t+m_0$	$(1-s'_1)Y'_t-s_0$	(6.25)
FR_t	$m'_1Y'_t+m_0-X_t$	$(kg'-s_1)Y'_t-s_0$	(6.26)

Source: Maizels (1968).

Notes: [a]Adding equation (6.11) to (6.14) with (6.15) to (6.17) and (6.19).
[b]Adding equation (6.11) to (6.14) with (6.15) to (6.18).

trade gap exists. The two gaps need not be equal *ex ante* except by chance. Usually, one of the gaps would be greater than the other. When the trade gap exceeds the savings gap the last equation, i.e. (6.19), operates, but not equation (6.18); contrariwise, when the savings gap exceeds the trade gap, equation (6.18) works, but not equation (6.19).

The basic solution of the Chenery and Strout model in the absence of any skill constraint has been well summarized in Maizels (1968) and this is illustrated in Table 6.1.

To find the relationship between the target growth rate g' and FR the following approximations could be used.

$$(1+g')^t = 1+g't \tag{6.27}$$

$$(1+x)^t = 1+xt \tag{6.28}$$

To find the net inflow of FR in the savings-limited growth path (FR_t^S) we obtain the following equation:

$$\mathrm{FR}_t^S = (ktY_0)g'^2 + Y_0(k - s'_1t)g' - (s'_1Y_0 + s_0) \tag{6.29}$$

Differentiating with respect to g' we obtain

$$\frac{\mathrm{dFR}_t^S}{\mathrm{d}g'} = Y_0[k + t(2p - s'_1)] \tag{6.30}$$

given $p = kg'$ or the necessary ratio of investment to Y. The model predicts a rise in FR_t^S even when planned propensity to save is equal to the necessary ratio of investment to income, if $s'_1 < 2p + k/t$.

In the trade-limited phase of growth the net inflow of FR (FR_t^T) is given by the following equation:

$$\mathrm{FR}_t^T = (m'tY_0)g' + [(m_0 + m'_1Y_o - X_0(1 + x + t)] \tag{6.31}$$

With a fixed x, FR_t^S rises at a rising rate while FR_t^T rises at a fixed rate as g' rises, given the quadratic form of the equation of FR_t^S.

With given FR_t^T, g' depends on x:

$$g' = \frac{X_0}{m'_t Y_0} x + \frac{1}{t}\left(\frac{X_0 + F_t - m_0}{m'_1 Y} - 1\right) \tag{6.32}$$

Some extensions of this basic model have been made. Maizels (1968), for example, tried to use the model by relating savings to exports. The model can be altered if some variables are converted into parameters and vice versa. Further, modification of some of the behaviouristic equations could change the model. The basic model suggests that when exports grow faster than national income, the trade gap will be smaller with given parameters even when FR get smaller because such FR form only a small fraction of exports. Further, should there be import substitution, the minimum import requirement will be smaller over time, and thus in the path of economic growth the savings gap is likely to be the dominant one, although at the outset the trade gap might have been the dominant one.

6.5.1 Evaluation of the dual-gap model

Dual-gap models have been criticized on two grounds. The model is criticized either because of its assumed adjustment mechanism or because of its assumptions which have engendered the idea of two separate types of constraints, or both. It is attempted to meet the first criticism by relaxing the assumption regarding saving. But such modifications do not destroy the existence of the two gaps.

More serious criticism of dual-gap analysis could be made on the grounds that such a model is based on the assumption that FR cannot be regarded as a substitute for domestic savings (Joshi 1970). To the extent that FR are substitutes for domestic savings, only one gap exists. Next, some of the assumptions about fixed savings and capital–output ratios in the dual-gap analysis cease to be valid if FR can alter the composition of output of the recipient country in a manner which would reduce the capital–output ratios. But if the rate of transformation of FR into domestic capital is zero or takes a long time, then two gaps exist. Figure 6.1 illustrates the problem.

In Figure 6.1 let TT_1 be the domestic transformation curve – the 'availability envelope' *à la* Baldwin in an open economy. Let the horizontal axis measure consumer goods X and let the vertical axis denote capital goods Y. Let us assume that OC_1 and C_1K_1 are the initial levels of consumption and investment respectively. To increase the rate of growth, suppose the planner has managed to reduce consumption (and increased saving) to OC_2 but finds it difficult to squeeze consumption (or raise savings) any more. This, then, is the 'savings constraint' which may be lower than the planned level of investment to achieve a target growth rate. Optimum welfare in the Paretian sense will be obtained where TT_1 is tangent to the highest possible social indifference curve Si_1, say, at K_2. Here consumption does not enter into the social welfare function of the planner; it only acts as a constraint. The savings constraint still exists given the nature of the transformation function and given the fact that the planner fails to raise investment by lowering consumption beyond OC_2. Also, in a pure savings constraint, trade is not a constraint and FR will be used for extra consumption. Likewise, in the case of a pure trade constraint, saving is not a constraint. Domestic savings are equal to domestic investment, but a higher growth

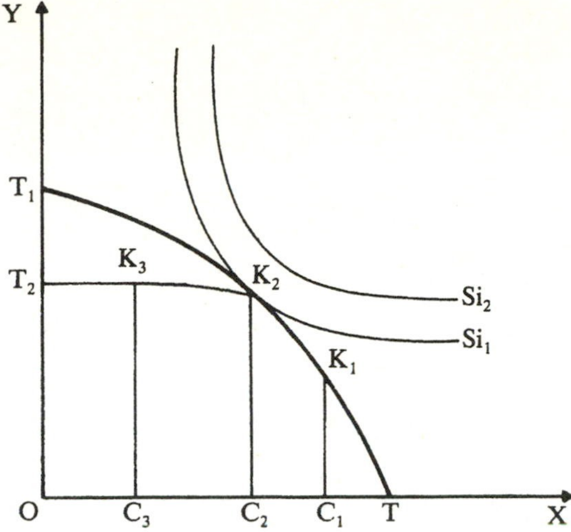

Figure 6.1

rate will be unattainable in the absence of some critical imports which underline the lack of FR. This trade constraint is shown in Figure 6.1 in the flat T_2K_2 section of the transformation curve TT_2. Clearly, T_2K_2 shows zero substitution possibility between X and Y. The savings constraint operated before at OC_2. Let us assume that this constraint does not hold any longer and consumption could fall to OC_3. But investment fails to rise. If the minimum consumption was OC_2 with the availability envelope TT_1, there is a savings constraint but no trade constraint. Given TT_2, at K_2 both the saving and the trade constraints operate. As long as a transformation curve like TT_1 slopes downwards monotonically, it is not possible to envisage a trade constraint. The advocates of the dual-gap analysis deny the existence of such a transformation curve in the LDCs, given rigidities in their economies (McKinnon 1964). Such rigidities are no doubt present in many LDCs partly owing to economic policies followed in the LDCs themselves, partly owing to the policies of the DCs and partly because of the present international economic order. As long as the substitution possibilities between foreign and domestic resources are limited, the empirical estimates of the sizes of the two gaps are not without their merits (see for example Chenery and Strout 1966; Adelman and Chenery 1966; Maizels 1968).

6.6 Gains and losses of investment by multinational corporations in less developed countries: some theoretical issues

The *direct benefits* from the transfer of technology by multinational corporations (MNCs) to the LDCs can be summarized as follows:

1 a higher amount and better quality of output available to host countries;
2 higher wages and salaries of local workers;
3 higher tax revenue for the host government from the investment income which can be utilized for development purposes.

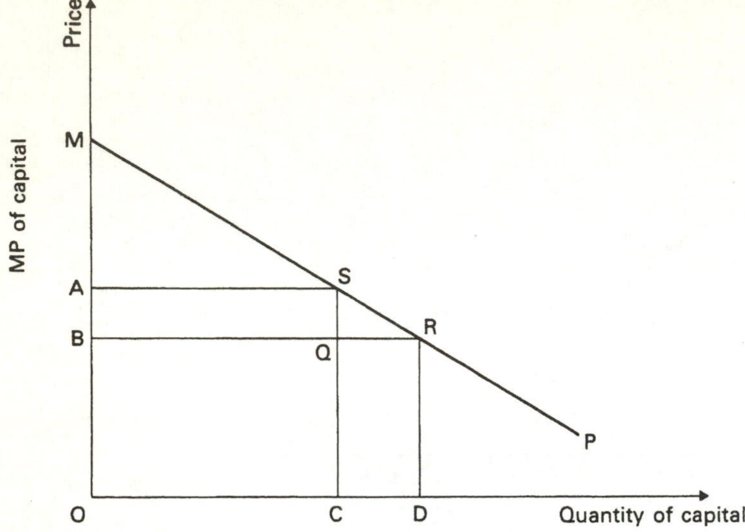

Figure 6.2

Figure 6.2 describes the direct gains from the transfer of technology to LDCs. The vertical axis measures the marginal product of capital and the horizontal axis measures capital. The MP line shows the falling marginal productivity of capital with its increasing use with a fixed supply of labour. Let OC be the initial stock of *domestic* capital. Total output is now equal to OMSC, and since the marginal product of capital will be equal to profit at the equilibrium, OASC is equal to profit and MAS is equal to wages. With the transfer of technology from abroad by the MNCs, the stock of capital rises to OD and total production increases by CDRS of which CDRQ is the profit of the MNCs. The domestic profit *decreases* to OBQC but wages increase to MBR. Such a change in profits and wages shows a *redistribution of income in favour of labourers* by ABQS. More social gains are shown by SQR. Further, the 'host' (i.e. LDC) governments can raise revenue for domestic capital formation by taxing foreign income from investment by the MNCs. Employment should rise as long as extra investment requires additional labour and as such some surplus labour will be absorbed. Other direct gains can be obtained due to a rise in exports and/or a fall in imports.

The *indirect gains* from the transfer of technology can be summarized as follows:

1 transfer of skills, know-how, management and marketing techniques;
2 supply of information about larger markets and cheaper sources of inputs;
3 provision of access to international capital markets where funds are usually supplied on the basis of complex negotiations and bargaining.

However, these benefits should be set against costs already mentioned in the text to reach final judgement about the *net* benefits.

It is suggested that one of the major reasons for the expansion of the MNCs is their possession of *intangible assets,* e.g. the new cost-minimizing technology or better quality products, patented processes or design, know-how and marketing skill.

Caves points out that when an MNC puts an intangible asset to work in its subsidiary abroad 'it is in a sense making use of an excess capacity in its roster of assets' (Caves 1982). Such a theory has received considerable support in statistical studies.

As regards the choice between exporting and direct foreign investment, it is possible to clarify the behaviour of a profit-maximizing MNC in the face of tariffs by using the model of Horst (see Horst 1973; Caves 1982). Let the MNC sell its product in two countries: home (H) and foreign (F). Let us also assume that it faces a downward-sloping demand curve for the product in each market. The cost of production depends upon the location of and amount of production. The base of production of the MNCs is H and this is shown in Figure 6.3. As regards the choice between export or local production we refer to the parts of Figure 6.3. Figure 6.3(a), which illustrates revenue and cost functions in the home country, describes the H market and the relevant demand (p_1), marginal cost (c_1) and marginal revenue (r_1) curves. If we assume that goods produced will be sold only at home, then production takes place at a point where $r_1 = c_1$. In Figure 6.3(c), intra-firm trade, *foreign* demand (p_2) and relevant cost curves (e.g. c_2) for MNCs are shown. In Figure 6.3(b), which illustrates revenue and cost functions in the foreign country, we synthesize the two sides of the analysis. When the MNC begins to export from H, MC will rise with a rise in production. As the domestic sale falls at H, MR will rise. Now let the MNC face a given price M to sell to F. It will then produce OQ_1. Home sales will be OS_1 and exports will equal S_1Q_1. Home prices will be OP_1 rather than the price lower than this which might have resulted in the absence of exports. In Figure 6.3(b), the line Mc_x depicts the marginal cost of exports from home and it shows the amount that will be exported for each price like M. In Figure 6.3(c) we obtain a similar curve by allowing the MNC the opportunity of importing different amounts of its goods for resale at prices like M_1. Should this price (i.e. M_t) be lower than the MNC's 'no imports level of marginal cost in local production', the MNC transfers a part of its imports and reduces home production. With the price at M_t, the MNC produces OQ_2 at home, sells OS_2 and imports Q_2S_2. Note that, when M_t falls, imports rise and production at F falls. The marginal revenue from importing into F is shown by r_m in Figure 6.3(b) by altering M_1.

When F imposes a tariff the price rises from Mc_x to $Mc_x + t$ in Figure 6.3(b). At the point of equilibrium total exports are OX. The MNC supplies F partly by home production and partly by exports from H. Should F raise tariffs, the MNC raises home production and reduces its exports. The locational judgements of MNCs also demonstrate the difference in real costs between the markets F and H. Also, the MNCs cannot set prices so wide that others can gain profits through arbitrage. The case of scale economies can also be shown with the help of downward-sloping MC curves (for details, see Horst 1973). Caves argues that many LDCs have followed the policy of attracting MNCs first with tariff protection and quantitative restrictions on imports and then inducing them to expand their investments through domestic content needs and other ways (Caves 1982: 41).

The policies which should be formulated to tackle some of the problems posed by the transfer of technology by the MNCs to LDCs are well documented in the text. One point that deserves to be emphasized here is that little attempt has so far been made to take into account the *environment damage* and *abatement costs* which are involved in the transfer of technology to the LDCs. Such environmental costs (economic and social) are involved both in the transfer of technology as well as in the transfer of

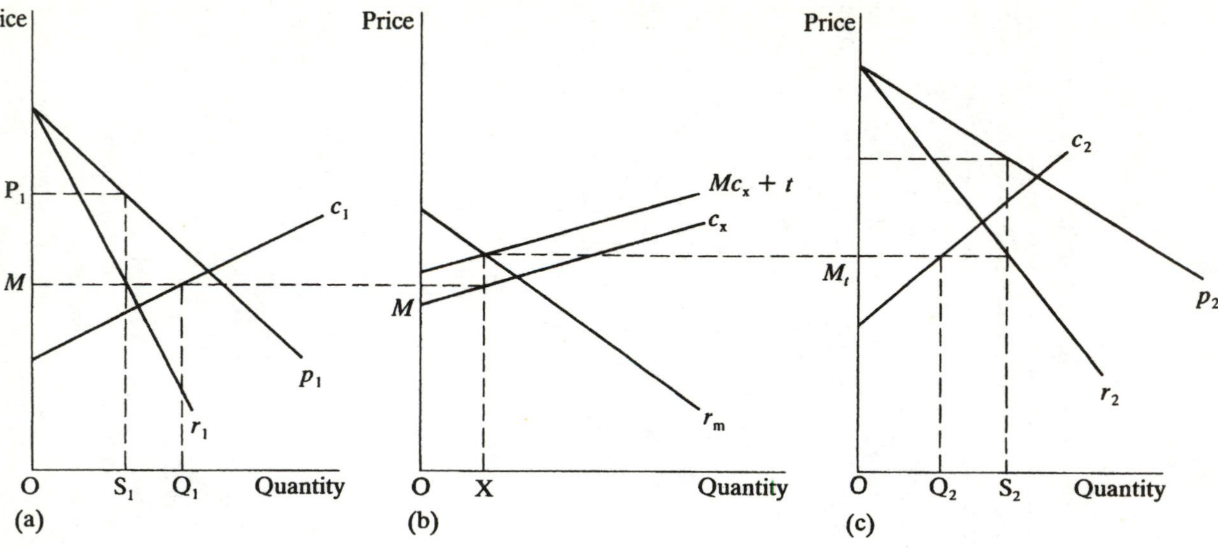
Price
P1
M
c1
p1
r1
O
S1
Q1
Quantity
(a)
Price
M
Mcx + t
cx
rm
O
X
Quantity
(b)
Price
Mt
c2
p2
r2
O
Q2
S2
Quantity
(c)

Figure 6.3

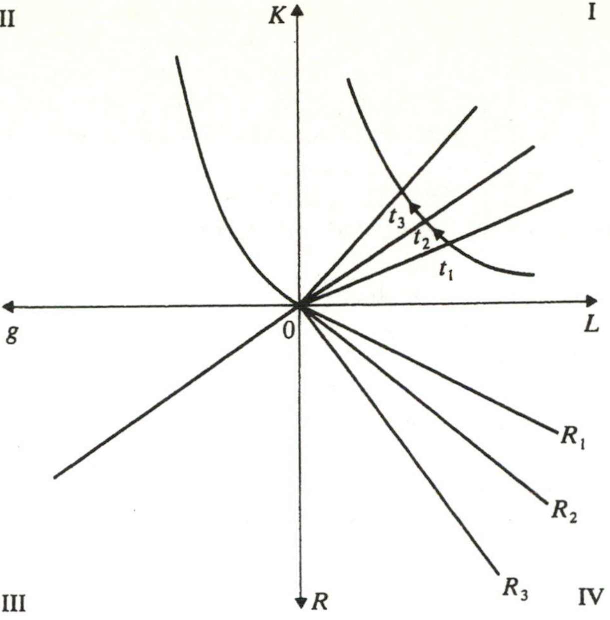

Figure 6.4

final product. The relationship between transfer of technology by the MNCs, growth and the environment can be stated with a diagram. Figure 6.4 illustrates this. Quadrant I shows the production isoquants against inputs of labour (L) and capital (K). It will be noted that, because we assume substitution possibilities between labour and capital, isoquants are convex to the origin. This assumption is made because we must assume that some range of substitution exists in the technology imported by LDCs.

Technical progress and an increase in capital intensity will lead to movements of the kind shown in the diagram, e.g. t_1 to t_2 to t_3 in quadrant I. Quadrant II shows the relationship between output growth (g) and capital, and an increase in intensity, the curve bending backwards due to lower productivity at high capital stock levels. Quadrant III assumes a linear, direct relationship between output growth and pollution R. However, the precise nature of this relationship is not always known. Quadrant IV postulates a relationship between pollution and population growth. This relationship requires some explanation. In general, we can expect high population levels to be associated with high pollution due either to increased waste disposal in absolute terms (assimilative capacity being fixed) or to congestion-style externalities. However, each capital–labour ratio in quadrant I is associated with a different pollution function since the amount of pollution is determined by the choice of technology as well as curve R_1 in quadrant IV, t_2 with curve R_2 and so on. The interesting point to emphasize is that an increase in capital intensity (without environmental safeguards) is likely to increase pollution (a social cost) and reduce the choice in favour of, say, capital-intensive techniques to maximize 'surplus' and growth. The size of social surplus is likely to fall given a rise in social cost.

Technical progress could be both 'embodied' and 'disembodied'. The technological gap of an 'embodied' type between DCs and LDCs can be due to the differences in the vintage of the respective production functions; when the technological gap occurs such that the same amount of inputs, say L and K, produce a higher amount of output in an advanced country in comparison with the LDC, the gap is 'disembodied'. The 'disembodied' gap can be measured by observing the difference between the two iso-products at given L/K ratios. The size of the 'embodied' technological gap is given by the difference in efficiency of capital use in the two countries. The 'disembodied' technical progress is usually reflected in superior knowledge, better quality of management, administration and marketing and greater strength in negotiations and bargaining.

It is obvious that to estimate marginal damage costs it is necessary to have some information about the costs of pollution. Several types of pollution indices are available depending upon the nature of the product/industry pollution.

In our analysis, it has been implicitly assumed that the transfer of technology mainly takes the form of transfers of capital goods from the DCs to the LDCs and this assumption is plausible. Moreover, it must be emphasized that a transfer of technology which is 'disembodied', i.e. which consists of the transfer of knowledge or skill, is rather unlikely to add to the problems of pollution. This explains why the transfer of 'disembodied' technology has not been taken into account in the analysis of environmental problems. It should be emphasized, however, that there are dangers in the global estimation of environmental costs and benefits because of the transfer of technology as LDCs are not a homogeneous group. There are considerable differences within the LDCs in their assimilative capacities, willingness to pay to protect their environment and in the types of technology they usually import. Also, the degree of pollution is not the same for all technologies. Hence, it is imperative to discuss the impact of the transfer of technology on growth and environment in a micro rather than a macro framework. It seems that country- and industry-wide studies may be quite useful in this regard to derive appropriate policies. Such an analysis should also be very rewarding in investigating the existence (if any) of *alternative technologies* wherever possible, the costs and benefits of developing and using such technologies, including the cost of pollution in the LDCs, and the areas where research and development activities should be concentrated (see Chapter 15).

The proportion of expenditure devoted by the MNCs and DCs to the invention of technologies which will minimize the social cost in the LDCs by taking care of their factor proportions and environmental hazards is pitifully low. It is both urgent and necessary for the DCs, the LDCs as well as the MNCs who are usually involved in the transfer of technology to direct research and development activities to invest in 'appropriate' (in both economic and social senses) technologies for the LDCs.

6.7 Private foreign investment and the transfer of technology to less developed countries

One of the crucial factors in promoting economic growth in the LDCs is technology. In one sense, here the LDCs of the present time have an advantage over the LDCs of the past because they can now choose from a 'menu' of technology available to them from past inventions and innovations. On the other hand, the availability of the menu of technology could pose problems for the LDCs. At the outset it is very important to decide the 'appropriate' technology for different LDCs. According to some economists, such appropriateness has to be judged in the light of the relative factor endowments and factor price ratios of the LDCs. Others have pointed out that such an argument would simply reinforce the *static* theory of comparative cost. Also, the existing factor prices may not reflect the true social costs and benefits because of distortions in the product and the factor markets. Next, it is necessary to analyse the effects of such a transfer of technology on the level of wages, employment and balance of payments of the LDCs. Fourth, the impact of transfer of technology on the pattern of income distribution of the LDCs should be examined carefully. Fifth, the transfer of technology may have important socio-political implications which could influence the power structure of the LDCs (Vernon 1971; Vaitsos 1974). Sixth, the transfer of technology has to be analysed along with the transfer of the product. It has been suggested that the choice of 'consumption' technology cannot be discussed in isolation from the problem of choice of product (Stewart 1974; OECD 1974; UNCTAD 1976b). It is true that where the final product is imported the foreign exchange cost can often be a heavy burden on LDCs. Where the technology is imported there may often be fears that technology 'dependence' is fostered and this could only be explained by the theory of imperialism (Radice 1975).

Thus, considerable debate has been observed about the transfer of technology and the role of MNCs regarding the net social benefits of such transfers to LDCs. It should be remembered that the transfer of technology and the role of the MNCs are two very complex issues. Notice that all MNCs are not involved in transfer of technology. It is equally noteworthy that since the technology-supplying industries, and even the final-product-supplying industries, are so often oligopolistic and multinational in character, technology dependence raises the further issue of the relationship between nation states and the giant corporations (Vernon 1971).

6.7.1 Transfer of technology and alternatives for less developed countries

To simplify the analysis of the effects of transfer of technology on the LDCs, let us list at the outset the options open to the LDCs. Thus the LDCs could

1 import the final product;
2 import the technology for producing the final product using
    (a) imported raw materials and
    (b) indigenous raw materials, or
    (c) adopt some combination of imported and indigenous raw materials;
3 import an intermediate product, using indigenous plant for the final mixing of the product;
4 develop indigenous technology similar to the imported technology;
5 develop indigenous alternative technology.

Most LDCs try to meet the gap between domestic demand and supply through imports of products of technology, or some combination of the two. Here the policies of the different governments are generally reflected regarding the import of the final product or technology. An LDC strongly in favour of import substitution would prefer to import technology rather than the final product. The difference in public policies could also reflect the differences in market size, expected economies of scale and the level of skill.

Some general remarks regarding transfer of technology in the LDCs are now in order. First, to the extent that LDCs suffer from the skill constraint to absorb technology, they would have to either import skilled labour or substitute capital for labour. Neither of them is inexpensive given the cost of training a highly skilled labourforce or the high cost of capital in LDCs. Second, many LDCs suffer from a high growth rate of population and consequent unemployment. If the transfer of technology is to contribute to the alleviation of the problem of unemployment, the burden of adjustment will fall to a substantial extent upon the industrial sector as the absorption of extra labour force will depend upon the growth of industrial output. Third, the market for technology is very imperfect and heterogeneous. It is generally characterized by monopolistic or oligopolistic situations with some MNCs operating on a large scale crossing national boundaries. Such monopolistic situations are accentuated with the systems of patents and export restrictions. The system of patents has the advantage of attracting FR; on the other hand, it gives rise to quasi-rents. Similarly, the parent firm, sometimes the big MNC, can stipulate many controls over the exports of the products produced by its wholly or partially owned subsidiary in an LDC. This, again, may adversely affect the benefits of foreign investment.

Fourth, the policy of import substitution via the imposition of tariffs or other forms of control generally leads to many forms of distortion. In such a situation, the transfer of technology is not the basic reason for such distortions though some of its effects could easily aggravate such distortions within the LDCs.

6.7.2 Types of transfer of technology

The transfer of technology can assume different forms. To summarize the major ones, we have:

1 *initiative* where the LDCs construct plants chiefly imitating the technology in the DCs;
2 *contractual* where an LDC obtains capital and know-how usually through licensing;
3 *joint ventures* where foreign firms collaborate with the home industries and could agree to minority holdings in assets;
4 *subsidiaries* where the foreign companies set up wholly or partly owned subsidiaries with the host country exercising little or some influence;
5 *turnkey projects* where the whole plant is transferred along with all the different stages of production to the point of final consumption through the marketing and distribution of the final products.

Contractual agreements, joint ventures and direct foreign investment are usually the major avenues of technological diffusion. Although direct foreign investment is probably the major route (UN 1975), contractual agreements also figure prominently as such agreements account for about 85 per cent of total foreign investment in India, 87 per cent in Korea and 66 per cent in Brazil. However, these data could be overestimated as the minority foreign equity participations are also included in the agreements. Joint ventures (with majority or minority participation) are also very common in LDCs as they account for 71 per cent of total foreign investments in Sri Lanka and 48 per cent of such investments in Colombia.

Foreign direct investment (FDI) is probably the most important way to effect transfer of technology and its impact is largely felt in the manufacturing sector. From the point of view of the technology-supplying country, FDI is preferable to other methods of transfer of technology if the nature of the product is important and durable, if the resources are available and if transfer of technology through other methods could give away secret information to potential rivals. The recipient country, usually anxious to be economically independent of the DCs, prefers collaborations or joint ventures usually with minority participation in the equity capital by the foreign companies. However, there are major problems in joint ventures and collaborations regarding division of operations, management and profits. Also, foreign firms apply export restriction clauses more to joint venture firms than to those wholly owned by them (Vernon 1971: 144). Nor do joint ventures rely less heavily on imports relative to their total needs than wholly owned subsidiaries. Thus, whether the local equity interest gives the recipient country any more effective control is sometimes doubted. Similarly, technical collaboration agreements do not always offer clear advantages (Balasubramanyam 1973: 35). For instance, foreign companies in the technical collaboration agreements rarely adjusted their production techniques in line with the Indian factor price ratios. It was only in joint ventures where the foreign firms had an equity interest that they modified technology to some extent. Interestingly enough, the Indian firms did not change the techniques either. From the point of view of the donor country, lack of control in management reduced the incentive to alter technology to the economic conditions of the LDCs. It could be argued that only a few LDCs have the administrative skill to choose 'appropriate' technology. But this is not always true (Streeten 1971). On the other hand, Singer and Shiavo-Campo (1970: 12) have advocated the establishment of an International Development Fund to support an agency which will help the LDCs in choosing an 'appropriate' technology. These different points of view highlight the necessity to undertake realistic appraisal of the difficult alternatives through a social cost–benefit analysis (Streeten 1971). Such a study could be facilitated by looking at the following benefits and costs of transfer of technology by MNCs.

6.7.3 Benefits and costs of transfer of technology to multinationals

The benefits of transfer of technology to the MNCs could be summarized as follows (see, in particular, Streeten 1973a).

1 The transfer of technology by the MNCs could ease the 'trade gap' in the LDCs.
2 When the transfer of technology takes the form of foreign direct investment (FDI) the difference between planned investment and planned savings could be reduced and to that extent the savings gap in the LDCs would also be minimized.
3 By supplying skilled personnel and labour the 'skill constraint' could also be eased.
4 To the extent that the MNCs contribute to the equity capital, the difference between planned expenditure on a project and domestic resources mobilized (say, through taxes or borrowing) would also be reduced.
5 The MNCs, through transfer of technology, transfer the knowledge, skill and entrepreneurship needed by the LDCs. Even if some of these technologies are highly sophisticated, they could be modified to suit the economic situations of the

LDCs. Also, the MNCs help the indigenous firms to establish contacts with the international capital markets.

6 The MNCs could increase competition in the economy of the host country and thereby improve the efficiency of the allocation of resources. In the absence of such competition it is argued that the indigenous firms, sheltered by protection, hardly feel the pressure of reducing cost by introducing technical progress and increase profitability.

7 The MNCs, through transfer of technology, could increase the level of output and employment within the recipient country. There is some evidence to suggest that MNCs had created about 5 million jobs in the LDCs by 1990 which accounted for about 0.8 per cent of their labour force. This is not insignificant if newly created jobs by the MNCs are taken as a proportion of the 54 million estimated to be in open unemployment in the LDCs. However, unemployment fell chiefly in a few industries and the degree of such reduction varied considerably. In some industries, technology was very capital intensive and the choice of alternative technology was rather small. In fact, in some extractive industries in Gabon employment actually fell from 14,800 to 8,400 between 1960 and 1970.

The major costs of the operations of MNCs can now be summarized as follows.

1 The MNCs usually transfer technology which tends to be capital rather than labour intensive and such a technology is regarded as generally 'inappropriate' for the labour-surplus LDCs.

2 Since technology is related to final product, it is contended that the transfer of technology from the DCs has led to the growth of 'Western' type 'elitist' consumption within a very small sector of the total market of the LDCs. A pattern of consumption which is related to the average standard of living of the DCs is not appropriate to similar standards in the LDCs because of the vast difference in their level of income.

3 The effects of the operations of the MNCs are not spread very evenly in the different sectors in the LDCs (e.g. between industry and agriculture or urban and rural areas). Further, the MNCs in the process of transferring technology have introduced or aggravated the distortions in the market of the LDCs. For instance, payment of high wages in the LDCs is a very good way of 'buying' industrial peace; on the other hand, such wages hardly reflect the social opportunity cost of labour in poor countries. They aggravate further the process of rural–urban migration as they accentuate the existing dichotomy between urban and rural wages. This, coupled with a higher capital intensity in the choice of technology, could lead to the aggravation of the inequalities in the distribution of income (Vaitsos 1974).

4 The MNCs with their vast resources could easily destroy their indigenous rivals. Far from promoting competition, the MNCs may actually make the market more imperfect by creating barriers to entry for their potential rivals.

5 If the MNCs supply inappropriate technology and/or products on the basis of resources partly obtained from the indigenous sources, then the diversion of such resources from socially desirable projects must be counted as a cost.

6 It is contended that the MNCs wield such strength with some host governments that they get away with large tax concessions, remittance facilities and royalties.

Such governments in LDCs grant input subsidies (e.g. low interest rates on capital) or output taxes or both. Coupled with the policy of protection pursued in many LDCs, profits extracted by the MNCs in such markets in LDCs are regarded as exploitative.

7 The existence of the MNCs in the LDCs could easily be the focus of political conflict between the DCs and the LDCs.

It is necessary to clarify certain major points regarding the 'exploitative' mechanism in the workings of the MNCs. Usually, such exploitative elements could be identified by looking at the difference between the price charged by the MNCs (P_m) and the world price (P_w) expressed as a proportion of the world price. More formally, the degree of 'overpricing' (P_o) will be given by the following formula:

$$P_o = \frac{P_m - P_w}{P_w}$$

Evidence suggests that the degree of overpricing is considerable in many LDCs. For example, in Chile, from fifty products for which the data for world prices were available, corresponding to the imports of thirty-nine firms, the figures shown in Table 6.2 were obtained (Vaitsos 1974).

In Colombia, in the field of pharmaceutical industries, the *average* rate of overpricing is an alarming 150 per cent. Such overpricing was found to be more among foreign-owned subsidiaries than local firms in Peru (Vaitsos 1974). Had all this overpricing been declared as profits, then the host country could have taxed away a part of these profits. Since such profits were not declared by the subsidiaries, the loss in revenue as well as in balance of payments must be considerable. Such losses would be higher if the crucial 'tie-in' clause in transfer of technology is also taken into account whereby the 'host' country is required to buy all the inputs from the same single source. If export restrictions operate, then the balance of payments losses would rise further.

The other element in the 'exploitative' mechanism is supposed to be patents. In theory, a patent reflects relative scarcity; its operation is supposed to ensure high price and profit and an inducement to further innovation. However, patents in LDCs are almost entirely of foreign origin. Also, a large proportion of these patents are now usually owned by the MNCs rather than by individuals. It should be noted that the ability of local firms in the LDCs to exploit the patents of the MNCs are severely

Table 6.2 Overpricing of imports, Chile

No of products	*Extent of overpricing (%)*
11	0
9	1–30
14	31–100
12	101–500
2	< 500

restrained partly because of the huge size of the MNCs. Thus, in Peru, only 1 per cent of the total patents granted in all sectors were exploited between 1964 and 1970 (UNCTAD 1972b).

Next, the operation of the 'transfer pricing' system has raised considerable criticism about the role of the MNCs in the LDCs. The concept is devised to avoid true tax liabilities by understatement of the 'real' profit level. Such understatement would take place because of 'transfer pricing' or the system within which the prices of goods (say, the output of one subsidiary flowing as an input to the other) passing between affiliated companies in different countries can be adjusted in a manner which enables a shift of financial resources from one country to another. Thus should the rate of taxes be higher in B than A, it pays the MNCs to overprice these transactions in B and shift profits to A, and should tariffs be higher in country B, then instead of overpricing these exports from B, it is more lucrative to underprice imports from the subsidiary into country B.

Transfer pricing is clearly a useful instrument to manipulate in those LDCs which impose restrictions on the remittance of profits and royalties. Similarly, the transfer-pricing mechanism could be used for the purpose of exchange rate speculation. For example, in an economy facing serious and chronic balance of payments deficits, the MNCs could use the transfer-pricing mechanism to shift profits out of such a country. Clearly, the implications of the transfer-pricing mechanism are quite serious from the viewpoint of LDCs.

6.7.4 Some policies to deal with the problems of transfer of technology and multinationals

In an ideal world, if all governments could get together and tax the MNCs jointly, then the dangers of transfer pricing or overpricing would be considerably reduced. Unfortunately, such a solution is hardly applicable in the real world. Hence, in an imperfect world, it is possible to suggest only some second-best remedies as follows.

1 Since evidence suggests that the LDCs are unlikely to alter the nature of technology developed mainly in the DCs simply by altering the factor price ratios, it is necessary to introduce a package of measures for increasing the competitive environment within the economy. Most empirical studies suggest that the MNCs are likely to choose the more appropriate technology for the LDCs whenever they face a more price-elastic demand curve for their product (UN 1974). This clearly implies the necessity to develop a more competitive economy.
2 Since indigenous entrepreneurs are likely to be weak rivals of the MNCs, governments in the LDCs could take measures to increase the countervailing power of the indigenous firms, through appropriate fiscal and monetary policies.
3 Within LDCs, inconsistencies could easily be observed in the policies pursued by the different ministries. For instance, the Department of Employment may be interested to maximize job opportunities while the Department of Industry could be anxious to import the most sophisticated and highly capital-intensive technology without due regard to the employment implications. The removal of such inconsistencies should be helpful to induce the MNCs to choose more appropriate technology for the economy.

4 Trade in selective second-hand capital goods could be encouraged by choosing suitable policies of tax subsidies. Here due care must be taken with regard to the availability of spare parts, servicing facilities and the period within which such machinery could be obsolete. It must be emphasized that here the choice may not be too great.

5 Governments facing a surplus-labour but capital-scarce situation should try to alter the existing factor price ratios between wages and interest rates in a manner which would reflect the real social opportunity costs of inputs. Since in most LDCs capital is generally underpriced as evidenced in low interest rates and wages are overpriced (given high unemployment, open or disguised), there is an important case for increasing interest rates and providing wage subsidies.

6 More resources should be spent on research and development to promote appropriate indigenous technology or to adapt imported technology to suit the local conditions. In most LDCs expenditure on research and development for developing indigenous technology is a very small proportion of the national income.

7 The host country should try to obtain different items of technology separately rather than in a 'package'. Such 'unpackaging' will tend to reduce the exploitation element in the transfer-price mechanism.

8 Protectionist policies in many LDCs provide a 'safe' market for the MNCs as well as domestic monopolies. Such tariff structures ought to be reviewed to foster greater competition. Although a tariff inflates the profits of the subsidiaries of the MNCs, it is not always a necessary condition for the establishment of such subsidiaries partly because they could be set up to take some special advantage of the economic conditions of the LDCs, e.g. low wages, and the gap between wages in the DCs and the LDCs (Posner 1961), or partly because of the nature of innovation, adaptation and export of a successful product in its different stages (i.e. the 'product life cycle' hypothesis, see Vernon 1966). At a more mature stage of the product which could be successfully imitated in the DCs, subsidiaries could be set up in the LDCs to take advantage of low average costs because of low wages and low cost of raw materials and the finished product could be exported from the subsidiary back to the country of origin or to other export markets. However, the 'product cycle' or the 'wage gap' theory does not explain why some vertically integrated MNCs are set up in LDCs with low capital still often using labour-intensive techniques (Helleiner 1973).

9 The MNCs should be induced to participate in training local people in co-ordination with the government. Also, local participation in management could remove some of the suspicions regarding the operations of the MNCs.

10 Greater information should be spread regarding the availability of technology, Here the international agencies (e.g. UNIDO, UNCTAD) could provide valuable guidelines to the LDCs.

11 Major criticisms of the different types of mechanisms used by the MNCs in the transfer of technology emanate because of the utmost secrecy observed in their financial and technical operations. One of the best ways to tackle the many criticisms and suspicions with regard to the workings of the MNCs would be to remove much of the secrecy, provide more relevant information and enable others to carry out more objective social cost–benefit analysis regarding the role of the MNCs in the transfer of technology in LDCs.

6.8 Special drawing rights and the 'link'

Special drawing rights (SDRs) were created by the IMF in July 1969, chiefly to meet the international liquidity crisis. This event could also be looked at as an important element of the 'New International Economic Order'. SDRs are 'paper' gold and they augment the volume of international liquid reserves. Originally an SDR account worth US$3.5 billion was set up. By 1972, its value rose to about $9.5 billion. Since 1 July 1974 the value of the SDR account is given every day by a 'basket' of sixteen major currencies. The functions of the SDR units are the same as those under gold and stable dollar standards. The SDRs are *liquid;* they are *convertible* in any other currency; their value is *stable;* they can be used as a *medium of exchange* to *settle international transactions.* It is easily seen that the SDRs can be regarded as the type of international currency which Keynes had in mind when he advocated the idea of issuing Bancors through an international clearing bank. The basic features of such a currency would be to promote international *liquidity, stability* and *confidence* in the international monetary system. The creation of SDRs has helped to achieve some of these objectives. Indeed, in some ways, the SDRs as reserve assets could be regarded as superior to gold holdings. For instance, the supply of SDRs could be augmented to meet an increased demand for international liquidity while the supply of gold is inelastic. Since the value of the SDRs is linked to an international basket of major currencies, the degree of fluctuation in their value is likely to be much less than for any other single currency. Just like gold, SDRs could be held as a store of value or spent to settle net deficits in international trade. The action of an individual country would not diminish the value of SDRs though this could easily happen with gold. As an international asset SDRs are durable: unlike, say, the dollar or pound they will not disappear if one country spends them, say, in the United States or UK. Indeed, if India spends SDRs to acquire goods from the UK the SDR *earnings* by the UK will *rise*. The SDRs are practically permanent assets because they will disappear only under the extreme assumption of their collective cancellation.

6.8.1 The principle of distribution of special drawing rights

Given the importance of the creation of SDRs as an international reserve asset, their distribution has attracted considerable attention, particularly in the LDCs. The existing principle allows the DCs (twenty-five) to obtain about $7.5 billion while ninety-three or more LDCs (with a huge population) can obtain only about $2.5 billion. This is because the SDRs are allocated on the basis of a country's quota with the IMF. Since the quota of the DCs is much greater than that of the LDCs, it is understandable that the DCs get a much larger proportion of the SDRs. This principle of distribution has caused resentment in the LDCs. Although the original quota with the IMF was fixed in line with a country's economic strength, it is undeniable that such quotas hardly reflect the needs of the poor countries. This apart, several other criticisms could be levelled at the present criterion for distributing the SDRs (Haan 1971).

1 The existing principle fails to economize the amount of reserves to be set up. SDRs could be accumulated indefinitely and eventually 'dehoarded' by a single country without any effective collective supervision.

2 Although the adjustment costs incurred by the LDCs (e.g. deflation and unemployment) in general are higher than those incurred by the DCs, the present system of SDR distribution does not take into account the distribution of adjustment costs *in proportion* to their disequilibria (Cohen 1966).
3 Since the global distribution of income and wealth is far from being equal, it may be argued that the collective saving in the form of SDRs should accrue to the LDCs in proportion to their needs (say, on a *per capita* basis) rather than on the basis of existing quotas.
4 To distribute the SDRs on the basis of quotas is to accept the static arguments for initial quota allocation among different countries with total disregard of the dynamic changes that have taken place so far in the world economy. This is considered unacceptable.
5 Triffin argues that 'internationally agreed SDRs should serve internationally agreed purposes' and thus SDR distribution on the ground of quotas is regarded as 'morally repugnant, economically wasteful and politically unviable' (Triffin 1971).

From these criticisms, it is clear that the existing principle of SDR distribution should be changed considerably from the standpoint of global redistribution of income and the needs of the LDCs. However, global redistribution of income is a noble principle which is rather difficult to achieve in practice, given the nature of present international relations. But if one of the major objectives of the international institutions is to establish a fairer system of existing international assets, then the present principle of SDR distribution on the basis of quotas is rendered very weak.

6.8.2 The link between special drawing rights and foreign resources

The idea of linking the SDRs to assist development plans and projects in the LDCs has received considerable attention (see Bauer 1973; Bird 1976; Helleiner 1974; Johnson 1972, 1977; Kahn 1973; Machlup 1968; Maynard 1973; Scitovsky 1966; Thirlwall 1976a; Triffin 1971; UNCTAD 1965; Williamson 1973). The main arguments for and against the 'link' could be summarized as follows (see, in particular, Maynard 1973).

Arguments in favour of the 'link':

1 Linking of the SDRs to aid development projects at a minimum cost would enable the LDCs not to resort to painful adjustment procedures (e.g. deflation, unemployment) to rectify persistent difficulties in their balance of payments.
2 The 'link' will ensure a smooth *long-term* flow of development finance along with global growth of output and trade.
3 When the 'link' would operate through an international agency, the delays in bilateral negotiations would be avoided.
4 The volume of *untied multilateral* flow of foreign resources is likely to rise in the event of a 'link' in such a way as to reduce the balance of payments and reserve costs of the donor countries substantially.

Arguments against the 'link':

1 Development finance and creation of international liquidity are regarded as two separate issues which are designed to realize separate objectives. But this criticism is not very compelling because the development within the LDCs could be achieved by the use of SDRs and no serious damage is likely to be inflicted on the international monetary system if one instrument (SDR creation) attains two objectives (meeting the shortage of international liquidity and aiding the development of the LDCs).
2 It is argued that since the SDRs are reserve monetary assets they should not be used for the transfer of real resources from the DCs, nor to finance spending within the LDCs. To the extent that deficits are historically financed by the creation of new money this argument loses some force. However, it is important to control the money supply firmly, particularly because in the LDCs supply tends to be rather inelastic.
3 The 'link' is supposed to be inflationary. This is a more serious criticism to the extent that the claims of the LDCs on the real resources of DCs could not be met without paying a high cost. Critics argue that most DCs try to acquire international reserve assets via export surpluses which does involve transfer of real resources. To the extent that the DCs have the capacity to meet demand, inflation is unlikely to occur. Further, the amount of SDR creation is so negligible as a proportion of total FR flow to LDCs that its additional impact is likely to be small – although it is sometimes maintained by the critics of the link scheme that the present global inflation is partly the result of too much international liquidity rather than too little (Johnson 1977). Here, it should be pointed out that the major reason for global inflation was the high rise in oil price in 1973–4 and again in 1978–9, not the creation of SDRs. Notice that the LDCs do not obtain SDRs simply to raise their demand and transfer of resources depends upon the net *use* rather than the allocation of SDRs. Some LDCs may decide to *accumulate* SDRs to guard themselves against uncertainties and evidence of SDR use by the LDCs up to 1977 seems to support this statement (see IMF 1970–82). Also it has been well argued that

> the burden on non-reserve currency countries implied by the transfer of real resource to LDCs through the link would be greater than in the pre-SDRs situation; the transfer would be made to the LDCs rather than to gold producers and reserve currency countries. The need for these countries to pursue appropriate demand management policies to make available the real resources for obtaining an increase in foreign exchange reserve would be no different.
> (Maynard 1973; see also Machlup 1968)

4 It is contended that in the presence of the 'link' DCs which offer foreign resources to LDCs will cut their individual or collective offer. This argument is difficult to accept, logically or empirically. To the extent that the allocation of SDRs is free of resource cost, some DCs may actually be induced to offer more.
5 The link scheme is sometimes criticized as undemocratic as its burden could be distributed over the taxpayers of the DCs without their assent. This point is also

very weak as it could be directed against all forms of untied or even tied aid which are not wholly effective.

6 It is maintained that link would reduce the confidence in SDRs as an asset. Further, the LDCs will be induced to put pressure upon the IMF to create more SDRs than would be indicated by the principles of international monetary policies. Neither of these two objections seems to be sound. The SDRs are safeguarded by the principle of acceptance; also no country is allowed to *accumulate* the SDRs by more than thrice the amount of its initial allocation or *spend* more than 70 per cent of its allocation. Moreover, when 85 per cent of the voting power in the IMF rests with the DCs, it is difficult to see how effective the pressure of LDCs on the IMF could be.

On balance, it seems that the arguments against the link are not very compelling. Indeed, it could be pointed out that if one of the major objectives of international monetary policy is to set up a fairer system of distribution of international assets on the basis of *needs,* then the arguments against the link clearly become rather weak. As regards the inflationary effect of the link, it can be mentioned that such an effect is likely to be smaller in comparison with, say, the dollar standard because, in the case of the link, collective supervision of liquidity will replace the decision made by a single country, say the United States. Further, the link may actually economize on SDR creation because, once the DCs are under pressure to 'earn' the SDRs by increasing their share in the world export market, they would be obliged to hold down the prices (Thirlwall 1976a).

The link could be developed in different ways. A *direct* link can be established by directly allocating more SDRs to the LDCs which would be greater than their long-run demand for reserves. This would imply, *inter alia,* an increase in LDCs' quotas with the IMF. The link could be *organic* if the SDRs are allocated to the LDCs through, say, an International Development Agency (IDA) for financing development programmes. Any DCs which would export to the LDC will earn SDRs in the credit account of the IDA while the LDCs' account will be debited by the value of such imports from the DC.

The link could be *inorganic* if the DCs decide to contribute voluntarily to any multilateral agency providing FR to the LDCs with every new allocation of the SDRs. In comparison with other forms of link, this plan has some major defects. For instance, since the scheme is voluntary, some DCs may decide not to provide anything. Also, if a DC, say the United States, suffers from a balance of payments deficit, it may decide not to contribute to the multilateral fund. It appears that either a *direct* or an *organic* link would be superior to an inorganic link.

6.8.3 Empirical evidence about the allocation, use and resource transfer of special drawing rights

Empirical evidence available so far provides some idea of the allocation, use and resource transfer of SDRs. On the basis of net acquisition of SDRs by the DCs and net use by the LDCs, Helleiner has argued that real resources were transferred from the DCs to the LDCs between 1970 and 1973. Out of the total allocation of $2,348 million SDRs by July 1973, the LDCs taken together used $835 million. By this time, the allocation to the DCs was $6,967 million and their net use was $308 million

(Helleiner 1974). It is true that the system of allocation and use of SDRs has resulted in an informal link between SDRs and aid, but the use of net acquisition data of the LDCs could be quite misleading for showing accurately the extent of such a link (Bird 1976). The permanent *potential* real resource gain over a period (G_p) should be equivalent to 70 per cent of the initial allocation of SDRs (A) minus interest charges for full *potential* SDRs net use (I). Thus

$$G_p = \frac{70}{100} Q(A) - I$$

where Q is the value of the quota. Notice that in the above equation G varies directly with Q and A and inversely with I. If r is the interest rate charged to *actual* net users of SDRs then I and r would vary directly. However, the *actual* real resource gain (G_a) should be equivalent to quota allocation of the SDRs $Q(A)$ minus the transfer to the general account of the IMF (T_g) to pay some charges or for repurchases and the proportion of SDRs which is to be added to reserves (Z). More formally,

$$G_a = Q(A) - T_g - Z$$

Helleiner assumed unrealistically that T_g or Z or both are equal to zero so that $G_a = G_p$. In practice, it turned out that $T_g = \$527.5$ million and $Z = \$1{,}512.8$ million by the end of July 1973, and therefore, recalculating Helleiner's figure, we obtain $G_a = \$307.7$ million. Thus, the overestimation of the actual resource transfer by Helleiner is wholly accounted for by the transfer to the general account by the LDCs (Bird 1976).

The use of the SDRs could be explained by both demand and supply factors. Assuming that the supply of SDRs is exogenous and given by the allocation of SDRs, the demand use of SDRs (S) could be stated in a simple form as follows (Leipziger 1975):

$$S = S(B_{t-1}, \mathrm{DR}, G, A)$$

where B_{t-1} is the net deficit in balance of payments with one-year lag since delays are involved in actual payments following trade flows; DR is the reserve variable expressed as the change in non-SDR reserves over the past year; G is the foreign exchange to gold ratio in a country's portfolio and A is the SDR allocation to a country in millions of US dollars.

In theory, if it is expected that

$$\frac{\partial S}{\partial B_{t-1}} > 0 \quad \frac{\partial S}{\partial \mathrm{DR}} < 0 \quad \frac{\partial S}{\partial G} \gtrless 0$$

(to test whether the SDRs are substitutes for either gold or foreign exchange) and $\partial S/\partial A > 0$. Linear least squares regression for forty-three LDCs in 1971 yielded the following equation (Leipziger 1975):

$$\begin{aligned} S &= 4.57 + 0.44A + 0.05B_{t-1} - 0.06\mathrm{DR} + 0.002G \\ &\quad\ (1.65)(7.97) \quad (3.24) \quad (-3.91) \quad (0.004) \\ \bar{R}^2 &= 0.63 \end{aligned}$$

(The figures in parentheses show the relevant t values.)

As hypothesized, most of the explanatory variables except G have the right signs and the estimated coefficients are statistically significant at 99 per cent confidence levels. The proportion of explained variation is 63 per cent and this is not very high. However, when the LDCs are divided between the Latin American and other LDCs, such a model fared well for the Latin American countries though it failed to explain very well the SDRs' use by the other LDCs. This is illustrated in the following two regression equations (Leipziger 1975):

Latin America:

$$S = 0.58 + 0.006B_{t-1} - 0.10\text{DR} + 0.11G$$
$$(11.64)^{**}\ (4.63)^{**}\ (-8.71)^{**}\ (2.45)^{*}$$
$$\bar{R}^2 = 0.89 \quad n = 19$$

Other LDCs:

$$S = 4.74 + 0.38A + 0.004B_{t-1} + 0.02\text{DR} - 0.09G$$
$$(1.54)(6.76)^{**}\ (1.73)^{**}\ (1.01)(-1.33)$$
$$\bar{R}^2 = 0.70 \quad n = 24$$

where ** indicates significance at the 95 per cent confidence level or better and * indicates significance at the 90 per cent confidence level or better; n is the number of observations.

The Chow test (Chow 1960) indicates that the determinants of the use of SDRs by the Latin American and the other LDCs are significantly different (the calculated F value being 9.12). Thus, although the above model has some interesting features, it fails to explain adequately the determinants of the SDRs' use by 'other' LDCs. Further, it is not very clear why SDR allocation has been dropped as an explanatory variable in the equation for the Latin American countries. Thus, more caution and further research are needed to analyse the pattern of SDRs' use by the LDCs. Since the LDCs are not a homogeneous group, it may be necessary to carry out country- or region-wide (within which LDCs show similar characteristics) studies to obtain more unbiased estimates by avoiding the problem of linear aggregation.

The 'link' is an important and useful idea for establishing a 'new international economic order'. Most of the arguments against the link are not very compelling. Internationally supervised, the scheme has considerable promise to assist the LDCs in their efforts to achieve a better standard of living. As Williamson observes:

> The international community has few instruments to improve the world distribution of income, and therefore it should utilize such opportunities as arise. One of these is the seigniorage resulting from the production of fiduciary reserve assets. There is a long and unfortunate tradition in economics of dismissing this type of argument just because it involves a value judgment additional to that embodied in the Pareto criterion. The degree of egalitarianism needed to justify preference for the link rather than neutrality is minimal, given the existing facts on world income distribution.
>
> (Williamson 1973: 278)

6.9 Foreign aid and economic growth

In theory, foreign aid should raise both consumption and investment in a developing country. Figure 6.5 illustrates. Without any foreign aid, an LDC can produce consumption and investment goods along the production possibility frontier TT′. The indifference curves in the figure define community tastes and preferences. If there is no inflow of FR, the optimal production of consumption and investment goods will occur at E where the social indifference curve I_1 is tangent to TT′. The economy produces C_1 of consumer goods and K_1 of capital goods. With the inflow of FR, line TT′ shifts to T_1T'' as the lending country offers EB of foreign 'aid'. With extra FR, optimal production now occurs at E′, i.e. the new point of tangency between T_1T'' and I_2. Consumption in the borrowing country rises to C_2 and investment rises to K_2. Hence, of the total foreign aid EB, EE_1 is invested and $E'E_1$ is consumed. However, if the economy has a very high preference for consumption, then most of the foreign aid could be consumed, i.e. points to the right of E_1, and as such the country's future investment will suffer. Note that some types of aid, e.g. food aid, could increase consumption rather than investment and project aid is usually designed to raise investment rather than consumption.

In the traditional Harrodian model discussed in Chapter 2 where $g = s/v$, i.e. the GDP growth rate g is given by the savings ratio s divided by the capital–output ratio v, an increase in foreign savings should raise the growth rate of the borrowing country by increasing its rate of investment. For some less developed countries like Bangladesh and Nepal in Asia and Mali and Senegal in Africa, foreign aid is a significant proportion of the GDP of these economies and thus the flow of FR should have an important impact on their growth rates. For countries like China and India, FR comprise only a small proportion of their GDP and hence the impact of FR may not be very high.

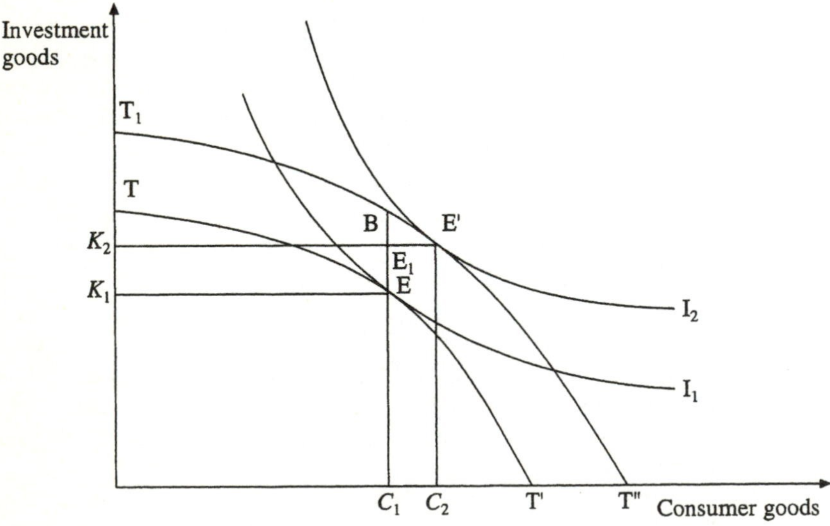

Figure 6.5 Foreign aid and economic growth

In the 1970s it was argued that the flow of FR had a positive effect on real output growth rate g in LDCs (Papanek 1972). The regression equations used in such studies were rather simple and can be stated as follows:

$$g = a_1 + a_2 \mathrm{FR}$$
$$a_2 > 0$$

As long as the value of a_2 is positive and significant, it was claimed that FR had an important positive role to play in stimulating economic growth. The other simple test that has been used to analyse the favourable effect of FR on economic growth rate is to assume a positive relationship between savings and FR. It is implicitly assumed that all savings S are invested and thus any incremental savings due to a rise in FR should increase the rate of investment and economic growth.

However, many economists (e.g. Bauer 1981; Griffin and Enos 1970; Mosley 1980; Mosley *et al.* 1987, 1991) argue that the flow of FR to LDCs may not increase domestic savings. Let us assume that

$$S/Y = b_1 + b_2 \mathrm{FR} + b_3 Z + v_t$$
$$b_2 > 0$$

where S is total savings, Y is real income, the Z are other variables which affect savings, FR is foreign resources and v is an error term.

In empirical analysis during the 1970s and 1980s, it turned out that $b_2 < 0$ and statistically significant. The implication of this type of result (on cross-section and time series) is that the flow of FR should *reduce* domestic savings! Indeed, some have observed a negative impact of FR on the economic growth rate of LDCs (Mosley *et al.* 1987).

The explanation of such negative effect of FR on growth rate is not difficult to understand. For one thing, LDCs are not homogeneous countries. Within the LDCs, there are substantial differences in the real *per capita* income levels as well as in absorptive capacity (measured by the levels of skill, administration, education, infrastructure etc.). When the LDCs are disaggregated according to the different levels of *per capita* income, it has been observed that FR could have a positive effect on growth rate for the *least* developed countries. Others point out that a rise in the flow of FR actually raises consumption at the expense of savings/investment and hence the overall growth rate suffers. A rise in domestic consumption due to a rise in FR actually raises imports and adds to the balance of payments problems of many LDCs. Moreover, many governments of LDCs use FR as a method to increase government consumption. If such public expenditures are unproductive, then clearly FR will have an adverse effect on economic growth.

Foreign aid can increase domestic economic growth rate by supplementing domestic savings and/or by releasing the constraint on foreign exchange reserves. In the aid literature (see, for example, Griffin 1967; Mosley 1980), the effectiveness of aid (A) is usually measured by testing the significance of the coefficient of the aid variable in the following single-equation model:

$$\mathrm{d}Y = a + bA + cS + eI_{\mathrm{f}}$$

where Y is domestic national income, A is aid inflows, S is domestic savings and I_f is inflows of private foreign capital.

The above equation has been expanded and tested by Mosley *et al.* (1987) to include *changes* in the literacy rate per annum (dL) and in export value (dX). Thus we have

$$\mathrm{d}Y = a_0 + bA + cS + eI_f + a_1\,\mathrm{d}X + a_2\,\mathrm{d}L$$

If the coefficient b is positive and significant, then aid is supposed to have a strong impact on domestic national income. As indicated above, the empirical estimates of b turned out to be *negative* and insignificant in many cases (see Mosley *et al.* 1987).

In this type of model specification, the aid variable is generally treated as given (exogenous). As regards the simultaneity problem, the point to remember is that aid could be an *endogenous* variable determined by the level of economic development, the rate of economic growth, the stock of human capital and the nature of the physical infrastructure of the recipient country. Thus, the causality could run from economic growth to aid rather than the other way round. The ordinary least squares estimates generally used in testing the aid–growth relationship could be misleading if aid and growth are simultaneously determined. The existence of such a relationship is quite plausible and a proper specification of the model may yield different results. In addition, the suppression of the constant term a in the estimated aid–growth equation could make the results dubious (see for example White 1991). A different model specification has actually shown that aid could exercise a positive and significant effect on the growth of some LDCs (White 1991).

Interestingly, the 'crowding out' effect of aid on private sector investment, observed as strong in the 1960s, disappeared completely in the 1970s in most LDCs (Mosley *et al.* 1987, 1991). Thus, it is difficult to discern any effect of aid on private sector investment once other determinants of investment (e.g. rate of return, cost and availability of credit, state of infrastructure etc.) have been taken into account. Hence the theory that the inflow of foreign aid generally strengthens the power of a regime which then retards the flow of private capital seems to have lost its force. This is not to deny that aid may not influence domestic national income, its growth rate and consumption through its influence on government *policies*. A corrupt government in a developing country, seeking to maximize its own 'utility function', can easily use aid money to expand non-productive expenditure, e.g. on military capability, corrupt bureaucracy and very inefficient parastatals. In such cases, the impact of aid on economic growth will be unsurprisingly negative.

Aid effectiveness sometimes depends on careful targeting of areas or projects in specific countries. It has been acknowledged that despite the absence of an overall and positive aid–growth correlation in India, aid inflows in the agricultural sector significantly helped to usher in the 'Green Revolution' in the late 1960s and early 1970s and to overcome India's acute problems of food security and famines. Such aid was utilized effectively apart from being targeted properly to specific areas in north-west India where irrigation facilities were available to reap the benefits of the new seeds–fertilizer revolution. The inflow of foreign aid to such specific rural areas helped India to import considerable amounts of new seeds and chemical fertilizers from abroad and increase yields of major food crops substantially within a short period.

As regards the impact of aid on domestic savings and investment, it has to be admitted that the determinants of domestic savings in LDCs are both economic (e.g. real income, real rate of interest, inflow of foreign capital, the expected rate of inflation etc.) and non-economic (e.g. family size, dependency ratio, social security and other welfare benefits, etc.). It would be interesting to endogenize domestic savings in LDCs (Stern 1989) and test the significance of the economic and non-economic factors including foreign aid.

The impact of foreign aid on overall economic growth rates of LDCs is expected to be different for different LDCs. More specifically, such effects will depend on:

1 the effective use of aid;
2 the state of economic development and its rate of growth;
3 the rates of return on investment;
4 the nature of the infrastructure and the availability of physical human capital;
5 the nature of economic regulation;
6 the political economy of the rent-seeking society (Krueger 1974).

Without a careful analysis of a complex set of dynamic socio-economic factors, it is difficult to draw a definitive conclusion about the real impact of foreign aid on LDCs.

Appendix 6.1 Less developed countries and world trade

Table A6.1.1 Direction of merchandise trade, 2000 (a) High-income importers (% of world trade)

Source of exports	*European Union*	*Japan*	*United States*	*Other industrial*	*All industrial*	*Other high income*	*All high income*
High-income economies	29.4	3.1	11.7	6.0	50.1	5.6	55.8
Industrial economies	27.9	2.1	9.8	5.7	45.4	4.3	49.7
European Union	22.3	0.6	3.4	2.0	28.3	1.5	29.7
Japan	1.2	–	2.3	0.3	3.8	1.4	5.2
United States	2.6	1.0	–	3.1	6.7	1.1	7.9
Other industrial economies	1.8	0.4	4.1	0.2	6.6	0.3	6.9
Other high-income economies	1.5	1.0	2.0	0.3	4.8	1.3	6.1
Low- and middle-income economies	6.0	2.3	7.0	0.8	16.1	4.2	20.3
East Asia and Pacific	1.7	1.7	2.3	0.4	6.1	2.3	8.4
Europe and Central Asia	1.7	0.0	0.1	0.1	1.9	1.1	3.0
Latin America and Caribbean	0.7	0.1	3.4	0.2	4.3	0.2	4.5
Middle East and N. Africa	1.0	0.3	0.4	0.1	1.8	0.3	2.1
South Asia	0.5	0.1	0.5	0.1	1.2	0.3	1.5
Sub-Saharan Africa	0.4	0.0	0.3	0.0	0.8	0.1	0.9
World	35.3	5.4	18.8	6.8	66.3	9.8	76.1

Table A6.1.1 Direction of merchandise trade, 2000 (b) Low- and middle-income importers (% of world trade)

Source of exports	*East Asia and Pacific*	*Europe and Central Asia*	*Latin America and Caribbean*	*Middle East and N. Africa*	*South Asia*	*Sub-Saharan Africa*	*All low and middle-income*	*World*
High-income economies	8.0	3.0	1.9	1.4	0.7	0.8	15.7	72.9
Industrial economies	4.2	2.9	1.8	1.3	0.4	0.7	11.2	63.2
European Union	1.0	2.5	0.6	0.8	0.2	0.5	5.7	35.9
Japan	1.7	0.1	0.2	0.1	0.1	0.1	2.2	7.5
United States	1.1	0.2	0.9	0.2	0.1	0.1	2.6	12.1
Other industrial economies	0.4	0.1	0.1	0.1	0.0	0.0	0.8	7.7
Other high-income economies	3.8	0.1	0.1	0.1	0.2	0.1	4.5	9.6
Low- and middle-income economies	2.6	1.7	1.1	0.6	0.5	0.4	6.9	27.1
East Asia and Pacific	1.6	0.2	0.2	0.2	0.2	0.1	2.6	11.1
Europe and Central Asia	0.2	1.3	0.0	0.1	0.0	0.0	1.7	4.8
Latin America and Caribbean	0.1	0.0	0.8	0.1	0.0	0.0	1.1	5.8
Middle East and N. Africa	0.5	0.1	0.0	0.1	0.1	0.0	0.9	3.1
South Asia	0.1	0.0	0.0	0.0	0.0	0.0	0.3	1.0
Sub-Saharan Africa	0.1	0.0	0.0	0.0	0.0	0.2	0.4	1.3
World	10.6	4.7	3.1	1.9	1.1	1.2	22.6	100.0

Source: World Bank 2002.

Table A6.1.2 Growth of merchandise trade, 1990–2000 (a) High-income importers (% p.a.)

Source of exports	*European Union*	*Japan*	*United States*	*Other industrial*	*All industrial*	*Other high income*	*All high income*
High-income economies	3.9	3.8	7.5	4.8	4.7	8.0	5.0
Industrial economies	3.7	2.5	7.4	4.7	4.5	7.6	4.7
European Union	3.7	2.9	7.4	2.4	4.0	8.2	4.2
Japan	2.9	–	4.7	0.7	3.7	7.5	4.6
United States	4.7	2.9	–	7.3	5.5	7.7	5.8
Other industrial economies	2.8	0.9	9.3	3.7	6.3	5.3	6.2
Other high-income economies	7.2	7.2	7.7	5.5	7.3	9.3	7.7
Low- and middle-income economies	8.7	7.6	13.2	10.6	10.3	13.5	10.9
East Asia and Pacific	12.9	9.4	13.5	13.2	12.0	10.3	11.5
Europe and Central Asia[a]	10.6	1.6	12.2	9.3	10.5	8.0	9.5
Latin America and Caribbean	3.2	1.1	16.0	11.0	11.8	11.2	11.8
Middle East and N. Africa	3.2	4.3	3.4	5.3	3.5	6.2	3.8
South Asia	7.6	2.6	14.0	9.2	9.4	12.7	9.9
Sub-Saharan Africa	4.7	10.0	6.6	4.6	5.6	21.3	6.2
World	4.4	5.1	9.2	5.3	5.7	9.0	6.0

Note: [a] Refers to 1993–2000.

Table A6.1.2 Growth of merchandise trade, 1990–2000 (b) Low- and middle-income importers (% p.a.)

Source of exports	*East Asia and Pacific*	*Europe and Central Asia*	*Latin America and Caribbean*	*Middle East and N. Africa*	*South Asia*	*Sub-Saharan Africa*	*All low and middle-income*	*World*
High-income economies	9.4	8.0	7.5	1.3	4.7	1.5	7.2	5.6
Industrial economies	8.3	7.9	7.5	1.1	2.9	1.1	6.2	5.1
European Union	7.3	9.0	6.4	1.0	3.5	0.8	5.7	4.4
Japan	8.8	−1.6	6.5	−1.6	1.4	−1.2	6.7	5.2
United States	9.2	3.9	9.0	3.0	1.5	3.8	7.5	7.0
Other industrial economies	6.4	1.2	4.9	1.3	4.1	3.3	4.4	6.0
Other high-income economies	10.9	12.7	8.0	3.3	9.6	5.4	10.3	9.1
Low- and middle-income economies	19.5	13.6	11.9	5.6	12.0	11.4	13.7	11.4
East Asia and Pacific	20.2	9.4	19.4	9.9	13.6	12.4	16.7	12.2
Europe and Central Asia[a]	3.4	10.4	8.4	2.5	6.0	8.7	8.6	9.2
Latin America and Caribbean	8.5	2.1	11.7	2.1	11.8	5.2	9.7	11.3
Middle East and N. Africa	20.6	−3.7	−2.2	1.2	7.7	7.2	7.1	4.8
South Asia	16.4	−6.6	28.1	7.4	12.3	15.3	7.5	9.1
Sub-Saharan Africa	23.8	5.2	16.3	5.7	18.7	11.9	14.3	8.0
World	11.6	7.9	8.9	2.1	6.6	3.8	8.3	6.5

Note: [a] Refers to 1993–2000.

Table A6.1.2 Balance of payments current account, 1990 and 2000 (US$ million)

	Goods and services						*Net*		*Current*		*Gross international*	
	Exports		*Imports*		*Net income*		*current transfers*		*account balance*		*reserves*	
Country	*1990*	*2000*	*1990*	*2000*	*1990*	*2000*	*1990*	*2000*	*1990*	*2000*	*1990*	*2000*
Afghanistan	–	–	–	–	–	–	–	–	–	–	638	–
Albania	354	704	485	1,499	−2	107	15	533	−118	−156	–	383
Algeria	13,462	22,359	10,106	9,842	−2,268	−3,075	333	–	1,420	–	2,703	13,556
Angola	3,992	7,945	3,385	6,195	−765	−1,843	−77	89	−236	−4	–	1,198
Argentina	14,800	30,934	6,846	32,722	−4,400	−7,482	998	289	4,552	−8,970	6,222	25,152
Armenia	–	447	–	966	–	53	–	188	–	−278	*1*	331
Azerbaijan	–	2,146	–	2,023	–	−346	–	73	–	−150	*0*	680
Bangladesh	1,903	6,611	4,156	9,060	−122	−221	802	2,672	−1,573	2	660	1,516
Belarus	*3,611*	7,980	*3,557*	8,257	*−1*	−42	*79*	157	*182*	−162	–	350
Benin	364	522	454	782	−25	−19	97	111	−18	−168	69	458
Bolivia	977	1,454	1,086	2,078	−249	−225	159	385	−199	−464	511	1,038
Bosnia & Herz	–	–	–	–	–	–	–	–	–	–	–	–
Botswana	2,005	*3,044*	1.987	*2,512*	−106	*−266*	69	*252*	−19	*517*	3,331	6,318
Brazil	35,170	64,469	28,184	72,739	−11,608	−17,884	799	1,522	−3,823	−24,632	9,200	33,008
Bulgaria	6,950	7,000	8,027	7,669	−758	−321	125	290	−1,710	−701	*670*	3,625
Burkina Faso	349	259	758	635	0	−39	332	350	−77	−65	305	244
Burundi	89	55	318	151	−15	−12	174	59	−69	−49	112	38
Cambodia	*314*	1,497	*507*	1,769	*-21*	−52	*120*	305	*−93*	−19	–	502
Cameroon	2,251	2,719	1,931	2,376	−478	−593	−39	97	−196	−153	37	212
Central African Rep.	220	110	410	149	−22	−12	123	51	−89	0	123	133
Chad	271	279	488	478	−21	−10	192	51	−46	−158	132	111
Chile	10,221	22,090	9,166	21,209	−1,737	−2,409	198	537	−485	−991	6,784	14,749
China†	57,374	279,562	46,706	250,688	1,055	−14,666	274	6,311	11,997	20,518	34,476	171,763
Hong Kong, China	100,413	244,004	94,084	236,311	0	2,766	–	−1,632	6,329	8,827	24,656	107,5060
Colombia	8,679	15,678	6,858	14,385	−2,305	−2,577	1,026	1,590	542	306	4,869	9,006
Congo, Dem. Rep.	2,557	–	2,497	–	−770	*−754*	−27	–	−738	*−583*	261	–
Congo, Rep.	1,488	2,714	1,282	1,332	−460	−839	3	–	−251	–	10	222
Costa Rica	1,963	7,628	2,346	7,265	−233	−1,176	192	*102*	−424	*−649*	535	1,318

Côte d'Ivoire	China	3,503	4,408	3,445	3,391	−1,091	−660	−181	−370	−1,214	−13	21
Croatia		–	8,651	–	9,597	–	−311	–	858	–	−399	*167*
Cuba		–	–	–	–	–	–	–	–	–	–	–
Czech Rep.		–	35,746	–	37,528	–	−752	–	298	–	−2,236	–
Dominician Rep.		1,832	8,964	2,233	10,852	−249	−1,041	371	1,902	−280	−1,026	69
Ecuador		3,262	5,987	2,519	4,998	−1,210	−1,412	107	1,352	−360	928	1,009
Egypt, Arab Rep.		9,151	15,975	13,710	22,756	−912	932	4,836	4,679	−634	−1,171	3,620
El Salvador		973	3,645	1,624	5,642	−132	−250	631	1,829	−152	−418	595
Eritrea		*88*	96	*278*	499	–	0	*171*	196	*−19*	−208	–
Estonia		*664*	4,791	*711*	5,040	*−13*	−204	*97*	138	*36*	−315	*198*
Ethiopia		672	984	1,069	1,960	−67	−60	220	701	−244	−335	55
Gabon		2,730	3,023	1,812	1,868	−617	−699	−134	−71	168	385	279
Gambia		168	262	192	321	−11	−5	59	15	23	−48	55
Georgia		–	1,136	–	1,410	–	13	–	100	–	−162	–
Ghana		983	2,403	1,506	3,339	−111	−108	411	631	−223	−413	309
Greece		13,018	29,440	19,564	41,727	−1,709	−885	4,718	3,352	−3,537	−9,820	4,721
Guatemala		1,568	3,892	1,812	5,584	−196	−226	227	868	−213	−1,049	362
Guinea		829	843	953	919	−149	−79	70	−10	−203	−165	*80*
Guinea-Bissau		26	70	88	106	−22	−13	39	–	−45	–	18
Haiti		318	530	515	1,333	−18	*−21*	193	*223*	−22	*−38*	10
Honduras		1,032	2,501	1,127	3,275	−237	−138	280	708	−51	−204	47
Hungary		12,035	31,618	11,017	31,948	−1,427	-1,574	787	410	379	−1,494	1,185
India		23,028	63,764	31,485	75,656	−3,753	−3,821	2,068	12,798	−10,142	−2,915	5,637
Indonesia		29,295	70,619	27,511	53,377	−5,190	−9,072	418	1,816	−2,988	7,986	8,657
Iran, Islamic Rep.		19,741	29,727	22,292	17,503	378	−200	2,500	621	327	12,645	–
Iraq		–	–	–	–	–	–	–	–	–	–	–
Israel		17,312	45,179	20,228	46,534	−1,975	−6,633	5,060	6,602	170	−1,416	6,598
Jamaica		2,217	3,580	2,390	4,340	−430	−336	291	821	−312	−275	168
Japan		323,692	528,751	297,306	459,660	22,492	57,623	−4,800	−9,831	44,078	116,883	87,828
Jordan		2,511	3,536	3,754	5,796	−215	−27	1,046	2,345	−411	59	1,139
Kazakhstan		*5,758*	10,751	*5,862*	8,705	*−175*	−1,179	*168*	207	*−111*	1,074	–
Kenya		2,228	2,741	2,705	3,768	−418	−133	368	922	−527	−238	236
Korea, Dem. Rep.		–	–	–	–	–	–	–	–	–	–	–
Korea, Rep.		73,295	205,645	76,360	192,499	−87	−2,421	1,149	680	−2,003	11,405	14,916
Kuwait		8,268	21,617	7,169	11,785	7,738	6,918	−4,951	−1,884	3,886	14,865	2,929
Kyrgyz Rep.		–	573	–	651	–	−80	–	82	–	−77	–
† Data for Taiwan,		74,175	167,907	67,015	160,457	4,361	4,468	−601	−2,602	10,920	9,316	77,653

Table A6.1.2 (continued)

	Goods and services											
	Exports		*Imports*		*Net income*		*Net current transfers*		*Current account balance*		*Gross international reserves*	
Country	*1990*	*2000*	*1990*	*2000*	*1990*	*2000*	*1990*	*2000*	*1990*	*2000*	*1990*	*2000*
Lao PDR	102	501	212	613	−1	−49	56	*240*	−55	*90*	8	144
Latvia	*1,090*	3,270	*997*	3,886	*2*	24	*96*	97	*191*	−494	–	919
Lebanon	511	2,141	2,836	6,228	622	932	1,818	90	115	−3,065	4,210	8,475
Lesotho	100	254	754	770	433	226	286	139	65	−151	72	418
Liberia	–	–	–	–	–	–	–	–	–	–	*1*	0
Libya	11,469	*6,813*	8,960	*4,914*	174	*289*	−481	*−204*	2,201	*1,984*	7,225	13,730
Lithuania	–	5,109	–	5,833	–	−194	–	243	–	−675	*107*	1,363
Macedonia, FYR	–	1,620	–	2,233	–	−45	–	551	–	−107	–	460
Madagascar	471	1,188	809	1,520	−161	−42	234	113	−265	−260	92	285
Malawi	443	487	549	934	−80	−83	99	6	−86	−523	142	250
Malaysia	32,665	111,261	31,765	94,024	−1,872	−9,282	102	−1,728	−870	*12,606*	10,659	29,844
Mali	420	705	830	1,060	−37	−28	225	–	−221	–	198	381
Mauritania	471	372	520	428	−46	−19	86	165	−10	90	59	*228*
Mauritius	1,722	2,630	1,916	2,699	−23	−28	97	64	−119	−33	761	914
Mexico	48,805	180,210	51,915	191,895	−8,316	−13,466	3,975	6,994	−7,451	−18,157	10,217	35,577
Moldova[a]	–	640	–	990	–	72	–	157	–	−121	*0*	230
Mongolia	493	607	1,096	772	−44	−3	7	*74*	−640	*−52*	*23*	202
Morocco	6,239	10,453	7,783	12,538	−988	−873	2,336	2,483	−196	−475	2,338	5,017
Mozambique	229	689	996	1,492	−97	−192	448	231	−415	−764	*233*	744
Myanmar	641	1,840	1,182	2,787	−61	−70	77	366	−526	−651	410	286
Namibia	1,220	*1,745*	1,584	*1,889*	37	*−42*	354	*390*	28	*204*	*50*	260
Nepal	379	1,279	761	1,782	71	34	60	175	−251	−293	354	989
Nicaragua	392	953	682	1,986	−217	−201	202	741	−305	−493	166	493
Niger	533	282	728	424	−54	−15	14	−10	−236	−168	226	80
Nigeria	14,550	23,047	6,909	14,124	−2,738	−3,287	85	1,348	4,988	6,983	4,129	*6,485*
Oman	5,577	11,602	3,342	6,094	−254	−705	−874	−1,456	1,106	3,347	1,784	2,460
Pakistan	6,217	9,575	9,351	11,762	−966	−2,018	2,210	1,997	−1,890	−2,208	1,046	2,087
Panama	4,438	7,666	4,193	8,164	−255	−612	219	177	209	−933	344	723

Papua N. Guinea	1,381	2,233	1,509	1,927	−103	−305	156	−9	−76	−8	427	326
Paraguay	2,514	2,801	2,169	3,307	2	32	43	175	390	−299	675	770
Peru	4,120	8,598	4,087	9,704	−1,733	−1,541	281	1,019	−1,419	−1,628	1,891	8,676
Philippines	11,430	41,468	13,967	36,465	−872	3,645	714	433	−2,695	9,081	2,036	15,035
Poland	19,037	46,294	15,095	57,210	−3,386	−1,461	2,511	2,380	3,067	−9,997	4,674	27,469
Portugal	21,554	33,166	27,146	45,544	−96	−2,041	5,507	3,406	−181	−11,012	20,579	14,262
Puerto Rico	–	–	–	–	–	–	–	–	–	–	–	–
Romania	6,380	12,133	9,901	14,701	161	−281	106	860	−3,254	−1,359	1,374	4,848
Russian Federation	*53,883*	115,200	*48,915*	62,290	*−4,500*	−11,154	*0*	90	*468*	41,846	–	27,656
Rwanda	145	131	359	403	−17	−15	145	281	−86	−7	44	191
Saudi Arabia	47,445	82,369	43,939	53,003	7,979	480	−15,637	−15,511	−4,152	14,336	13,437	20,847
Senegal	1,453	1,337	1,840	1,732	−129	−113	153	197	−363	−310	22	384
Sierra Leone	210	87	215	240	−71	−24	7	–	−69	–	5	51
Slovak Rep.	–	14,137	–	14,596	–	−355	–	120	–	−694	–	4,376
Slovenia	*7,900*	10,694	*6,930*	11,397	*−38*	−25	*46*	115	*978*	−612	*112*	3,196
Somalia	70	–	322	–	–	–	–	–	–	–	–	–
South Africa	27,742	36,522	21,016	32,818	−4,271	−3,247	−321	−926	2,134	−469	2,583	7,702
Sri Lanka	2,293	6,378	2,965	8,105	−167	−299	541	984	−298	−1,042	447	1,211
Sudan	532	1,892	1,453	1,921	−784	−1,264	407	319	−1,299	−974	11	*189*
Swaziland	658	885	768	1,098	59	77	102	96	51	−40	216	352
Syrian Arab Rep.	5,030	6,846	2,955	5,390	−401	−879	88	485	1,762	1,062	–	–
Tajikistan	*185*	800	*238*	839	*0*	−55	–	33	*−53*	−61	–	*56*
Tanzania	538	1,280	1,474	2,010	−185	−80	562	511	−559	−298	193	974
Thailand	29,229	81,817	35,870	71,652	−853	−1,381	213	586	−7,281	9,369	14,258	32,665
Togo	663	438	847	614	−32	−25	132	95	−84	−106	358	152
Trinidad and Tobago	2,289	4,769	1,427	3,823	−397	−610	−6	*22*	459	*−644*	513	1,403
Tunisia	5,203	8,607	6,039	9,311	−455	−942	828	824	−463	−821	867	1,871
Turkey	21,042	51,148	25,652	62,190	−2,508	−4,002	4,493	5,225	−2,625	−9,819	7,626	23,515
Turkmenistan	*1,238*	2,774	*857*	2,350	*0*	−177	*66*	166	*447*	412	–	*1,513*
Uganda	246	626	676	1,985	−77	−15	78	513	−429	−860	44	808
Ukraine	–	19,522	–	18,116	–	−942	–	1,017	–	1,481	*469*	1,477
United Arab Emirates	–	–	–	–	–	–	–	–	–	–	4,891	13,632
Uruguay	2,158	3,733	1,659	4,216	−321	−176	8	66	186	−593	1,446	2,776
Uzbekistan	–	3,383	–	2,962	–	−251	–	13	–	184	–	*1,242*
Venezuela, RB	18,806	34,272	9,451	19,746	−774	−1,204	−302	−211	8,279	13,111	12,733	15,899
Vietnam	1,913	17,107	1,901	17,344	−412	−597	49	1,341	−351	507	–	3,417

Table A6.1.2 (continued)

	Goods and services											
	Exports		*Imports*		*Net income*		*Net current transfers*		*Current account balance*		*Gross international reserves*	
Country	*1990*	*2000*	*1990*	*2000*	*1990*	*2000*	*1990*	*2000*	*1990*	*2000*	*1990*	*2000*
West Bank and Gaza	–	–	–	–	–	–	–	–	–	–	–	–
Yemen, Rep.	1,490	4,305	2,170	3,150	−372	−514	1,790	1,422	739	2,063	441	2,914
Yugoslavia, Fed. Rep.	–	–	–	–	–	–	–	–	–	–	–	–
Zambia	1,360	936	1,897	1,167	−437	−411	380	–	−594	–	201	245
Zimbabwe	2,012	2,101	2,001	1,991	−263	−242	112	–	−140	–	295	321
World	**4,252055 t**	**7,820,225 t**	**4,257,973 t**	**7,848,991 t**								
Low income	130,306	274,302	147,914	275,884								
Middle income	699,866	1,771,709	664,038	1,641,764								
Lower middle income	268,479	747,156	274,866	654,664								
Upper middle income	430,021	1,024,328	390,689	986,006								
Low and middle income	829,051	2,046,020	811,098	1,917,665								
East Asia and Pacific	239,776	817,861	240,892	730,851								
Europe and Central Asia	*187,852*	392,525	*187,180*	372,245								
Latin America and Carib	169,120	417,454	146,270	436,649								
Middle East and N. Africa	132,144	213,961	132,549	162,895								
South Asia	34,113	88,259	49,041	107,198								
Sub-Saharan Africa	81,284	116,295	74,679	106,577								
High income	3,419,212	5,774,700	3,432,886	5,933,098								
Europe EMU	1,530,965	2,256,837	1,495,268	2,215,062								

a. Includes Luxembourg.

Source: World Bank 2002.

Questions

1. What are the major criteria for distributing foreign resources for LDCs?
2. Explain carefully the strengths and weaknesses of the 'dual-gap' model.
3. How would you assess the gains and losses of investment by multinational corporations in LDCs?
4. What are the main types of technology transfer for LDCs?
5. What are the benefits and costs of technology transfer to LDCs?
6. Should there be a link between 'special drawing rights' (SDRs) and flow of foreign resources to LDCs?
7. Should LDCs receive foreign aid?

7 Industrialization, protection and trade policies

7.1 Major reasons for industrialization in less developed countries

Industrialization has been regarded as a major strategy for achieving a faster rate of economic growth and a higher standard of living in many LDCs. Several reasons are advanced to justify such a strategy. First, it is contended that economically advanced countries are usually more industrialized than the economically poor countries. The strength of this argument is derived from the lessons of economic history of developed countries. Second, industrialization is sometimes regarded as the major way to solve the problem of unemployment and underemployment in LDCs, many of which suffer from problems of a highly adverse man–land ratio. Third, the nature of trade of many LDCs prompts them to choose industrialization as an avenue to solve the problem of instabilities in the earnings from exports which chiefly consist of primary products. The demand for primary products in the international market is usually price and income inelastic. The LDCs also suffer from a chronic balance of payments deficit. Fourth, it is argued that industrialization alone can alter the present economic and social structure of many LDCs which is not conducive to achieving a higher level of economic development since dynamic externalities[1] concomitant with industrialization are necessary conditions for attaining a high level of growth. Some of the advocates of the 'big push' theory have actually emphasized the need for industrialization on the strength of dynamic externalities. Fifth, given the low level of productivity in most LDCs, particularly in agriculture, industrialization is supposed to improve productivity by increasing efficiency. Sixth, the desire to attain self-sufficiency has prompted many LDCs to choose the path of industrialization. Finally, industrialization is regarded as an important policy to affect fundamental economic *and* social changes in LDCs which are considered as necessary conditions to raise their growth potentials.

7.2 The role of tariffs in economic development

In economic history tariffs as an instrument of protection have played some part in the economic growth of industrially advanced countries though the exact extent of such a role has been debated considerably. Classical economists like Smith, Ricardo and Mill advocated the doctrine of free trade based on the theory of comparative advantage. Such a doctrine is an offshoot of the principles of *laissez-faire,* although it was soon realized that the principles of *laissez-faire* may not be the best for a country to follow, as some of the basic assumptions such as perfect competition and optimal income distribution may not hold. Several qualifications of the doctrine of free trade were made, and indeed Mill suggested the use of tariffs to protect infant industries. Some others (e.g. Bickerdike) have shown the case for tariffs to improve upon a country's terms of trade through trade restriction. This has now been regarded as the *optimum* tariff argument.

7.3 The optimum tariff argument

The point about optimum tariffs could be illustrated by a diagram. In Figure 7.1 let OV_1 be the offer curve of country 1 and OV_2 the offer curve of country 2 (for the derivation of offer curves, see Meade 1952). In a free trade situation OT is the terms of trade between the two countries. Imposition of a tariff by country 1 (assuming away any retaliation by country 2) will shift the offer curve to OV_1' and the terms of trade move in favour of country 1 as OT shifts to OT_1. Here country 1 acts like a monopolist and tries to realize higher gains through trade contraction. Such gains could not be made when the elasticity of foreign demand for imports is very high. Since this would imply a straight-line offer curve, the terms of trade would remain the same. In Figure 7.1 they will be the same at E′ as at E. It can easily be shown that country 2 can gain by imposing a tariff on the offer curve V_1' of country 1. But this could lead to further retaliation by country 1 and the final outcome is not easy to predict. It is only when equilibrium is reached (i.e. no country gains via the imposition of more tariffs) that it could be shown that either country 1 or 2 is actually better off. It is also hard to determine the exact significance of optimum tariff in commercial policies. Similarly, no positive conclusion has been drawn about the impact of commercial policy on Europe's terms of trade (Kindleberger 1956).

Johnson (1964) and Bhagwati and Ramaswami (1963) argue that as far as protection in the LDCs is concerned, only the optimum tariff argument is the valid one, and all others are really arguments for subsidies. The theory is derived from the principles of Paretian welfare maximization which requires that optimum welfare be reached at that point where the domestic marginal rate of substitution in consumption (DRS, i.e. the slope of the 'social' indifference curve) is equal to the domestic marginal social rate of transformation in production (DRT, i.e. the slope of the transformation

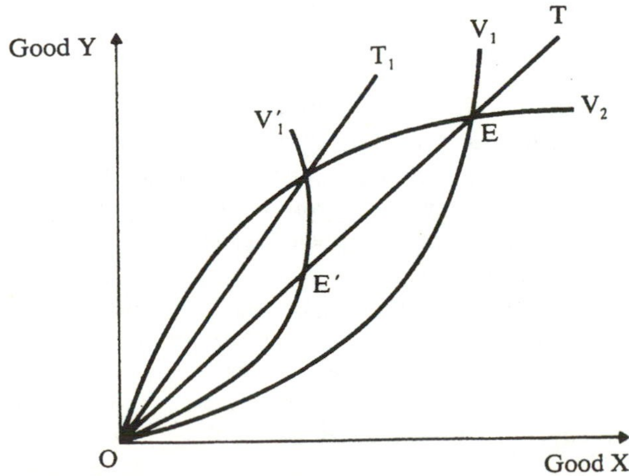

Figure 7.1

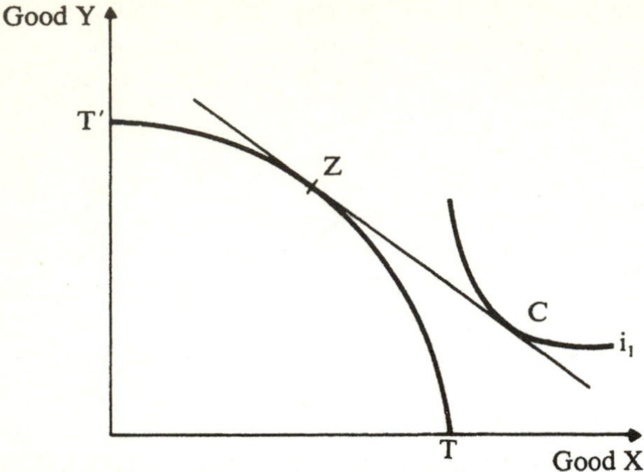

Figure 7.2

function for home production between any two goods) which is also equal to the foreign marginal rate of transformation (FRT, i.e. the slope of the price line which indicates the fixed world price ratio). This can easily be shown in Figure 7.2.

Let TT′ be the domestic transformation curve for two goods X and Y. In the absence of any distortion a country can produce at Z and consume at C, and since this would make DRS = DRT = FRT, welfare is maximized. Let us assume a domestic distortion (e.g. in the labour market of an LDC because, say, the social opportunity cost of labour is less than the private cost because of disguised unemployment – see Chapters 3 and 11). This would lead to a divergence between DRT and the ratio of marginal private costs of X to Y. These points are shown in Figure 7.3. The equilibrium for the producers is at Z and consumers will maximize their satisfaction at C because producers will produce according to the ratio of world prices (FRT) and marginal private costs whereas consumers will equate DRS to FRI. But optimum welfare in the Paretian sense is not obtained because FRT = DRS ≠ DRT. Here it is necessary to impose a tax on Y and subsidize the production of X which would lower the production of Y and raise the production of X until the point of optimum welfare is reached at Z_2 where DRT = DRS = FRT. On the other hand a tariff on X raises its domestic production.

This policy raises the production of X to Z_1. Equilibrium for production and consumption would now be given by the price line P_tP_t' which is steeper than the world price line since a tariff is now being included. Consumers attain a higher level of indifference curve at C_1 and they are better off in comparison with their previous point of equilibrium at C. (This need not always happen. Indeed, they may be worse off. See Bhagwati and Ramaswami 1963 for details.)

At C_1 optimum welfare is not obtained as the Paretian conditions are not fulfilled, i.e. DRT ≠ FRT ≠ DRS. Thus, the use of tariffs to correct domestic distortions is not an optimal policy. On the other hand, the use of domestic tax-cum-subsidy policy (in this case a tax on Y or a subsidy on X or both) clearly maximizes welfare since DRT = FRT = DRS when consumption takes place at C_2 and production takes place at Z_2.

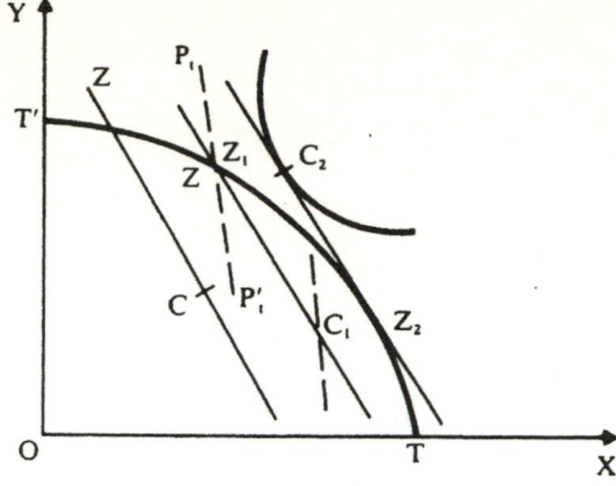

Figure 7.3

As Johnson concludes, 'Only the optimum tariff provides an economic justification for tariffs. All other arguments for protection are arguments for subsidies' (Johnson 1968: 353).

For most LDCs, the relevance of the optimum tariff is not much because few can exercise sufficient monopoly or monopsony power to cause an international income transfer by improving their terms of trade. The LDCs are actually the price takers, so their optimum tariffs are low or even zero, because alternative suppliers of foodstuffs generally exist, the economically rich nations are developing substitutes for natural raw materials, the size of an LDC's domestic market for a particular import is not large and its adaptability of demand and supply is not great.

7.4 The infant industry argument

It is contended that if free trade will not allow a country's true comparative advantage situation to develop, owing to a difference between marginal social and marginal private costs, then trade should be temporarily protected during its initial high cost period until the correct pattern of international specialization is established. The incurring of costs for a limited initial period in return for future benefits is normal investment procedure. To increase social welfare the infant industry must grow up and be able to compete on equal terms with foreign producers in domestic and world markets (Mill's test). It is a dynamic argument involving the lowering of production costs through learning by doing. The infant industry must be able to cover the costs of subsidizing its infancy by lowering production costs (Bastable's test).

As illustrated in Figure 7.4, under free trade, the country produces at P on the transformation curve TT′ and consumes at C, given that the terms of trade are P_wP_w. A tariff on industry will shift production and consumption to P′ with domestic prices P_hP_h. Social welfare has fallen since P′ is on a lower indifference curve (i.e. i_2) in comparison with C which is on i_1.

Protection could increase the output of cloth and shift the transformation curve outwards to TT″ where the country again operates under free trade, with the same terms of trade as before protection, $P'_wP'_w$. It will produce at P″ and consume at C′, which is Pareto better than T, so there is a higher level of welfare than before protection.

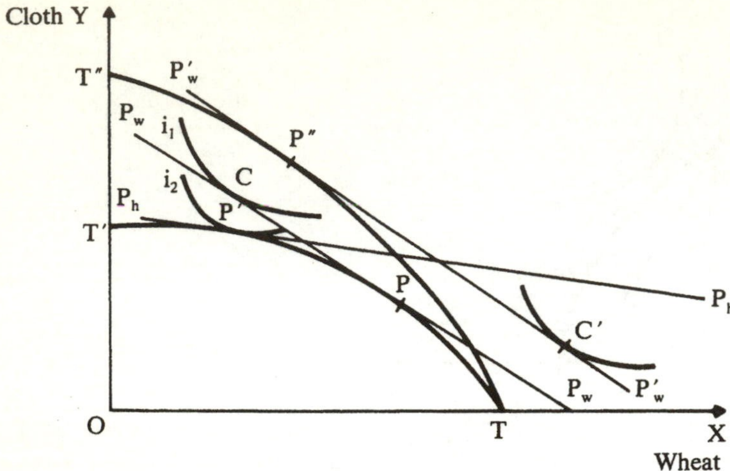

Figure 7.4

To provide an argument for government intervention, free traders require that the following two rules be satisfied.

1 The social rate must be greater than the private rate of return on an investment.
2 The private return necessary to induce the investment must exceed the private and social returns available on alternative investments sufficiently to make socially profitable investments privately unprofitable.

Here, two points should be made.

1 Producers may be pessimistic about future returns or unwilling to take risks in an unprotected market. Here the government should provide expert information on investment prospects in each sector.
2 Lack of perfection in the capital markets in LDCs make investment expensive, especially if an initial large scale is necessary for economic efficiency. The optimal policy is to subsidize the provision of capital.

To justify the infant industry argument, the whole of society must gain from the knowledge generated as the industry grows. Then it is reasonable for society to bear the costs of helping the industry mature. However, a tariff is not the optimal policy instrument, because the situation needs an alteration of loss in production, and not in consumption, and a tariff involves a loss in consumption which would not be the right impact of the subsidy. The existence of infant industries leads to FRT = DRS = DRT. A tariff would make FRT = DRT but DRT ≠ DRS. Only a policy of taxes and/or subsidies to the learning process can make FRT = DRS = DRT.

Advocates of free trade argue that protection is a selective method of granting differential price or cost advantage to particular industries, relative to other domestic industries. Protection to all industries means special protection to none. A policy of deflation or devaluation is generally preferred to tariffs or subsidies.

On the other hand, protectionists contend that it should apply to the whole infant economy, but the LDCs' manufacturing sector usually covers several import-substitute consumer goods industries matching the pattern of domestic demand, whereas the idea is to lower the future costs of the infant industries by the educative process. So their case is rather one for protection where there are potential economies of large-scale production.

The presence of distortions in the domestic commodity market has induced the supporters of the protectionist school to recommend the use of tariffs to correct such divergences. If the price of a commodity in which the country has a true comparative advantage is above its social cost, then it is argued that a tariff could rectify such a difference. Also, protection would enable the home market to expand and the industries could enjoy external economies (Scitovsky 1954). However, there could be external diseconomies as well. In such cases, private costs would be lower than social costs. Cultivators in LDCs, for example, do not take into account the (social) costs of soil erosion in their private profit calculation. Here a tariff may raise welfare as the production of agricultural goods would be discouraged, and allocation of resources would be more efficient because of a reduction in soil erosion. Thus, it is sought to rectify factor market divergences by the use of tariffs. However, gains in production via tariffs must be viewed against the loss of consumption to draw any conclusion about the overall impact of tariffs. Figure 7.5 illustrates this. A partial equilibrium analysis is used for simplification. Let DD′ be the domestic demand curve and SS′ the domestic supply curve of an importable product. Under free trade, QQ_1 would be the level of imports (because domestic demand is OQ_1 and domestic supply is OQ and $OQ_1 - OQ = QQ_1$).

Recalling the case for external economies, it may be argued that marginal social cost is less than marginal private cost. Since external economies represent social benefits, their value should be deducted from cost from the viewpoint of the community. We then obtain KK′. (Note that should there be external diseconomies, KK′ would lie

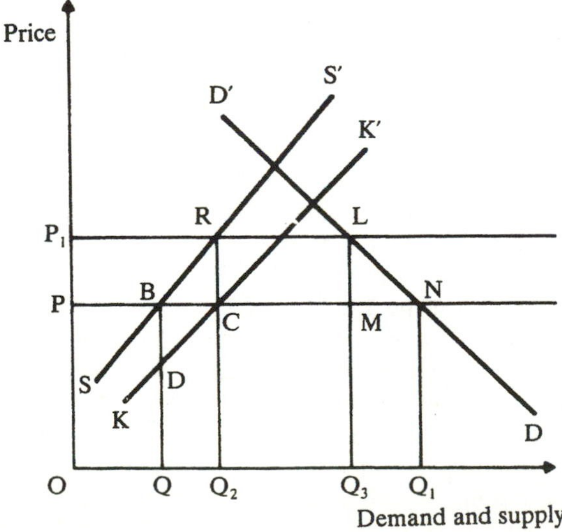

Figure 7.5

above SS′.) Should producers be given a subsidy of P_tP per unit of the commodity (i.e. P_tP/OP rate), then domestic production rises to OQ_2. The price remains at OP. Imports fall by QQ_2. The value of imports replaced ($QBCQ_2$) minus the social cost ($QDCQ_2$) is the gain for society which is shown by BCD. Note that a rate of subsidy higher than P_tP/OP will reduce the gains as prices will be lower than their social costs. Similarly, a rate lower than this would be inadequate to take full advantage of economies of scale.

A tariff at the same rate (i.e. P_tP/OP) could increase *production* by the same amount, i.e. QQ_2, but *consumption* will now suffer by Q_1Q_3. The loss of consumers' surplus is the area LMN. A subsidy does not inflict on society any such loss. Now the gain, i.e. area BCD, must be set against the loss, i.e. area MNL (see Corden 1974 for detailed analysis). The ultimate gain in terms of welfare will depend upon the relative sizes of the production gains and consumption losses. Here the weight of opinion seems to be in favour of the argument that domestic distortions should be corrected by domestic tax subsidy policies rather than by tariffs to achieve Paretian optimum welfare (i.e. DRS = DRT = FRT). Whenever there are domestic distortions, they should be dealt with directly (Ramaswami 1971).

7.5 Distortions in the factor markets

In many LDCs, distortions exist in the factor markets. For instance, in the presence of large-scale unemployed labour, particularly in agriculture, low wages in agriculture and high wages in industry, a tariff on importable industry is sometimes advocated as an offset against high cost of labour. The differences in wages between agriculture and industry overestimate the private cost of labour in industry since industrial wages exceed the social opportunity cost of labour. Such a situation shows inefficiency in resource allocation and underestimation of the benefits of industrial transformation. The aim is to increase real income over and above the level of suboptimal free trade by raising the relative price of industrial output via tariffs on industries, and a better allocation of resources (here, labour) is attempted by transferring labour from agriculture to industry (Myrdal 1956; Hagen 1958).

It is said that, given the imperfections of the labour market in the LDCs, a tariff can never be the optimal policy and a subsidy is better than the policy of imposing tariffs. Figure 7.6 illustrates this. Let TAT_1 be the transformation curve in the presence of distortions and TBT_1 the transformation curve in the absence of distortions. Actually, TBT_1 is derived if the country were producing along its contract curve in the Edgeworth box diagram. (For the derivation of such a contract curve, see for example, Staley 1970.) TAT_1 is inside TBT_1 because production is sub-optimal, given the distortions and the inefficiency in resource allocation (except at the extreme points of specialization).

Under free trade, the country operates on the TAT_1 curve (given the distortions in the labour market), produces at P and consumes at C. The line WW_1 indicates the terms of trade. A tariff on industrial output will take production to P_1 and this is a better situation (in terms of Paretian principles) than P. But such a tariff is not an optimal policy because DRT # FRT. Hagen's case for protection is derived from increased real income at P_1. But the policy is not the best. A subsidy, on the other hand, can take the economy to a point like C_1 which is better than P_1 or C. Again, a policy of subsidizing the use of labour inputs in industry is required for more efficient resource allocation.

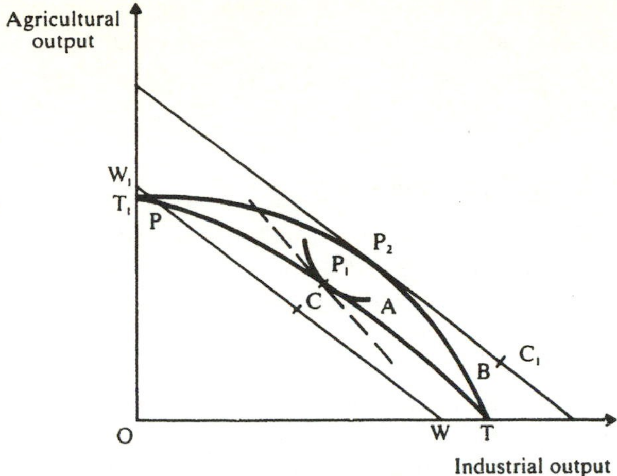

Figure 7.6

7.6 The balance of payments argument

Tariffs have been regarded as an effective weapon to reduce the balance of payments deficit. Both DCs and LDCs have taken resort to tariffs to reduce their trade deficits from time to time. The method is regarded as a simple one by some (Galbraith 1964). This is obvious if we consider Figure 7.5. The imposition of tariffs by the amount PP_1 reduces the deficit from QQ_1 to Q_2 Q_3. However, such a policy is not regarded as optimal by others (Johnson 1962) and a policy of a cut in domestic expenditure or devaluation is preferred to tariffs.

7.7 The employment argument

The use of tariffs to protect employment at home is advocated from time to time. In the LDCs, employment in more productive manufacturing industries is usually protected by tariffs in preference to labour utilization in low productivity sectors like agriculture. But this argument is not regarded as very convincing. Although a tariff may protect employment for some time, it creates distortions in both production (by favouring import substitution rather than export promotion) and consumption (by reducing consumer surplus). It is possible to envisage an *optimal* tariff in the event of a trade-off between distortion costs and unemployment, but this will be a second-best solution since the best solution is to allow devaluation of the currency which would avoid the costs of distortions introduced by tariffs (Corden 1974). However, in the past, many countries, both developed and less developed, have shown great reluctance to adopt devaluation as a policy variable and used tariffs chiefly for protecting the balance of payments, employment and capital flows. But in the mid-1970s, in an era of flexible exchange rates, such arguments for tariffs lost ground.

Despite the theoretical criticisms of the use of tariffs for import substitution and industrialization, their appeal still remains strong in many LDCs. However, it was soon realized that, in the process of stimulating domestic production, it is necessary not only to consider the impact of tariffs on domestic prices, but also equally important to consider the effects of tariffs on *inputs* which are used in domestic production. (A tariff on intermediate inputs does not alter the decision of the consumers.) This is the essence of the distinction between 'normal' and 'effective' tariffs, to which we now turn.

7.8 'Nominal' and 'effective' rates of protection

Import controls protect domestic firms from foreign competition, and the extent of protection can be measured by the degree to which import controls cause domestic prices of imports to exceed what their prices would be in the absence of such controls. When import control refers to an imported product and its price, it is known as the *nominal rate* of protection (NRP). When it refers to a stage of production and relates to the value added of the product at that stage of production it is known as the *effective rate* of protection (ERP). The NRP shows in percentage terms the extent to which the domestic prices of imported goods exceed what their domestic prices would be in the absence of protection. Thus, NRP is equal to the rate of tariff (*ad valorem*) over the domestic price. The ERP shows the percentage by which the value added at a stage of production in a domestic industry can exceed what this would be in the absence of protection. The NRP does not permit the analysis of the effects of a number of separate trade barriers upon a complex process of production. Thus, the concept of ERP is the more useful one, since it analyses the net effects on a plant or industry of controls on the imports of both its inputs and outputs.

There are some difficulties in the measurement of the rate of protection because of the use of non-traded inputs and methods used differ from each other. This point will be discussed later and, for the present, a more rigorous analysis of ERP is given.

Let us assume that cloth and yarn are imported and will continue to be imported after the imposition of tariffs and that there are two factors of production, i.e. yarn (a finished product) and a value-added product, which is the value added by the cloth industry. This product is produced by, say, labour, capital and natural resources. It is also assumed that

1 The input coefficients for domestic production are fixed for transforming yarn into cloth – this coefficient is equal for all firms.
2 The elasticities of foreign supply of imports of cloth and yarn are both equal to infinity (Corden 1971).

The effective rate of protection in a partial equilibrium model is shown in Figure 7.7; the assumption of fixed input coefficient is retained and both cloth and yarn are measured on the horizontal axis, so that one unit of yarn is required to make one unit of cloth.

The perfectly elastic foreign supply curves for yarn and for cloth are YY′ and CC′ respectively and OY and OC are free trade import prices of yarn and cloth respectively. The price for a unit of value added by the cloth industry – for the value-added product – is YC. This is the 'effective price' of cloth, as distinct from OC which is the 'nominal price' of cloth. If a nominal tariff of CT/OC is imposed on cloth, with no tariff on yarn, then the 'effective price' of cloth increases from YC to YT. This yields the 'effective rate of protection' or ERP for cloth CT/YC – the proportional increase in the effective price because of the imposition of the nominal tariff.

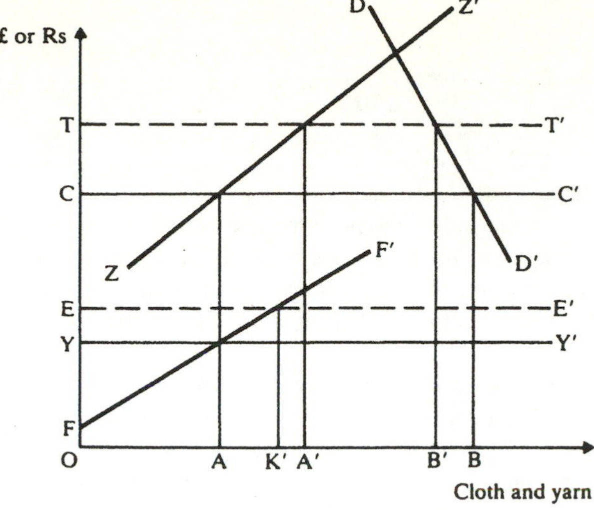

Figure 7.7

In the case of a tariff imposed on yarn of YE/OY, instead of the nominal tariff on cloth, the ERP of cloth would decrease from YC to EC. The ERP for cloth would be negative, −EY/CY.

Had a nominal tariff on cloth of CT/OC been combined with a nominal tariff on yarn of EY/OY, the 'effective' price of cloth would have altered from CY to ET, and the ERP would be equal to (CT − EY)/CY. Thus the proportion of CT to EY determines whether the effective price increases or decreases and whether the ERP is positive or negative.

Let DD′ be the domestic demand for cloth and ZZ′ be the domestic supply curve of cloth. Under free trade, consumption of cloth is OB. The domestic supply of yarn is FF′ and under free trade the domestic production of yarn is OA. A tariff on cloth raises domestic supply by AA′, cuts domestic demand by BB′ and reduces the deficit on the balance of payments to A′B′. Similarly, a tariff on yarn raises domestic supply of yarn by AK′.

The algebraic formulations of ERP and NRP could be stated as follows. If Z_v is the value added per unit of k in activity k in the absence of tariffs (i.e. free trade price), Z_{v1} is value added per unit of k in activity k made possible by the tariff structure ('effective price' after the imposition of tariffs), E_k is the proportional increase in the effective price of k because of the imposition of tariffs, P_k is the nominal price of a unit of k in free trade, a_{ik} is the share of i in the cost of k at free trade prices, t_k is the nominal tariff rate on k and t_i is the nominal tariff rate on i, the formula for calculating the ERP for the activity producing k – for the k value-added product – is given by the following equations:

$$Z_v = P_k(1 - a_{ik}) \tag{7.1}$$

$$Z_{v1} = P_k[(1 + t_k) - a_{ik}(1 + t_i)] \tag{7.2}$$

$$E_k = \frac{Z_{v1} - Z_v}{Z_v} \tag{7.3}$$

From (7.1), (7.2) and (7.3) we obtain

$$E_k = \frac{t_k - \sum_{i=1}^{n} a_{ik} t_i}{1 - \sum a_{ik}} \tag{7.4}$$

Equation (7.4) shows that the ERP (E_k) depends on t_k (nominal cloth tariff), t_i, (nominal yarn tariff) and a_{ik} (free trade input share).

It is clear that the ERP is a better index to measure protection than the rate of nominal tariffs because it takes account of the amount by which the prices of inputs are raised by tariffs, as well as the amount by which the price of the output is increased. However, there are some difficulties with this useful index of ERP (Helleiner 1972).

1 It was assumed at the outset that the input–output coefficients (the a_{ik}) are constant and not influenced by the tariff. If they were not, and indeed it is unlikely that they would be in reality, the measurement of ERP becomes very complicated. Variations from these assumed constant points could take place between intermediate and factor inputs as their relative prices change or because of economies of scale as production rises.
2 The other difficulty lies in one of the basic drawbacks of the index itself. The measurement of the ERP aims to estimate the impact of the tariff upon particular industries without including the indirect effects on other industries. This is a major limitation. But despite these difficulties it is a better index than the alternatives usually suggested.

There are other difficulties. Should tariffs be used to measure ERP rather than the difference between world prices and domestic prices, it is necessary to assume that tariffs are the only forms of trade controls, and also that the domestic price of an imported commodity is equal to the world price plus the tariff. Similarly, it will be assumed that the domestic price of an export good is the world price net of the export tax. This is only true if the country faces an infinitely elastic world demand for that product (Helleiner 1972: 127). Needless to say, such an assumption may not always be valid. Also, the value of the capital–output ratio may be different in different industries and capital can depreciate at different rates in different industries and as such, in any two industries with the same ERP, the net returns to capital could be different. Thus, the cost of depreciation should be deducted from the value added.

7.8.1 Non-traded goods

As regards non-traded goods, three different ways are suggested to tackle this problem: (1) the Corden method (1966); (2) the method proposed by Balassa *et al.* (1971); (3) the 'ideal' method of Scott (Little *et al.* 1970). Each of these methods will be discussed in turn.

1 The *Corden* method redefines value added to include non-traded inputs. Thus, what is measured is the percentage by which value added plus the payments for non-traded goods can be increased. The percentage ERP, then, is given by the following (Corden 1966):

$$\text{ERP} = 100\left(\frac{h_k - \sum a_{ik}h_i}{f_k - \sum a_{ik}f_i} - 1\right)$$

where h_k are home prices, f_k are foreign prices and a_{ik} is the input of the ith commodity for every unit of output k, the is being limited to traded commodities. Note that, whenever the ERP is high, the method underestimates the percentage by which value added alone is increased.

2 An alternative is to assume that there is no effect on the prices of non-traded inputs. Indeed, Balassa assumes that non-traded inputs are in infinitely elastic supply so that they can be treated the same as traded inputs. This method is not without criticisms since, if the index of the ERP is too high, it overestimates the amount by which the value added is increased because the negative effects of tariffs on export subsidies to indirectly traded inputs are ignored and none of the non-traded inputs is taken into consideration.

3 Scott measures the percentage by which domestic value added (DVA), given in domestic currency, is raised by protection above what it would be if the same process were operated at world prices (WVA) (Little *et al.* 1970). Thus

$$\text{ERP} = \left(\frac{\text{DVA}}{\text{WVA}} - 1\right)100$$

Alternatively,

$$\text{ERP} = \left(1 - \frac{\text{WVA}}{\text{DVA}}\right)100$$

which gives the proportion of value added at domestic prices because of protection.

The rate of protection can, however, be negative (Little *et al.* 1970). This can occur when the inputs of an activity are protected, but not the final output. Note that even when DVA $>$ 0 and WVA $>$ 0, ERP $<$ 0 if DVA $<$ WVA. Also, WVA could be negative which implies that, after considering only traded inputs and outputs, production costs foreign exchange for the economy.

In Table 7.1, it is shown that the treatment of non-traded inputs differs according to the method used. The Corden method includes non-traded inputs in the value added. Where protection is high this is likely to give a lower estimate than the Scott method. In the Balassa method, it is assumed that non-traded inputs in free trade would have the dollar or pound value given by their existing market value in domestic currency transformed at the official rate of exchange. Should the currencies be overvalued, it is likely to give too high a dollar or pound value. It is a better index if it is possible to estimate the value added at world prices to find out what the value added would be under free trade. Thus, dollar or pound prices of non-traded inputs are used. In the 'ideal' method of Scott, it is assumed that the proportionate difference between the actual and free-trade values of non-traded inputs is given by a weighted average of protection for manufacturing as well as agriculture. Reflection suggests that the Scott method is not exactly ideal but it is really a cross between the Balassa and the Corden methods minus their basic disadvantages (i.e. overestimation and underestimation).

Table 7.1 Effect of different treatment of non-traded inputs on the measurement of effective protection for manufacturing (%)

Country	*Year*	*Balassa method*	*Ideal method*	*Corden method*
Z				
Argentina	1958	247	174	162
Brazil	1966	155	98	118
Mexico	1960	28	27	27
India	1961	733	n.a.	313
Pakistan	1963–4	00	2,000	271
Philippines	1965	52	50	49
Taiwan	1965	50	38	33
U				
Argentina	1958	71	64	62
Brazil	1966	61	50	54
Mexico	1960	22	21	21
India	1961	88	n.a.	76
Pakistan	1963–4	100	95	73
Philippines	1965	34	33	33
Taiwan	1965	33	28	25

Source: Little *et al.* (1970: 431).

Notes:

$$Z = \frac{\text{Value-added manufactures at domestic prices expressed in terms of domestic currency}}{\text{Rate of exchange value added in manufactures at world prices expressed in dollars or pounds}}$$

$$U = 1 - \frac{\text{Rate of exchange value added in manufactures at world prices expressed in dollars or pounds}}{\text{Value-added manufactures at domestic prices expressed in terms of domestic currency}}$$

It can be seen from Table 7.1 that in all cases except Brazil and Pakistan the 'ideal' method gives results between the other two methods, and closer to the Corden method. It is also easy to check from the table how the ERP differed between different countries.

7.8.2 The effects of protection on exports

High rates of protection for industrialization could create a bias against the export sector of the economy. Discouragement of exports is conceivable under protectionist policy for the following basic reasons.

1 Import controls raise the exchange rate above its free trade level; therefore, the exporter receives less domestic currency than he would under free trade. Thus if the exchange rate is Rs 10 = £1 under import control rather than Rs 20 = £1 under free trade, the Indian exporters would be receiving Rs 10 rather than Rs 20 under a system of import restrictions. This implies that the size of an industry is likely to be smaller than it might be in the absence of such disincentives to exports.
2 The cost of production of export industries using inputs which come under import restriction is likely to rise. This has the effect of making exports less competitive on the international market.

In the post-Second World War period, the unfavourable treatment of primary exports may have contributed to the fall in their share in the world market of major exports of countries such as Brazil, Chile and Pakistan. Brazil's major primary commodity export, coffee, is a special case; while African producers increased plantings, Brazil reduced output to cushion against the drastic fall in prices. But she also experienced a decline in her market share for cocoa and lumber (Bergsman 1970).

There has been little rise for minor agricultural commodities such as bananas, tobacco, wool, processed oil and nuts. The policies adopted have not been very conducive to the development of new exports. In fact, in Pakistan both volume and value of major exports declined in absolute terms between 1950 and 1967 (Balassa *et al.* 1971: 226) and Pakistan's share in world exports of cotton and jute fell considerably. The import substitution of cotton and jute textiles by domestic production did not compensate for this loss.

In Malaya, the imposition of export taxes seems to have caused a similar fall in the country's share in the world exports of rubber. However, it has enjoyed substantial rises in the exports of some other primary products such as tin and tropical timber that are not subject to any discrimination (Balassa *et* at. 1971: 207).

Thus, where protection imparts a bias against exports, a fall in the share of exports of many LDCs has been observed. Discrimination against exports has also prevented the development of new types of exports. The limit to imports is usually set by exports and this has engendered a severe and chronic balance of payments deficit in many LDCs. Export industries are not usually protected but many inputs which are used by such export industries are subject to tariffs. This results in an inelasticity of the supply of primary goods in many LDCs following policies for import substitution. Thus the policy of imposing high tariffs for industrialization could easily dampen export promotion by taxing the primary sector.

7.9 The 'cost' of protection

An attempt has been made by Balassa to measure the cost of protection in some LDCs. Table 7.2 provides a comparison of the cost of protection in LDCs. The figures suggest that, except for Malaya, the net cost of protection as a percentage of GNP was quite significant. For Malaya, the negative cost is regarded as a reflection of the absence of discriminatory policies towards a large number of primary export products.

In Table 7.3 different ERPs on different types of industries in some selected LDCs are shown. Once again, the differences in the ERP for different types of industries in different countries are quite clear. Such differences partly reflect the different types of trade and industrial policies as well as different forms of ideologies. The lessons of the depression of the 1930s, the Second World War and the economic history of many rich countries have prompted a significant number of LDCs to build up a 'siege' economy by imposing tariffs, controls and quotas. Thus, it is not difficult to understand the desire for autarky in many LDCs. Further, given the pattern of trade between DCs and LDCs (i.e. LDCs chiefly being the exporters of primary products and the importers of finished goods from the DCs) and the nature of foreign trade in the LDCs, which too often suggests concentration in the production of too few goods (i.e. commodity concentration of trade), their exports to too few markets (i.e. geographic or market concentration) and very low price and income elasticities of world demand for their product, many LDCs have deliberately chosen protection

Table 7.2 The 'cost' of protection in individual countries (% of GNP)

	Brazil 1966	*Chile 1961*	*Malaya 1965*	*Pakistan 1963/4*	*Mexico 1960*	*Norway 1954*	*Philippines 1965*
Static (allocative cost of protection of import substitutes)[a]	0.6	1.4	0.6	1.5	0.6	0.5	2.0
Dynamic cost of protection of import substitutes[b]	9.5	9.6	0.4	5.4	2.2	2.0	2.6
Consumption effect[c]	0.1	0.6	0.1	0.2	0.1	0.1	0.4
Terms of trade effect[d]	−0.5	3.5	−1.4	0.6	−0.3	−0.7	−0.6
Cost of increased exports under free trade[e]	−0.2	1.9	−0.1	0.3	−0.1	−0.1	−0.7
Net cost of protection	9.5	6.2	−0.4	6.2	2.5	1.8	3.7

Source: Balassa *et al.* (1971: 82).

Notes: [a] Excess cost plus above-normal profits and wages in industries that would not survive under free trade. [b] Excess costs plus above-normal profits and wages in industries that would become competitive under free trade. [c] Consumer surplus on the increased consumption of imports. [d] Reductions in export prices in the event of free trade. [e] The rise in cost of exports under free trade under the assumption that export industries are subject to increasing costs.

for the industrialization and diversification of their economies. Although restrictive trade and tariff policies in the developed countries have been liberalized since the Second World War, the LDCs complain that they do not go far enough to give large access to their exports in the markets of the DCs. The system of tariffs used by some of the regional trading blocs within the DCs, e.g. the European Union which imposes a flat 30 per cent tariff on imports from the 'rest of the world', hits the LDCs particularly hard. Also, the LDCs complain about the existing international

Table 7.3 Average effective protection for manufacturing in relation to official exchange rates[a]

Country	*Year*	*Consumption goods*	*Intermediates*	*Capital goods*	*All manufactures*
Argentina	1958	164	167	133	162
Brazil	1966	230	68	31	118
Mexico	1960	22	34	55	27
India	1961	n.a.	n.a.	n.a.	313[b]
Pakistan	1963–4	883	88	155	271
Philippines	1965	94	65	80	49[c]
Taiwan	1965	n.a.	n.a.	n.a.	33[d]

Source: Little *et al.* (1971).

Notes: [a] For Brazil, the basic import rate of 2,220 cruzeiros. For Argentina, it is assumed that the average export exchange rate was used. [b] For one-sixth of large-scale manufacturing industry only. [c] Eighty-five for home market only. Other columns, home market only. [d] Very approximate.

economic system in general which does not help much to stabilize fluctuations in the income from exports by LDCs. It is in the light of these considerations that we shall discuss later the reasons for advocating trade, growth and a new international economic order (see Chapter 13).

7.10 Economic growth and trade

The Ricardian and the Hecksher–Ohlin models are modified in the current theories of trade to take into account the effects of growth. Since these developments are well covered in the literature (Johnson 1962, 1967), I shall mainly concentrate here on some of the major issues.

The effects of the growth of factor supplies can first be mentioned in the light of the Rybczynski theorem (Rybczynski 1955). Let us assume a rise in the supply of labour. If the terms of trade are given, then the Rybczynski theorem says that with an increase in the supply of labour relative to capital the production of a labour-intensive commodity will rise and that of a capital-intensive good will fall. This may be labelled the *pro-trade* bias at given terms of trade (TT). On the other hand, capital accumulation will imply an increase in the production of capital-intensive goods and a fall in the production of labour-intensive goods at given TT, and this impact on production has been labelled *anti-trade* bias. The impact on consumption can be measured by noting that at given terms of trade, and within fixed factor properties and marginal products, an increase in labour with fixed stock of capital will transfer income to labour. If the marginal propensity to consume by labourers is high for the labour-intensive good, then a larger proportion of society's income will be spent on the labour-intensive good in comparison with the capital-intensive commodity. This is 'anti-trade' bias because of consumption. However, the overall effect depends on the nature of assumptions made and the actual values chosen. Similarly, the reverse conclusion will follow in the face of capital accumulation. (For a detailed discussion see, for example, Johnson 1964. For a rigorous analysis of growth, trade and accumulation, see Bardhan 1970c.)

7.10.1 Welfare loss in trade through growth

A special case of *net* welfare loss through trade can be demonstrated with the help of Figure 7.8. This is sometimes known as 'immiserizing growth' (Bhagwati 1958). Let P_1P_1 be the transformation curve between two goods X and Y. Let X be an exportable whose improved production is shown by the new curve P_2P_2. Trade results in a decline of the TT and the point of equilibrium V_1 is on a lower indifference curve in comparison with V_0. Increased production results in welfare gains but this is more than offset by a loss of welfare because of the fall in TT so that there is a net welfare loss. Note that this result depends on the premises that the foreign demand curve for the exportables is inelastic and/or that a very high marginal propensity to import or an ultra-pro-trade bias exists in LDCs. Such a model also presumes mobility of resources between different industries. In many LDCs, this is the case in some sectors but not in others, as suggested by Kindleberger. Empirically, it is hard to say whether 'immiserizing growth' has actually taken place. In the United Nations Conference on Trade and Development (UNCTAD) in 1964, it was suggested that the TT declined by 17 per cent

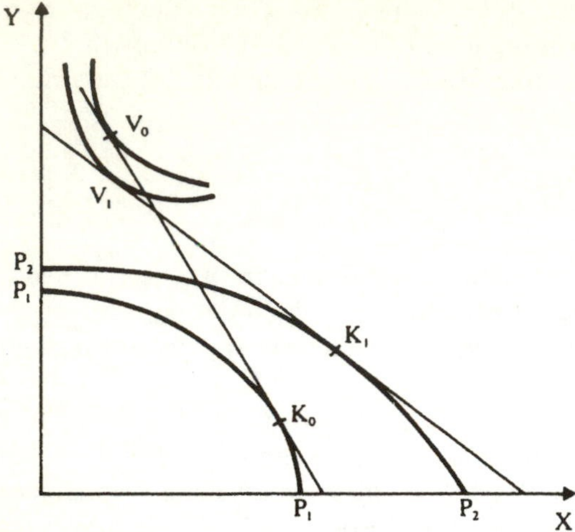

Figure 7.8

between 1950 and 1961 against the LDCs (leaving out the oil producers) *vis-à-vis* the DCs. But a fall in TT is not a sufficient condition to maintain the hypothesis about the net loss of welfare because such a fall should be viewed against the gains from production.

7.11 Terms of trade between developed countries and less developed countries

The TT between the DCs and the LDCs have been a major arena of debate and investigation in trade theory and policy (Prebisch 1959, 1964; MacBean 1966). The TT are generally defined as the ratio of export prices to import prices paid by the LDCs in their trade with DCs. If the TT move against the LDCs for some time, it would imply that the LDCs are losing out in their trade with the DCs. During the 1960s it was suggested that such an index of TT had actually moved against the LDCs *vis-à-vis* the DCs for a long time, and hence existing trade theory is inadequate to help the LDCs and a new economic order is called for both internationally (to help the LDCs) and nationally, chiefly via protection and industrialization.

The applicability of trade theory to the problems of LDCs had already been questioned during the 1950s (Myrdal 1956). Indeed, it has been suggested that strict adherence to the doctrine of Ricardian comparative cost theory would imply specialization in the production of primary goods by the LDCs, and this would eventually lead to a transfer of the gains of technical progress from the LDCs to the DCs (Prebisch 1959). Chenery (1961) points out that growth theories in LDCs do not usually accommodate the principles of comparative advantage. Trade is not relied upon as a method to optimize productivity since the premises upon which the traditional trade theory (i.e. the Ricardo and Heckscher–Ohlin models) rests have little relevance to the realities of the economies of LDCs. This is because (1) in LDCs the real social opportunity costs of factors are not given by the market prices of the different factors in view of market imperfections; (2) externalities and scale economies could be significant; (3) the supply of inputs and their nature could alter between different time periods; and (4) the demand of the buyers and the producers could be significantly influenced because of the nature of complementarities between different goods.

These distortions in LDCs, some of which have already been explained, create a divergence between money costs of factors and their real social opportunity costs. Since the LDCs trade on the basis of prices set by the distorted money costs rather than by the real social opportunity costs, the optimum rate of return from trade is likely to be lower. It is in the light of these considerations, plus the argument that the demand for exports from the LDCs is both price and income inelastic, that we will consider the basic points in the Prebisch thesis.

7.11.1 The Prebisch thesis

Prebisch has envisaged a global model with a developed centre and a backward periphery. Technical progress in DCs has resulted in improved income for their labourers, an improved standard of living and a high price for their goods, some of which are exported to the periphery, i.e. the LDCs. But such technical progress in LDCs has not raised wages of their workers. Indeed, prices have gone down and the prices of their exportables *vis-à-vis* their imports have decreased as the TT have moved against the LDCs. In other words, the fruits of technical progress have been transferred from LDCs to DCs. To alter the situation, Prebisch advocates industrialization via protection and import substitution.

Prebisch tries to explain such an adverse movement of the TT against LDCs by the following factors. First, the trade unions in DCs are more capable of raising wages for their workers than the trade unions in LDCs which are frequently very weak. Second, the increase in population in LDCs and the consequent rise in the labour supply have been absorbed mainly in those sectors where labour productivity is quite low and this has also resulted in a lower level of real wages. Next, in LDCs, given a low income elasticity of demand for the exports of LDCs and a high income elasticity for the exports of DCs in LDCs, with growth in both the DCs and LDCs, it is likely that LDCs will run into severe balance of payments deficits as their exports will tend to fall behind their imports. One way that has been suggested to overcome the problem is to reduce export prices, but here the danger is that, given the price inelasticity of demand for their exports which consist mainly of primary goods, the total earnings of LDCs are likely to fall. Prebisch suggests that the 'rational' policy for LDCs would be industrialization and import substitution.

Prebisch adds that LDCs generally suffer from significant price fluctuations in export earnings and the impact of such 'instabilities' is very damaging to growth and investment of LDCs. Here again, the proper policy for LDCs would be to diversify their economies in the line of industrialization.

7.11.2 An evaluation of the Prebiseh thesis

The Prebisch thesis has been questioned on both empirical and theoretical grounds. First, it may be argued that although the UNCTAD study between 1950 and 1961 has shown a relative decline of TT for the LDCs *vis-à-vis* the DCs, the choice of the base period (1950) is questionable as it was the boom year for primary goods because of the Korean War. On the basis of long-term information, Lipsey (1963) has shown that the TT have actually moved in favour of LDCs *vis-à-vis* the United

Box 7.1 Further reading on trade policy and economic growth

An influential paper from Jeffrey Sachs and Andrew Warner in 1995 suggested that the more a open a country was to trade, the better its economic growth. Sachs and Warner examined seventy-nine countries and gave each a rating of openness by measuring factors such as the existence of high tariff barriers, state monopolies and the use of a 'socialist system'. A discussion paper published in 1999 by Dani Rodrik and Francisco Rodriguez disputes the findings, however. Rodrik and Rodriguez argue that the two variables that are the most direct measures of trade policy, tariff barriers and non-tariff barriers, have very little effect on growth. They conclude that the Sachs–Warner indicator is a proxy for a wide range of policy and institutional characteristics, and that it yields a misleading estimate of the effects of trade restrictions proper.

One argument of the proponents of free trade has been that free trade generates technological and other positive spillovers to the rest of the economy. Rodriguez and Rodrik point to research that finds little evidence that firms in fact derive many technological or other benefits from exporting. On the contrary 'causality seems to go from productivity to exports, not the other way'.

States and Europe. But during the same period, starting with the last quarter of the nineteenth century, the TT have moved against LDCs *vis-à-vis* the UK. However, Lipsey's conclusion about the movement of the IT in favour of LDCs as opposed to Europe has been contradicted in the findings of Kindleberger (1956). Discussions about the IT are inconclusive one way or the other since the results crucially depend upon the base period and the nature of the index.

At the theoretical level, it has been argued that Prebisch's notion that the gains from technical progress should be distributed globally, independent of the countries of their origin, is of doubtful validity. If such distribution of gains means equalization of global real wages, then the realities of the present world (e.g. externalities, monopolies, economic and non-economic trade barriers) which rule out factor price equalization will also rule out any such global equalization of real wages (June-Flanders 1964). Also gains from technical progress could emerge from the expenditure on research and development and such gains are not for free global distribution. The value judgement about their equal distribution has also been questioned.

7.12 Export instability and economic growth in less developed countries

During the 1950s and the early 1960s, instability in the export earnings of the LDCs was highlighted. The reasons for such instability are supposed to be

1 the nature of the exports of LDCs;
2 low price and income elasticity of the demand for their products;
3 specialization in the production of only a few commodities, i.e. commodity concentration of exports;
4 a large proportion of exports to only a few markets which usually followed the pattern of colonial trade, i.e. market or geographical concentration.

It has been argued that such instabilities have serious adverse effects on growth, investment, balance of payments and planning in LDCs. Policies were recommended to iron out such instabilities to help LDCs in attaining higher growth (UN 1962).

During the 1960s, some of the above hypotheses were tested to find out their empirical validity. Most of these empirical studies have cast considerable doubt about the validity of the hypotheses. Thus, Coppock (1962), by using a log-variance index of instability (which comprises the dispersions from the trend line given by the first and last observations and thus makes it vulnerable to the specific period chosen for research) for exports of eighty-three countries between 1946 and 1958, has found that export instability was mainly correlated with price, terms of trade, volume of exports and imports. However, the statistical significance of these variables has not been mentioned. The interesting aspect in Coppock's findings is that export instability was *negatively* related with *geographical* concentration (as given by the Hirschman index, i.e. the square root of the sum of the squares of the percentage shares in given goods), was positive but very poor. However, Michaely's (1962) study of thirty-six countries for the period between 1948 and 1958 shows a *positive* and statistically significant association between commodity concentration and export *price* instability. It is noteworthy that Michaely has tried to explain changes in *export prices* rather than *export earnings*. On the other hand, for about the same period for the same number of countries, Massell (1964) failed to discover a significant relationship between instability and commodity concentration and geographic concentration. Further, by using the data of Coppock and Michaely, MacBean (1966) shows the absence of a significant difference between the levels of instability in export earnings for DCs and LDCs. MacBean then uses the indices of geographic and commodity concentration as well as the proportion of primary exports to total exports to account for the divergences in instability among different countries. His conclusion is: 'such theoretically proposed general factors as specialization in primary products or commodity concentration *per se* may have some slight instability, but their explanatory value in particular cases is very small' (MacBean 1966: 56). This view is also supported by Kingston (1976).

MacBean's study has been questioned by others, however (e.g. Sundrum 1967). When differences in time horizons are considered (i.e. 1946–58 and 1954–66), the divergences in the levels of instability tended to increase (Erb and Schiavo-Campo 1969). Massell (1970) found that the different levels of instability have been strongly influenced by the index of commodity concentration. Also, he observes that there is a 'slight suggestion that LDCs tend to experience greater instability than DCs net of other explanatory variables' (Massell 1970: 628).

As regards the effects of instability on growth and investment, empirical evidence tends to refute the view that such effects are *always* damaging to the LDCs (see, for example, MacBean 1966; Knudsen and Parnes 1975). Indeed, MacBean's study suggests that instability has a positive and significant effect on the rate of growth of investment. However, from MacBean's study, it does not follow that instability in export earnings has no detrimental effects on the LDCs. On the other hand, by using the normalized variance of transitory income – *à la* Friedman – Knudsen and Parnes (1975) have shown that increased instability reduces the propensity to consume and thus raises savings, investment and growth of the economy. But the same study has also shown that an increase in commodity concentration results in increased instability, with the implication that the decline in such concentration will reduce instability. This is similar to the view (Massell 1970: 629) that product concentration results in instability of exports. The study by Knudsen and Parnes (1975) should be accepted with caution, however, as the predictive power of their model is rather low.

On balance, empirical evidence available so far does not entirely rule out the relationship between instability and commodity concentration. But the adverse impact of such instability on the level of investment and growth of the LDCs has been doubted. Interestingly, despite the empirical findings most writers on the subject went on to suggest the means to stabilize export earnings of the LDCs because it has been gradually acknowledged that a sharp fall in export earnings in some period may produce a random shock to the economy which it may fail to absorb; thus severe balance of payments problems could mean inability to import not only capital goods but also food items in a period of harvest failure, accentuation of large-scale unemployment, particularly in labour-surplus economies, mass starvation and death, and the failure of planned economic growth. With these observations, it is now possible to turn attention to the different proposals which are put forward by UNCTAD and others to stabilize export earnings in the LDCs.

7.13 The role of the United Nations Conference on Trade and Development and some trade policies to help less developed countries

The role of UNCTAD to protect and champion the case for LDCs as against the trade policies of DCs has become increasingly prominent. Thus the UNCTAD meeting in 1964 specifically called for ironing out commodity price oscillations via commodity agreements, to reduce the non-tariff barriers such as quotas by DCs, to castigate the 'most favoured nation' clause and to give general preference to imports, particularly of manufactured goods from LDCs. It is clear from this list of demands that UNCTAD is chiefly interested in protecting the 'infant' industries in LDCs and in promoting their exports.

As regards the commodity agreement scheme, it has been observed that in theory the scheme is not likely to be effective because, if prices are raised, supply usually overtakes demand and it is very difficult to avoid a decline in prices. Also, the type of income transfer that it involves from the consumers of DCs to LDCs does not imply an optimal distribution of the burden of higher prices (Staley 1970).

It can be pointed out that a more efficient transfer of income from DCs to LDCs could be achieved by imposing direct taxes in DCs rather than by increasing commodity prices.

However, one of the important factors to account for a low world demand for the primary goods from LDCs is the high level of protection given to agriculture in some DCs. For example, the United States has offered considerable protection to her agriculture via a system of import quotas. The European Union, by following a Common Agricultural Policy (CAP), keeps the prices of agricultural goods artificially high (despite the rise of butter or beef mountains from time to time) within the Union by imposing 'variable levies' on imports. Such policies obviously discriminate against the exports of agricultural goods from the LDCs. Nor are these the best policies to help the agriculture of DCs (Colman and Mclnerney 1975), chiefly because an artificially higher price level (compared with world market prices) will involve considerable loss of consumers' surplus. Also, if the high prices are paid for running the buffer-stock scheme, there is no guarantee that such costs will be recovered from future sales. Further, income subsidies could be offered to the farmers in DCs. In the 1975 Lomé

Convention, it was decided that the system of subsidies within the EU via import levies should be modified.

Several Commodity Agreement Schemes (CAS) have been concluded, chiefly to guard against short-run oscillations in commodity prices, e.g. sugar, coffee, tin and wheat. From the consumers' point of view, it was expected that such agreements would help to maintain adequate supply at reasonable prices. However, quite a few of these schemes have failed to work successfully. Thus, the high rise in coffee prices from 1973 to 1977 caused major concern among the importing countries and the agreement was in danger of falling apart. Again, in the case of the International Wheat Agreement (1971), the council avoided the issues related to prices. Since many LDCs are net importers of wheat, the advantages of this agreement from their point of view is understandable, given the ready availability of wheat. But such a scheme also leads to a loss of incentive for producing wheat in LDCs because of limits on prices.

In the case of the International Tin Agreement (1971), a buffer stock has been set up and a maximum and a minimum price is laid down. This scheme has the advantage of smoothing out short-run price changes without altering the effects of long-run demand and supply. On the other hand, as has been argued before, buffer-stock schemes are criticized as inefficient on the grounds of loss of consumers' surplus and an increase in the cost of operations.

One of the main changes that the CASs face is the development of synthetics in DCs. Thus, although the price of Tanzanian sisal has been increased through negotiations, the scheme has failed to help Tanzania because synthetic substitutes for sisal are now being supplied in increasing quantities (Singer and Ansari 1977). One of the reasons why the Organization of Petroleum Exporting Countries (OPEC) has achieved a very significant increase in its export earnings from the huge increases in oil prices since 1973 is that the demand for oil is very inelastic and the substitutes are very few, at least in the short run. Thus, provided that the agreements reached within the cartels of the oil-producing countries hold, export earnings could be significantly increased. However, for the primary exports of most LDCs substitutes are available. Nor do all the primary producing countries have the political will to unite together.

The problem of eliminating major changes in the export earnings of the LDCs was once again highlighted in the UNCTAD conference of 1976 at Nairobi. More specifically, it called for (1) the setting-up of an international buffer-stock of commodities; (2) the creation of a common fund for financing the stock; (3) a method of multilateral assurances on individual goods; (4) an expansion of the transfer of technology from the DCs to the LDCs; (5) promotion of exports from the LDCs; and (6) debt relief.

The points raised in the UNCTAD (1976 and 1980) conferences are not novel and differences of opinion persist among economists about the effectiveness and desirability of the CASs and the buffer-stock schemes. More attention is now being paid to the Compensatory Financing Schemes (CFS), some of which were proposed in the 1950s. In some of these schemes, the exporters are compensated against any divergence from the trend lines of price or output which are mutually accepted between the exporting and the importing countries. The advantage of the CFSs over the CASs is that they do not interfere in the activities of the market. In practice, it has been observed that for deriving the gains from the CFSs the exporting country has reduced the volume of production (Singer and Ansari 1977). Another form of CFS proposed by the IMF (1966) requires that, should a country's earnings be less than its mean earnings for two years, the country would be entitled to draw up to 25 per cent of its quota with the IMF. This amount of drawing was later raised to 50 per cent. But the scheme did not find much favour with the LDCs since the possibility of ordinary drawings could be adversely affected because of the drawing under CFSs. Also, the LDCs have suspected that the IMF would get greater power to meddle with national economic matters.

In the Lomé Convention (1975), agreements were reached between forty-six LDCs, mostly from the Caribbean, African and Pacific regions, to include several commodities like cocoa and coffee, bananas, tea, wood products, sisal, palm products, iron ore, etc. and for the importing countries to offer to the producers a fixed sum of earnings subject to the proviso that the individual export formed only a small percentage of the whole export income of the exporting country. It was hoped that the scheme would help to stabilize export earnings of LDCs. However, LDCs like India, Pakistan, Bangladesh and Sri Lanka are not represented as full members of the Lomé Convention and, since these countries account for a very large proportion of the population in LDCs, CFSs envisaged in the Convention of Lomé would be inadequate and partial.

Another method to help the LDCs in stabilizing export income is the Supplementary Financing Scheme (SFS) innovated by the International Bank for Reconstruction and Development (IBRD or World Bank) in 1964. Under this scheme, if the actual export earnings are less than the projected earnings of the LDC then it would be entitled to obtain supplementary finance to bridge the deficit. But the administration of the SFS posed considerable problems. Moreover, doubts were raised about the validity of the projected earnings by LDCs. However, after the oil-price rise of 1973, some of the LDCs were most seriously affected (MSA) and in 1975–6 the IBRD took special steps to offer the SFS to the MSA poor countries.

7.14 Non-tariff barriers and the generalized system of preferences

Given the nature and level of protection offered to the primary and manufacturing sectors in DCs through tariff as well as non-tariff barriers like quotas (Balassa 1972), it has long been pointed out that LDCs would be able to increase their export earnings by the gradual removal of such restrictions. According to the General Agreement on Tariffs and Trade (GATT), such barriers could be removed on a reciprocal basis. In other words, both DCs and LDCs would be required to dismantle the protectionist policies. It was increasingly recognized that the removal of such restrictions would be much more harmful to the LDCs in comparison with the DCs. By the beginning of the 1970s, non-reciprocal agreement was reached under which DCs should remove or lower the barriers but the LDCs would not be required to reciprocate. Similarly, under the generalized system of preferences (GSP), preferences would be given for certain exports such as textiles and leather from LDCs which would be subject to a lower level of tariffs. The GSP scheme holds considerable hope for the future as it is flexible and subject to negotiation without significant detrimental effects on DCs. For an industry like textiles in DCs, the process of adjustment could be gradual and at the same time allocation could be more efficient by switching resources from declining to developing sectors. Further, to tide over the difficulties during the adjustment period, adjustment assistance could be offered. Indeed, in the United States such an Act was introduced in 1962 to offer direct financial help to those industries and labourers who were adversely affected. In the UK similar steps were taken by the Industrial Act of 1959 in the cotton industry.

The absorption of the resources made abundant in the process of adjustment in DCs should not pose great difficulties so long as their rate of economic growth is reasonable. However, to tide over the problems of resource mobility within the economy, fiscal and monetary policies (e.g. taxes, grants, subsidies, low interest rates) could be used effectively.[2]

7.15 Regional co-operation among less developed countries

The possibility of regional co-operation among the LDCs has been regarded as an alternative method of trade creation. The advocates of this scheme argue that such an integration among the LDCs would

1 expand the market;
2 enable them to enjoy the benefits of the economies of scale;
3 reduce the dependence of the LDCs on the DCs.

It is known that the creation of such trading blocs is based on the theory and practice of Customs Unions among the different DCs. The benefits of integration usually depend on the fulfilment of certain major conditions. For instance:

1 the member countries should mutually reduce tariff and non-tariff barriers.
2 There should be greater harmonization of monetary and fiscal policies.
3 The degree of trade between the member countries should be substantial, i.e. integration should increase the pro-trade bias given the complementarity in the production process among the member countries.
4 The countries within the trading bloc should follow a common external policy against the 'rest of the world', particularly with regard to tariffs.
5 The degree of trade dependence of the member countries on the rest of the world should not be very significant.
6 There should be a political will to unite.

Given the above conditions it is easy to see why regional integration among the LDCs is unlikely to be very successful. It is pointed out that 'more than 75 per cent of the LDCs' exports are to the rich countries and imports from the developed world into the LDCs are an even larger proportion of the LDCs' total imports' (Singer and Ansari 1977). The experience of the Latin American Free Trade Association (LAFTA) since its inception in 1961 has shown that the success of the integration scheme has been limited chiefly because of lack of complementary nature in trade and production as well as defective organization and administration. The gains in industrial production in the LAFTA have been very moderate. Similarly, the East African Community (EAC) consisting of Kenya, Uganda and Tanzania has confronted similar problems since its inception in 1967. Distribution of gains remains a bone of contention and political rivalry among these countries has been the cause of much concern despite some progress towards achieving a higher level of inter-regional trade. By 1977, trading blocs like the Association of South East Asian Nations (ASEAN), the Asian and Pacific Council (ASPAC) and the Central American Common Market (CACM) have come into existence. None of these trading blocs proved to be a great success given the low and oscillating level of trade among them.

However, one of the major reasons for setting up such trading blocs is political. Regional co-ordination among LDCs is supposed to provide them with greater bargaining power in their economic and political relationships with DCs.

7.16 Trade liberalization and industrialization

Trade liberalization and industrialization have been major strategies for accelerating the economic growth and standard of living in many LDCs in the 1980s. The policy is to raise exports in which the country has a comparative advantage (measured in terms of world to domestic cost price structure). This is also regarded as the export-led growth (ELG) strategy. Pricing rules should mirror both world prices and scarcity of domestic inputs. Exchange rates should clear the international markets.

Generally, LDCs following the ELG strategy must devalue domestic currencies to attain equilibrium rates. Exports will be promoted and underutilized resources will be employed. Commercial policy (e.g. a tariff *reduction*) could make production for exports incentive compatible as returns from domestic production made possible by tariffs and quotas would be less attractive. Such a policy would also reduce the biases in effective protection in favour of import-substituting industries. Despite such arguments for free trade, tariffs have historically played a significant role in economic growth (the import substitution industrialization or ISI policy). The doctrine of free trade is based on the theory of factor endowment and comparative cost advantage. Some of its basic assumptions, like perfect competition and optimal income distribution, have been called into question. Others have argued in favour of using tariffs to protect infant industries. Attention has been drawn to their beneficial effects on terms of trade (i.e. the optimum tariff argument; see Johnson 1968). Indeed, in the 1960s it was shown that, as far as protection is concerned, only the optimum tariff argument is the valid one; all others are really arguments for subsidies (Bhagwati and Ramaswami 1963). This line of argument is not very relevant to LDCs since few can exercise enough monopoly power to cause an international income transfer by improving their terms of trade. If countries are price takers, optimum tariffs are low or even zero. Also, the balance of payments argument is not regarded as optimal and a policy of a cut in domestic expenditure or devaluation is preferred to tariffs. Similar points have been made to dispose of the employment argument in favour of tariffs (Corden 1974).

The importance of LDCs as trading partners of the DCs has grown steadily throughout the 1970s and 1980s. According to one OECD report (1986), the share of all LDCs in industrial countries' total exports increased from 17 per cent in 1973 to about 25 per cent by 1985. Despite cyclical variations, the DCs' export surplus in manufactures with non-oil LDCs and OPEC nations is high, providing a substantial outlet for industrial activity in the OECD area. The DCs mopped up about two-thirds of the non-oil LDCs' exports of manufactures and a steadily rising share of their total exports. For many LDCs, demand conditions and access to DCs' markets for manufactures have become more important in determining their export earnings than has demand for their primary goods. The slowdown of growth in DCs in the early 1980s went hand-in-hand with the fall in LDC exports of manufactures and resulted in a massive debt crisis, chiefly in Latin America (see Chapter 14). Since 1982, with the impressive recovery in the United States (and in other DCs), anxiety regarding the debt crisis has eased somewhat (despite the persistence of high real interest rates) as LDC export earnings continued to rise along with an increase in debt-service capabilities. Some LDCs are still plagued by the debt problem and it is particularly acute in many African countries. Both tariff and non-tariff barriers in DCs (e.g. in agriculture) pose formidable problems for raising the share of primary exports by LDCs. To maintain export growth several newly industrialized countries (NICs) have set up production facilities in even lower-wage countries (e.g. 'South–South' trade between Malaysia, the Philippines and Thailand). Increasing risks in international investment have contributed to a rapid rise of offshore subcontracting initiated by the NIC firms (see, for example, OECD 1986). It has been estimated that an increase in protection beyond present levels could be very costly for *both* DCs and LDCs in terms of efficiency losses and feedback effects. A further rise of protection in DCs could lead to policy changes in LDCs (e.g. return to the ISI) as the credibility of a progressive reduction of trade barriers by DCs is undermined.

The years 1960–99 certainly witnessed a more 'interdependent' world as a larger proportion of world output is traded in world markets and the global capital market has been more integrated. Such a system has so far weathered major shocks, e.g.

1 the collapse of the Bretton Woods system of fixed exchange rates;
2 a massive rise in oil prices in the 1970s;
3 recessions in DCs in the early 1980s;
4 a phenomenal rise in real interest rates in the 1980s.

The likely impact of a crisis in the Middle East on an interdependent system is too early to predict. 'Nevertheless, the pessimistic perspective on the elasticity of trade with respect to output and income that coloured early development theorising and policy-making has been clearly belied by history' (Srinivasan 1988).

There were, of course, reasons for pessimism.

> The majority of the underdeveloped countries are monocultures, dependent for their earnings of foreign exchange on a single commodity (or at most two or three). These earnings are *highly inelastic* except when exports of the principal commodity form a small fraction of the world's consumption. At the same time, nearly all the plant and machinery that they require has to be imported, so that the scale of industrial development is limited by the foreign exchange available to pay for it.
>
> (Cairncross 1960)

Such ideas led to the growth of 'two-gap' models, i.e. a foreign exchange gap and a trade gap (see for example Chenery and Strout 1966), which are now widely studied in development economics. The central idea is:

> When the exchange gap was binding, which implied that there was a realisable but unrealised pool of domestic savings, foreign aid became twice blessed, once for relieving the constraint on imports of capital goods and once again by realising the potential domestic savings and converting it . . . into productive capacity in the form of plant and equipment.
>
> (Srinivasan 1988)

Around this theme, a number of multi-sector development models were developed which allowed for limited input substitution with *fixed* proportions (for a summary, see Blitzer *et al.* 1975). Production and consumption decisions at 'shadow prices' are the *effects* of some given objective functions of these models. Further, attempts were made to endogenize the price variable in a Walrasian general equilibrium model and to develop principles to compute its equilibrium value (see Robinson *et al.* 1982). Such an applied general equilibrium analysis has now been applied to analyse the impact of unilateral and multilateral trade liberalization in the context of a North–South model (Whalley 1984; see also Adelman and Robinson 1978; Shoven and Whalley 1991; Vines and Kanbur 1986). These models are useful for understanding the allocative efficiency implications of policies that alter the equilibrium prices and their effects on equilibrium returns to primary factors and income distribution. Given price expectation formation, accumulation and technical change, a *dynamic* set of (Hicksian temporary) equilibria can also be derived. The other useful tool for policy evaluation has been the social cost–benefit analysis (SCBA) of public investment (see Chapter 11). It is assumed that small open economies are world price takers. Thus, the 'shadow prices' for *traded* goods are their border (world) prices. Such 'shadow prices' for *non-traded* goods can also be derived from prices of traded goods. The results are fairly robust and can be rigorously derived from a general equilibrium model of the economy.

7.16.1 The theory of export-led growth

In an early work on trade orientation and economic growth in LDCs, Balassa *et al.* (1971) emphasized the need to alter the trade orientation of those LDCs which followed 'inward-looking' (i.e. ISI) policies. Balassa believed that ISI policies lead to a general misallocation of resources as they provide few incentives for maintaining cost–price discipline and improvement in productivity. The association between trade orientation and performance in productivity is sometimes derived from the well-known direct relationship between real output growth and productivity growth (i.e. the so-called Verdoon law). The validity of such a law has been observed in manufacturing and other secondary industrial activities by Kaldor (1967). The main cause behind such a positive correlation is supposed to be economies of scale gained with the expansion of the market. In LDCs, an important reason to account for economic growth and structural change is the size of the market. An LDC can experience substantial economies of scale and a fall in costs of production as a result of an expansion of the export market through trade. Thus, an ELG strategy is advocated for LDCs.

Second, dual-gap theories (Chenery and Strout 1966) offer another possible explanation of trade orientation and productivity performance. Due to the structural rigidities and production conditions in many LDCs, imports (of capital and intermediate inputs) are imperfect substitutes for domestically produced goods. Trade policies which reduce the availability of such critical foreign inputs for domestic production also reduce domestic capacity utilization and thus total factor productivity. An ELG strategy can increase the foreign exchange revenue, capacity utilization and growth of factor productivity.

Third, a more liberal trade policy, by opening up the domestic economy to foreign competition, enhances efficiency in domestic production as producers are forced to cut costs to retain their profit margins. Balassa (1989), in particular, argues that both 'export rivalry' and 'import competition' are necessary ingredients to raise domestic productivity because of the nature of a competitive market. In addition, ISI policies by imposing import restrictions break the important link between domestic and world prices. Producers at home are now 'protected' from the oscillations in world prices. Such a trade regime would allow rising costs to be passed forward to consumers via the pass-through effect. It is also argued that movements in world prices convey a lot of information on productivity trends in other countries of the world; policies and exchange rate distortions arising from them that prevent the transmission of the price signals can make the productivity performance inconsequential for policy analysis and reduce the dynamic comparative advantage in trade of an LDC.

Using a three-sector model, the relationship between the real exchange rate, trade and production can be shown as follows. Let the economy consist of three types of production sector: non-traded goods (N), exportables (X) and importables (Z). A simple production function comprising capital K and labour L is assumed to produce goods. Let the stock of capital be given in the short run. Each sector's profit (i.e. the marginal product of capital) and output are negatively correlated with the sectoral wage. Let W stand for such wage in the X sector, T the terms of trade (i.e. the ratio of export prices to import prices) and e the real exchange rate (i.e. the price of non-traded goods in terms of importables). Then the condition for clearing the labour market is

$$L_{\mathrm{dX}}(W) + L_{\mathrm{dZ}}(WT) + L_{\mathrm{dN}}(WT/e) = L \tag{7.5}$$

where L is the fixed labour supply and $L_{\mathrm{d}i}(\cdot)$ is the demand for labour in sector i with $L_{\mathrm{d}i},\ < 0$. Such a condition means that

$$\frac{\mathrm{d}W}{\mathrm{d}e} = \frac{L'_{\mathrm{dN}}WT/e^2}{L'_{\mathrm{dX}} + L'_{\mathrm{dZ}} + L'_{\mathrm{dN}}T/e} > 0 \tag{7.6}$$

Hence a fall in e (i.e. a real exchange rate depreciation) lowers W in the X sector and raises profits and production in the export sector. Further, owing to a rise in the marginal productivity of capital in the X sector, a *sustained* fall in the real exchange rate increases investment and production capacity in the export sector (Montiel 1990).

In theory, planners can of course try to raise productivity by expanding the market via intervention. In practice, it is almost impossible for planners to have 'ideal' models and information to replicate market solutions continuously. Many of the arguments mentioned by the advocates of trade liberalization policies for LDCs could be subject to some critical evaluation. For instance, the demand-oriented argument may not always be valid for LDCs as many contend that supply problems matter most in such countries. Technical progress, increasing returns to scale and growth of productivity via trade and exports could certainly be important sources of growth. In this context, the current work on 'endogenous growth theory' could be of relevance to examine the relationship between exports and economic growth (see, for example, Helpman 1989; Romer 1990; Lucas 1988; Barro 1991). In this class of models, exogenous labour supply growth on the traditional neoclassical growth model (Solow 1956) has been replaced by a human capital accumulation process which works as complementary input to physical capital. A further link could be established between trade-'acquired' comparative advantage and human capital accumulation.

Although the exact specification of such a link is very much in the area of useful future research, it is possible to see the nexus between trade, exports and economic growth as scale economies allow an LDC to take advantage of dynamic externalities. As an example, witness the South Korean economy which registered average economic growth rate in *per capita* income of 6.4 per cent per annum when the average export growth rate was 22.9 per cent per annum in real terms. Here scale economies seem to have contributed 38 per cent of the growth of total factor productivity over 1961–80 (Kwon 1986).

The dynamic impact of positive externalities due to the use of human capital can be stated with the following production function:

$$g = AK^{\alpha}H^{\beta} \tag{7.7}$$

where g is output per head, K is capital per head and H is human capital per worker. The term H^{β} represents the contribution of human capital where β is the elasticity of output with respect to human capital. Let the economy contain two sectors: (1) the export sector and (2) the non-export sector. In the export sector, let us assume that human capital grows at a rate proportional to the employment in that sector. Thus,

$$\Delta H_i/H_i = \lambda_i L_i(t) \qquad i = 1, 2 \ldots t \tag{7.8}$$

where λ_i is the coefficient of learning by doing (see, for example, Arrow 1962; Lucas 1988; Barro and Martin 1992) and L_i is the fraction of the labour force in the export sector.

Note that λ_i not only reflects Arrow's theory of learning by doing, i.e. the increase in labour productivity via the accumulated stock of physical capital, but also the knowledge of spillover effects between the different segments of human capital. In this way, the dynamic externalities are captured in equations (7.7) and (7.8). Since 'learning by doing' here is not subject to diminishing returns, the combination of equations (7.7) and (7.8) could measure the external effects of export growth on the overall economic growth. In theory, it is possible to relate export growth to a measure of trade orientation (i.e. a measure of openness) of an economy. It can be argued that, the greater the distortion in the exchange rate of the economy, the lower will be the growth rate of exports and hence the growth rate of output. In principle, it is not difficult to compute a simple index of trade orientation and exchange rate distortion by observing the extent of black market premia on the exchange rate of the domestic currency (see, for example, Edwards 1992; Kamin 1993; Ghatak and Utkulu 1994).

In the early stages of development during the 1950s and 1960s, following the Singer–Prebisch theorems, many LDCs adopted 'inward-looking' ISI rather than export promotion policies. Industrialization was sought through a protectionist environment, utilizing tariffs and quotas, foreign investment, technology transfer and foreign aid. In the mid-1960s, several LDCs abandoned such policies and liberalized their foreign trade and payments regimes. Some argue that in South Korea, Taiwan, Hong Kong and Singapore (and later in Malaysia), such liberalization policies have achieved remarkable success between 1968 and 1988 in terms of GDP growth rate, higher investment, greater employment creation and faster technological change (Balassa 1982; Bhagwati 1978; Krueger 1978). However, Srinivasan and Whalley (1986) have assessed the impact of trade liberalization in a Hicksian equivalent variation of income scale within the context of an applied general equilibrium analysis and found only modest global gains. These results should be treated with caution since the general equilibrium models are inadequate to capture the impact of *dynamic* capital accumulation and technical change; they also assume competitive markets and constant returns to scale.

Some believe that 'outward-looking' LDCs are generally more vulnerable to 'exogenous shocks' in the real world of incomplete markets. Balassa (1982, 1986, 1989) and Mitra (1986) try to quantify the effects on adjustment policies of the rise in oil price in the 1970s and of real interest rates in the 1980s by a number of indicators. Balassa's comparative study shows that LDCs following an outward-oriented development policy were more successful in their use of adjustment policies (i.e. regaining the pre-shock growth path of the economy). They comprised

1 deflation;
2 export promotion;
3 import substitution;
4 increased borrowing.

Using a macroeconomic structural model driven by gross national income (adjusted for terms of trade changes), Mitra (1986) argues that in many LDCs efforts to adjust to exogenous shocks were 'compromised' by domestic public sector profligacy and the use of exchange rate policy to attack inflation (due to public policy) has been counterproductive. The major response of the 'outward-oriented' LDCs has been external borrowing: for the NICs *deflation* has been used as the principal instrument of adjustment (Arida and Taylor 1989).

The use of the ISI strategy has prompted some to show its theoretical impact on 'rent-seeking' or 'directly unproductive profit' (DUP) activities due to diversion of resources (see, for example, Krueger 1974; Bhagwati 1978). These 'new theories', grafted on to some orthodox trade models, predict that given an existing distortion due to tariff or (non-optimal) taxes any increase in factor supplies due to accumulation or diversion of factors could *reduce* welfare by aggravating the effects of distortion (e.g. growth 'immiserization' or negative shadow factor price). The implication is that the gains to those policies that correct the distortion that engendered the rent-seeking could be significantly higher than the estimates of the cost of the same distortion in the absence of rent-seeking. When the resources devoted to lobbying for the adoption of a distortionary policy are included in the total cost of distortion, then welfare gains are substantial indeed.

But, if rent-seeking mitigated the distortion cost that engendered it, gains from removing distortions could be lower. The evidence tends to confirm the positive impact of an ELG policy on real income and output growth in many LDCs (see for example Kamin 1993). For Turkey and Malaysia, the use of cointegration analysis confirms a stable, positive, long-run relationship between a more liberal trade orientation and real output growth rate (Ghatak and Utkulu 1994).

7.17 The North–South models and intra-industry trade

In the North–South models (see Findlay 1980; Kanbur and Vines 1986), each region is specialized in producing its export commodity. The production function is neoclassical in both regions, but in the South labour supply is perfectly elastic with respect to wages. Saving is a fixed proportion of real income – the remaining portion is spent on home goods or imports from the South. Workers in the South consume their wages and capitalists save part of their profits. Relative prices determine total consumption on home goods and imports by workers and capitalists. Both regions grow at the steady state equilibrium given by the growth rate of effective labour supply in the North. In the comparative dynamic analysis, as the propensity to save rises and technology improves in the North, its *per capita* income and terms of trade improve but the South loses on both items. Some dubiously assume that capital is immobile and ignore the intertemporal gains or losses along the transitional path towards the new steady state. Kanbur and Vines (1986), however, show (with different assumptions, e.g. fixed capital–output ratio, long-run substitution between land and labour) that the two regions do not grow at the same rate; these growth rates are given by equilibrium terms of trade and a more favourable terms of trade for the South will lead to faster growth. In the medium term, the equilibrium terms of trade and capital stock are jointly determined. The growth rate of the effective stock of agricultural land is the same as the growth rate of the system in the long run. The model also analyses 'overshooting' adjustment behaviour in the face of exogenous shocks. In their simpler version (1986), the authors show that if Northern wages are sticky and the economy is Keynesian whereas Southern agricultural output is price inelastic, then price stabilization through buffer-stock operations should result in substantial macro benefits to the North – a result which contradicts previous findings that (micro) gains from agricultural price stabilization are very marginal indeed (see Newbery and Stiglitz 1981; Kanbur 1983). However, Kanbur and Vines do not consider the impact of price expectations and private costs of buffer-stock operations which could reduce the size of their estimated gains (for a neo-Ricardian and neoMarxian analysis see Evans 1989).

The other major development in the light of the marriage between trade and industrial organization theories has been to draw on models of a monopolistic or oligopolistic competition in an industry producing a set of differentiated products under *increasing returns to scale* to explain growing *intra-industry* trade. The useful result that has emerged is that, even when two countries are the same in all respects, exchanges will be beneficial because each country produces *differentiated* products from the same industry and consumers buy goods produced in both. Hence, welfare increases in both countries. Any difference between equilibrium price and marginal cost will induce countries to appropriate oligopolistic rent through strategic trade interventions.

Large-scale intra-industry trade takes place among LDCs (Greenaway and Milner 1987; Milner 1990). In one study on LDCs, it is observed that *per capita* income, diversity of manufactured exports, membership in a regional bloc and the *stage of development* account for a significant proportion of intra-industry trade. The penetration of the LDCs into the markets of DCs could spread over a number of products and hence the ultra-protectionist stance in the DCs is perhaps unwarranted (see Havrylshyn and Ciran 1983).

7.18 Conclusion

Trade policies in the LDCs, despite making some gains in industrialization and import substitution, have also caused some of their welfare loss in terms of negative value added at world prices in some of their industries. The ERP has remained quite high in many cases and the policy has promoted monopoly rather than competition and

Box 7.2 Venezuela: a case study in failed development strategies
Alan Mulhern

The foundation of the Venezuelan economy is oil production, typically constituting 80 per cent of total exports. Government revenues, the apparatus of state and the rest of the economy are dependent on its revenues. In the period up to 1978 Venezuela had low inflation and high economic growth. The percentage of the population in moderate poverty was 34.5 per cent, low by the standards of many developing countries. The Gini coefficient was an internationally respectable 33. Real incomes had seen substantial increases, for example 12.9 per cent in 1971 and 13.5 per cent in 1974 – the latter year saw the first hike in oil prices organized by the OPEC cartel of which Venezuela was a founding member. The non-oil economy responded with impressive increases in GDP of over 10 per cent per annum in 1974 and 1975. However, in the second part of this period (1974–8) supply-side constraints became evident with inflation on average almost three times higher than in the first half (1969–73). However, substantial gains were made – for example, a significant fall in the percentage of the labour force working in the informal sector.

The year 1979 was the dividing point in modern Venezuelan economic history. From that point onwards real incomes fell almost continuously, inflation accelerated, there was an alarming rise in the percentage of the population in poverty and the number and percentage of those working in the informal sector increased. The underlying structural weaknesses of the economy became evident. Despite the doubling of oil prices in 1979–80 the economy failed to respond in real terms. Instead the inflation rate tripled from 1978–81, real incomes fell and the Gini coefficient rose to 44 in 1982. This was all despite the immense oil revenues of the period. The period from 1985 to 1988 saw some recovery in non-oil GDP and an increase in real income; however, inflation remained high and the percentage of those in poverty increased to 53.5 per cent. The year 1989 saw a collapse of GDP (−9.4 per cent) and real income (−14.7 per cent) as well as rocketing inflation (84.5 per cent).

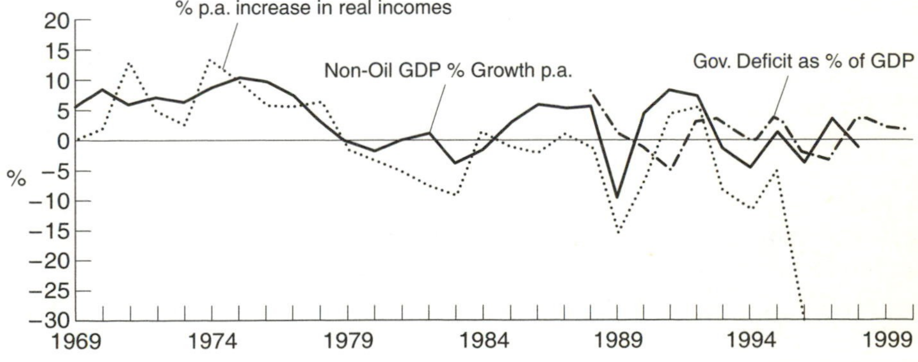

Figure 1

continued on next page

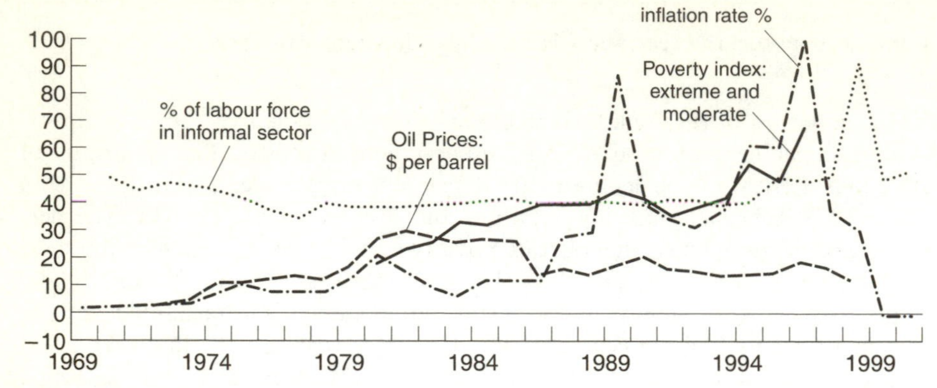

Figure 2

Up to this point the economy had been dominated by a development strategy dominated by government, large firms, oligopolistic sectoral interests and an ISI strategy. Corruption, elitism and 'insider' interests dominated the economy. This had proved disastrous and the government, in desperation, turned towards free market policies, opening up the economy, freeing its exchange rate, denationalizing state-run enterprises, engaging in free trade, ending subsidies and the like. This year was also known as the *Gran Viraje*, 'the great turnaround'. Figures 1–2 points to the real and immediate benefits of this free market experimentation. Real growth picked up in 1991–2 to the high levels of the mid-1970s. Inflation remained high, though it had halved from the 1989 rate, real incomes increased, the Gini coefficient improved, the percentage in poverty actually dropped and there was a decline in the percentage of those working in the informal sector between 1991 and 1993.

Nevertheless these policies were tremendously unpopular and were abandoned in 1993 with a government that returned to the failed policies of the past. The results were accelerating inflation, reaching almost 100 per cent in 1996 (fuelled by government budget deficits and a rising money supply), a serious decline in GDP and a catastrophic fall in real income (−30 per cent in 1996). The percentage of those in poverty increased to over 70 per cent and the number in the informal sector increased to almost half the labour force. By the end of the decade Venezuela was no nearer solving its economic problems and a new President had come to power with an extreme left-wing agenda.

inefficiency in many sectors. Exports of agricultural goods suffered and the policy of export promotion, until very recently, has generally been neglected. The trade policies used to correct domestic distortions are open to question. The problem of instability in export earning and its effect on growth and investment is also doubted on empirical grounds though the relationship between commodity concentration and export instability cannot be ruled out. However, such instability could stem from both world demand and domestic supply (for climatic and other reasons). Policies to stabilize export earnings such as regional integration or CASs do not hold much hope for the future of the LDCs. However, in schemes like the GSP, multilateral agreements, inter-governmental negotiations, expansion of domestic production, particularly of agriculture, and export promotion lie the best hopes for the LDCs. The policy of protection needs to be followed selectively in those cases where the benefits outweigh the losses.

Appendix 7.1 Indices of instability of exports

The index of instability in the exports of LDCs can be constructed in different ways and this could account for the differences in the results obtained. The main indices constructed so far can be summarized as follows.

Index used by the International Monetary Fund (IMF_I)

IME_I seeks to measure the divergences from a three-year weighted average of last year's income from exports, the distribution of weights being given as

$$X_t^* = 0.5X_t + 0.25X_{t-1} + 0.25X_{t-2}$$

where X_t is the actual income from exports at period t and X_t^* is the expected income from exports.

Index used by the United Nations (1952) (UN_I)

UN_I measures the sum of absolute divergences of income from exports per annum as a proportion of the higher of the two yearly incomes from exports. Notice that UN_1 fails to isolate the trends.

Index constructed on the basis of the moving average method (MA_I)

MA_I seeks to measure fluctuations as the sum of the absolute divergences of yearly income from exports from the moving average for n number of years where the value of n is subjectively chosen by the researcher. The value of n should be given by the theory that is applied as it influences the removal of fluctuations and difficulties could easily arise here, particularly in a cross-country analysis.

Percentage divergences of the average from the trend line observed by fitting the least squares method (A_I)

A_I consists of the derivation of the trend line by fitting the least squares method and then observation of the average percentage divergences from such a trend line.

Index of divergences front the linear least squares line (LLS_I)

LLS_I comprises the additions of the squared divergences from a trend line which is linear and obtained by minimizing the additions of squared residual elements.

Index of divergences from the exponential least squares line (ELS_I)

ELS_I comprises the additions of the squared divergences from a trend line which is exponential and obtained as for LLS_I.

Log-variance index of Coppock (LVC_I)

LVC_I comprises the divergences from a trend line given by the first and last period of the sample. Note that LVC_I is susceptible to the base period (Knudsen and Parnes 1975). Thus,

$$LVC_I = \text{antilog}\left[\frac{1}{n-1}\sum_{t=1}^{n-1}\left(\log\frac{V_{t+1}}{V_t} - r\right)^2\right]^{1/2}$$

and

$$r = \frac{1}{n-1}\sum_{t=1}^{n-1}\log\frac{V_{t+1}}{V_t}$$

or

$$r = \frac{1}{n-1}(\log V_n - \log V_1)$$

Transitory income index of Knudsen and Parnes (1975) (TKP_I)

TKP_I consists of the normalized variance of the transitory part of income. Notice the Friedmanian approach and its attendant comments. Let

$$C_t^* = K_y Y_t^* + K_x X_t^*$$

where C_t^* is permanent consumption, Y_t is actual domestic income, Y_t^* is permanent domestic income, X_t is actual income from exports, X_t^* is permanent income from exports, K_y is the propensity to consume out of Y_t^* and K_x is the propensity to consume out of X_t^*.

Let the index of export instability in transitory income be I_X where

$$I_X = \sum_{t=1}^{T}\frac{(X_t - X_t^*)^2}{X_t^{*2}}$$

Let the index of domestic instability in transitory income I_Y be

$$I_Y = \sum_{t=1}^{T}\frac{(Y_t - Y_t^*)^2}{Y_t^{*2}}$$

Notes

1 Dynamic externalities refer to the creation of some capital assets over time, for the use of which, firms in future will not be required to pay. Instances like the establishment of educational institutions or the development of transport facilities can easily be cited.

2 Some writers have recently argued that significant 'most favoured nation' (MFN) tariff cuts would provide the LDCs with more favourable access to world markets for unlimited trade volumes, as they cover more commodities and countries in comparison with the GSP, and hence MFN tariff cuts should be preferred to the GSP (see Baldwin and Murray 1977; sec also Grubel 1977).

Questions

1 Discuss the role of tariffs in promoting industrialization in LDCs.
2 Distinguish between 'nominal' and 'effective' rates of protection.
3 What are the major costs and benefits of protection of industrialization in LDCs?
4 Examine the relationship between trade and economic growth. How can trade 'immiserize' economic growth?
5 How do the 'terms of trade' move against primary-producing countries? What does the empirical evidence show?
6 Evaluate the relationship between trade liberalization, exports and economic growth.
7 What are the causes of export instability? What are its effects?

Part III

Sectoral development and planning

8 Sectoral allocation of resources: Agriculture

8.1 Introduction

Agriculture in most LDCs is the dominant sector of the whole economy. Indeed, it accounts for 40–90 per cent of the total output in LDCs and offers employment to 40–80 per cent of their working population. Given its overwhelming importance, the case for its improvement to promote economic growth can hardly be overemphasized. In this chapter, first, we discuss the role of agriculture in economic development. Next we examine the merit of the policies generally advocated for 'squeezing' agriculture for industrialization. An alternative model will then be formulated to analyse the problems of mobilizing surplus from agriculture. Finally, empirical evidence of farmers' response to economic incentives in LDCs will be provided (for a detailed analysis see Ghatak and Ingersent 1984).

8.2 The role of agriculture in economic development

Agriculture plays a crucial role in the economic growth of LDCs. We can summarize its role as follows.

1 Agriculture provides *labour* to the non-agricultural sector. It has been shown before (see Chapter 3) that many LDCs experience the existence of 'surplus' labour. Thus, availability of labour at a very low social opportunity cost could be an important factor to promote growth.
2 Food and raw materials are supplied by agriculture. Indeed, the cost of industrialization depends substantially upon low food and raw material prices. Since the industrial real wages would depend upon food prices, a steady food price is supposed to be imperative for achieving economic development. Further, in most LDCs the demand for food is high and is not expected to fall significantly partly because of 'population explosion' (i.e. high birth rate coupled with low death rate) and partly because of subsistence livelihood. In fact, the income elasticity of the demand for food is estimated to be much higher in LDCs in comparison with DCs. In most cases, it is 0.6 in LDCs while the comparative figure for DCs is about 0.2 (Johnston and Mellor 1961). The estimation of change in demand for food per annum could easily be made by using the following formula:

$$\mathrm{AD} = I + \varepsilon_y$$

where AD is changes in demand for food per annum, I is the population growth rate and ε is the elasticity of income (y) with respect to demand for agricultural products.

It must be borne in mind that since, in LDCs, consumption of food accounts for a high proportion of income, a rise in food prices, given an inelastic supply, could have an adverse impact on the whole economy.

3 Exports of agricultural products can help a country to earn valuable foreign exchange. When a country supplies only a small percentage of total exports chiefly in primary goods, it is likely to face an inelastic demand curve. However, if many LDCs try to export the same goods at the same time, prices may fall, given low income and low price elasticities of demand of these goods. The answer to this problem lies in not putting 'all the eggs in the same basket'. Diversification of export crops will help to reduce the risks.

4 The rate of capital formation in LDCs can be considerably improved by the agricultural sector. The process of capital accumulation and the role of agriculture in that process have already been discussed in the Lewis, Fei and Ranis, and Jorgenson models. It is enough to recall here that the process of accumulation depends upon the elasticity of food supply because, given the bottlenecks on the supply side, wages and costs will rise and profit margins are supposed to fall, leading to an overall decline in surplus and growth.

The process of capital formation will also depend upon fiscal and monetary policies to siphon off surplus from agriculture. The tax on agriculture in Japan accounted for about 80 per cent of total tax revenue during 1893–7 and 50 per cent between 1913 and 1917 (Johnston and Mellor 1961).

However, political factors often stood in the way of imposing an agricultural tax in many LDCs, including India, Pakistan and Burma. Frequently, simple inertia and weaknesses in the tax system have been major factors. Russian economic development illustrates vividly the price the agricultural sector had to pay for capital formation even when 'the birth pangs were sharp and the attendant midwifery was rough' (Dobb 1948). Whether the price was worth paying or not is another matter.

5 Agriculture in LDCs may play a crucial role in expanding the size of the home market. This can be achieved by enlarging the money and real income of the cultivators which will increase the demand for industrial products and thus will act as a stimulus to industrialization (e.g. Gold Coast, see Lewis 1953 for details; see also Nurkse 1959).

It is clear from the above analysis that agriculture can help or hinder the pace of economic growth and industrialization, given the considerable linkages between them in many LDCs. The next important issue is how to raise agricultural productivity to achieve a higher rate of growth. Here the main concern is how to raise 'surplus' (the difference between food production and food consumption) from agriculture to achieve a higher rate of capital formation. The problem is not new but important. In the following section we shall examine the nature of the debate between different schools about the ways of mobilizing surplus for reinvestment.

8.3 The concept of 'marketed surplus'

The concept and role of marketed surplus is hardly new in development economics. Adam Smith (1776), for example, observed: 'When by the improvement and cultivation of land . . . the labour of half the society becomes sufficient to provide food for the whole, the other half . . . can be employed . . . in satisfying the other wants and fancies of mankind.' Unfortunately, many Western economists have tended to ignore or seriously underestimate the importance of an agricultural surplus both in the earlier economic history of today's developed countries and in those countries which still remain at or near the bare subsistence level of food consumption (Nicholls 1963: 1). However, some have recognized its importance (Nicholls 1963; Owen 1966; Khusro 1967), and it is now argued that the size of the surplus is crucially related to the size of capital formation.

8.3.1 Marketed surplus and capital formation

It is generally stated that in a labour-surplus economy, without any loss of agricultural production, surplus population from agriculture can be transferred to other projects so long as consumption of agricultural output of agricultural and newly transferred non-agricultural labour remains constant. Defining marketed surplus as the difference between total food production and total food consumption, it may be argued that, if *per capita* consumption remains fixed, surplus could be mobilized for real capital formation. Obviously, the process involves leakages and the smaller the leakages the greater is the marketed surplus. It is also important that (1) those who still work in agriculture will refrain from consuming more agricultural goods; (2) the agricultural population, with expansion of marketed surplus and thus with rising capacity to consume more manufactured goods, should be prevented from consuming more agricultural goods at constant terms of trade.

The objectives are (1) to transfer marketed surplus and (2) to enforce savings on the agricultural population. To achieve these objectives, government may (1) impose taxes or levies or (2) try to persuade peasants to save more. The first policy *may* be successful in a command economy; the success of the second policy is questionable. It may require someone like Mao who may persuade the masses to swim, sometimes against the tide; or it may require a certain ideology and value judgement (e.g. everybody would be better off by giving up something). In any case, it is difficult to see the application *and* success of such a policy in all the LDCs. Alternatively, the terms of trade, i.e. the ratio of agricultural prices to industrial prices, could be changed against agriculture. This policy gained considerable favour in Russia in the 1920s. Originally advocated by Preobrazhensky (1965) and blessed by some key political leaders of the USSR at that time, the implications of this policy are interesting and deserve attention.

8.3.2 Marketed surplus and terms of trade

The method of turning the terms of trade against agriculture is supposed to be similar to that of a country's use of its favourable terms of trade with other countries for its capital formation. The terms of trade may be changed against agriculture in different ways (Narain 1957). For example:

1 The prices of agricultural goods may be prevented from rising in proportion to the prices of manufactured goods through price control.
2 Industrial goods entering into villagers' consumption could be taxed.
3 The prices of domestic manufactured goods may be allowed to rise by granting protection to the industries holding agricultural prices constant.
4 The state may trade in manufactured goods.

By adopting policies 1 and 3 the profit margins of private industry could be raised and fiscal policy may be used to mop up the surplus. Adoption of methods 2 and 4 should directly raise resources for financing development. It should be noted that the higher the percentage of surplus agricultural population to be transferred, *ceteris paribus*, the more will the terms of trade have to be moved against agriculture to absorb the potential savings. It is assumed that the required increase in marketed surplus is forthcoming.

However, the policy has limitations. It is plausible to think that when the surplus agricultural labour is transferred to the non-agricultural sector, those who would be left behind in the agricultural sector may consume more of their own produce than they did previously because they might be feeling better off. This may be regarded as the direct income effect and this may reduce marketed surplus. When the terms of trade are moved against agriculture, there would be two other effects. These are 'derived' income and substitution effects. When the terms of trade move against agriculture, the demand of agriculturists for everything including their own goods is thereby reduced by reducing this real income, This may raise the marketed surplus, but since agricultural goods become cheaper relative to industrial goods, it induces the agriculturists to substitute their own goods instead of industrial goods. If the direct income and substitution effects are more powerful than the derived income effect, then total marketed surplus *declines*.

There is an additional problem related to savings. The strength of the policy depends upon the compulsion under which the peasant should sell part of his production. Such compulsion exists in a command economy. But in a democratic society there is nothing to prevent a 'spite effect', i.e. as the terms of trade go against agriculture, a farmer might decide not to sell as much as he might have sold before any worsening of the terms of trade. In the extreme case, farmers may refuse to sell anything. These points are illustrated in Figures 8.1 and 8.2.

In Figure 8.1, the reactions of a farmer are described with changing terms of trade. The farmer's income in agricultural goods is given by OA and OB respectively, prior to and after the transference of surplus population. Since the diagram depicts every quantity as per head of agricultural population AB shows the addition per head of rural population after the transfer of surplus labour. The initial equilibrium is reached at E where AC – the slope showing the initial terms of trade – is tangent to the indifference curve i_1. The slope of BK passing through E shows the terms of trade that are required to absorb total potential savings (assuming that the appropriate rise in marketed surplus is forthcoming). As the slope of BK is greater than the slope of AC, and since indifference curves cannot intersect each other, it follows that E$'$, the point of new equilibrium, must lie above E and a decline in marketed surplus is observed. Could a more drastic change of terms of trade against agriculture raise marketed surplus? In theory, the answer is 'yes' at, say, E$''$, but the experience of some countries suggests that the consequences (both economic and social) could be very serious. It may

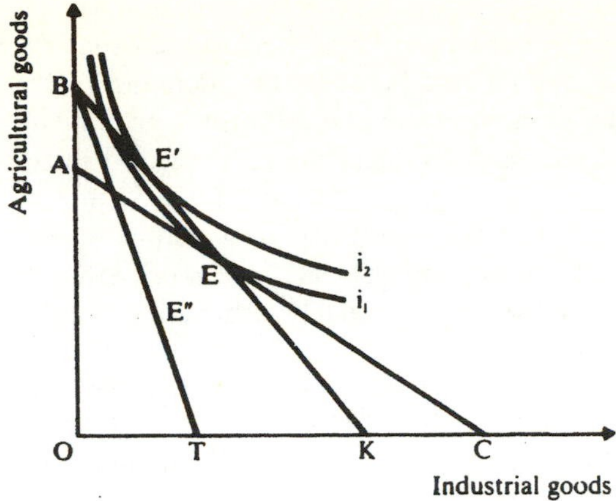

Figure 8.1

indeed be stated that marketed surplus will fall with significant decrease in agricultural prices.

In Figure 8.2 AB is the given amount of foodgrains, MM′ shows a declining marginal utility of foodgrains retained for consumption and PP' shows the declining marginal utility of sales. Equilibrium is reached at D and marketed surplus is CB. With a fall in the price of foodgrains, the curve PP′ shifts to pp′ and at the new equilibrium F marketed surplus falls to GB. (The arguments here rest on two assumptions: (1) separable utility; and (2) sufficient restrictions on the rate at which the marginal utility of non-foodgrains decreases in comparison with the price difference in the two events to make sure that PP′ and pp′ will not intersect one another. Relaxing either of these two assumptions might allow for the reappearance of negative price elasticity.) As long as production is positively elastic with respect to price changes, then even when consumption rises, marketed surplus must rise so long as the positive price elasticity of foodgrains is greater than the price elasticity of consumption (Bhagwati and Chakravarty 1969: 33).

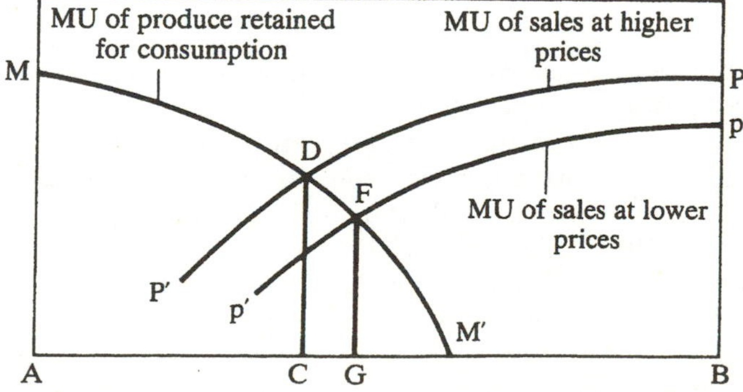

Figure 8.2

The point is made, however, that, if price falls, marketed surplus may rise (see Ghatak 1975b for a summary) for several reasons. Thus, it is argued that farmers wish to maintain the same level of money income because their demand for cash is fixed (Mathur and Ezekiel 1961). Such an assumption would imply very low income elasticity of the demand for non-foodgrains of the farmers as well as a zero substitution effect – an assumption which is hardly valid logically or empirically. Further, this model applies only to the very short run and does not show what happens when the initial equilibrium is disturbed. Indeed in Mathur and Ezekiel's model price movements could be explosive once the equilibrium is disturbed. Similarly, other advocates seemed to have ignored the substitution effect.

Several attempts have been made at an aggregative level (Krishnan 1965; Bardhan, K. 1970; Thamarajakshi 1969; Bardhan and Bardhan 1971) to estimate the marketed surplus in the Indian economy. Krishnan's method of estimation is of some interest. Let $\bar{Q}$ be the total output of foodgrains in the short run, P the price of foodgrains, $\bar{Q}P$ the farmer's income and r the proportion of output consumed by the cultivators themselves. Then we have

$$r\bar{Q} = AP^{-\alpha}(P\bar{Q})^{\beta}$$

Using the Rural Credit Survey data for the period between 1959–60 and 1962–3, Krishnan found that the elasticity of marketed surplus was −3,030 in India. But this finding is based upon the assumption that output is fixed. If that assumption is relaxed one might get positive elasticity (Bhagwati and Chakravarty 1969: 35). Second, in the equation the effects of factors affecting supply (e.g. input costs, land tenure, etc.), but not demand, are ignored. Further, it may be argued that the parameter in the demand function of Krishnan is not the price elasticity of demand of farmers. In fact, such elasticity is given by $\beta - \alpha$. Note that

$$r\bar{Q} = AP^{-\alpha}(P\bar{Q})^{\beta}$$

or

$$r\bar{Q} = AP^{\beta-\alpha}(\bar{Q})^{\beta}$$

Therefore

$$\frac{\partial r\bar{Q}}{\partial P}\frac{P}{r\bar{Q}} = \beta - \alpha$$

Redefined in this way, and using Krishnan's own estimation, the price elasticity of marketed surplus becomes positive (Macrae 1971).

But several criticisms can be made about almost all these empirical studies. First, no attempt has been made to look at the problem from the standpoint of the utility function of an individual farmer. Second, the data used in some of these studies are too aggregative (see Krishnan 1965; Thamarajakshi 1969). Third, the inverse relationship between price, terms of trade and marketed surplus observed at the national level may not be valid at the state level. Fourth, the variations of different crop prices are not usually considered. For example, the effects of changes in the price of one crop may be neutralized by changes in the price of other crops. In view of these criticisms, a formal model is set out in section 8.4 to examine the response of the marketed surplus to changes in the terms of trade; empirical estimates are also given. Section 8.8 draws some conclusions.

8.4 A model to mobilize agricultural surplus

Contrary to previous analysis, the problem of mobilizing surplus from agriculture is analysed in the following model, from the point of view of farmer's utility. Let the farmers' utility function be

$$U_a = U_a(a, i, L) \tag{8.1}$$

where U_a is the utility of the farmer, a is consumption of agricultural goods, i is consumption of industrial goods and L is leisure.

It is assumed that in a traditional society the farmer's demand for agricultural goods is given, i.e. $a = \bar{a}$. Hence rewriting equation (8.1) we have

$$U_a = U_a(\bar{a}, i, L) \tag{8.2}$$

The income of the farmer is given by the revenue from agricultural goods that could be sold in the market:

$$Y_a = p_a M \tag{8.3}$$

where Y_a is income from the sale of agricultural goods, p_a is the price of agricultural goods and M is the marketed surplus.

Marketed surplus is, in turn, regarded as a function of leisure; this simple assumption can be relaxed later. At the moment we are abstracting away from the product relationship not because it is unimportant but because it is another vast field of enquiry and because it facilitates diagrammatic exposition. Thus we have

$$M = f(L) \tag{8.4}$$

$$p_a M = p_i i + T + R \tag{8.5}$$

where p_i, is the price of industrial goods, T is taxes and R is rents. Equation (8.5) states that the income of the farmer is spent on industrial goods, as well as on taxes and rent that he pays in cash.

Substituting equation (8.4) into (8.5), we obtain

$$p_a f(L) = p_i i + T + R \tag{8.6}$$

or

$$p_a f(L) - p_i i - T - R = 0 \tag{8.7}$$

Expressing the Lagrangian for the maximization of the farmer's utility function subject to his income, we obtain

$$V = p_a f(L) - p_i i - T - R = 0 \tag{8.8}$$

$$\max V = U_a^*(\bar{a}, i, L) + \lambda[p_a f(L) - p_i i - T - R] \tag{8.9}$$

Setting the partial derivatives equal to zero, we obtain

$$\frac{\partial V}{\partial i} = \frac{\partial U_{\mathrm{a}}^{*}}{\partial i} - \lambda p_{\mathrm{i}} = 0 \qquad (8.10)$$

$$\frac{\partial V}{\partial L} = \frac{\partial U_{\mathrm{a}}^{*}}{\partial L} + \lambda p_{\mathrm{a}} f'(L) = 0 \qquad (8.11)$$

$$\frac{\partial V}{\partial \lambda} = p_{\mathrm{a}} f(L) - p_{\mathrm{i}} i - T - R = 0 \qquad (8.12)$$

Dividing (8.10) by (8.11) and eliminating λ we have

$$\frac{\partial U_{\mathrm{a}}^{*}/\partial i}{\partial U_{\mathrm{a}}^{*}/\partial L} = \frac{-P_{\mathrm{i}}}{P_{\mathrm{a}} f'(L)} \qquad (8.13)$$

Since

$$M = f(L) \qquad (8.4)$$

Therefore

$$\frac{\mathrm{d}M}{\mathrm{d}L} = f'(L) < 0 \qquad (8.4a)$$

Thus, $-p_{\mathrm{a}} f'(L)$ may be regarded as the unit price of leisure since $-f'(L) = \mathrm{d}M/\mathrm{d}L$ is the change in M resulting from a unit change of leisure, and the sign of the derivative is negative. Hence, equation (8.13) may be rewritten as

$$\frac{\text{Marginal utility of } i}{\text{Marginal utility of } L} = \frac{\text{Unit price of industrial goods}}{\text{Unit price of leisure}} \qquad (8.14)$$

The points are illustrated in Figure 8.3. In the north-east quadrant, the relationship between leisure and industrial goods is described by a family of indifference curves. Similarly, the relationship between consumption of industrial goods and terms of trade, i.e. $p_{\mathrm{a}}/p_{\mathrm{i}}$ is shown in the north-west quadrant. The curve indicates that, as the price of industrial goods falls relative to agricultural goods, demand for industrial goods will rise. In the south-west quadrant it is shown that, when the terms of trade move in favour of agriculture, marketed surplus will *rise*, though the rate of rise will decrease gradually. This is partly because of the limited role that terms of trade could play at a more developed stage, and also because there is an absolute limit after which peasants will be unwilling to sacrifice leisure, which also explains the nature of the relationship between leisure and marketed surplus in the south-east part of the diagram. It is implied that an indefinite increase in the relative prices of agricultural goods may not increase surplus because after a point farmers may wish to consume more leisure and the supply curve of labour may turn backwards. However, the case of the backward-bending supply curve of labour has never been well proved for agricultural systems in poor countries (Blake 1962). Similar doubts have been voiced about price responsiveness of peasants in poor countries. But almost all empirical studies show that farmers are responsive to economic incentives

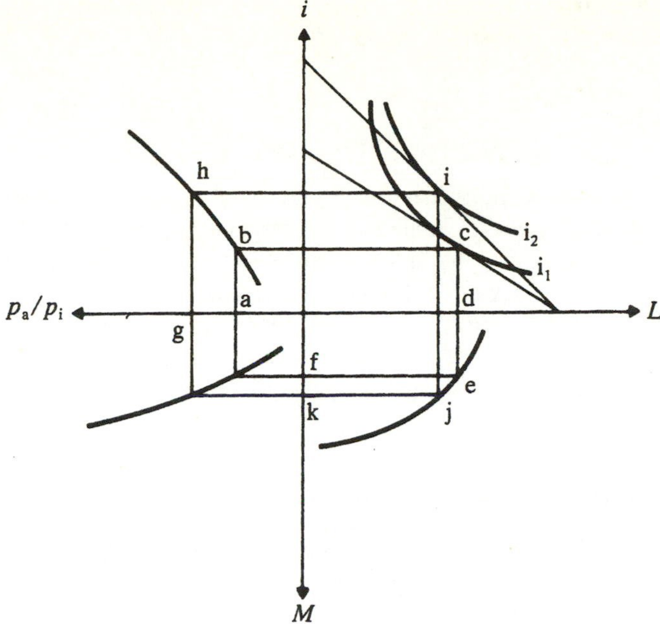

Figure 8.3

(Bauer and Yamey 1959; Krishna 1963; Behrman 1968). It may indeed be said that before branding the farmers as unresponsive they must be given the opportunities to respond.

In our model, price movements need not be divergent so long as the elasticity of the marketed surplus curve, i.e. the 'offer curve', is less than the elasticity of the urban demand curve. The stability of equilibrium in the Walrasian sense would be maintained when it could be shown that, at prices above the equilibrium, supply exceeds demand and that, when prices are lower than the level prevailing at equilibrium, demand exceeds supply. In order to evaluate conclusions what is useful is to test the price elasticities of marketed surplus and of urban goods of the farmers. Before the empirical estimates are made, it may be mentioned here that, contrary to the existing models, our model predicts that if the terms of trade are moved in favour of agriculture, surplus will rise rather than fall as long as farmers' consumption of agricultural goods remains stable and farmers' marginal utility of urban goods is high. Again, firm conclusions can be drawn only empirically. Suffice for the present to note that in countries like India income elasticity of demand for food is less than unity, while the income elasticity for industrial goods in the rural sector is very high. Similarly, the price elasticity of industrial goods in the rural sector is also very high (NCAER 1972). Hence, it is conceivable that a relative fall in the price of industrial goods may induce the farmer to sell more in the market. Indeed, the policy for mobilizing surplus by keeping agricultural prices rather low has repeatedly failed in many LDCs.

Rent and taxes may also explain the relationship between price and marketed surplus, depending on whether they are paid in cash or kind. For example, given fixed consumption of agricultural goods by the farmers in a bad year, if the rent is to be paid in kind, marketed surplus will fall. This may be true for a subsistence farmer who could reduce his demand for industrial goods rather than for food.

8.4.1 Empirical estimates

Empirical estimates of the relationship between terms of trade and marketed surplus do not yield any conclusive answer. While Krishnan (1965), Thamarajakshi (1969) and Bardhan, K. (1970) have found negative elasticity with respect to agricultural prices, Krishna (1965) found positive elasticity for a single crop. Using the data for wheat production and supply in Punjab–Haryana, Ghatak (1975a) also found positive elasticity with respect to both barter and income terms of trade (see also Bardhan and Bardhan 1971). Similarly, the long-run price elasticity is estimated as positive in Thailand (Behrman 1968). Also, both long- and short-run elasticities are shown as positive in Africa (Helleiner 1975).

8.5 Acreage response to prices

An alternative way that has been used by many economists to test the 'rational' behaviour of the peasants in LDCs was to examine the change in the distribution of acreage of land under cultivation because of price changes. It was sometimes held that the peasants in LDCs do not respond 'rationally', i.e. they do not respond to economic incentives. However, almost all the numerous studies which have been conducted so far confirm the hypothesis that the peasants in LDCs do respond to changes in economic incentives (Ghatak 1987). This is shown in Table 8.1. In only *one* case (sorghum in undivided Punjab) is the price elasticity negative and significant. But this was due to the fact that it was an inferior feed crop (Krishna 1968). Similarly, considerable evidence from African smallholders supply elasticities suggests the responsiveness of the African farmers to economic incentives (Helleiner 1975). This is shown in Table 8.2.

8.6 Marketed surplus, size-holdings and output

It has been suggested that size-holdings could affect the size of the surplus (Narain 1957; Krishna 1965). Empirical evidence suggests that the scale of holding is not a problem if only the *proportions* of output marketed are considered. Thus, the land-holdings in the size class of less than five acres supplied about 20.7 per cent of the value of their output as marketed surplus. This conclusion can be questioned, however, when the sale of individual crops is concerned. The following reasons can be offered to account for such inconsistencies:

1 different definitions of marketed surplus;
2 differences in the time and places covered;
3 while some have considered all the crops, others have considered only one crop.

It is worth noting that according to one survey of Indian agriculture (Narain 1961) the proportion of marketed surplus declines until size-holdings of ten to fifteen acres are reached but rises after that. If this is true, then the implication is that the break-up of large holdings may *increase* rather than diminish the marketed surplus, assuming

Table 8.1 Estimated price elasticities of acreage of specified crops, less-developed countries and regions

Crop and country or region	*Period*	*Elasticity*		*Source*
		Short run	*Long run*	
Rice				
Punjab				
(India–Pakistan)	1914–45	0.31	0.59	Krishna 1963
Pakistan	1948–63	0.05[a]		Hussain 1964
Indonesia (Java and Madura)	1951–62	0.30		Mubyarto 1965
Philippines	1947–63	[b]	[b]	Mangahas *et al.* 1965
Ilocos	1954–64	0.22	0.51	
C. Luzon	1954–64	0.13	0.62	
S. Tagalog	1954–64	0.24	0.42	
E. Visayas	1954–64	0.13	0.15	
Cagayan	1954–64	[b]	[b]	
Wheat				
Punjab				
(India–Pakistan)	1914–43	0.08	0.14	Krishna 1963
Pakistan	1944–59	0.20		Falcon 1964
Maize				
India–Pakistan	1914–43	0.23	0.56	Krishna 1963
Philippines	1911–41	0.02	0.04	Mangahas *et al.* 1965
Philippines	1947–64	0.07	0.42	Mangahas *et al.* 1965
Ilocos	1953–63	0.07	0.11	
C. Luzon	1953–63	[b]	[b]	
S. Tagalog	1953–63	0.42	0.47	
E. Visayas	1947–63	0.40[c]	0.57[c]	
W. Visayas	1947–63	0.03	0.04	
Cagayan	1953–63	[b]	[b]	
Bicol	1953–63	0.16	0.26	
Mindanao				
S. and W.	1953–63	[b]	[b]	
N. and E.	1947–63	[b]	[b]	
Barley				
Punjab				
(India–Pakistan)	1914–45	0.39[c]	0.50	Krishna 1963
Millet				
India–Pakistan	1914–45	0.09	0.36	Krishna 1963
Grain				
Punjab				
(India–Pakistan)	1914–45	–0.33[c]		Krishna 1963
Sorghum				
Punjab				
(India–Pakistan)	1914–43	0.58		Krishna 1963

continued on next page

Table 8.1 (continued)

Crop and country or region	Period	Elasticity		Source
		Short run	Long run	
Sugar cane				
Punjab				
(India–Pakistan)	1915–43	0.34	0.60	Krishna 1963
Cotton				
India–Pakistan	1922–43	0.59	1. 08	Krishna 1963
India	1948–61	0.64	1. 33	Krishna 1965
Pakistan				
(eight districts)	1933–58	0.41		Falcon 1964
Pakistan	1935–62	0.50[d]		Mohammad 1963
Egypt	1900–38	0.4–0.6[e]		Stern 1959
Egypt	1913–37	0.40		Stern 1962
Jute				
India–Pakistan	1911–38	0.46	0.73	Venkatamaranan 1958
Bengal				
(India–Pakistan)	1911–38	0.68	1. 03	Stern 1962
India–Pakistan				
(Bengal, Bihar, Orissa)	1893–1938	0.57–0.65		Stern 1962
Pakistan	1931–53	0.60		Clark 1957
Pakistan	1948–63	0.40		Hussain 1964
Rubber				
Malaysia				
Estates	1953–60	0		Stern 1965
Smallholders	1953–60	0.20		Stern 1965
Estates	1951–61	0.02[c, f]		Chan[g]
Smallholders	1948–61	0.12[f]		Chan[g]
Estates	1954–61	0.03[c, h]		Chan[g]
Smallholders	1953–60	0.34[h]		Chan[g]

Source: Krishna (1968).

Notes: [a] For summer and winter crops combined; elasticity for summer crop alone, 0.12. [b] Negative coefficient indicated. [c] Not significant at 10 per cent level. [d] Based on simple calculations from yearly variations. [e] Based on year-to-year arc elasticities. [f] Based on annual data. [g] Reported in Wharton (1964: tables 6.2, 6.3, 6.4). Wharton also reports (1963: 7) estimates of less than 0.21 for some other countries of South-east Asia. [h] Based on monthly data.

away any negative effect of any consequent change in output. But another study of Indian agriculture has shown that, in the absence of any change in the number of landholdings, changing output among different sized groups of land will not influence the amount of marketed surplus (Krishna 1965). However, this result could occur in the case of a single crop and not with the total agricultural output. On balance, it must be stated that in the absence of the availability of *time-series* data for most LDCs, no firm conclusion can be drawn.

The other important issue in agriculture in many LDCs is the relationship between farm size and output per acre of land. It has been observed on the basis of the Farm Management Surveys for some provinces of India between 1955 and 1957–8 that, as farm size increases, output per acre diminishes. In other words, smaller farms are

Table 8.2 Evidence on African smallholder supply elasticities[a]

Product and country	*Period*	*Short-run elasticity*	*Long-run elasticity*	*Positive response but no elasticity data*[a]	*Source*[c]
Cocoa					
Ghana	1930–40		0.43		Ady 1949
	1920–39	0.17			Stern 1965
	1920–46	0.15			*Ibid.*
	1946–62		0.32–0.87		Bateman 1965
	1946–62		0.77–1.28		*Ibid.*
	1947–64		0.71		Behrman 1968
Nigeria	1920–45		1.29		Stern 1965
	1947–64		0.45		Behrman 1968
	1948–67		0.20		Olayide 1972
Ivory Coast	1947–64		0.80		Behrman 1968
Cameroon	1947–64		1.81		*Ibid.*
Ghana	1947–64			•	Ady 1968
Nigeria	1947–65			•	*Ibid.*
Sierra Leone				•	Saylor 1967
Coffee					
Kenya, estates acreage	1946–64	0.16	0.47		Maitha 1969; Ford 1971
Kenya, smallholder acreage	1946–64	0.20	0.56		*Ibid.*
Kenya, estates yield	1946–64	0.66	0.71		Maitha 1970; Ford 1971
Kenya, smallholder yield	1946–64	0.64	1.01		*Ibid.*
Ethiopia	1964–70				Goering *et al.*
Uganda	1950–64			•	Ady 1968
Palm oil					
Nigeria	1950–64	0.81			Diejomaoh 1972
	1949–63	0.41			Helleiner 1966
	1948–67		0.22–0.26		Olayide 1972
Eastern Nigeria	1949–66	0.41–0.70			Oni 1969[a]
Palm kernels					
Nigeria	1950–64	0.25			Diejomaoh 1972
	1949–66	0.22–0.28			Oni 1969[a]
Sierra Leone				•	Saylor 1967
Cotton					
Nigeria	1950–64	0.67			Diejomaoh 1972
	1948–67	0.21–0.38			Oni 1969[b]
	1948–67	0.3			Olayide 1972
Tanzania	1953–69		2.44		Malima 1971

continued on next page

Table 8.2 (continued)

Product and country	*Period*	*Short-run elasticity*	*Long-run elasticity*	*Positive response but no elasticity data*[a]	*Source*[c]
Tobacco					
Malawi	1926–60	0.48			Dean 1966
Rubber					
Nigeria	1948–67	0.21	0.17–0.24		Olayide 1972
Haricot beans					
Ethiopia	1953–70	1.60			Goering *et al.*
Civet					
Ethiopia	1957–70	3.16			*Ibid.*
Pulses					
Ethiopia	1952–70	0.72			*Ibid.*
Lentils					
Ethiopia	1953–70	1.30			*Ibid.*
Sesame					
Ethiopia	1957–70	0.61			*Ibid.*

Source: Helleiner (1975: 401).

Notes: [a] It is difficult to summarize results in a number or two. A complete assessment of the meaning and value of these various estimates requires reference to the original source. [b] An asterisk indicates a statistically significant response. [c] Full references are given below in source notes.

more efficient than larger farms. Again from the point of view of policies, this finding has very important implications. Several explanations have been offered. We summarize here the major points.

1 While the larger farms are based on the capitalistic system of cultivation, the smaller farms are run on the principle of family farming. Hence, on the larger farms output is produced at a point where marginal productivity (MP) is equal to wages, whereas on smaller farms cultivation is carried out beyond this point as output could be extended up to the point where MP = 0. Small farms are thus regarded as more efficient on the basis of per acre productivity. But this explanation is not adequate.
2 Larger farms are less fertile than smaller farms because poorer peasants sell, frequently in distress, the inferior-quality land to rich peasants.
3 Larger farms may be scattered over a wide area particularly if the 'distress sale' hypothesis is true, and this could account for inefficiency emanating from fragmentation and distance. Also, since the smaller farms are in distress and may be operating close to the level of their survival, they would be more induced to use the inputs more efficiently, whereas the larger farms are not under compulsion to do so because of the higher marginal disutility from labour that they would now associate with marginal changes in income. Note that the point about the trade-

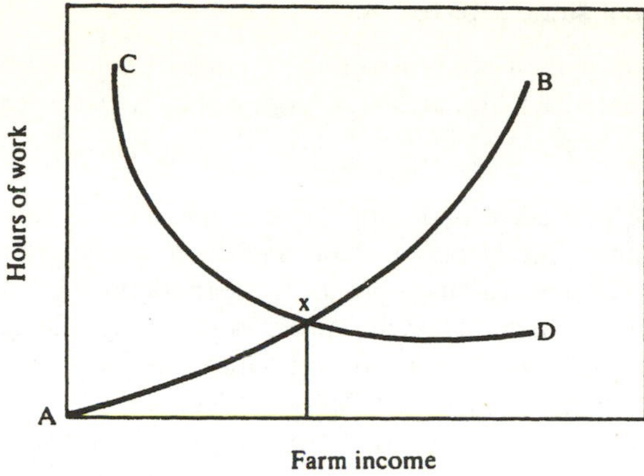

Figure 8.4

off between leisure and income is not new, as Chayanov (1966) has demonstrated (see Figure 8.4). The horizontal axis measures farm income. The curve CD shows the declining marginal utility of farm income whereas the curve AB depicts the marginal disutility of work associated with longer hours and higher income. The slope of the curve AB clearly shows that, as income rises, the marginal disutility after a point, say x, rises steeply. Equilibrium is reached at a point like x. However, Chayanov's argument that an increase in prices of crops will increase leisure preferences is open to question.

4 *Tenurial disincentives* on large farms may account for inefficiency. Nevertheless, empirical evidence to test this hypothesis has yielded conflicting results.
5 Poor managerial and innovative capacities are very frequently witnessed in many large farms which are often characterized by *absentee landlords*.
6 While large farms may wish to maximize profits, small farms may wish to maximize output or income. Figure 8.5 illustrates this point. The revenues (R) and costs (C) of the peasant farms are measured on the vertical axis whereas output of crops is measured along the horizontal axis. The large farm produces at a point like P where its marginal revenue is equal to marginal cost, whereas a small farm would produce at a point to the right of the point P (say M) as it is trying to maximize output. Thus, a small farm produces a larger output (q_2) than a large farm (q_1).

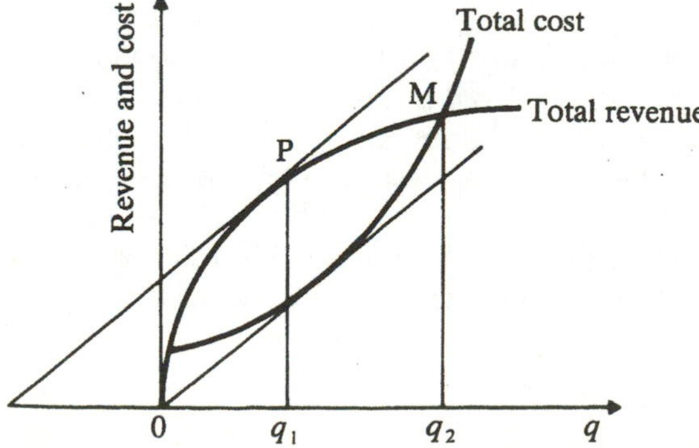

Figure 8.5

8.7 Limitations of price policy and some alternatives

It is not difficult to see that price policy, by itself, is not enough to mobilize the surplus. It is therefore necessary to point out some limitations of price policy and to suggest some alternatives.

1 Assuming that the necessary surplus is forthcoming, it is conceivable that farmers would like to buy more consumer goods rather than investment goods as their income rises. In order to induce farmers to buy more investment goods to promote productivity and growth in the agricultural sector, subsidies might be offered by the government on inputs like fertilizers, tube wells and pump sets for irrigation. This method achieved remarkable success in West Pakistan (Nulty 1972).

2 Attempts should be made to induce farmers to save more. This may be achieved by offering higher interest rates on savings. In LDCs the rates vary between 3 per cent and $4\frac{1}{2}$ per cent on savings (e.g. in the Post Office) in rural areas – rates which hardly reflect the opportunity cost of capital. Although savings are generally not regarded as very sensitive to changes in interest rates in poor countries (Williamson 1968), in India the interest elasticity is found to be positive and highly significant (Gupta 1970, 1971).

3 Fiscal policies may be required to supplement monetary policies to mobilize the surplus. Agricultural income is hardly taxed in LDCs, and land tax is almost non-existent. Indeed, direct taxes on land or on agricultural income form less than 1 per cent of total tax revenue. Thus there is scope to raise taxes on agricultural income. Since a very high level of taxes might impair the incentive of farmers to produce and sell, it may be necessary to introduce a differential system of taxation. That part of agricultural produce which is marketed may be taxed at a very low rate, or even be exempt for small farmers, whereas the part that is retained may be taxed at a higher rate.

In view of the difficulties in estimating agricultural income, it may be necessary to introduce land taxes. The advantage here is that while income sources could be concealed, it is difficult to conceal land. Second, if the tax has to be paid in any case, farmers would be induced to cultivate rather than to leave land fallow. Third, to make the system equitable, land tax could be made progressive, depending upon the minimum size of land holdings and on the proportion of the surplus marketed. It is possible to think of other methods as well, but these are outside the scope of the present analysis.

4 Marketed surplus may be affected by the sizes and types of land holdings. In India, it is argued (Narain 1957) that the proportion of output marketed declines until the size-holding of ten to fifteen acres is reached and then it rises. This implies that land ceilings leading to fragmentation of large holdings may raise the marketed surplus. But the point is debated and in the absence of necessary time-series data no firm conclusion can be drawn.

5 The present model deals primarily with the problem of mobilization of the surplus from the point of the farmer's utility. The model could be extended to accommodate the factors affecting production, e.g. land, capital, rainfall and temperature.

8.8 Conclusion

Given the role of agriculture in the economic development of the LDCs it is imperative to invest considerable resources for their agricultural development. Unfortunately, in many countries agriculture is synonymous with backwardness and planners too often equate development with urban industrialization. Lipton has noticed the presence of 'urban bias' in Indian planning (Lipton 1968a). It is doubtful whether the large-scale investment for urban industrialization would actually raise the living standard of the impoverished teeming millions among the peasantry, particularly when in terms of employment generation and income distribution the results in many countries have fallen short of expectations. The recent change in agricultural production in some parts of South and South-east Asia, a phenomenon often characterized as the 'Green Revolution', has demonstrated that farmers in the LDCs are quite willing to try new methods to raise their income and they are not unresponsive to economic incentives.[1] However, the gains from the 'Green Revolution' have not been distributed very equally (Bardhan 1970a, b, 1973; Dandekar and Rath 1971). But this is more a problem of distribution, and public policy may be used to rectify the situation. The crucial point to realize is that the role of agriculture in the economic development of LDCs can hardly be overemphasized. 'Whereas in the past, agriculture was often viewed as the passive partner in the development process, it is not typically regarded as an active and coequal partner with the industrial sector' (Thorbecke 1969). Also, the existing evidence conclusively shows that farmers do respond to economic incentives and changes in technology, though perhaps in a cautious way, in most LDCs and, given the necessary inputs to introduce technical change, they are not averse to adopting new technology. The analysis of the relationship between farm size and productivity shows that larger farms are not necessarily more 'efficient' than the smaller farms when efficiency is measured by productivity per acre. The Japanese experience also suggests the prospects of increasing output within small-scale farming (Okhawa and Johnston 1969). Radical land reforms involving the promotion of small-scale farming need not be ruled out, given the inefficiency of the larger farms, the preponderance of landless peasants and absentee landlords in many LDCs (see Chapter 9 for details).[2]

Notes

1 The literature on the 'Green Revolution' is huge. For a 'feel' of the subject, see, for example, Brown, D. (1971); Brown, L. (1970); Byres (1972), who includes an excellent bibliography; Griffin (1974, 1976); Harris (1971); Johnston and Cownie (1969); Sen, S. (1974, 1975).

2 On the economic theory of sharecropping, tenancy and some related issues, see Cheung (1969); Bardhan and Srinivasan (1971); Bardhan (1977); and Ghatak and Ingersent (1984).

Questions

1 Discuss the role of agriculture in economic development.
2 What is 'marketed surplus'? How could you promote the mobilization of such surplus for economic development?
3 Examine the relationship between marketed surplus, land size-holdings and output.
4 Evaluate the relationship between internal terms of trade and marketed surplus.
5 What are the major limitations on price policy in mobilizing 'surplus' from developing agriculture?

9 Green Revolution and income distribution

9.1 Introduction

The development of traditional agriculture on LDCs follows a few distinct phases. In stage I we find *subsistence farming* where farmers generally produce for their own consumption. Here the main objective of production is to maximize chances of survival rather than profit. In stage II we observe the growth of 'mixed farming'. Here the farmers produce partly for domestic consumption and partly for the market. Such production for the market marks the beginning of the process of commercialization of agriculture in LDCs. In the third phase, agriculture is fully 'commercialized' where production mainly takes place for the market. The main aim here is profit maximization by the modern farmers through a rise in productivity. While in some areas of LDCs we still observe subsistence farming, in many others a number of factors have led to the onset of 'mixed' and modern farming where the productivity, particularly yield per acre, of some types of agricultural crops has gone up sharply. Such an improvement in agriculture has been labelled the 'Green Revolution' (GR). In the next few sections the nature, causes and consequences of the GR are analysed in detail.

9.2 The nature of the Green Revolution

The GR can be explained by looking at the shift of the production function of any agricultural crop or crops. Consider Figure 9.1 where we measure production of a crop on the vertical axis and the use of inputs on the horizontal axis. Let the production function be given by $Q = f(I)$ where Q is equal to the output of agriculture and I equals inputs, e.g. land, labour, water, fertilizer, seeds etc. The production function $f(I)$ shows the relationship between output and input in a traditional agriculture. However, if $f(I)$ is shifted to be $f'(I)$, then such a shift can be regarded as quite substantial. If, for example, yield of rice is measured on the vertical axis, then with the use of OK inputs the rise in yield after the shift in the production function is bc. If bc is large then we have a GR after all.

The phenomenon of the GR was indeed observed in a phenomenal growth of yields of some foodgrains in parts of India, Pakistan, Thailand, parts of South and Central America and the Philippines during the late 1960s and 1970s. Some have argued that such a phenomenon is temporary and the hope for alleviating poverty, malnutrition and famines in LDCs is rather premature. Others have measured the trend lines of growth of some crops in India and Pakistan and expressed doubts about a significant,

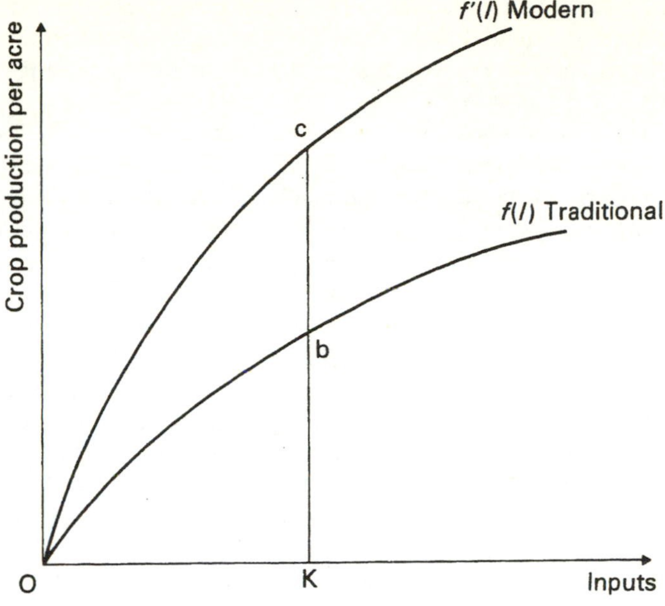

Figure 9.1

permanent shift in the production function (see Mellor 1976; Rudra 1978). However, during the last few years of the 1980s the foodgrain production in countries like India has surged ahead and yields of a number of foodgrains have indeed registered significant rises (151.6 million tons in 1983–4 from 128 million tons in 1978–9). India is also beginning to export rice to the world market. Needless to say, such a transformation of agriculture in LDCs makes a very important contribution to the overall rate of economic growth, speeds up the process of structural change, aids nutrition, efficiency and productivity of labour and leads to the general improvement of welfare. The GR has also facilitated the process of social modernization (including the extension of rural education and the decline of high birth and death rates in rural areas) by stimulating widespread changes of attitude among many farmers in LDCs.

It is useful to note at this stage that there are at least three elements of a change in *yield* in agricultural crop per unit of land:

1 a change in the output mix;
2 a change in cropping intensity;
3 a change in crop yield.

The empirical evidence available so far seems to suggest that, in underdeveloped agriculture, the differences in land productivity are mainly due to differences in output mix and cropping intensity rather than differences in crop yield (Berry and Cline 1979).

Technical change in underdeveloped agriculture can be classified into two broad kinds: (1) biological and (2) mechanical. Biological innovations usually refer to factors that raise land productivity. Better seeds and use of organic fertilizers in the right doses at the right time are useful instances. Mechanical innovation usually means the use of more machinery like tractors and is frequently referred to as 'tractorization'.

When the GR comprises biological innovation, more jobs can be created; if the GR implies tractorization, then the capital–labour ratio rises and employment falls. At this stage it may be useful to summarize the nature of the GR as follows (see Ruttan 1977 for a good summary).

1. The 'miracle seeds', i.e. the new wheat and rice varieties (sometimes referred to as the high yielding variety, HYV) have been adopted by farmers in some LDCs at high rates, especially in those regions where they are technically and economically superior to local types. Ruttan points out that in the Indian province of Punjab the proportion of total wheat area planted to the new HYVs of wheat increased from 3.6 per cent in 1966–7 (the first year of introduction) to 65.6 per cent in 1969–70. In the major wheat-producing regions of Pakistan, about 73 per cent of wheat acreage was sown with Mexican wheats during 1969–70. In the case of the Philippines, about 95 per cent of agriculturists in the barrios and nearly 60 per cent of the farmers in the municipality had adopted the HYV by 1969. In the case of rice, the highest rise in yields has been observed in relatively arid regions where farmers could easily have obtained irrigation water. It is interesting to note that, although differential rates of adoption by farm size and tenure have been observed in many LDCs, neither farm size nor tenure has been a very significant constraint to the adoption of new HYVs.

2. Existing evidence tends to suggest that in most cases neither tenure nor farm size has been considered as an important source of differential rates of growth in agricultural productivity. In the case of India, some have shown that the new wheat technology has been rather neutral to scale (i.e. neither capital saving nor labour saving) and both large and small farmers have gained roughly equal benefits (Sidhu 1974a). In the case of Pakistan, Azam notes 'that while the smaller farmers do face relatively more severe constraints on irrigation water and credit, the differences in the severity of these constraints are not serious enough to have caused any significant differences in the yields obtained by the small farmers as compared with the large farmers' (Azam 1973). Both Soejono for Indonesia and Managhas for the Philippines confirm the above findings (Soejono 1976; Managhas 1974). However, in the case of very poor farmers with little land and agricultural labourers, it is not clear how the constraints such as the lack of initial endowments, credit supply and other complementary inputs will cease to operate in their adoption of new technology.

3. There is some evidence from many LDCs to confirm the hypothesis that the introduction of the HYV technology has led to a rise in the demand for farm labour. In the case of Indian Punjab, some have shown that a rise in demand for labour has also resulted in a rise of real wages (see Sidhu 1974a, b; Johl 1975). There is also some evidence to confirm the net inflow of agricultural labour, particularly during the sowing and harvesting seasons, from the surrounding provinces like Uttar Pradesh and Rajasthan in the Indian Punjab and Haryana. This is in stark contrast to the evidence of static (or even falling) real wages in many other provinces of India, where the GR largely meant farm mechanization and 'tractorization', some loss of employment and a fall of real wages.

4. The adoption of the HYV technology has widened the existing disparity in income distribution in many instances. Typically, big landlords have gained relatively more than the tenants and landless labourers despite some rise in the level of real wages in HYV areas. Mellor, for example, concludes that although the percentage rise in labour income from a rise in employment and real wages has been quite significant

in a number of cases in India, the percentage rise of output for labour has been rather low (Mellor 1976). It is important to differentiate, however, between an absolute and a relative change in the pattern of income distribution. Many who analysed the nature of income distribution following the GR might have actually witnessed an increase in the income differential in *absolute* rather than in relative terms.

Another important problem that has characterized the GR is an increase in income differential between regions within the same country. For instance, because of the GR, many parts of the Punjab and Haryana states of India have become quite prosperous relative to other regions. The same kind of differences in regional growth rates have been observed in Pakistan, Thailand and the Philippines. The main reasons for the differential rates of growth in agriculture in these countries have been the following:

(a) differences in the availability of water and irrigation facilities;
(b) different levels of fertilizer use at the right time and in the right amount;
(c) a differential flow of information about the HYV seeds and other complementary inputs;
(d) differences in the availability of new varieties of seeds, fertilizer and pesticides;
(e) differences in the nature and attitude of farmers towards risks and uncertainties.

The last factor is important and deserves some elaboration. In a traditional and backward agriculture, average yields and output are usually very low. Farmers depend mainly on the vagaries of the weather. Farm output and income therefore mainly depend on random factors. Farmers are frequently exposed to dangers of starvation and famine. Hence, they may wish to maximize their chances of survival rather than current profit by following the orthodox textbook marginal principles. We have already discussed this topic in Chapter 8. The point worth noting here is that, when risks are high in the adoption of a new technology because of a greater variability in yield and income, a farmer may be reluctant to abandon the age-old technology which he at least understands. Given such risk aversion, farmers may actually prefer a technique which produces low *average* (mean) yield of crop (per unit of land) and income with low dispersion (variance) to an alternative method of crop production which combines larger average yield and income and a greater dispersion of variance (see Miracle 1968).

In Figure 9.2 time is measured on the horizontal axis and total crop output and consumption are measured on the vertical axis. The line MCN denotes the minimum consumption needs. It is fixed and parallel to the abscissa since the lower level of consumption will indicate famine and death. The line MDC stands for minimum desirable consumption which slopes gently upwards. This is due to changes in desired consumption patterns which accompany changes in attitudes in traditional societies because of economic growth and structural change. It may be argued that a small farmer's attitude towards risks and uncertainties will be determined by his traditional crop production with reference to these different sets of norms. In Figure 9.2 we have two types of farmers: advanced (A) and backward (B). The type B farmer's crop production has remained close to the MCN, but the type A farmer's crop production has increased steadily over time and remained well above MCN and close to MDC. It is then very likely that the type A farmer will be more willing to take risks and adopt new techniques of production than the type B farmer. Indeed, under the circumstances

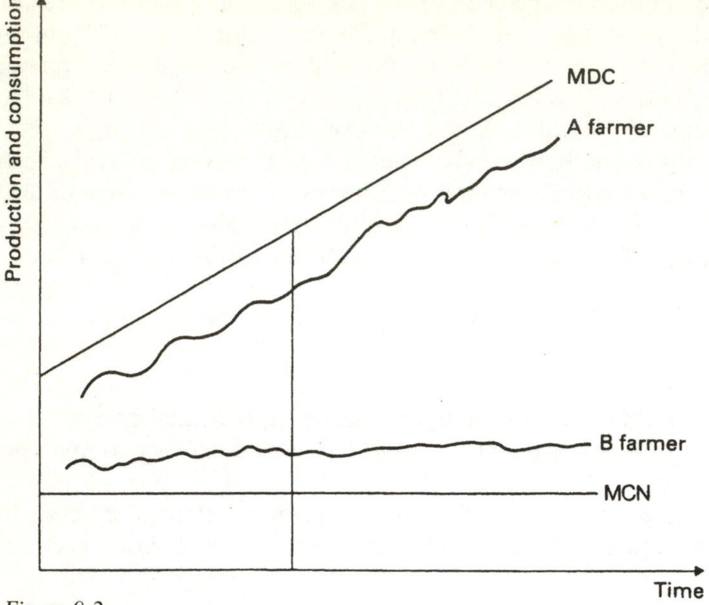

Figure 9.2

the unwillingness of the B type farmers to use new technology can hardly be regarded as 'irrational' as he cannot afford to take great risks so long as he lives a hand-to-mouth existence. It is necessary to mention at this stage that many governments of LDCs have failed to provide adequate cover against these types of risks so far (e.g. crop insurance) and hence a secure environment which is needed to introduce technical progress in backward agriculture has remained conspicuously absent. The other ingredients of a stable economic environment which enables farmers to innovate are the presence of good marketing and credit facilities. As Griffin (1973: 6) observes:

> If peasants sometimes appear to be unresponsive or hostile to proposed technical changes, it is probably because the risks are high, the returns to the cultivators are low – for example, because of local custom or land tenure conditions, or because credit facilities and marketing outlets are inadequate and the necessary inputs – including knowledge – are missing.

Needless to say, public policy can play a very useful role in creating a proper environment for a successful introduction of innovation in underdeveloped agriculture.

5. It has been observed that the introduction of the new HYVs has resulted in the decline of the rate of growth of foodgrain prices for consumers (Ruttan 1977). During the 1970s there has been a substantial increase in the areas under cultivation. There has also been a considerable rise in the double or even multiple cropping system. However, the distribution of gains among consumers clearly depends upon the amount consumed and the price elasticity of demand in different income classes. The greater the amount consumed and the larger the absolute value of the price elasticity of demand in the lower income class, relative to the higher income class,

the more equitable will be the system of distribution. The evidence from Colombia tends to suggest that during the late 1960s and early 1970s the lowest quartile of Colombian households which obtained only about 4 per cent of income gained 28 per cent of consumer benefits, owing to a significant increase in rice production in Colombia (Ruttan 1977). However, it should not be inferred from the above analysis that inflation has become a thing of the past in most LDCs. On the contrary, a number of LDCs still continue to suffer from general inflation and high price level of foodgrains.

9.3 Causes of the Green Revolution

A large number of factors individually *and* collectively have played roles, in varying degrees of importance, in the making of the GR. The literature is vast (see, for example, Byres 1972; Khan 1975; Sen, S. 1975; Mellor 1976; Day and Singh 1977; Ruttan 1977; Nulty 1972). Here we shall summarize the main reasons only.

1. The continuing high growth rates of population in most LDCs during the 1950s and early 1960s effectively reduced the growth of *per capita* real income and *per capita* food availability. As food production barely kept ahead of the population growth rate, the standard of living remained fairly static. In some regions a decline in *per capita* food availability has been recorded. Thus, necessity became the mother of invention. Faced with the urgent need of feeding a large number of extra mouths, there was very little choice but to introduce technical progress in agriculture.

2. With a limited stock of land, a fast growing labour force, a slow rate of growth of labour utilization in both the agricultural and the non-agricultural sectors and lack of a serious and active government policy for substantial investment in agriculture, food crises began to occur with regular frequency in some LDCs. Also countries like India and Pakistan launched ambitious development plans for a rapid industrialization of their economies. A large part of valuable foreign exchange resources has been spent on imports of capital goods and there were not enough reserves to pay for food imports. During the mid-1960s the Indian subcontinent was hit by one of the worst droughts of the century and famines began to spread in the countryside. A massive death from 'starvation' was averted by emergency supplies, distribution and American grain supply under PL 480 (though many died from 'malnutrition' – a euphemism for starvation). Shaken by the horrors of mass starvation, political and social disturbance, governments in South Asia, for instance, began to take serious steps for effective cures for low productivity in underdeveloped agriculture.

The answer was provided by the invention of a new high yielding variety of seed – sometimes called the 'miracle' seed – for the production of wheat and rice. The 'miracle' seed was first used in Mexico and hence it is also known as the Mexican seed or IR8. The results from the use of these new types of seeds showed remarkable success in Mexico and other LDCs. The productivity of these types of seeds was much higher than those of the traditional varieties and after trials and errors new seeds were invented to withstand different conditions of weather in different countries. The use of the *dwarf* varieties of new seeds became particularly successful in South and South-east Asia and farmers began to use them in large quantities. Dr Norman Borlaug, who invented this type of 'miracle' seed, eventually received the Nobel Prize in appreciation of his work for alleviating poverty and famine which still plagues more than a third of mankind.

3. The invention of new seeds went hand in hand with the *increase in cropping intensity*. Previously, in many LDCs the system of double cropping was rather uncommon owing to the length of the growing seasons of the traditional varieties of wheat and rice. For instance, in India, even in 1964–5, out of a total of 138 million hectares of *net* sown area, only 20.2 million hectares or less than 15 per cent were sown more than once. Further, the areas sown more than once were mostly double-cropped. The yield from the second crop used to be poor and a system of multiple cropping was virtually non-existent. As the Fourth Five Year Plan of the Government of India explains: 'In the absence of short-duration varieties, cropping intensity could not be made a focal point of agricultural strategy.' The arrival of the new dwarf varieties of seed opened up the possibility of double and multiple cropping on a large scale. The rise in cropping intensity was also enhanced by a system of relay cropping in India which consisted of the following four crops grown in quick succession: *moong* (pulse), hybrid maize, *toria* (*Brassica campestris*) and a dwarf wheat. Needless to say, a rise in cropping intensity raised substantially the yield per acre per year. Thus, farm income began to rise in the areas covered by the HYV projects. Farmers' attitude towards risks began to change (as explained before) when their production began to move well ahead of their minimum consumption needs.

4. The other important factor which substantially raised yield and food production in LDCs is a rise in the use of fertilizer. Various studies have confirmed that the use of chemical and other types of fertilizer in backward agriculture has been very little, particularly in relation to the fertilizer use of developed countries. (There are exceptions like Taiwan, Cuba, South Korea, Egypt and to some extent Sri Lanka: for a comprehensive summary, see Ghatak 1981.) Responses of crop yields to fertilizer use in both DCs and LDCs have been the subject of considerable research both past and present. These studies clearly indicate the positive relationship between fertilizer use and crop response, though the degree of response does vary between the crops and types of fertilizer. It has been demonstrated that the optimum rates of nitrogen fertilizer use for HYVs of rice and wheat are about three times greater than for traditional, native varieties. The *monetary return* to optimum fertilization of HYVs is estimated as one and a half times larger than for native varieties because of the greater marginal return for initial increments of applied nitrogen. Thus, through its effects on yields and by permitting multiple cropping, fertilizer application has had, and will continue to play, a vital role in promoting the GR in LDCs.

Government policies in many LDCs have played important parts in spreading the use of fertilizers. For instance, farmers were given large amounts in subsidies for the use of fertilizers and hence farm production costs have been kept low. The value–cost ratios (i.e. value of yield increases divided by cost of fertilizer) in the use of fertilizer for many LDCs (based on FAO data) already show the desirability of providing such incentives to farmers. One of the factors which could easily inhibit farmers from using more fertilizer is its high price. Evidence from LDCs suggests that the demand for fertilizer is inversely related to its price and in some cases (e.g. Brazil, 1949–71; India, 1958–64; Taiwan, 1950–66) price elasticity is greater than unity (see Ghatak 1981). The provision of subsidies for the use of fertilizers should induce farmers to demand more fertilizers despite their high prices. In fact, the use of fertilizer has played such an important part in the GR that many have described the phenomenon as a 'seed– fertilizer' revolution (see, for example, Johnston and Cownie 1969).

5. The next important element in spreading the GR has been the availability of irrigation facilities and controlled water supply. It has been well acknowledged that the use of fertilizer or other complementary inputs without *regular* and *timely* water supply is very likely to show signs of diminishing returns quite soon. Ishikawa, for example, has shown some instances of such growth of agricultural production in four regions of India and Japan with or without water supply. In the Indian states of Tamil Nadu and West Bengal, the use of more fertilizer without proper irrigation facilities led to a rise in food production first but then diminishing returns set in very quickly (see Figure 9.3; also Ishikawa 1967). But in the two regions of Japan with good irrigation facilities, the steady growth of production continued. In India and Pakistan, the yield of wheat rose most dramatically in Punjab – a state which has the highest proportion of irrigated land under cultivation. Average yields on irrigated land have been estimated to be 30 to 100 per cent higher than on unirrigated land (Nulty 1972). Indeed, given the voluminous evidence, the role of timely water supply in the spreading of the GR can hardly be overemphasized.

6. There are reasons to believe that the use of tractors and other machinery in agriculture has also aided the process of yield improvement in traditional agriculture. It is no doubt true that agricultural mechanization can raise yield per unit of labour and land substantially. The problem is that the growing use of tractors in agriculture has frequently been labour-displacing despite its advantages. The issue of farm mechanization in labour-surplus economies has been controversial. Many seem to think that the introduction of modern technology like tractors and combine harvesters, despite increasing profit for big capitalist farmers in LDCs, will create a large army of unemployed. This will depress real wages and the pattern of income distribution will tend to be more unequal. The increase in the income differential between the rich and poor farmers may be such as to create a deep division in the society. The conflagration within the society may not always come in the strict Soviet or Chinese style, but it will be a conflagration all the same. Thus, critics of the adoption of machinery on a large scale in labour-surplus agriculture fear that the GR may ultimately degenerate into a Red Revolution. It is thus important to analyse the relationship between

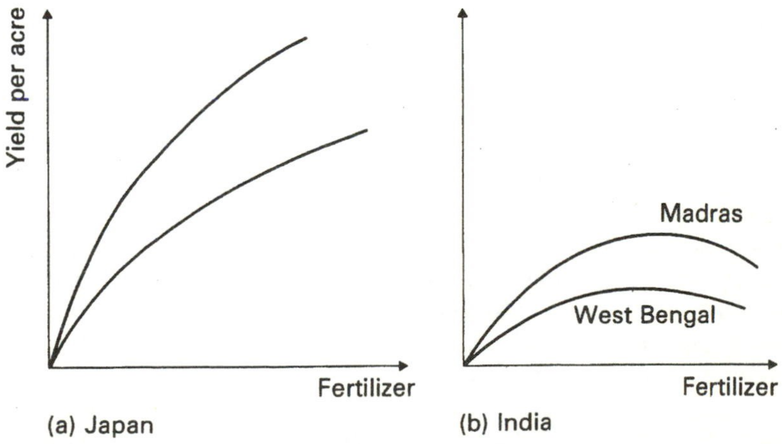

Figure 9.3

the GR and farm income distribution more rigorously. Such an analysis has been attempted later.

7. Some argue that a major inducement for the adoption of new technology in backward agriculture is the usual motive for profit maximization (e.g. Brown 1971; Nulty 1972). The following equations can explain such profit maximization behaviour. Let A denote the adoption level rate of new technology and (Y^{e}) indicate expected profit. We can then write

$$A = f(Y^{e})$$

Now

$$Y^{e} = R^{e}(q) - C^{e}(q)$$

where $R^{e}(a)$ is the expected revenue from the sale of a quantity of crop and $C^{e}(q)$ is the expected cost of such crop production.

Let the expected revenue function be given by the expected price in the next period, P^{e}_{t+1}, yield y and acreage a. Hence

$$R^{e}(q) = P^{e}_{t+1}ya$$

Let the cost function be the sum of autonomous cost b, the variable cost $\phi(q)$ and a risk factor associated with the adoption of the new technology.
Therefore

$$C^{e}(q) = b + \phi(q) + \theta$$

The profit-maximizing equation can now be written as

$$Y^{e} = R^{e}(q) - b - \phi(q) - \theta$$

Differentiating with respect to q we get

$$\frac{\mathrm{d}Y^{e}}{\mathrm{d}q} = R^{e\prime}(q) - \phi'(q) = 0$$

This gives us the standard neoclassical principle of profit maximization. It is claimed that in the case of Pakistan 'perhaps the most important lesson is that the adoption of new techniques requisite for higher levels of productivity in agriculture is very rapid when farmers can see a clear, substantial and unequivocal return from it' (Nulty 1972: 121). However, others claim that farmers in LDCs do not necessarily maximize profit within a neoclassical type of competitive economy (Junankar 1981).

It should be pointed out that, although the neoclassical model (with all its assumptions) may not be very appropriate to analyse the decision-making behaviour of farmers in LDCs, profits or income will remain an important determinant of the adoption of new technology. Farmers in LDCs may take decisions which can be logically inconsistent. But to assume that their willingness to adopt new techniques of agricultural production has very little correlation with the desire to raise, if not to maximize, gross or net income (profit) does not seem very realistic. However, farmers should be more aware of the relative merits of indigenous and exogenous technologies (Biggs and Clay 1983).

8. Public policy has played a significant role in the adoption of new technology in agriculture. We have already mentioned the case of subsidizing the purchase of fertilizers by farmers. Other policies which can be mentioned include the overvaluation of exchange rates, absence of any tariff on the purchase of tractors from abroad (as happened to be the case in Pakistan) and the provision of credit to farmers at a very low rate of interest (in capital-scarce economies!). Unfortunately, although these policies have succeeded in providing more inputs to farmers, they also led to a choice of a more capital-intensive technique of agricultural production in some regions of LDCs. Such a choice has inevitably led to the worsening of an already skewed system of income distribution. The other unfortunate implication of these types of public policies has been the concentration of income and power in fewer hands. This has taken place because resources tended to gravitate towards better-off farmers. The creditworthiness of the big landlords (sometimes called the 'kulaks') has always been rated highly. They also have a greater amount of land which has often been used as collateral to get more credit to buy more fertilizer, seeds and water. As a result, public policies have seldom been seen as neutral in their effects. Indeed, in some cases they might have resulted in concentration of wealth and power in fewer hands, a substantial rise in the proportion of landless labourers and increasing immiserization for quite a few people in rural areas (see Griffin 1976).

If the GR is to offer 'great opportunities for breaking the centuries-old chains of peasant poverty' (Wharton 1969), then it is necessary to understand its impact on factor shares and income distribution.

9.4 Effects of the Green Revolution on income: a simple theory

Let us assume that the GR can be both technological and biological. Whether the GR is labour-using or labour-displacing depends on the net effect of the forces released by two quite different kinds of technical progress. To analyse the exact impact on cost of production, it is necessary to know whether cost rises because of biological innovation (due to a greater use of complementary inputs) are greater or less than the cost reduction due to mechanical innovations (see Srivastava *et al.* 1971). Figure 9.4 illustrates total revenue (TR). Total output is measured on the horizontal axis and total revenue (TR) and total cost (TC_1 before and TC_2 after the innovation) on the vertical axis. Clearly, unit cost of production (of OQ_2 output) is lower with OC_2 (the new technique) than with OC_1 (the old technique). This is easily confirmed by the slope of OC with respect to OA. Assume that farmers want to maximize profits. Then the equilibrium will be obtained at a point where the total cost, total revenue and total output are given by Q_1A, Q_1B and OQ_1 respectively before the introduction of new technology. With the new technique, both total revenue and total cost rise and at equilibrium net profit CD is much greater than profit under the old technique (AB). It is evident that the new technology raises the net income or profit of farmers. Next, we shall discuss changes in relative factor shares after the introduction of new technology.

9.5 Effects of the Green Revolution on relative factor shares

As farmers realize the opportunity of raising their incomes through the adoption of new technology, the *absolute* income of all factors should rise as more inputs are

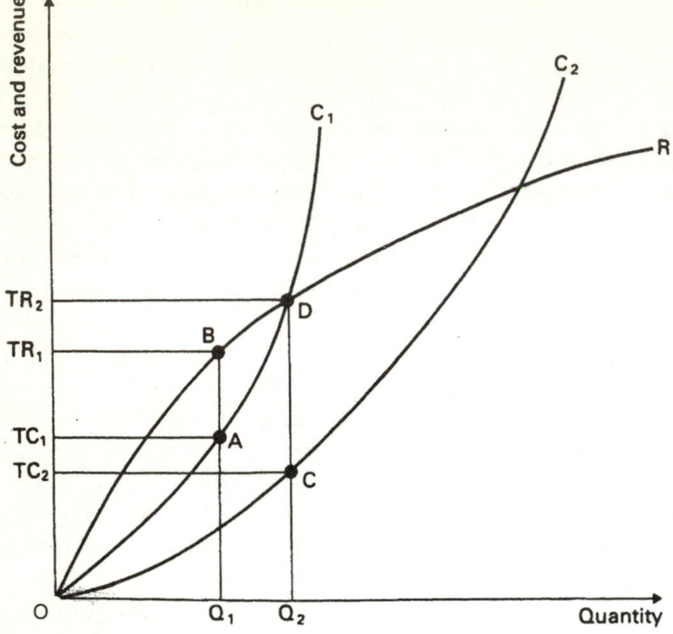

Figure 9.4

utilized for increasing production. However, the *relative* changes in factor shares depend on a number of factors such as (1) the neutrality or non-neutrality of technical progress; (2) changes in the sum of production elasticities under technical progress; (3) changes in the capital–labour ratios after the introduction of innovations in agriculture. In order to understand the process of changes in factor shares more clearly, we assume a Cobb–Douglas production function of the following form:

$$Q = AL^a B_1^b B_2^c C_1^d C_2^e$$

where Q is crop production, L is land, B_1 is human labour, B_2 is bullock labour, C_1 is machinery and equipment, C_2 is non-mechanical inputs, e.g. better seeds, fertilizers etc., and a, b, c, d, e are the relevant partial elasticities. It is useful to remember that ratios of partial elasticities show the relative factor shares between inputs. Note that with a Cobb–Douglas production function the elasticity of substitution r (the ratio of the percentage change of factors of production in any given production process and a percentage change in relative factor prices) is unity (see Figure 9.5). Hence r is independent of scale returns. Changes in factor shares are observed only when an extra new input, either as a substitute or as a complement to current inputs, incorporates a technical progress (see Brown 1966).

Now let us assume that the increasing use of C_1 and C_2 implies a technical progress. Let the new production function be written as follows:

$$Q^1 = A^1 L^{a^1} B_1^{b^1} B_2^{c^1} C_1^{d^1} C_2^{e^1}$$

Most evidence on the spread of the GR in LDCs suggests that C_1 is capital-using (i.e. labour-displacing) and C_2 is capital-saving (i.e. labour-using) (see Nulty 1972; Khan

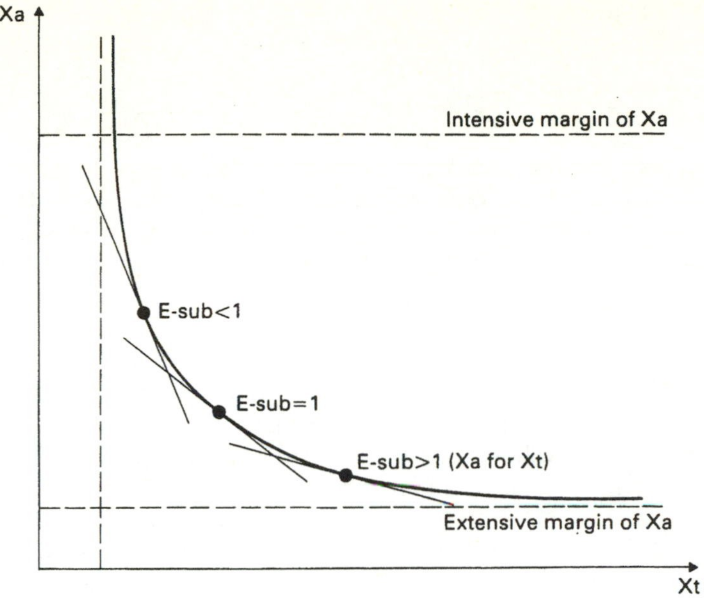

Figure 9.5

1975; Sen, S. 1975; Ruttan 1977). In view of the contradictory impact on labour use due to the difference in the nature of technical progress, the net result on labour utilization will depend on the empirical estimates of values of b, b^1, d, d^1, e and e^1. For instance, we should expect a fall in labour share with reference to C_1 (a labour-displacing input) when $b^1/d^1 > b/d$ Also, when C_2 is a complementary input (e.g. new seeds, fertilizer) to labour, it is to be hypothesized that $b/e \leq b^1/e^1$.

More formally, if the final impact of the GR is to lower the share of labour (wages) in total income, the net effect should be as follows:

$$\frac{b}{d}+\frac{b}{e}>\frac{b^1}{d^1}+\frac{b^1}{e^1}$$

On the basis of a large number of empirical estimates, it is difficult to draw any unambiguous conclusion regarding the movements of real wages in areas affected by the GR. However, it seems that in a large number of areas, *average* income and real wages have gone up more for most classes of farmers. Large farmers seem to have benefited relatively more than medium and small farmers. Note that to measure the income distribution impact of the relative rises in output on low or high income (Y) farms, we need to know about the price (P) elasticity of demand. Such elasticity can be either greater than or less than unity. Hence, we may have

$$\left|\frac{\mathrm{d}Y}{\mathrm{d}Py}\,\frac{Py}{Y}\right|>1$$

in the case of elastic demand or

$$0 < \left| \frac{\mathrm{d}Y}{\mathrm{d}Py} \frac{Py}{Y} \right| < 1$$

when demand is price inelastic. It is clear that when demand is price elastic an increase in crop production will increase total revenue, depending on the degree of elasticity of demand. Such a rise in supply will lower the price per unit of crop. If the small farmer fails to raise crop production, his total revenue will decrease. If he also fails to change the use of traditional inputs, his cost will remain the same and he will experience a fall in net income.

However, even a lower crop price may increase total income of the large farmer. Though his total cost will rise due to a rise in the use of inputs, the profit-maximizing farmer will purchase inputs up to the point where marginal revenue is equal to marginal cost. His profit (or net income) will increase (or it may remain the same). Hence, the income differential between large and small farmers will widen.

If the demand curve is price inelastic, a rise in supply reduces both farm price and total farm income. If the small farmer fails to contribute to an increase in supply or lowers the level of input utilization, his aggregate income and profit will fall. However, the large farmer does not necessarily experience a fall in total income in this case, although he might when farm total income declines faster than the aggregate income of small farmers. In fact, there may even be a rise in the income of the big farmers notwithstanding the fall in aggregate farm income. This will also lead to a widening of the income gap between different classes of farmers.

Although the initial impact of the technical progress due to the GR in underdeveloped agriculture may enlarge the income differential between adopters and non-adopters, eventually the traditional farmers will perceive gains through the adoption of new technology. This will help to spread the GR in remote areas of LDCs. After the GR, big farmers will find it profitable to invest their extra new income in non-land inputs like chemical fertilizer, pesticides, etc. As investment in land rises, productivity will rise. With a judicious use of farm price policy and agricultural marketing and dissemination of information among *all* classes of farmer, every kind of farmer should be able to reap gains from the GR.

9.6 Problems and prospects of the Green Revolution

Although the GR has not yet turned grey by the early 1980s and raised high hopes among many as a phenomenon which is likely to continue (as the record Indian food production of 151.6 million tons in 1984 suggests), a number of problems have attended its productive success. The ‘first generation’ problem of the GR has been to induce farmers to adopt the new technology to raise production. This problem is no longer considered very compelling. The ‘second-generation’ problem has been associated with the distribution of gains from increased farm income due to the GR. Here again real wages and employment have gone up in many areas and as such problems did not turn out to be very acute or insuperable – thanks to the seed–fertilizer (i.e. biological) revolution which resulted in an increase in labour demand. However, there are areas where real wages stagnated and even fell. This might have been due to the use of technological innovation which increased the capital–labour ratios. The distribution of income also worsened as wage share in total income fell with a rise in unemployment, particularly among unskilled workers and landless labourers. Evidence does suggest that, in many cases, big farmers took advantage of subsidized credit and an overvalued exchange rate to import large quantities of farm machinery including tractors. Although the use of farm machinery has quite a few advantages, in labour-surplus economies such a use has led to a rise in farm unemployment. In extreme cases many poor farmers, who failed to introduce new technology and reap gains from the GR because of either extreme risk aversion or a lack of initial endowment to buy necessary inputs, had to sell their small plots of land to rich landlords and migrate from villages only to be destitutes in most cases. It is therefore necessary to introduce the following policies to prevent such growing inequality in income distribution stemming from the GR.

9.6.1 Role of public policy

Public policies should be designed to increase the production and income levels of small and poor farmers. These may comprise:

1 subsidizing the purchase of new seeds, fertilizers and water, etc.;
2 a guaranteed price support system to provide incentives to farmers;
3 a progressive tax on agricultural income as the GR raises farm income, particularly of rich farmers;
4 a comprehensive system of income transfers from the rich to the poor farmers – such a transfer should be useful in providing more opportunities to poorer farmers in gaining greater access to resources;
5 bringing the domestic price of capital goods in line with world prices by a more appropriate use of exchange rate policy. It may also be necessary to impose tariffs on the import of agricultural machinery (e.g. tractors), particularly in labour-surplus economies, to prevent a rise in unemployment of landless labourers.

Evidence from LDCs suggests that rich farmers pay lower interest rates on credit (Day and Singh 1977; Ghatak 1975a, 1976, 1983) and this again promotes a 'wrong' choice of techniques which tends to displace labour. It may thus be necessary to *raise* interest rates as it will (1) prevent the use of credit for financing the introduction of labour-saving machinery; (2) shift some of the costs of socially developed new technologies onto those who use them; and (3) permit a rise in rural savings.

One of the most important sources of inequality in income distribution is the inequitable distribution of land ownership or of operational holdings. When the labour share in agricultural income rises, the income of tenants and landless labourers improves relative to landlords and owner-cultivators. The opposite happens when rent share in income rises. Hence, as Hayami and Ruttan argue, *land-saving* and *labour-using* technical progress that increases the return to labour relative to land should equalize the distribution of income between the landless and the land-owning classes (Hayami and Ruttan 1984). On the other hand, when technical progress comprises the use of labour-saving and land-using innovations, the inequality in income distribution will rise. Thus, a 'seed–fertilizer' revolution is expected to result in more equal distribution of income, but where the use of new technology has led to a stagnation or fall of real wages and a rise in rent, it may be necessary to manipulate taxes and subsidies to achieve a more equal income distribution. Where the socio-political conditions are favourable, a more egalitarian system of land ownership should be supported strongly to achieve greater equality in income distribution.

It is important to point out that many LDCs have experienced a rapid growth of population, particularly in the rural areas. It is possible that, in many cases, a shift in the supply of labour due to rapid growth of population has exceeded the shift in labour demand due to the 'seed-fertilizer' revolution. Under such conditions, it is possible to observe both a decline in real wage and a rise in inequality in income distribution as the rental share relative to wage tends to rise. The growth in rural wages can thus be a function of the growth of labour demand in the non-agricultural sector. It is also imperative to invent 'more productive biological and chemical technologies' to offset the adverse impact of growing population on real wages and income distribution (Hayami and Ruttan 1984). As far as the small farmers and landless labourers are concerned, the necessary conditions of reform have been well summarized by Grabowski (1981):

> Research activities must be directed at developing new seeds for the majority of farmers who lack irrigation. Research activities need to be oriented toward improving cultivation practices and irrigation techniques in order to increase cropping intensity. Credit must be available to allow farmers with small farms to irrigate their land and thus increase their cropping intensities. . . . Large farmers' privileged access to machinery must be eliminated. . . . All of these require an increase in the power and influence of farmers with small farms, relative to those with large farms, on government decisions concerning agricultural research and credit priorities. This could possibly be accomplished through land reforms, or a less radical solution, the organization of small farmers into groups which could put pressure on government agencies to recognize and respond to the interest of small farmers.

9.7 The basic needs approach

Though some argue that a more equal distribution of income will result in an increase in consumption at the expense of saving and a higher rate of economic growth, others point out that in LDCs an increase in consumption might actually *raise* the rate of growth by increasing the level of nutrition, efficiency and labour productivity (Leibenstein 1957; Mirrlees 1975). In Figure 9.6 we measure productivity on the vertical axis and consumption on the horizontal axis. Initially, a rise in consumption may add only a little to the growth of productivity. But with a gradual improvement in the health and efficiency of the labour force, productivity should rise significantly (as measured by the gradient of the productivity line between A and B). After B, the effect of an additional increase in consumption on productivity would show signs of diminishing returns. If the analysis is correct, then there is an urgent need to pay attention to the fulfilment of the 'basic needs' of the rural population. Health is after all wealth and an overall improvement of rural welfare cannot simply occur regardless of the environment in which rural people generally live in LDCs.

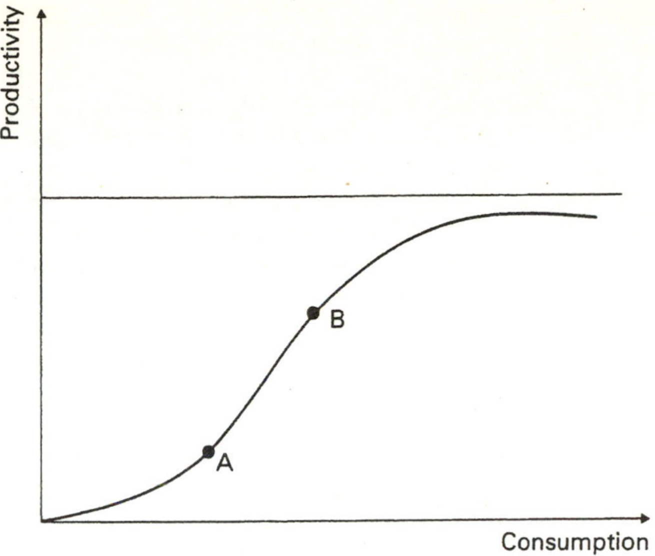

Figure 9.6

Sen has pointed out both theoretically and empirically that malnutrition and famine could occur on a massive scale despite considerable food availability. (Sen has labelled the food availability doctrine as the FAD. See, for example, Sen 1981b; for a summary, see Ghatak and Ingersent 1984.) This happens due to what Sen calls a failure in exchange entitlement or the inability to sell labour power by some groups at a real wage which will provide enough food to avoid starvation. Berg concludes that malnutrition is a problem of major proportion in many LDCs. The nutritional condition of the poor is no better today than it was a decade ago. In many LDCs it may be worse and the nutrition problem is unlikely to be resolved in most countries within a generation by simply raising incomes and agricultural production. The main problem is a deficiency in the intake of food and energy of a large proportion of the rural population and the main victims of such deficiencies are the very poor people in the rural areas. Once more, in many LDCs, public policies have been pitifully inadequate in redressing the pathetic living and working conditions of the rural people suffering from poverty and malnutrition. Evidence from Sahelian Africa, South Asia, Bangladesh, north-east Brazil, sub-Saharan Africa, parts of Central Africa and Central America seems to confirm Berg's analysis (Berg 1981; see also World Bank 1984: table on comparative social indicators; Srinivasan 1979).

If the direct relationship between health, efficiency and welfare is accepted, it is necessary to take steps to satisfy the basic needs of a large section of rural population. In order to meet these needs, it is necessary to provide better nutrition, education, health and housing facilities. The task of choosing the 'ideal' yardstick in each area is best taken up by experts in each field. Hicks and Streeten have suggested the following major indicators to prepare such indices in different fields (see Hicks and Streeten 1979).

	Indicators
(a) Health	(i) Life expectancy at birth
(b) Education	(i) Literacy
	(ii) Primary school enrolment (as a percentage of the population aged 5–14)
(c) Food and clothing	(i) Calorie supply per head or calorie supply as a percentage of requirements
(d) Water supply	(i) Infant mortality (per thousand births)
	(ii) Percentage of population with access to drinkable water
(e) Sanitation, drinking water and social security	(i) Infant mortality (per thousand births)
	(ii) Percentage of population with access to sanitation facilities
(f) Housing	
(g) Participation in government activities	

However, instead of trying to invent a composite index of basic needs (which can be quite complicated owing to the necessity of devising a rational system of weighting each type of need) it may be useful to concentrate on only a few (say two or three) indicators which correlate very strongly with basic needs development. Such an alternative will be quite helpful to assess the social performance quickly.

9.8 Growth theory and basic needs

Attempts have been made to incorporate the impact of basic needs on economic growth and equity within a macroeconomic model (see Boutros Ghali and Taylor 1980). Let us assume a single-sector economy which works at full capacity. The equilibrium between aggregate supply and demand is given by the following equation:

$$V = B + k(\Delta V) + f(\Delta L) \tag{9.1}$$

where ΔV and ΔL are rises in output and employment at each point of time (i.e. dV/dt, dL/dt), V is aggregate value added, B is total consumption to sustain a country's basic needs, L is total labour force, K is the capital–output ratio and f is investment in infrastructure for an extra unit of labour supply.

Let the labour–output ratio L/V be l; let b stand for the fraction of value added needed to satisfy the demand for basic needs (B/V). We can write the above equation as follows:

$$l = b + kV' + f1L' \tag{9.2}$$

where the prime indicates growth rates with reference to value added. Let c be the growth rate of labour productivity. Therefore,

$$L' = V' - c$$

We can solve the output growth rate as follows:

$$V' = \frac{1 - b + cf1}{k + f1} \tag{9.3}$$

The steady state solution can be devised from the above equation when b and $f1$ are inter-temporally stable. Now, let the growth rate at which the steady state solution is achieved be called the maximum technically feasible rate of growth subject to the constraint of basic needs (g^*) (equation 9.3). It is obvious that this rate is unattainable as we may have surplus consumption. Hence, it is useful to incorporate in our aggregate supply and demand equation a variable to stand for consumption of non-basic needs (S). Equation (9.1) can now be written as

$$V = B + S + k(\Delta V) + f(\Delta L) \tag{9.4}$$

If we carry out similar substitutions as before and calling the rate of growth g, we have

$$l = (S/V) + b + kg + f1(g - c) \tag{9.5}$$

Substituting this in equation (9.3), we obtain

$$g^* - \frac{g}{g^*} = \frac{S}{(1 - b + cf1)V}$$

In other words, a proportional fall in growth rate from its maximum level of basic needs (g^*) is equal to the ratio of surplus S to the amount of value added net of satisfaction of basic needs.

We know that the optimum feasible growth rate is $g^* = V'$. So from (9.3) we have

$$g^* = \frac{1 - b + cf1}{k + f1}$$

The optimal attainable growth rate rises as b falls, c rises and k falls. However, the effects of a change in f cannot be stated unequivocally and directly.

The above analysis implies that three factors can affect maximum investible surplus (for a definition, see Chapter 4): (1) the capital–output ratio, (2) the rate of technical progress and (3) the basic needs. The positive effect of growth due to a fall in the capital–output ratio is generally well known (see Chapter 4). In the present context, it is important to analyse the direction of change in the capital–output ratio when there is an increase in demand for more labour-intensive products following a redistribution of income in favour of the poorer section of the population. Evidence available so far tends to indicate such a rise in demand for labour-intensive products, though its size is not very substantial (see Cline 1982; Paukert *et al.* 1980). It also confirms that the incremental capital–output ratio tends to fall after an income redistribution.

As regards the impact of technical progress, Denison's study on post-war growth in Europe and the United States confirms its importance though some have questioned his measurement of units of production (see Denison 1967; Jorgenson and Griliches 1967). However, to understand clearly the impact of the basic needs approach it is imperative to develop theories which could specifically correlate changes in productivity to certain factors of production (Hopkins and Hoeven 1983). Bowman (1980) well observes:

> Whether growth is attributed to the new physical investment or to the available underutilised stock of human resources is a quibble: both are required. Economists can construct various sorts of 'aggregate production functions' to 'explain' growth,

> but the meaning of 'long-term equilibrium' itself becomes empirically elusive when what human beings do and might contribute to a changing scene is brought into the analysis.

It is needless to say that factors like better nutrition, health and education can considerably improve the quality of labour in the *long run*. However, the best way to analyse the impact of such factors on productivity is very much an area of future research.

As regards the impact of a loss of profit or surplus due to a rise in consumption for basic needs, it has been pointed out that most investments are usually made out of corporate or public rather than household savings (Bhat and Meerman 1978). Next, although a rise in consumption will reduce savings, it will also imply an increase in efficiency and productivity in LDCs (Cline 1982). *A priori* it is difficult to say whether the negative effects due to a fall in savings will be more than offset by a rise in productivity.

One of the major problems of these models is that the growth of population has been regarded as exogenous or given. It can, indeed, be argued that a radical system of asset (e.g. land) distribution can actually reduce the desire to have large families in LDCs. Many farmers in developing countries consider children as investment goods (see Chapter 7) plus an insurance for old age in the absence of a welfare state. A more egalitarian system of land reform can actually reduce fertility and lead to a greater provision of social and medical care for a relatively smaller number of the population. This again should improve the quality of labour and productivity.

An international cross-section analysis of *average* basic needs performance over the years 1960–75 among the major regions of the world reveals the following interesting points (Hopkins and Hoeven 1983).

1 Those countries performing well on one basic need are likely to perform well on another.
2 Per capita GNP is highly correlated with basic needs levels for most countries. Hopkins and Hoeven, for example, conclude on the basis of their extensive study that 'the most important variable explaining the average level of basic needs satisfaction in developing countries was gross national product per head. While this may seem obvious, it is worth emphasizing that material basic needs are ultimately satisfied out of national income and that in less developed countries these needs cannot be met without a major increase in the production of goods and services' (Hopkins and Hoeven 1983: 108–9).
3 The relationship between the basic needs indicators and *growth rate of GNP* per head has not been found to be significant (see also Morawetz, who reached a similar conclusion; Morawetz 1977). Nor has there been a consistent relationship between income distribution (as measured by the income share of the poorest 40 per cent of the population) and basic needs indicators. This finding is surely surprising and counter-intuitive. One explanation may be that the quality of data on income distribution in many LDCs is very poor. The other explanation is that there is no reason to assume that the overall income distribution should change the *average* level of basic needs satisfaction, since gains for the better-off simply offset the losses of the worse-off.

4 Countries which experienced more rapid rates of growth of population also registered inferior performance on a large number of the basic needs indicators. This result is not surprising for the reasons already given.
5 Between 1960 and 1967, improvements in basic needs seem to be mostly correlated with the following two variables: income *per capita* and past performance (Stewart 1979).
6 Out of a number of political indicators, the one most closely associated with basic needs performance was the Adelman and Morris composite participation index (see Adelman and Morris 1973 for the construction of such an index). Even so, no significant relationship has been observed in quite a few countries.

The above findings tend to suggest that a rise in *per capita* real income is one of the most important preconditions for satisfying basic needs, though the importance of income distribution and political participation should not be underemphasized. It is imperative to carry out more research in this field to reach more definite judgement.

Box 9.1 A Chinese example

The country that has been most successful among the LDCs in meeting the basic needs of its population has been China. The main reasons for such an achievement can be summarized as follows:

1 a radical land reform programme to raise food production and a programme for distributing benefits from such land reform among the largest number of rural population in China;
2 adoption of an imaginative method of raising the rate of rural capital formation and industrialization via a method of transfers of about a fifth of the total revenue of communes into an investible fund;
3 improvements of the internal terms of trade in favour of agriculture, diversification of rural economic activity and thereby mobilization and absorption of 'surplus' labour by increasing agricultural productivity;
4 provision of basic needs like health and education to *all* sections of the rural population;
5 decentralization of rural planning and optimum exploration of indigenous resources to meet local demand and the creation of a new political and ideological system which underlines the virtues of collective benefits rather than individual profits (see Aziz 1974).

It remains to be said that the 'Chinese lesson' for other LDCs is worthy of serious consideration.

9.9 A note on famines

It is almost ironical to reflect that despite the spread of the GR in many parts of LDCs, starvation and famines persist and seem to be affecting a large number of people over time. The Ethiopian famine of 1984, like the Great Bengal famine of 1943 when at least

2 million to 4 million people died (see Sen 1981b), seems to be a tragic reminder of the fact that, even in the midst of plenty, people perish. Thus, it may be useful to understand the nature and causes of famines.

Famine has been defined in the *Oxford English Dictionary* as an 'extreme and general scarcity of food'. An encyclopedia definition has it as 'a lack of food over a large geographical area sufficiently long and severe to cause widespread disease and death from starvation'. Others argue that the minimum acceptable definition should imply a wide and prolonged shortage of food resulting in an increased human death rate. Hence, famine implies widespread food shortage resulting in starvation of many people and a substantial increase in the mortality rate in a particular country or region (see Alamgir 1978 for a good summary). It should be noted that, while deaths from starvation occur mainly among the poor, epidemics might affect any section of the entire population.

9.9.1 Causes of famine

Famine could be caused by many factors of which the following deserve special emphasis.

Many argue that the decline in food availability *per capita* is the most important factor for the emergence of famine. Such a decline could be due to (1) a slow growth rate of foodgrain production; (2) a high rate of growth of population; or (3) a combination of (1) and (2). This type of explanation has been labelled as the FAD or the food availability doctrine. Its logic is very simple. If the *per capita* food availability falls substantially due to either a demand pressure (e.g. a significant rise in population relative to food supply) or a supply shock (because of a huge crop failure) then many people in LDCs are very likely to suffer from starvation and death. However, death is not simply related to a shortage of foodgrains. It is only when the shortage in foodgrain production leads to a *prolonged* fall in foodgrain intake that starvation on a massive scale leads to an excessive rise in the death rate and famine.

It is worth pointing out that a prolonged decline in foodgrain intake can directly and indirectly lead to an excessive rise in the death rate. For instance, the persistence of acute poverty and hunger in a region may substantially raise the rate of crime and death. Also, a serious fall in the level of nutrition may lead to a loss of body weight, eating of alternative poor quality 'famine foods', disease and death.

The causal sequences of the famine syndrome are given in Figure 9.7 (see Alamgir 1978 for details). The major causes of famines are stated to be the following:

1 foodgrain availability decline, total or *per capita*;
2 real income decline *per capita*;
3 foodgrain price increase which with a constant money wage will imply a decline in real wage;
4 absence of social security measures in most LDCs;
5 inefficient and imperfect mechanisms for storing and distributing foodgrains in the face of an acute supply bottleneck.

The causal sequences from these conditions leading to famine and death are described in Figure 9.7.

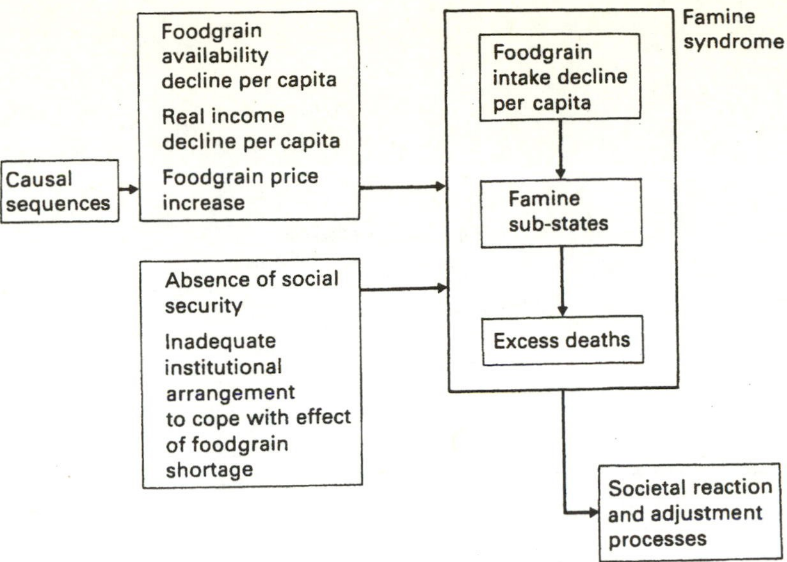

Figure 9.7

Figure 9.8(a) shows the relationship between the death rate and the foodgrain intake *per capita f*, the famine syndrome. This relationship should be inverse. However, when the natural death rate d_B is attained, the curve will be infinitely elastic as a rise in foodgrain intake beyond f_p will have no effect in reducing the death rate any further. Figure 9.8(b) measures the direct relationship between real income *per capita* (*Y*, on the vertical axis), and foodgrain intake *per capita*. The $f(y)$ line slopes upward and becomes vertical after a certain point like K as foodgrain intake does not respond any more with a further rise in *per capita* income beyond *Y*. The figure shows that with real income *per capita* at y_p, foodgrain intake *per capita* is f_p and the death rate stays at a natural level (d_n, in the top diagram). As y_p, falls to a very low level (y_f or the level of famine and real income), foodgrain intake *per capita* falls to f_t and the death rate exceeds the natural level (as shown by the difference between d_E and d_N).

However, A. K. Sen has put forward an alternative and interesting view to account for famines in different countries (Sen 1981a, b). Sen argues that in order to understand starvation it is necessary to understand the structure of ownership in an economy or society. Ownership relationships are regarded as one kind of *entitlement relationship*. Such entitlement relations can be based on (1) trade, (2) production, (3) labour power and (4) simple inheritance and transfer. It is obvious that the scope of ownership relations varies with economic systems.

Sen argues that in a standard market economy an individual can exchange what he owns for another bundle of goods via production and/or trading. The set of all the different collections of goods that he can obtain in exchange for what he owns has been labelled by Sen the *exchange entitlement* of what he owns. Sen then considers an exchange entitlement or E-mapping. This mapping denotes the set of exchange entitlements for each ownership bundle. An individual will be doomed to starvation if ‘for the ownership that he actually has, the exchange entitlement set does not contain any feasible bundle including enough food. Given the E-mapping it is then

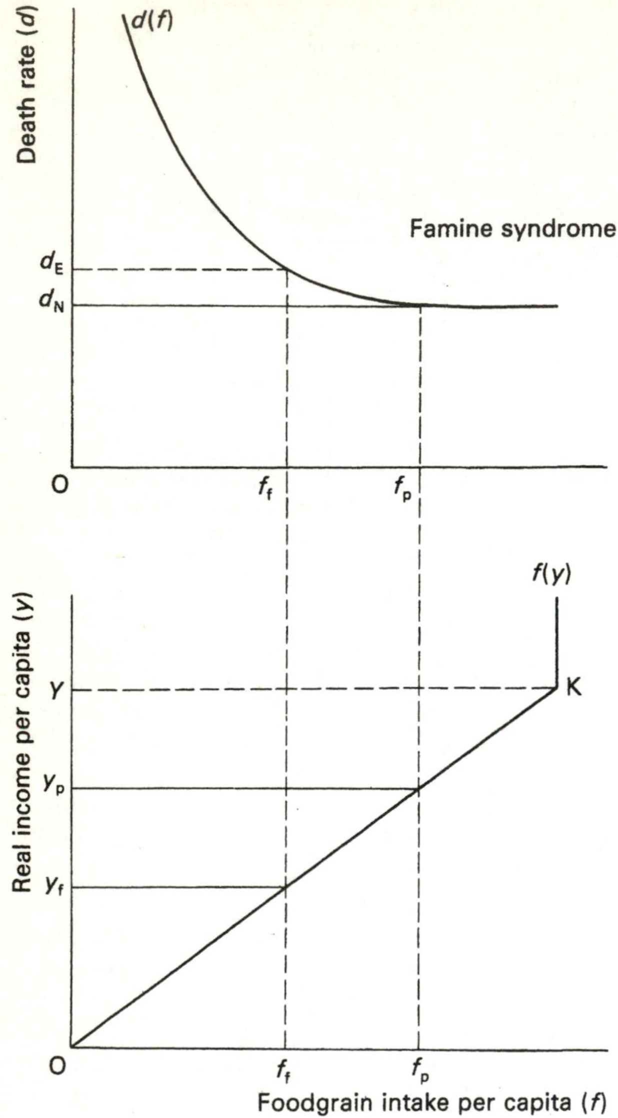

Figure 9.8

possible to identify those ownership bundles. . . . The starvation set – that must, thus, lead to starvation in the absence of non-entitlement transfers (e.g. charity)' (Sen 1981b: 3).

An individual's exchange entitlement can be affected by a number of factors, e.g. (1) the probability and the duration of a job; (2) the wage rate; (3) the price of goods to be bought; (4) the value of products he can sell and the cost of buying resources; (5) social security benefits.

It is obvious that a fall in food availability will raise food prices and, as such, an individual's exchange entitlement (EE) will be adversely affected. However, a person's EE may worsen for causes *other* than a general fall in the supply of food. Assume that the total supply of food is the same as before. Yet a person's EE may decline: some groups in society get richer and buy more food and thus drive up food prices beyond the reach of an average individual with a low income. Also, when the employment prospect worsens or nominal wages tend to lag behind prices considerably, EE declines. An individual can starve either because 'he does not have the ability to command enough food or because he does not use this ability to avoid starvation. The entitlement approach concentrates on the former, ignoring the latter possibility' (Sen 1981).

Figure 9.9 illustrates that an individual, say *i*, can suffer from starvation if his endowment collapses into the starvation set S_i, either because of a decline in the E bundle or owing to an adverse movement in the EE mapping. In the figure, food is measured horizontally and non-food is measured vertically. The EE assumes fixed-price terms of trade or exchange. When the price ratio is given by p and a minimum food requirement is OA, the starvation set S is given by OAB. When the endowment vector is x, an individual can avoid starvation. But he will suffer from starvation if either (1) he has a lower endowment vector, i.e. x^*, or (2) he faces an unfavourable EE mapping as given by p^*, when the starvation set expands to OAC.

Sen presents considerable evidence from Bengal (1943), Ethiopia (1972–4) and Bangladesh (1974) to claim that while the FAD fails to provide a good explanation of famine in a number of cases, e.g. the Bangladesh famine, a better understanding of such famines can be obtained through his EE approach.

Although Sen's analysis of famine is illuminating and provides deep insight into the causes of famines, for instance an imperfect system of distribution and very unfavourable terms of trade for weak and vulnerable groups in society (e.g. unemployed persons, agricultural labourers in the rural areas, unskilled workers etc.), it is necessary to point out some limitations of the EE approach. For example, it may be difficult to

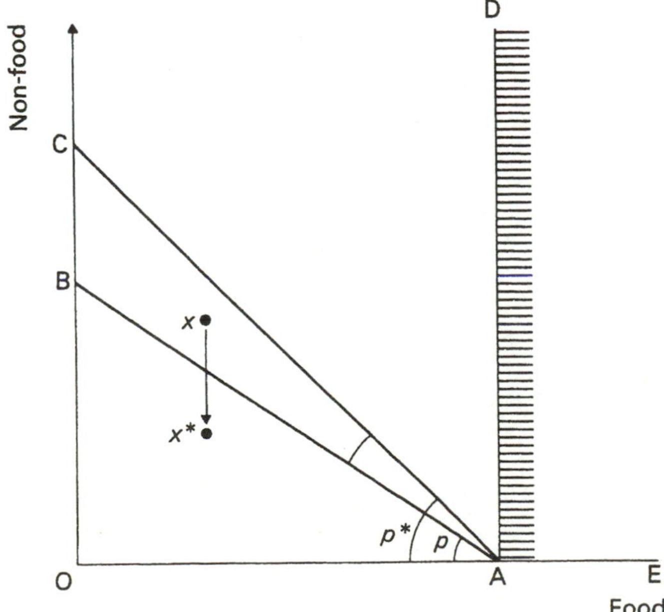

Figure 9.9

define EE clearly. Second, *lack of legal entitlement* can lead to famines even when economic entitlements are kept intact. Third, sometimes ignorance and apathy can cause actual food consumption to fall below what people are entitled to have. Also, many famine deaths are caused by diseases and epidemics rather than simple starvation. Fourth, in some cases, FAD may be the dominant cause of famine. Finally, sometimes the FAD and EE failure explanations of famines are not mutually exclusive (for a detailed analysis, see Ghatak and Ingersent 1984).

Sen (1999) has argued that freedom is an essential ingredient of human development. Five distinct types of freedom are investigated by Sen. They comprise (1) political freedoms, (2) economic facilities, (3) social opportunities, (4) transparency guarantees, (5) protective security. Each of these types of rights helps to advance the general capability of a person. They can also complement each other. Public policy can certainly play a useful and important role to foster human capabilities and EE.

Questions

1 What is the 'green revolution' in LDCs?
2 Account for the causes of the 'green revolution' in LDCs.
3 Analyse the effects of the 'green revolution' on income distribution.
4 Define the concept of 'basic needs'.
5 What are the major causes of famine in LDCs? How does an 'entitlement approach' offer greater insight into the causes of famine?

10 Population, poverty, income distribution, employment and migration

10.1 Population and economic development

The relationship between the growth of population and economic development could be regarded as a 'challenge' and a 'response'. Population growth against a given amount of resources at a certain point in time in economic history has posed the challenge of feeding extra mouths; the response has come from more economic growth. Thus, the relationship between population and economic growth can be viewed in two ways. From the standpoint of demand, the growth of population increases the demand for food, services and other resources: from the standpoint of supply, it implies the availability of more labour to produce more goods and services.

In the DCs, the long-run growth of the economy could be constrained by the supply of labour and here an increase in population growth rate might raise the rate of economic growth. Historically, if it is pointed out that the 'unprecedented rise in population' led to the emergence of the industrial revolution (Hicks 1957: 302). Since necessity is regarded as the mother of invention, the logic of such an argument is not difficult to understand.

Growth of population could have some beneficial effects on economic growth. First, a growing population enlarges the size of the market by raising aggregate demand. Second, a rising population supplies more labour for employment. Third, if the labour supply is a constraint on growth, then an expansion of the labour force will raise output and growth.

The major harmful effects of rapid population growth can be summarized as follows.

1 If the rise in *per capita* income or output growth is regarded as a rough indicator of the improvement of the *average* standard of living in the society, then it is obvious that in an economy with stagnant total income and rising population the *average* standard of living could only worsen. Similarly, if the population growth rate is faster than the growth rate of real income, again the average standard of living will fall. This is the famous 'Malthusian' picture of the population problem in LDCs. A backward economy with limited resources using primitive technology could only manage to register a slow growth of total output, and if the population growth rate outstrips the growth rate of output, *per capita* output is likely to fall. For many people living on the brink of subsistence in many LDCs, this picture may appear to be very real. The poverty, squalor, famine, epidemics, mass starvation and migration that are generally observed in many LDCs are regarded by many as the major 'Malthusian' effects of a rapid rise in population.

2 The positive effects of population growth on output growth could only be obtained if labour could be productively employed with the available resources. For most LDCs, the critical bottleneck in the path of economic development is regarded as the availability of capital, both physical and social. Given the paucity of capital, the availability of more labour does not add much to output growth. It is argued that in some cases the contribution of labour in the LDCs, particularly in agriculture, could be very low and even zero (Lewis 1954; Fei and Ranis 1964; see also Chapter 3).
3 The rise in population lowers the man–land or the man–resources ratios. This implies that a static, backward economy without any technical progress could only experience greater poverty with growing population pressure on available resources.
4 The lack of enough physical and social capital along with structural and technical rigidities in the LDCs render the curve for supply of output rather inelastic and a rise in population coupled with an increased supply of labour leads to greater underemployment and open unemployment, particularly in the agricultural sector. Where the level of population is very large (e.g. China, India), the population density per acre of land rises. Since the agricultural sector is backward and the industrial sector is generally small, additional labour could not be easily absorbed within the agrarian economy. Migration follows and unemployment in the rural areas turns into unemployment in the urban areas.
5 A high level of population or its rapid growth creates additional demands on social capital like education, housing and health services. Since the supply of such facilities is usually inadequate in LDCs, a growth in population tends to overstrain the existing limited supply.
6 If the supply of food is inelastic in LDCs, then a rising population with an increase in demand could lead to inflation. In order to cope with the problem, many LDCs import foodgrains from abroad and this causes an important drain on valuable foreign exchange which could have been used for better purposes. Since many LDCs suffer from serious inflationary and balance of payments problems, the concern about the population problem can easily be understood.
7 The rapid growth of population leads to a high dependency ratio, i.e. the proportion of non-working to working population. Also, the children below, say, 15–16 years tend to form a high proportion of the working population and the existence of such a young age group within the working population aggravates the problems of food supply and employment creation.
8 High population growth rates and/or a high level of population could lead to pollution and many environmental problems like the growth of shanty towns, juvenile delinquency, squalor, congestion, etc.
9 A rising population in a fairly static and poor economy could aggravate the problems of inequalities in income distribution. Since, on average, poor families tend to be larger than rich families, as long as there is only one bread-winner in both these income classes, *per capita*, real income and real consumption will clearly be lower in poor income groups in comparison with richer ones.

The above arguments show that the costs of population growth could be much greater than its benefits for the LDCs. Such costs would rise considerably if they experience what has come to be known as a 'population explosion' – a topic which will be discussed in section 10.2.

10.2 Population explosion in less developed countries and the theory of demographic transition

Population explosion is a phrase which is commonly used to describe the prevalence of high crude birth rates with low death rates in many LDCs. According to the theory of demographic transition, in the pre-industrial, backward society a high birth rate (BR) is generally accompanied by a high death rate (DR) with the result that the net growth rate of population remains low. Evidence from most countries seems to back up this argument. In the passage of economic growth, it is argued that BR remains high while DR falls resulting in a very rapid rise in population growth or 'population explosion'. In a more mature phase of economic development, BR tends to decline and DR falls to its lowest level and remains fairly stationary. Eventually, BR falls to a low level and the net growth of population becomes low and stable (see Figure 10.1). BR and DR are measured on the vertical axis and time is measured horizontally. At t_0, both BR and DR are high; at t_1, with economic development and say greater and better medical facilities, DR falls but BR remains much the same as before. The difference AB is the 'population explosion'. In the more mature period of economic growth, say at time t_2, BR falls and the population grows at a low and stable rate.

Although the *theory* of demographic transition is supposed to be a theory, it is noteworthy that it is not really a theory. Rather, it is a description of facts. Next, although parts of the movements of BR and DR in the way described above are observed in the passage of economic growth of the DCs, there is no way to suggest that the institutional conditions of the DCs of yesterday are the same as those of the LDCs of the present time. Also, if the implication of the 'theory' of demographic transition is that a higher *per capita* income over time leads to a fall in population growth rate, then this inference is not always substantiated by the evidence available so far (Cassen 1976). Indeed Kuznets has found a positive correlation between population growth

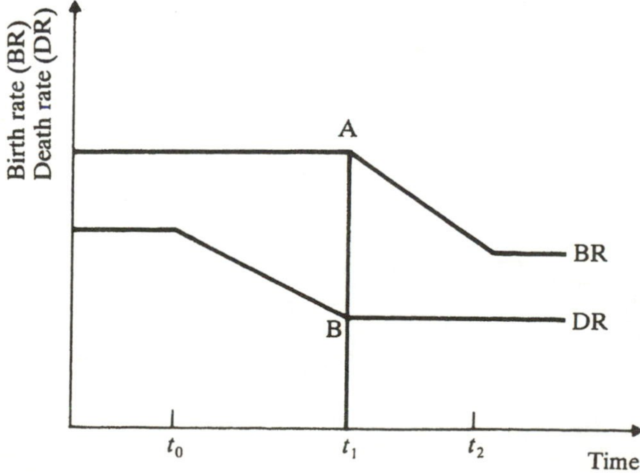

Figure 10.1

and economic growth (Kuznets 1967). Although correlation does not suggest causation, it is interesting to observe that no negative and statistically significant association was observed. Finally, the theory of demographic transition does not say much about the factors which affect the fertility and mortality *behaviour* which would explain some important demographic characteristics.

10.3 Low-level equilibrium trap

The other theory which is advanced to explain the relationship between population and income growth is known as the 'low-level equilibrium trap' (Nelson 1956). Basically, the theory suggests that, as long as *per capita* income remains below a critical level, a population growth rate that exceeds the income growth rate will always bring the economy back to a 'low-level equilibrium trap'. To avoid the trap, it is necessary to introduce technical progress so that the production function which accounts for the output or real income growth rate will lie above the population growth rate, and as long as that happens the trap will cease to operate (see Figure 10.2). The growth of population and the growth of income are measured vertically whereas *per capita* income (Y/N) is measured horizontally. The economy is at a low-level equilibrium at L because beyond L up to K population growth rate is faster than income growth rate and *per capita* income falls, bringing the economy back to L. The trap operates on any point between K and L. To avoid the trap it is necessary that the income growth rate curve should exceed the population growth rate curve; this occurs beyond K and *per capita* income rises. In order to attain sustained progress in *per capita* income, the policy implications are clear. First, the output growth curve must be shifted upwards by better allocation of resources or through the introduction of technical progress or both. Second, population growth rate must be controlled as far as possible.

Clearly, the shift of the output growth curve will require massive investments in the LDCs. This may call for greater effort by the government; here the *quality* rather than the quantity of government investment assumes importance. Public expenditure in most LDCs has grown over the last forty years but its effect on output growth has

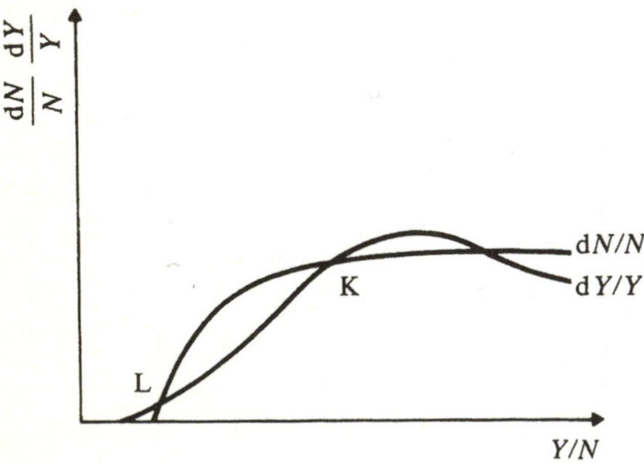

Figure 10.2

not always proved to be very encouraging. It is imperative to raise productive investment as far as possible and this could call for more technical progress in industry as well as in agriculture.

Evidence to support or reject the low-level equilibrium trap theory is rather scanty. One study indicates the possible existence of such equilibrium in the case of some Asian and Latin American countries (Moreland and Hazeldine 1974). More research is obviously necessary to draw firm conclusions.

The other important policy to raise *per capita* income is to control population growth rates. This is a complex issue and here the main problem of controlling fertility has received wide attention.

10.4 Fertility and population growth in less developed countries

Most evidence seems to confirm that the majority of LDCs are likely to experience high to moderate growth rates in population in the near future though for some larger countries like India and China the phases of highest growth rates seem to be over. In some countries there are now increasing signs of a decline in fertility (e.g. Singapore, Korea, Taiwan, Mauritius). But in general the fertility rates (as measured by BR per thousand) in LDCs are considerably higher than those in DCs. Since the mortality rates in most LDCs are unlikely to be reduced significantly in the future, the population growth rate could now be controlled mainly by reducing fertility rates. It has been suggested that the returns from fertility control and family planning in LDCs could be in excess of a hundred times the returns from other types of investment (Enke 1966). These estimates are, perhaps, exaggerated chiefly for two reasons. First, the estimates of social costs were very low as only the costs of contraceptive devices were considered. Second, the benefits from such prevention seem to have been overstated. Nevertheless, other estimates have shown that such social returns from family planning are not very low (Zaidan 1971). There seems to be a genuine and urgent necessity to increase expenditure for family planning. Since such expenditure is likely to be large, the government has to play a major role in financing these programmes. The problem here is to identify as accurately as possible the factors that affect fertility. Some of these factors are discussed in the next section.

10.4.1 Factors affecting fertility

Fertility could be influenced by a number of economic as well as non-economic variables. The economic factors in the LDCs include the need of the parents to have some sort of an insurance against old age while the non-economic factors include biological, psychological and social variables. It is argued that a decline in fertility could be achieved only when the following conditions are satisfied:

1 The parents must be conscious regarding the choice about fertility.
2 The net benefits from the fertility reduction should be considered as considerable by the parents.
3 The supply of effective family planning methods must be assured (Coale 1973).

The economic choice of the parents for children will no doubt depend on the above conditions. Clearly, it is assumed here that the parents are rational enough to calculate that the net benefits from family planning are significantly positive. In the urban and educated sector, it may be possible to apply such a model of economic choice for children. In the vast rural sector it is difficult to see how the model could be applied. However, many illiterate people living in the rural sector do not always show 'economic irrationality'. In fact, many parents in the villages consider children as an 'investment' rather than a consumption good since they can help the farming and other activities of the families. It is in this context that the relationship between fertility and mortality assumes some significance.

10.4.2 Fertility and mortality

Fertility could be significantly affected by mortality, particularly *infant mortality* (see Table 10.1). In LDCs, the chances of survival of a child are shown to be much less in comparison with DCs. From the point of view of a peasant family, if it is assumed that only two out of every three babies born are likely to survive, then the fertility rates are likely to remain high. In most LDCs social security and old-age assistance programmes are virtually non-existent. Thus the children are naturally regarded as some form of insurance in old age, and 'investment goods'. Evidence confirms that in most LDCs infant mortality and fertility are highly and significantly correlated. The interesting policy implication that follows from this is that, in order to reduce fertility, it is imperative to reduce infant mortality. Apart from this, social welfare systems should be extended wherever possible to help the old people.

10.4.3 Fertility and education: importance of female education

Higher education is generally expected to reduce fertility. Evidence available so far indicates a negative and statistically significant correlation between higher education and a decline in fertility in many LDCs. The Indian data strongly suggest such a negative correlation (Parikh 1976). What is important to emphasize here is that in almost all cases *female* education had a very strong *negative* impact on fertility. This implies the necessity to educate the female population in the LDCs to reduce population growth, since educated women are likely to see more clearly the logic of fertility control. Education also helps people to get over age-old customs and inhibitions, to change attitudes and motivations and to make a more rational choice. If education should enhance the income of the parents, the arrival of the babies can only diminish it: again, grounds for an 'economic choice' for babies can be seen.

An expansion of women's education may be a necessary but not a sufficient condition for reducing fertility. It is important to provide productive employment to the educated women's labour force and to raise their general status in the society to reduce fertility significantly.

10.4.4 Fertility and income

It is sometimes argued that fertility and *per capita* real income are inversely correlated so that a rise in *per capita* real income would tend to reduce fertility. In the 'economic choice' model if babies are treated as consumption goods then their demand will compete against the demand for all other items of consumption, and the benefits from having the babies ('consuming them') have to be viewed against the cost of bearing and rearing them. Such costs would include the allocation of more parental time to mind the babies and the possible loss of income. Thus, the demand for babies should be inversely correlated with income (see Schultz 1976; Becker and Lewis 1973).

It has been mentioned before that the children in the LDCs are also regarded as 'investment' goods. Casual observation seems to support this argument as many young children in LDCs, i.e. 'child labour' (Basu 1997), participate and help their families in different activities. It is also true that in the absence of a social security system parents expect their children to look after them in their old age, and if their children (generally their sons) do not, they are regarded as a disgrace to their families. On the other hand, it is doubtful whether children could be classified exactly as 'consumption' or 'investment' goods; perhaps they are regarded as a bit of both, and on the basis of available information it is hard to say whether the parents always calculate very carefully the discounted rates of return at the margin from a 'marginal' child! It is rather unlikely that parental decisions for having children would depend always on economic factors with utility or profit maximization being the overriding objective function. Psychological, social and biological factors also play important roles in determining fertility.

The statistical difficulty in assessing the impact of *per capita* real income growth on fertility is that it is not easy to establish the direction of causation. It is possible to argue that fertility decline tends to raise *per capita* real income. Also, it could be argued that parents usually want to provide better opportunities for their offspring, e.g. good health, better education, better nutrition, etc. Hence, if *per capita* real income rises, it is possible that parents will be less pessimistic about future costs of increasing the size of the family and the demand for babies will rise. In fact, there is some evidence in the LDCs which suggests a positive correlation between men's wages/earnings and fertility though the coefficients are not always statistically significant. Such results should be accepted with caution, however, because of limited samples and differences between institutions. More research is necessary, perhaps, in terms of simultaneous relationship models to draw firm conclusions.

In an interesting microeconomic model of choice, Schultz (1976) has shown that the overall positive or negative change in the demand for babies will depend upon price and income effects. Normally, a rise in the price of a baby should reduce its demand. If prices are given, a sudden rise in parental income could increase the demand for babies. A rise in the husband's income could increase the demand for babies whereas a rise in the wife's income could reduce such demand because of differences in the values assigned to time allocated for work and relative income earned by the parents, even when the same values (but different signs) are assigned to the price and income elasticities of demand for the babies (see Appendix 10.3).

Although Schultz's attempt to analyse the demand for children within an economic calculus is interesting, it is not clear whether such a model could be really applied to the LDCs where the vast majority of people are illiterate and unaware of the sophisticated techniques to evaluate at the *margin* the gains and losses from having children. As has been emphasized earlier, fertility is governed by a large number of biological, psychological, social and religious factors and the exclusion of these factors may weaken considerably the predictive power of the models which seek to explain fertility behaviour purely in terms of economic variables.

Table 10.1 Summary of empirical findings for low income countries on the determinants of fertility

Variable	*1*	*2*	*3*	*4*	*5*	*6*	*7*	*8a*	*8b*
Author (year; page)	Schultz (1969; 171)	Schultz (1970; 43)	Nerlove–Schultz (1970; 45)	Harman (1970; 29–30)	Schultz (1971; 61)	Da Vanzo (1972; 80)	Maurer *et al.* (1973; 209)	Schultz (1972; 36)	Schultz (1972; 38)
Population (time)	Puerto Rico (195–17)	Egypt (1960)	Puerto Rico (1950–60)	Philippines (1968)	Taiwan (1964–8)	Chile (1960)	Thailand (1960)	Taiwan (1964–9)	Taiwan (1964–9)
Observations (number)	Regions (75*7)	Regions (41)	Regions (78*11)	Individuals (250)	Regions (361)	Regions (50)	Regions (71)	Regions (361*7)	Regions (361*7)
Equation (estimators)[a]	Reduced form (OLS)	Reduced form (OLS)	Structural (TSLS/GLS)	Structural (TSLS)	Reduced form (OLS)	Structural (TSLS)	Solved reduced form (TSLS)	Reduced form (OLS)	Reduced form (GLS)
Dependent variable	Births per 1,000 population	Children (0–9) per 1,000 women (15–49)	Births per 1,000 population	Children ever born per 1,000 women aged 35–9	Normalized births per 1,000 women aged 35–9	Children ever born per 1,000 women aged 35–9	Children ever born per 1,000 women aged 35–9	Births per 1,000 women aged 35–9	Births per 1,000 women aged 15–0
Explanatory variables[b]									
1 Adult education	−1.58 (5.3) [0.15]		−1.95	–	–	–	–	–	-
2 Women's education	–	−65.2 (4.0) [0.087]		−0.092 (1.6) [0.094]	0.422 (1.97) [1.8][f]	–	−0.0926 [0.13][h]	98.2 (9.2) [0.37]	−45 4 (2.78) [0.17]
3 Women's wage	–	–	–	–	–	−1589 (1.84) [0.35][g]	−22.6 [0.16][h]	–	–

4 Men's education	–	–	–	–	–	–	0.526 [0.55][h]	−274 (16.0) [1.4]	−174 (7.9) [0.98]
5 Men's wage	–	–	–	–	–	170 (0.33) [0.054]	–	–	–
6 Death rate	1.18 (3.5) [0.27][d]	–	0.302 (1.6) [0.082][d]	5.76 (3.9) [1.0] [0.048][e]	5.61 (9.3) [5.5][f] [0.41][e]	7.65 (2.72) [0.28]	–	432 (17.9) [3.9] [0.28]e	172 (8.2) [15] [0.11][e]
R^2 (F; df)[c]	0.46	0.537	(27.3)	(3.5)	0.433[f]	(14.4; 6, 3)	(139; 7, 4)	0.461	0.809

Source: Schultz (1976).

Notes: After each regression coefficient the absolute value of the ratio is reported in parentheses and elasticities at regression means in brackets.

[a] Form of estimation equation such as reduced-form equations (only exogenous explanatory variables) which may be estimated by ordinary least squares (OLS), structural equations (including endogenous explanatory variables) estimated perhaps by an instrumental variable technique such as two-stage least squares (TSLS), solved reduced-form equations, derived from the simultaneous equations estimates of the related structural equations (generally without *t* statistics), and when a time series of cross-sections are pooled for either a reduced form or a structural equation, estimates may be reported using a generalized least-squares procedure (GLS) that assumes a Nerlovian two-component stochastic structure to the disturbances.For instrumental variable estimates asymptotic *t* statistics are reported.

[b] For definition of the explanatory variables, including those not reported in the table, see the original studies.

[c] Asymptotic significance of the entire equation can be evaluated with the *F* ratio when TSLS estimates are computed. For OLS and GLS of reduced-form equations, R^2 can be used to test the equation's overall statistical significance.

[d] Arithmetic sum of lagged coefficients, and averaged *t* statistics.

[e] Child death rate entered the regression as the reciprocal of child survival tale. For comparability and ease of interpretation, the second elasticity estimates are with respect to the child death rate.

[f] Arithmetic average of regression coefficients' *t* statistics, elasticities and R^2 from five annual cross-sectional regressions.

[g] The women's wage was treated as endogenous to this investigation and is therefore estimated as a linear function of exogenous variables such as women's education, etc.

[h] The solved reduced-form equations are reported without asymptotic standard error estimates. The elasticity estimates for education variables incorporate also the effect of an additional variable that is non-linear in male and female education, namely the educational attainment of women relative to that of men.

10.4.5 Fertility and urbanization

The hypothesis is often put forward that fertility should be inversely correlated with urbanization. To the extent that higher *per capita* real income, better education, greater employment opportunities, particularly for women, are all associated with greater urbanization in LDCs, the hypothesis seems to be valid, at least *theoretically*. On the other hand, the *independent* effect of urbanization on fertility is open to question as the statistical problem of multicollinearity among the explanatory variables like *per capita* real income, education, employment and urbanization is obvious. Although it is argued that urbanization could change 'attitudes', it is not quite clear how the mere transplantation of the village population into the urban society will lead to immediate changes in age-old customs. The process is thus likely to be slow. In fact, age-specific marital fertility differences between similar income groups in the rural and urban societies may not be significant. Indeed, evidence from Africa suggests that fertility in the urban areas is actually higher in comparison with that in the rural areas. In Latin America and India, it is just the opposite (see UN 1973; Opinion Research Group 1973). Thus, it is difficult to generalize from the existing evidence the likely impact of urbanization on fertility in LDCs. However, since the urban areas in LDCs have more access to education, information and supplies of the family planning devices, it is likely that fertility would be gradually lower in the urban areas in comparison with the rural areas.

10.4.6 Fertility, compulsory sterilization and incentive payments

One of the direct methods to reduce fertility could be compulsory sterilization. But the efficiency of such a method could be very much doubted, particularly in a democratic society. Perhaps in a regimented society (e.g. China), a more direct method to control fertility is likely to succeed. However, the Indian experience of 1975–7 shows how a high-handed compulsory sterilization programme could easily result in not only social unrest but also a dramatic political change. Few would genuinely doubt the necessity to pursue a vigorous family planning programme in India, but a *compulsory* sterilization programme seems to be an extreme and very unwise policy which could easily defeat the purpose. A more rational scheme should include a system of incentives and disincentives which could be provided to the parents. Economic sanctions (e.g. tax-cum-subsidies) could achieve substantial success as has been observed in the case of Singapore and China. Parents with one or two children could be given subsidies in cash or kind whereas families with more than three or four children could be penalized. Legislation may sometimes help to achieve a reduction in fertility. For instance, laws concerning an increase in the marriage age and a more liberal system of abortion may help to diminish fertility.

A rapid growth rate of population in a poor and static economy is one of the major reasons for poverty in the LDCs. Such poverty is observed in varying degrees in all the LDCs, although where the density of population is high, the existing resources are low, the population growth rate is high and income distribution is fairly unequal, poverty seems to beggar description. Instances of mass poverty are many in countries like Bangladesh, Ethiopia, Chad, Burkina Faso, India, Peru, etc. In section 10.5 we shall discuss poverty and income distribution.

10.5 Poverty and income distribution

The persistence of absolute poverty (see Appendix 10.1) and the increase in relative inequality in some developing countries in spite of comparatively rapid economic growth in the last two decades is a subject of increasing concern in recent discussions in development economics. The evidence of the maldistribution of past growth has led some to call into question the very idea of aggregate growth as a central aim of policy, believing that growth may have to be sacrificed for better distribution. Others, again, see no inevitable conflict between an increase in GNP and distribution. regarding growth as a necessary condition for better distribution but focusing attention on active policies to promote a more equal distribution of the fruits of growth.

We first deal with the facts as we know them about inequality and absolute poverty and their relationship with growth. Then the strategy of *Redistribution with Growth* will be outlined.[1]

10.6 Income inequality

From sample surveys there is now much more information than formerly on income distribution in a large number of developing countries; however, it is important to bear in mind the limitations of these data. Errors arise from a number of sources. First of all the income concept used is too restrictive. It is usually based on money income alone over a relatively short period such as a month or at most a year, rather than 'permanent income' allowing for income in kind and adjusted for tax incidence and transfer payments. Even where the income concept is properly defined it is difficult to measure in practice, particularly at the upper and lower ends of the scale. There is a likelihood that the highest income groups deliberately understate their income for fear of incurring a tax liability. At the other end it is difficult to value own consumption and investment in the rural subsistence sector. Also rural–urban price differentials tend to understate rural real income. The sample surveys used for estimating income distribution are frequently based on samples of insufficient size and representativeness.

Given these familiar weaknesses in the data, the following tentative picture emerges about income inequality. Using the method of measuring inequality by the extent to which the income share of groups of individuals or households differs from their population share and examining the problem in terms of the income shares of the lowest 40 per cent, the middle 40 per cent and the top 20 per cent of households, the following broad patterns emerge from the income share data of the sixty-six countries in Table 10.2.

The *socialist* countries have the highest degree of overall equality with the average income of the lowest 40 per cent amounting to about 25 per cent of total incomes. Income inequality in these countries derives mainly from inequality in wages and not from the ownership of capital which is largely in public hands.

Developed countries are next in income equality ranging equally between low and moderate inequality with the income share of the lowest 40 per cent averaging about 16 per cent of total incomes. But the use of pre-tax data understates the equalizing effect of progressive taxes and transfer payments that are relatively significant in developed compared with underdeveloped countries.

Table 10.2 Cross-classification of countries by income level and equality

High inequality *Share of lowest 40% less than 12%*					*Moderate inequality* *Share of lowest 40% between 12% and 17%*					*Low inequality* *Share of lowest 40%, 17% and abaove*				
Country (year)	*Per capita GNP (US$)*	*Lowest 40%*	*Middle 40%*	*Top 20%*	*Country (year)*	*Per capita GNP (US$)*	*Lowest 40%*	*Middle 40%*	*Top 20%*	*Country (year)*	*Per capita GNP (US$)*	*Lowest 40%*	*Middle 40%*	*Top 20%*
Redistribution with growth														
Income up to US$300														
Kenya (1969)	136	10.0	22.0	68.0	El Salvador (1969)	295	11.2	36.4	52.4	Chad (1958)	78	18.0	39.0	43.0
Sierra Leone (1968)	159	9.6	22.4	68.0	Turkey (1968)	282	9.3	29.9	60.8	Sri Lanka (1969)	95	17.0	37.0	46.0
Philippines (1971)	239	11.6	34.6	53.8	Burma (1958)	82	16.5	38.7	44.8	Niger (1960)	97	18.0	40.0	42.0
Iraq (1956)	200	6.8	25.2	68.0	Dahomey (1959)	87	15.5	34.5	50.0	Pakistan (1964)	100	17.5	37.5	30.0
Senegal (1960)	245	10.0	26.0	64.0	Tanzania (1967)	89	13.0	26.0	61.0	Uganda (1970)	126	17.1	35.8	47.1
Ivory Coast (1970)	247	10.8	32.1	57.1	India (1964)	99	16.0	32.0	52.0	Thailand (1970)	180	17.0	37.5	45.5
Rhodesia (1968)	252	8.2	22.8	69.0	Madagascar (1960)	120	13.5	25.5	61.0	Korea (1970)	235	18.0	37.0	45.0
Tunisia (1970)	255	11.4	53.6	55.0	Zambia (1959)	230	14.5	28.5	57.0	Taiwan (1964)	241	20.4	39.5	40.1
Honduras (1968)	265	6.5	28.5	65.0										
Ecuador (1970)	277	6.5	20.0	73.5										
Income US $300– $750														
Malaysia (1970)	330	11.6	32.4	56.0	Dominican Rep.					Surinam (1962)	394	21.7	35.7	42.6
Colombia (1970)	358	9.0	30.0	61.0	(1969)	323	12.2	30.3	57.5	Greece (1957)	500	21.0	29.5	49.5
Brazil (1970)	390	10.0	28.4	61.5	Iran (1968)	332	12.5	33.0	54.5	Yugoslavia (1968)	529	18.5	40.0	41.5
Peru (1971)	480	6.5	33.5	60.0	Guyana (1956)	550	14.0	40.3	45.7	Bulgaria (1962)	530	26.8	40.0	33.2
Gabon (1968)	497	8.8	23.7	67.5	Lebanon (1960)	508	13.0	26.0	61.0	Spain (1965)	750	17.6	36.7	45.7
Jamaica (1958)	510	8.2	30.3	61.5	Uruguay (1968)	618	16.5	35.5	48.0					
Costa Rica (1971)	521	11.5	30.0	58.5	Chile (1968)	744	13.0	30.2	56.8					
Mexico (1969)	645	10.5	25.5	64.0										
South Africa (1965)	669	6.2	35.8	58.0										

Income above US$750														
Venezuela (1970)	1,004	7.9	27.1	65.0	Argentina (1970)	1,079	16.5	36.1	47.4	Poland (1964)	850	23.4	40.6	36.0
Finland (1962)	1,599	11.1	39.6	49.3	Puerto Rico (1968)	1,100	13.7	35.7	50.6	Japan (1963)	950	20.7	39.3	40.0
France (1962)	1,913	9.5	36.8	53.7	Netherlands (1967)	1,990	13.6	37.9	48.5	UK (1968)	2,015	18.8	42.2	39.0
					Norway (1968)	2,010	16.6	42.9	40.5	Hungary (1969)	1,140	24.0	42.5	33.5
					Germany, Fed.Rep. (1964)	2,144	15.4	31.7	52.9	Czech. (1964)	1,150	27.6	41.4	31.0
										Australia (1968)	2,509	20.0	41.2	38.8
					Denmark (1968)	2,563	13.6	38.8	47.6	Canada (1965)	2,920	20.0	39.8	40.2
					New Zealand (1969)	2,859	15.5	42.5	42.0	USA (1970)	4,850	19.7	41.5	38.8
					Sweden (1963)	2,949	14.0	42.0	44.0					

Source: Chenery *et al.* (1974).

Note: Sources for these data are listed in Chenery *et al.* (1974: appendix to chapter 1). The income shares of each percentile group were read off a freehand Lorenz curve fitted to observed points in the cumulative distribution. The distributions are for pre-tax income. Per capita GNP figures are taken from the World Bank data files and refer to GNP at factor cost for the year indicated in constant 1971 US dollars.

Most *underdeveloped* countries have more inequality than developed countries with about half falling into the high inequality range and the average share of the lowest 40 per cent amounting to 12.5 per cent of total incomes. But there is a considerable variation around this range with a considerable group in the low inequality range with similar income shares to those of the most egalitarian developed countries.

10.7 Absolute poverty

While the degree of relative inequality is an important element in the problem of poverty in underdeveloped countries, it tells us little about the extent of absolute poverty. Our concern is with absolute standards of living in terms of nutritional levels, health, education, etc. To this extent using a monetary yardstick for measuring 'poverty datum lines' is extremely crude, particularly when making international comparisons. Nevertheless, bearing in mind the obvious limitations of using arbitrary money measures of 'poverty lines', it is still instructive to see the estimates of absolute poverty that emerge.

In Table 10.3 the forty-five countries listed cover about 60 per cent of the population of developing countries excluding China; about one-third of the population falls below a poverty line based on US$50 *per capita* and half falls below US$75 *per capita*.

Most of those living in absolute poverty are to be found in countries with low average levels of *per capita* income rather than in countries with very unequal income distribution patterns. India, Pakistan, Bangladesh and Sri Lanka, with 55 per cent of the total population in the table, alone account for about 75 per cent of the population living below US$50. Yet Pakistan, Bangladesh and Sri Lanka are characterized by low inequality with India displaying only moderate inequality. On the other hand there are some countries like Ecuador which, as in Sri Lanka, have one-third of their population below the US$50 level and yet have an average *per capita* income which is three times that of Sri Lanka. While low levels of *per capita* income may be the predominant cause of absolute poverty, unequal income distribution is also an important factor.

10.7.1 Growth, inequality and poverty

The above discussion only describes existing distributional patterns. Of more interest for assessing performance and guiding policy is the effect of growth on these patterns over time. Again data problems arise particularly with time series on the distribution of income. Based on data for only eighteen countries (Chenery *et al.* 1974: 14, figure 1.1), comparing rates of growth of GNP with rates of growth of income of the lowest 40 per cent between two points in time, what emerges is a considerable diversity of experience in developing countries in terms of changes in relative equality. (In Ahluwalia *et al.* 1979: 3 12–13, table 2, growth and distribution data are updated to 1975 for thirty-six countries. The conclusions in this study remain much the same as in the earlier study.) Countries like Sri Lanka, Taiwan and Colombia have seen an improvement in equality whereas in Peru, Mexico, Venezuela and Brazil inequality has increased. But even in countries like Mexico and Brazil where inequality has increased, the income of the lowest 40 per cent has still grown substantially (averaging about 6 per cent per annum) because of the high overall rate of growth of the economy.

Bearing in mind the weakness of the data, what does emerge is that there is no firm empirical basis for the view that high rates of growth inevitably generate greater

Table 10.3 Estimates of population below the poverty line in 1969

Country	1969 GNP per capita	1969 population (millions)	Population below $50 Millions	Population below $50 % of total population	Population below $75 Millions	Population below $75 % of total population
Latin America						
Ecuador	264	5.9	2.2	37.0	3.5	58.5
Honduras	265	2.5	0.7	28.0	1.0	38.0
El Salvador	295	3.4	0.5	13.5	0.6	18.4
Dominican Republic	323	4.2	0.5	11.0	0.7	15.9
Colombia	347	20.6	3.2	15.4	5.6	27.0
Brazil	347	90.8	12.7	14.0	18.2	20.0
Jamaica	640	2.0	0.2	10.0	0.3	15.4
Guyana	390	0.7	0.1	9.0	0.1	15.1
Peru	480	13.1	2.5	18.9	3.3	25.5
Costa Rica	512	1.7	–	2.3	0.1	8.5
Mexico	645	48.9	3.8	7.8	8.7	17.8
Uruguay	649	2.9	0.1	2.5	0.2	5.5
Panama	692	1.4	0.1	3.5	0.2	11.0
Chile	751	9.6	–	–	–	–
Venezuela	974	10.0	–	–	–	–
Argentina	1,054	24.0	–	–	–	–
Puerto Rico	1,600	2.8	–	–	–	–
Total	545	244.5	26.6	10.8	42.5	17.4
Asia						
Burma	72	27.0	14.5	53.6	19.2	71.0
Sri Lanka	95	12.2	4.0	33.0	7.8	63.5
India	100	537.0	239.0	44.5	359.3	66.9
Pakistan (East and West)	100	111.8	36.3	32.5	64.7	57.9
Thailand	173	34.7	9.3	26.8	15.4	44.3
Korea	224	13.3	0.7	5.5	2.3	17.0
Philippines	233	37.2	4.8	13.0	11.2	30.0
Turkey	290	34.5	4.1	12.0	8.2	23.7
Iraq	316	9.4	2.3	24.0	3.1	33.3
Taiwan	317	13.8	1.5	10.7	2.0	14.3
Malaysia	323	10.6	1.2	11.0	1.6	15.5
Iran	350	27.9	2.3	8.5	4.2	15.0
Lebanon	570	2.6	–	1.0	0.1	5.0
Total	132	872.0	320.0	36.7	499.1	57.2
Africa						
Chad	75	3.5	1.5	43.1	2.7	77.5
Benin	90	2.6	1.1	41.6	2.3	90.1
Tanzania	92	12.8	7.4	57.9	9.3	72.9
Niger	94	3.9	1.3	33.0	2.3	59.9
Madagascar	119	6.7	3.6	53.8	4.7	69.6
Uganda	128	8.3	1.8	21.3	4.1	49.8
Sierra Leone	165	2.5	1.1	43.5	1.5	61.5
Senegal	229	3.8	0.9	22.3	1.3	35.3

continued on next page

Table 10.3 (continued)

Country	*1969 GNP per capita*	*1969 population (millions)*	*Population below $50*		*Population below $75*	
			Millions	*% of total population*	*Millions*	*% of total population*
Ivory Coast	237	4.8	0.3	7.0	1.4	28.5
Tunisia	241	4.9	1.1	22.5	1.6	32.1
Rhodesia	274	5.1	0.9	17.4	1.9	37.4
Zambia	340	4.2	0.3	6.3	0.3	7.5
Gabon	547	0.5	0.1	15.7	0.1	23.0
South Africa	729	20.2	2.4	12.0	3.1	15.5
Total	303	83.8	23.8	28.4	36.6	43.6
Grand total	228	1,200.3	370.4	30.9	578.2	48.2

Source: Chenery *et al.* (1974: 12). See also Ahluwalia *et al.* (1979) for poverty data updated to 1975, including Kravis's adjustment factors for equivalent purchasing power conversion (pp. 302–3, table 1).

Note: –, negligible.

inequality. Cases of increases in equality are to be found in both high and low growth countries as are the reverse, but on balance there is a positive correlation between rate of growth of GDP and the share of the lowest 40 per cent, suggesting that the objectives of growth and equity may not be in conflict. There is some confirmation, however, for Kuznets's hypothesis as also applied to underdeveloped countries (Kuznets 1955). In his classic paper, based on long-run time-series data for three developed countries (the United States, England and Germany), Kuznets hypothesized a time path of inequality for nations undergoing economic development – with an increase in inequality in the early stages followed by a decrease in the later stages. This has come to be known as the Kuznets U-shaped curve hypothesis on the relationships between inequality and development. In the literature, based predominantly on cross-section analysis, the Kuznets hypothesis has not only received a great deal of attention (Adelman and Morris 1973; Paukert 1973; Ahluwalia 1974, 1976a, b; Ahluwalia *et al.* 1979) but has come to have acquired something of the force of an 'economic law' for developing countries. This literature has been subjected to substantial criticism by Anand and Kanbur (1978, 1981). They not only find serious weaknesses in the data base of the theory but also criticize it on the theoretical level, the econometric techniques used, and the policy implications of the analysis – in particular its deterministic bias.

While a theory explaining the causal relationship between different variables and the degree of inequality is still in its infancy, cross-section analysis is suggestive of certain relationships that are of particular interest because of their amenability to policy. For example, education is positively correlated to equality in terms of income shares, with primary school enrolment particularly significant in explaining the share of the lowest income group. Rate of growth of the population, on the other hand, is inversely related to equality. But broad cross-country analyses of the determinants of inequality are of limited usefulness either in capturing the complexity of the structural interrelations within a country or guiding policy. There is a need for a more disaggregated approach to the determinants of income distribution and one stage in this process which is emphasized in recent literature (ILO 1972a) is to identify the economic characteristics of poverty groups, It can be argued that the main purpose of studying income distribution is to give us better data on the sectoral distribution of the poor, their occupational characteristics, educational levels, ownership levels, ownership of productive assets and access to resources.

In most countries the poorest would be found among four identifiable economic groups. The rural landless, small farmers, the urban underemployed and the urban unemployed. Although the percentage engaged in agriculture varies considerably between developing countries, it is a general fact that the poor are disproportionately located in the rural areas. It is estimated (Chenery *et al.* 1974: 19) that at least 70 per cent of the poor are to be found in this sector, mostly landless farm workers and self-employed small farmers, but also including small traders and artisans located in the rural areas. The dimensions of this group have obvious implications for policies aimed at reducing poverty. But a mere shift in sectoral emphasis towards allocating resources to rural development is not sufficient if the benefits of policies aimed at this sector are slanted in favour of upper income groups in the rural areas. Policies will have to be designed that specifically favour the target group in question. In general terms this means physical investment in human capital to raise skill levels, increasing access to resources in the form of credit, etc., and in some cases land reform involving a redistribution of land ownership and security of tenure are essential elements in improving the productivity and income of the rural poor.

The next most important poverty group are the urban underemployed. These are the low earning self-employed or wage-based workers in the 'informal' urban sector. Until recently this rapidly growing sector comprising petty traders, providers of services, artisans and small-scale labour-intensive manufacturers have been given scant attention by investigators or policymakers in government. They share with their rural counterparts a lack of capital assets, limited access to resources and low levels of education and skill, It is a great merit of the Kenya Report (ILO 1972a) that it not only identified this sector but recommended specific policies for assisting it.

The urban unemployed, although a much smaller number than the 'working poor' in the rural and urban areas, are a poverty group of growing importance. This group is heavily concentrated among the young and recent migrants to the urban areas. More attention to this group will be given in a later section.

10.8 Redistribution with growth

The strategy of linking the problem of unemployment with that of the working poor with the objective 'of bringing every section (and if possible every member) of the population of working age up to a standard of employment productive enough to generate a reasonable minimum income (ILO 1972a: 104) was first put forward in a coherent form in the Kenya Report (ILO 1972a: 109). It was then generalized in the joint IBRD/IDS volume *Redistribution with Growth* (Chenery *et al.* 1974).

Redistribution with Growth describes a set of four basic approaches that can be used individually or in combination to increase the income of low income groups. The exact mix would depend on the economic and social structure of the country and the priority given to improving the welfare of the poorest. These approaches are: (1) maximizing GNP growth through raising savings and allocating resources more efficiently, with benefits to all groups in society; (2) redirecting investment to poverty groups in the form of education, access to credit, public facilities and so on; (3) redistributing income (or consumption) to poverty groups through the fiscal system or through direct allocation of consumer goods; (4) a transfer of existing assets to poverty groups, as in land reform (Chenery *et al.* 1974: 48).

1 Maximizing GNP growth may be a necessary but is not a sufficient condition for helping the poorest. Relying on growth alone would take too long to reach minimum income standards even if the poor participate fully in it. But it is more than likely that, because of the weak income linkages between poverty groups and the rest of the economy, their income will lag behind the general growth. Even though the poor may be better off in this case than with slower GNP growth, the welfare effects of a maximal growth strategy can usually be improved by some forms of redistribution as well.
2 Investing in the human and physical assets of poverty groups is likely to have a high pay-off in welfare terms as it will lead to income growth in groups that have higher welfare weights. But it may require some sacrifice of output in the short run in so far as returns on investment in human capital take longer to develop. To this extent it may involve a short-run cost to upper income groups but these may also benefit in the long run as the productivity and income of the poor improve.
3 The scope for redistributing *existing* income on any scale in developing countries, while having some positive welfare effects in the short run, is likely to be severely limited, Many developing countries are too poor for there to be any significant potential gain to the lower income groups from this strategy. There may be a high cost in terms of growth in the long term from its potentially damaging effect on the incentives, savings and investment of the upper income groups. It is also likely to encounter strong resistance from this group. It is therefore a political judgement of the authors of *Redistribution with Growth* that there will be less hostility from the rich if redistribution is confined to the *increment* to their income.
4 The same stricture applies to asset redistribution although in 'areas such as land ownership and security of tenure, some degree of asset redistribution may be an essential part of any programme to make the rural poor more productive' (Chenery *et al.* 1974: 49). But the preferred strategy is to divert a proportion of the annual investment resources of the rich towards the poor, in this way altering the distribution of the *increment* to the overall capital stock.

Some critics (e.g. Leys 1975) have criticized *Redistribution with Growth* for being essentially an incrementalist strategy almost always to be pursued in an evolutionary rather than a revolutionary way. They argue that it offers no theory of political change and underestimates the resistance that the rich would offer to its policies. In its defence Richard Jolly (Cairncross and Puri 1976: 48) argues that

> The four approaches of *Redistribution with Growth* are generalizations of strategic options each of which if adopted at all might be applied in a more or less incrementalist and less or more radical manner, depending on time and situation, and, no doubt, other factors too. But the essential point is that *Redistribution with Growth* is neither incrementalist nor radical but a framework for analysing the interconnections between economic growth and redistribution.

Box 10.1 Cuba

On 1 January 1959 Fidel Castro led a revolution to force the unpopular President Batista into exile. The new Castro-led government sought from the very beginning to improve economic growth. This in itself was extremely difficult, since Cuba's economy was heavily reliant upon sugar, a crop that depends hugely on good weather conditions. With the United States doing its best to rid Cuba of the Castro regime, the Cubans became heavily reliant upon the Soviet Union, thus further distancing themselves from any hope of valuable trade ties with America. There was no economic growth at all in the 1960s and the economy failed to reach its growth targets in the 1970s.

Despite these problems Cuba's economic performance was very impressive with respect to redistribution. There was a strong and largely successful policy of full employment and a rationing system to ensure access to goods at low prices. These policies meant that there was a dramatic reduction in inequality between social classes and the standard of living improved greatly for rural dwellers.

Following the collapse of Soviet Russia in 1989, Cuban exports slumped, owing to the country's heavy reliance on Soviet sales. The government responded by introducing new economic reforms in 1990, including the setting up of farmers' markets where surplus products could be sold at free market prices, allowing foreign investment, particularly in the tourist industry, and new rationing systems for food and energy. The reforms worked to a degree, but industry infrastructure remains poor and investment resources are in short supply.

Despite the many economic problems faced by Cuba, its population has benefited from higher levels of education, better health care and a lower infant mortality rate than many developed countries. Its economic successes and failures should be measured against those of states which have taken alternative routes to economic development.

Further reading

L. Bethell, *Cuba: a Short History*, Cambridge: Cambridge University Press (1993).

It is interesting to note, from the case studies included in the IBRD/IDS volume (Chenery *et al.* 1974: 253–5), that favourable trends in income distribution have taken place in countries with regimes as different in political ideology and approach as Cuba on the one hand and Taiwan on the other.

10.9 The employment problem

It is now widely held in the literature (see for example Cairncross and Puri 1976: 56–70; Jolly *et al.* 1973; Robinson and Johnston 1971; ILO 1972a; Chenery *et al.* 1974) that open unemployment in the urban areas must be viewed as only one aspect, and not necessarily the most serious one, of the wider problem of underemployment and poverty in developing countries. It is not obvious that the condition of unemployed educated youths (the vast majority of the open unemployed in developing countries), who are supported by the extended family system and pick up casual earnings in the urban informal sector while they seek relatively highly paid jobs in the modern sector, is worse than that of a fully employed peasant who works long hours for a meagre subsistence. Both in the analysis of this causation and the strategy to deal with it, open unemployment must be linked with the general problem of under-utilization of resources, poverty and inequalities in income distribution dealt with in the previous section.

Nevertheless, unemployment in the urban areas has become a problem of increasing seriousness in most developing countries. Again, statistics are notoriously inadequate but it is estimated that 15–25 per cent of the urban labour force is openly unemployed in many countries (Jolly *et al.* 1973: 9) and often much higher percentages for persons aged 15-24. The situation is more serious in the developing countries today than it ever was in the advanced countries in the worst period of the depression in the 1930s. The problem is chronic rather than cyclical, accompanying relatively high average rates of growth of GDP. Also in developing countries it disproportionately affects the young and better educated whereas in advanced countries it more seriously affects the old and unskilled. This phenomenon of growth without employment has exposed the weakness of conventional development strategies based on the Arthur Lewis type of labour surplus model with its heavy emphasis on modern sector industrialization and GDP growth. These models seriously overestimated the capacity of the modern sector to absorb the unemployed and underemployed and generate a spread effect to enable the population at large to share the benefits of growth. Worse than that, the form of modern sector development, with its urban bias, capital intensity, high productivity and wages, has exacerbated the situation by acting as a magnet to urban migration while not offering sufficient jobs.

On the supply side a number of factors have contributed to a rapid increase in the labour force. There is first of all the high rates of population increase already discussed in section 10.1. Then there is the 'education explosion' which has increased the proportion of the young leaving the rural areas to seek modern sector jobs. The nature of the educational system in developing countries carries a good deal of responsibility for this with its urban-academic bias. The rapid spread of universal primary education, seldom geared to the requirements of rural life, has raised the aspirations of the young to seek modern sector jobs, causing widespread unemployment among primary school leavers. In some countries like Sri Lanka (see ILO 1971), where secondary and higher education have been expanded over a longer period but where the educational system has also not been adapted to job opportunities, the employment problem is even more serious among high-school leavers and graduates.

There are also other structural weaknesses on the supply side, particularly in the rural areas, which contribute to the 'push' to the towns. Great inequalities in land-holdings in many developing countries result in large numbers of families being unable to provide sufficient work and income for their expanding numbers given their lack of capital and knowledge of techniques. At the same time land-holdings are often under-utilized and use capital-intensive techniques employing little labour. Low and unstable prices of agricultural products, poor transport facilities and poor general infrastructure turn the terms of trade against the rural sector and the small peasant in particular. The benefits of recent agricultural innovations in the form of the 'Green Revolution' have disproportionately favoured large farmers in particular areas and urban dwellers who enjoy lower food prices to the detriment of small peasants, who are unable to take advantage of these innovations because of their lack of resources for necessary inputs but have to suffer lower prices as producers.

On the demand side the capital-intensive nature of the modern sector has meant that output has grown faster than employment. Even where earnings in the modern sector are little above those in the rural sector, relatively capital-intensive methods of production are the general rule. There are a number of reasons for this. The importance of multinational corporations in the modern sector means that both the nature of the products and the technology are determined by conditions in the advanced countries rather than relative factor prices in developing countries. Even where more labour-intensive methods of production would be justified, these techniques are just not available. Most of the world's research and development takes place in the advanced countries where little attention is paid to intermediate technology. Capital intensity has also been artificially stimulated by policies adopted by governments in LDCs. High rates of protection, excessive tax concessions to foreign enterprises and overvalued exchange rates, all favour the importation of capital-intensive equipment.

In practice, however, earnings in the modern sector are generally well above the differential that may be required to equalize the net costs and benefits of urban modern sector life compared with rural life. A competitive labour market, crucial to the smooth working of the so-called labour surplus model of development where the price of modern sector labour is determined by average earnings in the rural sector, does not often obtain equilibrium. Government minimum wage legislation is widespread with the minimum usually based on criteria such as 'ability to pay' or 'requirements of civilized urban existence' rather than rural earnings. Western type trade unions have also interfered with the free market mechanism, raising wages above the 'minimum price of entry'. The new ruling elite in LDCs have inherited and reinforced an earnings structure based on expatriate Western standards rather than one more relevant to local conditions, Foreign enterprises, in order to avoid the stigma of being regarded as neo-colonialist exploiters, but also because of their superior resources, protected status and capital-intensive methods of production, have frequently set the pace by voluntarily paying wages above the free market level. This in its turn generates a vicious circle as far as employment is concerned by justifying the installation of even more capital-intensive methods of production.

As we shall show, this rural–urban differential is a vital factor explaining the continued high rates of rural–urban migration in the face of chronic and growing urban unemployment and underemployment.

10.10 The Todaro model

The fundamental contribution of the Todaro model (Todaro 1969, 1971b, 1976) to our understanding of the migration process and its links with unemployment is that

> migration proceeds primarily in response to differences in 'expected' urban and rural real incomes and that as a result of this the observed accelerated rates of internal migration in developing countries in the context of using urban unemployment are not only a plausible phenomenon but are in fact entirely rational from the private 'expected' income maximization viewpoint of individual migrants.
>
> (Todaro 1976: 45)

The two principal economic factors that are involved in the decision to migrate are the existing rural–urban real wage differential and the degree of probability of finding a modern urban sector job. The rural–urban differential alone would not explain the migration given high levels of urban unemployment. The positive stimulus of the differential is likely to be restrained by the negative effect of the risk that a migrant may not find a modern sector job. But even if the probability of finding a highly paid job in the short term is low, it may still be a perfectly rational decision to migrate even though expected urban income in the short period is less than expected rural income. If the migrant takes a longer term view of his permanent income prospects (which is realistic in view of the fact that the vast majority of migrants are young) and if he expects the probability of finding a job to increase over time as he improves his urban contacts, then as long as the present value of the net stream of expected urban income over his planning horizon exceeds that of expected rural income, the decision to migrate is justified.

10.10.1 Mathematics of the Todaro model

The Todaro model can be summarized mathematically as follows (see Todaro 1976: 32–5). If $V(0)$ is the discounted present value of the expected 'net' urban–rural income stream over the migrant's time horizon, $Y_U(t)$, $Y_R(t)$ are the average real incomes of individuals employed in the urban and the rural economy, n is the number of time periods in the migrant's planning horizon, i is the discount rate reflecting the migrant's time preference, $C(0)$ is the cost of migration and $p(t)$ is the probability that a migrant will have secured an urban job at the average income level in period t then the decision to migrate or not depends on whether

$$V(0) = \int_{t=0}^{n} [p(t)Y_U(t) - Y_R(t)]e^{-it}\mathrm{d}t - C(0) \tag{10.1}$$

is positive or negative.

In any one time period the probability of being employed in the modern sector, $p(t)$, will be related to the probability Π of having been selected in that or any previous period from a given stock of unemployed job seekers. If it is assumed that for most migrants the selection procedure is random, then the probability of having a job in the modern sector within x periods after migration, $p(x)$, is

$$p(1) = \Pi(1) \tag{10.2}$$

and

$$p(2) = \Pi(1) + [1 - \Pi(1)]\Pi(2) \tag{10.3}$$

so that

$$p(x) = \Pi(x - 1) + [1 - \Pi(x - 1)]\Pi(x) \tag{10.4}$$

or

$$p(x) = \Pi(1) + \sum_{t=2}^{x} \Pi(t) \prod_{s=1}^{t=1}[1 - \Pi(t)] \tag{10.5}$$

where $\Pi(t)$ equals the ratio of new job openings relative to the number of accumulated job seekers in time t.

Expressing the probability variable in this way means that the longer the migrant has been in the urban area the higher is the probability p of his finding a modern sector job and therefore his expected income in that period. This is realistic in that migrants improve their contacts and are better informed as time passes. It also avoids having to assume that the migrant earns either nothing or the average urban income, and therefore allows for the probability that many migrants will earn some income in the informal urban sector while looking for a modern sector job.

From the above an aggregate dynamic equilibrium model of urban labour demand and supply is developed as follows.

The rural labour force L_R is assumed to grow at a natural rate r less migration m, or

$$\dot{L}_R = (r - m)L_R \tag{10.6}$$

where L_R is the time derivative of L_R.

The urban labour force L_U also grows at a rate r plus migration from rural areas:

$$\dot{L}_U = rL_U + mL_R \tag{10.7}$$

Substituting $M = mL_R$ where M represents the actual amount of rural–urban migration, equation (10.7) can be written as

$$\dot{L}_U = rL_U + M \tag{10.8}$$

The growth of urban employment opportunities (the demand for urban labour) is assumed to be constant at a rate g, so that

$$\dot{E}_U = gE_U \tag{10.9}$$

where E_U is the level of urban sector employment.

To this standard model Todaro adds his migration function which assumes that the rate of rural–urban migration m

$$m = \frac{M}{L_R} \tag{10.10}$$

is a function of:

1 the *probability* of finding a modern sector job, which can be expressed as some simple positive monotonic function of the urban employment rate

$$E_U/L_U \tag{10.11}$$

or a negative function of the urban unemployment rate $(L_U - E_U)/L_U$;

2 the *urban–rural real income differential* expressed as a ratio

$$\frac{Y_U}{Y_R} = W \tag{10.12}$$

where $W > 1$ and is assumed fixed;

3 other factors, Z, such as personal contacts, travel distance, urban amenities etc., which influence the migrant's view of the worth of migrating.

The basic Todaro migration equation can be stated as

$$m = F\left(\frac{E_U}{L_U}, W, Z\right) \tag{10.13}$$

where

$$F'\left(\frac{E_U}{L_U}\right) > 0 \quad F'(W) > 0 \quad F'(Z) \gtrless 0$$

Assuming W and Z as fixed, the function F can be stated as

$$F\left(\frac{E_U}{L_U}, W, Z\right) = f\left(\frac{E_U}{L_U}\right) \tag{10.14}$$

where $f' \geq 0$ for all values of E_U/L_U between 0 and 1.

Substituting equation (10.13) and (10.14) in (10.7) yields the basic differential equation for urban labour force growth in the Todaro model:

$$\frac{\dot{L}_U}{L_U} = r + \frac{L_R}{L_U} f\left(\frac{E_U}{L_U}\right) \tag{10.15}$$

Although the Todaro model has been criticized for assuming a 'too simple and exclusively economic motivation for migration' (Jolly *et al.* 1973: 13) its virtue lies in the readily quantifiable form that it handles the major, even if not the exclusive, factors determining migration.

Among the several modifications of the basic Todaro model that have been suggested so far, the following deserve special consideration.

10.10.2 Harris–Todaro model (1970)

An attempt has been made in the Harris–Todaro (HT) model (1970) to distinguish between the rural and urban sectors and to analyse the effects of migration on rural and urban output, income and welfare. The model can be stated algebraically as follows.

Let

$$E(W_U) = W_U \frac{E_U}{L_U}$$

where $E(W_U)$ is expected urban income, W_U is urban wages, E_U is the amount of urban employment and L_U is the current size of urban labour.

Assuming that W_R is rural wages, $E\ (W_R)$ is the expected rural wage. Let

$$E(W_R) = W_R$$

and the rural–urban migration M be

$$M = \dot{L}_U$$

Assume that $\dot{L}_U$ is a function of the urban–rural expected wage differential, so that we have

$$M = \dot{L}_U = f[E(W_U) - E(W_R)]$$

In equilibrium,

$$E(W_U) = E(W_R)$$

By substitution, we now have

$$W_U \frac{E_U}{L_U} = W_R$$

An equilibrium unemployment rate is then given by dividing the above equation by W_U and subtracting each side from 1, i.e.

$$1 - \frac{E_U}{L_U} = 1 - \frac{W_R}{W_U}$$

That is, the rate of *employment* is given by

$$\frac{E_U}{L_U} = \frac{W_R}{W_U}$$

The final equation illustrates the negative relationship between expected urban–rural wage differences and the rates of equilibrium unemployment.

The modified HT model implies that an increase in the rate of creation of urban employment could raise the unemployment levels. The impact on social welfare is measured by the HT model in terms of output gains or losses, given the different avenues (e.g. sectoral wage subsidies, demand creation etc.) to create urban employment. Harris and Todaro have also shown the situation where compulsory prohibition of migration could *reduce* the net welfare of the rural sector (see Appendix: p. 304).

10.10.3 Bhagwati and Srinivasan model

In the model of Bhagwati and Srinivasan (1974), it has been contended that a second-best solution in the HT model, which required control of migration plus an urban wage subsidy to obtain the most efficient production, is unnecessary because a first-best solution could be obtained via a judicious use of tax/subsidy policies. This would render the physical control of migration of labour irrelevant to the HT argument.

10.10.4 Fields's model

In addition to the quantity adjustment as the major instrument to obtain equilibrium in the urban labour market in LDCs (a point which has been suggested by Harris and Todaro), Fields (1975a, b) has considered some other variables. For example (1) the high probability of an educated person being able to obtain a job in the modern sector; (2) the rate of labour turnover in the urban sector and the difference in attitudes towards risks among the migrants; (3) the presence of underemployed workers in the urban informal sector and the lower probability of their obtaining a job in comparison with those who are wholly occupied in searching for a job; and (4) an urban job search process where people living in rural areas have a reasonable chance of obtaining jobs in the city without first going there, On the basis of these more realistic assumptions in comparison with those made in the HT model (1970), Fields has demonstrated that an urban equilibrium unemployment rate will be lower than the one predicted by the HT model.

Fields has also suggested some policies to tackle the problem of unemployment in the light of his analysis. These include (1) the setting up of an urban–rural job centre to reduce the cost (both private and social) of job search and thus raise output; and (2) 'overeducation' of labour, which would appear paradoxical in countries suffering from educated unemployment.

Some other criticisms of the HT model could also be mentioned. For instance, the HT model ignores the possibility of inter-sectoral capital mobility between the urban and rural areas. Once such possibilities are included, some of the results of the HT model have to be modified (Corden and Findlay 1975). It could also be argued that Harris and Todaro have unrealistically assumed labour to be homogeneous. Different types of labour respond differently to migration opportunities. Landless workers tend to migrate more frequently than other types of agriculturists in many parts of Asia. Moreover, migrants' income does not wholly accrue to the village sector in many parts of Asia. The HT assumption regarding immobility of capital stock could be doubted, Further, the welfare effect of migration should also include the possibility of transfers of human capital between different sectors (Corden and Findlay 1975).

10.11 Migration theory and evidence: an assessment

In Figure 10.3 we present a standard HT class of models which exemplify the gap between W_U and W_R. Let the curves for the rural agricultural and urban industrial sectors demand (derived) for labour be $D_RD'_R$ and the $D_UD'_U$ respectively. At C, wages are equalized at W^* and the process of labour allocation between the two sectors is optimal (we ignore costs of migration for the time being). However, if wages in industry are set at W_U a wage gap of AB arises. Wages in the agricultural sector will be depressed to W_R, say, and 'surplus labour' of L^*L occurs. The 'Harberger' triangle ABC shows the efficiency loss to the economy due to labour misallocation. This 'wage gap' can be as much as 30 per cent according to Lewis (1954). However, a survey of deadweight loss (i.e. triangle ABC) has been found to be a small proportion of the GDP (Williamson 1988). The actual empirical measurement of a gap like AB has been difficult (Kanappan 1985; Williamson 1988). Others have shown that the inclusion of educational quality differences among the standard factors which account for the difference between W_U and W_R leads to the elimination of wage gaps. Indeed, the presence of a wage gap, so crucial to the HT model, has been questioned by some (Kanappan 1985). However, the reason for the persistence of the wage gap could lie in unbalanced production and population growth rates – neither of which has been tackled in the HT class of models.

Given such interesting predictions, while development economists extend the HT model by relaxing the labour market assumptions (e.g. Todaro 1976; Fields 1975b), trade theorists concentrate their attention on factor market distortions in open econo-

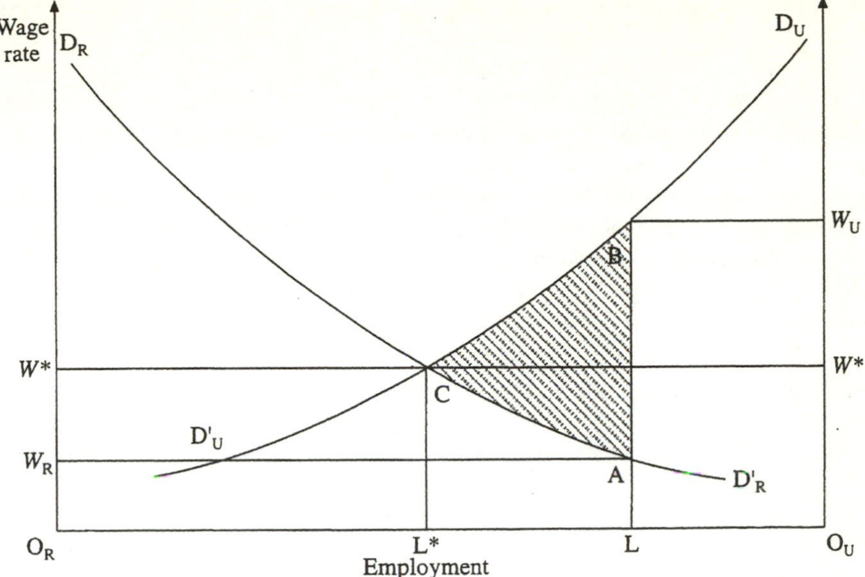

Figure 10.3

mies (Bhagwati and Srinivasan 1974; Corden 1974; Corden and Findlay 1975). While some looked at the welfare gains and losses of the HT model in the context of factor-market distortions (e.g. Bhagwati and Srinivasan 1974) others relaxed a key assumption of the HT model about the lack of capital mobility (e.g. Corden and Findlay 1975), thereby linking the HT model with the Samuelson–Heckscher–Ohlin theories of trade and factor price equalization. Neary (1981) also allows for inter-sectoral capital mobility and derives the dynamic behaviour of the model. After all, urban–rural migration and inter-sectoral capital allocation are 'dynamic phenomena'. Neary argues that with sector-specific capital the HT model is always stable; however, if capital is inter-sectorally mobile, the stability condition is violated. As regards supply response, the Neary (1981) model predicts that a rise in minimum wage in the manufacturing (modern) sector can raise manufacturing output. Other extensions of the HT model for skilled labour suggest:

1 a higher probability of employment of an educated person;
2 the different types of impact on the rate of migration due to different attitudes towards risk among migrants (note that Harris and Todaro assume risk-neutrality among migrants) and the rate of labour turnover in the modern sector;
3 the presence of underemployed workers in the *modern informal sector* and the lower probability of their obtaining a job in comparison with those who are wholly occupied in job search (Bhattacharya 1993). Bartlett (1983) points out that if the share of rural population in an economy is large, then its growth rate dominates the change in unemployment rates which calls for a sectoral allocation of labour. Such allocation is expected to be sluggish.

It is useful to point out that a large number of relatively uneducated and unskilled people do migrate and work, which cannot be explained by the HT model. Further, the model predicts that policies to promote industrialization and urban job creation will lead to urban unemployment. Ironically, the market must be perverse because 'decisions that are rational from the point of view of individuals appear disastrous for society' (Cole and Sanders 1985). Many unskilled people could migrate to the cities owing to excessive pressure of population on fixed land or because of a rise in the demand for urban exports resulting in a big difference between the urban and rural subsistence wage. Migration is socially desirable as long as it transfers labour from low (rural) to high (urban) productivity areas (Ghatak 1991). However, in the HT model urban employment is fixed and no net transfer of employed labour occurs.

Unlike the HT model, where a marginal amount of rural development reduces the rate of migration, it may be argued that a marginal rural development may not provide enough incentive for some people to stay behind, People who wish to migrate generally face liquidity/borrowing constraints and a marginal rise in rural income simply eases such constraints and raises the rate of migration (Kanbur 1981). Thus, as far as migration policy is concerned, a marginal improvement of real wages W_R in the rural sector (i.e. a reduction of the differential between W_U and W_R), as suggested by the HT model, is not good enough to reduce the rate of migration. What is necessary is to impact a 'big push' to the investment projects in the rural/backward sector.

10.12 Stark's model

Four major points stand out prominently from the research on migration by Stark (1991). First, Stark shifts the focus of migration research from individual independence (as in the HT class of models) to *mutual interdependence*. Remittances from migrants to their families at home and a number of overt and covert inter-family exchanges are thus results of *collective* migration decisions. Thus the activities of the migrants in the recipient areas can mostly be explained not only by their endowments and characteristics but also by their preferences and constraints (see for example Rosenzweig and Wolpin 1985).

Next, migration in the absence of a significant wage gap between the advanced and the backward region, or the lack of migration in the face of a substantial wage gap, does *not* mean irrationality. Decisions to migrate could depend on wage uncertainty and relative deprivation at home which could force families to pool risks and alter the pattern of human capital investments in children.

Third, migration could be the product of *imperfect and incomplete markets* and financial institutions, particularly in LDCs. Informational asymmetries and lower income variance aid gains from migration and the 'established' inverse correlation between distance and migration can weaken considerably.

Fourth, migration can also be regarded as the child of inequality and relative deprivation! Migration takes place because people who live in backward areas feel 'relatively deprived' and want to keep up with the Joneses. Migration thus stems from people's desire for improving their relative position on the economic ladder. Evidence from village studies seem to confirm the positive and significant correlation between the rate of migration and the degree of inequality in the distribution of land holdings (as proxies for wealth/income) in India. In a way, Stark's evidence (1991) seems to confirm the conclusion reached in the IDS studies some time ago (Connell *et al.* 1976).

According to Stark's *portfolio investment theory*, families spread their labour assets over geographically dispersed and structurally different markets to reduce risks. Evidence suggests that, after migration, members of the family combine and share their incomes. Such pooling is regarded as a form of insurance against uncertain income flows from specific markets to smooth the family consumption growth path. Thus, if future earnings are uncertain and imperfectly but positively related in a geographically specific area, the migration policy of a member of the income-pooling family diversifies risk (Stark 1991).

10.13 Employment policy

A number of important implications for employment policy follow from Todaro's analysis of the migration process.

An attempt to solve the urban unemployment problem by relying only on increasing the number of modern sector jobs may actually make the situation worse, given a positive rural–urban earnings differential, in so far as the increased demand for urban labour raises the probability of finding a modern sector job and so encourages even higher rates of migration. There is evidence to show that this can occur as in the case of the 1964 and 1970 Tripartite Agreements in Kenya. The agreement between government, industry and the trade unions to tackle unemployment by expanding employment in exchange for wage restraint proved self-defeating.

Of crucial importance is narrowing the expected rural–urban income differential. This involves a broad strategy to get at the root causes of the employment problem at both the rural and urban end, linking it with the wider problem of under-utilization of resources, poverty and inequality discussed earlier. The chief elements in the strategy are as follows.

1 Rural development with all that is involved in improving rural incomes and job opportunities is seen to be the most important way of reducing the push' from the countryside. A note of caution about the efficacy of rural development in reducing the rate of rural–urban migration has been sounded, however, by Kanbur (1981). Unlike Todaro where any amount of rural development, no matter how small, will always reduce the rate of migration, he argues that the short-run effects of rural development are more complex than the literature suggests and that policymakers may encounter increased rates of migration, at least in the early stages of a rural development programme. His basic argument is that rural development will give some people the resources with which to migrate while a small amount of rural development may not provide sufficient incentive for some people to stay behind. He assumes that migration has costs and the rural sector is non-homogeneous, being divisible into at least three income categories:

   (a) those who are too poor to migrate although they may wish to do so;
   (b) those whose income level is below that which is thought attainable in the city but sufficient to migrate;
   (c) those whose income level is such that migration offers no attraction.

The problem as Kanbur sees it is that with small amounts of rural development, at least in the short run, the numbers moving out of category (a) to category (b) (the migrants) may exceed the number moving from (b) to (c) and thus migration rates may still rise. His analysis is not an argument against rural development as such but that it may have to be in the nature of a 'big push' and take time to have the effect of reducing migration rates. Countering the attraction of cities has proved an enormous problem in developing countries in practice (Yap 1977).

2 Positive policies should be introduced to increase productivity and incomes in the informal urban sector. This sector is small scale, labour intensive, competitive and economical in its use of imported inputs, and yet it has been generally neglected by government and frequently discriminated against by severe licensing restrictions and a range of measures that favour the modern sector. Increasing attention has been given to this sector in the reports of ILO employment missions (see for example ILO 1972a).
3 An incomes policy to reduce or at least prevent a widening of the gap between earnings in the modern sector and in the rest of the economy is widely stressed in the literature (see for example ILO 1967, 1972a, b). Governments in a few developing countries like Tanzania and Kenya have paid serious attention to this problem in their policies and plans (e.g. Tanzania 1967; Kenya 1973, 1974). Tanzania has been something of a pioneer in being one of the first to link an incomes policy with a programme for rural development as part of a broad strategy to deal with employment and poverty.

Besides the above, a comprehensive and integrated strategy dealing with the employment problem would also have to include

1 a population policy to control fertility and labour supply;
2 an education policy which gives less emphasis to the quantitative link between occupation and formal education and more attention to the structure and content of education, making it more relevant to the environment in which most of the pupils and students are going to live and work; there is a trend in developing countries away from concentrating expansion on secondary and higher education in favour of improving basic education for the very young and giving a second chance via informal educational institutions to those who dropped out of the educational system or did not get in it in the first place;
3 a policy regarding choice of techniques which encourages the use of labour-intensive methods of production and the development of intermediate technology without sacrificing output for employment (see for example Morawetz 1974).

10.14 Poverty, inequality and financial development

10.14.1 Recent evidence on growth, distribution and poverty reduction

Economic growth is regarded as the major factor for achieving improvements in *per capita* income and standard of living. In the past, it was believed that economic growth affected poverty through a 'trickle down' effect through a rise in investment and employment.

According to the World Bank (2001), economic growth is the main motor for reducing poverty and the income of the poor grows in proportion with the economy as a whole (Dollar and Kraay 2000). However, it has been shown that 'for a given rate of growth, the extent of poverty reduction depends on how the distribution of income changes with changes in growth and on initial inequalities in income, assets and access to opportunities to allow the poor to share in growth' (World Bank 2001: 52). Cross-country evidence shows that when initial inequality is low, growth reduces poverty nearly twice as much as when inequality is high. It is clear, therefore, that economic growth will have different relationships with poverty reduction, depending upon the *pattern* of growth (see also Allen and Thomas 2001).

The causal links between economic growth and distribution, therefore, need to be integrated into the analysis of poverty reduction policy (see Kanbur 2000: 794). Regarding the causal links between distribution and growth, Barro (1991) argues that inequality is likely to retard the growth of the economy. Inequalities in wealth imply significant inequalities in access to productive assets (both physical and financial), resulting in underutilization of the productive potential of the poor. Other empirical evidence also suggests that the link between inequality and growth can be approximated by an inverted U curve (the Kuznets hypothesis). This implies that economic growth will first raise inequality but then reduce it.

Most recent studies confirm an overall positive impact of growth on poverty reduction, with some exceptions. The reason for the inverse causal link from growth to income inequality is the initial skewed ownership of resources and lack of access to various forms of productive capital. Gradually those who are in possession of financial, physical and human capital assets are likely to benefit most from economic growth. As the economy develops and market imperfections lessen, access to capital in its various forms may be expected to broaden, as inequality begins to lessen with continued economic growth (Jalilian and Kirkpatrick 2002).

Most empirical studies of the growth and inequality relationships do provide cross-country evidence of a negative *relationship between inequality and income* per capita *below certain level of development, as proxied by income* per capita.

In sum, wealth distribution significantly affects economic growth and poverty reduction. Both theory and empirical evidence suggest that inequality affects, and is affected by, economic growth. Hence, as economies grow, poverty is likely to be reduced but the rate of reduction will be adversely affected owing to increased inequality, and, depending on the magnitude of poverty reduction elasticity with respect to growth and inequality, the net effect of growth on poverty reduction could be positive or negative (Jalilian and Kirkpatrick 2002).

10.14.2 Financial market development, inequality and poverty reduction

Financial development through the development of an array of financial assets and institutions enables economic agents to transform their production and employment activities, thereby fostering economic growth.

However, capital market failures could occur in LDCs owing to the problems of moral hazard and adverse selection in credit markets (Stiglitz and Weiss 1981; Stiglitz 1998). Imperfect or inefficient capital markets result in unequal access to credit, whereby a group of people are unable to invest productively, simply because they do not have sufficient collateral or are caught in a low return–high borrowing rate situation. The poor are prevented from choosing the most productive activity because imperfect information and incomplete contracts cause a credit market failure.

The form and severity of capital market failures could be linked, therefore, with wealth and income inequality. Banerjee (2001) observes large differences within a single sub-economy, and asks 'Why is intermediation so inefficient with some people and so efficient with others? Why are the rich borrowers and those who borrow more favoured by the market?' Answers to these questions may be given in terms of the skewed distribution of income and wealth in most developing countries. Those who are in possession of financial, physical and human capital resources are likely to benefit most from any general improvement in financial market efficiency, as reflected in growth in financial development. Market behaviour will allocate credit to those who can provide collateral, and to those with whom the financial institutions have an established relationship. This can boost the economy's growth rate through improving the productivity of endowed resources and increased accumulation. However, given the unequal distribution of the gains from growth, the income gap between those who have access to the formal financial system and those who do not can be expected to widen, particularly when there are fixed costs of monitoring (Banerjee 2001: 27).

Credit market imperfections can thus be regarded as an important determinant of inequality. In the absence of credit markets, or when such markets are imperfect, investment in both human and physical capital is likely to be determined by individuals' wealth and income. Development of the financial system and the growth in average income levels, however, may eventually weaken the link between asset ownership and productive investment activity. At the initial phase of development of an economy, there are few financial markets and economic growth is slow. As the economy develops, the financial system also develops but transaction costs and credit market failures are such that only those with command over a certain level of assets are likely to be engaged with the financial system and to benefit from it. As the financial system approaches maturity, the transaction costs of using financial services decline and there is improved access to its use for a wide section of society.

Gradual development of the financial system can be expected, therefore, to weaken the link between asset ownership and investment. During this process, the dynamics of income distribution will change. In the early stages inequality is likely to increase as financial development takes place and benefits are unequally shared in favour of the relatively wealthy. Gradually, as further development takes place and the benefits from such development are more widely shared, inequality will begin to decline.

Theoretical and empirical research indicates a simultaneous relationship between economic growth and inequality; we can expect, therefore, that the impact of financial development on poverty will be influenced by, and have an influence on, the distribution of income and wealth.

In the past, governments of developing countries actively intervened in financial markets to influence the allocation of credit to priority needs, including moving households out of poverty. By the early 1970s this interventionist approach was replaced by financial liberalization, which emphasized a market-led approach to financial development policy (Levine 1997; World Bank 2001). Policy has been intended to improve the efficient operation of financial markets, by privatizing state-owned financial institutions and encouraging new, private institutions to enter the market, by removing controls on interest rates and credit allocation, and by strengthening the prudential regulation and supervision of financial institutions (see Chapter 5).

Research suggests that financial liberalization in the presence of severe information imperfections combined with a inadequate regulatory framework will result in a less efficient and more unstable outcome. The implication for policy is that liberalization has to be carefully managed, and that the appropriate bank regulatory and supervisory structures must be in place before liberalization is attempted.

Inappropriate economic liberalization policies and premature deregulation measures could destabilize the financial system, with adverse impacts on the real economy. Financial liberalization has increased the probability of a banking crisis occurring, even when it is carried out in a stable macroeconomic environment (Kaminsky and Reinhart 1999; Demirgüz-Kunt and Detragiache 1998). However, King and Levine (1993) argue: 'higher levels of financial development are significantly and robustly correlated with faster current and future rates of economic growth, physical capital accumulation and economic efficiency improvements' (pp. 717–18); and 'finance does not only follow growth; finance seems importantly to lead to economic growth' (p. 730).

The problems associated with cross-country regression analysis are well known, particularly in its use for causal inference. Using data for sixty-three countries averaged over the period 1960–95, Levine *et al.* (2000) find that after controlling for country-specific effects and potential endogeneity bias, 'the data suggest a strong, positive link between financial intermediary development and economic growth' (p. 54). In sum, the empirical evidence from econometric studies confirms the positive relationship between financial development, poverty reduction and growth, but demonstrates that this relationship is likely to reflect, *inter alia*, differences in institutional development and in levels of economic development.

10.4.3 Conclusion

The following conclusions can be drawn from the most recent evidence:

1 Economic growth is good for the poor, albeit with some exceptions. The causality runs from growth to poverty reduction and not the other way round.
2 Financial development is good for growth and hence good for poverty reduction, albeit indirectly.
3 Inflation affects poverty reduction policies negatively.
4 Financial development affects economic growth positively in LDCs but only up to a point. This indicates the presence of a threshold.
5 Financial development and human capital are important determinants of the inverted U relationship between inequality and economic development.

Once again, a threshold effect is detected. It is argued that economies with a ratio of private credit to GDP of less than 40 per cent would experience a positive relationship between inequality and growth. Similar impact is noted in the context of globalization (Jalilian and Kirkpatrick 2002). Greater trade openness in LDCs tends to increase inequality first and then be reduced in countries with *per capita* income greater than US$6,000.

Appendix 10.1 The definition of a poverty line

An *absolute* index of poverty is a 'head-count' ratio P_h, as Sen (1976) puts it, which shows the *percentage* of people in poverty. Thus

$$P_h = q/n$$

where q is the number of people in poverty with $y_i \leq Z$, n is the total population, y is income and Z is the poverty line. Note that P_h does not consider the *extent* by which the incomes of the poor fall short of the poverty line.

The relative index of poverty P_g is the total income necessary to bring all the poor people up to the line of poverty, i.e. Z. Thus we have

$$P_g = \sum_{i=1}^{q} g_i$$

where

$$g_i = Z - y_i \qquad 1, 2, 3 \ldots \text{persons}$$

and

$$g = \sum_{i=1}^{q} (Z - y_i) = q(Z - M)$$

where M is the mean income of the poor. The *average* gap in poverty is $Z - M$. The proportion of shortfall of average income from the line of poverty is $(Z - M)/Z$.

Note that the relative index of poverty, P_g, is insensitive to the *number* of people in poverty. Also, both P_h and P_g are independent of income transfer *among the poor*.

The Sen index or P_s is actually a composite yardstick which includes the features of both P_g and P_h and takes into account the distribution of income among the poor (Sen 1976). Here the nature of poverty is assumed to be a 'normalized weighted sum of the income gaps of the poor'. An income weighting scheme is described and then a method of normalization is suggested by Sen. A rank-order weighting scheme is chosen where the weight in the income difference of a poor person is equal to the rank in ordering of income below the line of poverty. Such a method of weighting naturally involves the Gini coefficient of the distribution of income among the poor. In the normalization axiom of Sen, it is necessary that when every poor person has the same level of income, the value of the index is given by the proportion of persons in poverty multiplied by the proportion of the average gap between the line of poverty and the income of the poor.

The normalized value of the index of Sen is

$$\frac{q}{n} \frac{Z - M}{Z}$$

In the rank-order weighting scheme, a weight $q + 1 - I$ on $g_i(= Z - y_i)$ is suggested because we have $q - i + 1$ people among the poor whose income would be at least equivalent to that of individual i. Now we have the index of Sen or P_s as

$$P_s = A\sum_{i=1}^{q}(q+1-i)(Z-y_i)$$

where A is a parameter which may be defined as

$$A = \frac{2}{(q+1)nZ}$$

If $y_i = M$, then the normalized value of the Sen index may be written as

$$\frac{q}{n}\frac{Z-M}{Z} = A(Z-M)\frac{q(q+1)}{2}$$

because

$$\sum_{i=1}^{q}(q+1-i) = \frac{q(q+1)}{2}$$

Now G or the Gini coefficient of income distribution among the poor may be defined as

$$G = \frac{q+1}{q} - \frac{2}{q^2M}\sum_{i=1}^{q}(q+1-i)y_i$$

Hence

$$P_s = \frac{q}{n}\frac{1}{Z}\left(Z-M+\frac{q}{q+1}GM\right)$$

For large numbers of poor, i.e. for large q, $q/(q+1) \approx 1$, P_s is simply given by

$$P_s = \frac{q}{n}\frac{1}{Z}[Z-M(1-G)]$$

When the index of relative poverty, as defined above, is given by the income–gap ratio or

$$I = \sum_{i\in S_{(Z)}}\frac{g_i}{qZ}$$

then, for large numbers of poor, we have

$$P_s = P_h[I+(1-I)G]$$

P_s should vary between 0 and 1. When every individual earns an income above Z, $P_s = 0$ as $q = 0$. Similarly, $P_s = 1$ when nobody earns anything so that $M = 0$ and $q = n$. (For a further discussion, see Sen 1976; see also Anand 1977 for a comparison between the Sen index and the other indices, e.g. Atkinson 1970, and the application of the Sen index to the Malaysian economy.) Anand reports that $P_s = 0.20$ in peninsular Malaysia. Since the estimates for other countries are not available, it is difficult to state its relative significance. Clearly, in absolute terms the figure is quite substantial, As usual, the use of P_s reveals that the incidence of poverty in Malaysia is highest among agriculturists and illiterates.

Appendix 10.2 Migration

In this section, we show a simple way of measuring the welfare gains or loss from migration in a two-bloc, say East–West model. Unlike the H–T model, where wages are fixed in the host country and unemployment adjusts, here we assume that wages are flexible. Assume that West (W) and East (E) produce the same commodity and the labour forces are equal. Both physical and human capital are given and are higher in the West. Hence, both marginal and average product is higher in the West. Figure A10.2.1 illustrates what happens when migration from East to West takes place. The E labour force falls from OA by HA, raising the W labour supply by the same magnitude as HA = AB. The area under the MPL curves depicts total output.

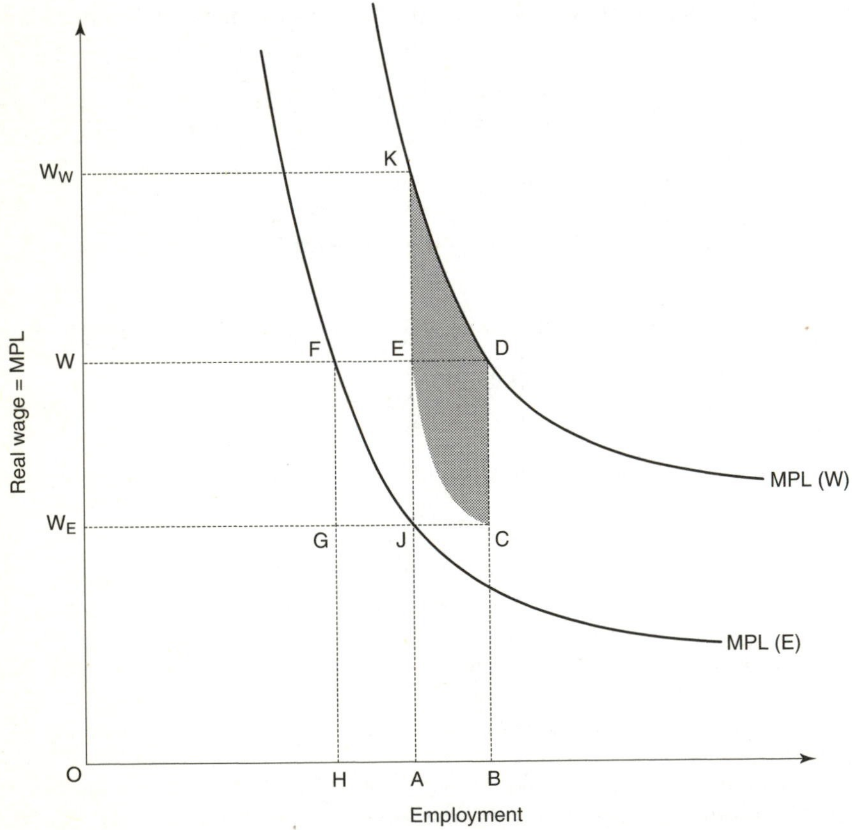

Figure A10.2.1 Migration and welfare: employment and real wage after migration.
Source: Adapted from Paul Levine (1999) and Ghatak *et al.* (1996)

The MPL(W) is clearly higher than that of the E. If differences in human capital are assumed away, then there is no difference between two labour units in the W and E. After migration, production increases in the West by KDBA and falls by FJAH = ECBA in the East. The net rise in output (therefore welfare) is given by KDCE, the shaded area. The real wage rises in the East but falls in the West. If we assume that migration has its costs and migrants maximize income net of costs (as is assumed in the migration research studies), then migration will stop before wages are equalized. Figure A10.2.1 shows the classic factor–price equalization where there is no migration cost. In the model, the winners are migrants and Western capitalists and the losers are the original West workers and East capitalists. If, however, the East migrant has a lower human capital than the West worker, then MPL(W) shifts inwards and the welfare gains are reduced. In practice, the overall welfare gains will depend on the semi-elasticity of real wages with respect to unemployment. The higher the elasticity and the greater the flexibility of the labour market in the host country, the higher will be the welfare gains. The earnings differential between the migrants and the indigenous workers depends on many factors like experience, age, education and command of the language (see for details Borjas 1987; Ghatak *et al.* 1996; Levine 1999; Shields and Wheatley Price 2000, 2002).

Appendix 10.3 Schultz's model of the household production approach to fertility

Several attempts have been made to analyse rigorously the demand for children by households. One interesting model is that of Schultz. Let U be the utility function of the parents, Z the bundle of final consumption commodities and f the production function using market goods X. The utility function is defined as

$$U = U(Z_1 \ldots Z_n)$$

and

$$Z_1 = f_1(X_i, M_i, F_i) \quad \text{for} \quad i = 1, 2 \ldots n$$

where M is the husband's time and F is the wife's time.

Let Y be total money income, P the prices of market goods, N_{m} the husband's time devoted to earning income, N_{f} the wife's time devoted to earning income, W_{m} the income of the husband, W_{f} the income of the wife, K the return to families' non-human wealth and T the total available time that could be devoted to market and non-market activities by the parents.

We have

$$Y = \sum_i P_i X_i = W_{\mathrm{m}} N_{\mathrm{m}} + W_{\mathrm{f}} N_{\mathrm{f}} + K$$

$$\sum_i M_i + N_{\mathrm{m}} = \sum_i F_i + N_{\mathrm{f}} = T$$

Now, let there be two non-market goods, the number of babies (B), and all other goods (G), and assume that the production functions are linear, homogeneous and independent of each other. The total price of the ith good is given by

$$Q_i Z_i = M_i W_m + F_i W_f + P_i X_i$$

where $i = B, G$ and Q is the price for B and G. The total income I of the family is given by

$$I + Q_d B + Q_d G = TW_f + TW_m + K$$

Note that total price elasticity of the demand for the jth good is

$$\eta_j Q_j = \frac{dZ_j}{dQ_j} \frac{Q_j}{Z_j}$$

Similarly, the total income elasticity of the demand for the jth good is given by

$$\eta_{ji} = \frac{dZ_j}{dQ_j} \frac{I}{Z_j}$$

Assuming that j is not an inferior good, η_{ji}will be positive. With given income, price elasticity will be negative. As regards non-human wealth K, the elasticity of demand for babies will be given by

$$\eta_{bk} = \frac{K}{B} \frac{dB}{dK} = \eta_{bi}$$

The expression η_{bk} will be positive as long as the babies are not considered as inferior goods.

The elasticity of the demand for babies with regard to the income of the husband and wife can be stated as follows (see also Ben Porath 1973):

$$\eta BW_m = \frac{W_m}{B} \frac{\partial B}{\partial W_m}$$

$$\eta BW_f = \frac{W_f}{B} \frac{\partial B}{\partial W_f}$$

The overall positive or negative change in the demand for babies will depend upon price and income effects. Normally, a rise in the price of a baby should reduce its demand. If prices are given, a sudden rise in parental income could raise the demand for babies. A rise in the husband's income could raise the demand for babies whereas a rise in the wife's income could reduce such demand because of differences in the values assigned to time allocated for work and relative income earned by the parents, even when the same values (but different signs) are assigned to the price and income elasticities of demand for the babies.

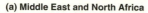

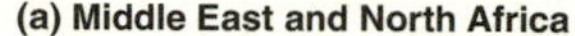

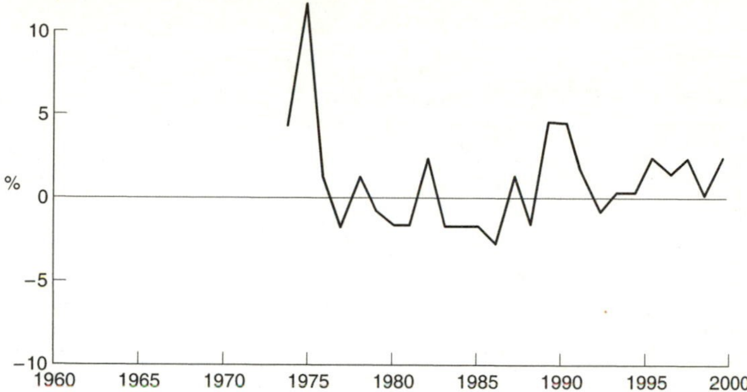

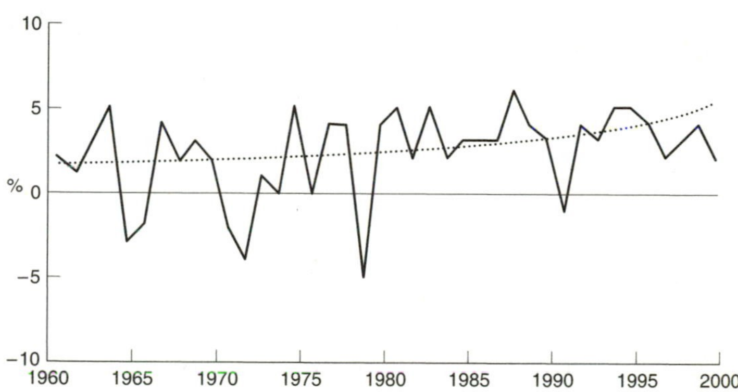

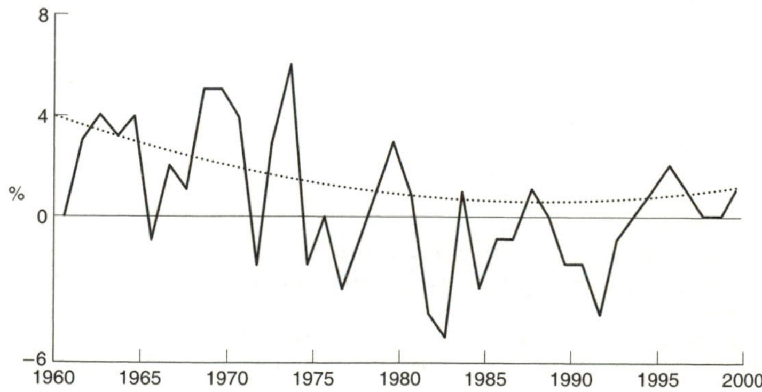

Figure A10.4.1 Annual growth of GDP *per capita* and long-term trends, by region, 1960–2000.

Source: World Bank data

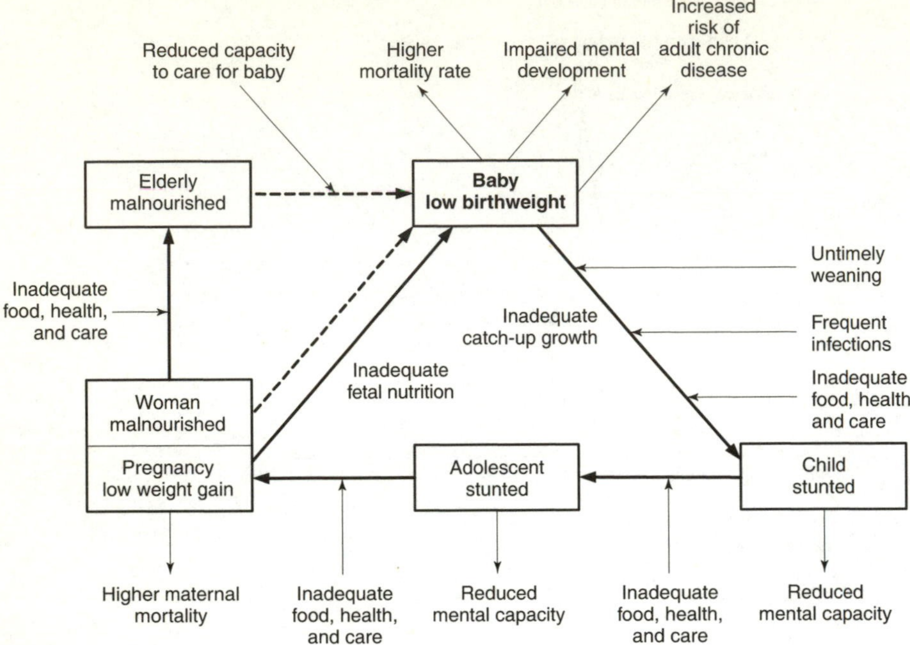

Figure A10.4.2 Nutrition throughout the life cycle.

Source: UN ACC/SCN 2000

Appendix 10.4 Poverty and nutrition

Figure A10.4.1 shows how the annual growth of GDP *per capita* interacts with the reduction of poverty in less developed regions of the world. Figure A10.4.2 illustrates the vicious circle of undernourishment and malnutrition throughout the life cycle of the world's poor.

Note

1 This section draws heavily on the material in Chenery *et al.* (1974).

Questions

1 (a) What are the costs and benefits of population growth to LDCs?
  (b) What are the major reasons for the 'population explosion' in LDCs?
2 Evaluate critically the concept of 'low level equilibrium trap'.
3 What are the major determinants of the fertility rate in LDCs?
4 Examine the relationship between growth, inequality and poverty.
5 How far would you advocate a policy of redistribution with economic growth?
6 Assess the major determinants of rural–urban migration in LDCs.

11 Development planning

11.1 Concept of economic planning

Economic planning has become one of the main instruments of achieving a higher growth rate and better standard of living in many LDCs. Planning can be defined as a conscious effort on the part of any government to follow a definite pattern of economic development in order to promote rapid and fundamental change in the economy *and* society. Such a concept of planning is fairly broad as it seeks to promote not only a fast growth rate but also significant structural socioeconomic changes via public intervention. However, the degree of state intervention defines the nature of different types of planning.

11.2 Types of planning

Planning could be of various types. For example, it could be *totalitarian* when all the means of production are usually owned and manipulated by the state. In the Soviet Union or China, all the 'commanding heights' of the economy are governed by the state. Here the degree of state intervention is the highest. At the other extreme planning could be democratic. In France, for example, the state does not own all the means of production. But it sets out some guidelines for the private sector to follow. Thus, planning here takes place through *inducement* rather than through *control*. This kind of democratic planning is sometimes known as *indicative* planning. In between these two extremes there are cases of mixed planning. Here both the public and the private sector operate side by side. Some means of production (usually the basic and strategic industries) are owned by the state while the free private sector is expected to attain the targets laid down by the government in the plan document. Social welfare takes precedence over private welfare although the private sector is free to operate on the basis of the principle of private maximization. The price mechanism is far less constrained in the mixed systems and does have a real resource allocation role to play (see Turner and Collis 1977).

Planning horizons can vary considerably. Thus, short-term planning can be undertaken which would last up to, say, one to two years. Similarly, medium-term planning would last for three to five years. The duration of long-term planning could be ten, fifteen or even twenty years. These are generally regarded as *perspective plans* which set out the long-term targets and the likely instruments to achieve these targets.

Emergency planning is usually drawn up for a short period to deal with specific problems arising from, say, famine, flood, drought, civil war and earthquakes. Many countries adopt *cyclical planning* mainly to tackle the cyclical problems emanating from fluctuations in growth rate, prices and unemployment. Here the main objective is to achieve stability in the movements of the major economic variables. These planning measures require a degree of state intervention in the market economy and the degree of intervention is generally determined by public policies.

11.3 Economic models and economic planning

Economic models are frequently used to construct economic planning. These economic models are useful to set out: (1) the objective function or the targets that should be achieved; (2) the interrelationships among the different economic variables which would indicate the general structure of the economy; and (3) the constraints (e.g. capital, labour, foreign exchange) which should be overcome to realize the objective function. Sometimes the models set out the objectives; sometimes these objectives are derived from some political process.

Economic models should have the dual characteristics of *clarity* and *consistency*. Some other properties of the model can also be stated. For instance, models must be *selective* so that only the behaviour of the major variables is analysed. Minor factors may account for some disturbances in the economic system, but they are not regarded as very significant. It may be contended that the best way to describe an economic system would be to set out a general equilibrium model, but such models could be unmanageable and their testing very difficult, given the data constraint and the statistical problem of identification. Further, models should be *closed* i.e. given the assumptions, the conclusions must follow logically. Finally, models should be *quantifiable* as far as possible.

The limitations of such models clearly follow from the above analysis. First, models may not be wholly comprehensive. Second, the validity of the models could be questioned if they rest on very dubious assumptions. Third, within the economic system, there may be many non-quantifiable variables. For example, it is not easy to evaluate in money terms the worth of a life or the cost of pain or suffering. Thus it is easy to realize that any particular economic model in the context of overall planning cannot provide all the answers. Hence the practical economist tries to isolate some variables for developing a model which are regarded as important. Such a model may rest on some simplifying assumptions but they should be based upon the economic realities. Models thus developed should be operational, i.e. they should be tested, accepted, modified or rejected. However, a model based on sound logic need not be castigated if it runs counter to the available evidence because, very frequently in LDCs, information about the relevant variables is not always available, and even if it is available it is not very reliable. Indeed, the need to improve the database of most LDCs can hardly be overemphasized. Economic planning based on economic models would not be very effective as long as wide gaps remain between the required and available information. In brief, economic models provide systematic and logical frameworks for economic planning to obtain feasible and optimal solutions in the light of the available information.

11.4 The case for and against planning

Planning in different forms has been accepted as an important policy instrument to attain specific targets in most LDCs. It is thus necessary to examine carefully the arguments for planning.

1 Since the product and the factor markets in most LDCs are usually imperfect, market forces fail to attain efficient allocation of resources. Hence, state intervention in the form of planning is necessary to obtain an efficient allocation of resources, since prices are 'wrong' signals to the decision makers.
2 Private investors usually do not pay much attention to the dynamic externalities (see Chapter 7, note 1) which could be generated in the process of development and which would account for the differences between marginal net social benefit (MNSB) and marginal net private benefit (MNPB). To obtain optimal allocation of resources, planning is necessary to remove the difference between MNSB and MNPB.
3 Private investors are usually interested in maximizing short-term and not long-term profits and this again may lead to a resource allocation which is less than socially optimal in the long run.
4 The path to economic progress via reliance upon market forces is considered very long and, given the present differences between rich and poor countries, the task of achieving a high rate of growth in the shortest possible time is considered to be of paramount importance. It is believed that planning would accelerate the rates of growth in LDCs.
5 Rapid economic growth would be retarded if necessary institutional and structural reforms were not carried out simultaneously. Planning is supposed to achieve the necessary institutional reforms to allow for more rapid growth. Also, planning may exert some such psychological impact upon the nation as a whole which is conducive to the attainment of a higher standard of living (Todaro 1971a).
6 Since many LDCs have very limited resources, it is necessary to utilize such resources (e.g. capital, skilled manpower, foreign exchange, etc.) in the most productive way and this can only be achieved if the whole economy, including the different sectors and subsectors, is brought under an overall planning mechanism.

The arguments against planning can now be analysed.

1 It is argued that if planning is necessary to avoid the imperfections of the market mechanism, then what is necessary is to make the market more perfect, not planning.
2 When there are differences between MNSB and MNPB because of externalities, the best way to solve the problem would be to tax or to provide subsidies and information to the producers so that the differences could be removed. 'Imperfect operation of the market in an underdeveloped country can be attributable to ignorance in the sense of lack of familiarity with market mechanisms and of awareness of relevant information, or to the prevalence of other modes of behaviour other than rational maximization of returns from effort' (Johnson 1962).
3 It is argued that many LDCs have lacked the skilled manpower necessary to tackle the problem of preparing and executing an efficient planning mechanism. Given

wide intervention by the state in the decision-making process, an inefficient and corrupt bureaucracy may easily increase the waste of resources that would otherwise have resulted in the operation of the imperfect market. Also, planning requires a large amount of information about many branches of the economy. The availability and reliability of such information is doubtful. Further, once power is concentrated within the hands of a few bureaucrats, vested interest could inhibit further growth and technical change.

4 The costs of planning are quite large for LDCs. Apart from the costs of running the planning administration, government intervention and planning for promoting industrialization via protection, industrial licensing and quotas have increased the real cost (in terms of net value added at world prices) enormously for LDCs (Little *et al.* 1970; Bhagwati and Desai 1970).

Most LDCs have shown a tendency to adopt planning as an important policy to achieve a higher rate of growth. However, apart from China, in very few LDCs have all the means of production been owned by the state. Few LDCs have resorted to totalitarian forms of planning and the private sector is allowed to operate alongside the growing public sector, even in the People's Republic of China. It is interesting to observe that in most cases the price mechanism is not suppressed and market prices are sometimes relied upon by the planners for allocating resources. Perhaps the desire to accelerate the economic growth rates, promotion of self-reliance, the inadequacy of the imperfect market mechanism, the inefficiency of the existing private sector and the need for structural reforms are the main reasons for the adoption of planning in most LDCs.

11.5 Development planning models

Development planning models can be *aggregative*. Here the entire economy is taken into account and the behaviour of some of the major variables such as output, income, saving and capital are taken into consideration. These are also regarded as macro models and as an example, the use of the Harrod–Domar model can be cited. Sometimes macroeconometric models are constructed for the whole economy to achieve some specific targets. The applications of these models will be shown later.

In many LDCs, relevant data for the entire economy may not be available although enough information could be obtained for a single project. In such cases *sectoral* models are developed and different sectoral plans are combined together to form an overall sectoral-project plan (e.g. Ghana 1958–64; Kenya 1964 to 1969–70; Pakistan 1956; Nigeria 1963–8). The main defect of the sectoral plans lies in the lack of co-ordination among them. Thus the heterogeneous collection of plans for different projects may be neither consistent with each other nor feasible when they are taken together. Also, in the absence of a unified contour of analysis, different rules could be applied to assess different sectors.

As aggregative models do not provide a detailed description of the inter-industry relationships between supply and demand, to achieve greater balance or consistency between various sectors, inter-industry models are now being used to determine the demand for intermediate goods plus imports. Relationships among different sectors are described by *linear* equations between output produced by a sector and its input requirement, and the model can only be applied where some industrialization has taken place and the information about the linkages between inputs needed to produce outputs is known and available. These models are useful

1 to achieve consistency between demand and supply in different sectors;
2 to know whether investment demand will be enough to produce a target output;
3 to determine intermediate demand for inputs including capital and labour;
4 to provide the basis for the use of programming models in which, apart from achieving consistency, the planner can test the feasibility and optimality of different projects within a plan.

11.5.1 Aggregate models: the Harrod–Domar model

In the aggregate models only a few crucial variables are taken into consideration. The model which is most used is the one developed by Harrod and Domar (HD) in the context of growth theory. In a simple form, the model could be set out as follows:

$$S_t = I_t \tag{11.1}$$

$$I_t = K_{t+1} - K_t \tag{11.2}$$

$$S_t = sY_{t-1} \tag{11.3}$$

$$K_t = vY_{t-1} \tag{11.4}$$

where S is savings, I is investment, K is capital stock, Y is income, v is the capital–output ratio or capital coefficient and s is the propensity to save.

After making the necessary substitutions from (11.1), (11.2) and (11.3) we get

$$sY_{t-1} = vY_t - vY_{t-1} \tag{11.5}$$

i.e.

$$sY_{t-1} = v(Y_t - Y_{t-1}) \tag{11.6}$$

i.e.

$$\frac{Y_t - Y_{t-1}}{Y_{t-1}} = \frac{s}{v} \tag{11.7}$$

Since growth of income (g) is defined as

$$g = \frac{Y_t - Y_{t-1}}{Y_{t-1}}$$

we get the familiar HD equation

$$g = s/v \tag{11.8}$$

The model helps the planner to predict the required savings rate once the target growth rate and the capital–output ratio v are given. In any economy, if the actual growth rate is 3 per cent per annum, given $s = 9$ per cent and $v = 3 : 1$, then in order to achieve a target g of 5 per cent, the planner will have to recommend a rise of s to 15 per cent with given v(3 : 1). Thus, fiscal (e.g. high taxation) and/or monetary policies have to be used to acquire a desired rate of saving. The model is also helpful to find out the extent of foreign resources that would be necessary to realize the target growth rate should domestic savings be inadequate. For example, if the use of fiscal and monetary policies yields only 12 per cent rather than 15 per cent savings, then the difference between planned savings and actual savings would be 3 per cent (i.e. 15 per cent − 12 per cent) and this amount of resources could represent the amount of foreign resources necessary to realize the target.

11.6 Application of the Harrod–Domar model in development planning: India's first five year plan

The HD model has been applied as a basis to develop more comprehensive plans for some LDCs. In India, for example, the HD model has been used to formulate the First Five Year Plan (1950–1 to 1955–6). The following equations illustrate the use of the HD model; most of the notation has already been explained in the previous section.

$$I_t = S_t \tag{11.9}$$

$$S_t = aY_t - c \tag{11.10}$$

$$Y_t = vK_t \tag{11.11}$$

$$I_t = \dot{K}_t \tag{11.12}$$

where K_t is the incremental capital stock (i.e. dK/dt).

Substituting we get

$$\dot{K}_t = avK_t - c \tag{11.13}$$

The time-path of capital accumulation is thus

$$K_t = \left(K_0 - \frac{c}{av}\right) e^{avt} + \frac{c}{av} \tag{11.4}$$

Unlike the HD model, the growth rate in this model can be increased from period to period if $a > S_0 > Y_0$, i.e. if the marginal rate of savings is higher than the average rate of savings. The asymptotic relative growth rate is given by the expression av.

The use of the HD model has its advantages. Its clarity and simplicity deserve attention. Also, the model is complete in the sense that it covers the entire economy; it is selective and fairly realistic. Moreover, the model does not suffer from any internal inconsistencies. However, it is highly aggregated and does not provide any idea about the internal relationships between different sectors. Thus it fails to give us any idea about the consistency between different sectors. The use of the concept of capital–output ratio has its limitations. For one thing, it is necessary to distinguish between *marginal* and average capital–output ratios (v). For another, planned v and realized v may not be the same and global v may be different from local (i.e. regional) v. The estimation of capital in LDCs is always a rather difficult task. However, the HD model has been disaggregated into two sectors for planning purposes in Kenya and this is shown in the next section. Recently, Easterley (1999) found very little empirical support for the HD model from the evidence of LDCs between 1960 and 1996.

11.7 A two-sector Harrod–Domar model for planning: the Kenyan case

Let the total output Y be divided into two forms: consumer goods Y_1 and capital goods Y_2. Thus we have

$$Y = Y_1 + Y_2 \tag{11.15}$$

Let

$$Y_1 = m(Y_1 + Y_2) \tag{11.16}$$

where m is the marginal propensity to consume. The ratio of the outputs of the two sectors would then be given by

$$\frac{Y_1}{Y_2} = \frac{m}{1 - m} \tag{11.17}$$

If $m = 0.80$ the ratio of consumer goods output (Y_1) to capital goods output is fixed at 4 : 1. If m falls because of a rise in savings, output of Y_2 will tend to grow at a higher rate. However, more of Y_2 (capital goods) would have to be used in order to release the bottleneck in the production of more consumer goods, and the production of capital goods is then given by the following relationship:

$$Y_2 = v_1 \Delta Y_1 + v_2 \Delta Y_2 \tag{11.18}$$

where v_1 is the capital–output ratio in Y_1 and v_2 is the capital–output ratio in Y_2. Then the overall growth would be given by[1]

$$g = \frac{\Delta Y_1 + \Delta Y_2}{Y_1 + Y_2} = \frac{1 - m}{m v_1 + (1 - m) v_2} \tag{11.19}$$

Given the values of m, v_1, v_2 and the productive capacity of the Y_1 and Y_2 sectors at the base level, it is possible to work out the rate of economic growth for the whole economy.

The type of disaggregation described above is not sufficient for planning for LDCs. More comprehensive sectoral planning has been attempted in some other countries. Such a case of sectoral planning is described in the next section.

11.8 Feldman–Mahalanobis sectoral planning and the Indian second five year plan

In India's Second Five Year Plan (1955–6 to 1960–1), an interesting attempt was made to develop sectoral planning as a basis for more comprehensive planning. The model developed by Feldman (1928) and Mahalanobis (1953) (FM) deserves special attention as it provides a contrast to the HD model. The main difference between the two types of model lies in the fact that, whereas a Keynesian flow analysis is accepted in the HD model which emphasizes the desirability of raising savings that could be channelled into higher investment, a 'structuralist' view is adopted in the FM model. Here it is emphasized that important bottlenecks can appear in the process of this type of transformation of savings into investment and the only way in which such constraints can be released is to alter the structure of the economy in such a way as to allow the economic system to produce more capital goods to maintain a higher rate of investment. In the FM model, it is assumed that there are real bottlenecks in the channelling of savings into investments which are ignored in the HD model, since the structural rigidities and the inter-temporal choice between present and future consumption benefits are assumed away in the HD model. The argument is important, since in the HD model it is indeed assumed that the marginal propensity to consume or save remains unchanged.

The following assumptions are usually made in the FM model.

1 The economy is divided into two sectors – one produces consumer goods C and the other produces capital goods K.
2 Once a machine is installed in one sector it cannot be transferred to the other sector, i.e. capital is not shiftable.
3 The technological coefficients in both sectors are fixed.
4 Capital is the only scarce factor.
5 Depreciation of capital stock is ruled out and thus incremental capital stock is equal to total investment. However, such an assumption is not strictly necessary for the analysis of the FM model (Bose 1968).
6 Trade is assumed away in the model and as such capital goods cannot be imported from abroad.
7 Production of capital goods is independent of the production of consumer goods.

Given these assumptions the FM model can be shown with the following equations. Let λ_k be the proportion of investment in capital goods, λ_c the proportion of investment in consumer goods, β_k the output–capital ratio in the capital goods sector and β_c the output–capital ratio in the consumer goods sector. Then

$$1 = \lambda_k + \lambda_c \tag{11.20}$$

and

$$\beta = \lambda_k\beta_k + \lambda_c\beta_c \tag{11.21}$$

Let K_t be the capital stock at time t. We have

$$K_{t+1} - K_t = \lambda_k\beta_k K_t \tag{11.22}$$

$$C_{t+1} - C_t = \lambda_c\beta_c K_t \tag{11.23}$$

$$K_t = (1 + \lambda_k\beta_k)^t K_0 \tag{11.24}$$

Then

$$Y_t = \left(1 + \alpha_0 \frac{\lambda_k\beta_k + \lambda_c\beta_k}{\lambda_k\beta_k}\right)[(1 + \lambda_k\beta_k)^t - 1] \tag{11.25}$$

where $a_0 = I_0/Y_0$, i.e. the initial investment–income ratio. Given a_0, β_k and β_c, λ_k is the instrumental variable and, since the asymptotic growth rate is given by $\lambda_k\beta_k$, choice of a higher value of λ_k will produce a higher growth rate and a higher level of consumption eventually. This is because, by allocating more investible resources to the production of capital goods, a higher marginal savings rate and a higher output or consumption growth rate would be obtained. The greater emphasis on the production of capital goods for industrialization in the early Soviet plan and in the Second Five Year Plan of India is not difficult to understand in the light of the above analysis. However, the precise amount of investment in the production of capital goods has not been stated and the optimal choice would depend upon both domestic and foreign transformation constraints. (See also Appendix 11.1.)

11.8.1 Evaluation of the Feldman–Mahalanobis model

Despite the ingenuity of the FM model, the following criticisms are usually made against it.

1 The absence of the role of foreign trade is regarded as a very unsatisfactory part of the FM model since capital goods can be imported instead of being produced at home at a high cost, chiefly behind the protectionist wall which could sometimes lead to a welfare loss to the economy. The limited role that exports usually played in India's economy might have prompted Mahalanobis to neglect foreign trade, but it is doubtful to what extent such a neglect of the export sector is justified for many LDCs today.

2 The FM model is aggregative. Though Mahalanobis disaggregated the model later into four sectors, Komiya (1959) has shown that the value which Mahalanobis chose for λ_k yielded inefficient resource allocation as it lay within the feasibility locus between an increase in employment and a rise in output. In other words, reallocation of the investment among the three sectors apart from the capital goods sector would have resulted in higher output and employment.

3 In the FM model, the problem of unemployment has not received due emphasis. The choice of more capital-intensive methods of production usually increases the problem of unemployment, particularly in a labour-surplus economy. Brahmananda and Vakil (BV) (1956), in their planning model, have tried to focus attention on wage-goods rather than fixed capital and have pointed out the need to promote employment, However, in the BV model the basic problem of capital accumulation that FM encountered has not been solved satisfactorily as the supply of abundant labour alone is not enough to achieve a higher level of capital formation. It is, of course, true that the problem of employment creation in labour-surplus countries can hardly be exaggerated, and such a problem has not really been solved in the FM model.

4 Given the predominant role of agriculture in LDCs, the planner is generally expected to consider the dynamic development of agriculture within the model. Unfortunately the FM model does not take into account the role of agriculture and public policies based on such models have led to the growth of 'urban bias' (Lipton 1968a) in the planning of many LDCs. It is argued that a policy of industrialization on the basis of the recommendation of the FM model has resulted in the neglect of the rural sector and has widened the development gap between the

modern, urban industrial sector and the backward, rural agricultural sector within LDCs.

In view of the aggregative nature of the HD and the FM models, methods have been devised to include sectoral details within the macro models to obtain greater information for the whole economy. Some of these methods are described in the next section.

11.9 Macroeconometric models in development planning

The use of macroeconometric models is now popular in the planning exercises for the LDCs. One way to demonstrate the application of such models is to use a simple Keynesian framework of analysis as described by Hicks and Lange. More formally, let C_t be consumer expenditure, I_t capital formation, Y_t national income, r_t the interest rate, M_t the money supply (exogenous or determined outside the system), t time and u_t, v_t, z_t, error terms. We can write

$$C_t = a_0 + a_1 Y_t + a_2 r_t + u_t \tag{11.26}$$

$$I_t = b_0 + b_1 Y_t + b_2 r_t + v_t \tag{11.27}$$

$$Y_t = C_t + I_t \tag{11.28}$$

$$M_t = c_0 + c_1 Y_t + c_2 r_t + z_t \tag{11.29}$$

However, such a model is not dynamic; it does not determine prices; it ignores foreign trade; also, public policy (i.e. changes in government taxes and spending) is not allowed to play any role. A more sophisticated model has been set out by Klein and this is illustrated below (see Klein 1965):

$$C_t = a_0 + a_1 \frac{Y_t - T_t}{p_t} + a_2 C_{t-1} + u_{1t} \tag{11.30}$$

$$I_t = b_0 + b_1 \frac{Y_{t-1}}{p_{t-1}} + b_2 K_{t-1} + b_3 r_{t-1} + u_{2t} \tag{11.31}$$

$$F_t = c_0 + c_1 \frac{Y_t - Y_{t-1}}{p_t} + c_2 F_{t-1} + c_3 \frac{p_{ft}}{p_t} + u_{3t} \tag{11.32}$$

$$E_t = d_0 + d_1 T_{wt} + d_2 \frac{p_{et}}{p_t} + u_{4t} \tag{11.33}$$

$$\frac{Y_t}{p_t} = C_t + I_t - F_t + E_t + G_t \tag{11.34}$$

$$T_t = e_0 + e_1 Y_t + u_{5t} \tag{11.35}$$

$$I_t = K_t - K_{t-1} \tag{11.36}$$

$$\frac{Y_t}{p_t} = g_0 + g_1 L_t + g_2 K_t + u_{6t} \tag{11.37}$$

$$p_t = h_0 + h_1 \frac{w_t L_t}{Y_t p_t} + h_2 \frac{p_{ft}}{p_t} + u_{7t} \tag{11.38}$$

$$\frac{w_t - w_{t-1}}{w_{t-1}} = j_0 + j_1 \frac{N_t - L_t}{N_t} + j_2 \frac{p_t - p_{t-1}}{p_{t-1}} u_{8t} \tag{11.39}$$

$$N_t = k_0 + k_1(N_t - L_t) + k_2 w_t / p_t + u_{9t} \tag{11.40}$$

$$\frac{M_t}{p_t} = l_0 + l_1 \frac{Y_t}{p_t} + l_2 r_t + u_{10t} \tag{11.41}$$

$$p_e = m_0 + m_1 p + u_{11t} \tag{11.42}$$

The endogenous variables (i.e. variables which are determined within the system) in the Klein model are as follows: C, real consumer expenditures; Y, national income (in current prices); T, taxes less transfer payments; p, an index of the general price level; I, net real investment; K, real capital stock; r, interest rate; F, real imports; E, real exports; p_e, export prices; L, employment; w, wage rate; N, labour supply.

The exogenous variables may be stated as follows: p_f, import prices; T_w, volume of world trade; G, real government expenditures; M, money supply.

The above model describes a set of *linear* relationships among the variables and it now determines both absolute and relative price levels. Foreign trade has been included. The role of taxes and expenditures by the government has been described and lags are introduced to make the model dynamic. However, the practical economist will have to determine different types of interest rates, consumption, investment, taxes, expenditures and trade to render such a model applicable to the special problems of LDCs. The actual econometric techniques to be used will depend upon initial specifications of the equations and the subjective judgement of the planner in the light of the actual state of information. (For a discussion of different types of econometric models and their applications to LDCs, see Ghosh 1968; Agarwala 1970; Chenery *et al.* 1971; Ghosh *et al.* 1974.)

It is important to remember some of the difficulties that the planners are likely to encounter in their attempts to build up the econometric models. First, the testing of the model will usually depend upon the *availability* of *reliable* data. It is generally accepted that such data are not always available. Second, it is assumed in the application of linear least squares regression analysis that the explanatory variables should be independent of one another to avoid the problem of multicollinearity and the disturbance terms should not be serially correlated with one another to avoid the problem of autocorrelation. However, many macro models for LDCs suffer from the difficulties involved in what is called 'misplaced aggregation and illegitimate isolation' (Streeten 1966). Misplaced aggregation occurs in the economic models for LDCs mainly because of market imperfection. 'If there is excess demand in one sector and excess supply in another, but the supply in one cannot be used to meet the demand in the other, there is no sense in talking of aggregate demand or aggregate supply' (Streeten 1966). Illegitimate isolation occurs in the opposite case, i.e. when the explanatory variables are not independent of one another or what is known as the problem of multicollinearity in econometrics. 'Violins, however fine, cannot produce a melody without skilled violinists, nor can violinists without violins. The appropriate unit is violin plus violinist, and to talk of a violin/melody ratio is to commit both the fallacies, misplaced aggregation and illegitimate isolation' (Streeten 1966). Thus the case for the proper specification of equations to test the econometric models for planning can hardly be overemphasized. Third, relationships between the variables could be non-linear. Finally, it must be borne in mind that the results of regression analysis by themselves do not establish causation. Causality comes from economic theory. Here it is important to remember that, in choosing an 'appropriate' model for a less developed country, the realities should dominate the technique instead of the converse.

Given the need for analysing many important sectors of the economy and their interrelationships to provide greater consistency between aggregate supply and aggregate demand, development planners have increasingly turned their attention to the application of the input–output technique originally invented by Leontief (1951). Such a technique is described in the next section.

11.10 Input–output analysis in development planning

Usually the input–output technique (IO) delineates the general equilibrium analysis and the empirical side of the economic system of production of any country. Its use in development planning has become quite noticeable and, in the following paragraphs, its salient features will be described.

11.10.1 The assumptions of the IO analysis

It is important to note the basic assumptions of IO analysis.

1 No substitution takes place between the inputs to produce a given unit of output and the *input coefficients are constant*. The linear input functions imply that the marginal input coefficients are equal to the average.
2 Joint products are ruled out, i.e. each industry produces only one commodity and each commodity is produced by only one industry.
3 External economies are ruled out and production is subject to the operation of *constant* returns to scale.

These assumptions require that to produce one unit of the jth good the required ith input would be constant; let us call it a_{ij}. Thus, the production of each unit of the jth good would need, say, a_{1j} of the first commodity, a_{2j} of the second and a_{nj} of the nth input. Note that the first subscript refers to the input and the second subscript refers to the output. Hence, if $a_{ij} = 0.20$p, this means that 20p worth of the first commodity is necessary as an input to produce £1 worth of the jth good. The symbol a_{ij} is regarded as the input coefficient.

Let there be n industries in the economy. The input–output table in the form of the matrix $A = [a_{ij}]$ would state the input coefficients. The availability of the input–output table is thus an important condition for any calculation. Actually, the table shows the inter-industry flows where each column shows the necessary input for producing one unit of the output of a certain industry. If any element in the matrix is zero, it shows that the input demand is zero. The input coefficients can be written as

$$a_{ij} = \frac{x_{ij}}{X_j} \qquad i + 1, 2, \ldots n \quad j = 1, 2, \ldots n$$

where X_j is the total output of the jth industry and x_{ij} is the number of units of the ith good used by the jth industry.

The IO table is usually given in the following matrix:

$$A = \begin{array}{r} \\ \text{Input} \\ \text{I} \\ \text{II} \\ \\ N \end{array} \begin{array}{c} \text{Output} \\ \hline \end{array} \begin{bmatrix} \text{I} & \text{II} & \ldots & \text{N} \\ a_{11} & a_{12} & \ldots & a_{1n} \\ a_{21} & a_{22} & \ldots & a_{2n} \\ \vdots & \vdots & & \vdots \\ a_{n1} & a_{n2} & & a_{nm} \end{bmatrix}$$

However, the IO table in the above form considers only inter-industry flows and ignores final demand. An 'open' IO table can be easily constructed where a final demand for the product of each industry is included. Note that corresponding to the *demand* for the products, the IO table should now be expanded to include *supplies* of primary inputs. For example, if the household sector's final demand for output is now included it is also necessary to include the labour supplied by the households as inputs. It is now obvious that, because of the supply of labour inputs, the sum of the elements in each column of the matrix A will be less than one because in the absence of primary input costs (e.g. labour supply) the sum of each element in any column will be exactly equal to one. Thus:

$$\sum_{i=1}^{n} a_{ij} < 1 \qquad j = 1, 2, \ldots n$$

It follows that the value of primary input required to produce one unit of the jth good is given by

$$1 - \sum_{i=1}^{n} a_{ij}$$

Now for industry 1, to produce enough output to cater for the final demand plus the input demand of n industries, the following equation must hold:

$$x_1 = a_{11}x_1 + a_{12}x_2 + \ldots + a_{1n}x_n + D_1$$

or

$$(1 - a_{11})x_1 - a_{12}x_2 - \ldots - a_{1n}x_n = D_1$$

where D_1 is the final demand for the output of industry 1.

Similarly, for the second industry, the equation can be set out as below:

$$-a_{21}x_1 + (1 - a_{22})x_2 - \ldots - a_{2n}x_n = D_2$$

Thus

$$-a_{n1}x_1 - a_{n2}x_2 - \ldots + (1 - a_{nn})x_n = D_n$$

The system of equations can be written in the following matrix form:

$$[I - A]x = D \begin{pmatrix} 1 - a_{11} & -a_{12} & -a_{1n} \\ -a_{21} & 1 - a_{22} & -a_{2n} \\ \vdots & \vdots & \vdots \\ -a_{n1} & -a_{n2} & 1 - a_{nn} \end{pmatrix} \begin{pmatrix} x_1 \\ x_2 \\ \vdots \\ x_h \end{pmatrix} = \begin{pmatrix} D_1 \\ D_2 \\ \vdots \\ D_h \end{pmatrix}$$

where the identity matrix I is given by

$$I = \begin{pmatrix} 1 & 0 & 0 & \ldots & 0 \\ 0 & 1 & 0 & \ldots & 0 \\ 0 & 0 & 1 & \ldots & 0 \\ \vdots & \vdots & \vdots & & \vdots \\ 0 & 0 & 0 & \ldots & 1 \end{pmatrix}$$

That is, all the elements in the principal diagonal are 1 and all other elements are zero.

Now solving for x we have

$$x = [I - A]^{-1}D$$

The rule for matrix inversion, i.e. $[A]^{-1}$, can be given as

$$A^{-1} = \frac{1}{|A|}A^*$$

The following example can be given. Let

$$A = \begin{pmatrix} a_{11} & a_{12} \\ a_{21} & a_{22} \end{pmatrix}$$

Then

$$|A| = a_{11}a_{22} - a_{12}a_{21}$$

and

$$A^* = \begin{pmatrix} a_{22} & -a_{12} \\ -a_{21} & a_{11} \end{pmatrix}$$

$$A^{-1} = \frac{1}{|A|}\begin{pmatrix} a_{22} & -a_{12} \\ -a_{21} & a_{11} \end{pmatrix}$$

$$= \begin{pmatrix} \frac{a_{22}}{|A|} & \frac{a_{12}}{|A|} \\ -\frac{a_{21}}{|A|} & \frac{a_{11}}{|A|} \end{pmatrix}$$

A numerical example can help one to understand the solution more clearly. To simplify the analysis we are concerned with only two sectors, agriculture (X_1) and textiles (X_2). Let the IO table be given as

	Agriculture	*Textiles*
Agriculture	0.6	0.2
Textiles	0.4	0.3

Then

$$A = \begin{pmatrix} 0.6 & 0.2 \\ 0.4 & 0.3 \end{pmatrix}$$

Now

$$I - A = \begin{pmatrix} 1 & 0 \\ 0 & 1 \end{pmatrix} - \begin{pmatrix} 0.6 & 0.2 \\ 0.4 & 0.3 \end{pmatrix} = \begin{pmatrix} 0.4 & -0.2 \\ -0.4 & 0.7 \end{pmatrix}$$

$$[I - A]^{-1} = \begin{pmatrix} 0.7/0.2 & 0.2/0.2 \\ 0.4/0.2 & 0.4/0.2 \end{pmatrix} = \begin{pmatrix} 3\frac{1}{2} & 1 \\ 2 & 2 \end{pmatrix}$$

Let the final demand be given by

$$D = \begin{pmatrix} 10 \\ 5 \end{pmatrix}$$

Recall that

$$x = [I - A]^{-1} D$$

Thus we have

$$x = \begin{pmatrix} 3\frac{1}{2} & 1 \\ 2 & 2 \end{pmatrix}\begin{pmatrix} 10 \\ 5 \end{pmatrix} = \begin{pmatrix} 40 \\ 30 \end{pmatrix}$$

Thus the agricultural sector (X_1) would produce forty units and the textile sector (X_2) would produce thirty units. Note that the effects of change in final demand on the production of X_1 and X_2 can easily be found. Further, given the employment coefficient, the effect on employment can be traced out. The IO analysis can be extended to include many other sectors like foreign trade and the balance of payments. It is now easy to see how the IO tables are used for comprehensive development planning in many sectors, to find total output in different sectors, to obtain certain demand targets, the size and direction of inter-industry flows, the amount of imports and the level of use of different inputs like capital and labour.

11.10.2 The limitations of the use of the input–output model

The assumptions set out at the outset of the discussion of IO analysis help us to understand the major limitations of this analysis.

1 It is assumed in the IO analysis that the input coefficients remain unchanged. However, these coefficients may not remain constant when growth is taking place. In the long run the validity of the assumption of a constant coefficient is all the more questionable as technical progress gains momentum, substitution possibilities arise and returns to scale might be rising instead of being constant. Thus, marginal input coefficients might no longer be equal to the average.
2 If the linkages among the different sectors are rather weak or non-existent, then the IO table will give us only very limited information.
3 The IO analysis assumes that the composition of demand is constant. In the long run this is unlikely to be valid and any change in demand composition is likely to change input coefficients.

However, it should be pointed out that some of these limitations in the application of the IO analysis can be removed by continuously updating the IO tables to incorporate any effects of changes in technical progress and/or demand pattern on sectoral input coefficients. Also, if the IO analysis is used to make short-run rather than long-run predictions, and if the data are reliable, then the margin of error is unlikely to be large.

Finally, IO analysis further assumes that each industry has only one way of producing a given product. But it is conceivable that there could be more than one process or activity to produce a commodity. IO analysis cannot help to find out which process among two or more activities would use the minimum amount of resources. In short, IO analysis cannot help to solve the choice of optimal technique of production. This would necessitate the use of linear programming analysis to which we now turn.

11.11 Linear programming and development planning

Linear programming (LP) is really a mathematical tool which is now being increasingly used in economic analysis. Its use in the field of development planning is of much interest chiefly because it helps the planner to allocate resources optimally among alternative uses within the specific constraints. At the micro level, the technique could be used to find out optimal and efficient (least expensive) methods of production. Actually, LP can be regarded as a powerful and complementary tool which can be used to analyse the IO tables in order to solve the problems of choice of techniques on the supply side as well as the problem of choice of final demand. It is important to emphasize that the LP technique helps to tackle the major problems of investment planning: (1) *consistency* between sectors; (2) *feasibility* of plans; and (3) *optimality* in resource allocation. However, it should be pointed out that the important assumption that is made in LP analysis is that variables are interrelated in a *linear* way. This assumption may not be very realistic in all cases. But if it is, then LP is indeed very useful for planning. On the other hand, if the relationships among the variables are non-linear, then non-linear programming can be used to solve the problems.

11.11.1 General formulation of linear programming problems

In an LP exercise, usually the objective is to *maximize* or *minimize* some linear function of the variables given, say, r variables. The programmer seeks to obtain non-negative values of these variables subject to the constraints and maximize (or minimize) the objective function. More formally

$$\max V = c_1x_1 + \ldots + c_rx_r$$

with m inequalities or equalities in r variables, i.e.

$$a_{i1}x_1 + \ldots + a_{ir}x_r \{\geq, =, \leq\} b_i \qquad i = 1, \ldots m$$

and

$$x_j \geq 0 \qquad j = 1, \ldots r$$

where a_{ij}, b_i and c_j are given constants.

The problem is sometimes written in a more compact way, e.g.

$$\max Z = \sum_{j=1}^{n} c_{ij}x_i$$

subject to

$$\sum_{j=1}^{n} a_{ij}x_j \leq r_i \qquad i = 1, 2, \ldots m$$

$$x_j \geq 0 \qquad j = 1, 2, \ldots n$$

where c_j and a_{ij} are the given coefficients and r_i are the constraints. Note that in matrix form a_{ij} helps us to find the exact location of each coefficient.

Let us assume a simple case of two variables to illustrate diagrammatically the LP solution. Let the objective function be

$$\max V = 5X_1 + 3X_2$$

subject to

$$3X_1 + 5X_2 \leq 15$$

$$5X_1 + 2X_2 \leq 10$$

$$X_1, X_2 \geq 0$$

The graphical solution of this LP problem will be shown first and then the numerical solutions will follow. (See, for example, Hadley 1962.)

11.11.2 The graphical solution

Let us first convert the inequalities into equalities, i.e.

$$3X_1 + 5X_2 = 15 \tag{11.43}$$

$$5X_1 + 2X_2 = 10 \tag{11.44}$$

Accordingly we get lines like AB for equation (11.43) and CD for (11.44) (see Figure 11.1).

Any point *on* or *below* AB satisfies the inequality $3X_1 + 5X_2 \leq 15$, just as any point *on* or *below* CD satisfies the inequality $5X_1 + 2X_2 \leq 10$. Also, there is no point above, say, AB (or CD) which satisfies the above inequalities. The points which will satisfy both the non-negativity restrictions are given by the area OAKD. This area is then regarded as a feasible region. Any point such as P is regarded as feasible because production of X_1 and X_2 at point P does not violate the constraints. A *feasible* solution could lie at a point like O (at the origin). But such a feasible solution should imply that *no* production of X_1 and X_2 would take place! In order to obtain the *optimum* feasible solution it is necessary to find the point at which the iso-profit curve is tangent to any point lying on AKD. Any iso-profit line such as V_1 which lies *inside* the area OAKD does not yield the optimum profit because profit could always be increased by moving further away to a higher iso-profit line like V_2 which just touches the area AKD at K. Similarly, the iso-profit line V_3, although indicating higher profit, is not attainable. Thus, the optimum profit is given at the point K where OM of X_1 and ON of X_2 will be produced. Thus at K the objective function $V = 5X_1 + 3X_2$ is at a maximum. It is necessary to point out here that, given the above profit equations, iso-profit lines are straight lines. Since constant returns to scale operate, the further we move away from the origin along the iso-profit line, the greater is the level of profit. The iso-profit lines, i.e. V_1, V_2 etc., are parallel to one another because the slope of V_1, V_2 etc. is $-5/3$ and is independent of V_1, V_2. To obtain the optimal values of X_1 and X_2, it is necessary to solve the two equations for lines AB and CD at K. Thus, we have

$$3X_1 + 5X_2 = 15$$

$$5X_1 + 2X_2 = 10$$

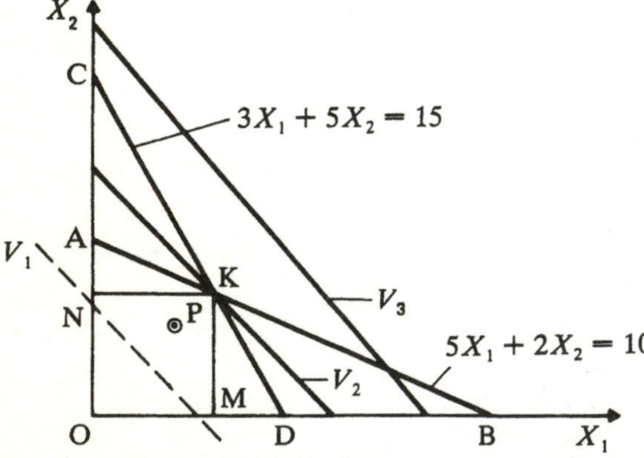

Figure 11.1

Solving for X_1 we have $X_1 = 1.053$; $X_2 = 2.368$. The maximum profit now is $V = 12.37$.

The line V could lie along one edge of the polygon AKD. In such a case, no unique values of X_1 and X_2 would maximize V. Indeed, there will be more than one optimal solution which would imply that there exists more than a single way to juxtapose resources to obtain the highest profit.

The above example of solving the LP problem is highly simplified. In reality, it is generally found that an optimum solution has to be found subject to some inequalities in the constraints. These inequalities are usually converted into equalities by adding extra or 'slack' variables for solving the equations. Optimum solutions are then derived by using the 'simplex' method. In the simplex method, the optimum solution is reached via an iterative procedure. According to the rules of LP, any corner solution such as O, A, K, D in the figure is a basic solution. In the simplex method, starting from any basic solution (e.g. O), we move to the adjacent corner solution (e.g. either A or K) to improve upon the value of the objective function until the optimum is reached (i.e. any further move will worsen the situation). At each corner the simplex procedure states whether the corner point is optimal, and if not, what the next corner point will be.

To show the use of the slack variables, we first state the system of inequalities, i.e.

$$\max V = 5X_1 + 3X_2$$

$$3X_1 + 5X_2 \leq 15$$

$$5X_1 + 2X_2 \leq 10$$

$$X_1, X_2 \geq 0$$

With the slack variables, we can now write

$$3X_1 + 5X_2 + X_3 = 15$$

$$5X_1 + 2X_2 + X_4 = 10$$

where X_3 and X_4 are the slack variables.

After the choice of a 'pivot', the optimum solution is found in successive steps. (For the choice of 'pivot' and solution, see Hadley 1962; Panne 1976; Baumol 1977.)

11.11.3 Duality

LP problems are also solved by the application of the principle of *duality*. Previously we have observed how to maximize an objective function, e.g. profit. Corresponding to every maximization of profit problem, which is regarded as a *primal*, a *dual* involves minimization, say, of cost. Note that if the constrained equations are given by $\leq$ signs, the dual would imply $\geq$ signs. The profit constraints r_i will be replaced by the capacity constraints C_i and a different set of variables appears in the dual. More formally, we can write the primal as

$$\max V = r_1X_1 + r_2X_2 + \ldots + r_nX_n$$

subject to

$$b_{11}X_1 + b_{12}X_2 + \ldots + b_{1n}X_n \leq L_1$$

$$b_{m1}X_1 + b_{m2}X_2 + \ldots + b_{mn}X_n \leq L_m$$

$$X_1 \geq 0, \ldots X_n \geq 0$$

The dual can be written as

$$\min \gamma = L_1C_1 + L_2C_2 + \ldots + L_mC_m$$

subject to

$$a_{11}C_1 + a_{21}C_2 + \ldots a_{m1}C_m \geq r_1$$

$$a_{1n}C_n + a_{2n}C_n + \ldots + a_{mn}C_m \geq r_n$$

$$C_1 \geq 0, C_2 \geq 0, \ldots C_m \geq 0$$

Note that, in the constrained inequalities, while the coefficients appear in the *rows* in the primal, they are observed in the *columns* in the dual. Also a new set of variables $C_1, C_2, \ldots C_m$ appears in the dual.

If the slack variables are introduced, the system of *equations* can be written as follows:

Primal:

$$\max V = r_1X_1 + \ldots + r_nX_n$$

subject to

$$b_{11}X_1 + \ldots + b_{1n}X_n + S_1 = L_1$$

$$b_{m1}X_1 + \ldots + b_{mn}X_n + S_m = L_m$$

$$X_1 \geq 0, \ldots X_n \geq 0, S_1 \geq 0, \ldots S_m \geq 0$$

Dual:

$$\min \gamma = L_1C_1 + \ldots + L_mC_m$$

subject to

$$a_{11}C_1 + \ldots + a_{n1}C_m - K_1 = r_1$$

$$a_{1n}C_1 + \ldots + a_{mn}C_m - K_n = r_n$$

$$C_1 \geq 0, \ldots C_m \geq 0, K_1 \geq 0, \ldots K_n \geq 0$$

The economic interpretation of the dual is not difficult. The structural variables $C_1, C_2, \ldots$ etc. of the dual are really the 'shadow prices' assigned to each input or resource. They represent the marginal product of each resource included in the optimal solution. The link between the shadow price of an input as its marginal yield to profit can be seen through changes in profit resulting from the subtraction of a single unit of an input from its use. Also, in the dual, the objective function, i.e.

minimization of cost, shows the total value of the inputs as it is the product of shadow prices of the inputs ($C_1, C_2, \ldots$) and their respective input capacities. The constrained inequalities in the dual suggest that profits made from the production of goods must be wholly imputed to the resources used in their production. At the point of optimal solution, all inputs would be valued according to their marginal product and the total profit will be exhausted. Should the value of an input used in the production of an additional unit of any output be greater than the unit profit of that output, a loss will be indicated and the size of this loss is given by the slack variable in the constrained equations of the dual. It is now easy to see the main argument in one of the major theorems of the duality in relation to the primal solution. First, at the optimal point of the feasible solution, the shadow prices of each unit of resources should be such that there would not be any profit which could be made from anywhere and hence, at the optimal point, the highest profit V is equal to the minimum cost of resources, i.e. γ, in the dual. The other duality theorem states that should the 'shadow' cost of inputs to produce a unit of output exceed the unit profit that could be made from that output, then at the optimal point such a product should not be produced as its production means a loss. At the optimal point, those goods should be produced whose loss is nil. It is now clear that wherever the values of the slack variable $K_1, K_2, \ldots K_n$ are positive (which would mean loss), such activities should be excluded from the optimal solution. Thus, LP shows the utility of the use of shadow prices for inputs for efficient allocation within the context of planning.

It should be mentioned, however, that in an LP solution prices are regarded as the indicators of the marginal worth to society. But in LDCs, where the market is mostly imperfect, prices will usually be higher than the marginal cost. Second, the relationships in the LP analysis are assumed to be linear. On the other hand, many constraints in the LDCs are non-linear functions of the structural variables. However, here the problem is not insuperable as non-linear programming methods could be used. Finally, if the society attaches considerable weight to the growth objective and if the market price of labour is overestimated (because wages are artificially high despite the abundance of labour) and/or that of capital is underestimated (since the interest rate is kept low despite capital scarcity), then some necessary corrections ought to be made by using some 'accounting' prices for a more efficient allocation of resources. In practice, some such corrections are attempted using cost–benefit analysis (CBA) and this will be examined in the next section.

11.12 Micro-planning: aims of cost–benefit analysis

The reasons for undertaking *social* CBA can be stated at the outset. Whereas a private producer is generally interested in the maximization of private profit, a project evaluator of, say, a fertilizer plant, or of an underground railway system, would like to maximize the *social* net benefits of the project. The distinction between private profit and social benefit is usually made because of the presence of externalities. Thus while the firm producing cigarettes would only be interested in the pure economic gains, the project evaluator would have to know about the possible costs to society arising out of the danger of lung cancer. Further, while the private owner of the fertilizer plant would be interested in maximizing his private profit, the economist in charge of evaluating such projects for the public should also calculate the costs to society because of effluent discharges and water pollution. Thus the problem of choosing appropriate prices (or shadow prices) to reflect social gains or losses becomes important. Further, since the project may last for several years, it is necessary to discount the benefits and costs. Here again, while the commercial firm would be inclined to use the existing market interest rate (at which it can borrow) to discount the future benefits and costs, the project planner would have to choose a *social* rate of discount or opportunity cost of capital to the society as a whole. The task of the project planner is not easy as he will have to decide about the relative valuation of the *social* preference between consumption today or consumption at some future point in time. In short, 'The main reason for doing social cost–benefit analysis in project choice is to subject project choice to a consistent set of general objectives of national policy' (Sen *et al.* 1972: 11). In order to realize such an objective, the project planner tries to choose some 'shadow' prices (which could be different from market prices) which would be relevant for measuring net *social* benefits. Such a measurement is supposed to be more useful for taking decisions regarding project choice as it is not based upon some purely subjective judgements on which decisions could sometimes be made.

11.12.1 Some basic principles of cost–benefit analysis

Some of the basic principles of CBA are generally derived from welfare economics (for a general discussion see, for example, Dasgupta and Pearce 1972; Layard 1974; Mishan 1975). The objective is to choose the project which yields positive net *social* benefit (NSB) where NSB is defined as

$$\text{NSB} = \text{Benefits (willingness to pay)} - \text{Costs (compensation needed)}$$

All benefits and costs are expressed in monetary units. The *willingness* to pay is given by the area under the demand curve, but the actual total price paid is given by the price multiplied by the quantity. In other words, the amount of consumer surplus reflects the size of gains. Thus in Figure 11.2, although the consumers are willing to pay ODSM for quantity OM, they actually pay OPSM and hence the area DPS measures consumers' surplus. Now suppose that a cost-saving device is used in a project (e.g. time is saved because of the construction of a new highway), prices fall to OP_1 from OP, *ceteris paribus*, and an increase in the goods provided is shown by MM_1. Now the total willingness to pay is given by ODS_1M_1 which is greater than ODSM by MSS_1M_1 out of which MM_1S_1E accounts for actual payments and thus the change

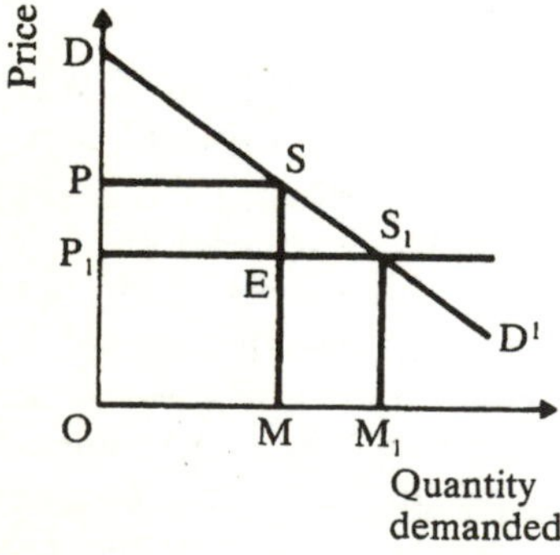

Figure 11.2

in consumer surplus is given by the shaded area ESS_1. This is equivalent to NSB for society. However, its actual estimation is beset with many problems. For example, the demand curve is assumed to be linear; marginal utility of income is supposed to remain fixed; utility is supposed to be measurable cardinally; the prices of all other goods are expected to remain unchanged; there are some intangibles which cannot be measured (e.g. scenic beauty). Hicks tried to tackle some of these problems by allowing changes in the marginal utility of income and by using the indifference curve analysis. Also, Kaldor and Hicks pointed out that to increase social welfare it is only necessary to show that the gainers should be able to compensate the losers and still remain gainers. But difficulties arise if these compensations are potential, rather than actual. Moreover, as Scitovsky points out, if the gainers can compensate the losers in accepting a change and the losers can 'bribe' the gainers back to the *status quo*, then a clear contradiction emerges as there is no way to tell whether social welfare has increased or decreased (Arrow and Scitovsky 1969). Critics of CBA further argue that market preferences shown in the demand curve are not equivalent to voting preferences; it is thus undemocratic. Since projects affect not only the present but also future generations, it is regarded as ethically immoral to pass judgement today on behalf of future generations (for details, see Dasgupta and Pearce 1972; Mishan 1975). Despite these criticisms, some of which are tackled in subsequent literature, CBA retains its appeal as an important analytical and rational framework for the formulation of public policies.

11.12.2 The decision rules in CBA

To take decisions regarding project choice, the project planner confronts the following sets of problems:

1 the problem of identification of the benefits and costs;
2 the problem of valuation of these benefits and costs at prices which would be relevant to society;
3 the problem of choosing an appropriate rate of discount for evaluating such benefits and costs;
4 the problem of identifying the actual constraints;
5 the problem of uncertainty.

After carefully solving these problems, the planner tries to find the net present value (NPV) discounted by a certain rate of discount, and if NPV > 0 then the project should be accepted. If the projects are mutually exclusive, then the one which yields the highest NPV should be accepted. Note that NPV means present discounted value of benefits less present discounted value of costs. More formally, if the net benefits are given by $P_1, P_2, \ldots$

$$\text{NPV} = \sum_{t=0}^{n} \frac{P_t}{(1+i)^t}$$

where i is the rate of discount. This could be a social rate of discount or the opportunity cost of capital or a synthesis of the two (see Marglin 1967). In practice, the choice is rather difficult. It is obvious that, the higher the rate of discount, the lower will be

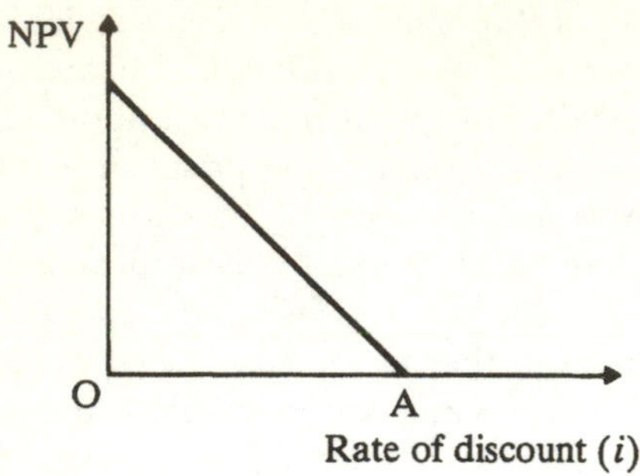

Figure 11.3

the NPV (see Figure 11.3) and at a certain rate of discount NPV = 0. Such a rate is called the internal rate of return (IRR) or OA in Figure 11.3.

More formally,

$$\sum_{t=1}^{n} \frac{P_t}{(1+\lambda)^t} = 0$$

where λ is the IRR. If $\lambda > i$, then the project should be accepted; if not, the project should be rejected.

In practice, the use of the NPV criterion rather than the IRR rule has gained preference (for an exception, see Mishan 1975) for a number of reasons. First, the IRR rule simply provides a rate greater than the size of total gains to the project planner. In many cases, it would be important to know the total size of gains rather than a single rate. Second, the use of the IRR rule can yield multiple roots without any unique solution. The number of roots will be given by the number of times the benefits change signs. For example, there are projects which could incur losses in the first year, yield benefits in the next two years and show losses again for the subsequent year followed by benefits in the next year; then we would find three values of λ. Third, IRR tends to favour short-life projects in comparison with those with longer lives. Fourth, projects which have long fruition lags or gestation periods will be discriminated against under the IRR rule. Similarly, projects which involve larger capital costs would be discriminated against under the IRR rule (for a reconciliation between the two, see the normalization criterion proposed by Mishan 1975).

After briefly explaining the major principles of CBA, the special reasons for undertaking CBA for LDCs in particular will be discussed in the next section.

11.12.3 Reasons for undertaking cost–benefit analysis in LDCs

Several reasons are given for undertaking CBA for LDCs to make a realistic estimate of the NSB (see Little and Mirrlees 1968, 1974).

1 *Inflation*. Inflation in many LDCs, emanating chiefly from the supply inelasticities, alters the relative prices and government's intervention in the form of price controls results in the distortion of NSB.

2 *Overvaluation of currency*. In most LDCs, exchange rates of the domestic currencies are kept artificially high. This again leads to an excess demand for foreign exchange, and when the government imposes import restrictions market prices of goods exceed their world price and such market prices tend to overestimate the NSB within the country.
3 *Wages and unemployment*. Given the imperfections of the labour market in LDCs, different modes of production (e.g. use of family labour rather than wage labour and the absence of a unique relationship between marginal productivity of labour and wages) and the presence of large-scale unemployment, it is argued that wages paid to labourers in LDCs tend to overestimate their true social opportunity costs. Hence a 'shadow' wage rate should be calculated to work out the true cost of labour to society.
4 *Capital market and interest rate*. Given the imperfections of the capital market in most LDCs, the interest rate is kept artificially low, particularly when capital is in very scarce supply. Here again, a 'shadow' rate of interest should be calculated to remove the underestimation of the cost of capital to society.
5 *Large projects*. Since large projects are likely to yield significant *secondary* benefits to the economy, it is not enough to count only the primary benefits of a project.
6 *Protection: tariffs, quotas, etc*. Since many LDCs have decided to industrialize their economies behind protectionist walls by using tariffs, quotas, exchange controls etc., market prices within the economy would fail to reflect the NSB.
7 *Saving deficiency and public income*. Given the dearth of savings in LDCs, the government can value an extra unit of saving more than the extra unit of consumption and impose appropriate taxes (which of course imposes some costs) to raise such savings. It is assumed that money at the disposal of the government of any country is worth more than private consumption because, while money in the hands of the government could be invested to produce future consumption, it would be wasteful if left in the hands of private individuals who have very high propensity to consume.
8 *Wealth distribution*. The problem of inequalities in the distribution of income and wealth is very much present in the LDCs. Such a problem would be lessened if public savings could substitute for private savings by the rich in LDCs.
9 *Externalities*. It is argued that whenever externalities are present (say, in the presence of diminishing costs in certain industries with a large investment project), such externalities should be fully taken into account in the project appraisal for LDCs.

11.13 The Little and Mirrlees method of project evaluation in less developed countries

Given the nature of distortions in the product and factor markets in LDCs, Little and Mirrlees (LM) have suggested a novel way to measure the costs and benefits of projects in LDCs. Fundamental to the understanding of the LM method for project appraisal are two points.

1 Foreign exchange, rather than domestic price, measures the true costs and benefits of commodities produced. Therefore, the net value of all the goods produced

should be converted into its foreign exchange equivalent, i.e. foreign exchange is used as the numéraire. As Little and Mirrlees say: 'It is present uncommitted social income measured in terms of convertible foreign exchange of constant purchasing power' (Little and Mirrlees 1974). In practice, the rate of conversion is equal to convertible foreign exchange at the official rate of exchange.

2 Since total saving is less than socially optimal in LDCs, one additional unit of investment is more valuable than an extra unit of consumption at the margin. Note that, on the basis of these principles, Little and Mirrlees have altered the usual procedure of revaluing foreign resources in terms of domestic ones; in contrast, they convert all domestic costs into 'border' prices. The choice of the numéraire and the nature of its measurement have enabled Little and Mirrlees to derive the special rate of discount which they have called the accounting rate of interest (ARI) and the cost of labour which they have tried to measure with the shadow wage rate (SWR).

The arguments for using the foreign exchange rate rather than market prices to evaluate net benefits are supposed to be as follows.

1 Every domestic demand and supply has a balance of payment effect.
2 The rate of free foreign exchange is the true yardstick of costs and benefits to society.
3 Foreign exchange is a reasonable unit of account.
4 Foreign exchange could be used to satisfy domestic demand and supply.

These reasons are not without criticisms. But before we state these criticisms, we will describe the actual methods of estimation as suggested by Little and Mirrlees.

11.13.1 LM methods of estimation

Let the income of the public project be given by Y, V the value added, c the consumption per worker and N the number of labourers employed in the project. Then we have

$$Y = V - cN \tag{11.45}$$

But Y is not the only benefit, as additional consumption would not be without any social value. Hence not all extra consumption should be regarded as a cost. Also there are externalities which should be included within the concept of benefits.

Additional consumption is accounted for by the excess of industrial wages over the marginal product of rural labour (m). If the industrial worker consumes all his wage and if c denotes the consumption of the labour employed in the new industrial project, then the total effect *in terms of consumption* for employing N labourers in a project would be $(c - m)N$. As mentioned before, the whole of this extra consumption should *not* be treated as a cost. Accordingly, it has to be evaluated in terms of public income or the numéraire. Here, Little and Mirrlees have argued in favour of weighting government income with reference to consumption arising out of new employment. This is the parameter s. Since LDCs are likely to suffer from a savings constraint, an extra unit of government income is regarded as more valuable than an extra unit of private consumption. Thus, £1 of current savings or investment is worth s (say £10) of present consumption. Hence, consumption has $1/s$ or one-tenth of the value had the same resources been saved and invested. In principle, s would depend upon the following factors:

1 social returns earned on marginal investment;
2 the time horizon within which savings are regarded as less than socially optimal;
3 the rate of decline of extra consumption over time or what Little and Mirrlees consider as the 'consumption rate of discount'. This is usually known as the social rate of discount.

Given the above concepts, NSB is given by the following:

$$\text{NSB} = (V - cN) + (c - m)\frac{N}{s} \tag{11.46}$$

Note that $V - cN$ is the net benefit which arises because of a rise in the government's income. Next, $(c - m)N/s$ shows the value of extra consumption measured in terms of income by the government. Alternatively, we have

$$\text{NSB} = V - \left[c - \frac{1}{s}(c - m)\right]N \tag{11.47}$$

and the shadow wage rate W is given by

$$W = c - \frac{1}{s}(c - m) \tag{11.48}$$

This is exactly the term in brackets in equation (11.47). Equation (11.48) could also be written as

$$W = m + (c - m)\left(1 - \frac{1}{s}\right) \tag{11.49}$$

It is clear that W is given by m (the marginal product of rural labour or the opportunity cost of labour measured in terms of additional output forgone) plus $c - m$ or the cost of providing extra consumption because of the employment of a new worker *net* of the *benefit* of such additional consumption given in terms of government income, i.e. $(c - m)1/s$. If there is no difference in the value of public income and private consumption, $s = 1$ and $W = m$ (check equation 11.49). If no value is attached to additional consumption, the value of s would be equal to infinity and the market wage would be equal to W.

11.13.2 The accounting rate of interest

The ARI or i is the rate at which the value of government income falls over time. In principle, it can be determined by the social rate of return on the marginal public investment (r), the fraction of it that is saved (λ) and s. In practice, r could be determined by the weighted average of 'social' rates of profit earned from present investments. The value of λ could be derived from the information on saving propensities and tax rates. The ARI can now be defined as

$$i = r[\lambda + (1 - \lambda)/s] \tag{11.50}$$

where

$$s = [1 + \tfrac{1}{2}(i - k)]^T \tag{11.51}$$

k is the social rate of discount, T is the time when savings and consumption are regarded as equally valuable,

$$k = (1 + v_t)^e - 1 \tag{11.52}$$

v_t is the *per capita* consumption growth rate and e is the elasticity of marginal social utility with respect to consumption, usually given by the ratio of income and price elasticity of demand.

Since the social rate of discount describes the social time preference between present and future consumption and since, in the growth process, future consumption is expected to be greater than at present leading to a decline in marginal utility of future consumption, we therefore require information on the consumption growth rate v_t and e as defined above (for the derivation of equation 11.52 see, for example, Dasgupta and Pearce 1972).

After substituting (11.50) into (11.51) we get

$$s = \left\{1 + \frac{1}{2}\left[r\left(\lambda + \frac{1-\lambda}{s}\right) - k\right]\right\}^T \tag{11.53}$$

Given the values of λ, r, k and T, s could be determined. Of these T is difficult to estimate and projections of income and savings growth rates are necessary to arrive at the most likely year when savings would be enough for achieving a sufficient long-run growth rate and that year will determine the value of T.

For the evaluation of output and input, Little and Mirrlees classify all the items as *traded* or *non-traded* goods. However, they acknowledge that there could be *partially traded goods*. According to Little and Mirrlees, *traded goods* are

1 goods which are actually imported or exported;
2 goods which would be exported or imported if the country had followed policies which resulted in *optimum industrial development* (author's italics).

Definition 2 would take account of tax and subsidy policies and hence departures from free trade policies to accommodate the external effects arising from domestic industries.

The non-traded goods are defined as those goods which would not enter world trade even if there was no tariff or quota, simply because of high costs of transport and lack of physical mobility (e.g. unskilled labour, transport, power, etc.).

The concept of 'partially traded goods' is introduced by Little and Mirrlees in the second edition of their manual (1974) and the definition is as follows:

> Only if domestic production (if there is any) and consumption are unaffected can one strictly say that the commodity is wholly traded; and similarly a good is wholly non-traded only if imports and exports (if any) are unaffected. All other commodities can be said to be partially traded.

The exact classification of any item depends very much upon the nature of the commodity concerned and the judgement of the project planner.

After classifying the different goods in different ways, all traded goods should be evaluated at their world (or 'border') prices. All exportables should be valued at f.o.b. prices; likewise, all importables should be valued at c.i.f. prices. All domestic (e.g. distribution and transport) costs should be converted into world prices. Here the fundamental principle of the LM analysis remains the same. In an open economy the actual value of a commodity produced in a public project is equal to the foreign exchange earned in the case of the exportables or foreign exchange saved in the case of the importables.

For evaluating non-traded goods, it is necessary to break down such items into their different components, i.e. traded items, other non-tradeables, unskilled labour. Since the aim is to evaluate the non-tradeables at their marginal social costs, these items should be split further into traded items and unskilled labour; finally, all tradeables should be valued at their 'border' prices while shadow wage rates should be used to calculate the costs of unskilled labour. In practice, difficulties may arise in the estimation procedures in the above-mentioned way. A standard conversion factor (SCF) can then be used to transform domestic costs of non-tradeables into their world prices where the SCF is the mean of the proportions by which home prices of all home-produced commodities are in excess of their world prices. However, excise taxes should be excluded from the domestic prices. Actually, the SCF is a rough guide to show the excess of domestic price over world price.

Several criticisms are made against the LM method.

1 The principle of using the world price as the shadow price is only valid in an economy which is open, fairly competitive in the context of world markets and not suffering from excess capacity. If, for example, a commodity has restricted access to the world market, then it would be improper to use world prices for its evaluation. Similarly, in the presence of excess capacity within the economy, a rise in demand for its product because of the setting up of a project is unlikely to influence the trade balance (Joshi, H. 1972). Little and Mirrlees here argue that it is very hard to predict the occurrence of excess capacity and hence it is reasonable to assume full capacity working.
2 The determination of world price is not easy, given the large number of heterogeneous goods, different forms of transactions, different supplies, bilateral agreements and the monopolistic structure of the market. Further, world prices may be influenced by the project's supply or demand of a commodity if less than perfect elasticities in the supply of and demand for the product are assumed away. Little and Mirrlees here advocate the use of marginal export revenue and marginal import cost. But in practice, such revenues and costs are not easy to estimate.
3 Little and Mirrlees have not paid much attention to the linkages and externalities because of the problems involved in the measurement of such external economies.

The LM assumption that public projects would affect trade only and not domestic economic activities is valid only when the linkages and externalities are completely assumed away – an assumption which to some would be regarded as very restrictive (see, for example, Stewart and Streeten 1972).

4 Little and Mirrlees have assumed that governments will follow 'sensible' or 'optimal' economic policies, but this would be incongruous with 'the assumption – and the fact – that governments lack the full powers assumed in classical welfare economies' (Little and Mirrlees 1972).
5 The problems of inequalities in income distribution are not highlighted in the LM analysis. This argument is not compelling as attempts have been made by Little and Mirrlees (1974) and others (Squire and Tak 1975) to deal with the problems of income distribution within the LM framework of analysis.
6 The evaluation of non-tradeables in terms of world prices poses both conceptual and practical difficulties. However, in the second edition of the manual (1974) Little and Mirrlees have recognized this difficulty and suggest the use of the 'willingness to pay' principle to evaluate social benefits.

In the light of some of these criticisms it is now possible to describe the alternative method of project appraisal which has been set out by UNIDO (Sen *et al.* 1972).

11.14 The United Nations Industrial Development Organization (1972) guidelines

The basic difference between the LM and UNIDO guidelines stem from the facts that, while Little and Mirrlees have tried to convert all benefits and costs to an index of government income, UNIDO translates all such benefits and costs to an index of present consumption. The difference in the choice of numéraire accounts for the divergences in the two methods in the estimations of discount rate, shadow wage rates and the social value of investment. Like Little and Mirrlees, UNIDO recognizes that in LDCs the social value of a marginal unit of consumption is *less* than that of a marginal unit of investment. But instead of converting all the consumption benefits into government income as in the LM procedure, UNIDO recommends the conversion of all investment into present consumption since the UNIDO report uses present consumption rather than public income as the numéraire. Thus UNIDO tries to find the NPV of all the consumption flows because of an additional unit of investment. The concept of the accounting price of investment (API) is introduced by UNIDO to imply the worth of the present value of the discounted consumption emanating from an additional unit of investment. Thus, there will be no difference between the social rate of discount and the opportunity cost of capital where API = 1, and at the margin present consumption will be as valuable as investment. There is no reason why the API cannot change over time with changes in the social productivity of investment, different weights given to consumption at different periods and different rates of reinvestment from profits.

The shadow wage rate W^* in the UNIDO procedure is defined in a way which is similar to the one observed in the LM procedure. Thus,

$$W^* = m + \alpha(\beta - 1)W$$

where m the marginal product of labour in rural areas, estimated in terms of consumption (i.e. the direct opportunity cost of labour), α is the marginal propensity to save from the income of the project and $\beta ==$ API (as defined above). Note that the second term on the right-hand side of the above equation is derived from the following relationship (see Sen *et al.* 1972: ch. 15 for details):

$$[(1-\alpha)-\beta\alpha]W - W = \alpha(\beta - 1)W$$

where $(1-\alpha)$ W is equal to the present fall in aggregate consumption and $\beta\alpha W$ shows the aggregate consumption value of the fall in investment. However, this loss would be offset by increased consumption of extra labour and therefore W is subtracted. It is possible to make adjustments for the problems of income distribution in W by choosing appropriate weights for the extra consumption of industrial labourers.

UNIDO uses the social rate of discount for calculating the NPV and this is different from the API used by Little and Mirrlees. Further, since UNIDO recognizes that the stated foreign exchange rates in many LDCs do not estimate the actual benefit to society, it derives 'shadow exchange rates' (SERs) given by the value to consumers of the commodities which one extra unit of foreign exchange makes available to them. Thus, if an additional unit of a domestic currency (pesos or rupees) buys foreign exchange (pounds or dollars) which will provide a commodity to the consumer whose domestic value (i.e. the price at which it is sold domestically) is equal to five pesos or rupees, then SER = 5. According to UNIDO, the SER is equal to the weighted average (where weights are the proportions in which foreign exchange is expected to be distributed at the margin to different types of imports) of the ratio of domestic prices at which markets are cleared and the world prices (c.i.f.) at the government-stated rates of foreign exchange. Unlike the LM method where the world price is used to revalue the domestic costs and benefits, in the UNIDO method the domestic currency is used to evaluate the costs and benefits of foreign resources by using the SER.

However, the use of the LM and UNIDO methods is likely to achieve the same result. In the LM analysis, given the lower level of shadow prices, production of non-tradeables would be disfavoured (although their domestic use would be favoured); similarly, the use of SER under UNIDO would promote exports or those projects which would save imports. In the estimation of SWR, the differences between the two approaches are also minimal. This can be easily shown. Let ϱ_t be equal to the shadow price of savings and let the total wage for unskilled labour be equal to W_t under the UNIDO principle. Under the LM rule this wage bill would be W_t/ϱ_t simply because $1/\varrho_t$ is the shadow price of consumption in terms of investment at period t (Dasgupta 1972).

In working out the NPV under the LM and UNIDO rules, a difference could arise for $\varrho > 1$ because of the choice of different numéraires in the two methods – present consumption under UNIDO and present investment under LM. However, as long as the decision rule is to accept the projects whose NPV > 0, the choice of different numéraires will not lead to a difference in the prediction of final results. But there could be a difference in the estimation of shadow prices as well as in the classification of the different outputs and inputs of the project. The scope of UNIDO is larger as it emphasizes the objectives rather than maximization of the sum of total consumption.

Also, it seeks to incorporate the importance of the principle of income distribution in project selection. However, in the second edition of the LM manual (1974), some principles have been discussed to adjust for differences in income distribution and Squire and Tak (1975) have tried to highlight the adjustment principles to account for changes in income distribution in project appraisal within the framework of LM analysis. It is necessary to point out that while UNIDO distinguishes between consumption and investment, Little and Mirrlees have distinguished between private and public funds. The latter is regarded as superior by Little and Mirrlees since public investment is considered as more valuable than private investment and a 'rational' government should try to equate the social value of public consumption and investment. Further, the SER as defined by UNIDO is regarded as a 'very slippery concept and treacherous parameter' (Lal 1974a). The formula for calculating the SER under UNIDO is as follows:

$$\text{SER} = \sum_{i=1}^{n} \text{fi}\frac{P_i^{\text{D}}}{P_{i\text{c}}} + \sum_{i=n+1}^{n+h} \text{xi}\frac{P_i^{\text{D}}}{P_{i\text{f}}}$$

where fi is 'the fraction of foreign exchange allocated to imports of the *i*th of *n* commodities at the margin', P_i^{D} is the domestic market clearing prices of imports and exports (inclusive of taxes and subsidies), xi is the 'rupee amount by which each of *h* exports falls in response to earnings of foreign exchange', $P_{i\text{c}}$ is world prices of imports and $P_{j\text{f}}$ is world prices of exports (see Lal 1974a; for details see also Sen *et al.* 1972).

It is argued that the proper values of the weights that should be attached to the ratio of domestic prices to world prices are not easy to define in principle and sometimes very hard to determine in practice. Also, it is not easy to classify the commodities over which the averaging should be carried out. Because of these difficulties, different SERs can be observed for the same country. Here the use of multiple conversion factors as recommended by the LM method can solve the problem of obtaining a unique SER. The use of the LM method is thus regarded as less difficult to apply; it is also supposed to yield more accurate estimates. Further, since many governments do not like the idea of working out the SER for their country, it is claimed that there are 'diplomatic advantages' in not finding out the SER for any LDC.

It may be argued that the use of SCF as prescribed by the LM method to evaluate the non-traded inputs in terms of world prices would raise the familiar problems of averaging over a large number of goods as well as the problems of using a system of proper weighting. Further, when the commercial policy of the government of any LDC renders the project output as a non-tradeable item, then the production of such a commodity would alter domestic supply. Here, the proper method to evaluate the social value of such a non-tradeable commodity would be to use the principle of willingness to pay as recommended by UNIDO. Also, it is worth remembering that the concept of a world price is not always very clear. The practical project planner should thus be guided by the realities of the situation before choosing one technique or the other.

The application of the two methods could lead to significant divergences in the ranking of projects because of the differences in the rules as to when the domestic or world price should be applied to evaluate the costs and benefits and also because of differences in the methods for translating domestic values and world prices into domestic currencies. In practice, the use of these two methods is unlikely to alter the ranking of projects substantially. Both approaches emphasize the need to use shadow prices to correct for market distortions. Both recognize the importance of savings and foreign exchange bottlenecks in the process of economic development. Both stress the need for using different weights to adjust for income distribution, given massive unemployment and poverty in LDCs.

11.15 Social accounting and development planning by Barbara M. Roberts

11.15.1 Social accounting matrices

The input–output technique focuses on intersectoral interdependence arising from the flow of intermediate goods among sectors. Issues such as income distribution and structural adjustment, vital for development planning, require analysis that goes beyond sectoral production to include income and expenditure flows. The circular flow of income between production, factors of production and institutions in the economy has to be adequately reflected. The production sphere generates demand for factor services. Factor incomes flow to domestic institutions and this leads on to the demand for products and hence back to the demand for output from the production sphere. The framework that captures full flow of income is provided by a social accounting matrix (SAM). A SAM is a generally approved tool of development planning and Pyatt and Round (1985) present the methodology as well as review numerous applications.

A SAM is a square matrix with the rows and columns representing the income and expenditure accounts of various economic agents. The convention is that entries are to be interpreted as receipts for the row account in which they are located and outlays for their column accounts. The row and column sums for a given account must be equal because all income must be accounted for by a total outlay. Data to fill in the SAM come from the input–output tables, national income statistics and household income and expenditure statistics.

A representative SAM in aggregated form is given in Table 11.1. There are accounts for production (activities and commodities), factors of production, domestic institutions (enterprises, households, government), saving–investment operations (capital account) and transactions with the rest of the world. The activities column represents the cost of production, including the purchase of intermediate inputs, factor payments and indirect taxes. The activities row shows how total production is divided between domestic sales and exports. The commodity account represents the domestic product market, where demand comes from domestic purchasers, as can be seen from the commodity row. Total supply is given by goods supplied by the domestic activities and those imported from the rest of the world. The factors account shows the allocation of factor payments to domestic institutions. Households' factor income is supplemented by distributed profits and transfers. This income is later divided between consumption, taxes and savings. The allocation of the total income of enterprises (gross profits and transfers from government) is shown in the enterprise column. Government income is derived from taxes and tariffs and is spent on government consumption, transfers and savings. Capital account combines savings of domestic institutions and net capital inflow to give total savings for financing investment. The

Table 11.1 A representative social accounting matrix

	Production			*Institutions*					
	1	*2*	*3*	*4*	*5*	*6*	*7*	*8*	*9*
	Activities	*Commodities*	*Factors*	*Enterprises*	*Households*	*Government*	*Capital account*	*Rest of world*	*Total*
1 Activities		Domestic sales						Exports	Total sales
2 Commodities	Intermediate demand				Household consumption	Government consumption	Investment		Total demand
3 Factors	Factor payments								Value added
4 Enterprises			Gross profits			Transfers			Enterprise income
5 Households			Wages	Distributed profits		Transfers		Transfers from abroad	Household income
6 Government	Indirect taxes	Tariffs	Factor taxes	Enterprise taxes	Direct taxes				Government receipts
7 Capital account				Retained earnings	Household savings	Government savings		Net capital inflow	Total savings
8 Rest of world		Imports							Imports
9 Total	Total payments	Total supply	Value added	Enterprise expenditure	Household expenditure	Government expenditure	Total investment	Foreign exchange	

transactions between the domestic economy and the rest of the world are given in the last row and column of the SAM.

The general framework in Table 11.1 makes it possible to cover a wide range of problems, provided that various accounts have been disaggregated to a satisfactory level. Usually, activities accounts are disaggregated in the same way as the input–output tables. For the study of income distribution, additional disaggregation of the household sector and factor accounts is necessary. On the other hand, if the focus is on tax incidence, it would be important to provide details of the tax flows by creating additional accounts for different types of taxes.

11.15.2 Social accounting multipliers

The uses of a SAM fall into two categories. A SAM can provide a framework for the organization of information about the economic and social structure of a country. The second broad category of uses includes applications where a SAM serves as a database for a model of the economy under consideration. Multiplier analysis will be considered here as a modelling application of SAMs.

Keynesian multipliers show how exogenous changes affect the economy. They have their sectoral counterparts in the input–output multipliers, whereby an endogenous vector of sectoral production can be predicted from a matrix of input–output coefficients and a vector of exogenous final demand, using the Leontief inverse matrix $(I - A)^{-1}$. Similarly, it is possible to trace the economy-wide impact of exogenous changes within a SAM.

To move from a social accounting matrix to a multiplier model requires that each account should be designated as endogenous or exogenous. Usually it is assumed that the accounts for production, factors, households and enterprises are endogenous. The accounts for government, investment and transactions with the rest of the world are considered exogenous. Table 11.2 shows an aggregated SAM for multiplier analysis. Injections include transfers to households and enterprises (from government and from abroad) as well as the demands placed on production through government consumption, investment and exports. Direct and indirect taxes, savings, imports and income transfers abroad constitute the leakages. For practical applications, endogenous accounts have to be disaggregated far more than the classification in Table 11.2 suggests.

Following the approach of input–output models the relationship between endogenous and exogenous accounts can be derived. First, all the expenditure coefficients in the columns of a SAM are assumed to be constant. Then each entry in the endogenous partition of the SAM is divided by the corresponding column total to give the matrix of average propensities to consume, S. The income (and expenditure) of the endogenous accounts y can be expressed in terms of the coefficients of matrix S and exogenous accounts x:

$$y - Sy + x = (I - S)^{-1}x = M_a x$$

where y is a vector of incomes of endogenous accounts, S is the matrix of average propensities to consume, x is a vector of incomes of exogenous accounts, I is the identity matrix, $(I - S)^{-1}$ is the inverse of matrix $(I - S)$ and $M_a = (I - S)^{-1}$ is the social accounting multiplier.

Table 11.2 Aggregated social accounting matrix for multiplier analysis

	Production	*Factors*	*Institutions*	*Exogenous accounts*
Production	Intermediate consumption		Institutions' consumption	↑
Factors	Value-added payments			Injections from exogenous accounts
Institutions		Factor income	Transactions between institutions	↓
Exogenous accounts	← Leakages from endogenous accounts →			Transactions between exogenous accounts

A simple example explains how to calculate social accounting multipliers and interpret the results. Let us assume that the SAM in Table 11.3 represents an imaginary economy. Using the notation introduced above, the social accounting multipliers can be calculated in the following steps:

$$S = \begin{vmatrix} 0.45 & 0.00 & 0.70 \\ 0.40 & 0.00 & 0.00 \\ 0.00 & 0.95 & 0.14 \end{vmatrix}$$

$$I - S = \begin{vmatrix} 0.55 & 0.00 & -0.70 \\ -0.40 & 1.00 & 0.00 \\ 0.00 & -0.95 & 0.86 \end{vmatrix}$$

The inverse of $(I - S)$ gives the multiplier matrix M_a:

$$(I - S)^{-1} = M_a = \begin{vmatrix} 4.15 & 3.21 & 3.28 \\ 1.66 & 2.29 & 1.35 \\ 1.84 & 2.52 & 2.66 \end{vmatrix}$$

Table 11.3 SAM for an imaginary economy

	Production	*Factors*	*Institution*	*Exogenous accounts*	*Total*
Production	45		35	20	100
Factors	40				40
Institutions		38	7	5	50
Exogenous accounts	15	2	8	7	32
Total	100	40	50	32	

Matrix M_a measures the income accruing to endogenous accounts as a result of a unit injection. For example, an exogenous increase in the demand for goods generates a 4.15 unit increase in the production sphere. The impact on other endogenous accounts is much weaker and expansion in production leads to increases in the incomes of factors and institutions by 1.66 and 1.84 units respectively. Other entries can be interpreted in a similar fashion. Thus, factor income increases by 1.35 units as a result of an injection into the institutions account.

Social accounting multipliers, like input–output models, are based on fixed coefficients and do not allow for any substitution. The multiplier models are demand driven and do not incorporate any supply constraints. For this reason they are Keynesian in spirit. Moreover, they correspond to a fixed-price response to an exogenous change. In order to capture substitution possibilities in supply and demand as well as price adjustments, a computable general equilibrium (CGE) framework is needed. CGE models have been used in development planning (Dervis *et al.* 1982) but their introduction is beyond the scope of this text.

Appendix 11.1 The Feldman–Mahalanobis model

The basic Feldman–Mahalanobis (FM) model can be described easily. Assume that the economy consists of two sectors (1 and 2) and a proportion λ of the current output of capital goods is allocated to sector 1 and the remainder to sector 2. Let Q_1 be the total output of capital goods and Q_2 the total output of consumption goods. Let K_1 and K_2 be the quantities of capital goods allocated to sectors 1 and 2 respectively. Let V_1 and V_2 be the capital coefficients. Labour is not regarded as a constraint on economic growth. With fixed technologies we have

$$Q_1 = \frac{K_1}{V_1} \quad Q_2 = \frac{K_2}{V_2} \quad Q = Q_1 + Q_2 \tag{A11.1.1}$$

With no depreciation the rate of change of the capital stock K is equal to total investment I. This implies

$$I = Q_1 = \frac{K_1}{V_1} \tag{A11.1.2}$$

or

$$\dot{I} = \dot{Q}_1 = \frac{1}{V_1}\dot{K}_1 \tag{A11.1.3}$$

The above equation gives us the rate of change in total investment.

Since the rate of change in capital stock is given by the proportion of the total output of investment goods allocated to sector 1, we can write

$$\dot{K}_1 = I_1 = \lambda I \tag{A11.1.4}$$

If we substitute (A11.1.4) into (A11.1.3), we get

$$\dot{I} = \frac{1}{V_1}\lambda I \tag{A11.1.5}$$

Hence,

$$\frac{\dot{I}}{I} = \frac{\lambda}{V_1} \tag{A11.1.6}$$

Equation (A11.1.6) shows clearly that a rise in the proportion of current investment goods allocated to the production of more investment goods, i.e. λ, will raise the growth rate of total investment. We would obtain the same result via a reduction of V_1 (i.e. a fall in the capital–output ratio). However, in the FM model V_1 is fixed.

We can also demonstrate that the rate of growth of consumption $\dot{C}/C$ will depend positively upon the growth rate of investment. By definition

$$C = Q_2$$

and

$$Q_2 = \frac{K_2}{V_2} \tag{A11.1.7}$$

Hence

$$\dot{C} = \dot{Q}_2 = \frac{1}{V_2}\dot{K}_2 \tag{A11.1.8}$$

Since

$$\dot{K}_2 = I_2 = (1 - \lambda)I \tag{A11.1.9}$$

we obtain the following by substitution:

$$\dot{C} = \frac{1 - \lambda}{V_2} I \tag{A11.1.10}$$

Dividing (A11.1.10) by C, we get the growth rate of consumption, i.e.

$$\frac{\dot{C}}{C} = \frac{1 - \lambda}{V_2}\frac{I}{C} \tag{A11.1.11}$$

It is clear from equation (A11.1.11) that the rate of growth of consumption is positively related to I. But the growth rates of C and I will not be equal. Domar has shown that $\dot{C}/C$ rises with time and its long-run growth rate is given by λ/V_1. It has also been shown in the Feldman model that the growth rate of national income ($\dot{Q}$) will *not* be equal to the growth of total investment. Like consumption growth rate, it will tend to be equal to λ/V_1 in the long run. (For a lucid numerical analysis, see Jones 1975; see also the table, p. 20 in the same reference. In the table, we can see how the theory, i.e. 'steel to produce steel to produce steel' works rather well with a higher value for λ to raise the growth rate of *consumption goods* after the fourteenth year of planning.)

Note the similarity between the FM type model and the Harrodian model in the long run, If the economy follows the balanced growth path $\lambda = K_1/K$. We know that

$$\frac{K_1}{K} = \frac{V_1 Y_1}{V_1 Y_1 + V_2 Y_2} = \frac{V_1 I}{V_1 Y_1 + V_2 Y_2} \tag{A11.1.12}$$

In Harrod, $V_1 = V_2 = V$. Therefore

$$\lambda = \frac{VI}{V(Y_1 + Y_2)} = \frac{VI}{VY} = \frac{I}{Y} = \frac{S}{Y} = s \qquad \text{(A11.1.13)}$$

Since $\lambda = s$, the FM growth rate

$$\frac{\lambda}{V_1} = \frac{s}{V} \qquad \text{(A11.1.14)}$$

The Mahalanobis model

Assume a one-period lag between investment and resultant capacity creation and let K_t^{u} and C_t^{u} denote the capacity of production in time t in the capital and consumer goods industries respectively. Let β_{k} and β_{c} stand for incremental capacity–capital ratio. Then we have

$$K_t^{\mathrm{u}} = K_{t-1}^{\mathrm{u}} + K_{t-1}\lambda_{\mathrm{k}}\beta k \qquad \text{(A11.1.15)}$$

$$C_t^{\mathrm{u}} = C_{t-1}^{\mathrm{u}} + C_{t-1}\lambda_{\mathrm{c}}\beta c \qquad \text{(A11.1.16)}$$

In a closed economy with full capacity utilization in the capital goods sector, whatever is produced will be absorbed in capital formation. Thus, the capacity to produce capital goods should be equal to domestic capital formation. Hence, we have

$$K_t^{\mathrm{u}} = K_t \qquad \text{(A11.1.17)}$$

Then from (A11.1.15)

$$K_t = K_{t-1} + K_{t-1}\lambda_{\mathrm{k}}\beta_{\mathrm{k}} \qquad \text{(A11.1.18)}$$

or

$$K_t = K_{t-1}(1 + \lambda_{\mathrm{k}}\beta_{\mathrm{k}})$$

This difference equation has the following solution:

$$K_t = K_0(1 + \lambda_{\mathrm{k}}\beta_{\mathrm{k}})^t \qquad \text{(A11.1.19)}$$

Substituting equation (A11.1.19) into (A11.1.16) yields

$$C_t^{\mathrm{u}} = C_{t-1}^{\mathrm{u}} + K_0\lambda_{\mathrm{c}}\beta_{\mathrm{c}}(1 + \lambda_{\mathrm{k}}\beta_{\mathrm{k}})^t - 1 \qquad \text{(A11.1.20)}$$

The solution for equation (A11.1.20) is

$$C^{\mathrm{u}} = C^{\mathrm{u}} + K\lambda\beta\frac{(1 + \lambda_{\mathrm{k}}\beta_{\mathrm{k}})^t - 1}{\lambda_{\mathrm{k}}\beta_{\mathrm{k}}} \qquad \text{(A11.1.21)}$$

Since

$$Y_t^{\mathrm{u}} = C_t^{\mathrm{u}} + K_t^{\mathrm{u}}$$

we add equation (A11.1.19) to equation (A11.1.21) to obtain

$$Y^{\mathrm{u}} = Y^{\mathrm{u}} + K\frac{\lambda_{\mathrm{k}}\beta_{\mathrm{k}} + \lambda_{\mathrm{c}}\beta_{\mathrm{c}}}{\lambda_{\mathrm{k}}\beta_{\mathrm{k}}}[(1+\lambda\beta)^t - 1] \tag{A11.1.22}$$

Assuming full capacity output for the whole economy and $_0$ as the rate of investment in the base period, we get

$$Y_t = Y_0\left\{1 + \alpha_0\frac{\lambda_{\mathrm{k}}\beta_{\mathrm{k}} + \lambda_{\mathrm{c}}\beta_{\mathrm{c}}}{\lambda_{\mathrm{k}}\beta_{\mathrm{k}}}[(1+\lambda\beta)^t - 1\right\} \tag{A11.1.23}$$

Note

1 Since $s = 1 - m$, $v = mv_1 + (1-m)v_2$ and $g = s/v$.

Questions

1 Discuss the case for and against planning in developing countries.
2 Show the use and abuse of the Harrod–Domar model as an instrument of planning in LDCs.
3 Explain the major features of the Feldman–Mahalanobis model of planning. What are its limitations?
4 What are the major ingredients of macroeconomic models in development planning?
5 Discuss the role played by input-output analysis in development planning.
6 What are the main reasons for undertaking cost–benefit analysis in LDCs?
7 Discuss the Little and Mirrlees method of project evaluation in LDCs and compare it with the UNIDO method.
8 Discuss the use of social accounting method (SAM) in project planning in LDCs.

12 Structural adjustment and development

12.1 Structural adjustment and economic growth

Many LDCs in the last two decades – particularly in Latin America, Africa and some parts of Asia – experienced serious macroeconomic instability. Such instability comprised:

1 huge public sector deficit (i.e. savings gap) as a percentage of GDP;
2 large and chronic balance of payments deficit sometimes bordering on insolvency (foreign exchange gap);
3 accumulation of huge and non-sustainable external debt;
4 high inflation and currency overvaluation.

Faced with such problems, many debtor countries had to deal with the International Monetary Fund (IMF) and the World Bank (WB) to seek new loans and to extend the loan repayment period for principal and interest. Some LDCs had to renegotiate loans with private international banks and financial agencies to cover a domestic budget or external balance of payments deficit. In response, the IMF/WB strongly advocated their 'conditionality' clauses, i.e. structural adjustment and stabilization policies (SAS) before they first agreed to advance further loans to countries suffering from serious macroeconomic instability. The SAS policies required countries to adopt appropriate monetary, fiscal and trade policies to reduce internal (fiscal) and external (balance of payments) deficit and bring down the rate of inflation from a high level. The overall objective was to promote economic growth by pursuing prudent microeconomic reform policies to improve economic efficiency and productive capacity. Policies are also designed to promote enough flexibility in the economic systems of LDCs to absorb the adverse impact of any negative shocks (Agenor 2001). At the same time, some macroeconomic stabilization policies like reduction of public sector deficit and money supply are supposed to bring down the rate of inflation and increase the competitiveness of the economy. In the next section, we discuss the different types of SAS policies generally recommended by the IMF and the WB.

12.2 The structural adjustment and stabilization policies of the IMF

IMF SAS programmes generally seek to address serious balance of payments problems whilst retaining price stability, stability of public sector deficit and encouraging the resumption of economic growth. The main planks of typical IMF-sponsored SAS policies are as follows:

1 economic liberalization of the economy via the reduction or elimination of controls, privatization of public sector assets, deregulation and promotion of competition to promote efficiency and economic growth;
2 monetary contraction – restrictions on credit to the public sector and increases in real interest rates (i.e. nominal interest rates the rate of inflation) and reserve requirements to end a state of 'financial repression', reward savers and reduce the rate of inflation.
3 fiscal contraction, which implies a reduction of public sector deficit through cuts in public expenditure/rises in taxation. The overall aim of fiscal stability is to pursue sustainable economic growth by enhancing the credibility and reputation of government policy. However, control of government deficit implies a massive cut in social services for the poor and staple food subsidies;
4 trade liberalization via the dismantling of tariff barriers, quotas, reduction of distortions in exchange rates and other forms of trade controls. Devaluation of the exchange rate has often been a precondition for the serious negotiation of a SAS programme, rather than a part of the programme as such.
5 incomes policy – wage restraint and removal of subsidies and reduction of transfer payments.
6 a general opening up of the economy to international finance to promote globalization, which is supposed to benefit LDCs via a freer flow of goods, capital, labour, knowledge and organization.

12.2.1 The SAS programme: theory

Most of the policies involved in the IMF stabilization programmes have been of a deflationary nature. Given the fact that the IMF is mainly concerned with high inflation prompted by huge excess demand within the country, the rationale of the policies is easy to understand. Using Figure 12.1, we can see that the impact of the deflationary measures would lead to the shift of the aggregate demand (AD) curve from AD_1 to AD_2, thus reducing the price level from p_1 to p_2 but also reducing output from q_2 to q_1. Thus the debtor country may be made more competitive in its exports and import-substitute sectors, benefiting its balance of payments and reducing its debt, but at the cost of lost output and employment. This phenomenon is also known as the 'contractionary' impact of SAS policies.

Sometimes, the main effect of the SAS policies has been to decrease the labour share in income distribution. A wage freeze has often been involved, reducing the real value of all income from labour, especially of those employed in the public sector where a wage freeze can be applied most effectively. Stabilization has often been found to be associated with a decline in public sector employment. To some extent, this has been due to very low efficiency as evidenced by the low labour productivity in the public sector in many LDCs.

Cuts in public expenditure to reduce public sector deficit have been an important part of many SAS programmes, such as health and education, with disproportionate effects on the poor. Stabilization has had different effects on the urban and the rural poor. Most of the World Bank's structural adjustment and lending (SAL) projects have sought to improve the supply side of the economy. This results in the downward shift of the aggregate supply (AS) curve from AS_1 to AS_2, thus reducing the price level

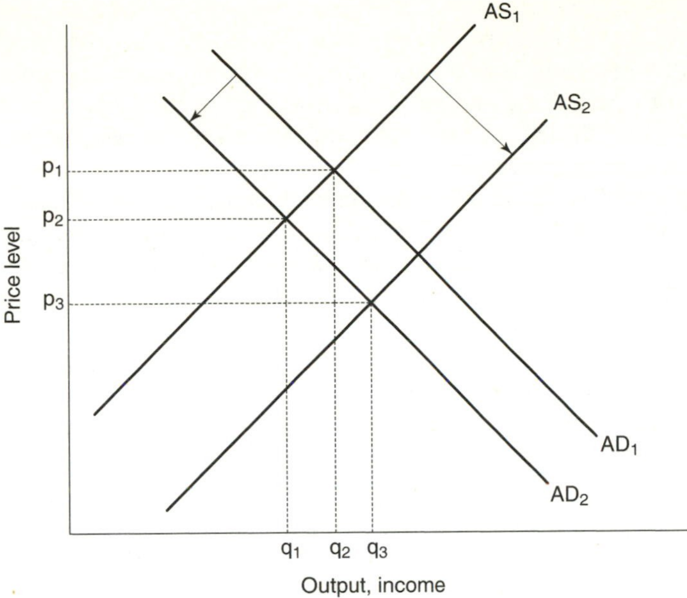

Figure 12.1 Stabilization and structural adjustment

from p_2 to p_3 and raising output from q_2 to q_3. Clearly, the medicine via SAS programmes is more acceptable when output and employment rise but only after difficult changes in labour and capital market practices.

12.3 Trade adjustment

It is well known that international trade allows each economy to use its resources most efficiently, concentrating on the activities it is best suited to pursue, and reap significant economies of scale. Thus, trade raises the real income of each country. Further, improvements in technology developed in one country are shared with other countries.

By affecting the allocation of domestic resources, trade affects the distribution of domestic income. A change in the level or composition of a country's trade can require a reallocation of resources and thus redistribution of income. International trade creates strong links between national economies. An increase in one country's income will raise its demand for imports This will raise other countries' exports and thus raise their incomes via the operation of the foreign trade multiplier.

Classical economists (e.g. Ricardo) measured gains from trade by the increase in efficiency that could be achieved by concentrating on the activities in which an economy had a competitive advantage. They also urged the state to abstain completely from regulating trade.

Modern economists who advocate SAS measures pay more attention to the role of government. Trade and other international transactions are influenced by many economic policies, including those adopted for domestic reasons. Similarly, international transactions impinge on the conduct of domestic policies. Furthermore, the tasks of domestic policies are complicated by international disturbances – by changes in incomes, prices and interest rates in other countries (Kenen 2000).

According to Ricardo, differences in prices between countries are the basic cause of trade. Prices reflect differences in costs of production. Therefore, free trade serves to minimize the real value of production by allocating worldwide resources most efficiently. Trade does so by permitting and inducing producers in each trading country to concentrate on adopting those economic activities that make the best use of their country's physical and human resources.

Hence, trade must reflect systematic international differences in the structures of costs and prices. This proposition is known as the *law of comparative advantage*. The Ricardian law states that in a world of competitive markets, trade will occur and will be beneficial whenever there are international differences in relative costs of production.

However, the Heckscher and Ohlin (H–O) theorem assumes that all countries have the same technologies. The approach of H–O in trade theory, which is also known as the factor-endowments approach, is based on two suppositions (see any good textbook, e.g. Krugman and Obstfeld 2002):

1 Goods differ in their factor requirements. Some products require more capital per worker than other products. Hence, goods can be ranked by factor intensity.
2 Countries differ in their factor endowments. Some have much capital per worker and others have little. Therefore, countries can be ranked by factor abundance. Building on these two suppositions, a country with abundant capital will tend to specialize in capital-intensive goods (e.g. the United States) and will therefore export those goods in exchange for labour-intensive goods. By so doing, it relieves the scarcity of labour. Likewise, the labour-abundant country always exports the labour-intensive goods (e.g. India), and relieves the scarcity of capital. Thus, trade is based on differences in factor abundance and reduces the principal effects of these differences.

12.4 Structural adjustment, stabilization and trade policies

In the presence of trade, structural adjustment in the domestic economy requires appropriate economic policies. Most approaches to economic policy follow Meade in seeing the twin objectives of economic policy as being internal and external balances.

As regards exchange rate policy, in the short run it is possible to cover any foreign exchange shortfall by running down foreign exchange reserves. But in the longer run, there were believed to be three broad approaches for assuring external balance. First, policy makers might adopt quantitative restrictions (quotas, import licensing etc.) to reduce actual imports to a level consistent with available foreign exchange. Second, policy makers could tighten monetary and fiscal policy to reduce demand for imports and increase the supply of exports, thus restoring external balance. Third, policy makers could change the nominal/real exchange rate, thus reducing imports and making exports more profitable.

It is argued that monetary and fiscal policy should be used to achieve internal balance, while the exchange rate could float in order to achieve external balance. If the current account is in surplus and domestic demand is 'too low', monetary and fiscal policy could be relaxed and move the economy towards both internal and external balance. Likewise, with inflationary pressures and a current account deficit, restrictive monetary and fiscal policies could serve to move towards both targets. Sometimes, there is an inadequate level of domestic demand and current account deficits, or excess domestic demand and current account surplus. In these situations, monetary and/or fiscal policy alone could achieve only one target. The case for flexible exchange rates rested on the proposition that monetary and fiscal policy should (or would) be geared towards internal balance, leaving the exchange rate as the policy instrument for external balance.

In most LDCs, policy makers believed they had three objectives: internal balance, external balance, and economic growth. In most cases, LDCs had fixed their nominal exchange rates during the 1960s. However, they were experiencing inflation while world prices were constant, and simultaneously, greatly increasing demand for internationally traded goods as efforts were made to raise investment levels, levels which had a relatively high import content. With appreciating real exchange rates, and high protection through tariffs and import restrictions pulling resources into import-competing activities, export earnings failed to grow rapidly. Both these factors contributed to a growing excess demand for foreign exchange at fixed nominal exchange rates.

Therefore, there were three policy choices: (1) the exchange rate could be altered; (2) domestic macroeconomic policy instruments could be adjusted to levels designed to eliminate excess demand for foreign exchange; or (3) quantitative restrictions (QRs) on imports could be adopted. With rising inflation and falling foreign exchange reserves, policy makers in most LDCs rejected the devaluation alternative. Likewise, restrictive monetary and fiscal policy could only result in recession and because of policy makers' determination that development plans should not be cut back, the second alternative was also ruled out.

That left QRs on imports as the only way to manage external accounts. Since it was, at that time, widely believed that import substitution would in any event be desirable as the means to achieve industrialization (rationalized by the infant industry argument) and rapid growth, there was little resistance to QRs (Krueger 1997).

However, throughout the 1950s and 1960s, evidence mounted of the high costs of closed economies, import licensing and the necessary accompanying exchange controls (see Chapter 7). It was acknowledged that those costs could be avoided *only* with a floating exchange rate or an exchange rate regime that kept the real exchange rate at realistic levels for a sustainable current account position. Many LDCs continued to maintain a fixed exchange rate system, and hence found their currencies increasingly overvalued with respect to exports and imports.

A 'stop–go' pattern of growth gradually became recognizable in many LDCs. As import demand exceeded export supply growth, authorities at first restricted 'unnecessary'/'luxury' imports, tightened (and delayed) import licensing, and otherwise attempted to restrict the quantity of imports. Over time, however, the restrictive effect on economic activity caused by the lack of spare parts, raw materials and capital goods imports mounted (see Bhagwati 1978). But countries would eventually encounter a severe balance of payments crisis. Thus, their policy makers would approach the IMF and agree on a stabilization programme under which the exchange rate would be devalued, credit and other ceilings could be imposed to bring down the rate of inflation and a structural adjustment and stabilization programme (SASP) would begin.

Following the implementation of the SASP, it has been observed, in many LDCs the rate of growth of output would slow markedly or, in some cases, be followed by a recession and a drop in output. Government investment plans would be cut back, and private domestic spending would drop. In response to the slowdown in domestic economic activity and to the restrictive effects of the monetary and fiscal contraction associated with devaluation, exports would increase while imports would fall. Hence, the early response to devaluation would be an improvement in the trade balance. Policy makers would therefore begin increasing public investment and expenditure, and the growth of output would resume or accelerate.

As that happened, imports would increase more rapidly, while increased domestic demand could reduce export growth. As inflation picked up, appreciation of the real exchange rate would also affect exports, imports and the current account balance. Foreign exchange reserves would once again be run down. Countries would attempt to persuade donors to increase foreign aid and delay issuing foreign exchange to domestic importers. But as the costs of the 'foreign exchange shortage' mounted, the strength of the import licensing regime failed to keep pace with flagging export receipts. In addition, importers would attempt to 'speculate' against devaluation, despite capital controls, by trying to delay payments on imports and build inventories, while would-be exporters delay exporting and try to keep their foreign exchange receipts abroad. Ultimately, another 'foreign exchange crisis' would ensue, and the stop–go pattern would repeat itself.

Though there are obvious differences between developing countries, this sequence took place in many of them. Almost invariably, pressure to go to the IMF became irresistible when countries' foreign exchange obligations exceeded their ability to pay, and restrictions on imports resulting from 'foreign exchange shortage' were seen to be sufficiently harmful to the growth and development objective.

The East Asian 'tigers' – Hong Kong, Singapore, South Korea and Taiwan – shifted away from the inner-oriented trade strategies, and began focusing on export-led growth. To achieve this, they rapidly found that a realistic exchange rate was an essential prerequisite to an outer-oriented trade strategy. Evidence tends to suggest that an outward-looking, export-oriented policy had a positive effect on the economic growth rates of the East Asian 'tiger' economies, including Malaysia and Singapore plus Turkey (Ghatak *et al.* 1995, 1997).

While the negative experience with QRs did not substantially alter views regarding the desirability of import substitution in developing countries, the success of the East Asian 'tigers' began raising questions about the overall desirability of an inner-oriented trade strategy. As policy makers became convinced that they could achieve more under a less restrictive trade and payments regime, more and more countries began changing their exchange rates and their exchange rate regimes, in an effort to open their economies (Krueger 1999).

12.5 Exchange rate and trade reforms

With the oil price increases of the 1970s and the lessons of QR regimes learned, exchange rates were increasingly seen as the policy instrument used to provide incentives for exporting. With the debt crisis of the early 1980s this trend accelerated. In some instances QRs were removed and tariffs reduced in an effort to switch to an

Table 12.1 Real effective exchange rate indices for some LDCs, 1985–97 (1990 = 100)

Year	*Argentina*	*Chile*	*Malaysia*	*Mexico*	*Thailand*
1985	121.78	129.13	154.43	126.50	121.28
1986	104.48	111.28	126.36	90.17	103.09
1987	92.58	105.78	188.74	92.92	96.88
1988	103.27	98.64	106.06	112.30	97.40
1989	87.97	101.88	103.48	107.57	100.37
1990	100.01	100.00	100.00	100.00	99.99
1991	115.43	106.10	98.79	106.16	102.33
1992	113.41	113.80	106.42	107.74	98.67
1993	114.94	113.86	109.51	116.58	100.13
1994	111.40	113.93	106.30	112.19	99.44
1995	108.86	120.22	106.10	78.88	97.71
1996	112.76	126.38	110.98	89.77	105.33
1997	120.29	134.80	108.26	102.67	96.59

Source: Krueger (1999), table 6.3, p. 84.

outer-oriented trade regime. In other instances, the exchange rate became more realistic, although protection and import substitution policies still prevailed.

In the early 1980s, most Asia–Pacific countries were still on a fixed exchange rate system, with the occasional devaluations. As the 1980s progressed, more and more LDCs switched to a regime in which their exchange rates were adjusted more frequently or were permitted to float freely. But frequent adjustment does not imply constancy of the real exchange rate (see Table 12.1). But the underlying fact remains: many LDCs had realized the problems of an increasingly overvalued real exchange rate between nominal devaluations, and had adopted exchange rate regimes which permitted less abrupt changes in the time path of the real exchange rate.

Exchange rate adjustment is considered a central feature of the stabilization and SASP which a large number of developing countries were urged to adopt during the 1980s and 1990s. Evidence suggests that the exchange rate policies followed by developing countries in the 1970s and early 1980s contributed significantly to the build-up of unmanageable foreign debt burdens, contributing to the global debt crisis. Poor exchange rate policies have been identified as a major cause of the dramatic deterioration in the economies of sub-Saharan Africa, particularly the collapse of agricultural production and exports, and the region's chronic and increasing dependence on imports, even of food. Devaluation, and indeed overall adjustment efforts, have generally worked better and more quickly in developing countries which are relatively more advanced, i.e. generally those which have a diversified modern industrial sector which is export-oriented or can easily switch from imported to domestic intermediates in the production process. Supply responses to exchange rate adjustment measures have been much slower in the least developed economies, where linkages between price signals and output response have been weak. These realities have supported the view in many low-income developing countries, particularly in Africa, that devaluation is not particularly effective in addressing the special problems they face (Ajayi 1994).

Prices of imports measured in domestic currency are expected to increase as a result of devaluation. The market prices of imported products will have risen relative to those of home-produced products. If there is any possibility of substitution between home products and imported products, purchasers in the importing country will shift their demand from imported products to home-produced products. This will cause an improvement in the balance of trade of the importing country. Such an improvement in trade balance clearly needs the fulfilment of the Marshall–Lerner condition, i.e the sum of the elasticities of the demand for imports and exports must be greater than 1. However, if the elasticity of demand for a country's exports is less than unity, the decline in its export prices may reduce the total amount which purchasers in the other countries will spend on its products. In this case export subsidies or import restrictions are in a sense more effective than exchange rate depreciation.

Trade policy can play a powerful part in bringing about a desired change in the economy through its effects on the overall balance of payments (Okorie and Colman 1995). Further, it can be used to bring about changes in particular sectors. In addition, trade policy can affect the quantities and prices of imports and exports.

Trade theory suggests that exporters should benefit from a real devaluation, at least in the short run, as a result of high domestic prices received from the exportables. It is argued that in the majority of the sub-Saharan Africa countries the trade policies were biased (Acharya 1981). They favoured industrial and commercial activities and were against agriculture. The bias could be seen with regard to producer and consumer pricing, the exchange rate, foreign trade taxes, subsidies and controls, and domestic indirect taxes. In most sub-Saharan countries the state sets producer prices for most important food and export crops. A similar tendency existed for export crops because they provided administratively easy tax handles. For Africa, high and non-uniform domestic taxation in selected agricultural sectors is the most important distortion. It is argued that Africa can make enormous gains from a reduction of these distortions.

Although external balances had improved in many LDCs, and reliance on quantitative restrictions was greatly diminished, there was one significant negative effect of devaluation, i.e. a high rate of inflation, e.g. Turkey. Table 12.2 gives data on the average rate of inflation among LDCs for five-year intervals since 1960. The table shows that the average rate of inflation was below 10 per cent in the 1960s. It jumped to about 68 per cent in the late 1980s before it came down to about 55 per cent in the first half of the 1990s. It decreased even lower to 13.5 per cent during the period 1996–8.

Whereas SASP in both the first and second phases were motivated in large part by balance of payments difficulties, many of the reforms of the 1980s were motivated by the desire to reduce inflation. However, the ultimate impact of trade liberalization

Table 12.2 Rates of inflation in developing countries (average annual inflation rate for wholesale prices)

	1961–65	*1966–70*	*1971–5*	*1976–80*	*1981–5*	*1986–90*	*1991–5*	*1996-8*
Inflation rate (%)	9.4	8.8	20.3	30.0	40.6	67.8	54.5	13.5

Source: IMF, *International Financial Statistics, Yearbook*, 1990, 1999.

(TL) on balance of payments is theoretically ambiguous. In the partial equilibrium frame of the elasticities approach, the impact depends on the extent to which import and export duties change and on the price elasticities of imports and exports. Export revenue rises if the price elasticities are greater than unity. With price elasticity of demand greater than zero, import payments will rise. This approach is unsuitable when TL does not imply price changes. In the absorption approach, the impact of TL depends on how real income is influenced relative to real absorption or expenditure. A fall in export taxes will shift expenditure to home-produced goods, thereby increasing income. But a fall in import taxes does the opposite. Despite a rise in real income, the balance of payments will deteriorate as long as the propensity to absorb is greater than unity. In the monetary approach to balance of payments, the effect of TL depends on how real demand for money changes relative to supply. To examine precisely the effect of a fall in taxes on the trade and balance of payments it is necessary to normalize for differences in country size. After making such adjustments, it has been claimed, pure liberalization worsened the balance of trade and balance of payments of twenty-two selected LDCs of Asia, Africa and Latin America between 1972 and 1998 because imports increased more rapidly than exports. The study applies dynamic panel data and time-series/cross-section analysis. The effect of TL, of course varied according to the regions and type of existing trade policy regime (Santos-Paulinos and Thirlwall 2002).

12.6 Structural adjustment programmes: the experience of sub-Saharan African countries

Many African countries are undergoing a period of economic transition under the aegis of SASP as prescribed by the IMF and the World Bank. It would be sad if, at a time when most African countries are in the midst of implementing difficult economic changes, vital and much needed external support were either to slow down or be reduced. The short-run costs of dislocation and disruption in economic reforms should not be underestimated. The majority of African countries are suffering from acute difficulties with debt servicing. If these remain without being settled urgently, any future improvement in economic performance will come under serious challenge.

It is said that the poorer the country, the greater the efforts required for undertaking SAS, and also the more resources required. Since these resources are not available internally, the more the external support needed. Ironically, countries with better economic conditions attract more resources. The poorer ones get even less. Therefore it is necessary to design strategies which ensure the distribution of foreign resources on the basis of need. This moral argument has recently been put by NGOs like Christian Aid.

Many lessons have been learnt about SASP in sub-Saharan Africa (Ajayi 1994). The first lesson is that no quick fix will occur in the African countries that adopted these programmes. In some cases, the situation had deteriorated very badly before the programmes were undertaken. In reality, the programmes have not succeeded in turning the economy around as quickly as was planned. On the contrary, in most cases the economic situation became worse than before the programmes were applied. The second lesson is that the issue of getting prices right as the dictum of policy effectiveness has not worked in an environment where the structural facilities and institutions and laws of governance leave much to be desired, as in the case of many sub-Saharan countries. Thirdly, the external circumstances surrounding many African countries, such as trade, have been no more favourable to African countries in the 1990s than they were in the 1970s.

The other important lesson is that the heavy external burden of debt had a detrimental effect on growth in sub-Saharan Africa. Africa's external debt tripled between 1980 and 1999. Debt service actually paid in 1999 was equivalent to 28-30 per cent of total exports of goods and services. This situation might seriously affect the ability of African countries to finance their investment needs. A fifth lesson possibly to be learnt about SASP is that of the need from time to time to adopt compensatory policies to reduce the undesirable effects of such programmes. Policy instruments and resources to deal with these negative effects are often limited in sub-Saharan countries.

The main reasons for the poor economic performance of those sub-Saharan countries that applied SASP may be summarized as follows (Mustapha 2001):

1 Only a few adopted SASP in a half-hearted manner. The uncertainty produced by such policies stifled supply response in production.
2 The decline in external terms of trade increased the dependence of the sub-Saharan countries on commodity trade, and led to quantitative and non-quantitative restrictions on trade.
3 The inadequate or complete absence of new financing failed to compensate for the deterioration in the terms of trade.
4 The massive drain of resources due to debt servicing implied that most African countries were compelled to reduce their imports with a significant detrimental effect on growth and investment.
5 An important cause of the failure of the SASP in sub-Saharan countries is often the wrong assumption that African markets are fully competitive and institutions are well developed. It is well known that markets are imperfect in Africa and economic and legal institutions are poorly developed.

Many SSA countries are indeed characterized by poor infrastructural facilities, low levels of education, low levels of health services, etc. Investments in infrastructure, institutions, legal and accounting systems, human capital and technology are crucial for African prosperity. It has been found that investment in education and health, the effects of which are not immediately felt, has not been dealt with properly during the course of SAP. Some sub-Saharan countries, as part of reducing public expenditure in the SAS, have reduced investment in these areas. Furthermore, a massive devaluation of the currency raised rapidly the cost of imported productive inputs, eroding the competitiveness of domestic enterprises and intensifying inflationary pressures (Ajayi 1994).

The SASP, successful as currently measured in only a limited number of cases, may not be a sufficient instrument to meet today's challenges. Moreover, it may not be an adequate tool in dealing with the severe institutional and policy deficiencies besetting many African societies. The major emphasis of structural adjustment was on relative prices, privatization, financial and trade liberalization. These procedures generated extremely modest supply responses which are much smaller than those anticipated at the beginning. More recently, using the computable general equilibrium model for Cameroon, the Gambia, Niger and Madagascar, Dorosh and Sahn (2000) examine the consequences of macroeconomic policy reforms on real incomes of poor households in sub-Saharan Africa. The results imply that, compared with alternative policy options, trade and exchange rate liberalization tends to benefit poor households in both rural and urban areas as rents on foreign exchange are eliminated, demand for labour rises and returns to tradeable agriculture rise. The small sizes of the gains in average real incomes imply that macro-policy reforms alone are inadequate to significantly reduce poverty in Africa.

12.7 Conclusion

This chapter highlights the complex issues involved in different facets of economic adjustment in LDCs – the short-run macroeconomic adjustment to correct distortions and promote efficiency, e.g. changes in the real exchange rates and interest rates and SASP aimed at boosting long run economic growth. The structural features of an economy play a crucial role in both the transmission of the policy shocks and the response of the economy to SASP policies (Agenor 2001). The SASP policies achieved success in some countries; in others, chiefly in many African countries, the adjustment policies were far from successful. Such evidence clearly calls for more country-specific studies and the need to be sceptical about 'quick fixes'. The 'magic' of the market may not work unless laws, ownership, accountability, governance, transparency and institutions play a major role in the proper enforcement of policies.

To ensure effective institutions in many LDCs, it is imperative to:

1 Design them to complement what exists in terms of other supporting institutions, human abilities and available techniques to maximize efficiency gains.
2 Innovate to design institutions that work, like the 'grameen' (village) banks.
3 Improve trade and information flows to connect communities of market players.
4 Promote competition among jurisdictions, firms and individuals as more competition improves the strength of present institutions, changes people's incentives and behaviour for the better and generates demand for better institutions.

Questions

1 What are the objectives of structural adjustment programmes of the World Bank and the IMF?
2 What are the major ingredients of structural adjustment lending (SAL)? How successful has it been?
3 Critically examine the impact of trade liberalization on the economic growth of LDCs.
4 What are the major problems in the implementation of structural adjustment programmes in sub-Saharan Afrca?
5 What are the criticisms against the IMF in its SAP policies to support LDCs?

Part IV

A new deal in commodity trade?

13 The new international economic order

13.1 Introduction

In this chapter we discuss the major issues that have been highlighted in the last three decades to promote mutual co-operation and economic welfare of the rich and poor countries. In order to understand the problems of cooperation between the rich (or the 'North') and the poor (once again, loosely labelled the 'South') countries of the world, it is important to pay special attention to the main reasons behind creating a new international economic order (NIEO). Many LDCs now argue that only an NIEO would be able to alleviate problems of poverty and inequality in income distribution among different countries. Despite some development in many LDCs, they face continuing, if not worsening, hardships on many fronts. One of the prime reasons for such hardship is supposed to be the decline in export income of the LDCs. A part of this problem has already been discussed in Chapter 8. It has already been shown that the relationship between export instability and economic growth is not always very clear cut. However, the following points are usually made in favour of an NIEO.

1 An NIEO is supposed to provide the proper framework for stabilizing commodity prices and export income earnings for LDCs.
2 The idea of income stabilization should be viewed in the context of primary product price fluctuations as LDCs depend chiefly upon the export of primary products for earning foreign exchange.
3 A secular decline in the terms of trade for many LDCs should be compensated by the creation of new international institutions.
4 Since production, trade and financial flows have all become much more international, the interdependence of nations and interaction between economic transactions in many areas have risen considerably. For example, protection of agriculture in the north has an adverse impact on trade in agricultural goods. It also adversely affects the economic growth of the south and its capacity to repay the debt. A failure of debt repayment by Mexico or any other LDC can easily be a dangerous development for some DCs. The type of change that can be observed today simply underlines the need for a 'new look' at the financial and trading system as a whole. An NIEO is supposed to incorporate such changes. An alteration of the framework of finance and trade and the role of the major institutions has thus become unavoidable to buttress the management of the world economy.

5 The dramatic rise in oil prices and the recession of the major industrialized countries in the 1970s once more raised the problems of a shortage of world liquidity, inflation, high interest rates, adjustments in the balance of payments, large fluctuations in exchange rates and mass unemployment. The least developed countries have been particularly hit by the rise in oil price and recession in the rich countries. Special provisions are called for to help such countries in an NIEO. A radical system of aid, commercial lending and debt management for these poor countries should be evolved within the new order. The other important ingredient of the NIEO is a transfer of technology from the rich to the poor countries to enable them to raise their productivity and economic growth. Although some successes have been observed in post-war international economic co-operation in the field of technology and resource transfer through the bilateral and multilateral agencies, there have evidently been a number of failures. Important changes have taken place during the 1970s, partly due to the rise of the Organization of Petroleum Exporting Countries (OPEC) and partly due to the rise of the newly industrialized countries (e.g. Brazil, Mexico, Taiwan, Venezuela, Malaysia, South Korea). The problem of recycling 'petro-dollars' from the oil-rich countries to the non-oil developing countries has also been brought to the fore consistently. Doubts have been raised about the present role of the current institutions like the International Monetary Fund (IMF) and the International Bank for Reconstruction and Development (IBRD or World Bank). Among the suggestions that have been put forward to improve the global economic prospect is to set up 'another Bretton Woods' (see, for example, Commonwealth Secretariat 1983).

6 A major element of the NIEO is the issue of appropriate power sharing in international economic institutions. It has been acknowledged that in the framework of growing interdependence and the need to evolve a more co-operative international system, continuing progress in power sharing is an important objective. An important ingredient of interdependence between the north and the south is supposed to be shared management. Thus, many LDCs are asking for a greater share in the management of the international institutions and in the formulation of global policies.

It has been well observed by the Commonwealth Secretariat (1983) that

> a sound longer-run international economic system would not normally encounter problems as severe as those which have characterised the past few years; on the infrequent occasions when it nevertheless did, it would not impose such heavy costs upon those nations and people least able to protect themselves against externally created shocks. Prime objectives within a reformed international system must be improved stabilisation mechanisms and contra-cyclical policies, together with improved protection for those most affected when instabilities and shocks nevertheless persist . . . what is required is a more deliberate construction of the elements of a more stable and equitable global economy.

13.2 The evolution of the new international economic order

The structure of trade with LDCs in the post-Second World War period retained its colonial origins. The IMF and the General Agreement on Tariffs and Trade (GATT) were viewed as institutions primarily for rich countries. Industrialization and development planning in LDCs were preoccupied with domestic efforts to maximize domestic economic growth rates. Little attention was given to structural reform of the international economic system until 1964, when UNCTAD was created by an original group of seventy-seven LDCs (known as the Group of 77).

During the period from UNCTAD I in 1964 to UNCTAD III in 1972, tariff and non-tariff barriers in developed countries constituted a variety of obstacles to the expansion and diversification of exports from LDCs. These sessions concentrated on the development of commodity agreements. The other aim of the UNCTAD meetings was to promote the liberalization of trade exports of LDCs to DCs on a generalized scheme of preference, which would grant preferential tariffs to LDCs, giving them advantageous access to the rich markets in DCs. These repeated attempts by the Group of seventy-seven countries to obtain trade concessions from DCs resulted in failure and confrontation, except for the generalized scheme of preference which GATT later adopted. However, the actual tariff concessions granted little visible benefit to LDCs.

There still remained frustrations in the LDCs over the development process, international economic relations and the limited control of LDCs over their own destiny. With the increase in oil prices in 1973, the oil-importing LDCs were hard hit by the new levels of foreign exchange they would now have to find to pay for their oil import. The LDCs were asked to accept these new higher oil prices as the vanguard of an NIEO that would seek to improve the terms of international trade for other primary products (all of which had been declining in relation to DCs' manufactured exports), along the lines of cartelization of their primary products such as OPEC had done to improve their bargaining position with the DCs.

Prebisch argued that the terms of trade for the primary commodity exports of LDCs are deteriorating in the long run. The reason is that the gains in productivity occurring in the DCs, which ought to lead to lowered prices, remain in these countries because of strong trade unions with high pay claims. But the gains in productivity in LDCs are transferred to the consumers in the DCs. Other elements of the theory are that the demand for primary commodities grows slowly, partly because of the increasing use of synthetic materials and the more effective utilization of natural raw materials. Singer pointed out that the extraction of minerals in LDCs is often in the hands of multinationals and this implies that the diffusion effects are small (see Chapter 8).

Thus, the main rationale for an NIEO is that sustained domestic development in the Third World cannot be achieved until the existing system of international trade is restructured drastically to promote equitable global distribution of incomes and resources. NIEO is the product of the Sixth Special Session of the General Assembly of the United Nations, incorporating past UNCTAD proposals into a 'Declaration on the Establishment of a New International Economic Order' and a 'Programme of Action' to carry it out. This Sixth Special Session of the United Nations was held in 1974.

The NIEO declaration covers a great number of issues, e.g. commodity price stabilization schemes, indexation of the prices of primary products, compensatory financing to offset the oil deficits of poor countries, and trade liberalization advantages to LDCs. The LDCs now want a larger role in working out their aspirations for development progress through greater and more stable access to markets of the DCs. They also want to have an international system which will be more responsive to their requirements to attain a higher level of economic welfare.

The detailed proposals for an NIEO include the following:

1 the indexation of export prices of LDCs to import prices of the DCs;
2 for development finance of the LDCs, the attainment of the target of 0.7 per cent of the GNP of DCs;
3 a package programme of price supports at levels higher than historical trends for a group of export commodities of LDCs;
4 some kind of tie between foreign development aid and the creation of international reserves in terms of special drawing rights (for details, see Chapter 9);
5 a special framework for the transfer of technology to LDCs and codes of conduct for multinational corporations for helping LDCs in obtaining 'appropriate' technology and products.

An NIEO is thus seen as a vehicle for the LDCs to get important concessions from the DCs in matters such as trade, aid and debt relief. It is also regarded by some as a mechanism to change existing biases in income, wealth and power distributions (Meier 1984).

Haq (1981), for instance, says:

> The basic purpose of the current demand for a new international economic order is to restructure the prevailing market rules, largely fashioned by the financial power of the rich nations and their multinationals; to obtain a greater voice in international financial institutions; and to break the age-old patterns of economic and political dependency of the poor nations on the goodwill of the rich nations. The main objective, however politely or skillfully stated, is restructuring of power; whether political, economic, financial, or intellectual.

It has been argued by some that such demands by the LDCs, if granted, are very likely to diminish the power of rich countries. A state of confrontation, rather than co-operation, may spoil the relationship between the rich and poor countries. It has also been pointed out that the authors of the NIEO seem to believe in a zero-sum game where only LDCs win. The proponents of the NIEO thus fail to emphasize the possible gains from a positive-sum game where all the players can win. As such, the desire for having an NIEO is unlikely to be achieved.

13.3 The main objectives of a new international economic order

In simple terms, there are four main aims of an NIEO for LDCs:

1 stabilize the commodity trade and export earnings of primary producers – UNCTAD IV in 1976 adopted a programme for commodities agreements to cater for this.
2 international monetary reform, and linking it to the development financing needs of LDCs – as provided by the special drawing rights from the IMF in 1969 to tackle debt burdens and increases in the oil price, plus development financing (the section on compensatory finance schemes explains some of this);
3 reform of the activities and power of multinational corporations (MNCs) in the LDCs – it is well known that the MNCs pursue global profit maximization,

through pricing and marketing policies and production techniques, which often clash with development policies of host LDCs; MNCs have had charges of neo-imperialism made against them, all designed to exploit the resources of LDCs and harm their efforts of achieving sustained domestic development;

4 the evolution of an international mechanism to affect the transfer of 'appropriate' technology and products for the LDCs.

To understand the complex nature of gains or losses in a zero or a positive sum game, we will discuss a few major issues emphasized in the NIEO. Some of the issues are not exactly 'new'. Even so, a close examination is required to understand the real gains and losses. Since the issue of commodity price stabilization has received major attention, we examine it in detail in the next section.

13.4 The theory of commodity price stabilization: demand/supply shifts

The gains from commodity price or income stabilization have been discussed at length in recent literature. It is sometimes contended that the stabilization of export income is probably of more interest to LDCs than the stabilization of prices for their products; however, it is also harder to bring about than price stabilization by international commodity agreements (ICAs). Nevertheless it is still used as a complement to the ICAs in the form of compensatory finances and such like.

Following the analysis of Behrman (1979) it is possible to demonstrate the result of price stabilization on producer revenues theoretically. Here we use the simple supply and demand curves for a purely competitive international commodity market (see Figure 13.1). Figure 13.1 represents a shift in demand only – unstable prices are caused by a shift in demand from DD_1 to DD_2; at DD^* buffer stocks are in action. The supply curve SS gives the average quantity supplied for each possible price. The demand curve (DD) therefore gives the average quantity demanded for each possible price. In Figure 13.1, P^* is the equilibrium price, at which the quantity demanded

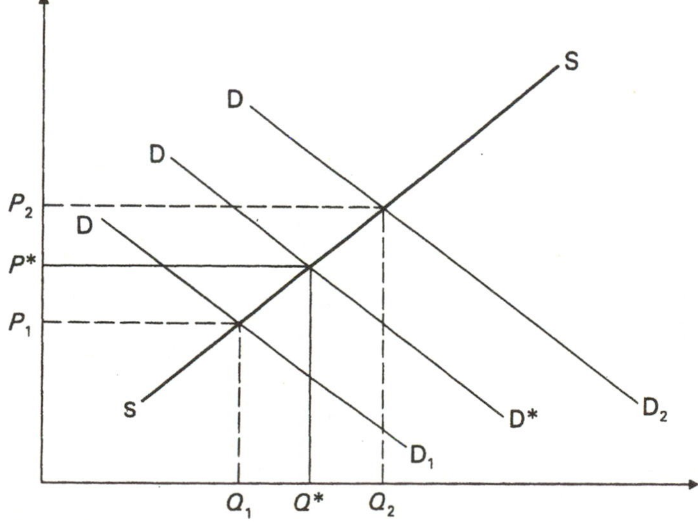

Figure 13.1

equals the quantity supplied, where both equal Q^*. P^* is also the price at which a buffer stock is assumed to stabilize prices by purchasing the excess commodity, if otherwise the price would fall, and in turn selling it if the price were to rise, thus ensuring price stability.

The buffer stock comes into operation when instability results due to a shift in the demand curve downwards by selling $Q^2 - Q^*$ units in order to keep the price at P^*. Whether the demand curve shifts to the right or the left, producers receive P^*Q^* when the buffer stock operates. As a result, price stabilization implies revenue stabilization as well in this case. But it will imply a fall in revenue when P^*Q^* is smaller than

$$\frac{P_1Q_1 + P_2Q_2}{2}$$

Now we should consider instability due to supply shifts alone. This will depend on the supply and demand elasticities to price changes. The price elasticity of a curve indicates by what percentage the quantity changes along a curve when the price changes by 1 per cent. If the quantity change is greater than the percentage price change, then price elasticity for that curve is greater than 1 and the curve is price elastic for that range of price changes (e.g. Figure 13.2a). If the opposite were to hold true, then the curve is price inelastic for that range of price changes (e.g. Figure 13.2b). Also if the price elasticity is zero, then the curve is completely inelastic.

Without price stabilization average producer revenues are

$$\frac{P_2Q_2 + P_3Q_3}{2}$$

whilst with stabilization they are

$$\frac{P^*(Q_1 + Q_4)}{2}$$

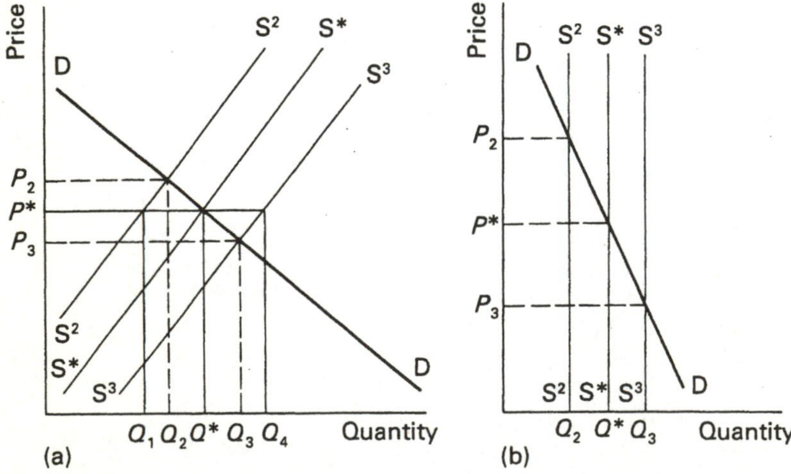

Figure 13.2

Here, price stabilization has meant a rise in the producers' revenue. But what about the stability of those revenues under price stabilization when the supply curve alone shifts? In the case of the price elasticity of the supply and demand curves, price stability increases the instability of revenue. When both the supply and demand curves shift, the net result depends on the size of the two shifts as well as the size of price elasticity.

It is now clear that even absolute stabilization of the price received by producers will not completely stabilize the revenue of producers, even as a body, quite apart from individuals. Variations in the quantity of commodities exported have caused at least as much instability of export proceeds as have variations in world prices. This is obvious from our analyses of the causes of instability. Not only may stabilization of producer prices fail to produce stable revenues; it may on occasion destabilize them. Whenever variations in the volume of exports would normally cause a compensatory change in price, a fixed price will increase instability unless it in turn reduces fluctuations in supply.

We can illustrate the point with a simple numerical example. If the volume of the exported commodity this year was 10 million tons, and the price was US$10/ton, revenue received would be $100 million. If in the next year the crop happened to be a bad one and exports fell to 8 million tons, the price could rise to, say, $11/ton, giving an income of some $88 million. But if the price had been fixed by policy at $10.50/ton, the revenue received would have been $105 million and $84 million respectively in the two years. Although total revenue was $1 million better because of a fixed price agreement, in the first case the percentage change is 12.0 and in the second 20.0, showing greater instability of income with stable prices. Thus, the lower the price elasticity of demand for the commodity, and the larger the autonomous fluctuations in output, the more relevant and significant is this point.

But for many countries, destabilization of income is unlikely to be caused by a fixed price; a relatively high elasticity of demand for one country's output is normal, and price variations are more often the consequence of fluctuations in demand. It is thus necessary to examine the possible gains to be had from price stabilization (see the next section) and who is liable to benefit from it.

13.5 Commodity price stabilization: gains and losses

Fluctuations of commodity prices and stabilization arrangements for them have been of considerable importance in international trade for a long time. In this section, we try to analyse whether more stable prices would be beneficial to LDCs by helping to maintain their foreign exchange earnings which would therefore facilitate fiscal planning and economic management, as well as the benefits it would, in turn, bring to the DCs – the consumers of the commodity. There is of course a problem of co-operation between the producers and the consumers. Also the storage and transaction costs for the buffer stock scheme should be included in the estimation of net benefits. A measure has to be taken as to the derived benefits which are going to accrue to each partner in the scheme. An index of the net benefits (or losses) to the producers by the additional (or lessened) revenues they receive, plus a measure of benefits (or losses) to consumers by the extra (lessened) consumer surplus they receive, must be constructed.

Consumer surplus is measured by the sum, for all units of a commodity, of the difference between what consumers would be willing to pay for each unit and what they

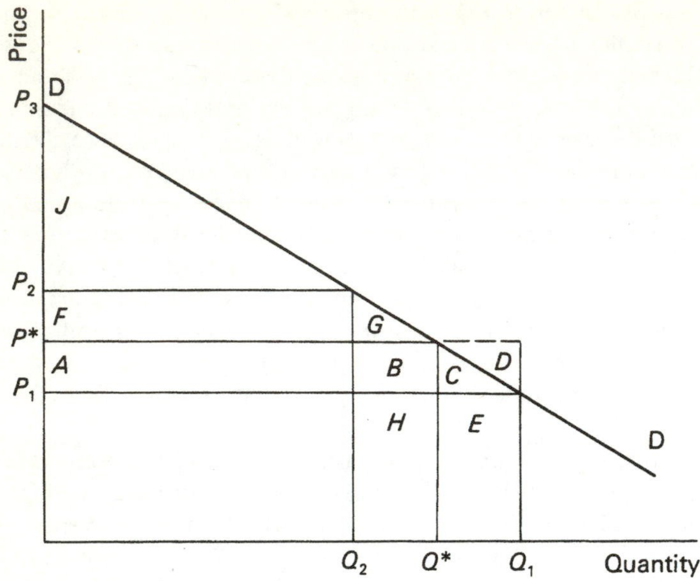

Figure 13.3

actually pay. Figure 13.3 (shifts in inelastic supply curve only) illustrates that in order to buy the first unit the consumer is willing to pay P_3, whilst to buy the next unit the consumer is willing to pay slightly less than P_3. In order to buy the Q_2 unit, the consumer's willingness to pay is P_2. If the market price is P_2, then P_2 must be paid for each of the Q_2 units demanded. To measure the consumer surplus at price P_2, subtract P_2 from what consumers would be willing to pay for each of the Q_2 units actually purchased. Here, the difference between the demand curve and the horizontal line at P_2, or the area indicated by the triangle J, is the area of consumer surplus. If the market price happened to be P^*, then the consumer surplus would be $J + F + G$. Assume that the demand curve is fixed. Then the only source of instability is the shifting supply curve. P^* is the average price, and is the one at which the buffer stock stabilizes the price when in operation.

When the supply curve is at Q_1, buffer stock purchases will be $Q_1 - Q^*$ units. The change in consumer surplus as a result of paying P^* instead of price P_1, which would have prevailed had there been no buffer stocks, is negative: $-A - B - C$. The producer's revenue gain due to the higher prices is positive, $A + B + C + D$. The cost to the buffer stock of buying $Q_1 - Q^*$ units is $-C - D - E$, and as a result the total benefit is $-C - E$.

When the supply curve shifts to Q_2, $Q^* - Q_2$ units are sold by the buffer stock at P^*, thus stopping the price from rising to P_2. The benefit to consumers is $F + G$, due to the lower price and larger quantity. The benefit, or loss in this case, to the producers is $-F$ since they receive a lower price for their Q_2 units than they would do without the buffer stock. Therefore, the financial inflow to the buffer stock is $B + H$, and the total benefit is $B + G + H$.

If the sequencing over time of the supply shifts is ignored, the total benefits to each of the three groups is the sum of those obtained from buffer stock operation with supply at Q_1 and at Q_2. For the consumers, the sum is $F + G - A - B - C$; for the producers the sum is $A + B + C + D - F$. For the buffer stock the sum is $B + H - C - D - E$. And for the total overall benefit, the sum is $B + G + H - C - E$. Under these assumptions, the sum for the buffer stock is zero and the overall sum is positive. Whether or not the consumers or producers benefit depends upon the exact shape of the curves. If the supply and demand curves are of constant price elasticity, consumers will always benefit from price stabilization, while producers will only benefit if demand is elastic; otherwise they will suffer lower welfare. This is basically an empirical issue. Newbery and Stiglitz (1981), on the basis of their extensive investigations, have argued that the micro gains from price stabilization are probably very low. On their calculations, the size of the optimal buffer stock seems to be rather small. These conclusions are obviously tentative and initially depend on the unbiased estimation of the relevant parameters. Kanbur has argued that the macro benefits of stabilization schemes in terms of investment and growth are, perhaps, a lot larger than those suggested by Newbery and Stiglitz (see Kanbur 1983).

Another possible welfare gain from price stabilization is the reduction of risk, for what price the producer is going to receive. This will enable the producer to increase his capital stock and the rate of investment will now be higher. The supply curve will shift to the right because lower risks will prompt producers to sell at a lower price than before, resulting in an increase in consumer surplus. The producer's welfare has increased because of the reduction in the risks.

A similar effect operates on the demand side. If the consumers of a commodity are risk-averse, they will, at the margin, substitute a more price-stable alternative for the commodity. If the price of the commodity is now stabilized, risk-averse consumers will wish to purchase more of it, and the demand curve will shift to the right. If market prices rise, the increase in producers' surplus is an additional welfare gain. However, if both consumers and producers are risk-averse, the rightward shift of supply and demand curves indicates the revealed preferences of both groups for price stability, and welfare will have been increased.

The major cause of the instability though is the fluctuations in price of the primary products. Therefore, it is reasonable to conclude that the desire to stabilize export earnings and the efforts to establish international institutions with this objective in mind is rational from the exporter's point of view. As a result under the initiative of UNCTAD IV in 1976 an Integrated Programme for Commodities was adopted which incorporated the establishment of ICAs. This is examined in the next section.

13.6 Implications of international commodity agreements, buffer stocks and compensatory finances

The argument for international schemes for stabilizing primary product prices rests on the assumption that the governments of LDCs are afflicted with severe problems of economic planning and management owing to fluctuations in their export earnings associated with the dominance of primary products in their exports. The facts responsible for this assumption are well known and have been discussed in previous sections: the variability of supply of and demand for individual primary products, the low elasticities of both supply and demand, the specialization of LDCs on one or a few primary product exports, and the concentration of their exports on one or a few developed country markets.

The ICAs basically have two purposes: (1) to reduce the fluctuations in world commodity prices, whilst also trying to set output levels, and (2) to raise the long-term trend of prices to compensate for what is perceived to have been deteriorations in LDC terms of trade.

The ICA will provide greater protection to individual exporting countries against excessive competition and the overexpansion of world production. The overexpansion of supply will drive down prices and, consequently, curtail the growth of earnings for all countries. Commodity agreements, as a result, will guarantee particular nations a relatively fixed share of world export earnings for the commodity along with a more stable price.

In order to establish the ICAs and get them working effectively UNCTAD advocated the establishment of a US$6 billion Common Fund to support the prices of some eighteen primary products produced by LDCs. This money in the Common Fund is for financing the creation of buffer stocks as the major price stabilization weapon. The idea of the Common Fund is that of risk spreading, among those nations who are part of it. It is to be financed by contributions from exporting countries, OPEC and developed importing countries plus some from multilateral agencies, and by borrowing in private capital markets.

Therefore, the ICAs involve the establishment of buffer stocks which are designed to keep the market price of a commodity within certain maximum and minimum limits whenever supply and demand become grossly imbalanced. When the price falls to the lower limit the buffer stock agency will buy up the surplus goods at the floor price in order to check the decline in prices. If the price happens to rise above some agreed maximum, the stocks which have been accumulated will be sold on the market thus exerting a downward pressure on prices. But, as can be seen, the scheme is only viable for non-perishable commodities.

The advantages of this scheme are that it need not include all major producing or consuming countries, an advantage over the traditional quota system which requires all countries to participate if it is to work, nor does it involve the restriction of production or exports by the producing countries, also required by quotas. It allows the efficient producers scope for expansion, whereas the quota system keeps inefficient producers in the market at the expense of the efficient ones.

Its disadvantages are the capital and storage costs of operating the stock, which are substantial. If the stock's resources are inadequate, as they may be if tendencies towards high or low prices are persistent, and necessarily must be if the long-run equilibrium price falls outside the selected range of stabilization prices, the buffer stock will exhaust either its capital or its power to stabilize price. If the selected price range is too low, the stock will end its phase of stabilization with a profit and can be reconstituted to stabilize prices within a higher price range. If, on the other hand, the price range is too high, the stock will end its stabilization phase with a stock of the commodity bought at prices above the current market price, and hence will have suffered a capital loss. The risk of such a loss, which might well be substantial, is a major deterrent to the participation of consuming countries in buffer stock schemes.

If the aim of the ICA is to increase commodity prices over the long term, it is important to consider the price elasticity of demand for the product. It can cause some export earnings to decline, particularly in commodities where there are close natural or synthetic substitutes. But if demand is price inelastic extra revenue can be raised; an example would be OPEC and oil. The success of OPEC has tempted other LDCs to establish similar cartels for other inelastic demand goods, but this has resulted in little success, with bauxite coming a very distant second to oil.

In order for ICAs to work, it would need co-operation between producers and consumers – something which has been lacking in recent UNCTAD meetings. But the ICAs by themselves would not provide all the answers to the problems faced by exporting countries, it would need a complement, that of compensatory finance schemes.

Compensatory finance schemes do not attempt to regulate international trade in the commodity, but provide a sort of insurance payment to countries that have had an unexpected and severe fall in their export earnings.

In 1963, the IMF introduced a form of compensatory financing, under which LDCs could borrow a certain proportion of their quota from the fund if their export earnings were reduced for reasons beyond the country's control and if the shortfall was large enough to require compensation. The drawings on the IMF Compensatory Financing Facility between 1976 and 1979, according to the Brandt Report (1980), were almost half the total credit extended by the IMF to LDCs.

In addition to the IMF facility, there is also an export earnings stabilization scheme, known as Stabex, under the Lomé Convention between the European Union and the African, Caribbean and Pacific (ACP) countries. The scheme at the moment does not cover minerals, but they are to be introduced in due course. Stabex provides compensation in the form of grants rather than loans, on a very soft basis to the least developed of the ACP countries.

It is hoped that the ICAs and various compensatory finance schemes do go a long way towards reducing the instability in export earnings and stabilizing prices, but there are still gaps in these policies which will result in some instability in exports for LDCs.

13.7 Conclusion

More than twenty-five years after the UN decisions on an NIEO, many of the components of the Action Programme are far from being implemented. Looking back on what the LDCs have achieved so far, one can record that a larger number of negotiations have been set in motion in many spheres, e.g. the Uruguay Round. However, few concrete results have been achieved through these negotiations, and it may be too early to expect any. International negotiations can be very complicated and time consuming. Many proposals also require careful preparatory work, such as those on price stabilization and codes of conduct for multinational corporations and the transfer of technology. Only time will tell – especially as the economic well-being of the DCs is increasingly dependent on the LDCs and that may change the basis for future negotiations.

There is a deep consensus among economists that a major stress on agriculture holds the best hope for alleviating the Third World's problems. Many reports stressed the fact that government protection of agriculture in much of the DCs had created major problems for LDCs.

This is because farmers in most DCs are heavily protected by government subsidy or other means which enables them to sell their produce more cheaply. But at the same time, most of the LDCs depend on earnings from farm exports to pay for their economic growth. Developed agricultural countries have unloaded huge farm surpluses on to world markets, thus resulting in depressed commodity prices. Importers in LDCs, such as those in sub-Saharan Africa, might enjoy temporary bargains, but in the long term low-priced farm goods reduce the incentive to produce food locally and create a demand for food which often cannot be grown locally.

By contrast, though, many of the LDCs have unwittingly hampered their own farm output with food price controls that cramp farmers' incentives to grow more (see Ghatak and Ingersent 1984 for details).

Protectionism itself still poses a grave threat to world trade, but the more immediate danger may he that it will trigger a severe disturbance in the already troubled international financial system. It could result in an international liquidity shortage, one severe enough to produce a series of insolvencies. This is why there should be a review of the quotas in the IMF and new special drawing rights allocations.

These policies are important to any prospect of real improvement in the economic conditions of the LDCs, but can only be achieved by an increase in the resources made available to the multilateral financial institutions. An expansion of IMF resources through quota increases (instead of through commercial flows) would make it possible for the agency to lend at 'softer' rates of interest. Additionally, the balance of payments support from the IMF could be larger and more effective.

At the moment, however, most LDCs lack the means by which to develop and expand their exports. Many are faced with significant current account deficits being financed largely by private inflows (bank lending), thus increasing the problem of debt servicing. The mobilizing of the excess liquidity in the international banking system into a facility to offer trade credits could have an important impact on production for exports. For example, sustained growth in agricultural production requires a substantial outlay on infrastructural development, and if trade credits were forthcoming these would enable the financing of much larger imports for this purpose.

There are a number of issues on which the LDCs should press for positive action in their trade relations with DCs. The worsening position of the LDCs was in part attributed to the steady deterioration in the volume of world trade; consequently one main demand should be for a lifting of tariff and non-tariff barriers to trade imposed by DCs. Other demands should be for improvements in access to markets for the exports of LDCs, structural adjustments in DCs which would enable the raw-material-producing countries to develop their processing industries; and new approaches to ensure less volatility in the international market.

The non-oil exporting countries have felt the impact of the sharp decline in export commodity prices, and the unstable market conditions prevailing globally. The problem, of course, has been intensified as a result of the protectionist policies imposed by the DCs, which coupled with the world recession have meant a severe shrinkage of the markets for the products of major export interest to the LDCs. World prices for the primary products of LDCs, including agricultural and mining sector exports, have declined by as much as 40 per cent, thus affecting the level of foreign exchange earnings.

But these prescriptions are not new. The topic has appeared repeatedly on the agenda of UNCTAD and World Trade Organization (WTO), and the discussions with the DCs have made little or no progress, ending inconclusively all the time.

In the meantime, the economic position of the non-oil developing world has worsened. According to the UNCTAD report on developing countries, in 1999 economic growth in the Third World oil-importing countries declined to 3 per cent from 5 per cent in 1990. Unfavourable terms of trade, and high interest payments, helped to erode any gains of LDCs from increased production in DCs during 1983–94. Therefore, the decline in commodity prices, plus the crisis in the debt servicing which has pushed many countries to the brink of default – Mexico being a good example – are crucial elements in the present difficulties (see Chapter 14). It becomes even more distressing when it is realized that the increase of US$60 billion in the combined debts of the LDCs was absorbed largely by consumption rather than investment in development. Perhaps a restructuring of the international trade and finance through an NIEO is overdue for enhancing global welfare.

Questions

1 What are the major reasons in favour of NIEO? What are its main objectives?
2 Explain the theory of commodity price stabilization. What are the gains and losses of such stabilization plans?
3 What are the main implications of international commodity agreement schemes?
4 Should LDCs stabilize commodity prices or export income?

14 The international debt crisis

With Nigel M. Healy

14.1 Introduction

The so-called 'international debt crisis' first came to public attention on 13 August 1982 when Mexico unilaterally announced that it could no longer service its $80 billion external debt. Although individual countries like Ghana, Turkey and Indonesia had suffered debt servicing problems in the 1970s, these had essentially been isolated incidents of internal policy mismanagement. In contrast, during the second half of 1982, it became apparent that dozens of other developing countries shared Mexico's problems. Squeezed between world recession and high real interest rates, and suffering capital flight on an unprecedented scale, the developing world found itself incapable of servicing the external debt it had accumulated during the 1970s. As its major creditor, the international banking system faced the prospect of collapse in the event of a generalized default by the developing countries. In this sense, the international debt crisis was initially a *banking crisis* and the solutions advanced for its management were primarily directed at maintaining the solvency of the international banks (Lever and Huhne 1987).

By the late 1980s, however, the threat of financial disaster had receded despite the onset of 'Asian' financial crisis in 1997. The international banks had set aside sufficient 'loan-loss' provisions to secure their balance sheets against the possibility of default. The developing countries, on the other hand, had refocused their economies on servicing external debt, compressing imports with serious repercussions for economic growth and development (Warner 1992; Cohen 1992). The international debt crisis gradually evolved from a banking crisis into a *development crisis* and new initiatives by the International Monetary Fund (IMF) and the International Bank for Reconstruction and Development (IBRD or World Bank) were launched with the aim of ending what was widely perceived as 'debt slavery' (but see Vogl 1990). This chapter explores the changing nature of the international debt crisis. It begins with an overview of the changing debt position of the developing world. It then considers the reasons why developing countries become indebted and the causes of the post-1982 crisis. It finally discusses events since 1982, critically assessing the management of the crisis.

14.2 The evolving debt position of the developing world

Table 14.1 provides an overview of the debt position of the developing world over the ten years to 1993. It shows that total external debt grew steadily, from US$879 billion

Table 14.1 The evolving picture of developing country debt (all developing countries, excluding Eastern Europe and former USSR)

	1984	*1985*	*1986*	*1987*	*1988*	*1989*	*1990*	*1991*	*1992*	*1993*
Total external debt ($billion)	879	949	1050	1173	1194	1222	1281	1348	1388	1451
Total external debt ($ of exports)	137.0	154.5	180.4	167.0	148.2	135.3	126.0	125.7	119.5	112.5
Debt service payments ($ billion)	124	128	131	141	151	147	145	152	169	170
Debt service payments ($ of exports)	19.3	20.9	22.5	20.1	18.8	16.3	14.3	14.2	14.5	13.2

Source: IMF World Economic Outlook.

in 1984 to $1451 billion by 1993. Over the same period, debt service payments (i.e. payments of interest and scheduled capital repayments) also rose by a similar factor, from $124 billion per annum in 1984 to $170 billion per annum by 1993. These crude data must be adjusted in some way, however, to allow for changes in the developing countries' ability to pay, in order to get a truly meaningful picture. One possible approach is to focus on external debt (or debt service payments) as a percentage of developing countries' GDP. However, the binding constraint on the ability of developing countries to manage external debt is not their GDP *per se*, but rather their capacity to generate the export revenues necessary to meet their debt servicing obligations. For this reason, external debt (and debt service payments) is conventionally expressed as a percentage of export revenues, in order to give a clearer picture of the underlying position of the developing countries.

Expressed in this way, Table 14.1 shows that there appears to have been a marginal improvement in the situation of the developing countries over the ten years. As a percentage of exports, total external debt fell from 137.0 per cent in 1984 to 112.5 per cent by 1993. Over the same period, debt service payments as a percentage of exports (also known as the debt service ratio or DSR) showed an even sharper decline, from 19.3 per cent in 1984 to 14.2 per cent by 1993.

Whilst Table 14.1 suggests some marginal improvement in the developing countries' position since 1984, disaggregating the data by region reveals worrying differences. Table 14.2 shows that in the developing countries of Asia, where external debt was never a particularly serious problem, DSRs more than halved from their peak in 1986. For the 'Asian tigers' (Hong Kong, Singapore, South Korea and Taiwan), the improvement in the debt situation was even more impressive, with the DSR dropping from 9.1 per cent in 1984 to 2.8 per cent by 1993. For the developing countries of Africa, and those of sub-Saharan Africa in particular, however, the ten years saw almost no change in their debt position. And while the Latin American countries enjoyed a decline in their DSRs, debt servicing continued to absorb almost one-third of total export earnings. In other words, at a regional level the marginal improvement

Table 14.2 Debt service ratios by region

	1984	*1985*	*1986*	*1987*	*1988*	*1989*	*1990*	*1991*	*1992*	*1993*
Africa	26.0	27.6	27.8	23.4	25.8	25.1	25.5	26.7	28.3	24.6
of which sub-Saharan Africa	23.5	22.4	24.7	21.6	22.9	21.6	21.4	22.0	22.7	21.8
Asia	12.7	14.3	15.1	14.6	10.9	10.4	8.8	7.9	7.7	7.7
of which four NICs[a]	9.1	9.3	9.6	10.5	5.6	4.6	3.3	3.0	2.9	2.8
Latin America	40.5	42.2	46.1	39.5	43.9	31.4	27.3	31.5	35.3	29.4

Source: JMF World Economic Outlook.

Note: [a] Newly industrializing countries of Hong Kong, Singapore, South Korea and Taiwan.

in the debt situation of the developing countries as a group is very unevenly shared out. While Asia brought an initially modest debt problem under control, Africa made almost no headway and, despite some progress, the position in Latin America is still bleak.

Moreover, these data on debt cannot be taken in isolation from the economic circumstances in which they arise. A DSR of, say, 25 per cent in 1993 may actually be more worrying than a DSR of 30 per cent in 1984. The obvious reason is that the developing world has undergone a sustained period of adjustment since 1982, as their economies have been refocused on the need to service external debt. To the extent that this adjustment has typically involved deflation (in order to compress imports and free export revenues to service debt), the political capacity of many developing countries to endure continuing high DSRs may be in doubt. This point is explored further below. Second, high DSRs in the mid-1980s coexisted with positive net resource transfers to the developing world. Net resource transfers may be defined as

Net resource transfers =

New loans *less* debt service payments *less* other net capital outflows

where 'other net capital outflows' includes capital flight. Unsurprisingly, the willingness of the international banking system to lend to developing countries has been reduced by the latter's debt servicing difficulties and, as a result, new loans (and so net resource transfers) have fallen sharply. Table 14.3 shows that while net resource transfers have remained modestly positive for the smallest and least developed economies (mainly African states), the larger middle-income economies (mainly in Latin America) have suffered reverse transfers on a massive scale. For the so-called 'Baker 15' (i.e. the fifteen most heavily indebted countries which were singled out for special assistance under the Baker Plan – see below), cumulative net resource transfers between 1984 and 1993 amounted to approximately $300 billion. This raises important issues about the incentive compatibility of debt servicing, an issue which is explored in more detail below.

Table 14.3 Net resource transfers to developing countries ($ billion)

	1984	*1985*	*1986*	*1987*	*1988*	*1989*	*1990*	*1991*	*1992*	*1993*
Small low-income countries	3.5	3.5	2.8	3.5	4.6	4.8	5.5	4.9	4.9	4.7
Least developed countries	2.6	2.1	1.6	1.5	2.2	1.8	2.9	3.1	3.1	2.8
Fifteen heavily indebted countries	−45.6	−44.7	−22.4	−29.7	−33.1	−40.7	−42.1	−16.7	−8.0	−11.5
Countries with recent debt servicing difficulties	−41.5	−44.4	−14.7	−30.6	−30.9	−40.3	−46.8	−21.2	−10.2	−14.5

Source: IMF World Economic Outlook.

14.3 Why do developing countries become indebted?

The practice of resorting to overseas capital as a means of promoting economic growth is far from new. The United States, for example, succeeded in transforming itself from a colonial outpost into an international superpower after less than a century of importing European capital. Moreover, there are sound theoretical reasons why it may be entirely rational for developing countries to borrow from abroad.

1 *The 'savings gap'.* Economic theory suggests that poorer societies may be unable to save enough to finance the level of investment necessary for self-sustaining growth. Overseas borrowing can fill this savings gap by providing the resources that domestic savers are unable or unwilling to sacrifice. In time, growth should increase the volume of domestic savings, eventually generating a surplus over investment which can be used to repay the original borrowing. By altering the inter-temporal pattern of saving in this way, a developing country can therefore increase its average level of consumption over the long term.

2 *The 'forex gap'.* The second argument for borrowing from overseas concerns the 'foreign exchange (forex) gap'. For many developing countries, the real brake on growth stems from the fact that the bulk of the investment crucial to economic development requires foreign, rather than domestically produced, plant, equipment and expertise. If export earnings are insufficient to earn the forex necessary to finance this investment, overseas borrowing may be the only means of gaining access to the technology vital for rapid growth. Again, over time, rising output should produce the net exports required to pay back earlier debt.

3 *The marginal efficiency of capital.* A third feature of developing countries which may encourage borrowing from overseas is that in poorer countries where capital is relatively scarce the marginal efficiency of capital (MEC) tends to be higher than in the developed world where it is relatively abundant. Assuming that interest rates broadly reflect MECs, it follows that lending rates in Western financial centres are below MECs prevailing in developing countries. Hence, economic efficiency –

and commercial logic – dictate that capital should flow from the relatively less-profitable First World to the relatively more profitable Third World.

14.4 Sources of external finance

The form in which external finance is received by borrowing countries is critically important. It is important to distinguish between both the type of creditor and debtor (private or public sector) and the nature of the external liability incurred. In practice, most developing countries have relied on some mix of the following four means of finance.

1 *Bond finance*. In the period before 1939, the governments of developing countries (particularly Latin America) relied heavily on the sale of fixed-interest bonds to foreign citizens and financial institutions. In recent years, this form of finance has again become more popular, providing a means of insulating the borrower from variations in interest rates.
2 *Bank loans*. During the 1970s, commercial bank lending to sovereign governments rose very sharply, for reasons discussed below. This lending was normally arranged on a syndicated basis by a group of banks and the loans carried a variable interest rate linked to the London interbank offer rate (LIBOR) on dollar deposits.
3 *Official loans*. External financing is available from several different types of public sector organization, including multilateral development banks like the World Bank, the Inter-American Development Bank, the European Bank for Reconstruction and Development, the IMF and bilateral official agencies (e.g. the British Overseas Development Administration). Such lending is often 'concessional' (i.e. offered at below market interest rates), although in the case of bilateral agencies the value of loans may be reduced if they are 'tied' to the purchase of goods and services from the donor nation.
4 *Foreign direct investment (FDI)*. The acquisition of local capital, whether by the purchase of existing physical assets or 'greenfield site' investment in new plant and equipment, is an important source of external finance for many developing countries. In the eighteenth and nineteenth centuries, North America and the Commonwealth relied heavily on FDI from Europe to finance their economic development. In contrast to the other three sources of external finance, FDI may be categorized as 'equity' rather than 'debt'; i.e. foreign owners take a share in the economic prosperity of the country in which they have invested, rather than a prior claim on its resources as in the case of debt financing. The disadvantage for the developing country is the potential loss of economic sovereignty which may follow from allowing foreign owners to control a significant proportion of its domestic capital stock.

The relative importance of these four sources of external finance for developing countries as a group has varied over time. There is also a systematic bias in the type of external finance which different groups of countries are likely to use. The poorest developing countries, notably in sub-Saharan Africa, are forced to rely very heavily on official lending, since they are insufficiently creditworthy to borrow in the market place on their own account. The middle-income countries, in contrast, are much better placed to borrow on commercial terms, thereby avoiding the 'strings' (e.g. in terms of contingent policy reforms, etc.) which often accompany official loans. Politically stable market economies (e.g. Singapore, South Korea etc.) are more likely to attract, and to be receptive to, FDI than centrally planned countries.

14.5 Why do debt servicing problems arise?

Successfully exploiting the opportunities offered by overseas capital requires that three conditions be fulfilled: first, that the savings gap can in due course be reversed (in technical terms, this means that the marginal propensity to save must be greater than the average propensity to save); second, that the forex gap can be reversed (either by increasing exports or 'compressing' imports); and finally, that the funds are invested in projects which yield a rate of return in excess of the interest rate on the debt.

By implication, debt servicing problems necessarily arise when one or more of these conditions is not fulfilled (see also Bird 1992). Domestic policy making by the developing country government concerned is clearly an important factor in this regard. Failure to develop local capital markets and a reluctance to push domestic interest rates above the rate of inflation (so that *real* domestic interest rates are negative) may militate against closing the savings gap, for example. The temptation to maintain an overvalued exchange rate (in order to keep down the domestic price of imported goods) may reduce international competitiveness and so prevent countries from turning around their current accounts. And using borrowed funds for uses which do not promote growth means that, even if the savings and forex gaps can be closed, overseas borrowing still ultimately constitutes a drain on the economy. Such uses include expenditure on military hardware and prestige capital projects which turn out to be 'white elephants', as well as channelling the borrowed funds into the forex market to support an overvalued exchange rate, thereby allowing urban elites to import luxury consumer goods or export their savings (i.e. engage in 'capital flight'). Table 14.4 shows the scale of capital flight in Mexico during the 1980s, which accelerated to staggering proportions as the government announced its inability to meet its debt servicing obligations in 1982.

The conditions necessary for successful debt repayment may also be violated by developments wholly external to – and hence beyond the control of – the developing country debtors. A marked deterioration in the developing countries' terms of trade (i.e. the value of their exports *vis-à-vis* their imports) or a sharp rise in the interest rate charged on overseas borrowing would both have far-reaching effects on the Third World's capacity to service its debt. The key difference, moreover, between externally and internally induced debt problems is that the former are likely to affect large numbers of developing countries simultaneously, whereas examples of the latter should tend to be spread more or less evenly across the world and over time. The most striking characteristic of the debt situation is that, when it broke in 1982, almost all developing

Table 14.4 Estimated capital flight from Mexico ($ billion)

1980	*1981*	*1982*	*1983*	*1984*	*1985*	*1986*	*1987*	*1988*	*1989*	*1990*
5.4	6.6	6.8	9.2	2.7	4.7	0.1	7.0	−1.0	−5.7	−5.8

Source: World Development Report.

countries experienced difficulties at the same time. The implication must be that the main cause of the 1982 crisis was external to the developing countries themselves.

14.6 The external dimensions of the 1982 crisis

In searching for external causes of the debt crisis, a useful starting point is the unprecedented role played by commercial banks in lending to developing countries during the 1970s and early 1980s. Indeed, the history of international banking in its present form dates back only to the 1960s, when technological developments – cheap, reliable air travel, transcontinental telephone and telex communications and the spread of computerization – allowed innovative US banks to escape stifling domestic regulations by establishing branches in Europe. These offshore subsidiaries initially accepted deposits from, and made loans to, US customers denied access to domestic facilities by the Federal Reserve Bank's monetary policy – and in so doing gave birth to today's 'Eurodollar' market.

In the 1970s, US regulations eased, but by then these new international banks had discovered the competitive edge that their offshore status and early, forced specialization gave them over more conventional rivals. Unencumbered by national balance sheet regulations, secure in a low-overhead world of wholesale, large denomination business and freed from the need for expensive high street branching networks, the international banks found themselves able to operate on much narrower margins, offering lending rates that undercut, and deposit rates that outbid, their competitors.

14.6.1 The first oil-price 'shock'

The growth of the Euro-markets apart, the other special contributory factor in the present international debt crisis was the pair of oil-price shocks which rocked the international economy in 1973 and 1979. The first more than quadrupled the price of oil, reshaping overnight the international pattern of balance of payments surpluses and deficits: the oil-exporting nations, especially the Middle Eastern states with small populations, enjoyed huge surpluses, while the oil-importing nations suffered a sharp deterioration in their trade balances (see Table 14.5). Because oil is almost universally priced and traded in US dollars, the so-called 'oil surpluses' manifested themselves in a rapid build-up of dollar balances with the ultra-competitive international banks, which they in turn sought to invest.

Table 14.5 The current account effects of the two oil-price shocks (current account balances, $ billion)

	1973	*1974*	*1975*	*1976*	*1977*	*1978*	*1979*	*1980*	*1981*	*1982*
Major oil exporters	6.7	68.3	35.4	40.3	29.4	−1.3	56.8	102.4	45.8	−17.8
Other developing countries	−11.3	−37.0	−46.3	−32.6	−29.6	−33.2	−49.7	−74.4	−95.0	−73.2
Industrial countries	20.3	−10.8	19.8	0.5	−2.4	14.6	−25.6	−61.8	−18.9	−22.2

Source: IMF World Economic Outlook.

Because Western governments typically responded to the oil-price shock by deflating their economies in an attempt to restore external balance, investment opportunities in the developed world proved scarce in the latter half of the 1970s. In contrast, the international banks found willing borrowers in the Third World. Amongst the oil-importing developing countries, the trade imbalances caused by the sharp rise in oil prices were exacerbated by the slump in primary export sales to the depressed industrialized world. Borrowing from the banks to fill their burgeoning forex gaps appeared the only way of maintaining growth. And for the oil-exporting developing countries with large populations like Mexico, Nigeria and Indonesia, the anticipation of even larger oil price rises in future encouraged more ambitious growth programmes financed by foreign bank debt. Reflecting the terms on which the deposits were accepted, the loans made by the international banks were predominantly in US dollars, at variable interest rates and on a short-term basis, although the normal practice was to 'roll over' loans (i.e. to pay off a maturing loan by extending another).

14.6.2 The second oil-price 'shock'

In 1979 oil prices doubled, with much the same effects on the global economy as the 1973 shock; indeed, until 1982 history seemed to be repeating itself, with both the oil-importing and the large-population, oil-exporting developing countries increasing their borrowing from the international banking system. The important difference lay in the West's reaction to the second price shock. Years of electorally unpopular inflation and the rise of monetarism as a political force caused many Western governments to respond to the surge in OPEC-induced inflation by sharply tightening monetary policy. In the United States, where this change in policy stance took place against the background of loosening fiscal policy, the effect was particularly dramatic: interest rates, which in real terms had been negative during the 1970s, soared in both nominal and real terms between 1979 and 1982; with the bulk of developing country debt short-term and denominated in dollars, the impact on debt servicing costs was almost immediate.

The huge stocks of overseas bank debt, which had been accumulated in the expectation of continuing low or negative real interest rates, simply became unmanageable by mid-1982. One after another, Third World countries were inexorably squeezed into financial crisis. Against this background, it is clear that the fundamental cause of the present debt crisis was not an epidemic of internal debt mismanagement across the Third World, but rather a combination of largely external factors which affected the developing countries as a group (see also Sachs 1989). In assessing the measures used to contain the crisis since 1982, it is important to bear this analysis firmly in mind.

14.7 Phase one: 'muddling through' the debt crisis, 1982–9

The IMF played the key role in managing the early stages of the debt crisis. Its approach was predicated on the underlying assumption that the developing countries' external debt *should*, and with appropriate policy changes *could*, be repaid in full and was driven by the overriding need to prevent a generalized default which could threaten the stability of the international banking system. The Fund adopted a twin-track strategy, seeking to maintain the net flow of capital to the developing countries in the short term to allow them a breathing space, while at the same time promoting 'structural adjustment' within the debtor countries in order to increase their debt servicing capacity in the longer term (see also Healey 1990 for a critique of muddling through).

In relation to the scale of the debt crisis, the Fund's resources were (and remain) so limited that direct financial assistance to all but the smallest developing countries is, of itself, little more than symbolic. Total quota subscriptions by the Fund's members, for example, currently amount to approximately $120 billion – little more than the outstanding debt of Brazil alone. For this reason, the Fund was forced to enlist the reluctant support of the international banks in dealing with the crisis. Its *modus operandi* for the more heavily indebted developing countries was to negotiate three-sided deals: the banks (often through the so-called 'London Club') agreed to 'reschedule' (i.e. roll over) existing debt and provide additional loans to maintain economic development, provided the developing country government undertook to implement an IMF package of policy 'reforms' (see Chapter 12).

14.7.1 The Baker Plan

The Baker Plan marked the high-water mark of the 'muddling through' approach to the debt crisis. In October 1985 the then US Treasury Secretary, James Baker, announced a plan which effectively formalized muddling through and the twin-track approach taken by the IMF to date. It emphasized, on the one hand, the need for the banks to continue lending to the developing world (the Baker Plan called for a further $20 billion over three years to the fifteen most heavily indebted countries) and, on the other, growth-oriented structural reform programmes in the debtor countries. New money was, as hitherto, to be highly contingent on adherence to IMF-orchestrated adjustment policies. The only novel feature of the Baker Plan was the inclusion of the World Bank as a joint partner with the IMF. The plan was thus predicated on the clear assumption that, with appropriate policy reforms, the developing world could be induced to repay its external debt in full.

In the event, the Baker Plan failed to take into account the changing nature of the debt crisis. Even as it was announced, the crisis was turning from a banking to a development crisis. As the banks managed to reduce their exposure and the threat of insolvency receded, their willingness to commit new money was sharply curtailed. At the same time, years of deflation and economic stagnation were taking their toll in the developing world. The Baker Plan was further undermined by the weakening of commodity prices and the collapse of oil prices in 1985–6, which led to further economic dislocation in many developing countries. Not only was new lending by the commercial banks not forthcoming on the scale envisaged, but net lending by the multilateral development banks, the IMF and bilateral official creditors also fell well below projections.

While muddling through 'succeeded' in averting the banking crisis, in the sense that it headed off wide-scale defaults and consequent bank collapses, it suffered from two major flaws which became increasingly apparent in the latter half of the 1980s: first, it ran directly counter to the objective of the banks, which was to reduce their exposure to the developing countries rather than increase it further; and it forced the burden of adjustment on the poorest countries of the world, locking them into apparently unending 'debt slavery'.

14.7.2 Muddling through: the view from the banks

Initially, the Fund's strategy appeared to be successful, to the extent that the banks continued to 'lend' to the developing countries throughout 1983 and 1984. In reality, they had little choice. Under US banking regulations, to which the majority of the most heavily exposed banks were subject, a loan which is not serviced for ninety days must be declared 'non-performing' and may no longer be booked as an asset. Writing off assets in this fashion in 1982 would have led to almost all the major banks being rendered insolvent. The only way of remaining *technically* solvent, therefore, was for them to keep alive the fiction that their developing country loans were performing, by 'lending' non-paying debtors the funds they needed to service their loans (Gottlieb and Change 1992).

Such forced or 'involuntary' lending basically involved the bank adding the overdue payments to the developing countries' outstanding debt, thereby avoiding short-term difficulties at the cost of further weakening their balance sheets in the longer term. Suppose developing country X has a \$100 billion debt and, this year, \$10 billion interest and \$20 billion repayment of capital are due. If X can only pay \$5 billion, the banks concerned have to accept the \$5 billion against the \$10 billion interest due and add the remainder to the outstanding debt. They then reschedule the \$20 billion capital due, charging an arrangement fee of \$1 billion which is also added to the total owed. To satisfy banking regulations, therefore, the banks were forced to 'lend' a non-paying debtor developing country a further \$6 billion, so increasing their exposure from \$100 billion to \$106 billion.

So long as the banks lacked the reserves to admit that developing country debt was non-performing, such involuntary lending was unavoidable. But the IMF's plan envisaged the banks continuing to supply the developing countries with 'new' capital to allow them to grow out of their difficulties, and this the Fund failed to achieve. (Note that, in the numerical example outlined above, the banks would have had to lend developing country X at least \$11 billion of new money to keep capital flowing into X in net terms.) The Fund's efforts to orchestrate so-called 'new lending' (i.e. lending net of debt service payments) were dogged by the 'free rider' problem. While it could argue convincingly that new lending was rational from the point of view of the international banking community as a whole – in the sense that it maximized the probability of the Third World repaying its debt – it was in the interests of each individual bank to lend only what was absolutely necessary to keep its own assets performing, taking advantage of new lending by other banks to cut its own involuntary lending.

Not only was new money largely unforthcoming, but by the late 1980s the banks began making stringent efforts to reduce their involuntary lending as well (see Bird 1989). Led by the US bank Citicorp, which set aside \$3 billion of its profits in 1987 to cover future losses on its developing country debt, all the other international banks dramatically increased their loan-loss reserves. Between 1987 and 1989, for example, the 'big four' British banks made loan-loss provision equal to 50 per cent of their Third World debt. This development increased the ability of the banks to wash their hands of the developing countries, either by writing off the debt altogether or, more usually, disposing of it at a discount (see below), so further weakening what little incentive there ever was for the banks to lend new money in the interests of eventually getting back their early loans (Armendariz de Aghion 1990).

Table 14.6 Debt and growth in severely indebted countries (%)

Country	*Outstanding debt.1990 ($ billion)*	*Debt/GDP, 1990*	*Interest/exports, 1990*	*Average GDP growth, 1982–90*	*Average import growth, 1982–90*	*Average investment growth, 1982–90*	*Average growth of per capita consumption, 1982–90*
Algeria	26.8	52.9	15.1	1.9	−2.2	−1.2	−0.6
Argentina	61.1	61.7	18.4	−0.0	1.2	−8.3	−1.1
Bolivia	4.3	101.0	15.9	1.0	2.2	−10.5	−1.7
Brazil	116.2	22.8	8.6	2.5	−0.1	1.3	0.5
Bulgaria	10.9	56.9	6.4	1.0	−0.2	3.0	3.8
Congo	5.1	203.6	9.3	1.1	0.7	−18.9	−0.7
Côte d'Ivoire	18.0	203.9	13.3	−0.4	2.8	−12.4	−4.7
Ecuador	12.1	120.6	14.5	2.0	−1.5	−4.1	−0.5
Mexico	96.8	42.1	16.7	1.6	5.0	−2.6	−1.1
Morocco	23.5	97.1	11.7	4.0	5.4	1.4	0.9
Nicaragua	10.5	–	3.0	−3.8	−0.8	−7.5	−6.5
Peru	21.1	60.1	5.2	−1.4	−1.8	−9.3	−3.5
Syria	16.4	118.1	3.9	1.8	−2.6	−9.1	−1.7
Venezuela	33.3	71.0	15.6	1.1	−7.7	−10.7	−1.2
Nigeria	36.1	117.9	12.1	1.9	−8.4	−9.6	−2.3

Source: World Development Report

14.7.3 Muddling through: the view from the developing world

From the point of view of the developing countries, 'muddling through' meant falling living standards and continuously rising debt: growth was sacrificed to make the switch from capital importer to capital exporter, while the stock of outstanding debt continued to mount (Fieleke 1990). Table 14.6 summarizes the experience of the 1980s for the most heavily indebted developing countries. It shows the scale of the cumulative compression of imports (which declined by as much as 8.4 per cent per annum over the period 1982–90 in Nigeria) and the knock-on effects this had for investment, which contracted sharply. The starkest statistics are for the growth of *per capita* consumption. In twelve of the fifteen cases, *per capita* consumption fell between 1982 and 1990, with countries like Côte d'Ivoire (−4.7 per cent per annum) and Nicaragua (−6.5 per cent per annum) recording declines of catastrophic proportions.

The Fund's early approach to managing the crisis, moreover, was vulnerable to criticism in several other respects. The first was its refusal to view the debt situation as the result of an external shock and its consequent preoccupation with internal adjustment policies. Even if there were scope for adjustment within an individual country, the same could not logically be true of the developing world taken as a whole. One country's imports are another's exports. If Argentina cuts its imports, it buys less from Chile, Brazil and Mexico, which in turn must embark on further rounds of austerity themselves – leading to an endless downward spiral.

A second problem was that many Third World countries export the same raw materials, for which world demand is both price and income-inelastic. The huge IMF-inspired increases in the Third World's output of basic commodities such as cotton, coffee, cocoa and copper depressed prices, often leading to lower export revenues despite the higher export volumes. Table 14.7 shows the steady deterioration in the terms of trade (the value of exports relative to the value of imports) for the developing countries, with Africa and Latin America suffering particularly damaging declines.

These 'fallacies of composition' apart, the logic of internal adjustment was also dangerously misconceived for a third reason. There is no escaping the stark fact that cutting imports and increasing exports meant reducing the real living standards of the world's poorest peoples to generate the surpluses needed to service debt. In many cases, the depth of the cuts required was so socially unacceptable, and the political structures so weak, that this form of adjustment proved simply unworkable. In the latter half of the 1980s, twenty-five of the developing countries which had sought assistance from the Fund experienced serious civil disorder as public hostility to the IMF-imposed austerity measures spilled over into violence. The worst disturbances were in Venezuela, where so-called 'IMF riots' led to hundreds of deaths in 1989.

14.7.4 The emergence of market-based debt reduction

Towards the end of Phase One, secondary markets began to emerge in developing country debt (Barston 1989). These markets were particularly attractive to smaller banks, which could reduce their exposure by selling their claims on developing countries at a discount. The price at which the debt traded was a function of the debt service payments the buyer *expected* the debtor country to make over time (in technical terms, the price of the debt was equal to the discounted or 'present value' of expected debt servicing payments to maturity). Discounts were expressed in terms of 'cents on

Table 14.7 Changes in terms of trade (annual changes, %)

	1974–83	*1984–8*	*1988*	*1989*	*1990*	*1991*	*1992*	*1993*
Africa	3.9	−7.0	−5.0	−0.8	3.7	−6.3	−3.0	−0.1
Asia	–	−0.2	0.3	0.7	−1.3	0.6	−0.4	−0.1
Latin America	1.4	−3.6	−0.7	−0.4	−1.2	−5.2	−0.6	1.1

Source: IMF World Economic Outlook.

the dollar' (e.g. debt trading at 60 per cent of its face value was said to be priced at '60 cents on the dollar'). The buyers of discounted debt initially comprised other small banks which had low exposure to sovereign debt, but the practice quickly spread to embrace multinational companies and the debtor countries themselves. By the late 1980s, several distinct transactions had become commonplace (Helpman 1989).

1 *Debt buybacks*. While the secondary market offered a way for banks to reduce their exposure, interbank transactions made no difference to the debtor country. It was still contractually obliged to service the debt at its full face value, even though the new owner had acquired it at a discount. Debt buybacks allowed debtor countries to capture the benefits of this discount by repurchasing their own debt in the secondary market. For example, if a country's debt were trading at 50 cents on the dollar, it could buy back its outstanding obligations at 50 per cent of their face value. One difficulty with debt buybacks is that they necessarily affect the price of such debt in the secondary market (i.e. by reducing its stock of outstanding debt, the debt servicing capacity of a developing country is increased, leading to a rise in the price of its debt). Large-scale buybacks were therefore unattractive to developing countries as a way of significantly reducing their debt.
2 *Debt-for-equity swaps*. Multinational companies became significant buyers of debt in the secondary markets in the late 1980s, normally with the intention of exchanging the debt acquired with the debtor government for local assets. In some cases the debtor country would swap local currency for its debt (with which the multinational could finance purchases of shares in local companies); in others the debtor government would swap shares directly (e.g. by transferring control of a former state-owned enterprise to the multinational).
3 *Debt-for-debt swaps*. Some developing countries attempted to buy back debt in exchange for 'senior' debt, rather than hard currency. The principle of senior debt is that it commands a first claim on the debtor country's reserves. Suppose its existing debt were trading at 50 cents on the dollar. The debtor country could buy back debt with a face value of $2 million in exchange for new senior debt with a face value of $1 million. Because the preferential terms of the senior debt imply that it will be paid in full, the market value of the senior debt would be exactly the same as the old debt which had been retired, so that the lender would be unaffected (although it would have to accept the formal write-down of its book assets). For the debtor, its contractual debt servicing costs would have been halved. Although a secondary market price of 50 cents on the dollar reflects a market expectation that the debtor will only meet half of its debt service costs in the long run, in the short run the developing country may actually be paying

most or all of its debt service costs; in this case, the saving from the debt-for-debt swap would be a real one. Moreover, there are other penalties which may stem from being in arrears or partial default, not least the denial of access to new loans. A successful debt-for-debt swap may unlock new money in the future. Variations on this basic theme included the swapping of collateralized debt for existing debt (i.e. debt that was guaranteed in some way, for example because it was underwritten by a third country).

14.8 Phase two: debt forgiveness and the Brady Plan

By the late 1980s it had become clear that the banking crisis had been successfully averted. The international banks had greatly strengthened their balance sheets, to the extent that a generalized default no longer threatened the stability of the system. On the other hand, evidence of a growing development crisis was mounting (Fischer and Husain 1990). In aggregate, the developing countries had a higher debt–export ratio in 1988 than in 1982, while their DSR was only 1 per cent lower. For the severely indebted low-income and middle-income countries the position was much worse. Arrears grew to $52 billion by December 1988, while the failure of many debtors to carry through adjustment policies was reflected by the decline in secondary market prices: between 1986 and 1989, the weighted average of debt for the major developing countries halved from 70 cents in the dollar to 35 cents in the dollar.

In March 1989 the then US Treasury Secretary, Nicholas Brady, advanced a new approach to managing the debt crisis (Fried and Trezise 1989). Unlike the Baker Plan, which was based on the assumption that sovereign debts would be repaid in full, the Brady Plan argued that debt forgiveness rather than further borrowing was the key to restarting economic growth in the developing world (see also Krugman 1988). A key feature of the Brady Plan was its use of the newer, market-based debt reduction techniques as a means of easing the debt burden. The Brady Plan had three main dimensions:

1 It urged commercial banks to develop a broader range of alternatives for financial support, to include debt service reductions and debt forgiveness.
2 It called on Western governments to amend national banking regulations, so that accounting rules did not impede debt forgiveness by their banks (e.g. see the rules of performing loans above).
3 It encouraged the IMF and the World Bank to provide funding for debt and debt service reduction purposes (e.g. by lending money which developing countries could use to buy back their debt in the secondary market).

At the heart of the Brady Plan was the proposition that developing countries should be able to capture the benefits offered by the discounted price of their debt in the secondary market. In May 1989 the IMF and the World Bank adopted guidelines for lending in support of debt and debt service reduction and a number of such packages were agreed, including agreements with the Philippines, Costa Rica, Venezuela, Uruguay and Niger. By far the largest was the agreement involving Mexico, under which $49 billion of debt was restructured. The package was highly complex, involving all the market-based debt reduction techniques outlined above. The banks were offered a menu of options: they could swap old debt (at 65 cents on the dollar) for new debt bearing market interest rates; they could swap old debt at par for fixed interest rate bonds (where the fixed rate was below the prevailing market rate); or they could swap old debt for equity. In the case of the debt-for-debt swaps, the new debt was partly collateralized with US Treasury bonds (the purchase of which was financed by the IMF and the World Bank to guarantee the principal on the new bonds) and backed by a special pool of earmarked foreign exchange reserves which provided a rolling eighteen month guarantee that interest payments would be met.

After the deal was completed, Mexico's IMF programme remained broadly on course and the secondary market price of its debt increased sharply. Nevertheless, the complexity of the deal and the length of time it took to arrange similar, less ambitious agreements for other debtors suggests that the impact of the Brady initiative is likely to remain limited (Unal *et al.* 1993; Rogoff 1992). Moreover, it is easy to overstate the value of the Brady deal to debtor countries. In the case of Mexico, for example, although $49 billion of debt was involved, it has been calculated that the actual value of the debt relief to Mexico was only $ 12–13 billion, from which must be deducted the $7 billion cost to Mexico of providing collateral for the new bonds (Bank of England 1991).

14.8.1 The Paris Club and the 1988 Toronto economic summit

The Brady Plan's analysis of the emerging development crisis was shared in the late 1980s by an important subset of the developing world's creditors, namely the so-called 'Paris Club' of official lenders. At the 1988 Toronto economic summit, the British Chancellor of the Exchequer, Nigel Lawson, pre-empted his US counterpart by calling on official lenders to grant debt relief to the poorest debtor nations (i.e. those with *per capita* GDP of less than $600). Under the Toronto terms (since amended by the 1990 Trinidad Agreement), debt may be rescheduled at concessional interest rates in cases where DSRs exceed 25 per cent. Some twenty countries have taken advantage of these arrangements, all of them African with the exception of Bolivia and Guyana. Given the small relative size of the countries so far involved, however, these initiatives have made only a marginal impact on the overall debt situation.

14.8.2 The case for and against debt forgiveness

The Brady Plan and the Toronto Agreement have been widely criticized, on the grounds that debt forgiveness rewards developing countries for their past profligacy and undermines their incentive to pursue internal adjustment policies. The basic argument follows 'moral hazard' lines and suggests that widespread debt forgiveness may actually prove counterproductive, increasing the likelihood of further debt servicing problems in the future. This critique implicitly assumes that the cause of debt problems is internal mismanagement, rather than some external combination of unforeseeable circumstances, and may be effectively challenged on this basis. There are compelling reasons to consider debt forgiveness as a solution to debt servicing difficulties, however, regardless of their ultimate causation.

The calculus of debt repudiation (i.e. complete unilateral default on debt obligations) suggests that, with rising adjustment costs and negative net resource transfers, debtor

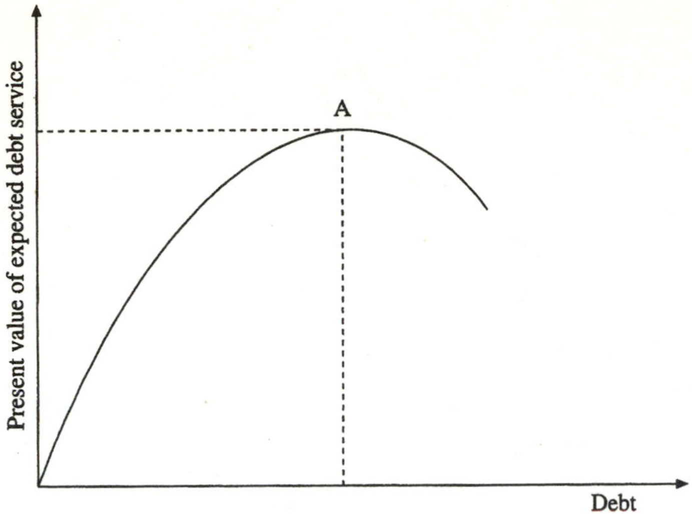

Figure 14.1

countries face an increasing incentive to renege on their obligations. Knowing that the banks are better able to withstand the balance sheet losses that would follow such action may further embolden some debtors, since they may expect the hostile reaction by lenders (and their national governments) to be less muted than hitherto. It may be, therefore, that if developing country debt is allowed to exceed a certain level, the flow of debt service payments may decline. Under these circumstances, debt forgiveness could actually increase the flow of interest and capital payments to the lenders. This concept is captured by the 'debt relief Laffer curve' (see Figure 14.1). It shows that, as the stock of outstanding debt rises, so the present value of expected debt servicing payments also increases, but at a decreasing rate. If point A is exceeded, the debtor countries will find it increasingly attractive to default, sacrificing the opportunity of future credit for the immediate savings in debt service costs. It follows that, if countries are allowed to accumulate debt beyond point A, debt forgiveness by the banks will actually increase the present value of expected debt servicing payments. (As noted above, the price of debt in the secondary market is simply the capitalized value of future expected debt service payments, so debt forgiveness should lead to a rise in the price of a country's debt for countries to the right of point A.)

The economics of debt repudiation may be more formally explored within the framework of the simple model developed by Krugman and Obstfeld (1988); see also Schwartz and Zurita (1992). In judging whether or not to default, a debtor country must weigh the benefits of default (namely, the savings in foreign exchange earnings which will no longer be diverted into debt service) against the costs (i.e. the loss of access to new loans).

For a given stock of external debt, D, a given interest rate on this debt, r, and scheduled repayment of principal, D^*, the benefit of default is given by total debt service payment due in the current period, i.e. $rD + D^*$. Against this benefit from default must be set the cost of default, namely the loss of new loans, L. The net

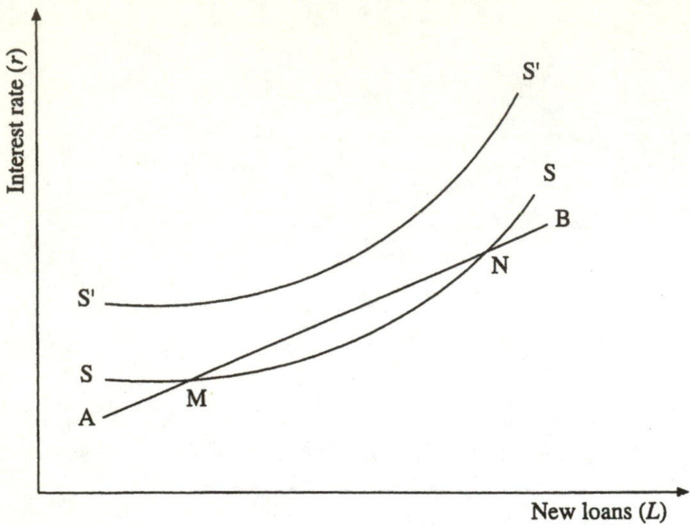

Figure 14.2

benefit from default is the net resource transfer (RT) from the debtor to the creditor country (see above), i.e.

$$\mathrm{RT} = D^* + rD - L$$

If RT is positive (i.e. if $D^* + rD > L$), then there is a positive benefit from default. Conversely, all other things equal, a negative RT eliminates the incentive to default. From this basic relationship may be derived schedule AB in Figure 14.2, which shows combinations of L and r at which the benefits of default are equal to the costs for a given D, D^*; i.e. along the length of AB

$$\mathrm{RT} = 0$$

or equivalently

$$D^* + rD = L$$

The AB schedule is upward-sloping because an increase in r increases the debt service obligations, requiring an offsetting increase in L to maintain a zero RT. At combinations of r, L above AB, the debtor country is likely to default (i.e. $\mathrm{RT} > 0$). On the other hand, at combinations below AB, the debtor country will continue to service its debt (i.e. $\mathrm{RT} < 0$).

While AB represents the combinations of r and L at which the debtor country will be indifferent between defaulting and servicing its debt, SS represents the supply of new loans from the international banks (i.e. the feasible combinations of r, L open to the debtor country). The SS schedule slopes upwards because, for a given market rate of interest, the banks will charge individual borrowers a higher rate of interest as the supply of loans increases (see also Thapa and Mehta 1991). The reason is that, as the supply of loans to an individual borrower increases, the likelihood of default in the long run is increased, inducing banks to demand a higher return to compensate for the increased risk. Thus while an increased flow of funds reduces the probability of default in the current period, it raises the likelihood of default in subsequent periods by increasing the stock of outstanding debt *D* (and so future debt service payments).

Provided that some portion of the SS schedule is below AB, there exist feasible combinations of *r*, *L* at which the debtor country has an incentive to continue servicing its debt. For example, in Figure 14.2, SS intersects AB at points M and N. At any point along the section of SS between M and N, the debtor country will choose to continue to service its debt rather than default. Suppose, however, that the SS schedule were to shift to the left to S′S′. With the new loan supply schedule, there is no feasible combination of *r*, *L* at which the debtor country has an incentive to continue servicing its debt. Under such circumstances, default is inevitable.

This model suggests that there is a strong likelihood of debt repudiation on the part of certain debtor countries. In the early 1980s, the SS curve shifted sharply to the left (e.g. to S′S′ in Figure 14.2), as monetary conditions in the United States levered up the prevailing market interest rate on dollar-dominated instruments (thereby driving up the marginal cost of funds to the international banks). The result was to force many developing countries temporarily into a position where default became attractive. Although market interest rates have subsequently eased from the levels reached in 1982, a rightward shift in the loan supply schedule from S′S′ (i.e. back towards SS) has been inhibited by two factors. First, banks have revised their judgement of the riskiness of lending to the developing countries, so that they are less willing to advance new funds at any given interest rate. And second, their willingness to lend has been further reduced by the loan-loss provisioning of the international banks, which has strengthened their capacity to write off existing debt. The result is that, despite the easing in market interest rates, the loan supply function remains at S′S′ (i.e. above the AB schedule) for many developing countries, making default incentive-compatible.

Debt forgiveness would have the effect of reducing the debtor's external debt *D*, shifting the AB schedule upwards (until eventually it cuts the S′S′ schedule). This is because, at any given interest rate, the debtor country would require a smaller flow of new loans to ensure a zero RT. Under circumstances in which default is incentive compatible, therefore, some form of debt forgiveness may be the only way of preventing outright default and ensuring that debt service payments continue to be paid (in part, at least).

14.8.3 The role of the IMF: change of policies in 2002

The scars left by successive financial crises from 1997 to 2002 in some LDCs were evident for all to see at the spring meetings of 2002 of the IMF. From the 1997 currency devaluations in South East Asia to Argentina's debt default at the end of 2001, the events of those five years were a sobering experience that prompted a wholesale rethink of the fund's approach.

The Fund has found itself under attack from every side over the past few years. It has been criticized for its economic prescriptions (which intensified the depth of the recession in South East Asia), its multi-billion-dollar bail-out packages (which largely benefited the Wall Street creditors of emerging market economies) and the inadequacies of surveillance mechanisms that failed to forecast financial market upheavals. Its traditional role as a supposed 'lender of last resort' became increasingly untenable as private-sector capital flows dwarfed any rescue package that the IMF could conceivably offer, while the attitude of Fund officials alienated all but its staunchest supporters.

Criticism of the Fund began to gather ground in the late 1990s, after the Asian devaluations and subsequent Russian debt default exposed the extent of the institution's failings. At first, the response of the IMF was simply to bury its head in the sand. It took another couple of years, and another couple of emerging market upsets before the IMF began to see that in a fast-changing world reinventing itself was the key to survival. Its policies began to alter after the departure of M. Camdessus when Germany's pragmatic Horst Kohler was named as his replacement. The IMF has started to take a more flexible approach to dealing with emerging market crises.

In the past, the Fund's starting point was adherence to orthodox economic policy. Countries were encouraged to defend fixed exchange rate regimes with higher interest rates, an approach that often had substantial financial and human cost. The IMF has since taken a more pragmatic stance, tailoring its policy prescriptions to individual country circumstance, and taking on board new thinking from the economic literature.

The Clinton administration of the 1990s blocked discussions about how the Fund should address country debt defaults, preferring to deal with them case by case. Although there were benefits – for example, flexibility – in this approach, there were also substantial costs. Under the Clinton administration's case-by-case strategy the IMF agreed many multi-billion-dollar bail-outs that largely ended up in the hands of Wall Street creditors. These rescue packages, dubbed a 'welfare system for Wall Street' in Washington, infuriated Congress, which threatened to block the IMF's access to US financial resources. There were other drawbacks of the case-by-case approach too, not least the uncertainty it generated in the markets and for the recipients of IMF aid.

It became increasingly clear that the international community needed to agree a common approach on how to deal with actual, or threatened sovereign bankruptcies. The existing approach failed to meet the needs of either global policy makers or developing countries. The debate moved along with the aid of Anne Krueger at the IMF. The first result was a new action plan on sovereign debt restructuring, published after the meeting of the Group of Seven finance ministers. In 2002, among others matters, the plan proposed the introduction of fixed limits on the size of IMF bail-outs, agreed the need for well defined rules on restructuring and suggested that LDCs introduce so-called 'collective action' clauses into bond contracts that would require creditors to work together in the event of a debt default.

The plan was a sensible step forward in the debate about how to deal with sovereign bankruptcies, and outlined a potential role for the IMF in a world that has changed beyond all recognition since the institution was set up in 1944. Evidently, the IMF can no longer act as a lender of last resort that averts sovereign bankruptcies with a combination of plenty of cash and a set of orthodox policy prescriptions. For the Fund to survive, and to prosper, it needs to hone its economic skills, to improve its surveillance role and, crucially, to work out a sensible and sustainable approach to debt defaults. The IMF has a long and difficult path ahead of it, but has at long last taken important first steps on the road towards carving out a sustainable role in a fast-changing financial world.

14.8.4 Conclusion

Since the debt crisis first began in 1982, the threat of widespread default and the collapse of the international banking system has receded. However, by the end of the 1980s it had become clear that 'muddling through' had led to the creation of a *development* crisis, with an increasing number of Third World countries facing years of economic stagnation and internal unrest, during which income and wealth would flow massively – and regressively – to the industrialized world. For a large group of developing countries, the benefits of formal debt repudiation, namely the retention of debt service payments for domestic uses, now outweigh the costs, namely exclusion from overseas credit markets. Several Latin American nations, notably Bolivia and Peru (but also on occasions Brazil), have been in *de facto* default for some years.

It is now generally recognized that the ultimate solution to the debt crisis must be through economic growth rather than austerity. Demand-side adjustment policies have not been successful and are logically misconceived. Longer-term supply-side adjustment policies are the only way forward, and for such policies to succeed the restoration of positive net capital transfers from the West to the developing countries is essential. Given the scale of the problem, some form of generalized 'debt forgiveness' is a *sine qua non* of a lasting solution, but such measures can only ease the negative resource transfers – debt and debt service reduction cannot, *per se*, bring about a resumption of positive capital flows to the developing world. Herein lies the real danger.

The experience of the Baker and Brady Plans highlights the difficulties of levering new money from a commercial banking system that has seen its faith in the security of sovereign lending terminally damaged. The multilateral agencies, including the IMF and the World Bank, have also experienced difficulties in setting in place structural adjustment projects on the scale needed, and Western governments have strongly resisted further quota increases in the resources of such agencies. With the governments of the major industrialized countries dealing with serious fiscal deficits, the prospect of a spontaneous recovery in bilateral aid flows is remote. Finally, the creation of new regional trade blocs (e.g. the European Union's single market and the North American Free Trade Area) and the opening up of Eastern Europe are attracting flows of FDI away from the developing world. Nor is it clear that there is any strong political will in the industrialized world to tackle the new development crisis. Unlike the earlier banking crisis, which threatened the stability of the international financial system, the consequences of developing country debt for economic development command little public interest. The most likely outcome is that defaults and arrears will quietly mount, while economic development in the world's poorest nations will continue to be retarded in the twenty-first century.

Questions

1 Why do developing countries become indebted?
2 What are the sources of external finance for LDCs?
3 Why do debt servicing problems arise?
4 What is the role of International Monetary Fund (IMF) in solving the debt crisis in LDCs?
5 What are the reasons in favour and against 'debt forgiveness'? Can countries borrow too much?

15 Environment and development

15.1 Introduction

The literature on political economy shows a broad area of 'government failure' in the efficient use of natural resources. The implications of such government failure could be as damaging to the economy as those of 'market failure'. Such failures comprise:

1 intervention in markets and present wrong price signals which distort allocation (Agarwala 1983);
2 marketing controls;
3 land use controls;
4 inappropriate fiscal policies (e.g. taxes and subsidies);
5 the general failure of bureaucracies to formulate and implement rational national resource policies in LDCs.

Some of these failures will have a clear impact on natural resource degradation (NRD) in LDCs. It is now acknowledged that relative prices matter; otherwise there will be a natural desire to exhaust the lowest priced resource first regardless of its true scarcity and environmental benefits. It is also clear that underpricing of, say, fuelwood and charcoal is linked with severe fuelwood depletion in some LDCs. However, in Ethiopia, fuelwood prices are very high, partly reflecting severe depletion of forest areas and partly showing the results of government policy. Rent-seeking behaviour (Krueger 1974) of the government can also encourage unsustainable natural resource use. The specific aims of this chapter are:

1 to examine some *macro* variables which could influence the process of NRD, like deforestation (since distortions can generate NRD, there is a case for examining the impact of *price* distortions, e.g. overvaluation of exchange rates and currency controls, on the use of natural resources at the macro level);
2 to analyse some economic policies to prevent NRD in LDCs;
3 to describe the determinants of demand for and supply of fuelwood in some African countries and suggest an alternative farming system for protecting the environment in LDCs.

15.2 Deforestation and macroeconomic environment

At a *macro* level, it is possible to conceptualize the impact of a number of variables to explain NRD in general and deforestation in particular. Here, some major candidates are:

1 population growth rate;
2 arable land availability *per capita*;
3 an index of food sufficiency;
4 movements in the terms of trade or real exchange rates;
5 fiscal policy, the debt–export ratio or an index of debt service;
6 *per capita* income.

The area of closed broad-leaved forests industrially logged can be used as an indicator of tropical forest degradation as it is highly correlated with the available data on deforestation. In theory, there are reasons to argue that significant terms of trade losses, severe foreign exchange constraints, tax/subsidies policies, rises in debt–export or debt–income ratios and subsequent exchange rate depreciation made deforestation 'incentive compatible' in many LDCs. Where land shortage seriously constrains arable agriculture, continual devaluations are likely to make governments more inclined to permit logging and colonization as a prelude to forest land conversion to agriculture. Further, a rise in incentives for agricultural production invites illegal cultivation of public forests under a condition of virtual open access.

Pooled cross-section and time-series data can be used fruitfully to understand the nature of relationships between deforestation (Y) and the movements of some major variables in a linear model as follows:

$$\text{I: } Y = XB + U$$

$$\text{II: } Y = XB + DA + U$$

$$\text{III: } Y = XB + CT + U$$

where X is an $n\text{X} \times 6$ (as per our example) matrix of explanatory variables with the first column consisting of the unit vector, U is an $n \times 1$ vector of residuals with $E(U) = 0$ and $E(UU') = \sigma^2 I$ where I is the identity matrix, D is an $n \times k$ matrix of dummy variables for region, income group and international credit standing and C is an $n \times 1$ vector denoting the interaction of the rate of devaluation and the dummy variable for a country's international credit standing. A, B and T are the respective regression coefficient vectors. In each model, the first element of the B vector is the intercept term.

Note that model I assumes common intercept and slope coefficients for all countries whilst model II assumes common slope coefficients but allows the intercept term to vary differently by region, income group, credit standing, etc. Model III assumes common intercept and slope coefficients on all variables except real devaluation. Countries belonging to different types of indebtedness are allowed to respond differently to real devaluations in model III (Capistrano and Kiker 1990).

Macroeconomic variables by themselves are not adequate to explain the complex phenomenon of deforestation. It is thus necessary to examine the specific micro

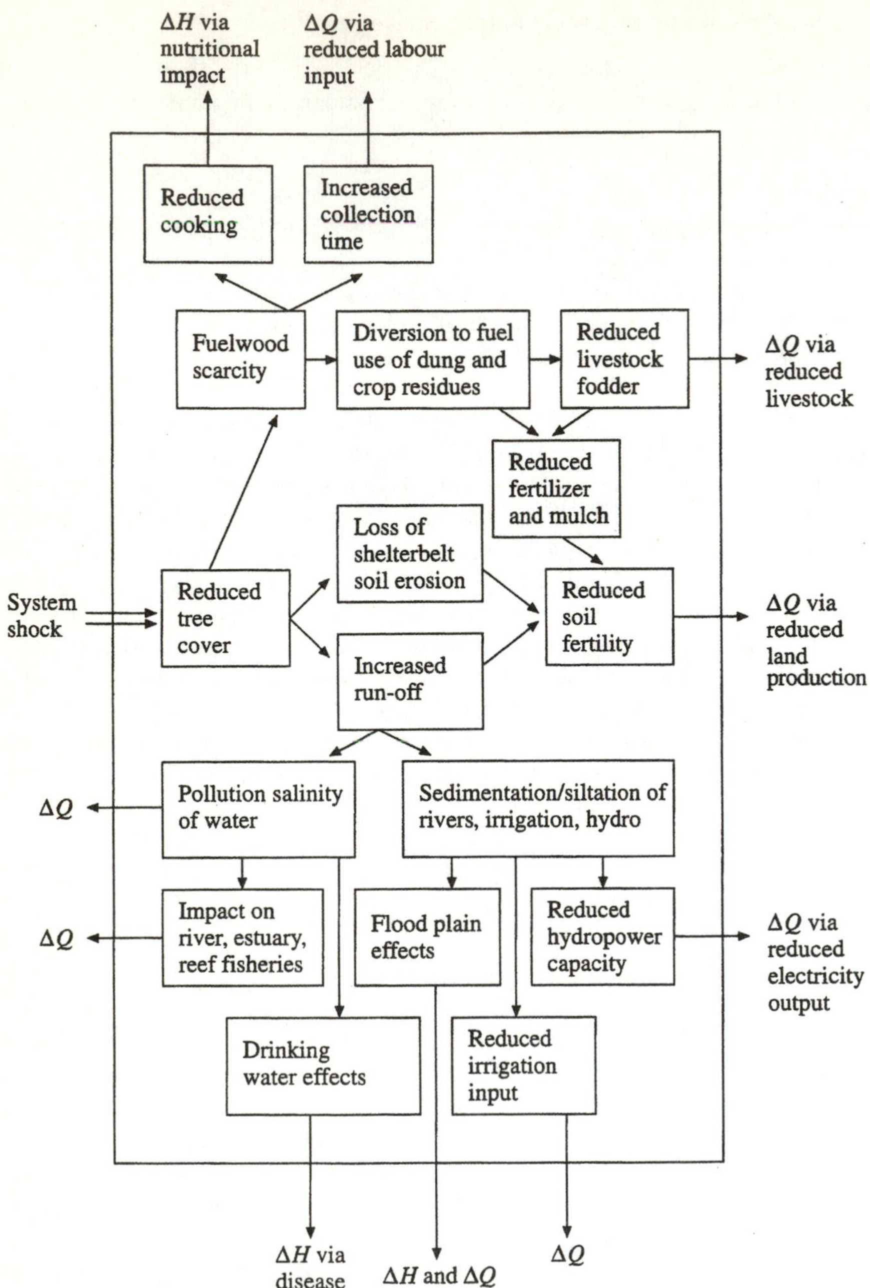

Figure 15.1 Resources interconnections in developing countries. Q agricultural output, H an index of health.

Source: Adapted from Pearce and Turner (1990)

factors which could explain the different facets of NRD and deforestation. However, in small open economies, it is very likely that producers' prices in agriculture could be influenced by movement in exchange rates. Thus, macro policy changes could alter the system of incentives and disincentives for a predominantly agrarian economy. Such linkages need more careful analysis (see Figure 15.1).

15.3 The 'tragedy of the commons'

In the absence of general economic policies to prevent the over-use of physical and economic resources, it is very likely that resource use will be inefficient. Such inefficiencies are quite common in LDCs with *common property resources* or *open access resources* and the effect on the environment could be very damaging. The final result could be tragic when a common property, say in parts of Africa or Asia, is overgrazed.

> Picture a pasture open to all. Each herdsman tries to keep as many cattle as possible on the commons. This works well for centuries because wars, poaching, and disease keep the numbers well below the carrying capacity of the land. But eventually the day of reckoning arrives. Each herdsman seeks to maximize his personal gain; he concludes that the only sensible course is for him to add another animal to his herd. And another. But this is the conclusion reached by each and every rational herdsman sharing a common. Herds are increased without limit in a world that is limited. Therein is the tragedy: Freedom in a common brings ruin to all.
>
> (Hardin 1968)

This brilliant statement of Hardin implies that in the absence of a tariff or rent on scarce resources, serious misallocation in their uses could result. In some cases, common property resources will not just be used but abused because of overgrazing and destruction of soil fertility. The same tragedy occurs when everyone 'fishes and overfishes' and each firm/farmer pollutes and over-pollutes the air or water to maximize profit in a competitive economy.

One simple question arises. Why are scarce resources so underpriced in LDCs? The main reasons could be as follows:

1 For common property/open access resources, since everyone's property belongs to no one, no owner is interested in preventing air/water pollution to keep the private cost of clearing the environment down to the minimum. Sometimes, we observe the same phenomenon in highly congested motorways, as the price of using such highways is zero.
2 The cost of *monitoring* the use of common property resources is high; so are the costs of collecting tariffs. Hence, governments sometimes decide to stay away from the duty of protecting the environment.

However, rising concern for environmental problems has forced economists, scientists and politicians to discuss practical policies for preserving the environment. The general economic solution to achieve 'efficiency' in the Paretian sense (i.e. it is impossible to make an economic situation better in terms of production, consumption and allocation without making someone worse off) could be achieved only in an ideal world of a fully competitive market economy. Problems arise because many LDCs suffer from 'distortions' as they experience both market and policy failures. Markets may be quite imperfect – sometimes dominated by monopolies or oligopolies – or they may be incomplete, even missing, in LDCs. As regards policy failures the World Bank observes: 'the perception that government has shifted during the past decade; where government was commonly seen as catalyst of development, many now think it an obstacle'.

Policy failures, i.e. government failures, occurred in the context of (1) trade regimes, (2) population growth, (3) fiscal policies (i.e. taxes and subsidies), (4) the definition and enforcement of property rights, (5) inadequate environmental information and (6) misuse of government expenditure.

Market failures contribute to 'distortions' and environmental degradation – such failures are common in the face of 'externalities'. An externality is present whenever an agent's (e.g. X) utility or production processes incorporate real variables whose values are chosen by other agents (e.g. governments) without much attention to the impact on X's welfare. Externalities can affect both producers and consumers.

When spraying with pesticides upstream reduces fish catches and thus the production and consumption of fish downstream, such externalities are negative. When trees provide wind shelter and shade one's neighbour's crops, externalities are positive. In the face of NRD, we are mainly concerned with negative externalities. They assume great importance when property rights are poorly defined in a resource-abundant economy managed by communal practices. However, the correlation between the two is not always perfect. 'Farmland may not always be individually owned although it may be quite scarce (e.g. China) and trees may not be privately controlled although near extinction (e.g. Lesotho).' Nevertheless, externalities are at the heart of the matter when *rational* individual decisions may lead to catastrophic social results, as exemplified before in the 'tragedy of the commons': 'Ruin is the destitution toward which all men rush, each pursuing his own best interest in a society that believes in the freedom of the commons' (Hardin 1968).

Note that, in the 'tragedy of the commons' drama, the price of the herd may be inadequate to lead to over-stocking. Besides, if we follow Hardin's 'logical' policy, i.e. privatization, then former land users could be destitute (Dasgupta 1982). Besides externalities, in poor agrarian LDCs, distortions could arise because the notion of risk can be different for an individual and the society. Sometimes, the markets for risks to insure against possible crop damage are not available at all, i.e. the 'missing markets'. Such a problem is generally explained by the existence of high transaction costs for drawing up contracts for many millions of farmers. Also, the insurance may 'adversely' influence an agent's behaviour, i.e. the problem of *moral hazard* – farmers may sell inputs and seed corn and claim full compensation for crop loss.

15.4 Externalities, natural resource degradation and economic policies

Suppose an upstream farmer pollutes a river flowing into a downstream farm. The upstream farmer can abate the pollution, shown in his or her marginal abatement cost (MAC) (see Figure 15.2). Since water pollution causes damage to crops for the downstream farmer, he or she decides to control such damage and MDC shows the marginal damage cost. The principle of cost minimization (i.e. the sum of MAC and

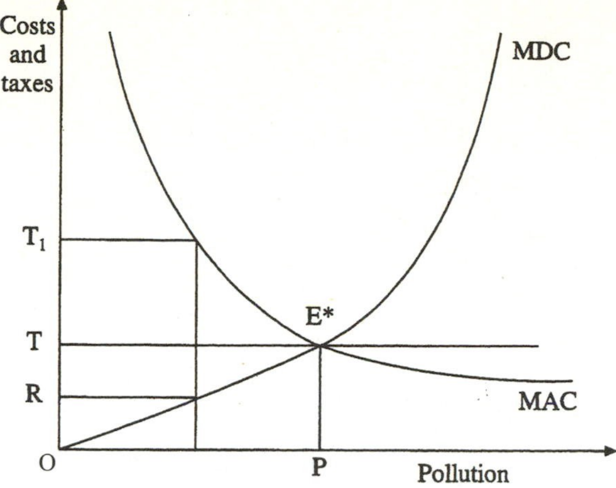

Figure 15.2

MDC) implies that the optimal level of pollution is E* because an agreement at that point is the most beneficial to both farmers in terms of overall net gains.

15.4.1 The pollution tax: the 'polluter pays' principle

In economic theory, the simple way to solve the problem of pollution from an industry would be to equate the marginal abatement cost MAC (i.e. the cost of abating or controlling pollution, also known as marginal control cost which lowers marginal private net benefits, MPNB) to the marginal benefits from abating pollution. When the latter benefits are regarded as the cost of the damage avoided, they can also be regarded as marginal damage or external cost (MDC or MEC; see Figures 15.2–3) which rises with increasing pollution. The socially optimal level of pollution occurs at a point where MAC = MDC. For industry in the private sector, the marginal private cost (MPC) is likely to be less than the marginal social cost (MSC) because the private manufacturer is unlikely to consider the social cost of pollution when he or she seeks to maximize profit and equates the marginal revenue (MR) with the marginal private cost. In order to induce a firm to move to the socially optimal level, a tax (T) equivalent to the marginal costs of pollution (MCP) could be imposed. This is the 'polluter must pay' principle. Symbolically, then, for a firm producing fertilizer, say, the profit maximization principle is

$$\text{MR} = \text{MPC} + \text{MCP}$$

If

$$\text{MCP} = T$$

then

$$\text{MR} = \text{MPC} + T$$

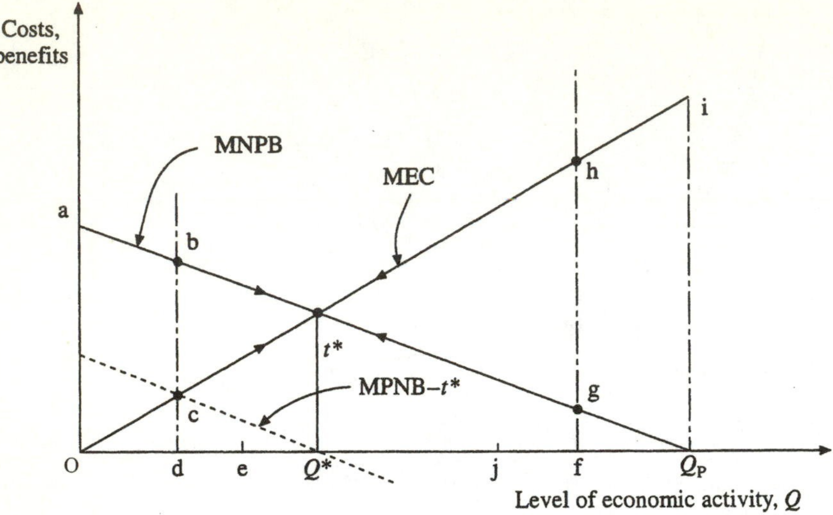

Figure 15.3 Optimal pollution through bargaining. When t^* is the pollution tax to attain Q^*, MPNB shifts downward to MPNB $-t^*$

Note that MSC = MPC + MCP = MPC + T. Thus

$$\text{MR} = \text{MSC}$$

It has to be recognized that the imposition of a tax on the fertilizer industry is likely to reduce output and raise prices as firms tend to internalize the 'external' cost of pollution and include it as part of the private cost. Under market imperfection this is very likely to be the case, and the size of 'social' surplus would fall in comparison with the situation before tax. If the fertilizer industry is under the public sector operating according to the principle of equalizing marginal cost (MC) to price P, i.e. MC = P, and the difference between private output and 'social' output is negligible in the pre-tax situation, then the imposition of a pollution tax is unlikely to make a significant difference. Second, when the taxes are introduced in an imperfect market, it should be remembered that we are actually in a 'second-best' world and there are, in fact, two distortions: the first arises out of the imperfection of the market and the second arises out of externalities (i.e. pollution). Thus, to obtain a socially 'optimal' level of output, imperfections in the market have to be corrected *before* the introduction of taxes.

There are other problems, however, in the practical application of pollution taxation of which the most important one is actually estimating the monetary cost of pollution. Otherwise, the calculation of the marginal pollution cost (MPC) would be rough and crude. This task is particularly difficult in the LDCs where the money value of some products is not usually known. The problem could be overcome by using 'surrogate', i.e. shadow, prices.

In principle, the derivation of a tax to achieve an optimum solution could be explained in a diagram (see Figure 15.2). Let costs be measured on the vertical axis and pollution be measured on the horizontal axis. The Pareto optimum is reached at a point such as E* where MDC = MAC. If the economy operates at a suboptimal level, a tax equivalent to OT will make MDC = MAC at level of pollution OP. If the *ex ante* damage function is unknown, an iterative principle could be adopted. A tax rate like OT_1 could be imposed; since it would be regarded as too high in comparison with MDC = MSC since $OT_1 > OR$, a lower rate of tax should be chosen to induce a move towards E*. Conversely if the tax is too low in comparison with MSC then such a tax should be raised. The difficulty in the application of this principle is that to achieve equality between MAC and MDC one has to know about the range of the damage function rather than the value at a point, as the estimation of points is not helpful for assessing *marginal* changes.

15.4.2 The fixed standard, bargaining and the Coase theorem

Other principles to achieve a socially desirable level of pollution involve the least cost method of a *fixed standard of environmental quality,* the principle of bargaining (under which victims of pollution negotiate directly with the polluters and a 'deal' is struck where the victims' marginal damage is equal to the firm's marginal benefit) and regulations to achieve a certain standard. It has been persuasively argued that a competitive market economy can reach an 'optimum' level of pollution through bargaining among the affected parties when the property rights are well defined, regardless of who holds the property rights. This proposition – discussed under the 'Coase theorem' – if valid will render government regulation to correct for externalities superfluous. The market simply takes care of itself. An unregulated polluting farmer will try to maximize profits by operating at Q_p. The 'social optimum' output is Q^* (see Figure 15.3). If the suffering farmer has the property right, he or she would prefer to have zero pollution. Otherwise, the polluting farmer must pay compensation. In a bargaining model, at the pollution level Od, the welfare loss for the polluted farmer is area Ocd but the compensation he receives is the area Oabd. Hence it is incentive compatible for both parties to find an 'optimal' level of pollution at Q^*. At any point to the right of Q^*, the victim of pollution 'compensates' the polluter to 'sacrifice' a certain amount of polluting activity. A little reflection suggests that, once again, under the 'victims pay for pollution' (VPP) principle, it is 'optimal' for both parties (given the relative net gains) to reach Q^*.

The difficulties of the applications of these principles can be easily understood. First, the principles involve subjective judgement about the standards and some of them could only operate within a given set of political mandates which may or may not be optimal. Also, the distribution effects of taxes and regulations are unlikely to be the same.

Efforts to reduce pollution by taxes, quality standards and regulations have at least one major impact which should be acknowledged: collectively or individually, they may foster attempts to invent or switch over to less polluting technology. If this happens, the overall social benefit will depend upon the marginal social cost of such a switch and the marginal benefits from reduced pollution. Where a developing country depends very much upon imported technology which has substantial pollution content, then a switch to alternative technology has the important effect that more is spent on research and development for inventing such a technology both within the home country and abroad. Where domestic innovation is encouraged along with the objective of achieving efficiency in resource allocation (by minimizing the relative factor–cost ratios) in LDCs, the effects on indigenous research, output, employment and distribution are likely to be favourable. However, an accurate estimation of net social benefit along the lines suggested is very much in the lap of future research. In the context of the fertilizer and pesticide industries in the LDCs, since fertilizer and pesticides are regarded as vital inputs for agricultural and income growth, the detrimental effects of its production on the environment have hardly figured in the literature. This could partly be explained by the basic need to survive at any cost, partly by the lack of awareness of the problems of the environment and partly by the general willingness to pay for the pollution as a necessary evil.

15.5 A case study: the importance of fuelwood in household energy consumption

Fuelwood and other biomass materials are the most important household fuels in developing countries (Cline-Cole *et al.* 1990). This is mainly because of their low cost, ready availability and the extremely modest cooking facilities needed to convert them into useful energy. Estimates of worldwide consumption of fuelwood indicate that in 1978 2 billion people relied on fuelwood and biomass as their primary source of household energy. The potential demand for fuelwood, however, exceeds the supply in many locations. According to de Montalembert and Clement (1983), a total of 96 million people experienced an acute fuelwood deficit of 1 m^3 *per capita* per year in 1980.

Given population growth, fuel use and forest conversion trends, LDCs faced a potential deficit of 100 million m^3 per year by 2000. Overall, by the year 2000, a total of 2.4 billion people were expected to be using fuelwood at a rate faster than it could be generated (Eckholm *et al.* 1984).

Fuelwood, bagasse, coconut shells and husks, bamboo, sawdust, agricultural residues and dung provide the major share of household energy in fourteen of the fifteen cases shown in Table 15.1. Nairobi, a large urban area, is the only exception. None the less, fuelwood accounts for 47 per cent of total household energy in Nairobi. Low quality biomass fuels are important sources of household energy in countries where fuelwood resources have already been severely depleted, e.g. India, where agricultural residues and dung are the only fuel sources available.

The quantity of fuelwood consumed by households varies greatly from continent to continent, country to country and even between neighbouring villages. Table 15.2 shows the wide variation in fuelwood consumption throughout the world. Fuelwood consumption ranges from 2.6 million tonnes *per capita* per year in Kwenzitu, Tanzania, to just 0.1 million tonnes *per capita* per year in Hyderabad, India. Household income and the availability of wood resources are strong determinants of the quantity of fuelwood consumed in most South Asian and Central American countries (Alam *et al.* 1985).

A clearer picture of household energy consumption is presented in Table 15.1. Fuelwood is the most important sources of household energy in six of the fifteen cases. Fuelwood and kerosene are used at every location. A wide variety of biomass sources other than wood, of both high quality (bamboo) and low quality (bagasse, coconut husks and sawdust), are used in Indonesia and the Philippines (see, for example, Thomsen 1988).

Table 15.1 Percentage contribution of woodfuels, other biomass and petro-fuels and electricity to village energy needs

Location	*Wood fuels*	*Other biomass*	*Petro-fuels and electricity*
Bundilya, Tanzania[a]	98.8	0	1.2
Machackos, Kenya[b]	98.9	0	1.1
Nairobi, Kenya[c]	47.3	0	52.7
Taruyan, Jndonesia[d]	76.7	1.3	22.0
Bukit Apit, Indonesia[d]	67.7	2.0	30.3
Ilocos Norte, Philippines[c, f]	84.7	10.6	4.7
Jogeshwari, India[g]	41.0	51.6	7.4
Satwad, India[g]	43.8	53.4	2.8
Chandanagar, India[g]	32.3	64.3	3.4
Reddypalle, India[g]	35.2	60.7	4.1
Gopularam, India[g]	19.4	77.2	3.4
Pemmadapalle, India[g]	39.0	57.9	3.1
Gunnikuntla, India[g]	40.7	56.1	3.2
Doolavariapalle, India[g]	24.5	71.1	4.4
St Lucia[h]	53.1	0	46.9

Sources: [a] Nkonoki and Sorensen (1984); [b] Openshaw (1981); [c] Hughes-Cromwick (1985); [d] Down (1983); [e] Hyman (1985); [f] Bowonder *et al.* (1985); [g] Wilkinson (1984); [h] all these references are cited in Thomsen (1988).

15.5.1 Economic factors

Household income and size. Household income is regarded as an important determinant of the demand for energy and individual fuels in LDCs. As household income increases, the tendency is for the consumption of primary energy to increase but not in direct proportion. A household fuel consumption study of Nairobi demonstrates this tendency (Hughes-Cromwick 1985). Energy is clearly used more efficiently as incomes increase. In India the income elasticity of demand or primary energy consumption is estimated as –0.054 (Alam *et al.* 1985).

The impact of household size is to increase the efficiency of fuel use for larger households. Increasing family size, in effect, lowers the cost *per capita* of energy used. Such economies of scale in household energy consumption have been observed in the rural village of Kwenzitu, Tanzania (Fleuret and Fleuret 1978). A high growth rate of population also leads to a rise in the demand for fuelwood as the dependency ratio rises.

Urban/rural location. The availability of a particular fuel in a location is a major determinant of the fuel choice (Wilkinson 1984). Fuelwood is used most frequently in rural areas because it is readily available at a very low or even zero monetary cost. However, charcoal is a more economical form of energy than fuelwood in an urban setting when transport costs are considered because of its higher energy content per unit weight (Wood and Baldwin 1985).

15.5.2 Fuel prices and opportunity costs of labour

The relative prices of fuels have been important determinants of the demand for individual fuels. The elasticity of substitution between, say, fuelwood and kerosene could be different owing to the difference in the methods required for using the two fuels.

Table 15.2 Quantity of woodfuel energy consumed in various locations around the world (per capita)

Location	*GJ*	*MT*	*Location*	*GJ*	*MT*
Tanzania[a]	21.76	1.40	Bundilya, Tanzania[a]	19.20	1.24
Kwemzitu, Tanzania[b]	40.38	2.61	Machakos, Kenya[c]	13.86	0.89
Nairobi, Kenya[d, n]	14.68	0.95	Bamako, Mali[c]	8.37	0.54
Ouagadougou, B.F.[f]	7.88	0.44	Costa Rica[g]	8.46	0.55
El Salvador[g]	13.18	0.85	Guatemala[g]	10.09	0.65
Honduras[g]	12.10	0.78	Mexico[g]	7.79	0.50
Nicaragua[5]	8.66	0.56	Panama[5]	6.79	0.44
Haiti[g]	9.29	0.60	Dominican Republic[g]	3.56	0.23
St Lucia[h]	2.47	0.16	Bolivia[g]	1.69	0.11
Brazil[g]	4.97	0.32	Colombia[g]	4.91	0.32
Ecuador[g]	4.28	0.28	Peru[g]	5.78	0.37
Uruguay[g]	6.68	0.43	Bangalore, India[i]	2.82	0.18
Hyderabad, India[i]	1.57	0.10	Bangladesh[j]	4.51	0.29
Ilocos Norte, Philippines[k]	9.38	0.61	Taruyan, Indonesia[l, m]	5.94	0.38

Sources: [a] Nkonoki and Sorensen (1984); [b] Fleuret and Fleuret (1978); [c] Openshaw (1981); [d] Hughes-Cromwick (1985); [e] Foley (1985); [f] Chauvin (1981); [g] Sanchez-Sierra and Umaña-Quesada (1984); [h] Wilkinson (1984); [i] Alam *et al.* (1985); [j] Prior (1986); [k] Hyman (1985); [l] Down (1983); [m] Thomsen (1988).

Note: [n] Total household consumption.

Fuelwood gathering, however, can require a large amount of time in areas where wood is scarce. Table 15.3 shows that the fuelwood gathering in households in Kwenzitu, Tanzania, occupies eleven hours a week. The amount of time spent collecting fuelwood varies widely and has been reported to reach a level as high as two or three man-hours per day in wood-scarce areas of Nepal and Sahelian Africa (Leach *et al.* 1986; Pearce *et al.* 1990).

In such cases the price (cost) of fuelwood is the opportunity cost of the gatherer's time. The opportunity cost of the time spent collecting fuelwood depends on the seasonal variation in the demand for labour in agriculture, potential returns from cottage industry opportunities and the demand for labour at home. When labour is scarce, the time spent collecting fuelwood has a high opportunity cost. In Kwemzitu, Tanzania, women, the traditional gatherers of fuelwood, spent 11 per cent of their

Table 15.3 Amount of time spent by households gathering fuelwood

Location	*Time spent (per week)*
Kwemzitu, Tanzania[a]	11.0 hours
Machakos, Kenya[b]	0.2 man days[e]
Ilocos Norte, Philippines[c]	6.4 hours
Taruyan, West Sumatra, Indonesia[d]	6.3 hours
Kukit Apit, West Sumatra, Indonesia[d]	1.5 hours

Sources: [a]Fleuret and Fleuret (1978); [b] Openshaw (1981); [c] Hyman (1985); [d] Down (1983).

Note: [e] The number of hours in a man-day was not given.

work week gathering fuelwood. In a subsistence economy the shortage of labour limits the production of cash goods, like beer and charcoal, which were traditionally produced by women (Fleuret and Fleuret 1978; Thomsen 1988).

15.5.3 Fuel energy content and conversion efficiency

The energy content of the fuel and the efficiency of the conversion device have important effects on both primary and useful energy consumption. Usually, about three tonnes of fuelwood are needed to obtain the equivalent energy of one tonne of LP gas. However, the efficiency of the conversion system, the ability of the stove-pot system to capture and deliver heat energy to cook food, must still be considered (Gill 1987; Hughes-Cromwick 1985).

15.5.4 Real exchange rates and the price of fuelwood

Fuelwood and petro-fuel are *potential* substitutes. When petro-fuel prices increase relative to fuelwood prices, the demand for and the price of charcoal may increase, affecting demand for fuelwood. Given such indirect linkages, exchange rates could alter relative prices in determining demand for fuelwood.

15.5.5 Supply of forest area

Several perennial supply response studies postulate supply relationships in which the expected price of alternative crops affect the perennial planting decisions. For new plantings, theory suggests that agents invest in new trees up to the point where the stream of discounted net revenues acquired over the productive period of the stock compensates the initial investment for the establishment of the grove. Hence, agents take into account output prices and production costs in appraising the flow of net revenues and the costs of land and capital in evaluating the initial investment. The optimality conditions further suggest that new planting investment in any period depends on the tree stock of the previous period as well as past new plantings. Changes in the expected prices and production costs are assumed to sufficiently approximate changes in the expected profitability of trees and changes in the weather (e.g. severe drought) can affect replantings.

The following supply equation was specified:

$$Q_t = \alpha_0 + \alpha_1 \frac{P_{t-1}}{P^0_{t-1}} + \alpha_2 W_t + \alpha_3 T_t + \alpha_4 P_{t-2} + \varepsilon_t$$

where Q_1 is the tree output, P_{t-1}/P^0_{t-1} is a price ratio representing the effects of deviations of actual prices on the short-run output adjustment of the firm, P_{t-2} is a lagged price which allows for the possible effects of past input utilization levels on current yields, W_t is a dummy weather variable reflecting output reductions from drought occurrences and T is a trend variable to capture productivity gains. All prices in the supply equation are constructed as the ratio of nominal price to production costs. Expectations can be static, adaptive or rational and are assumed here to be adaptive.

Given the large-scale deforestation occurring in many LDCs, it is imperative to devise alternative systems of farming for underdeveloped agriculture. In humid West

Africa, agro-forestry has been promoted as an interesting alternative farming system as a pragmatic solution to the serious problems of deforestation, soil erosion and loss of land productivity. Such an alternative farming system is discussed briefly in the next section.

15.5.6 Role of economic policies

Economic policies – at both the macro and micro level – can play a significant role in increasing supply and reducing the demand for fuelwood in LDCs. Here, it is imperative to be aware of the total economic value (TEV) of forests and fuelwood. Such TEV comprises actual use value (AV) plus an option value (OV) plus existence value (EV). Thus

$$\text{TEV} = \text{AV} + \text{OV} + \text{EV}$$

Generally speaking, AVs and OVs are obtained from the direct and indirect use of the forest environment (e.g. the use of trees for fuelwood and the restoration of soil fertility via nitrogen-fixing properties). If agriculturists in LDCs are risk-averse and prefer to preserve the soil conservation attributes of trees in the current period as insurance against the risk of losing these functions in the future, then surely trees have some option values. These OVs assume great importance within certain communities whose culture and heritage depend on the unique characteristics of the natural environment around them (Pearce *et al.* 1991). Existence values are not related to any use of a resource. Such values usually arise when agents derive utility because of its sheer existence (e.g. tropical forests). Inability to understand the role of the different components of the TEV frequently causes environmental degradation in many LDCs because distorted prices send wrong signals to producers and consumers and the private costs of fuelwood collection culminating in environmental degradation fail to reflect the true social cost in terms of forgone environmental values. The problem of a mismatch between fuelwood demand and supply and consequent resource degradation in West Africa has also been aggravated by government failure, which is quite different from market failure. Market failures occurred because of the inadequacy of the incomplete/imperfect or missing markets to reflect TEV. Where government policies failed to take into account the full incidence of the different sections of the TEV, we have examples of government failure. Such failures have been quite serious in the following cases:

1 output and input pricing policies;
2 the introduction of land and forest resource rights as incentives to their protection;
3 inappropriate monetary policies (e.g. cheap credit to exploit forest and fuelwood supply) and fiscal policies (e.g. tax concessions);
4 faulty and insecure land titling and registration;
5 inappropriate exchange rate policies, sometimes at the behest of international agencies.

The last point is of considerable interest to policy makers as it tends to suggest that a frequently recommended remedy (for the necessary 'adjustment' in some African countries) like devaluation makes deforestation incentive compatible for a country which earns substantial amounts of foreign exchange by exporting wood and other timber products. The problem of market failure becomes acute when the main use of fuelwood is cooking – a phenomenon which is observed in most parts of rural Africa. With growing paucity of fuelwood, cooking habits can alter, to affect the level of nutrition adversely. An inadequate supply of fuelwood can hinder the introduction of a nutritious product like soya beans as the development of such food needs extra cooking time. Besides, with a growing shortfall in the supply of fuelwood, more crop residues and animal dung are burned rather than applied to the soil as fertilizers. The additional food production due to dung use can be estimated with a crop response function. The product of the extra food grains and the market price will yield the shadow price of dung (see for example Pearce and Turner 1990). Thus, reflection suggests that the pricing and the economic policies for fuelwood in many African countries do not really reflect its actual cost to society.

15.5.7 The political economy of rent-seeking behaviour in fuelwood

The phenomenon of rent seeking usually arises as a result of the inability of the governments of LDCs to levy market-clearing prices for fuelwood (Krueger 1974). In economic theory, economic rent is the difference between the willingness to pay of the farmer and the actual payment. The existence of administered prices (i.e. price controls) for fuelwood can make such rents very substantial for LDC governments. Figure 15.4 illustrates. Let DD′ be the demand curve for fuelwood and SS′ the supply curve. The price of fuelwood is artificially fixed by the government at PP′. Let OQ be the given access to land for fuelwood collection. Rent is very high, as shown by PMRD, the shaded area – the gap between the demand curve and the

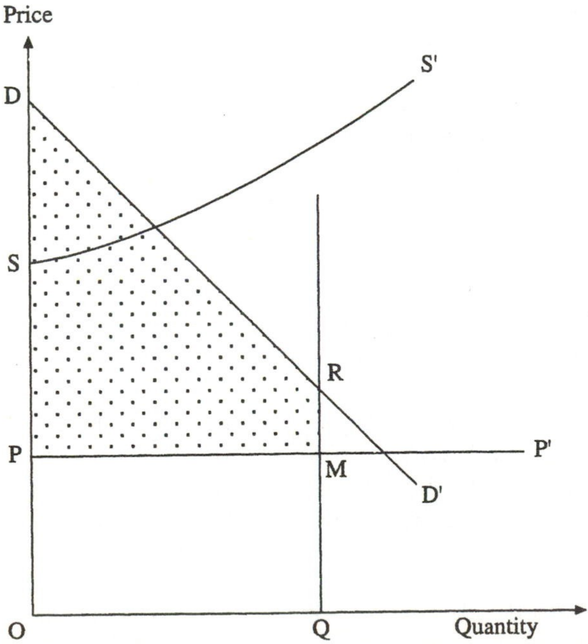

Figure 15.4 Fuelwood supply and demand in a rent-seeking company

price charged. Clearly, the deliberate underpricing of fuelwood leads to a substantial misallocation of resources.

15.6 An alternative farming system: alley cropping in humid West African agriculture

West African agricultural productivity has been sustained through shifting cultivation methods (i.e. cultivating a piece of land for a year or two and then shifting to fields that have been in long-term fallow). However, owing to an increase in population pressure on arable land, fallow periods have been shortened with adverse consequences on the natural restoration of the physical, chemical and biological properties of soils (Lal *et al.* 1985; Juo and Kang 1987, cited in Thomsen 1988). The long forest and bush fallow have been replaced by short grass fallow. The result has been a decline in crop productivity and the availability of food *per capita* over the last decade or so.

A set of new technologies developed elsewhere is most often inappropriate to the unstable soils found in much of sub-Saharan Africa (Matlon and Spencer 1984). Of the various technologies developed by scientists, alley cropping has shown the most promise. Alley cropping mimics the natural land management system by introducing leguminous trees/shrubs in hedgerows with crops grown between the alleys. The leguminous trees contribute by fixing nitrogen, recovering nutrients leached in subsoil, recycling nutrients by returning tree prunings to the surface soil and reducing soil erosion (Kang *et al.* 1984). The long-term use reduces demand for idling of land and thus enables an increased proportion of the land to remain in cultivation. The replacement of bush fallow cultivation methods by a semi-permanent cultivation system is a desirable strategy to meet the growing food needs of tropical sub-Saharan Africa (Ashraf 1990).

Although some economic analysis of alley cropping technology has been performed (Ehui *et al.* 1988; Ngambeki 1985; Raintree and Turry 1980; Sunberg *et al.* 1987; Verinumbe *et al.* 1984), none of them is used for a complete farm system analysis and they have largely ignored the economic efficiency consideration of farmers' limited resources. Since the decision to accept or reject new technology rests with the farmer, the unit of analysis is a farm household. A whole farm analysis can be made by using a linear programming model adapted to a farm system. Alternatively, it is possible to use a *social* cost–benefit analysis of alley cropping. This approach can be used to identify costs and benefits at appropriate prices and discount rates in order to gain some knowledge of the viability of such projects in specific (e.g. humid or sub-humid, labour surplus) areas. Results of such a study would be of use to authorities interested in sustainable economic development (Anderson 1987; see also Ruitembeck 1989).

The industrially developed countries should try to conserve the tropical forests, genetic species and biodiversity out of self-interest as the 'greenhouse effect' begins to take its toll and the depletion of non-renewable resources buttresses the case for 'sustainable supplies' from the LDCs. Besides, the existence of species and a cleaner environment in LDCs should command a fair market value for the tourists from the DCs, not to mention the option and bequest values that could be obtained from conserving living forest resources. Sustainability of the supply of raw materials from LDCs at lower cost should increase producers' surplus. Similarly, the size of the consumers' surplus of tourists from DCs visiting LDCs should rise from forestry conservation

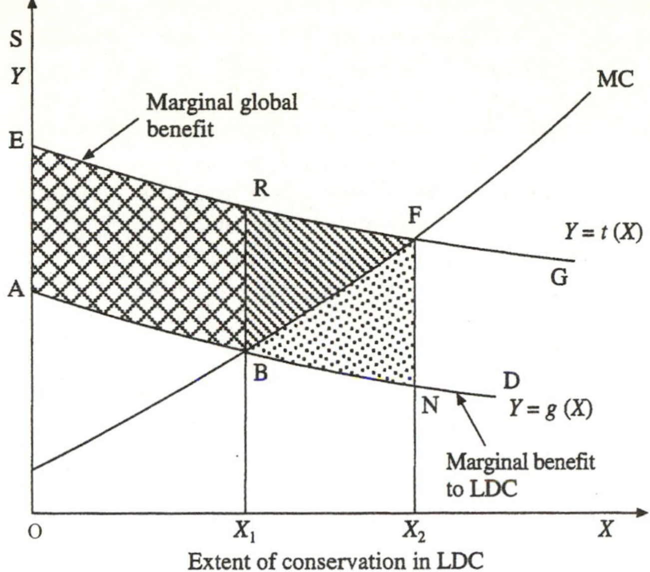

Figure 15.5 International spillover benefits from conservation in an LDC as illustrated by the theory of public goods; see Tisdell 1990.

projects. Sometimes, aid effectiveness in agricultural projects could be seriously reduced owing to a lack of environmental impact assessment. In the following we show the international gains from forestry conservation with a simple theory.

Assume that the function AD in Figure 15.5 measures the marginal benefit of forest conservation in an LDC, i.e. $Y = g(X)$, and EG measures the global benefit, $Y = t(X)$. Clearly, the difference between AD and EG measures marginal external benefits to the rest of the world. Let MC denote the marginal costs of forest conservation in an LDC. In the absence of any attempt to absorb the external benefits, equilibrium is obtained at B and conservation will be OX_1. Here, the 'spillover' effect for the rest of the world (ROW) is ABRE. To conserve forest up to X_2 at F, a point which is optimal for ROW, an LDC will find it 'incentive compatible' only if it receives a transfer payment of area BFN. In a bargaining model, an LDC should then try to obtain as much as possible of the area ABRE + BFR + BFN = AEFN, the maximum amount ROW is willing to pay an LDC (see Tisdell 1990). Since DCs are likely to benefit from such conservation, they have an incentive to support such policies by using aid, debt forgiveness and proper exchange rates for LDCs. DCs may also assist in setting up suitable institutions which would promote greater conservation of forests in LDCs (see Chapters 12 and 13).

15.7 Conclusion

Evidence available so far clearly suggests a close nexus between economic policies and deforestation in LDCs in general and West Africa in particular. The arbitrary prices of fuelwood, timber and other forest products have frequently distorted the long-run 'real' and social costs of deforestation. Present prices of forest products seldom include the forgone timber rentals, direct forestry services, e.g. tourism, and future ecological costs. Besides, *ad hoc* microeconomic setting of forestry product prices could have made deforestation 'incentive compatible'. Similarly, interest rate policies have kept the real cost of borrowing artificially very low owing to a regime of 'financial repression' (Ghatak 1995) and have provided incentives to destroy virgin forests and promote 'new frontier' land for non-forestry activities. Together with the expanding credit system, a low real interest rate policy could also affect investors' planning horizons. Appropriate population policies, at both micro and macro level, given their impact on food, fuel and other types of energy and land use, could help or hinder the pace of deforestation considerably. Commercial policies which directly affect the demand for forest products and energy pricing for switching demand towards the substitutes of fuelwood are urgently needed.

Questions

1 What is the 'tragedy of the commons'?
2 What are 'externalities'? How are they regarded as problems in environmental management in LDCs?
3 What is a pollution tax? Should polluters pay?
4 Evaluate the role of economic policies for the conservation of firewood in LDCs.

Bibliography

Acharya, S. (1981) 'Perspectives and problems of development in sub-Saharan Africa', *World Development* 9: 109–47.

Adelman, Irma (1962) *Theories of Economic Growth and Development*, Stanford: Stanford University Press.

—— (1968) 'An econometric model of socio-economic and political change in underdeveloped countries', *American Economic Review* 58: 1184–1218.

—— (1975) 'Growth, income distribution and equity-oriented development strategies', *World Development* February–March: 67–73.

Adelman, Irma and Chenery, H. (1966) 'Foreign aid and economic development: the case of Greece', *Review of Economics and Statistics* 48: 1–19.

Adelman, I. and Robinson, S. (1978) *Income Distribution Policy in Developing Countries: A Case Study of Korea*, London: Oxford University Press.

Adelman, Irma and Taft Morris, Cynthia (1967) *Society, Politics and Economic Development: A Quantitative Approach*, Baltimore: Johns Hopkins University Press.

—— (1968) 'Performance criteria for evaluating economic development potential; an operational approach', *Quarterly Journal of Economics* 37 (2): 260–80.

—— (1973) *Economic Growth and Social Equity in Developing Countries*, Stanford: Stanford University Press.

Adelman, I. and Taylor, J.E. (1990) 'Is structural adjustment with a human face possible? The case of Mexico', *Journal of Developed Studies* 22 (3): 387–407.

Adelman, Irma and Thorbecke, E. (eds) (1966) *The Theory and Design of Economic Development*, Baltimore: Johns Hopkins University Press.

Adler, John H. (1958) 'Fiscal policy in a developing country', in A.N. Agarwala and S.P. Singh (eds) *The Economics of Underdevelopment*, New York: Oxford University Press.

Agarwala, Ramgopal (1970) *An Econometric Model of India 1948–1961*, London: Frank Cass.

—— (1983) *Price Distortions and Growth in Developing Countries*, World Bank Paper 575.

Agenor, R.P. (2001) *The Economics of Adjustment and Growth*, London: Academic Press.

Agenor, R.P. and Montiel, P. (1996) *Development Macroeconomics*, Princeton: Princeton University Press.

Aghion, P. and Howitt, P. (1998) *Endogenous Growth Theory*, Cambridge MA: MIT Press.

—— (1992) 'A model of growth through creative destruction', *Econometrica* 60: 323–51.

Ahluwalia, Montek S. (1974) 'Income inequality: some dimensions of the problem', in H. Chenery, M.S. Ahluwalia, C.L.G. Bell, J.H. Duloy and R. Jolly (1974) *Redistribution with Growth*, London: Oxford University Press.

—— (1976a) 'Inequality, poverty and development', *Journal of Development Economics* 3: 307–42.

—— (1976b) 'Income distribution and development: some stylized facts', *American Economic Review* May: 128–35.

—— (1985) 'Rural poverty, agricultural production and prices: a re-examination', in J. Mellor and G. Desai (eds) *Agricultural Change and Rural Poverty*, Baltimore: Johns Hopkins University Press.

Ahluwalia, Montek S. and Chenery, H.B. (1974) 'A model of distribution and growth', in H. Chenery, M.S. Ahluwalia, C.L.G. Bell, J.H. Duloy and R. Jolly (1974) *Redistribution with Growth*, London: Oxford University Press.

Ahluwalia, M.S., Carter, N.G. and Chenery, H.B. (1979) 'Growth and poverty in developing countries', *Journal of Development Economics* 6: 299–341.

Ahmad, A. and Kwan, C.C. (1991) 'Causality between exports and economic growth', *Economics Letters* 37: 243–8.

Ahmad, E. and Stern, N. (1984) 'The theory of reform and Indian indirect taxes', *Journal of Public Economics* 25: 259–95.

—— (1989) 'Taxation for developing countries', in H. Chenery and T.N. Srinivasan (eds) *Handbook of Development Economics*, Amsterdam: North-Holland, vol. II, ch. 20.

Ajayi, S. (1994) 'The state of research on the macroeconomic effectiveness of strutural adjustment programme in sub-Saharan Africa', in R.D. Hoeven and F.V.D. Kraaji (eds) *Structural Adjustment and Beyond in sub-Saharan Africa*, Westport, CT: Greenwood Press.

Alam, M., Dunkerley, J., Gopi, K.N. and Ramsay, W. with Davis, E. (1985) *Fuel-wood in Urban Markets: A Case Study of Hyderabad*, New Delhi: New Concept Publishing.

Alamgir, M. (1978) 'Towards a theory of famine', University of Stockholm, 103 (mimeo).

Alesina, A. and Rodrik, D. (1994) 'Redistributive politics and economic growth', *Quarterly Journal of Economics* 109: 465–90.

Alesina, Alberto and Rodrick, Dani (1991) 'Redistributive Politics and Economic Growth', mimeo, Cambridge MA: Harvard University.

Allen, F. (1985) 'On the fixed nature of sharecropping contracts', *Economic Journal* 95: 30–48.

Allen, I. and Barnes, D. (1985) 'The causes of deforestation in developing countries', *Annals of the Association of American Geographers* 75: 1963–84.

Allen, T. and Thomas, A. (2001) *Poverty and Development*, Oxford: Oxford University Press.

Amano, M. (1980) 'A neo-classical model of the dual economy with capital accumulation in agriculture', *Review of Economic Studies* 47: 933–44.

—— (1983) 'On the Harris–Todaro model with inter-sectoral migration of labour', *Economica* 50: 311–23.

Amemiya, T. (1973) 'Regression analysis when the dependent variable is truncated normal', *Econometrica* 41: 977–1016.

Amin, Samir (1969) 'Levels of remuneration, factor proportions and income differentials with special reference to developing countries', in A.D. Smith (ed.) (1976) *Wage Policy Issues in Economic Development*, London: Macmillan.

Anand, R., Chibber, A., Rocha, R. and van Wijnbergen, S. (1990) 'External balance and growth in Turkey: can they be reconciled?', in T. Aricanli and D. Rodrik (eds) *The Political Economy of Turkey: Debt, Adjustment and Sustainability*, London: Macmillan.

Anand, Sudhir (1977) 'Aspects of poverty in Malaysia', *Review of Income and Wealth* 23 (1): 1–16.

Anand, S. and Kanbur, S.M. (1978) 'Inequality and development: a reconsideration', St Catherine's College, Oxford (mimeo).

—— (1981) 'Inequality and development: a critique', St Catherine's College, Oxford (mimeo).

—— (1985) 'Poverty under the Kuznets process', *Economic Journal* 95.

—— (1986) 'Inequality and development: a critique', symposium paper, Yale University Growth Center.

Anderson, D. (1987) *The Economics of Afforestation: A Case Study in Africa*, Baltimore: Johns Hopkins University Press.

Arestis, P. and Demetriades, Panicos (1997) 'Financial development and economic growth: assessing the evidence', *Economic Journal*, 107: 783–99.

Aricanli, T. and Rodrik, D. (eds) (1990a) *The Political Economy of Turkey: Debt, Adjustment and Sustainability*, London: Macmillan.

—— (1990b) 'An overview of Turkey's experience with economic liberalisation and structural adjustment', *World Development* 18 (10): 1343–50.

Arida, P. and Taylor, L. (1989) 'Short-run macroeconomics', in H. Chenery and T.N. Srinivasan (eds) *Handbook of Development Economics*, Amsterdam: North-Holland, vol. II.

Armendariz de Aghion, B. (1990) 'International debt: an explanation of the commercial banks' lending behaviour after 1982', *Journal of International Economics* 28: 173–86.

Arrow, K.J. (1962) 'The economic implications of learning by doing', *Review of Economic Studies* 29: 155–73.

Arrow, K. and Scitovsky, T. (eds) (1969) *Readings in Welfare Economics*, London: Macmillan.

Arslan, I. and van Wijnbergen, S. (1993) 'Export incentives, exchange rate policy and export growth in Turkey', *Review of Economics and Statistics* 75 (1): 128–33.

Aschauer, D.A. (1985) 'Budget deficits and aggregate demand', *American Economic Review* 75: 117–27.

Aschauer, David (1989) 'Is public expenditure productive?' *Journal of Monetary Economics* 23: 177–200.

Ashraf, M. (1990) 'Economics of alley-cropping in humid West Africa: a linear programming analysis', Food and Resource Economics Department, University of Florida, Gainesville (mimeo).

Asikoglu, Y. and Uctum, M. (1992) 'A critical evaluation of exchange rate policy in Turkey', *World Development* 20: 1501–14.

Askari, H. and Cummings, R. (1976) *Agricultural Supply Response: The Econometric Evidence*, New York: Praeger.

Atkinson, A.B. (1970) 'On the measurement of inequality', *Journal of Economic Theory* 2: 244–63.

Ayre, P.C.I. (ed.) (1977) *Finance in Developing Countries*, London: Frank Cass.

Azam, K.M. (1973) 'The future of Green revolution in West Pakistan: a choice of strategy', *International Journal of Agrarian Affairs* 5, March.

Azariadis, Costas and Drazen, Allan (1990) 'Threshold externalities in economic development', *Quarterly Journal of Economics* 105: 501–26.

Aziz, S. (1974) 'The Chinese approach to rural development', *World Development* 2: 87–91.

Bagchi, Amiya (1962) 'The choice of the optimum techniques', *Economic Journal* 72 (3): 658–76.

Bahmani-Oskooee, M. (1993) 'Black market exchange rates versus official exchange rates in testing purchasing power parity: an examination of the Iranian rial', *Applied Economics* 25: 465–72.

Bahmani-Oskooee, M. and Alse, J. (1993) 'Export growth and economic growth: an application of cointegration and error-correction modelling', *Journal of Developing Areas* 27: 535–42.

Bahmani-Oskooee, M. and Payesteh, S. (1993) 'Budget deficits and the value of the dollar: an application of cointegration and error-correction modeling', *Journal of Macroeconomics* 15 (4): 661–77.

Baker, Arnold B. and Frank, Falero, Jr (1971) 'Money, exports, government spending and income in Peru, 1951–66', *Journal of Development Studies* 7 (4): 353–64

Balassa, Bela (1972) *The Structure of Protection in Industrial Countries*, Report EC-152, Washington DC: IBRD.

—— (1982) *Development Strategies in Semi-industrial Economies*, Baltimore: Johns Hopkins University Press.

—— (1986) 'Policy responses to exogenous shocks in developing countries', *American Economic Review, Papers and Proceedings* 75–8.

—— (1989) 'Outward orientation', in H. Chenery and T.N. Srinivasan (eds) *Handbook of Development Economics*, Amsterdam: North-Holland, vol. II.

Balassa, Bela and Associates (1971) *The Structure of Protection in Developing Countries*, Baltimore: Johns Hopkins University Press.

Balasubramanyam, V.N. (1973) *International Transfer of Technology to India*, New York: Praeger.

Baldwin, Robert F. (1972) *Economic Development and Growth*, New York: Wiley.

Baldwin, Robert E. and Murray, T. (1977) 'MFN tariff reductions and LDC benefit under the GSP', *Economic Journal* 87: 30–46.

Balkir, C. (1993) 'Turkey and the European Community: foreign trade and direct foreign investment in the 1980s', in C. Balkir and A.M. Williams (eds) *Turkey and Europe*, London: Pinter.

Balogh, T. (1967) 'Multilateral versus bilateral aid', *Oxford Economic Papers* 19 (3): 328–44.

Bandyopadhyay, S. and Deverajan, S. (1993) 'Using Project Rates of Return to inform Project Allocation Decisions', mimeo, Washington DC: World Bank.

Bandyopadhyay, T. and Ghatak, S. (1982) 'Some remarks on agricultural backwardness under semi-feudalism', *Indian Economic Review* 20: 27–35.

—— (eds) (1990) *Current Issues in Monetary Economics*, Brighton: Harvester; New York: Barnes & Noble.

Banerjee, Abhijit (2001), 'Contracting Constraints, Credit Market and Economic Development', mimeo, Cambridge MA: MIT.

Banerjee, Abhijit, and Duflo, E. (2000) 'Reputation effects and limits to contracting', *Quarterly Journal of Economics* 115: 989–1019.

Banerjee, Abhijit, Besley, T. and Guinnane, T. (1992) 'Thy neighbour's keeper: the design of a credit co-operative with a theory and a test', *Quarterly Journal of Economics* 109: 491–515.

Banerjee, A., Dolado, J., Galbraith, J.W. and Hendry, D.F. (1993) *Cointegration, Error Correction and the Econometric Analysis of Nonstationary Data*, Oxford: Oxford University Press.

Banerjee, A., Dolado, J., Hendry, D.F. and Smith, G. (1986) 'Exploring equilibrium relationships in econometrics through static models: some Monte Carlo evidence', *Oxford Bulletin of Economics and Statistics* 48: 253–77.

Bank of England (1991) 'The LDC debt crisis', *Bank of England Quarterly Bulletin* 31: 498–507.

Banuri, T. and Schor, J.B. (1992) *Financial Openness and National Autonomy*, Oxford: Clarendon Press.

Bardhan, Kalpana (1970) 'Price response of marketed surplus of foodgrains: a cross-sectional study of some north Indian villages', *American Journal of Agricultural Economics* 52: 51–61.

Bardhan, Kalpana and Bardhan, Pranab (1971) 'Price response of marketed surplus of foodgrains: an analysis of Indian time series data', *Oxford Economic Papers* 23: 255–67.

Bardhan, Pranab Kumar (1970a) 'Green revolution and agricultural labourers', *Economic and Political Weekly* 5 (29–31): 1239–46.

—— (1970b) *Economic Growth, Development and Foreign Trade*, New York: Wiley.

—— (1973) 'On the incidence of poverty in rural India of the sixties', *Economic and Political Weekly* 8.

—— (1977) 'Variations in forms of tenancy in a peasant economy', *Journal of Development Economics* 4 (2): 105–18.

—— (1984) *Land, Labour and Rural Poverty: Essays in Development Economics*, New York: Columbia University Press.

—— (1985) 'Poverty and "trickle down" in rural India: a quantitative analysis', in J. Mellor and G. Desai (eds) *Agricultural Change and Rural Poverty*, Baltimore: Johns Hopkins University Press.

—— (1987) 'Optimum foreign borrowing', in K. Shell (ed.) *Essays in the Theory of Optimal Economic Growth*, Boston: MIT Press.

—— (1988) 'Alternative approaches to development economics: an evaluation', in H. Chenery and T.N. Srinivasan (eds) *Handbook of Development Economics*, Amsterdam: North-Holland, vol. I.

Bardhan, Pranab Kumar and Srinivasan, T.N. (1971) 'Crop-sharing tenancy in agriculture: a theoretical and empirical analysis', *American Economic Review* 61: 48–64.

—— (eds) (1975) *Poverty and Income Distribution in India*, Calcutta: Statistical Publishing House.

Barel, Ann and Lichtenberg, Frank (1987) 'The comparative advantage of educated workers in implementing new technology', *Review of Economics and Statistics* 69: 1–11.

Barker, R.W. and Cordova, V. (1978) 'Labour utilization in rice production', in R.W. Barker and Y. Hayarni (eds) *Economic Consequences of the New Rice Technology*, Manila: IRRI.

Barro, Robert (1990) 'Government spending in a simple model of endogenous growth', *Journal of Political Economy* 98: S103–S125.

Barro, Robert (1991) 'Economic growth in a cross-section of countries', *Quarterly Journal of Economics* 106: 407–443.

Barro, Robert and Becker, Gary (1988) 'A reformulation of the economic theory of fertility', *Quarterly Journal of Economics* 103: 1–25.

Barro, Robert and Sala-i-Martin, Xavier (1992) 'Convergence', *Journal of Political Economy* 100: 000–00.

Barro, Robert and Sala-i-Martin, Xavier (1995) *Economic Growth*, New York: McGraw-Hill.

Barston, R. (1989) 'The international debt crisis: evolving management methods', *Journal of World Trade* 23: 69–82.

Bartlett, W. (1983) 'On the dynamic instability of induced migration unemployment in a dual economy', *Journal of Development Economics* 13: 85–95.

Bartsch, W.H. (1977) *Employment and Technology Choice in Asian Agriculture*, New York: Praeger.

Basu, K. (1983) *The Less Developed Economy: A Critique of Contemporary Theory*, Oxford: Blackwell.

—— (1997) *Analytical Development Economics*, Oxford: Oxford University Press.

—— (1997) 'Economics of child labour', *Journal of Economic Literature*.

Bator, F.M. (1957) 'On capital productivity, input allocation and growth', *Quarterly Journal of Economics* 71: 86–106.

Bauer, P.T. (1971) *Dissent on Development: Studies and Debates in Development Economics*, London: Weidenfeld & Nicolson.

—— (1973) 'Inflation, SDRs and aid', *Lloyds Bank Review* 25: 31–5.

—— (1981) *Equality, the Third World, and Economic Delusion*, Cambridge, MA: Harvard University Press.

Bauer, P.T. and Yamey, B.S. (1957) *The Economics of Underdeveloped Countries*, Chicago: University of Chicago Press.

—— (1959) 'A case study of response to price in an underdeveloped country', *Economic Journal* 69: 800–5.

Baumol, William J. (1968) *Economic Dynamics*, 3rd edn, New York: Macmillan.

—— (1977) *Economic Theory and Operations Analysis*, 4th edn, London: Prentice Hall.

Baysan, T. and Blitzer, C. (1991) 'Turkey', in D. Papageorgiou, M. Michaely and A.M. Choksi (eds) *Liberalizing Foreign Trade: New Zealand, Spain and Turkey*, Cambridge: Blackwell.

Becker, G. (1981) *A Treatise on Family*, Cambridge MA: Harvard University Press.

Becker, G.S. and Lewis, H.G. (1973) 'On the interaction between the quantity and quality of children', *Journal of Political Economy* 81 (2): S279–88.

Becker, Gary, Murphy, Kevin and Tamura, Robert (1990) 'Human capital, fertility, and economic growth', *Journal of Political Economy* 98: S126–S150.

Beckerman, Wilfred (1966) *International Comparisons of Real Incomes*, Paris: OECD Development Center.

—— (1974) *In Defence of Economic Growth*, London: Jonathan Cape.

Beckerman, Wilfred and Bacon, Robert (1970) 'The international distribution of incomes', in P. Streeten (ed.) *Unfashionable Economics: Essays in Honour of Lord Balogh*, London: Weidenfeld & Nicolson.

Behrman, Jere (1979) *Development, the International Economic Order and Commodity Agreements*, London: Addison Wesley.

Behrman, J.R. and Deolalikar, A. (1987) 'Will developing country nutrition improve with income? A case study for rural south India', *Journal of Political Economy* 95: 492–507.

—— and ——(1988) 'Health and nutrition', in H. Chenery and T.N. Srinivasan (eds) *Handbook of Development Economics*, Amsterdam: North-Holland, vol. I.

Behrman, J. and Wolfe, B. (1987) 'How does mother's schooling affect the family's health, nutrition?', *Journal of Econometrics* 36: 185–204.

Behrman, R.L. (1968) *Supply Response in Underdeveloped Agriculture: A Case Study of Four Major Annual Crops in Thailand 1937–1963*, Amsterdam: North-Holland.

Bell, C. (1988) 'Credit markets and interlinked transactions', in H. Chenery and T.N. Srinivasan (eds) *Handbook of Development Economics*, Amsterdam: North-Holland, vol. I.

Benhabib, Jess and Jovanovic, Boyan (1991) 'Externalities and growth accounting', *American Economic Review* 81: 82–113.

Ben Porath, Y. (1973) 'Economic analysis of fertility in Israel: point and counterpoint', *Journal of Political Economy*, supplement 81, 2: S202–33.

Berg, A. (1973) *The Nutrition Factor*, Washington DC: Brookings Institution.

—— (1981) *Malnourished People: A Policy View*. Washington DC: World Bank.

Bergan, A. (1967) 'Personal income distribution and personal savings in Pakistan', in K. Griffin and A. Khan (eds) (1972) *Growth and Inequality in Pakistan*, London: Macmillan.

Bergsman, J. (1970) *Brazil: Industrialization and Trade Policies*, Paris: OECD; London: Oxford University Press.

Berill, K. (ed.) (1964) *Economic Development with Special Reference to East Asia*, London: Macmillan.

Berry, A. and Cline, W.R. (1979) *Agrarian Structure and Productivity in Developing Countries*, Baltimore: Johns Hopkins University Press.

Berry, Albert and Soligo, Ronald (1968) 'Rural–urban migration, agricultural output and the supply price of labour in a labour surplus economy', *Oxford Economic Papers* 20 (2): 230–49.

—— (1975) 'Presumptive income tax on agricultural land', in R. Bird and O. Oldman (eds) *Readings on Taxation in Development Countries*, 3rd edn, Baltimore: Johns Hopkins University Press.

Besley, T. and Burgess, R. (2000) 'The Political Economy of Government Responsiveness: Theory and Evidence from India', discussion paper, London School of Economics, November.

Bhagwati, Jagdish (1958) 'Immiserizing growth: a geometrical note', *Review of Economic Studies* 25: 201–5.

—— (1964) 'The pure theory of international trade: a survey', *Economic Journal* 74: 1–56.

—— (ed.) (1970) *International Trade*, London: Penguin.

——(1978) *Foreign Trade Regimes and Economic Development*, Cambridge MA: Ballinger.

—— (ed.) (1979) *The New International Economic Order*, Boston: MIT Press.

Bhagwati, Jagdish and Chakravarty, S. (1969) 'Contributions to Indian economic analysis: a survey', *American Economic Review*, September supplement: 2–73.

Bhagwati, Jagdish and Desai, Padma (1970) *India: Planning for Industrialization*, Oxford and Paris: OECD.

Bhagwati, J. and Hansen, B. (1973) 'A theoretical analysis of smuggling', *Quarterly Journal of Economics* 87: 172–87.

Bhagwati, Jagdish and Ramaswami, V.K. (1963) 'Domestic distortions, tariffs and the theory of optimum subsidy', *Journal of Political Economy* 71: 44–50.

Bhagwati, Jagdish and Srinivasan, T.N. (1974) 'On re-analysing the Harris–Todaro model: policy ranking in the case of sector-specific sticky wages', *American Economic Review* 64: 502–8.

—— (1983) *Lectures on International Trade*, Boston: MIT Press.

Bhalla, A.S. (1964) 'Investment allocations and technological choice: a case of cotton-spinning techniques', *Economic Journal* 74: 611–22.

—— (1965) 'Choosing techniques: hand-pounding versus machine-milling of rice: an Indian case', *Oxford Economic Papers* 17: 147–57.

—— (ed.) (1975) *Technology and Employment in Industry: A Case Study Approach*, Geneva: ILO.

Bharadwaj, K. (1978) *Production Conditions in Indian Agriculture*, Cambridge: Cambridge University Press.

Bharadwaj, V.P. and Dave, P.K. (1973) 'An empirical test of Kaldor's macro-model of income distribution for Indian economy', *Indian Economic Journal* 20 (3): 515–20.

Bhat, V.V. and Meerman, J. (1978) 'Resource mobilisatiom in developing countries', *World Development* 6 (7).

Bhattacharya, P. (1993) 'Rural-urban migration in economic development', *Journal of Economic Surveys* 7 (3): 243–81.

Biggs, S. and Clay, F. (1983) *Technology Diffusions in Developing Countries*, Geneva: ILO.

Bigsten, A. (1987) 'Poverty, inequality and development', in N. Gemmell (ed.) *Surveys in Development Economics*, Oxford: Blackwell.

Billings, M. and Singh, A. (1969) 'Labour and the Green Revolution', *Economic and Political Weekly*, Review 4, December.

Binswanger, H.P. and Ruttan, V. (eds) (1978) *Induced Innovation: Technology, Institutions and Development*, Baltimore: Johns Hopkins University Press.

Bird, Graham (1976) 'The informal link between SDR allocation and aid: a note', *Journal of Development Studies* 12 (3): 268–73.

—— (1989) 'Loan loss provisions and Third World debt', *Essays in International Finance 176*, Princeton: Princeton University Press.

—— (1992) 'Ten years older and deeper in debt: the developing country debt problem in retrospect and prospect', *Economics* 28: 19–26.

Bird, Richard M. (1977) 'Land taxation and economic development: the model of Meiji Japan', in P.C.I. Ayre (ed.) *Finance in Developing Countries*, London: Frank Cass.

—— (1982) Taxation and employment in developing countries', *Finanzarchiv* 40: 211–39.

—— (1983) 'Taxation and income distribution in Latin America', *IMF Staff Papers* 20: 639–82.

Bird, Richard M. and Oldman, Oliver (1975) *Readings on Taxation in Developing Countries*, 3rd edn, Baltimore: Johns Hopkins University Press.

Birdsall, N. (1988) 'Economic approaches to population growth', in H. Chenery and T.N. Srinivasan (eds) *Handbook of Development Economics*, Amsterdam: North-Holland, vol. I.

Blackburn, K. and Hung, Y. (1998) 'A theory of growth, financial development and trade', *Economica* 65: 107–24.

Blake, J.D. (1962) 'Labour shortage and unemployment in northeast Sumatra', *Malayan Economic Review* 7 (2): 106–18.

Blangiewicz, A. and Charemza, W.W. (1990) 'Cointegration in small samples: empirical percentiles, drifting moments, and customized testing', *Oxford Bulletin of Economics and Statistics* 52: 303–15.

Bleaney, M. (1996) 'Macroeconomic stability, investment and growth in developing countries', *Journal of Development Economics* 48: 461–77.

Blejer, M. (1978) 'Exchange rate restrictions and monetary approach to exchange rates', in J.A. Frenkel and H.S. Johnson (eds) *The Economics of Exchange Rates*, Reading MA: Addison Wesley.

Bliss, C.J. and Stern, N.H. (1976) 'Economic aspects of the connection between productivity and consumption', Discussion Paper 67, University of Essex.

—— (1982) *Palanpur: The Economy of an Indian Village*, Oxford: Clarendon Press.

Blitzer, C. *et al.* (1975) *Economy-wide Models and Development Planning*, London: Oxford University Press.

Blough, S.R. (1988) 'On the impossibility of testing for unit roots and cointegration in finite samples', Working Paper 211, Department of Economics, Johns Hopkins University.

Bober, M.M. (1950) *Karl Marx's Interpretation of History*, Cambridge MA: Harvard University Press.

Boeke, J.H. (1953) *Economics and Economic Policy of Dual Societies*, Haarlem: Tjeenk Willink.

Bolnick, Bruce R. (1975) 'Interpreting Polak: monetary analysis in dependent economies', *Journal of Development Studies* 11 (4): 325–42.

Boone, P. (1996) 'Politics and the effectiveness of foreign aid', *European Economic Review* 40: 289–329.

Borjas, J.G. (1987) 'Self-selection and the earnings of immigrants', *American Economic Review* 77: 531–53.

Bose, Arun (1975) *Marxian and Post-Marxian Political Economy*, London: Penguin.

Bose, Sanjit K. (1968) 'Optimal growth and investment allocation', *Review of Economic Studies* 35: 465–80.

Bose, Swadesh R. (1972) 'Trend of real income of the rural poor in East Pakistan', in Keith Griffin and Azizur Rahrnan Khan (eds) *Growth and Inequality in Pakistan*, London: Macmillan.

Boserup, B. (1965) *The Conditions of Agricultural Growth*, London: Allen & Unwin.

Bottomley, A.C. (1965) 'Keynesian monetary theory and the developing countries', *Indian Economic Journal* April–June: 95–105.

—— (1971) *Factor Pricing and Economic Growth in Underdeveloped Rural Areas*, London: Crosby Lockwood.

Boutros Ghali and Taylor, Lance (1980) 'Basic needs macroeconomics: is it manageable in the case of Egypt?', *Journal of Policy Modeling* 2 (3), September.

Bowman, M.J. (1980) 'Education and economic growth: an overview', in T. King (ed.) *Education and Economics*, World Bank Working Paper 402, Washington DC: World Bank.

Bowonder, B., Rao, N.P., Dasgupta, B. and Prasad, S.S.R. (1985) 'Energy use in eight rural communities in India', *World Development* 13: 1363–86.

Brahmananda, P.R. and Vakil, C.N. (1956) *Planning for an Expanding Economy*, Bombay: Vora.

Brandt, W. (1980) *North–South: A Programme for Survival*, London: Pan.

Braverman, A. and Guasch, L. (1986) 'Rural credit markets and institutions in developing countries', *World Development* 13.

Braverman, A. and Stiglitz, J. (1982) 'Sharecropping and the interlinking of the agrarian markets', *American Economic Review* 72: 695–715.

Brown, Doris (1971) *Agricultural Development in India's Districts*, Cambridge MA: Harvard University Press.

Brown, Lester R. (1970) *Seeds of Change: The Green Revolution and Development in the 1970s*, New York: Praeger.

Brown, Murray (1966) *On the Theory and Measurement of Technical Change*, Cambridge: Cambridge University Press.

Bruton, H. (1987) 'Technology choice and factor proportions problems in LDCs', in N. Gemmell (ed.) *Surveys in Development Economics*, Oxford: Blackwell.

Buchanan, N.S. (1945) *International Investment and Domestic Welfare*, New York: Henry Holt.

Buiter, W. and Patel, V. (1992) 'Debt, deficits and inflation: an application to the public finance in India', *Journal of Public Economics* 47 (2): 171–205.

Bulow, J. and Rogoff, K. (1986) *A Constant Recontracting Model of Sovereign Debt*, Working Paper 2088, Washington DC: NBER.

Burgess, S.Z. and Stern, N. (1993) 'Taxation and development', *Journal of Economic Literature* 31.

Burnside, Craig (1995) 'What do Production Regressions tell us about Increasing Returns and Externalities?' Mimeo, Washington DC: World Bank.

Byres, T.J. (1972) 'The dialectic of India's green revolution', *South Asian Review* 5 (2): 99–116.

—— (ed.) (1983) 'Sharecropping and sharecroppers', *Journal of Peasant Studies* 10 (2–3): 102–25.

Byres, T.J. *et al.* (1980) *The Green Revolution in India*, Milton Keynes: Open University Press.

Caballero, Ricardo and Lyons, Richard (1992) 'The role of externalities in US manufacturing', *Journal of Monetary Economics* 29: 209–25.

Cairncross, A. (1960) 'International trade and economic development', *Kyklos* 13: 4.

Cairncross, A. and Puri, Mohinder (eds) (1976) *Employment, Income Distribution and Development Strategy*, London: Macmillan.

Capistrano, A. and Kiker, C. (1990) 'Global economic influences on tropical, closed broad-leaved forest depletion 1967–1985', Food and Resource Economics Department, University of Florida, Gainesville (mimeo).

Cardosa, B. and Dornbusch, R. (1989) 'Foreign private capital flows', in H. Chenery and T.N. Srinivasan (eds) *Handbook of Development Economics*, Amsterdam: North-Holland, vol. II.

Carroll, Christopher, Byung-Kun Rhee and Changyong Ree (1994) 'Are there cultural effects on saving? Some cross-sectional evidence', *Quarterly Journal of Economics* 109: 685–700.

Cassen, Robert (1976) 'Population and development: a survey', *World Development* 4 (10–11): 785–830.

—— (1978) *India: Population, Economy and Society*, London: Macmillan.

—— Cassen, R., Toye, J. *et al.* (1989) *Does Aid Work?*, Oxford: Clarendon Press.

Casson, M. (1984a) 'The theory of vertical integration', University of Reading Discussion Paper (mimeo).

—— (1984b) 'A theory of the international division of labour', University of Reading Discussion Paper (mimeo).

Casson, M. and Pearce, R. (1987) 'Multinational enterprises in LDCs', in N. Gemmell (ed.) *Surveys in Development Economics*, Oxford: Blackwell.

Caves, R.E. (1982) *Multinational Enterprise and Economic Analysis*, Cambridge: Cambridge University Press.

Cecelski, E., Dunkerley, J. and Ramsay, W. (1979) *Household Energy and the Poor in the Third World*, Washington DC: Resources for the Future.

Celasun, M. and Rodrik, D. (1989) 'Debt, adjustment and growth: Turkey', in J. Sachs (ed.) *Developing Countries' Debt*, Chicago: University of Chicago Press; Washington DC: NBER.

Chakravarty, Sukhamoy (1959) *The Logic of Investment Planning*, Amsterdam: North-Holland.

—— (1969) *Capital and Development Planning*, Cambridge MA: MIT Press.

Charemza, W.W. and Deadman, D.F. (1997) *New Directions in Econometric Practice*, Aldershot: Edward Elgar.

Charemza, W.W. and Ghatak, S. (1990) 'Demand for money in a dual-currency quantity-constrained economy: Hungary and Poland, 1956–1985', *Economic Journal* 100: 1159–72.

Chayanov, A.V. (1966) 'The peasant economy', in Daniel Thorner *et al.* (eds) *The Theory of Peasant Economy*, Homewood: Irwin.

Chelliah, Raja J. (1969) *Fiscal Policy and Underdeveloped Countries*, London: Allen & Unwin.

—— (1971) 'Trends in taxation in developing countries', *IMF Staff Papers* 18: 254–327.

—— (1991) 'The growth of Indian public debt', IMF Working Paper WP/91/72, Washington DC: IMF.

Chelliah, R.J. *et al.* (1975) 'Tax ratios and tax efforts in developing countries', *IMF Staff Papers* 22: 187–205.

Chenery, Hollis B. (1953) 'The application of investment criteria', *Quarterly Journal of Economics* 67: 76–96.

—— (1961) 'Comparative advantage and development policy', *American Economic Review* 51: 18–51.

Chenery, Hollis B. and Bruno, M. (1962) 'Development alternatives in an open economy: the case of Israel', *Economic Journal* 72: 79–103.

Chenery, H. and Srinivasan, T.N. (eds) (1988–9) *Handbook of Development Economics*, Amsterdam: North-Holland, vols I and II.

Chenery, Hollis B. and Strout, A. (1966) 'Foreign assistance and economic development', *American Economic Review* 56: 680–733.

Chenery, Hollis B. and Taylor, Lance (1968) 'Development patterns among countries over time', *Review of Economics and Statistics* 50: 391–416.

Chenery, Hollis B. *et al.* (eds) (1971) *Studies in Development Planning*, Cambridge MA: Harvard University Press.

Chenery, Hollis B., Ahluwalia, Montek S., Bell, C.L.G., Duloy, John H. and Jolly, Richard (1974) *Redistribution with Growth*, London: Oxford University Press.

Cheung, S. (1969) *The Theory of Share Tenancy*, Chicago: University of Chicago Press.

Chichilnisky, G. and Cole, S. (1978) 'Growth of the north and growth of the south: some results on export-led policies', University of Essex Discussion Paper (mimeo).

Cho, Y.J. (1986) 'Inefficiencies from financial liberalization in the absence of well functioning equities markets', *Journal of Money, Credit and Banking* 18 (2): 191–9.

Chow, G.C. (1960) 'Tests of equality between sets of coefficients in two linear regressions', *Econometrica* 28: 591–605.

Christiano, L.J. (1992) 'Searching for a break in GNP', *Journal of Business and Economic Statistics* 10 (3): 237–50.

Clark, C. (1967) *Population Growth and Land Use*, London: Macmillan.

Cline, W.R. (ed.) (1977) *Policy Alternatives for a New International Economic Order*, New York: Praeger.

—— (1982) *Potential Effects of Income Redistribution on Economic Growth*, New York: Praeger.

Cline, W.R. *et al.* (eds) (1981) *World Inflation and the Developing Countries*, Washington DC: Brookings Institution.

Cline-Cole, R.A. *et al.* (1990) 'On fuelwood consumption, population dynamics and deforestation in Africa', *World Development* 18: 513–27.

Coale, A.J. (1973) 'The demographic transition reconsidered', in International Union for the Scientific Study of Population, *International Population Conference*, Liège: IUSSP, vol. 1.

—— (ed.) (1976) *Economic Factors in Population Growth*, London: Macmillan.

Coale, A.J. and Hoover, E.M. (1958) *Population Growth and Economic Development in Low Income Countries*, Princeton: Princeton University Press.

Coats, W.L. and Khatkhate, D. (eds) (1980) *Money and Monetary Policies in Less Developed Countries*, Oxford: Pergamon Press.

Cohen, Benjamin J. (1966) *Adjustment Costs and the Distribution of New Reserves*, Princeton Studies in International Finance 18, Princeton University.

Cohen, D. (1987) 'External and domestic debt constraints of LDCs . . . Brazil and Mexico', in R. Bryant and R.C. Portes (eds) *Global Macroeconomics*, London: Macmillan.

—— (1992) 'The debt crisis: a post-mortem', Centre for Economic Policy Research Discussion Paper 692, London: CEPR.

Cohen, D. and Sachs, J. (1986) 'Growth and external debt under risk of debt repudiation', *European Economic Review* June.

Cole, W.E. and Sanders, R.D. (1985) 'Internal migration and urbanization in the Third World', *American Economic Review* 75: 481–93.

Colman, David and McInerney, John (1975) 'The economies of agricultural policy', in R.M. Grant and G.K. Shaw (eds) *Current Issues in Economic Policy*, Oxford: Philip Allan.

Commonwealth Secretariat (1983) *Towards a New Bretton Woods*, London.

Connell, J. *et al.* (1976) *Migration from Rural Areas*, Delhi: Oxford University Press.

Coppock, Joseph D. (1962) *International Economic Instability*, New York: McGraw-Hill.

Corbo, V. and J. de Melo (eds) (1985) 'Liberalization with stabilization in the southern core of Latin America', special issue, *World Development*, August.

Corden, W.M. (1966) 'The structure of two tariff systems and the effective protective rate', *Journal of Political Economy* 74: 221–37.

—— (1971) *The Theory of Protection*, Oxford: Clarendon Press.

—— (1974) *Trade Policy and Economic Welfare*, Oxford: Clarendon Press.

Corden, W.M. and Findlay, R. (1975) 'Urban unemployment, intersectoral capital mobility and development policy', *Economica* 42: 37–78.

Crawford, M. (1978) 'Back to the energy crisis', *Science* 235: 626–7.

Culbertson, W.P. (1975) 'Purchasing power parity and black-market exchange rates', *Economic Inquiry* 13: 287–96.

Cuthbertson, K., Hall, S.G. and Taylor, M.P. (1992) *Applied Econometric Techniques*, New York: Philip Allan.

Dandekar, V.M. (1964) 'Prices, production and marketed supply of foodgrains', *Indian Journal of Agricultural Economics* 19: 186–95.

Dandekar, V.M. and Rath, N. (1971) 'Poverty in India', *Economic and Political Weekly* 6: 1–2, 25–48, 106–46.

Dasgupta, Ajit K. and Pearce, D.W. (1972) *Cost–Benefit Analysis: Theory and Practice*, London: Macmillan.

Dasgupta, Partha S. (1972) 'A comparative analysis of the UNIDO guidelines and the OECD manual', *Bulletin of the Oxford University Institute of Economics and Statistics* 34 (1): 33–52.

—— (1982) *The Control of Resources*, Oxford: Blackwell.

Dasgupta, P. and Ray, D. (1987) 'Inequality as a determinant of malnutrition and unemployment: theory and policy', Parts I and II, *Economic Journal* 97.

Dasgupta, Partha, Sen, Amartya K. and Marglin, Stephen (1972) *Guidelines for Project Evaluation*, Vienna: UNIDO.

Day, R. and Singh, I. (1977) *Economic Development as an Adaptive Process: The Green Revolution in the Indian Punjab*, Cambridge: Cambridge University Press.

Deadman, D. and Ghatak, S. (1981) 'On the stability of the demand for money in India', *Indian Economic Journal* 29 (1): 41–54.

Dean, F. (1966) *Supply Response of African Farmers*, Amsterdam: North Holland.

Deaton, A. (1988) 'Quality, quantity and spatial variation in price', *American Economic Review* 78 (3): 418–31.

De Gregorio, Jose (1996) 'Borrowing constraints, human capital accumulation and growth', *Journal of Monetary Economics* 37: 49–72.

De Long, Bradford and Summers, Lawrence (1991) 'Equipment investment and economic growth', *Quarterly Journal of Economics* 106: 445–502.

Demetriades, P. and Hussein, H. (1996) 'Does financial development cause economic growth? Time series evidence from sixteen countries', *Journal of Development Economics* 51: 387–411.

Demetriades, P. and Luientel, K. (1997) 'The direct costs of financial repression: evidence from India', *Review of Economics and Statistics* 79: 311–19.

Demirguc-Kunt, A. and Detragiache, E. (1999) 'The determinants of banking crisis in developed and developing countries', *IMF Staff Papers* 45: 81–109.

Demirguc-Kunt, Astli and Levine, R. (2001) *Financial Structures and Economic Development*, Cambridge MA: MIT Press.

Denison, E.F. (1967) *Why Growth Rates Differ: Post-war Experiences of Nine Western Countries*, Washington DC: Brookings Institution.

Dernburg, T.F. and McDougall, Duncan M. (1976) *Macroeconomics*, 5th edn, New York: McGraw-Hill.

Dervis, K., de Melo, J. and Robinson, S. (1982) *General Equilibrium Models for Development Policy*, Cambridge: Cambridge University Press.

Desai, Meghnad and Mazumdar, Dipak (1970) 'A test of the hypothesis of disguised unemployment', *Economica* 37: 39–53.

Dhar, E.N. and Lydall, H.F. (1961) *The Role of Small Enterprises in Indian Economic Growth*, Bombay: Asia Publishing House.

Diaz, Alejandro, C. (1985) 'Good-bye financial repression: hello, financial crash', *Journal of Development Economics* 19: 112.

Dickey, D.A. and Fuller, W.A. (1981) 'Likelihood ratio statistics for autoregressive time series with a unit root', *Econometrica* 49: 1057–72.

Dixit, Avinash (1968) 'The optimal development in the labour surplus economy', *Review of Economic Studies* 35: 23–34.

—— (1969) 'Theories of the dual economy: a survey', University of California, Berkeley (mimeo).

—— (1971) 'Short-run equilibrium and shadow prices in the dual economy', *Oxford Economic Papers* 23 (3): 384–99.

—— (1973) 'Models of dual economies', in J. Mirrlees and N. Stern (eds) *Models of Economic Growth*, New York: Wiley.

Dobb, Maurice (1948) *Soviet Economic Development since 1917*, London: Routledge.

—— (1955) *On the Economic Theory of Socialism*, New York: McGraw-Hill.

—— (1960) *Economic Growth and Planning*, London: Routledge.

—— (1965) *Soviet Economic Development since 1917*, London: Routledge.

Doessel, D.P. and Gounder, R. (1994) 'Theory and measurement of living levels: some empirical results of the human development index', *Journal of International Development* 6 (4): 415–35.

Dolado, J.J. and Jenkinson, T. (1987) 'Cointegration: a survey of recent developments', Applied Economics Discussion Paper Series 39, University of Oxford.

Dolado, J.J., Jenkinson, T. and Sosvilla-Rivera, S. (1990) 'Cointegration and unit roots: a survey', *Journal of Economic Surveys* 4 (3).

Dollar, D. (1992) 'Outward-oriented developing economies really do grow more rapidly', *Economic Development and Cultural Change* 40: 523–44.

Dollar, D. and Kraay (2000) 'Growth is good for the poor', Development Research Group, World Bank.

Domar, E.D. (1947) 'Expansion and employment', *American Economic Review* 37: 34–55.

—— (1957) *Essays in the Theory of Economic Growth*, New York: Oxford University Press.

Dornbusch, R. (1992) 'The case for trade liberalization in developing countries', *Journal of Economic Perspectives* 6 (1): 69–85.

Dornbusch, R., Dantas, D.V. *et al.* (1983) 'The black market for dollars in Brazil', *Quarterly Journal of Economics* 98: 25–40.

Dorosh, Paul A. and Sahn, D.E. (2000) 'A general equilibrium analysis of the effect of macroeconomic adjustment on poverty in Africa', *Journal of Policy Modeling* 22 (6): 753–76.

Down, S. (1983) 'Household energy consumption in west Sumatra: implications for policy makers', *Energy* 88: 821–33.

Drazen, A. and Grilli, V. (1993) 'The benefits of crises for economic reforms', *American Economic Review* 83: 59–607.

Dreze, J. and Sen, A.K. (1990) *Hunger and Public Action*, Oxford: Oxford University Press.

Due, John F. (1970) *Indirect Taxation in Developing Countries*, Baltimore: Johns Hopkins University Press.

—— (1976) 'Value-added taxation in developing economies', in N.T. Wang (ed.) *Taxation and Development*, New York: Praeger.

Duggar, Jan W. (1968) 'International comparisons of income levels: an additional measure', *Economic Journal* 78: 109–16.

Dunning, John H. (ed.) (1971) *The Multinational Enterprise*, London: Allen & Unwin.

Easterlin, R.A. (1980) *Population and Economic Change in Developing Countries*, Chicago: University of Chicago Press.

Easterlin, R.A. and Crimmins, B. (1985) *The Fertility Revolution: A Supply–Demand Analysis*, Chicago: University of Chicago Press.

Easterly, W. and Rebelo, S. (1993) 'Fiscal policy and economic growth: an empirical investigation', *Journal of Monetary Economics* 32: 417–58.

Easterly, W. (1999) 'The ghost of financing gap', *Journal of Development Economics* 60: 423–38.

Easterly, W., *et al.* (1993) 'Good policy or good luck?' *Journal of Monetary Economics* 32: 459–83.

Easterly, William, King, Robert, Levine, Ross and Rebelo, Sergio (1994) 'Policy, technology adoption and growth', in Robert M. Solow and Luigi L. Pasinetti (eds) *Economic Growth and the Structure of Long-term Development*, International Economic Association.

Eaton, J. (1989) 'Foreign public capital flows', in H. Chenery and T.N. Srinivasan (eds) *Handbook of Development Economics*, Amsterdam: North-Holland, vol. II.

Eaton, J. and Gersovitz, M. (1981) 'Debt with potential repudiation: theoretical and empirical analysis', *Review of Economic Studies* 48 (2): 289–309.

Eaton, J. and Taylor, L. (1986) 'Developing country finance and debt', *Journal of Development Economics* 22 (1): 209–65.

Eckaus, R.S. (1955) 'The factor proportions in underdeveloped countries', *American Economic Review* 45 (4): 539–65.

—— (1970) 'Economic criteria for foreign aid for economic development', in J. Bhagwati (ed.) *International Trade*, London: Penguin.

Eckaus, R.S. and Parikh, Kirit S. (1968) *Planning for Growth*, Boston: MIT Press.

Eckholm, B. (1975) *The Other Energy Crisis: Firewood*, Washington DC: World-watch Institute.

Eckholm, B., Foley, G., Barnard, G. and Timberlake, L. (1984) *Fuelwood: The Crisis that Won't Go Away*, Washington DC: Earthscan.

Eckstein, O. (1957) 'Investment criteria for economic development and the theory of intertemporal welfare economics', *Quarterly Journal of Economics* 71: 56–85.

Edwards, S. (1984) *The Order of Liberalization of the External Sector in Developing Countries*, Princeton Essays in International Finance 156, Princeton: Princeton University.

—— (1992) 'Trade orientation, distortions and growth in developing countries', *Journal of Development Economics* 39: 31–57.

—— (1993) 'Openness, trade liberalization and growth in developing countries', *Journal of Economic Literature* 31: 1358–93.

—— (1998) 'Openness, productivity and growth: what do we really know?' *Economic Journal* 108: 383–98.

Ehui, S. and Hertel, T.W. (1989) 'Deforestation and agricultural productivity in Côte d'Ivoire', *American Journal of Agricultural Economics* 71: 703–11.

Ehui, S.K., Kank, B.T. and Spencer, D.S.C. (1988) *Economic Analysis of Soil Erosion Effects in Alley Cropping, No-till and Bush Fallow Systems in South West Nigeria*, Ibadan: International Institute of Tropical Agriculture.

Eichengreen, B. and Portes, R. (1989) *Dealing with Debt: the 1930s and 1980s*, London: Centre for Economic Policy Research.

Elkan, Walter (1973) *An Introduction to Development Economics*, London: Penguin.

Emmanuel, A. (1972) *Unequal Exchange*, London: New Left Books.

Energy Information Administration (1987) *International Energy Outlook 1986*, Washington DC: US Government Printing Office.

Engle, R.F. and Granger, C.W.J. (1987) 'Cointegration and error-correction: representation, estimation and testing', *Econometrica* 55: 251–76.

—— (eds) (1991) *Long-run Economic Relationships: Readings in Cointegration*, New York: Oxford University Press.

Engle, R.F. and Yoo, B.S. (1987) 'Forecasting and testing in cointegrated systems', *Journal of Econometrics* 35: 143–59.

Enke, Stephen (1966) 'The economic aspect of slowing population growth', *Economic Journal* 76: 44–56.

Erb, Guy and Schiavo-Campo, Salvator (1969) 'Export instability, level of development and economic size of less developed countries', *Bulletin of the Oxford Institute of Economics and Statistics* 31 (November): 263–83.

Eshag, B. (1983) *Fiscal and Monetary Policies and Problems in Developing Countries*, Cambridge: Cambridge University Press.

Eswaran, M. and Kotwal, A. (1985) 'A theory of contractural structure in agriculture', *American Economic Review* 75: 352–67.

Evans, D. (1989) 'Alternative perspectives on trade and development', in H. Cheney and T.N. Srinivasan (eds) *Handbook of Development Economics*, Amsterdam: North-Holland, vol. II.

Evenson, R. (1988) 'Technology, productivity growth and economic development', in L. Ranis and T.P. Schutz (eds) *The State of Development Economics*, Oxford: Blackwell.

Faaland, J. and Parkinson, J.R. (1976) *Bangladesh: The Test Case for Development*, London: Hurst.

Falcon, W.P. (1970) 'The Green Revolution: generation of problems', *American Journal of Agricultural Economics* 52: 698–710.

Fan, L.S. (1970) 'Monetary performance in developing economies: a quantity theory approach', *Quarterly Review of Economics and Business*, summer: 475–81.

Federal Energy Administration (1979) *Energy Interrelationships: A Handbook of Tables and Conversion Factors for Combining and Comparing International Energy Data*, Washington DC: Federal Energy Administration.

Feenstra, Robert *et al.* (1999) 'Testing endogenous growth in South Korea and Taiwan', *Journal of Development Economics* 60: 317–41.

Fei, J.C. and Ranis, G. (1961) 'A theory of economic development', *American Economic Review* 51: 533–65.

—— (1964) *Development of the Labour Surplus Economy: Theory and Policy*, Homewood: Irwin.

Feldman, G.A. (1928) 'On the theory of growth rate of national income – I', in N. Spulber (ed.) (1964) *Foundations of Soviet Strategy for Economic Growth: Selected Soviet Essays 1924–1930*, Bloomington: Indiana University Press.

Fellner, William (1957) 'Marxian hypotheses and observable trends under capitalism', *Economic Journal* 67: 16–25.

Fields, Gary S. (1975a) 'Rural–urban migration, urban unemployment, and job-search activities in LDCs', *Journal of Development Economics* 2 (2): 165–87.

—— (1975b) 'Higher education and income distribution in a less developed country', *Oxford Economic Papers* 27 (2): 245–59.

—— (1980) *Poverty, Inequality and Development*, Cambridge: Cambridge University Press.

Fieleke, N. (1990) 'Economic adjustment in heavily indebted developing countries', *Contemporary Policy Issues* 8: 18–35.

Findlay, R. (1966) 'Optimal investment allocation between consumer goods and capital goods', *Economic Journal* 74: 70–83.

—— (1980) 'The terms of trade and equilibrium growth in the world economy', *American Economic Review* 70: 291–9.

Fischer, Stanley (1993) 'The role of macroeconomic factors in growth', *Journal of Monetary Economics* 32: 485–512.

Fischer, S. and Husain, I. (1990) 'Managing the debt crisis in the 1990s: the resumption of sustained economic growth should take priority', *Finance and Development*, June: 24–7.

Fischer, Stanley and Thomas, V. (1990) 'Policies for economic development', *American Journal of Agricultural Economics*, August: 809–14.

Fishelson, G. (1988) 'The black market for foreign exchange', *Economics Letters* 27: 67–71.

Fleming, Marcus (1955) 'External economies and the doctrine of balanced growth', *Economic Journal* 65: 241–56.

Fleuret, P.C. and Fleuret, A.K. (1978) 'Fuelwood use in a peasant community: a Tanzanian case study', *Journal of Development Areas* 12: 35–22.

Foley, G. (1985) 'Wood fuel and conventional fuel demands in the developing world', *Ambio* 14: 253–8.

Foxley, A. (1976) 'Redistribution of consumption: effects on products and employment', *Journal of Developmental Studies* 12 (3): 171–90.

Frank, André Gunder (1969) *Capitalism and Underdevelopment in Latin America*, New York and London: Monthly Review Press.

—— (1975) *On Capitalist Underdevelopment*, Bombay: Oxford University Press.

Frankel, Francine R. (1971) *India's Green Revolution: Economic Gains and Political Costs*, Princeton: Princeton University Press.

Fried, E. and Trezise, P. (1989) 'Third World debt: phase three begins', *Brookings Review* 7: 24–31.

Fry, M. (1997) *Money, Interest and Banking in Economic Development*, 2nd edn, Baltimore: Johns Hopkins University Press.

—— (1989a) 'Financial development: theories and recent experience', *Oxford Review of Economic Policy* 5 (4): 13–28.

—— (1989b) 'Foreign debt instability', *Journal of International Money and Finance* 8: 315–44.

—— (1997) 'In favour of financial liberalisation', *Economic Journal* 107: 754–70.

Fulbright, W. (1966) *Congressional Record;* 89th Congress, 2nd Session, 112, 120, pp. 16020–4, Washington DC.

Furtado, C. (1970) *The Economic Development of Latin America*, Cambridge: Cambridge University Press.

Gaiha, R. (1985) 'Poverty, technology and infrastructure in rural India', *Cambridge Journal of Economics* 9: 221–43.

—— (2001) 'Decentralisation and Poverty Alleviation in Asia', mimeo, Delhi: Management Studies, University of Delhi.

Galbis, Vicente (1977) 'Financial intermediation and economic growth in less developed countries: a theoretical approach', in P.C.I. Ayre (ed.) *Finance in Developing Countries*, London: Frank Cass.

Galbraith, John K. (1964) 'The balance of payments: a political and administrative view', *Review of Economics and Statistics* 46 (2): 120.

Galenson, W. and Leibenstein, H. (1955) 'Investment criteria, productivity and economic development', *Quarterly Journal of Economics* 69: 343–70.

Geary, R.C. (1951) 'A note on a constant-utility index of the cost of living', *Review of Economic Studies* 18: 65–6.

Gelb, A. (1989) *Financial Policies, Growth and Efficiency*, PPR, June, Washington DC: World Bank.

Gemmell, N. (ed.) (1987a) *Surveys in Development Economics*, Oxford: Blackwell.

—— (1987b) 'Taxation and development', in N. Gemmell (ed.) *Surveys in Development Economics*, Oxford: Blackwell.

Ghai, D. (ed.) (1977) *The Basic Needs Approach to Development*, Geneva: ILO.

Ghai, D. and Radwan, S. (1979) *Agrarian Systems and Rural Development*, New York: Holmes.

Ghatak, A. and Ghatak, S. (1985) 'Output response in underdeveloped agriculture: a case study in West Bengal Districts', *Indian Journal of Economics* 66 (260), July.

Ghatak, A. and Ghatak, S. (1996) 'Budgetary deficits and Ricardian equivalence: the case of India, 1950–1986', *Journal of Public Economics* 60: 267–282.

Ghatak, Subrata (1975a) 'Rural interest rates in the Indian economy', *Journal of Development Studies* 11 (3): 190–201.

—— (1975) 'Marketed surplus in Indian agriculture: theory and practice', *Oxford Bulletin of Economics and Statistics* 37 (2): 143–53.

—— (1976) *Rural Money Markets in India*, New Delhi: Macmillan.

—— (1978) 'Growth, technology transfer and environment', *Indian Journal of Economics* 59: 73–85.

—— (1981) *Transfer of Technology to Developing Countries: The Case of the Fertilizer Industry*, Greenwich, CT: JAI Press.

—— (1983) 'On inter-regional variations in rural interest rates in India', *Journal of Developing Areas* 18: 21–34.

—— (1987) 'Agriculture and economic development', in N. Gemmell (ed.) *Surveys in Development Economics*, Oxford: Blackwell.

—— (1991) 'Development economics: a survey', *British Review of Economic Issues*, February: 1–60.

—— (1995) *Monetary Economics in Developing Countries*, 2nd edn, London: Macmillan.

—— (1997) 'Financial liberalisation: the case of Sri Lanka', *Empirical Economics* 22: 117–29.

Ghatak, S. and Charemza, W. (1994) 'Financial dualism and virtual interest rates: the case of India', *Economic and Political Weekly* 23, April.

Ghatak, S. and Deadman, D. (1989) 'Money, prices and stabilization policies in some developing countries', *Applied Economics* 21: 853–65.

Ghatak, S. and Ingersent, K. (1984) *Agriculture and Economic Development*, Brighton: Harvester; Baltimore: Johns Hopkins University Press.

Ghatak, S. and Levine, P. (1994) 'The adjustment towards national solvency in developing countries: the case of India', *Journal of International Development* 6 (3): 399–414.

Ghatak, S. and Sassoon, A. (2001) *Migration and Mobility: The European Context*, Basingstoke: Palgrave.

Ghatak, S. and Seale, J., Jr (2001) 'Rice, risk and rationality: supply response in west Bengal, India', *European Research Studies Journal* 4: 155–69.

—— (2001) 'Supply response and risk in Chinese agriculture', *Journal of Development Studies* 37: 141–50.

Ghatak, S. and Siddiki, J. (2001) 'The use of the ARDL approach in estimating virtual exchange rates in India', *Journal of Applied Statistics* 28 (5): 573–83.

Ghatak, S. and Utkulu, U. (1994) 'Trade liberalization and economic development: the Asian experience', in V.N. Balasubramanyam and D. Greenaway (eds) *Essays in Honour of Professor Jagdish Bhagwati*, Aldershot: Edward Elgar.

Ghatak, S. and Wheatley Price, S. (1997) 'Export composition and economic growth: cointegration and causality evidence for India', *Weltwirtschaftliches Archiv* 00: 538–53.

Ghatak, S., Levine, P. and Wheatley Price, S. (1996) 'Migration theories and evidence: an assessment', *Journal of Economic Surveys* 10 (2): 159–96.

Ghatak, S., Milner, C. and Utkulu, U. (1995) 'Trade liberalisation and endogenous growth: some evidence from Turkey', *Economics of Planning* 28: 147–67.

—— (1997) 'Exports, export composition and growth: cointegration and causality evidence from Malaysia', *Applied Economics* 29: 213–23.

Ghosh, Ambika (1968) *Planning, Programming and Input–Output Analysis*, Cambridge: Cambridge University Press.

Ghosh, Ambika, Chakravarty, D. and Sarkar, H. (1974) *Development Planning in South East Asia*, Rotterdam: Rotterdam University Press.

Gilbert, C.L. (1986) 'Professor Hendry's econometric methodology', *Oxford Bulletin of Economics and Statistics* 48 (August): 283–303.

Giles, D.E.A., Giles, J.A. and McCann, E. (1993) 'Causality, unit roots and export-led growth: the New Zealand experience', *Journal of International Trade and Economic Development* 1: 195–218.

Gill, J. (1987) 'Improved stoves in developing countries: a critique', *Energy Policy* 10: 135–44.

Gillis, M. (1980) 'Energy demand in Indonesia: projections and policies', Development Discussion Paper 92, Cambridge MA: Harvard Institute for International Development.

—— (1985) 'Micro and macroeconomics of tax reform: Indonesia', *Journal of Development Economics* 19: 221–56.

Gillis, M., Perkins, D., Roemer, M. and Snodgrass, D.R. (1999) *Economics of Development*, London and New York: Norton.

Goode, R. (1984) *Government Finance in Developing Countries*, Washington DC: Brookings Institution.

Gottlieb, C. and Change, C. (1992) 'Sovereign debt: avoiding the nightmare scenario', *International Financial Law Review* 11: 19–22.

Grabowski, R. (1981) 'Induced innovation, Green Revolution and income distribution', *Economic Development and Cultural Change* 30: 177–81.

Granger, C.W.J. (1981) 'Some properties of time series data and their use in econometric model specification', *Journal of Econometrics* 16: 121–30.

—— (1986) 'Developments in the study of cointegrated economic variables', *Oxford Bulletin of Economics and Statistics* 48 (3): 213–28.

—— (1988) 'Some recent developments in a concept of causality', *Journal of Econometrics* 39: 199–211.

Gray, Clive S. (1963) 'Credit creation for Nigeria's economic development', *Nigerian Journal of Economic and Social Research* 5 (3).

Greenaway, D. (1984) 'A statistical analysis of fiscal dependence on trade taxes and economic development', *Public Finance* 20: 70–89.

Greenaway, D. and Milner, C. (1987) 'Trade theory and less developed countries', in N. Gemmell (ed.) *Surveys in Development Economics*, Oxford: Blackwell.

Greenaway, D., Morgan, W. and Wright, P. (1998) 'Trade reform, adjustment and growth: what does the evidence tell us?' *Economic Journal* 108: 1547–61.

Greenwood, Jeremy and Smith, Bruce (1994) 'Financial markets in development and the development of financial markets', *Journal of Economic Dynamics and Control* 21: 145–82.

Griffin, Keith (1969) *Underdevelopment in Spanish America*, London: Allen & Unwin.

—— (1974) *The Political Economy ofAgrarian Change*, London: Macmillan.

—— (1976) *Land Concentration and Rural Poverty*, London: Macmillan.

Griffin, K. and Enos, J. (1970) *Planning Development*, Reading MA: Addison Wesley.

Griffin, Keith and Khan, Azizur R. (eds) (1972) *Growth and Inequality in Pakistan*, London: Macmillan.

Grossman, Gene and Helpman, Elhanan (1991) *Innovation and Growth in the Global Economy*, Cambridge MA: MIT Press.

Grubel, Hebert G. (1977) 'The case against the new international economic order', *Weltwirtschaftliches Archiv* 113 (2): 284–307.

Guha, Ashok (1969) 'Accumulation, innovation and growth under conditions of disguised unemployment', *Oxford Economic Papers* 21 (3): 360–72.

—— (1981) *An Evolutionary View of Economic Growth*, Oxford: Clarendon Press.

Gupta, K.L. (1970) 'Personal saving in developing nations', *Economic Record* 46: 243–9.

Gupta, S.G. (1971) 'Interest sensitiveness of deposits in India', *Economic and Political Weekly* 20: 2357–63.

Gurley, J.G. and Shaw, E.S. (1960) *Money in a Theory of Finance*, Washington DC: Brookings Institution.

—— (1967) 'Financial structure and economic development', *Economic Development and Cultural Change* 15 (3): 257–68.

Haan, Roelf L. (1971) *Special Drawing Rights and Development*, Leiden: Stenfert Kroese.

Hadley, G. (1961) *Linear Algebra*, Reading MA: Addison Wesley.

—— (1962) *Linear Programming*, Reading MA: Addison Wesley.

Hagen, Everett E. (1958) 'An economic justification of protectionism', *Quarterly Journal of Economics* 72 (4): 496–514.

Hahn, F.H. (ed.) (1971) *Readings in the Theory of Growth*, London: Macmillan.

Hahn, F.H. and Matthews, R.C.O. (1964) 'The theory of economic growth: a survey', *Economic Journal* 74: 779–902.

Hall, P. (1983) *Growth and Development*, Oxford: Martin Robertson.

Hall, R.E. and Jones, C. (1999) 'Why do some countries produce so much more output per worker than others?' *Quarterly Journal of Economics* 114: 83–116.

Hall, S.G. and Henry, S.S.B. (1988) *Macroeconomic Modelling*, Amsterdam: North-Holland.

Hansen, B. (1968) 'The distributive shares in Egyptian agriculture, 1897–1961', *International Economic Review* 9: 175–94.

Haq, M. Ul. (1965) 'Tied credits: a quantitative analysis', in J. Alder (ed.) *Capital Movements and Economic Development*, London: Macmillan.

—— (1981) 'Beyond the slogan of south–south co-operation', in K. Haq (ed.) *Dialogue for a New Order*, New York: Pergamon Press.

Hardin, G. (1968) 'The tragedy of the commons', *Science* 162: 13.

Harris, Barbara (1971) 'Innovation adoption in Indian agriculture: the high yielding varieties programme', *Modern Asian Studies* 6 (1): 78–98,

Harris, J.R. and Todaro, M.P. (1970) 'Migration, unemployment and development: a two sector analysis', *American Economic Review* 60: 126–42.

Harrod, Roy F. (1948) *Towards a Dynamic Economics: Some Recent Developments and their Applications to Policy*, London: Macmillan.

—— (1970) 'Harrod after twenty-one years: a comment', *Economic Journal* 80: 737–41.

Hasan, P. (1960) 'The investment multiplier in an underdeveloped economy', *Economic Digest* (Karachi) 3: 75–84.

Havrylyshyn, O. and Ciran, E. (1983) 'Intra-industry trade and stage of development', in P.K. Thakaran (ed.) *Intra-industry Trade: Empirical and Methodological Issues*, Amsterdam: North-Holland.

Havrylyshyn, O. and Wolf, M. (1983) 'Recent trends in trade among developing countries', *European Economic Review* 21: 333–62.

Hayami, Y. (1981) 'Induced innovation, green revolution and income distribution: comment', *Economic Development and Cultural Change* 30: 169–76.

Hayami, Yujiro and Ruttan, Vernon W. (1971) *Agricultural Development: An International Perspective*, Baltimore: Johns Hopkins University Press.

—— (1984) 'The Green Revolution: inducement and distribution', *Pakistan Development Review* 23 (1): 37–63.

—— (1985) *Agricultural Development: an International Perspective*, Baltimore: Johns Hopkins University Press.

Hayter, Teresa (1971) *Aid as Imperialism*, London: Penguin.

Heal, G.M. (1973) *The Theory of Economic Planning*, Amsterdam: North-Holland.

Healey, N. (1990) 'The international debt crisis eight years on: an interim report', *Journal of Regional Policy* 10: 170–81.

Helleiner, G.K. (1972) *International Trade and Economic Development*, London: Penguin.

—— (1973) 'Manufactured exports from less developed countries and multinational firms', *Economic Journal* 83: 21–47.

—— (1974) 'The less developed countries and the international monetary system', *Journal of Development Studies* 10 (3): 347–71.

—— (1975) 'Smallholder decision making: tropical African evidence', in L. Reynolds (ed.) *Agriculture in Development Theory*, New Haven: Yale University Press.

—— (1989) 'Transnational corporations and direct foreign investment', in H. Chenery and T.N. Srinivasan (eds) *Handbook of Development Economics*, Amsterdam: North-Holland, vol. II.

Helpman, E. (1989) 'The simple analytics of debt–equity swaps', *American Economic Review* 79: 440–51.

Hicks, John R. (1957) *Value and Capital*, London: Oxford University Press.

—— (1965) *Capital and Growth*, Oxford: Clarendon Press.

Hicks, Norman and Streeten, P. (1979) 'Indicators of development: the search for a basic needs yardstick', *World Development* 7: 568–79.

Higgins, B. (1968) *Economic Development*, 2nd edn, London: Constable.

Hill, T.P. (1964) 'Growth and investment according to international comparisons', *Economic Journal* 74: 287–304.

Hirschman, Albert O. (1958a) *The Strategy of Economic Development*, New Haven: Yale University Press.

—— (1958b) 'Investment criteria and capital intensity once again', *Quarterly Journal of Economics* 72: 469–71.

Ho, Yhi-Min (1972) 'Development with surplus-labour population – the case of Taiwan: a critique of the classical two-sector model, *à la* Lewis', *Economic Development and Cultural Change* 20: 210–34.

Holden, K. and Thompson, J. (1992) 'Cointegration: an introductory survey', *British Review of Economic Issues* 14 (June): 1–55.

Hopkins, M. and Hoeven, Rolph van der (1983) *Basic Needs in Development Planning*, London: Gower Press.

Horst, T. (1973) 'The simple analytics of multinational firm behaviour', in M.B. Connolly and A.K. Swoboda (eds) *International Trade and Money*, London: Allen & Unwin.

Hughes-Cromwick, E.L. (1985) 'Nairobi households and their energy use – an economic analysis of consumption patterns', *Energy Economics* 7: 265–78.

Husted, S. (1992) 'The emerging US current account deficit in the 1980s: a cointegration analysis', *Review of Economics and Statistics* 74 (February): 159–66.

Hyman, E. (1985) 'Demand for woodfuels by households in the province of Iloe Norte, Philippines', *Energy Policy* 8: 581–91.

International Bank for Reconstruction and Development (IBRD) (1969) *The Problem of Stabilization of Prices of Primary Products*, Washington DC: IBRD.

International Labour Office (ILO) (1967) *Report to the Government of United Republic of Tanzania on Wages, Incomes and Prices Policy*, Government Paper 3, Dar es Salaam: Government Printer.

—— (1971) *Matching Employment Opportunities and Expectations: A Programme of Action for Ceylon*, Geneva: ILO.

—— (1972) *Employment, Incomes and Equality: A Strategy for Increasing Productive Employment in Kenya*, Geneva: ILO.

—— (1973) *Sharing in Development: A Programme of Development, Equity and Growth for the Philippines*, vol. 1, Main Report, Geneva: ILO.

—— (1976a) *The Impact of Multi-national Enterprises on Employment and Training*, Geneva: ILO.

—— (1976b) *Wages and Working Conditions in Multi-national Enterprises*, Geneva: ILO.

International Monetary Fund (IMF) (1966) *Compensatory Financing of Export Instability*, Washington DC: IMF.

—— (various years) *International Financial Statistics*, Washington DC: IMF.

Ishikawa, Shigeru (1967) *Economic Development in Asian Perspective*, Tokyo: Kunokuniya.

Ishimine, T. (1984) 'Food, energy and debt servicing as reserve and development constraints of less developed countries', *Revista Internazionale di Scienze Economiche e Commerciali* 31: 371.

Jain, S. (1975) *Size Distribution of Income: A Compilation of Data*, Washington DC: World Bank.

Jalilian, H. and Kirkpatrick, C. (2002) 'Financal Development, Inequality and Poverty Reduction in Developing Countries', paper presented at the ESRC conference, Birmingham, August.

deJanvry, A. (1981) *The Agrarian Question and Reformism in Latin America*, Baltimore: Johns Hopkins University Press.

Jarvis, L. (1973) 'The relationship between unemployment and income distribution in less developed countries', in *Employment Processes in Developing Countries*, Bogota: Ford Foundation.

Johl, S.S. (1975) 'Gains of the Green Revolution: how they have been shared in Punjab', *Journal of Development Studies* 11: 178–89.

Johnson, G.E. (1971) 'The structure of rural–urban migration models', *Eastern Africa Economic Review*, June: 21–8.

Johnson, Harry G. (1962) *Money, Trade and Economic Growth*, London: Allen & Unwin.

—— (1964) 'Tariffs and economic development', *Journal of Development Studies* 1 (1): 3–30.

—— (1967) *Economic Policies towards Less Developed Countries*, London: Allen & Unwin.

—— (1968) 'Tariffs and economic development: some theoretical issues', in J.D. Theberge (ed.) *Economics of Trade and Development*, New York: Wiley.

—— (1969) Hearing before the Sub-committee on International Exchange and Payments of the Joint Economic Committee, Congress of the United States, 28 May, p. 16.

—— (1972) 'The link that chains', *Foreign Policy*, autumn.

—— (1977) 'The new international economic order', *Boletin International, Banco de Vizcaya* (Spain) 5: 4–9.

Johnston, B.F. and Cownie, John (1969) 'The seed–fertilizer revolution and labour force absorption', *American Economic Review* 59: 569–82.

Johnston, J. (2000) *Econometric Methods*, 4th edn, New York: McGraw-Hill.

Jolly, Richard (1974) 'International dimensions', in Hollis B. Chenery, Montek S. Ahluwalia, C.L.G. Bell, John H. Duloy and Richard Jolly (eds) *Redistribution with Growth*, London: Oxford University Press.

Jolly, Richard, Emanuel, Kadt, Singer, H. and Wilson, F. (eds) (1973) *Third World Employment*, Oxford: Penguin.

Jones, Charles (1991) 'Economic Growth and the Relative Price of Capital', mimeo, Cambridge MA: MIT.

Jones, Hywel (1975) *An Introduction to Modern Theories of Economic Growth*, London: Nelson.

Jones, J.D. and Joulfaian, D. (1991) 'Federal government expenditures and revenues in the early years of the American republic: evidence from 1792 and 1860', *Journal of Macroeconomics* 13 (1): 133–55, esp. 146.

Jones, Lawrence and Marinelli, Rodolfo (1990) 'A convex model of equilibrium growth: theory and policy implications', *Journal of Political Economy* 98: 1008–38.

Jorgenson, D.W. (1961) 'The development of a dual economy', *Economic Journal* 71: 309–34.

—— (1966) 'Testing alternative theories of the development of a dual economy', in I. Adelman and E. Thorbecke (eds) *The Theory and Design of Economic Development*, Baltimore: Johns Hopkins University Press.

—— (1967) 'Surplus agricultural labour and the development of a dual economy', *Oxford Economic Papers* 19 (3): 288–312.

Jorgenson, D. and Griliches, Z. (1967) 'The explanation of productivity changes', *Review of Economic Studies* 34 (3): 249–83.

Joshi, Heather (1972) 'World prices as shadow prices: a critique', *Bulletin of the Oxford University Institute of Economics and Statistics* 34 (1): 53–73.

Joshi, Vijay (1970) 'Saving and foreign exchange constraints', in P. Streeten (ed.) *Unfashionable Economics: Essays in Honour of Lord Balogh*, London: Weidenfeld & Nicolson.

—— (1972) 'The rationale and relevance of the Little–Mirrlees criterion', *Bulletin of Oxford University Institute of Economics and Statistics* 34 (1): 3–32.

Journal of Economic Dynamics and Control (1988) Special issue on cointegration.

Journal of Policy Modeling (1992) Special issue on cointegration.

Junankar, P.N. (1981) 'Do Indian farmers maximise profit?', *Journal of Development Studies* 17 (1).

June-Flanders, M. (1964) 'Prebisch on protectionism: an evaluation', *Economic Journal* 74: 305–26.

Juo, A.S.R. and Kang, B.T. (1987) 'Nutrient effect in modification of shifting cultivation in West Africa', *Proceedings of an International Symposium on Nutrient Cycling in Tropical Forest and Savanna Ecosystems*, Stirling University, Scotland.

Kahn, A.E. (1951) 'Investment criteria in development programs', *Quarterly Journal of Economics* 65: 38–61.

Kahn, R. (1973) 'SDRs and aid', *Lloyds Bank Review* 110: 1–18.

Kaldor, N. (1955) *An Expenditure Tax*, London: Allen & Unwin.

—— (1956a) *Indian Tax Reform*, Delhi: Ministry of Finance, Government of India.

—— (1956b) 'Alternative theories of distribution', *Review of Economic Studies* 23: 83–100.

—— (1957) 'A model of economic growth', *Economic Journal* 67: 591–624.

—— (1965) 'The role of taxation in economic development', in R. Robinson (ed.) *Industrialization in Developing Countries*, Cambridge: Cambridge University Press.

—— (1972) 'The irrelevance of equilibrium economics', *Economic Journal* 82: 1237–55.

Kaldor, N. and Mirrlees, James A. (1962) 'A new model of economic growth', *Review of Economic Studies* 29: 174–92.

Kamin, S.B. (1993) 'Devaluation, exchange rate controls, and black markets for foreign exchange in developing countries', *Journal of Development Economics* 40: 151–69.

Kanappan, S. (1985) 'Urban employment and the labour market in developing countries', *Economic Development and Cultural Change* 33: 669–730.

Kanbur, Ravi S.M. (1981) 'Short-run growth effects in a model of costly migration with borrowing constraints: will rural development work?', in D. Currie *et al.* (eds) *Microeconomic Analysis*, London: Croom Helm.

—— (1983) 'How to analyse commodity price stabilisation: a review article', *Oxford Economic Papers* 35.

—— (2000) 'Income distribution and development', in A. Atkinson and F. Bourguignon (eds) *Handbook of Income Distribution*, Amsterdam: Elsevier.

Kanbur, R. and McKintosh, J.P.L. (1987) 'Dual economy models: a survey', *Bulletin of Economic Research.*

Kanbur, R. and Vines, D. (1986) 'North–south interaction and commodity control', *Journal of Development Economics*, 371–87.

Kang, B.T., Wilson, G.F. and Lawson, T.L. (1984) *Alley Cropping: A Stable Alternative to Shifting Cultivation*, Ibadan: International Institute of Tropical Agriculture.

Kapur, B. (1976) 'Alternative stabilization policies for less developed economies', *Journal of Political Economy* August.

Katrak, H. (1981) 'Multi-national firms' exports and host country commercial policy', *Economic Journal* 91.

—— (1983) 'Multi-national firms' global strategies, host country ownership policies and welfare', *Journal of Development Economics* 9.

Kawagoe, T., Hayami, Y. and Ruttan, V. (1985) 'The intercountry agricultural production function and productivity differences among countries', *Journal of Development Economics* 19: 113–32.

Kay, Geoffrey (1975) *Development and Underdevelopment: A Marxist Analysis*, London: Macmillan.

Kazgan, G. (1993) 'External pressures and the new policy outlook', in C. Balkir and A.M. Williams (eds) *Turkey and Europe*, London: Pinter.

Kelly, Allen C., Williamson, Geoffrey G. and Cheetham, Russel J. (1972) *Dualistic Economic Development: Theory and History*, Chicago and London: University of Chicago Press.

Kenen, M. (2000) *International Economics*, 4th edn, Cambridge: Cambridge University Press.

Kenya (1973) *Sessional Paper on Employment*, Nairobi: Government of Kenya, 10.

—— (1974) *Third Economic Plan* (1974–78), Nairobi: Government of Kenya.

Keynes, John Maynard (1930) *A Treatise on Money*, London: Macmillan.

—— (1936) *The General Theory of Employment, Interest and Money*, London: Macmillan.

Khan, A. (1975) *Green Revolution in Pakistan*, New York: Praeger.

Khan, M.S. (1974) 'Export and import demand in developing countries', *IMF Staff Papers* 21: 3.

Khusro, A.M. (1967) 'The pricing of food in India', *Quarterly Journal of Economics* 81: 271–85.

Killick, A. (1980) *Policy Economics*, London: Heinemann.

Kindleberger, Charles P. (1956) *The Terms of Trade: A European Case Study*, New York: Technology Press/Wiley.

—— (ed.) (1970) *The International Corporation*, Boston: MIT Press.

—— (1977) *Economic Development*, 3rd edn, New York: McGraw-Hill.

King, Robert and Levine, Ross (1993) 'Finance and growth: Schumpeter might be right', *Journal of Monetary Economics* 32: 513–542.

King, Robert and Rebelo, Sergio (1993) 'Transitional dynamics and economic growth in the neoclassical growth model', *American Economic Revieew* 83: 908–931.

Kingston, Jerry L. (1976) 'Export concentration and export performance in developing countries, 1954–67', *Journal of Development Studies* 12 (4): 311–19.

Kleenow, P. (1997) 'Economic growth', *Journal of Monetary Economics* 40: 597–617.

Klein, L. (1965) 'What kind of macro-econometric model for developing economies?', *Indian Economic Journal* 13 (3): 313–24.

Kletzer, K. (1988) 'External borrowing by LDCs; a survey of some theoretical issues', in G. Ranis and T.P. Schultz (eds) *The State of Development Economics*, Oxford: Blackwell.

Knack, Stephen and Keefer, Philip (1994) 'Institutions and Economic Performance: Cross-country Tests using Alternative Institutional Measures', mimeo, Baltimore: University of Maryland.

Knudsen, Odin and Parnes, Andrew (1975) *Trade Instability and Economic Development*, Lexington: Heath.

Komiya, R. (1959) 'A note on Professor Mahalanobis' model of Indian economic planning', *Review of Economics and Statistics* 41: 29–35.

Kravis, J.B., Heston, A. and Summers, R. (1978) 'Real GDP *per capita* for more than one hundred countries', *Economic Journal* June: 88.

Krishna, Raj (1962) 'A note on the elasticity of the marketable surplus of a subsistence crop', *Indian Journal of Agricultural Economics* 17: 79–84.

—— (1963) 'Farm supply response in India–Pakistan: a case study of the Punjab region', *Economic Journal* 73: 477–87.

—— (1965) 'The marketable surplus function for a subsistence crop: an analysis with India data', *Economic Weekly* 17: 309–20.

—— (1968) 'Agricultural price policy and economic development', in H. Southworth and B.F. Johnston (eds) *Agricultural Development and Economic Growth*, Ithaca NY: Cornell University Press.

—— (1975) 'Measurement of the direct and indirect employment effects of agricultural growth with technical change', in L. Reynolds (ed.) *Agriculture in Development Theory*, New Haven: Yale University Press.

Krishnan, T.N. (1965) 'The marketed surplus of foodgrains: is it inversely related to price?', *Economic Weekly* 17: 325–8.

Krueger, A. (1974) 'The political economy of rent seeking society', *American Economic Review* 64: 291–303.

—— (1978) *Foreign Trade Regimes and Economic Development*, Cambridge MA: Ballinger.

—— (1983) *Exchange Rate Determination*, Cambridge: Cambridge University Press.

—— (1990) 'Comparative advantage and development policy twenty years later', in A. Krueger (ed.) *Perspectives on Trade and Development*, Brighton: Wheatsheaf.

—— (1997) 'Trade policy and economic development', *American Economic Review* 87: 1–22.

—— (1999) 'Exchange rate policies for developing countries', in G. Ranis and I. Raut (eds) *Trade Policy and Economic Development*, Amsterdam: North-Holland.

Krugman, P. (1985) 'International debt problems in an uncertain world', in G. Smith and J. Cuddington (eds) *International Debt and the Developing Countries*, Washington DC: IBRD.

—— (1987) 'The narrow moving band, the Dutch disease, and the competitive consequences of Mrs Thatcher: notes on trade in the presence of dynamic economies of scale', *Journal of Development Economics* 27: 41–55.

—— (1988) 'Financing versus forgiving a debt overhang: some analytical notes', *Journal of Development Economics* 29: 253–68.

Krugman, P. and Obstfeld, M. (2002) *International Economics: Theory and Policy*, 6th edn, Harlow: Addison Wesley.

Kuznets, Simon (1955) 'Economic growth and income inequality', *American Economic Review* 45: 1–28.

—— (1965) 'Demographic aspects of modern economic growth', *World Population Conference*, Belgrade.

—— (1966) *Modern Economic Growth: Rate, Structure and Speed*, New Haven: Yale University Press.

—— (1967) 'Population and economic growth', *Proceedings of the American Philosophical Society* 3: 170–93.

—— (1971) *Economic Growth of Nations: Total Output and Production Structure*, London: Oxford University Press.

—— (1974) *Population, Capital and Growth: Selected Essays*, London: Heinemann.

Kwiatkowski, D., Phillips, P.C.B., Schmidt, P. and Shin, Y. (1992) 'Testing the null hypothesis of stationarity against the alternative of a unit root: how sure are we that economic time series have a unit root?', *Journal of Econometrics* 54: 159–78.

Kwon, J.K. (1986) 'Capital utilization, economies of scale and technical change in the growth of total factor productivity: South Korea', *Journal of Development Economics* 24: 1.

Lal, Deepak (1972) *Wells and Welfare*, Paris: OECD.

—— (1974a) *Methods of Project Analysis: A Review*, Baltimore: Johns Hopkins University Press; London: IBRD.

—— (1974b) *Appraising Foreign Investment*, London: Heinemann.

—— (1983) *The Poverty of Development Economies*, London: Hobart.

Lal, R., Sanchez, P.A. and Cummings, R.W., Jr (1985) *Land Clearing and Development in the Tropics*, Rotterdam: Balkema.

Langham, M. and Ahmed, I. (1981) 'Factor productivity differences in different regions', *American Journal of Agricultural Economics* 73.

—— (1983) 'Measuring productivity in economic growth', *American Journal of Agricultural Economics* 75: 445–51.

Lau, L. and Yotopoulos, P.A. (1989) 'The meta-production function approach to technological change in world agriculture', *Journal of Development Economics* 31: 241–69.

Layard, Richard (ed.) (1974) *Cost–Benefit Analysis*, London: Penguin.

Layard, R. and Walters, A. (1978) *Microeconomics*, New York: McGraw-Hill.

Leach, G., Jarass, L., Obermair, G. and Hoffman, L. (1986) *Energy and Growth: A Comparison of Thirteen Industrial and Developing Countries*, London: Butterworth.

Lee, K., Pesaran, H. and Smith, R. (1997) 'Growth empirics', *Quarterly Journal of Economics* 113: 319–23.

Leibenstein, Henry (1957) *Economic Backwardness and Economic Growth*, New York: Wiley.

Leipziger, Danny M. (1975) 'Determinants of use of special drawing rights by developing nations', *Journal of Development Studies* 11 (4): 316–24.

Lele, U. (1985) 'Terms of trade, agricultural growth and rural poverty in Africa', in J.S. Mellor and G. Desai (eds) *Agricultural Change and Rural Poverty: Variations on a Theme by Dharm Narain*, Baltimore: Johns Hopkins University Press.

—— (1986) 'Women and structural transformation', *Economic Development and Cultural Change* 34 (2): 195–22 1.

—— (1988) Comparative advantage and structural transformation: a review of Africa's development experience', in G. Ranis and T.W. Schultz (eds) *The State of Development Economics*, Oxford: Blackwell.

Leontief, W.W. (1951) *The Structure of the American Economy 1919–1939*, 2nd edn, New York: Oxford University Press.

Lever, H. and Huhne, C. (1987) *Debt and Danger: The World Financial Crisis*, Harmondsworth: Penguin.

Levine, P. (1999) 'The welfare economics of immigration control', *Journal of Population Economics* 12: 23–43.

Levine, Ross (1997) 'Financial development and economic growth', *Journal of Economic Literature* 35: 688–726.

Levine, R. *et al.* (2000) 'Financial intermediation and growth', *Journal of Monetary Economics* 46: 31–77.

Levine, Ross and Renelt, David (1992) 'A sensitivity analysis of cross-country growth regressions', *American Economic Review* 82: 942–63.

Lewis, Arthur W. (1953) *Industrialization and the Gold Coast*, Accra: Gold Coast Government.

—— (1954) 'Economic development with unlimited supplies of labour', *Manchester School of Economic and Social Studies* 22: 139–91.

—— (1955) *The Theory of Economic Growth*, London: Allen & Unwin.

—— (1966) *Development Planning*, London: Allen & Unwin.

—— (1979) 'The dual economy revisited', *Manchester School* 47: 211–29.

Leys, C. (1975) *Underdevelopment in Kenya: The Political Economy of Neocolonialism*, London: Heinemann.

—— (1977) 'Underdevelopment and dependency: critical notes', *Journal of Contemporary Asia* 2: 92–107.

Lipsey, Robert E. (1963) *Price and Quantity Trends in the Foreign Trade of the United States*, Princeton: National Bureau of Economic Research and Princeton University Press.

Lipton, Michael (1962) 'Balanced and unbalanced growth in underdeveloped countries', *Economic Journal* 72: 641–57.

—— (1968a) 'Strategy for agriculture: urban bias and rural planning', in Paul Streeten and Michael Lipton (eds) *The Crisis of Indian Planning*, London: Oxford University Press.

—— (1968b) 'The theory of the optimizing peasant', *Journal of Development Studies* 3: 327–51.

—— (1969) *Supply Problems Matter Most in the Economy*, Brighton: Institute of Development Studies.

—— (1977) *Why Poor People Stay Poor: A Study of the Urban Bias in World Development*, London: Temple Smith.

Lipton, M. and Longhurst, R. (1989) *New Seeds, Poor People*, London: Allen & Unwin.

Little, I. (1982) *Economic Development: Theory, Policy and International Relations*, New York: Basic Books.

Little, I.M.D. and Clifford, J. (1965) *International Aid*, London: Allen & Unwin.

Little, I.M.D. and Mirrlees, J.A. (1968) *Manual of Industrial Project Analysis*, Paris: OECD.

—— (1972) 'A reply to some criticisms of the OECD Manual', *Bulletin of the Oxford University Institute of Economics and Statistics* 34 (1): 153–68.

—— (1974) *Project Appraisal and Planning for Developing Countries*, London: Heinemann.

Little, I., Scitovsky, T. and Scott, M. (1970) *Industry and Trade in Some Developing Countries: A Comparative Study*, London: OECD and Oxford University Press.

Livingstone, I. (ed.) (1981) *Development Economics and Policy*, London: Allen & Unwin.

Loehr, W. and Powelson, J.P. (1981) *The Economics of Development and Distribution*, New York and London: Harcourt Brace Jovanovich.

Lucas, R. (1988) 'On the mechanics of economic development', *Journal of Monetary Economics* 22: 3–42.

Mabro, Robert (1967) 'Industrial growth, agricultural underemployment and the Lewis model: the Egyptian case, 1937–1965', *Journal of Development Studies* 3 (4): 322–51.

MacBean, Alasdair I. (1966) *Export Instability and Economic Development*, London: Allen & Unwin.

Machlup, Fritz (1968) *Remaking the International Monetary System*, Baltimore: Johns Hopkins University Press.

Macrae, John (1971) 'The relationship between agricultural and industrial growth with special reference to the development of the Punjab economy from 1950–1965', *Journal of Development Studies* 7 (4): 397–422.

Maddala, G.S. (1992) *Introduction to Econometrics*, 2nd edn, London: Macmillan.

Mahalanobis, P.C. (1953) 'Some observations on the process of growth of national income', *Sankhya (Indian Journal of Statistics)* 14: 307–12.

—— (1955) 'The approach of operational research to planning in India', *Sankhya (Indian Journal of Statistics)* 16: 3–13D.

Maizels, Arthur (1968) *Exports and Economic Growth of Developing Countries*, Cambridge: Cambridge University Press.

Managhas, M. (1974) 'Economic aspects of agrarian reform under new society', *Philippine Review of Business and Economics* 11: 175–87.

Mankiw, Gregory, Romer, David and Weil, David (1992) 'A contribution to the empirics of economic growth', *Quarterly Journal of Economics* 107: 407–37.

Manne, A.S. (1974) 'Multi-sector models for development planning: a survey', *Journal of Development Economics* 1 (1): 43–70.

Marglin, Stephen A. (1967) *Public Investment Criteria: Studies in the Economic Development of India*, London: Allen & Unwin.

—— (1976) *Value and Price in the Labour Surplus Economy*, London: Oxford University Press.

Marx, Karl (1853) 'The British rule in India', *New York Tribune*, 25 June, reprinted in A. Burns (1970) *A Handbook of Marxism*, New York: Haskell.

—— (1906) *Capital*, vol. 1, revised by E. Untermann, Chicago: Kerr.

Massell, Benton F. (1964) 'Export concentration and export earnings', *American Economic Review* 54: 47–63.

—— (1970) 'Export instability and economic structure', *American Economic Review* 60: 618–30.

Mathur, Ashok (1964) 'The anatomy of disguised unemployment', *Oxford Economic Papers* 16 (2): 161–93.

—— (1966) 'Balanced versus unbalanced growth: a reconciliatory view', *Oxford Economic Papers* 18 (2): 137–57.

Mathur, P.N. and Ezekiel, H. (1961) 'Marketed surplus of food and price fluctuations in a developing economy', *Kyklos* 14: 396–408.

Matlon, P.J. and Spencer, D.S. (1984) 'Increasing food production in sub-Saharan Africa: environmental problems and inadequate technological solutions', *American Journal of Agricultural Economics* 66: 671–6.

Maynard, Geoffrey (1973) 'Special drawing rights and development aid', *Journal of Development Studies* 9 (4): 518–40.

McDermott, C.J. (1990) 'Cointegration: origins and significance for economists', *New Zealand Economic Papers* 24: 1–23.

McIntosh, J.P. (1975) 'Growth and dualism in less developed countries', *Review of Economic Studies* 42 (3): 421–33.

—— (1978) 'The economics of growth and underdevelopment: a test of the dual hypothesis', *Review of Economic Studies* 45 (2): 285–98.

McKinnon, Ronald I. (1964) 'Foreign exchange constraints in economic development', *Economic Journal* 74: 388–409.

—— (1973) *Money and Capital in Economic Development*, Washington DC: Brookings Institution.

McKinnon, R. (ed.) (1976) *Money and Economic Development*, New York: Dekker.

Meade, James E. (1952) *A Geometry of International Trade*, London: Allen & Unwin.

—— (1961) *A Neo-classical Theory of Economic Growth*, London: Allen & Unwin.

—— (1964) 'International commodity agreements', *Lloyds Bank Review* 73: 28–42.

Mehra, S. (1966) 'Surplus labour in Indian agriculture', *Indian Economic Review* 1: 1; reprinted in Pramit Chaudhuri (ed.) (1972) *Readings in Indian Agricultural Development*, London: Allen & Unwin.

Meier, Gerald (2001) *Leading Issues in Economic Development*, 6th edn, New York: Oxford University Press.

Mellor, J.W. (1976) *The New Economics of Growth: A Strategy for India and the Developing World*, Ithaca NY: Cornell University Press.

Mellor, J. and Desai, G. (eds) (1985) *Agricultural Change and Rural Poverty*, Baltimore: Johns Hopkins University Press.

Michaely, Michael (1962) *Concentration in International Trade*, Amsterdam: North-Holland.

Michaely, M., Papageorgiou, D. and Choksi, A.M. (eds) (1991) *Liberalizing Foreign Trade: Lessons of Experience in the Developing World*, Cambridge: Blackwell.

Miller, S.M. (1991) 'Monetary dynamics: an application of cointegration and error-correction modeling', *Journal of Money, Credit and Banking* 23 (2): 139–54.

Milner, C. (1990) *Trade Policy and Industrialization in Developing Countries*, London: Allen & Unwin.

Miracle, M.P. (1968) 'Subsistence agriculture: analytical problems and alternative concepts', *American Journal of Agricultural Economics* 50: 292–310.

Mirrlees, James A. (1975) 'A pure theory of underdeveloped economies', in Lloyd Reynolds (ed.) *Agriculture in Development Theory*, New Haven: Yale University Press.

Mishan, E.J. (1975) *Cost–Benefit Analysis*, 2nd edn, London: Allen & Unwin.

Mitra, P. (1986) 'A description of adjustment to external shocks: country groups', in D. Lal and M. Wolf (eds) *Stagflation, Savings and the State of Perspectives on the Global Economy*, Oxford: Oxford University Press.

Modigliani, Franco (1970) 'The life cycle hypothesis of saving and intercountry differences in the savings ratio', in W.A. Eltis, M.F.G. Scott and N.J. Wolfe (eds) *Induction, Trade and Growth: Essays in Honour of Sir Roy Harrod*, Oxford: Oxford University Press.

Montalembert, M.R. de and Clement, J. (1983) *Fuelwood Supplies in the Developing Countries*, FAO Forestry Paper 42, Rome: FAO.

Morawetz, David (1974) 'Employment implications of industrialization in developing countries: a survey', *Economic Journal* 84: 491–542.

—— (1977) *Twenty-five Years of Economic Development*, Washington DC: World Bank.

Moreland, R.S. and Hazeldine, A. (1974) 'Population, energy and growth: a world cross-section study', paper presented to the European Econometric Society meeting, Grenoble.

Morss, Elliott R. and Peacock, Alan T. (1969) 'The measurement of fiscal performance in developing countries', in Alan T. Peacock (ed.) *Quantitative Analysis in Public Finance*, New York: Praeger.

Moses, John (1957) 'Investment criteria, productivity and economic development: comment', *Quarterly Journal of Economics* 71: 161–4.

Mosley, P. (1980) 'Aid, savings and growth revisited', *Oxford Bulletin of Economics and Statistics* 42: 79–95.

Mosley, P., Harrigan, J. and Toye, J. (1991) *Aid and Power*, vols I and II, London: Routledge.

Mosley, P., Hudson, J. *et al.* (1987) 'Aid, the public sector, and the market in less developed countries', *Economic Journal* 97: 616–41.

Mundell, Robert (1965) 'Growth, stability and inflationary finance', *Journal of Political Economy* 73 (2): 97–109.

Myint, Hla (1971) *Economic Theory and the Underdeveloped Country*, New York: Oxford University Press.

Myrdal, Gunnar (1956) *An International Economy*, New York: Harper & Row.

—— (1957) *Economic Theory and the Underdeveloped Regions*, London: Duckworth.

—— (ed.) (1968) *Asian Drama*, vols I–III, London: Penguin.

Nakamura, J.I. (1965) 'Growth of Japanese agriculture 1875–1920', in W.W. Lockwood (ed.) *The State and Economic Enterprise in Japan*, Princeton: Princeton University Press.

Narain, D. (1957) 'Ratio of interchange between agriculture and manufactured goods in relation to capital formation in underdeveloped economies', *Indian Economic Review* 3: 46–55.

—— (1961) *Distribution of the Marketed Surplus of Agricultural Produce by Size-level of Holding in India* 1950–1951, Bombay: Asia Publishing House.

—— (1965) *Impact of Price Movements on Areas under Selected Crops in India*, Bombay: Asia Publishing House.

Nath, S.K. (1962) 'The theory of balanced growth', *Oxford Economic Papers* 14 (2): 138–53.

National Council of Applied Economic Research (NCAER) (1972) *All-India Household Survey of Income, Saving and Consumer Expenditure*, New Delhi: NCAER.

Neary, P.J. (1981) 'On the Harris–Todaro model with intersectoral capital mobility', *Economica* 48: 219–34.

Nelson, Richard R. (1956) 'A theory of low-level equilibrium trap in underdeveloped economies', *American Economic Review* 46 (5): 894–908.

Newbery, David (1974) 'The robustness of equilibrium analysis in the dual economy', *Oxford Economic Papers* 26 (1): 32–44.

Newbery, D.M.G. and Stern, N. (eds) (1987) *The Theory of Taxation for Developing Countries*, Oxford: Oxford University Press.

Newbery, D.M.G. and Stiglitz, J.E. (1981) *The Theory of Commodity Price Stabilization: A Study of the Economics of Risk*, Oxford: Oxford University Press.

Newlyn, W.T. (1967) *Money in an African Context*, Nairobi: Oxford University Press.

—— (1969) 'Monetary analysis and policy in financially dependent economies', in I.G. Stewart (ed.) *Economic Development and Structural Change*, Edinburgh: Edinburgh University Press.

—— (1977) 'The inflation tax in developing countries', in P.C.I. Ayre (ed.) *Finance in Developing Countries*, London: Frank Cass.

—— (1983) *Measuring Tax Effort in Developing Countries*, Warwick University Discussion Paper 28.

Ngambeki, D.S. (1985) 'Economic evaluation of alley cropping with maize–maize and maize–cowpea in southwest Nigeria' *Agricultural Systems* 17: 243–85.

Nicholls, William H. (1963) 'An "agricultural surplus" as a factor in economic development', *Journal of Political Economy* 71: 1–29.

Niho, Y. (1974) 'Population growth, agricultural capital, and the development of a dual economy', *American Economic Review* 64 (6): 1077–85.

Nkonoki, S. and Sorensen, B. (1984) 'A rural energy study in Tanzania: the case of Bundilya village', *Natural Resources Forum* 8: 51–62.

North, D. (1990) *Institutions, Institutional Change and Economic Performance*, New York: Cambridge University Press.

Nowshirvani, F.H. (1967) 'A note on the fixed cash requirement theory of marketed surplus in subsistence agriculture', *Kyklos* 20: 772–3.

Nulty, Leslie (1972) *The Green Revolution in West Pakistan*, New York: Praeger.

Nunnenkamp, P. (1986) *The International Debt Crisis of the Third World*, Brighton: Wheatsheaf.

Nurkse, R. (1953) *Problems of Capital Formation in Underdeveloped Countries*, Oxford: Blackwell.

—— (1959) *Patterns of Trade and Development*, Stockholm: Almqvist & Wiksell.

Okhawa, Kazushi and Johnston, Bruce F. (1969) 'The transferability of the Japanese pattern of modernizing traditional agriculture', in E. Thorbecke (ed.) *The Role of Agriculture in Economic Development*, New York: National Bureau of Economic Research.

Okita, S. (1964) 'Choice of techniques: Japan's experience and its implications', in K. Berill (ed.) *Economic Development with Special Reference to East Asia*, London: Macmillan.

Openshaw, K. (1981) 'Rural energy consumption with particular reference to the Machakos District of Kenya', *L'Energie dans les communautés rurales des pays du Tiers Monde*, Talence: Ministère des Universités, Centre National de la Recherche Scientifique, Centre d'Etudes de Geographie Tropicale.

Opinion Research Group (ORG) (1973) *An All-India Survey of Family Planning Practices*, Baroda: ORG.

Organization for Economic Co-operation and Development (OECD) (1974) *Choice and Adaptations of Technology in Developing Countries: An Overview of Major Policy Issues*, Paris: Development Centre.

—— (1986) *Protectionism and Developing Countries*, Paris: OECD.

Osmani, R.S. (1987) *Social Security Systems in Developing Countries*, Helsinki: WIDER.

Owen, Wyn F. (1966) 'The double development squeeze on agriculture', *American Economic Review* 56 (2): 43–70.

Oxford Bulletin of Economics and Statistics (1986, 1992) Special issue on cointegration.

Oyejide, Amemda T. (1972) 'Deficit financing, inflation and capital formation: an analysis of the Nigerian experience 1957–1970', *Nigerian Journal of Economic and Social Research*, March.

Pack, Howard and Todaro, Michael (1969) 'Technological transfer, labour absorption and economic development', *Oxford Economic Papers* 21 (3): 395–403.

Palmedo, P.F., Nathans, R., Beardsworth, E. and Hale, S. (1978) *Energy Needs, Uses, and Resources in Developing Countries*, Upton NY: Brookhaven National Laboratory.

Panne, van de C. (1976) *Linear Programming and Related Techniques*, 2nd edn, Amsterdam: North-Holland.

Papanek, G. (1972) 'The effect of aid and other resource transfers on savings and growth in less developed countries', *Economic Journal* 82: 934–50.

Papps, I. (1987) 'Techniques of project appraisal', in N. Gemmel (ed.) *Surveys in Development Economics*, Oxford: Blackwell.

Parikh, A. (1971) 'Farm supply response: a distributed lag analysis', *Oxford Bulletin of Economics and Statistics* 33.

Parikh, J.K. (1980) *Energy Systems and Development*, Delhi: Oxford University Press.

Parikh, K.S. (1976) 'India in 2001', in A.J. Conic (ed.) *Economic Factors in Population Growth*, London: Macmillan.

Parkinson, J.R. (ed.) (1983) *Food Aid and Poverty*, Oxford: Blackwell.

Pasinetti, Luigi (1962) 'Rate of profit and income distribution in relation to the rate of economic growth', *Review of Economic Studies* 29: 267–79.

Patinkin, Don (1968) *Money, Interest and Prices*, 2nd edn, New York: Harper & Row.

Paukert, F. (1973) 'Income distribution at different levels of development', *International Labour Review* 108.

Paukert, F. *et al.* (1980) *Income Distribution: Structure of Economy and Employment*, London: Croom Helm.

Peacock, Alan T. (ed.) (1969) *Quantitative Analysis in Public Finance*, New York: Praeger.

Peacock, Alan T. and Shaw, G.K. (1974) *The Economic Theory of Fiscal Policy*, 2nd edn, London: Allen & Unwin.

Pearce, D.W. and Turner, R. Kerry (1990) *Economics of Natural Resources and the Environment*, Hemel Hempstead: Harvester Wheatsheaf.

Pearce, D.W. *et al.* (1990) *Sustainable Development: Economics and Environment in the Third World*, Aldershot: Edward Elgar.

—— (1991) *Blueprint 2: Greening the World Economy*, London: Earthscan.

Pearson, Lester B. (1969) *Partners in Development*, report of the Commission on International Development, New York and London: Praeger.

Pen, Jan (1971) *Income Distribution*, London: Penguin.

Pereira, A., Ulph, A. and Tims, W. (1987) *Socio-economic and Policy Implications of Energy Price Increases*, Brookfield VT: Gower.

Perron, P. (1989) 'The great crash, the oil price shock, and the unit root hypothesis', *Econometrica* 57: 1361–1401.

—— (1990) 'Testing for a unit root in a time series with a changing mean', *Journal of Business and Economic Statistics* 8 (2): 153–62.

Persson, Torsten and Tabellini, Guido (1994) 'Is inequality harmful for growth? Theory and evidence', *American Economic Review* 84 (3): 600–21.

Pesaran, M.H. and Pesaran, B. (1991) *Microfit 4: An Interactive Econometric Software Package (User Manual)*, Oxford: Oxford University Press.

Phylaktis, K. (1991) 'The black market for dollars in Chile', London: City University Business School (mimeo).

Pincus, John (1967) *Trade, Aid and Development*, New York: McGraw-Hill.

Polak, J.J. (1943) 'Balance of payments problems of countries reconstructing with the help of foreign loans', *Quarterly Journal of Economics* 57: 208–40.

—— (1957) 'Monetary analysis of income formulation and payment problems', *IMF Staff Papers* 6: 1–50.

Polak, J.J. and Boissonneult, L. (1959) 'Monetary analysis of income and imports and its statistical application', *IMF Staff Papers* 7: 349–415.

Posner, Michael V. (1961) 'International trade and technical change', *Oxford Economic Papers* 13 (3): 323–41.

Prais, S.J. (1961) 'Some mathematical notes on the quantity theory of money in an open economy', *IMF Staff Papers* 8: 212–26.

Prebisch, Raul (1959) 'Commercial policy in the underdeveloped countries', *American Economic Review*, Papers and Proceedings 49 (2): 251–73.

—— (1964) *Towards a New Trade Policy for Development*, New York: United Nations.

Preobrazhensky, E. (1965) *The New Communism*, Oxford: Clarendon Press.

Prest, A.R. (1972) *Public Finance in Underdeveloped Countries*, London: Weidenfeld & Nicolson.

Prior, M.J. (1986) 'Fuel markets in urban Bangladesh', *World Development* 14: 865–72.

Psacharopoulos, G. (1985) 'Returns to education: a further international update and implications', *Journal of Human Resources*, 20: 597.

Pyatt, G. and Round, J. (eds) (1985) *Social Accounting Matrices: A Basis for Planning*, Washington DC: World Bank.

Radice, Hugo (ed.) (1975) *International Firms and Modern Imperialism*, London: Penguin.

Raintree, J.B. and Turry, R. (1980) 'Linear programming model of an experimental Leucaena rice alley cropping system', *Research Briefs* 1: 5–7 (International Institute of Tropical Agriculture, Ibadan).

Ram, R. and Schultz, T.W. (1979) 'Life span, health, saving and productivity', *Economic Development and Cultural Change* 27 (3): 399–421.

Ramanathan, R. (1967) 'Jorgenson's model of a dual economy: an extension', *Economic Journal* 77: 32 1–7.

Ramaswami, V.K. (1971) 'Optimal policies to promote industrialisation in less developed countries', in *Trade and Development*, London: Allen & Unwin.

Rao, V.K.R. (1958) 'Investment income and the multiplier in an underdeveloped economy', in A.N. Agarwala and S.P. Singh (eds) *The Economics of Underdevelopment*, New York: Oxford University Press.

Ravallion, M. (1987) *Markets and Famines*, Oxford: Oxford University Press.

Ravallion, M. and Dearden, L. (1988) 'Social security in a moral economy: an empirical analysis for Java', *Review of Economics and Statistics* 70: 36–44.

Rebelo, Sergio (1991) 'Long-run policy analysis and long-run growth', *Journal of Political Economy* 99: 500–21.

—— (1996) 'The Determinants of Economic Growth', mimeo, IEA conference, Tunis.

Reddy, A.K.N. and Reddy, B.S. (1983) 'Energy in a stratified society: case study of firewood in Bangalor', *Economic and Political Weekly* 8: 1757–70.

Repetto, R. (1987) 'Creating incentives for sustainable forest development', *Ambio* 16: 94–9.

—— (1990) *Macroeconomic Policies and Deforestation*, Helsinki: WIDER.

Reynolds, Lloyd George (ed.) (1975) *Agriculture in Development Theory*, New Haven: Yale University Press.

Rivera-Batiz, Luis and Romer, Paul (1991) 'International trade with endogenous technical change', *European Economic Review* 35: 971–1001.

Robinson, Joan (1956) *The Accumulation of Capital*, London: Macmillan.

Robinson, R. (ed.) (1965) *Industrialization in Developing Countries*, Cambridge: Cambridge University Press.

Robinson, R. and Johnston, P. (eds) (1971) *Prospects for Employment Opportunities in the Nineteen Seventies*, London: HMSO.

Robinson, S. (1972) 'Sources of growth in less developed countries: a cross-section study', *Quarterly Journal of Economics* 85: 391–408.

Robinson, S. *et al.* (1982) *General Equilibrium Models for Development Policy*, Oxford: Oxford University Press.

Rodrik, D. (1990) 'Some policy dilemmas in Turkish macroeconomic management', in T. Aricanli and D. Rodrik (eds) *The Political Economy of Turkey: Debt, Adjustment and Sustainability*, London: Macmillan.

—— (1992) 'The limits of trade policy reform in developing countries', *Journal of Economic Perspectives* 6 (1): 87–105.

—— (1996) 'Understanding economic policy reform', *Journal of Economic Literature* 34: 9–41.

Rodrik, D. and Rodriguez, F. (1999) 'Trade Policy and Economic Growth', CEPR Discussion Paper, London: Centre for Economic Policy Research.

Rogoff, K. (1992) 'Dealing with developing country debt in the 1990s', *World Economy* 15: 475–86.

Romer, David (2001) *Advanced Macroeconomics*, 2nd edn, New York: McGraw-Hill.

Romer, Paul (1986) 'Increasing returns and long run growth', *Journal of Political Economy* 94: 1002–37.

—— (1990) 'Endogenous technological change', *Journal of Political Economy* 98: S71–S102.

—— (1993) 'Dynamic Competitive Equilibria with Externalities, Increasing Returns and Unbounded Growth', unpublished Ph.D. thesis, University of Chicago.

—— (1993) 'Idea gaps and object gaps in economic development', *Journal of Monetary Economics* 32: 543–74.

—— (1994) 'New goods, old theory and the welfare costs of trade restrictions', *Journal of Development Economics* 43: 5–38.

—— (1994) 'The origins of endogenous growth', *Journal of Economic Perspectives* 8 (1): 322.

Rosenstein-Rodan, Paul N. (1943) 'Problems of industrialization of Eastern and South Eastern Europe', *Economic Journal* 25: 202–11.

—— (1961) 'International aid for underdeveloped countries', *Review of Economics and Statistics* 43 (2): 107–38.

Rosenzweig, M. and Schultz, T.P. (1985) 'The demand and supply of births: fertility and its life cycle consequences', *American Economic Review* 75 (5) (December).

Rosenzweig, M. and Wolpin, K.I. (1982) 'Government interventions and household behaviour in a developing country', *Journal of Development Economics* 10 (2): 209–26.

—— (1985) 'Specific experience, household structure and intergenerational transfers', *Quarterly Journal of Economics* 100: 961–88.

Rudra, A. (1978) 'Relative rates of growth', *Economic and Political Weekly* 7 (February).

Ruitembeck, H. (1989) *Social Cost–Benefit Analysis of the Korup Project, Cameroon*, London: World Wide Fund for Nature.

Ruttan, V. (1977) 'The Green Revolution: seven generalizations', *International Development Review* 19: 16–23.

Ruttan, V.W. and Thirtle, C. (1989) 'Induced technical and institutional change in African agriculture', *Journal of International Development* 1 (1): 1–45.

Rybczynski, T.N. (1955) 'Factor endowment and relative commodity prices', *Economica* 22 (4): 336–41.

Sachs, J. (1986) *Managing the LDC Debt Crisis*, Brookings Paper, 397–443. Washington DC: Brookings Institution.

—— (ed.) (1989) *Developing Country Debt and the World Economy*, Chicago: University of Chicago Press.

Sah, R. and Stiglitz, J. (1984) 'The economics of price scissors', *American Economic Review* 74: 125–38.

Saint-Paul, Gilles and Verdier, Thierry (1992) 'Education, Democracy and Growth', Center for Economic Policy Research working paper 613.

Samuelson, Paul (1994) *Economics*, 14th edn, New York and London: McGraw-Hill.

Samuelson, Paul and Modigliani, Franco (1966) 'The Pasinetti paradox in neo-classical and more general models', *Review of Economic Studies* 33: 269–301.

Santos-Paulino, Amelia and Thirlwall, A.P. (2002) 'Trade Liberalisation and the Balance of Payments in Selected Developing Countries', University of Kent DP. (Forthcoming *Economic Journal*.)

Sara, Tejinder Singh (1975) 'Cost–benefit analysis in developing countries: case study of a fertilizer plant in India', unpublished Ph.D. thesis, University of Massachusetts.

Sato, K. (1967) 'Taxation and neo-classical growth', *Public Finance* 22 (3): 346–70.

Sato, R. (1963) 'Fiscal policy in a neo-classical growth model', *Review of Economic Studies* 30: 16–23.

Sato, R. and Niho, Y. (1971) 'Population growth in the development of a dual economy', *Oxford Economic Papers* 23: 418–36.

Schotta, Charles, Jr (1966) 'The money supply, exports and income in an open economy: Mexico 1939–1963', *Economic Development and Cultural Change* 14: 458–70.

Schultz, P.T. (1976) 'Determinants of fertility: a micro-economic model of choice', in A.J. Coale (ed.) *Economic Factors in Population Growth*, London: Macmillan.

—— (1988) 'Economic demography and development: new directions in an old field', in G. Ranis and P.T. Schultz (eds) *The State of Development Economics*, Oxford: Blackwell.

Schultz, T.W. (1964) *Transforming Traditional Agriculture*, New Haven: Yale University Press.

Schwartz, F. and Zurita, S. (1992) 'Sovereign debt: optimal contract, underinvestment and forgiveness', *Journal of Finance* 47: 981–1004.

Scitovsky, Tibor (1954) 'Two concepts of external economies', *Journal of Political Economy* 17: 143–51.

—— (1959) 'Growth: balanced or unbalanced', in M. Abramovotz (ed.) *The Allocation of Economic Resources: Essays in Honour of B.F. Haley*, Stanford: Stanford University Press.

—— (1966) 'A new approach to international liquidity', *American Economic Review* 54.

Sen, Amartya Kumar (1966) 'Peasant and dualism with or without surplus labour', *Journal of Political Economy* 74: 425–50.

—— (1967) 'Surplus labour in India: a critique of Schultz's statistical test', *Economic Journal* 77: 154–61.

—— (1968) *Choice of Techniques: An Aspect of the Theory of Planned Economic Development*, 3rd edn, Oxford: Blackwell.

—— (ed.) (1970) *Growth Economics*, London: Penguin.

—— (1972) 'Control areas and accounting prices: an approach to economic evaluation', *Economic Journal* 82: 486–501.

—— (1973) *On Economic Inequality*, Oxford: Clarendon Press.

—— (1975) *Employment Technology and Development*, Oxford: Clarendon Press.

—— (1976) 'Poverty: an ordinal approach to measurement', *Econometrica* 44 (2): 219–31.

—— (1981a) 'Ingredients of famine analysis: availability and entitlements', *Quarterly Journal of Economics* 95.

—— (1981b) *Poverty and Famines: An Essay on Entitlement and Deprivation*, Oxford: Clarendon Press.

—— (1999) *Freedom and Development*, Oxford: Oxford University Press.

Sen, Amartya Kumar, Dasgupta, P. and Marglin, S. (1972) *Guidelines for Project Evaluation*, Vienna: UNIDO.

Sen, Sudhir (1974) *A Richer Harvest: New Horizons for Developing Countries*, New York: McGraw-Hill.

—— (1975) *Reaping the Green Revolution: Food and Jobs for All*, New York: McGraw-Hill.

Sengupta, A. (ed.) (1980) *Commodities, Finance and Trade: Issues in North–South Negotiations*, London: Pinter.

Shaw, Edward S. (1973) *Financial Deepening in Economic Development*, New York: Oxford University Press.

Shetty, M.C. (1963) *Small-scale and Household Industries in a Developing Economy*, Bombay: Asia Publishing House.

Shields, M. and Wheatley Price, S. (1998) 'The earnings of male immigrants in England', *Applied Economics* 30: 1157–68.

Shoven, A. and Whalley, J. (1991) *Applied General Equilibrium Analysis*, Oxford: Blackwell.

Shukla, Tara (1965) *Capital Formation in Indian Agriculture*, Bombay: Vora.

Sidhu, S.S. (1974a) 'Economics of technical change in wheat production in the Indian Punjab', *American Journal of Agricultural Economics* 56 (May): 221.

—— (1974b) 'Relative efficiency in wheat production in the Indian Punjab', *American Economic Review* 64: 742–51.

Simon, J. (1977) *The Economics of Population Growth*, Princeton: Princeton University Press.

—— (1981) *The Ultimate Resource*, Princeton: Princeton University Press.

Singer, Hans W. (1965) 'External aid: for plans or projects?', *Economic Journal* 75: 539–45.

Singer, Hans W. and Ansari, Javed (1977) *Rich and Poor Countries*, London: Allen & Unwin.

Singer, Hans W. and Schiavo-Campo, S. (1970) *Perspectives of Economic Development*, New York: Houghton Mifflin.

Sinha, Radha P. (1969) 'Unresolved issues in Japan's early economic development', *Scottish Journal of Political Economy* 16: 109–51.

Sinha, R.P. and Drabek, A.G. (1978) *The World Food Problem: Consensus and Conflict*, Oxford: Pergamon Press.

Smith, A.D. (ed.) (1976) *Wage Policy Issues in Economic Development*, London: Macmillan.

Smith, P. (1993) 'The quality of life', *Economic Review*.

Soejono, D. (1976) 'Growth and distributional changes in paddy farm income in central Java', *Indonesian Journal of Social and Economic Affairs*, May: 26–32.

Solow, Robert (1956) 'A contribution to the theory of economic growth', *Quarterly Journal of Economics* 70: 65–94.

—— (1957) 'Technical change and the aggregate production function', *Review of Economics and Statistics* 39: 312–20.

—— (1960) 'Investment and technical progress', in K. Arrow *et al.* (eds) *Mathematical Methods in Social Sciences*, Stanford: Stanford University Press.

Southgate, D. (1989) 'The causes of tropical deforestation in Ecuador: a statistical analysis', LEEC Paper 89–09, London: London Economic and Ecological Centre.

Southworth, Herman M. and Johnston, Bruce F. (eds) (1967) *Agricultural Development and Economic Growth*, Ithaca NY: Cornell University Press.

Spraos, J. (1980) 'The statistical debate on the net barrier terms of trade between primary commodities and manufacturers', *Economic Journal* 90: 107–28.

Spulber, N. (ed.) (1964) *Foundations of Soviet Strategy for Economic Growth: Selected Soviet Essays 1924–1930*, Bloomington: Indiana University Press.

Squire, L. (1981) *Employment Policy in Developing Countries: A Survey of Issues and Evidence*, Oxford: Oxford University Press.

Squire, Lyn and Tak, H.G. van der (1975) *Economic Analysis of Projects*, Baltimore: Johns Hopkins University Press.

Srinivasan, T.N. (1962) 'Investment criteria and choice of techniques of production', *Yale Economic Essays* 2 (1).

—— (1979) *Malnutrition: Some Measurement and Policy Issues*, Washington DC: World Bank.

—— (1988) 'International trade and factor movements in development theory, policy and experience', in G. Ranis and T.P. Schultz (eds) *The State of Development Economics*, Oxford: Blackwell.

Srinivasan, T.N. and Bardhan, P.K. (eds) (1975) *Poverty and Income Distribution in India*, Calcutta: Statistical Publishing Society.

Srinivasan, T.N. and Whalley, J. (1986) *General Equilibrium Trade Policy Modelling*, Cambridge MA: MIT Press.

Srivastava, Uma, Crown, R.W. and Heady, E.O. (1971) 'Green Revolution and farm income distribution', *Economic and Political Weekly*, December: A 163–72.

Stark, O. (1991) *Economics of Migration*, Oxford: Blackwell.

Stern, N. (1989) 'The economics of development: a survey', *Economic Journal* 99 (397): 597–685.

Stevens, R.D. and Jabara, C.L. (1988) *Agricultural Development Principles: Economic Theory and Empirical Evidence*, Baltimore: Johns Hopkins University Press.

Stewart, F. (1972) 'Choice of techniques in developing countries', *Journal of Development Studies* 9 (1): 99–121.

—— (1974) 'Technology and employment in LDCs', *World Development* 2 (3): 17–40.

—— (1975) 'Manufacture of cement blocks in Kenya', in A.S. Bhalla (ed.) *Technology and Employment in Industry: A Case Study Approach*, Geneva: ILO.

—— (1979) 'Country experience in providing for basic needs', *Finance and Development* 16 (4): 23–36.

—— (1984) *Structural Adjustment with a Human Face*, London: Pinter.

Stewart, Frances and Streeten, Paul (1971) 'Conflicts between output and employment objectives in developing countries', *Oxford Economic Papers* 23 (2): 145–68.

—— (1972) 'Little–Mirrlees methods and project appraisal', *Bulletin of the Oxford University Institute of Economics and Statistics* 34 (1): 75–91.

Stiglitz, J. (1976) 'The efficiency wage hypothesis, surplus labour, and the distribution of income in LDCs', *Oxford Economic Papers* 28: 185–207.

—— (1988) 'Economic organization, information and development', in H. Chenery and T.N. Srinivasan (eds) *Handbook of Development Economics*, Amsterdam: North-Holland, vol. I.

—— (1998) 'The role of the state in financial markets', *Proceedings of the Annual Conference on Development Economics*, 19–52.

Stiglitz, J. and Weiss, A. (1981) 'Credit rationing in markets with imperfect information', *American Economic Review* 71: 393–410.

Stock, J.H. (1987) 'Asymptotic properties of least squares estimators of cointegrating vectors', *Econometrica* 56: 1035–56.

Stokey, Nancy (1988) 'Learning by doing and the introduction of new goods', *Journal of Political Economy* 96: 702–17.

Stone, R. (1964) 'Linear expenditure systems and demand analysis: an application to the pattern of British demand', *Economic Journal* 74: 511–27.

Streeten, Paul (1959) 'Unbalanced growth', *Oxford Economic Papers* 11 (2).

—— (1966) 'Use and abuse of planning models', in K. Martin and J. Knapp (eds) *Teaching of Development Economics*, London: Frank Cass.

—— (ed.) (1970) *Unfashionable Economics: Essays in Honour of Lord Balogh*, London: Weidenfeld & Nicolson.

—— (1971) 'Costs and benefits of multinational enterprises in less developed countries', in John H. Dunning (ed.) *The Multinational Enterprise*, London: Allen & Unwin.

—— (1973a) 'The multinational enterprise and the theory of development policy', *World Development* 1 (10): 1–14.

—— (1973b) *Trade Strategies for Development*, London: Macmillan.

—— (1979) 'Basic needs: premises and promises', *Journal of Policy Modeling* 1 (1): 1–22.

Summers, A. and Heston, A. (1984) 'Improved international comparisons of real product and its composition 1950–1980', *Review of Income and Wealth* 30 (2): 207–62.

—— (1988) 'A new set of international comparisons of real product and price level estimates for 130 countries, 1950–1985', *Review of Income and Wealth* 34 (1): 1–25.

—— (1991) 'Penn World Tables Mark 5: 1950–1988', *Quarterly Journal of Economics:* 340–67.

Summers, Robert and Heston, Alan (1991) 'The Penn World Table (Mark 5): an expanded set of international comparisons, 1950–1988', *Quarterly Journal of Economics* 2: 327–68.

Sunberg, J.E., McIntire, J., Okali, C. and Atta-Krah, A. (1987) *Economic Analysis of Alley Farming with Small Ruminants*, Bulletin 28, Addis Ababa: International Livestock Centre for Africa.

Sundrum, R.M. (1967) 'The measurement of export instability', mimeo, June; cited in Odin Knudsen and Andrew Parnes (1975) *Trade Instability and Economic Development*, Lexington: Heath.

—— (1983) *Development Economics*, New York: Wiley.

Swan, Trevor (1956) 'Economic growth and capital accumulation', *Economic Record* 32 (November): 334–61.

Sweezy, Paul M. (1942) *The Theory of Capitalist Development*, London: Dennis Robson.

Tait, A. (1988) *Value Added Tax: International Practice and Problems*, Washington DC: IMF.

Tanzania (1967) *Wages, Incomes, Rural Development, Investment and Price Policy*, Government Paper 4, Dar es Salaam: Government Printer.

Taylor, Lance (1979) *Macro Models for Developing Countries*, New York: McGraw-Hill.

—— (1983) *Structuralist Macroeconomics*, New York: Basic Books.

Thamarajakshi, R. (1969) 'Intersectoral terms of trade and marketed surplus of agricultural produce 1951–2 to 1965–6', in Pramit Chaudhuri (ed.) (1972) *Readings in Indian Agricultural Development*, London: Allen & Unwin.

Thapa, S. and Mehta, D. (1991) 'An empirical investigation of the determinants of the supply of bank loans to less developed countries', *Journal of Banking and Finance* 15: 535–57.

Theberge, James D. (ed.) (1968) *Economics of Trade and Development*, New York: Wiley.

Thirlwall, A.P. (1974) *Inflation, Saving and Growth in Developing Economies*, London: Macmillan.

—— (1976a) *Financing Economic Development*, London: Macmillan.

—— (1976b) 'Reconciling the conflict between employment and saving and employment and output in the choice of techniques in developing countries', University of Kent, Discussion Paper 19 (mimeo).

—— (2003) *Growth and Development: with Special Reference to Developing Economies*, 6th edn, London: Macmillan.

Thomsen, M. (1988) 'Demand for charcoal in Jamaica', unpublished M.Sc. thesis, Gainsville: University of Florida, Food and Resources Economics Department.

Thorbecke, Eric (1969) *The Role of Agriculture in Economic Development*, New York: National Bureau of Economic Research.

Thraen, C.S., Hammond, J.W. and Buxton, B.M. (1978) 'Estimating components of demand elasticities from cross-sectional data', *American Journal of Agricultural Economics* 60: 674–7.

Timmer, C.P. (1986) *Getting Prices Right: The Scope and Limits of Agricultural Price Policy*, Ithaca NY: Cornell University Press.

—— (1988) 'The agricultural transformation', in H. Chenery and T.N. Srinivasan (eds) *Handbook of Development Economics*, Amsterdam: North-Holland, vol. I.

Tisdell, C. (1990) *Economics of Environment*, New York: Praeger.

Tobin, James (1965) 'Money and economic growth', *Econometrica* 33: 671–84.

Todaro, Michael P. (1969) 'A model of labour migration and urban unemployment in less developed countries', *American Economic Review* 59 (1): 138–48.

—— (1971a) *Development Planning: Models and Methods*, London and Nairobi: Oxford University Press.

—— (1971b) 'Income expectations, rural–urban migration and employment in Africa', *International Labour Review* 104 (5): 387–413.

—— (1976) *Internal Migration and Economic Development: A Review of Theory, Evidence, Methodology and Research Priorities*, Geneva: ILO.

—— (2001) *Economics for a Developing World*, 6th edn, London: Longman.

Toye, J. (ed.) (1979) *Taxation and Economic Development*, London: Frank Cass.

Triffin, R. (1971) 'The use of SDR finance for collectively agreed purposes', *Banca Nazionale de Lavoro Quarterly Review*.

Turner, R. Kerry (ed.) (1988) *Sustainable Environmental Management*, London: Belhaven Press; Boulder, CO: Westview Press.

Turnham, David and Jaegar, Ian (1971) *The Employment Problem in Less Developed Countries*, Paris: OECD.

Unal, H., Demirgue-Kunt, A. and Leung, K. (1993) 'The Brady Plan 1989: Mexico debt-reduction agreement and bank stock returns in United States and Japan', *Journal of Money, Credit and Banking* 25: 410–29.

UNDP (1990) *United Nations Human Development Index*, New York: UNDP.

United Nations (1952) *Instability in Export Markets of Underdeveloped Countries*, New York: UN Secretariat.

—— (1961) *International Compensation for Fluctuations in Commodity Prices*, New York: Department of Economic and Social Affairs.

—— (1962) *The Capital Developing Needs of the Less Developed Countries*, New York: UN.

—— (1973) *The Determinants and Consequences of Population Change*, New York: UN.

—— (1974) *The Acquisition of Technology from Multinational Corporations by Developing Countries*, ST/ESA/12, New York: UN.

—— (1975) *Multinational Corporations in World Development*, ST/ECA/ 190, New York: UN.

United Nations Conference on Trade and Development (UNCTAD) (1965) *International Monetary Issues and the Developing Countries*, New York: UN.

—— (1968) *Proceedings of the Conference, New Delhi.*

—— (1972a) *Proceedings of the Conference, Santiago.*

—— (1972b) *Merchandise Trade*, New York: UN.

—— (1975) *Major Issues arising from the Transfer of Technology to Developing Countries*, TD/B/AC11/10/Rev. 2, New York: UN.

—— (1976a) *The Role of Transnational Corporations in the Trade in Manufactures and Semi-Manufactures of Developing Countries*, Support Paper TD/185/ Supp. 2, Nairobi: UN.

—— (1976b) *Transfer of Technology: Technological Dependence: its Nature, Consequences and Policy Implications*, 12, TD/190, Nairobi: UN.

Uzawa, H. (1962) 'On a two-sector model of economic growth', *Review of Economic Studies* 29: 40–7.

Vaitsos, C.V. (1974) *Inter-country Income Distribution and Transnational Enterprises*, London: Oxford University Press.

Verinumbe, I., Knipscheer, H.C. and Enabor, E.E. (1984) 'The economic potential of leguminous tree crops in zero tillage cropping in Nigeria: a linear programming model', *Agroforestry Systems* 2: 129–38.

Vernon, Raymond (1966) 'International investment and international trade in the product cycle', *Quarterly Journal of Economics* 80 (2): 190–207.

—— (1971) *Sovereignty at Bay: The Multinational Spread of US Enterprise*, London: Longman.

Vines, D. and Kanbur, S.M.R. (1986) 'North–south interaction and commodity control', *Journal of Development Economics* 23 (2): 371–87.

Vogel, F. (1990) 'Who cares about Third World debt?', *Asian Finance* 16: 39–40.

Vogel, R. and Buser, S. (1976) 'Inflation, financial repression and capital formation in Latin America', in R. McKinnon (ed.) *Money and Finance in Economic Growth and Development*, New York: Marcel Dekker.

Wai, U. Tun (1957) 'Interest rates outside the organized money markets in underdeveloped countries', *IMF Staff Papers* 6: 1.

—— (1972) *Financial intermediates and National Savings in Developing Countries*, New York: Praeger.

Wald, Haskell P. (1958) 'Taxation of agriculture in developing economies', in A.N. Agarwala and S.P. Singh (eds) *The Economics of Underdevelopment*, New York: Oxford University Press.

Wallich, H.C. (1969) 'Money and growth: a country cross-section analysis', *Journal of Money, Credit and Banking* 1: 281–302.

Wang, N.T. (ed.) (1976) *Taxation and Development*, New York: Praeger.

Warner, A. (1992) 'Did the debt crisis cause the investment crisis?', *Quarterly Journal of Economics* 107: 1161–86.

Whalley, J. (1984) 'The north–south debate and the terms of trade: an applied general equilibrium approach', *Review of Economics and Statistics* 66: 224–34.

Wharton, C., Jr (1969) 'The Green revolution: cornucopia or Pandora's box?', *Foreign Affairs* 47: 464–76.

Wheatley Price, Steve (2000) 'The employment adjustment of male immigrants in England', *Journal of Population Economics* 14: 193–220.

White, H. (1991) 'Foreign aid, savings and economic growth: a critical survey', *Journal of Development Surveys* 3.

Wijnbergen, Sweder Van (1983a) 'Interest rate management in less developed countries', *Journal of Monetary Economics* 12 (3): 433–52.

—— (1983b) 'Credit policy, inflation and growth in financially repressed economies', *Journal of Development Economics* 13: 45–65.

—— (1984) 'Exchange rate management and stabilization policies in developing countries' (mimeo).

Wilkinson, P.F. (1984) 'Energy resources in a Third World microstate: St Lucia Household Energy Survey', *Resources and Energy* 6: 305–28.

Wilkinson, R.G. (1972) *Poverty and Progress*, London: Methuen.

Williamson, Jeffrey G. (1968) 'Personal savings in developing nations', *Economic Record* 44: 194–209.

Williamson, John H. (1972) 'SDRs, interest and the aid link', *Banca Nazionale del Lavoro Quarterly Review* June.

—— (1973) 'International liquidity: a survey', *Economic Journal* 83: 685–746.

Williamson, J.W. (1988) 'Migration and urbanization', in H. Chenery and T.N. Srinivasan (eds) *Handbook of Development Economics*, Amsterdam: North-Holland, vol. I.

Wood, T. and Baldwin, S. (1985) 'Fuelwood and charcoal use in developing countries', in J.M. Hollander (ed.) *Annual Review of Energy*, Palo Alto CA: Annual Reviews, vol. 10.

World Bank (1980–2002) *World Development Report*, various issues, Washington DC: World Bank; New York: Oxford University Press.

—— (2002) *World Development Indicators*, Washington DC: World Bank.

Yap, L.Y.L. (1977) 'The attraction of cities: a review of migration literature', *Journal of Development Economics* 3 (4).

Yotopoulos, P. and Nugent, J. (1976) *Economics of Development: Empirical Investigations*, New York: Harper & Row.

Young, Alwyn (1991) 'Learning by doing and the dynamic effects of international trade', *Quarterly Journal of Economics* 106: 396–405.

—— (1992) 'A Tale of Two Cities: factor accumulation and technical change in Hong Kong and Singapore', *NBER Macro Annual, 1992*, Washington DC: National Bureau of Economic Research.

—— (1994) 'The Tyranny of Numbers: Confronting the Statistical Realities of the East Asian Growth Experience', mimeo, Cambridge MA: MIT.

Zaidan, George C. (1971) *The Costs and Benefits of Family Planning Programs*, Baltimore: The Johns Hopkins University Press; London: IBRD.

Zellner, A. (1988) 'Causality and causal laws in economics', *Journal of Econometrics* 50: 7–21.

Index

absorption of surplus labour 81
absorptive capacity of an economy 148–9
accounting rate of interest (ARI) 337–41
Adelman, Irma 265
Africa, sub-Saharan 359–61
Aghion, P. 62, 73
agriculture 19, 229–45; basic needs approach to 260–5; limitations of price policy for 244; role in economic development 229–30; role of public policy 255, 259–60
Ahmad, E. 139
aid programmes 146–7; and economic growth 176–9
alley cropping 412
Anand, S. 286, 305
anti-trade bias 205
Arrow, K. 56, 76, 218
Aschauer, D. 65, 143, 145
Asian and Pacific Council 213
Asian 'tiger' economies 356, 379
assimilative capacity 162
Association of South East Asian Nations (ASEAN) 213
Ayre, P.C.I. 123
Azam, K.M. 248
Azariadis, Costas 67

babies, demand for 277, 308
Baker Plan 380, 386, 397
balance of payments 358–9; statistics of 184–8; and tariffs 197
balanced budget multiplier (BBM) 127–8
balanced growth (BG) theory 109–12
Balassa, Bela 200–3, 216–19
Banerjee, Abhijit 302
bank loans 382
Barro, Robert 57, 69, 141, 301
basic needs, satisfaction of 260–5
Bastable's test 193
Bauer, P.T. 110
Becker, G. 67
Behrman, J. 369
Berg, A. 261
Bergan, A. 93–4
Berry, A. 86
Bhagwati, J. 191
Bhagwati–Srinivasan model of migration 295
bilateral flows of foreign resources 152–3
Bird, R.M. 138
bond finance 382
Borlaug, Norman 251
Brady Plan 391–2, 397
Brahmananda, P.R. 319
Brandt Report 375
Brazil 203
Buchanan, N.S. 100
budgetary deficits 141–5
buffer stocks 369–74
Buiter, W. 142–3
Burgess, S.Z. 140–1

Cairncross, A. 215
Camdessus, M. 396
capital intensity 102, 107–8, 291
capital-labour ratio 71–3
capital markets 22, 30–2, 335
capital-output ratio 45–6, 89, 100, 121, 129, 132, 200, 316
capital turnover criterion 100
capitalism 51–2
'catching up' effect 70
Caves, R.E. 159
Central American Common Market 213
Chenery, H. 101, 154, 206
children as 'consumption' and 'investment' goods 276–7
Chile 167
China 265, 311
Chow test 175
Christian Aid 359
Citicorp 387
Clinton, Bill, administration of 396
Coase theoren 405
Cobb–Douglas production function 31–3, 56, 73–4
Colombia 167, 251

commodity agreement schemes (CASs) 211, 222
commodity markets 23
commodity price stabilization 369–71; gains and losses from 371–3
Commonwealth Secretariat 366
comparative advantage, theory of 190, 354
compensatory financing schemes (CFSs) 211–12, 375
conditionality clauses 351
consortiums for foreign resourcing 153
convergence 57–8, 68–70; conditional 69
Coppock, J.D. 209, 224
Corden, W.M. 200–2
corruption 178
cost-benefit analysis: basic principles of 332–3; decision rules for 333; reasons for application of 334–5; *see also* social cost-benefit analysis
'creative destruction' 62, 66
cropping intensity 252
'crowding out' effects 141–3, 178
Cuba 289
customs duties 136
customs unions 213

debt 214–15, 357–60, 378–97; reasons for problems with 381–4
debt buybacks 390
debt-for-equity and debt-for-debt swaps 390–2
debt forgiveness 391; cases for and against 392–7
deficit financing (DF) 131–2, 143
deforestation 399–401
De Long, B. 64
demand structure by country 14–17
demographic transition, theory of 273
Denison, E.F. 263
deregulation 303
devaluation 357–8
development planning models 314–16; macroeconomic 320–2
direct taxation 133–4
directly unproductive profit (DUP) 219
diversification 230
Dixit, A. 92–3
Dixit–Marglin model 90–1
Dobb, M. 103, 108, 230
Dobb-Sen model 107
domestic resources for development 115
Drazen, Allan 67
dual economy models 79–81; criticisms of 81–2, 91–4; empirical tests of 82–3; extension of 90
dual-gap models 154–6, 216; criticisms of 156–7
Dutch Republic 130
dynamic economies 60–1

East African Community 213
Easterly, W. 63, 65, 67
Eckaus, R.S. 150
Eckstein, O. 102–3
economic growth *see* growth
economic planning: cases for and against 313–14; concept of 311; types of 311–12; use of economic models 312
economies of scale in agriculture 241–3
education 62–4, 67, 276, 290, 300, 360
Egypt 83
E-mapping 267–9
employment and growth 94–5
employment policy 299–300
'employment problem' 289–91
endogenous growth theories 56–60, 73–8, 217; 'old' and 'new' 60–1
endogenous population growth 67
entrepreneurship 22
European Bank for Reconstruction and Development 382
European Union 204, 210, 375, 397
exchange entitlement (EE) 267–70
exchange rate policy 354–8
excise duties 137
exploitative mechanisms 167
export-led growth (ELG) 216–19
exports: effects of protection on 202–3; instability of 208–10, 223–4, 365
external finance, sources of 382–3
externalities 62, 109, 218, 335
Ezekiel, H. 234

factor markets, distortion in 196–7
famines 265–70
Fan, L.S. 117
Fei-Ranis model 83–7, 94; criticisms of 86–7, 92
Feldman–Mahalanobis model 317–20, 347–9
fertility 67–8, 275–80; determinants of 278–9; household production approach to 307–8
fertilizers, use of 252, 406
Fields, G.S. 295–6
financial intermediation 65
financial markets: development of 302; intervention in 302
financial revolution 130
financially repressed regimes (FRRs) 125
fiscal contraction 352, 356
fiscal deficits 122–3
fiscal policy 102, 244, 354–5; and growth 127–31; objectives of 126–7; in open economies 128–9

Fischer, S. 64
Fleming, M. 110
food availability doctrine (FAD) 261, 269–70
foreign direct investment (FDI) 165, 382–3
foreign resources for promoting economic development 146; criteria for distribution of 147–50; different types of 150–3; and special drawing rights 171–2
forex gap 381–5
France 311
free trade doctrine 65, 190–1, 214
fuelwood 406–12

Galenson, W. 101–2
Gemmell, N. 138
General Agreement on Tariffs and Trade (GATT) 212, 366–7
Generalized System of Preferences (GSP) 212, 222–3
Ghana 124
Gini coefficient 29–30, 304–5
government spending, modelling of 142–5
Grabowski, R. 260
Green Revolution 87, 99, 133, 135, 178, 246–51, 290; causes of 251–5; effects on factor shares 255–8; effects on income 255; problems and prospects for 258–60
Griffin, K. 250
Grossman, G. 62, 73
growth: and aid programmes 176–9; balanced and unbalanced 109–12; country statistics of 6–8; differences in rates of 60–71; and employment 94–5; and export instability 208–10; and fiscal policy 127–31; and human capital 77–8; and income inequality 284–7, 300–3; indicators of speed of 63; and inflation 117–24; and money supply 116–17; motors of 61–3; *per capita* real income as an index of 23–6; and population growth 271–4; and redistribution 287–9; and satisfaction of basic needs 262–5; and standards of living 300–1; 'stop-go' pattern of 355–6; and trade 205
'growth menu' 66
growth models: classical 37–9; endogenous 56–61, 73–8, 217; Harrod-Domar 42–3, 100, 129; Kaldor-Mirrlees 52–5; Keynesian 39–41; Marxist 47–52; neoclassical 43–7, 55–6, 68–73
Guatemala 135

Hagen, E.E. 196
Haq, M.Ul. 368
Hardin, G. 401–2
Harris-Todaro model 294–8
Harrod-Domar model 42–3, 100, 129, 314–16; applied to India 316–17; applied to Kenya 317
Heckscher-Ohlin theorem 354
Helleiner, G.K. 173–4
Helpman, E. 62, 73
Heston, A. 63
Hicks, J.R. 333
Hicks, N. 261
Hirschman, A.O. 111
Hoeven, R. van der 264
Honduras 135
Hopkins, M. 264
household production theory 306–9
Howitt, P. 62, 73
human capital 40, 62, 67–8, 303; and growth 77–8
human development index (HDI) 26–8

import substitution industrialization (ISI) policy 214–19
income distribution 18, 66–7, 281–4; in agricultural sector 249, 257–9; measurement of inequality in 28–30; and poverty 281
income *per capita* 1; as an index of growth and development 23–6
income tax 133
India 82, 133, 141–5, 178, 234, 248–9, 253, 316–19
indicative planning 311
indirect taxation 135–7, 141
industrial revolution 130
industrialization 214; reasons for 190
infant industries 102, 193–6, 355
infant mortality 276
inflation 64, 117–18, 122–4, 132, 334, 358; and economic growth 117–24; and investment 121; and special drawing rights 172
infrastructure investment 65
input–output analysis 322–6
institutional factors 66, 70–1
intangible assets 158–9
Inter-American Development Bank 382
interest rates 123–6, 335; *see also* accounting rate of interest
internal rate of return 334
International Bank for Reconstruction and Development *see* World Bank
international commodity agreements (ICAs) 369, 374–8
International Labour Organization (ILO) 300
International Monetary Fund (IMF) 150, 170, 173, 223, 351–9, 366–8, 382–97
International Tin Agreement 211

International Wheat Agreement 211
investible surplus, creation of 101–3
investment 63–4; allocation of 108; criteria for 99–100; and inflation 121; in infrastructure 65; rewards for 70; and technology transfer 162–9; *see also* foreign direct investment
Iran 124
iron law of wages 38
irrigation 253
Ishikawa, S. 253

Japan 134
Johnson, H.G. 191–3
joint ventures 165
Jolly, Richard 288–9
Jones, C. 64
Jorgenson model 87–92

Kahn, A.E. 101
Kaldor, N. 133, 216, 333
Kaldor-Mirrlees growth model 52–5
Kanbur, R. 220, 299–300, 373
Kanbur, S.M. 286
Kelly *et al.* growth model 91
Kenya 317
Kenya Report 287
Keynesian theory 39–41, 131–2
Kindleberger, C.P. 205, 208
King, R. 65, 126, 303
Klein, L. 320–1
knowledge: accumulation of 75–6; and capital 76
Knudsen, O. 209–10, 224
Kohler, Horst 396
Komiya, R. 319
Krishnan, T.N. 234
Krueger, Anne 396
Krugman, P. 393
kulaks 133, 255
Kuznets, S. 273–4, 286, 301

labour intensity 107–9, 300
labour markets 22
Lal, D. 342
land ownership 259–60, 264
land taxes 134–5, 244
Latin American Free Trade Association 213
Lawson, Nigel 392
learning by doing (LBD) theory 76–7, 218
Leibenstein, H. 101–2
Leontief, W.W. 322
less-developed countries: characteristics of 1–20; economic performance of 2–3; macroeconomic indicators for 4–5; production conditions in 20–1
Levine, R. 65–6, 126, 303

Lewis, A.W. 79, 94, 110
liberalization, financial 124–6, 30–3; of trade 214–17, 352, 358–9
linear programming 326–31
Lipsey, R.E. 207–8
Lipton, M. 245
Little–Mirrlees method of project evaluation 335–43
loans, official 382
Lomé Convention 210–12, 375
London Club 386
Lorenz curve 28–9
low-level equilibrium trap 274–5
Lucas, R. 57, 62
luck, role of 67
luxury goods 136, 355

MacBean, A.I. 209
machinery, agricultural 253
macroeconomic instability 351
macroeconomic models 320–2
Mahalanobis, P.C. *see* Feldman–Mahalanobis model
Maizels, A. 154, 156
Malaya 203
malnutrition *see* nutrition
Malthusian theory 37–9, 67–8, 271
Managhas, M. 248
Mankiw, G. 69
marginal analysis in economics 99
marginal efficiency of capital (MEC) 381–2
marginal growth contribution (MGC) 102–3
marginal net social benefit (MNSB) and marginal net private benefit (MNPB) 313
marketed surplus: concept of 231; mobilization of 235–8; in relation to size-holdings and output 238–43; and terms of trade 231–5
markets in less-developed countries, types of 20
Marshall–Lerner condition 358
Marxist growth theory 47–52
Massell, B.F. 209–10
Mathur, P.N. 234
Maynard, G. 172
Meade, James 354
Mellor, J. 248–9
Mexico 378, 383, 391–2
Michaely, M. 209
migration 70; mathematical models of 291–9; theory of and evidence on 296–8; welfare gains or loss from 306–7
Mill, John Stuart 190–1
minimum wage legislation 291
Mirrlees, J.A. 109; *see also* Little–Mirrlees method
Mitra, P. 219

modelling, economic 312; aggregative 314–15; macroeconomic 320–2
monetary contraction 352
monetary policy 354–5
money markets 115–16, 124–6
money supply 116–17
Morris, Taft 265
Mosley, P. 178
MRIS (maximization of rate of creation of investible surplus) criterion 101–4
multilateral flows of foreign resources 152–3
multinational corporations 368–9; technology transfer by 157–62, 165–8
Mundell, R. 118–21

national plans 151–2
Neary, P.J. 297
neoclassical growth model 43–6, 55–6, 68–70; applied to less-developed countries 46–7; basic equations of 71–3
neo-Marxist theory of development 50–2
net present value (NPV) 333–4
net resource transfers (NRTs) 380–1
net social benefit (NSB) 332–7
new international economic order 170; arguments for 365–6; evolution of 366–8; objectives of 368–9
Newbery, D.M.G. 373
newly industrialized countries (NICs) 63–4, 215, 366, 377
Nicaragua 135
non-tariff barriers 212
non-traded goods 200–2, 338
North American Free Trade Area 397
North-South models 219–20
Nulty, L. 254
Nurkse, R. 110, 112
nutrition and malnutrition 261, 310

Obstfeld, M. 393
oil-price shocks 384–5
open economies 64–5; fiscal policy in 128–9
optimum tariff argument 191–3, 197
organization, economic 22–3
Organization of Petroleum Exporting Countries (OPEC) 211, 366, 374, 385
output structure by country 10–13
overpricing 167
overshooting adjustment 220
overvaluation of currency 335

Pakistan 203
Paretian efficiency 401–2
Paris Club 392
Parnes, A. 209–10, 224
partially traded goods 338–9
Pasinetti, L. 54
patents 167
Peacock–Shaw model 129–31
Penn World Tables 26
Persson, T. 66–7
planning *see* development planning models; economic planning
planning horizons 311
Polak, J.J. 100
'polluter pays' principle 403–5
population growth 1–9, 251, 260, 264, 290; and economic expansion 271–4; endogenous 67; and fertility 275; harmful effects of 271–3
portfolio investment theory 299
poverty 18, 281, 301, 361; absolute 284–7
poverty line, definition of 304–6
poverty traps 67–70
Prebisch, R. 207–8, 367
Preobrazhensky, E. 231
Prest, A.R. 133
production functions 30–2, 59; with constant elasticity of substitution (CES) 32–4; *see also* Cobb–Douglas
productivity 9, 59–60, 63–4; agricultural 248
profit maximization behaviour in agriculture 254
protection 52, 102, 169, 193–7, 205, 376; costs of 203–5, 215; effects on exports of 202–3; nominal and effective rates of 198–203

quantitative restrictions (QRs) on imports 355–6

Ramaswami, V.K. 191
rational expectations hypothesis 144–5
Rebolo, S. 65
redistributive policies 287–9
regional co-operation 213–14
reinvestible surplus criterion 103–6; criticisms of 106–9
Renelt, D. 66
rent-seeking behaviour 219, 411–12
research and development (R&D) 62, 73
Ricardian equivalence (RE) theorem 141–5
Ricardo, David 353–4
Rivera-Batiz, L. 64
Robinson, Joan 65
Robinson, R. 59–60
Rodriguez, Francisco 208
Rodrik, Dani 208
Romer, P. 61–5, 73
Rosenstein-Rodan, P.N. 109–10
Russia 230
Ruttan, V. 248, 259
Rybczynski theorem 205

Sachs, Jeffrey 208
Saint-Paul, G. 66–7
Sala-i-Martin, Xavier 69
sales tax 137–8
savings 64, 75, 112–13
savings gap 147, 154–5, 381–3
Schultz, P.T. 277, 307–8
Schultz, T.W. 82
Schumpeter, J. 62
Scitovsky, T. 333
seeds, new varieties of 248, 251–2
Sen, Amartya 103–8, 261, 267–70, 304–5
'shadow cost' model 105
shadow exchange rates (SERs) 341–2
shadow prices 216, 330–2, 339, 343
shallow finance 123
Shiavo-Campo, S. 165
Singapore 60–1
Singer, H.W. 165
Smith, Adam 231
social accounting matrices 343–6
social accounting multipliers 345–7
social cost-benefit analysis 216, 331–5
social marginal productivity (SMP) criterion 101–4
social welfare functions 139
Soejono, D. 248
Soligo, R. 86
Solow, Robert 61
Solow, Minhas, Arrow and Chenery (SMAC) production function 32–4
South Korea 218
special drawing rights (SDRs) 170–2, 368, 376; empirical evidence on 173–5
spillover effects 218
Squire, L. 342
Sri Lanka 133, 290
Srinivasan, T.N. 108, 215, 218–19; *see also* Bhagwati–Srinivasan model
Stabex scheme 375
stagnant economies 67
Stark, O. 298
Stern, N. 139–41
Stewart, F. 106
Stiglitz, J.E. 373
'stop-go' pattern of growth 355–6
Streeten, P. 106, 111–12, 261, 321–2
Strout, A. 154
structural adjustment and lending (SAL) projects 352
structural adjustment and stabilization (SAS) 351–8; experience in sub-Saharan Africa of 359–61; theory of 352–3; and trade policies 354–6
Summers, A. 63
supplementary financing schemes (SFS) 212
surplus labour 79–83; and economic growth 80–1
sustainable growth 61

Tabellini, G. 66–7
Taiwan 83
Tak, H.G. 342
tariffs 135, 169, 335; and balance of payments 197; employment argument for 197–8; optimum level of 191–3, 197; role in economic development 190–1
taxation 129–41, 358; of companies 134; and domestic resource mobilization 138–9; reform of 140–1; structure of 132–8; *see also* fiscal policy
technological progress 59–62, 66; in agriculture 247–8; embodied and disembodied 161–2; small farmers' response to 245, 250, 254, 258; transfer of benefits from 207
technology, choice of 108–9, 249–50
technology transfer 366; benefits and costs of 165–8; by multinational corporations 157–62; policies for 168–9; and private foreign investment 162–9; types of 164
terms of trade 206–8, 290–1, 367, 383; and marketed surplus 231–5
Thailand 124
Thorbecke, E. 245
tied resources 150–1
Tobin, J. 142–3
Todaro model of migration 291–6, 299
Toronto Agreement (1988) 392–3
trade 19–20; country statistics of 180–3; and economic growth 205; net welfare loss resulting from 205–6; *see also* liberalization of trade
trade adjustment 353–4
trade policy 64–6
trade reform 356–9
traded goods 338–9
trading blocs 213–14
'tragedy of the commons' 401–2
training 62
transfer pricing 168
'trickle-down' effect 300–1
Triffin, R. 171
two-gap model (of foreign exchange and trade) 215

unbalanced growth theory (UBG) 109–12
underdevelopment 50–2
underdevelopment and dependency theory (UDT) 51–2
underemployment 9
unemployment 9, 287, 290, 296–8, 319, 335; disguised 79, 82–3

United Nations 53, 223; Conference on Trade and Development (UNCTAD) 210–11, 367, 373–6; Development Programme (UNDP) 26–7; General Assembly 367; Industrial Development Organization (UNIDO) 340–3
urbanization 280
Uruguay 124
Uruguay Round 375

Vakil, C.N. 319
value-added tax (VAT) 137–8, 141
Venezuela 221–2, 389
Verdier, T. 66–7
Verdoon law 216
'victims pay for pollution' principle 405
Vines, D. 220

Warner, Andrew 208
Whalley, J. 218–19
World Bank 65, 153, 212, 301, 351–2, 359, 366, 378, 382, 386, 391–2, 397, 402
writing-off of debt 387

Yamey, B.S. 110
Young, A. 63–4